THE
RECKONING

THE
RECKONING

David Halberstam

WILLIAM MORROW AND COMPANY, INC.
NEW YORK

Library of Congress Cataloging-in-Publication Data

Halberstam, David.
The reckoning.

Bibliography: p.
Includes index.
1. Automobile industry and trade—United States.
2. Automobiles—United States—Fuel consumption.
3. Petroleum industry and trade—United States.
4. Energy consumption—United States.   I. Title.
HD9710.U52H28   1986   338.4′76292′0973   86-16427
ISBN 0-688-04838-2

A Thomas Congdon Book

Printed in the United States of America

First Edition

1 2 3 4 5 6 7 8 9 10

BOOK DESIGN BY BETH TONDREAU

For Alan U. Schwartz

CONTENTS

PART
ONE

1.
MAXWELL'S
WARNING

There had been plenty of warnings. Some experts had pointed out that the sources of oil were not limitless, that consumption was rising faster than production. Some noted that certain of the oil-producing countries were politically unstable and hostile to the United States. The men of the auto industry had never heeded the warnings. They dismissed them as veiled criticisms of the cars they were making.

In June 1973, a young man named Charley Maxwell flew from New York to Detroit to talk to the top executives of the three main auto companies. A decade later astute observers would mark that particular time, mid-1973, as the last moment of the old order in the industrialized world. It was a time when energy was still remarkably cheap and in steady supply, a time when the great business captains could still make their annual forecasts with some degree of certainty. Detroit was still Detroit in those heady days. It regularly sold eight million cars a year, and in a good year, a boomer's year, the kind loved by everyone in the business from the president of a company to the lowliest dealer, it sold ten or eleven million. More, these were precisely the kind and size of cars Detroit wanted to sell—big, heavy cars loaded with expensive options. In those days no one talked about energy conservation except a few scholarly types. The average American car got about thirteen miles per gallon then, a figure far below that expected of cars in most other modern countries. Detroit's cars were large, weighty, and powerful. Comfort and power, rather than economy, seemed important in the marketplace. Americans were a big people, and they liked to drive long distances. If the cars were no longer of quite the quality many of the company engineers and manufacturing men wanted, this was deemed a matter of no great consequence, for they still sold.

Anyone who complained about the quality of the cars was a quibbler, more than likely an egghead who subscribed to *Consumer Reports*. After all, a car need last no more than the three years before the owner turned it in for a brand-new model, which would be equally large, or, given the American presumption of rising social status, even larger. As the new car reflected the owner's climb, so the old car now began its own journey down the social scale, ending up an owner or two later in some ghetto inhabited by members of the American underclass. There, patched and repatched, it would consume even greater quantities of gas.

The intelligentsia of America, much given to driving small, fuel-efficient, rather cramped foreign cars, often mocked Detroit for the grossness and gaudiness of its product. To many liberal intellectuals Detroit symbolized all that was excessive in the materialism of American life (just as to many small-town American conservatives, the companies' partner, the United Auto Workers, symbolized everything that was excessive about the post –New Deal liberal society). None of this carping bothered Detroit. It was a given that Americans preferred big cars—and only Detroit made big cars. There was a seldom-spoken corollary to this axiom: Big cars meant big profits, and small cars meant small profits. In early 1973 the fact that Detroit was selling what it wanted to sell was considered proof that Detroit, rather than its critics, truly understood the American customer. The future looked brighter than ever. An ugly war in Southeast Asia which had sapped the nation's strength and resources was finally ending, and Detroit was bullish about the auto economy just ahead. That bullishness seemed to be based on good reason. For if there was one benign economic certainty, as far as American industrialists and American consumers were concerned, it was the low price of gas and oil, a price that seemed almost inflation-proof in the postwar era. In 1950 the price of a gallon of gas at the pump had been 27 cents, 20 cents of it for the gas itself and the rest for taxes. Twenty years later, the price of virtually every other basic consumer commodity had approximately doubled, but the price of gas had remained, tantalizingly, almost the same. At the moment that Charley Maxwell set out for Detroit, in 1973, a gallon of gas cost 37 cents at the pump, 26 of it for the gas itself. The price seemed a blessing so constant that everyone had come to take it for granted.

That was the premise of the city to which Charley Maxwell was traveling. He was thirty-five years old and had spent all of his adult life in the oil business, mostly with Mobil in the Middle East and Nigeria. He was by nature scholarly, and those long years in the field had added practical experience to his theoretical expertise, a rare combination. In the late sixties, when Mobil had started replacing its American overseas employees with foreign nationals, Maxwell had been sent back to the United States. It seemed to him that his career opportunities in the oil industry had been drastically reduced, and, looking around for a way to exploit his knowledge, he had become an oil analyst for a Wall Street firm called Cyrus Lawrence.

Every field has its awesome experts, but there was something about Charley Maxwell's professional authority that was almost chilling. Part of it was his appearance, the hair plastered down over his forehead and parted in the middle, the old-fashioned, almost prim wire-rimmed glasses, the slightly stooped posture, the preoccupied manner; he looked like the sort of person who as a sixth-grader had been doted upon by his teachers because he had always gotten the right answer to every question, who had been good at what his teachers wanted rather than at what mattered to his peers.

He was an obsessed, intellectually passionate man. It was clear that what he was thinking about at any one moment he thought about to the exclusion of all other things. When Charley Maxwell started talking about energy, it was as if he might never stop, that meals might be missed, engagements forgotten. He answered questions thoroughly, his control of material was total, his voice was quietly confident, his judgments were clearly devoid of bias. He seemed to pursue the truth with so much intensity he made other men nervous. Eventually he would become one of the country's most prominent experts on oil prices, a man whose opinions would be eagerly sought. He would win many professional awards, in fact would be named the number-one institutional analyst in the field of energy, and his firm would permit him to speak to business groups at a fee of $2000 a hour. By then when he would walk to lunch along Wall Street he would often be hailed by colleagues—and when one of them lightly asked him a question, this most serious and thorough of men would reply at length, his answer becoming an exposition lasting ten or fifteen minutes, as he jumped quickly from one century to another, one American administration to another. He seemed destined to be late to every appointment on his calendar. Reporters interviewing Maxwell would find him always a little short of time, and their interviews would of necessity continue as they walked with him to his subway stop or even rode the Lexington Avenue line uptown with him, Maxwell shouting his answers above the subway's roar.

In those June days of 1973, however, he was not yet well known outside his field, and his field was not yet a hot one. Americans believed that their own domestic supplies of oil were plentiful and that there were virtually limitless sources in the Persian Gulf. What Charley Maxwell intended to tell the top-level auto executives he believed he would meet in Detroit was what he had been telling his superiors for some time now—that there would soon be dramatic, indeed revolutionary, changes in the price of energy. The assumption of the past, that energy would remain cheap because it had always been cheap and its price would increase only at small, acceptable, noninflationary increments, had to be discarded. America's own resources were rapidly proving inadequate, and the nation would thus become far more dependent upon the oil-producing nations of the Middle East. But the American oil companies would no longer be able to control the prices set for Arab oil, as they had so easily in the past. The Arabs would set the prices themselves. Since oil was in those days significantly underpriced in terms of its true market value, the loss of that control would have serious consequences for American heavy industry in general and Detroit in particular.

Maxwell had seen all this coming for a number of years. As early as 1970 he had started using the phrase "energy crisis"—apparently his coinage. He used it to refer to a crucial, ominous shift in the supply and demand of oil. He calculated that worldwide oil consumption was climbing 5 to 6 percent annually, and there was no reason to believe the surge would abate. If anything, it was likely to accelerate. New nations, recently graduated from their colonial past, were fast becoming both industrialized and urbanized and demanding far greater amounts of energy. Throughout the underdeveloped world, people were leaving their tribal huts and moving into cities, and, as they did, they took new jobs in factories which required energy, they lived in apartments which required energy, and to get to work they used transportation which also required energy. It was revolution taking place, a revolution of people who were changing their way of life and of nations that were expanding and modernizing their economies. The world, Maxwell concluded, had changed dramatically and was going to continue to change as more and more nations moved toward industrial economies. Ten and sometimes fifteen additional countries were leaving the preindustrial age each year and coming into the mechanical age. But there had not as yet been any reflection of this trend in the price of the ingredient most precious to the modern industrialized state, oil. There was going to be one terrible moment, Maxwell was sure, when the price would simply shoot up, out of anyone's control, the oil seeking its true market value.

By 1973, Maxwell was expecting the breakaway to come fairly soon, perhaps in three years, at the most in five. He was, he later ruefully noted, far too optimistic. His projections had not given adequate weight to rising Arab nationalism, though he was well aware that as the economic power of the oil-producing Arab nations increased, their awareness of their political power would increase as well. That so finite a resource as oil was remaining so inexpensive in a world that was demanding more and more of it constantly amazed him. Under normal conditions, Maxwell believed, the post–World War II era would have seen the price of oil go up steadily as the Arab nations, finally free of their colonial and semicolonial bondage, took direct control of their resources. But for some twenty years that had not happened. Instead there had been a vast postwar expansion of the Middle East oil reserves, because geologists, using more modern technology in their explorations, were finding more oil. The expansion of these reserves, particularly in places like Saudi Arabia, had temporarily neutralized the political and economic power of the producing states—the Arabs had so much oil to sell that they had not been able to push the price up. Now that was about to change.

Maxwell knew that he was not alone in his pessimism, that a number of other energy experts, using much the same research, had come to similar conclusions. But most of these experts worked for the large oil companies, where the darker view had not yet been accepted. Maxwell's own superiors at the Wall Street investment firm of Cyrus Lawrence, however, had been greatly impressed by his estimates and the dispassionate way in which he presented his evidence. Both as a courtesy and also out of their own self-interest, for it would not hurt to lend out so brilliant a man with such original and important perceptions, they decided to send him to Detroit. There, the Cyrus Lawrence people proposed, he would talk to executives at the highest level, who surely would be more than anxious to hear these findings that had such fateful implications for their companies.

Maxwell himself was not so sure. He knew Detroit and he knew it well. He had grown up there, his stepfather had been employed at a middle level by Ford, he himself had even gone to Cranbrook, the city's elite prep school, where many of his classmates were sons of auto titans. Maxwell knew how stratified the city was, how isolated and insular. It was, he believed, a place of bedrock beliefs, a place where new truths did not seep easily from the bottom to the top. In Detroit, truth moved from the top to the bottom.

Maxwell had been promised meetings with the high auto executives, people who operated at the ultimate level of power. He was dubious about that. He might be well known in the world of oil, but he was young, and Detroit did not readily listen to junior people. Detroit believed in hierarchy and seniority rather than in individual brilliance. One advanced in Detroit not necessarily by being brilliant—brilliance meant that someone might be *different* and implied a threat—but by accommodating oneself to the attitudes of those above one. Maxwell, because of his age and the nature of his message, would almost surely be looked upon as impertinent. These men would have their own sources of information, among them the men who headed the great oil companies, the men still resistant to the pessimistic vision of Maxwell and his kind. Powerful, successful, and conventional, typical of the corporate class, they believed that tomorrow would be like today because it had always been like today and because they wanted it to be like today. In their view, if the price of oil went up, it would go up slowly over many decades. They had controlled the oil world—and thus the price of energy—in the past. They would control that world and the price of energy in the future. So Charley Maxwell had been skeptical from the start that he would get the very top people as promised. If his superiors thought so, he knew better, and he had automatically translated his prospects downward. He would be lucky, he decided, to meet people at the 65 percent level of power. That, he soon learned, was too sanguine an expectation.

He did not do badly at the start. He went first to Chrysler, where Tom Killefer, the senior financial officer, had assembled a group of upper-middle-level executives. They listened quietly as Maxwell made his solemn little speech, saying in effect that all their estimates about what kind of cars Americans could and would drive were about to fly out the window. Killefer himself had been pleasant; he was a Rhodes scholar, different from the average Detroit executive, less narrow, in better touch with the outside world. When Maxwell finished, Killefer thanked him and said, "Well, what you say is very, very impressive, very impressive indeed, and of course if it's true, then we're going to have to give it a hard, hard look." There were questions, and the bright young men in the group, perhaps less complacent because Chrysler was already a shaky company, were clearly interested. But even as he was finishing his presentation, Maxwell had a sense that it was all to no end, that these men would leave the meeting and shake their heads and say how interesting it had been, what a bright fellow Maxwell was, maybe a bit rash, something of an alarmist, didn't they think, but bright and interesting nonetheless. Worth thinking about. That would be it, Maxwell thought, possibly a letter or two thanking him, but no real penetration of the process.

Chrysler, unfortunately, turned out to be by far the best of the three meetings. He had been taken seriously there, and Killefer was, whatever else, a representative of top management. Ford was a good deal worse. At Ford he met two people at the lower planning level. They were junior executives, making, he suspected, about $25,000 a year, which was a very small salary in executive Detroit. They were, he knew instantly, completely without power, and they had been sent there because a steadily descending series of Ford executives had told their immediate subordinates that someone had to go and cover the meeting, until finally, far down the line, there had been two men so unimportant that they had no subordinates to send. These two were there precisely because they were powerless. Maxwell felt a bit odd, standing in that room saying that Detroit was going to have to change its whole line of cars and that an entire era had ended, and saying this to men who could not change the design of an ashtray. Somehow that thought made his presentation more impassioned than ever.

General Motors, of course, was the worst. There were no high-level meetings scheduled. In fact, there were no meetings scheduled at all. Someone very junior asked Maxwell if he would like to drive out to the testing grounds and meet with some GM people there. He did, encountering no one in any position of responsibility, though for his troubles he was able to see some of GM's new models. They looked rather large to him, cars that would surely use a great deal of gas.

Such was Charley Maxwell's trip to Detroit. He had not even gotten across the moat. Detroit was Detroit, and more than most business centers it was a city that listened only to its own voice. But he left town worried about what he was sure was going to happen to a vital American industry. Maxwell did not think that the coming change in price would necessarily be so great that even a Detroit that was prepared for change would be severely damaged. Rather, he was worried because Detroit was unprepared—because no one in America seemed willing to practice even the most nominal kind of conservation, which suggested that the country was psychically unready for major increases. A big jump in price might trigger a panic, which would compound the difficulty of entering a new economic order. Those who were set up for change could deal with it, he suspected; those who were not were likely to come apart. Detroit, he feared, was going to have to learn its new truths the hard way.

A few months later, on October 6, 1973, on the eve of Yom Kippur, the holiest of Jewish holy days, Egypt tried a military strike on Israel. Eventually Israel struck back and once again, for the third time since World War II, defeated the Egyptians. To the Arab world this humiliation was one more demonstration of its powerlessness. The Arabs blamed Israel's existence on its American sponsorship. Thwarted both militarily and politically, the Arabs now turned at last to their real strength, their economic leverage. They began an oil embargo on the West. Before it was over, the price of oil had rocketed from $3 a barrel to $12 a barrel. The United States, long accustomed to cheap energy, was completely unprepared to respond to the Arab move. Unwilling to increase the taxes on gasoline and oil and thus at least partially stabilize the price of energy, it had in effect permitted the Arabs to place a tax not just on the American oil consumer but on the entire country. The effects on the American economy at every level were dramatic. The era of the cheap energy upon which so much of America's dynamism and its broad middle-class prosperity was premised was beginning to end. A new era with profound implications for the industrial core of America, the great Middle Atlantic and Midwestern foundry of the nation, had arrived. Occasionally in later years Charley Maxwell would run into Tom Killefer, who by then had left Chrysler to become the chairman of the United States Trust Company, and when he did, Killefer would shake his head and say, "You—you're the one man I hate to see. God, I still remember that warning."

At almost the same time that Charley Maxwell went to Detroit, a man named David E. Davis, Jr., was also given a special mission. Davis—David E., as he was more commonly known in Detroit—was a prominent and ubiquitous figure in the city. He was a certified car nut, and far more than most senior auto executives, who lived for their careers, he lived for cars. He loved them, he was always to be found tinkering with them, or racing them, or hanging around the men who designed them. In a previous Detroit incarnation he had been the editor of *Car and Driver*, a magazine by and for car nuts.

Davis was a close friend of Tom Adams, a major Detroit shaker who headed the local office of Campbell-Ewald, a New York advertising agency that handled the GM account. Campbell-Ewald had hired Davis not so much because it needed his advertising expertise but, it was widely believed, because it was doing a subtle favor for GM, finding a place for a talented car man whose instincts were clearly first-rate but whose style was too outrageous for that most conservative of American business institutions, General Motors. Thus though his salary was laundered through Campbell-Ewald, Davis in effect worked for GM. At the agency, his manner, his clothes, his beard, his passion for the truth would not offend his superiors, and their manners and dress would not offend him. For as far as Davis was concerned, the GM executives all wore the same suit, spoke the same language, lived in the same Detroit suburb, even, he believed, drank the same wine, which, he was convinced, was Blue Nun. (Davis claimed that GM tours of Europe—rewards for executives who had surpassed their quotas—were carefully arranged so that all the inns along the way would be sure to serve thick steaks and Blue Nun.)

Tom Adams of Campbell-Ewald was glad to take Davis in. Adams knew that if his agency was to serve its huge client well, it would not only have to show GM's products to the world, through advertising, but keep the cloistered executives of the gigantic corporation in some kind of touch with that world. Between GM and the world a man like Davis was a good bridge.

Adams himself had played the role of bridge before, not always with complete success. During the late sixties, when John DeLorean was the *enfant terrible* of GM—at once a very able car man and a violator of all unwritten codes for GM executives, in dress, length of hair, and youthfulness of female companions—Adams had found himself constantly mediating between DeLorean and his older, more traditional superiors. Once in those years, in the middle of a high-level Campbell-Ewald meeting, Adams had been obliged to take an urgent phone call. A few minutes later he returned to the meeting.

"I will never," he said, shaking his head, "be able to explain to my grandchildren the business I have been in all my life."

"What happened, Tom?" one of his colleagues asked.

"Well," he replied, "that was Roger Kyes, the head of General Motors, the largest corporation in the world, and he asked me if I was a good friend of John DeLorean's. I said yes, I was. Then he asked me if I had any influence with John. I said that was a completely different matter, but what could I do for them? Roger said that he and the top executives of GM were all concerned about the way John dressed. Very concerned.

"I told Roger I thought John dressed very nicely. 'No,' he said, 'we're all very upset with the boots he's wearing—you know, John has started wearing very high, very fancy boots.' They wondered if I might talk him back into wearing regular shoes of a normal height and style."

Thus it was not surprising to Tom Adams that Pete Estes, one of the top executives of General Motors, wanting to keep David E. Davis around but not in his hair, had placed him under Adams's wing at Campbell-Ewald.

In the spring of 1973, Estes, who was soon to become GM's president, had called Davis in and asked him to undertake an important assignment for General Motors. Davis's mission was to go to Europe and take a look at the new front-wheel-drive cars that were just coming out there and to check on their suitability for the American market, a market, which because it was composed of larger sized cars, had always favored rear-wheel drive. Volkswagen had just brought out the Rabbit, and the Rabbit and comparable European front-wheel-drive cars were generating excitement as no small cars had done in years. The excitement was not just among customers but among auto professionals, who saw in these cars a significant break from the past. They not only used less fuel but, because they had front-wheel drive, which saved weight, they achieved it without sacrificing performance. By contrast, when Detroit had brought out small cars in the past, they had been merely sawed-off versions of the industry's larger cars. What they gained in economy they always lost in performance.

Estes told Davis he wanted him to see how good these cars really were, and above all to find out whether front-wheel drive was the kind of product innovation that GM might be able to charge extra for as an option. "Our people are telling us that it's going to be very expensive—a whole new engine, a whole new power train," Estes said. "They think it will cost us about eighty-five or ninety dollars a car. So if we put it on our small cars, will we be able to charge extra and make it work?" The question struck Davis as precisely the wrong one, but at the same time typical of what he had come to expect in the new Detroit, where car people and their standards no longer dominated the industry. The proper question, Davis believed, was not whether this could be a new option for which a little extra could be charged. On an innovation of this magnitude, the right questions were whether it worked, whether it was as good as everyone said, and, if so, how quickly it could be introduced. Davis believed that in the old Detroit, the Detroit of car men, no one would have asked what it might cost as an option but simply whether it made the car better. If the answer was yes, the manufacturers would have gone ahead and done it.

To Davis the old auto executives were men who had little financial sophistication but trusted their almost primal instincts. The new Detroit, he thought, was more cautious, a place of people who had made their way up by taking as few risks as possible and never letting their eyes waver from the bottom line. Innovation cost money and entailed risk, and they had little stomach for it. The three main Detroit companies believed that they were fiercely competitive with each other, and in a sense, he thought, they were, though mostly on trivial matters. The more important the issue, the less they competed and the longer they waited for someone else to take the first step, lest it be a mistake. It was, in the words of another Detroit journalist, Pat Wright, "a shared monopoly." Davis agreed; he did not see them as they saw themselves, three intense rivals flying the banner of free enterprise and fighting against one another at every level of operation. He saw them as one big company with three divisions, in which everyone played it safe and no division tried something new unless it was reasonably sure that the other two were going to try it as well. In the new Detroit, it was mainly the engineers who still cared about in-novation and whose principal pleasure came from changing and improving and probing into the future; and the engineers, he had seen, were almost completely stymied by the power of the financial people, and were frustrated and angry. The auto industry was static. Its member corporations changed hemlines every year to give the illusion of change, but in truth they were more concerned with preserving their positions than with improving their products.

Davis undertook the assignment from Pete Estes with a certain ambivalence. He liked the idea of scouting the new European models, but he doubted that Detroit would commit itself to genuinely new small cars. Its heart had always belonged to big cars. The cars he found in Europe were an auto enthusiast's dream. By having the engine drive the front wheels instead of the back, the designers had eliminated the drive shaft that had always run through the rest of the car, creating weight and a hump in the floor. Without the drive shaft the car, though smaller, could be roomier. It was also lighter. Because it was smaller and lighter, the engine could be smaller, and the cars demanded less gas. They cost less and demanded less fuel than anything comparable which Detroit had yet produced. Davis was immediately converted, not just because the cars were more fuel-efficient, though that was important, but also because they responded better to the driver's touch. Driving them provided something that had long been missing in the small-car range in America—fun.

A few weeks later, Davis was back in Detroit reporting to Estes, telling him everything he had learned. They were better cars, he said, better engineered and better built than those Detroit was making. Front-wheel drive, he declared, was a breakthrough of immense significance. It was not a question that could be debated anymore, because it had already happened. It was the state of the art. It was the way all cars would be built in the future, not just small ones. There was, he emphasized, no turning back. The European market was extremely competitive, and thus the cars were likely to get better and better. Eventually Detroit would have to respond.

Davis tried to be dispassionate in his report, but it was difficult, because he felt such enthusiasm for what he had just seen. Pete Estes listened to him patiently, but when Davis was finished, he shook his head. "When I was at Oldsmobile," he said, "there was something I learned that I've never forgotten. There was an old guy there who was an engineer, and he had been at GM a long time, and he gave me some advice. He told me, whatever you do, don't let GM do it first."

That was it, Davis thought later—the Detroit line, the symbol of the protected industry. Don't let GM do it first, let the other guy make the early, expensive mistakes. Right then, he was sure, at Ford and Chrysler there were people who were also deciding not to do it first because some-how someone else should do it first. It was, he thought, management by default. He knew there were businesses in America, typically smaller ones in various fields of technology and medical science, that were authentically competitive. There, companies lived on the edge, their survival depending on innovation and technological advantage. But in the auto industry, as in most big industries, it was not like that. It was a protected world, the shares of the market already apportioned, GM big, Ford moderate, Chrys-ler small, with the government watching to see that GM did not put either of the others out of business. It was not a vibrant industry anymore, he thought, because the top people were no longer doing things simply be-cause they were the right thing. Those who had the most power had the least passion.

He told Pete Estes that he believed he was making a major mistake, and that eventually the customers would let him know. Privately he felt even more strongly about it. Someday, and probably soon, Detroit was going to pay for this attitude. As it turned out, David E. Davis was right. The American auto industry was completely unready when the oil embargo hit, its products suddenly very wrong for the marketplace. The manufac-turers had squandered a decade in which they could have created cars suited to the new nature of the industrialized world.

That was the first oil shock. Some six years later, in 1979, just as the American auto industry was beginning to recover from the trauma of the first one and its customers were becoming accustomed to the higher gas prices and beginning to return to big cars, there was a second shock. This one resulted from the disintegration of the government of the Shah of Iran.

If there had been a keystone of American economic policy in the Middle East, it had been support of the Shah. The Shah, in fact, had been installed by the Americans, after a CIA coup in 1953 had overthrown the leftist prime minister, Mohammed Mossadegh. "I owe my throne," the Shah later told Kermit Roosevelt of the CIA, who organized the coup, "to God, my people, my army—and to you!" For almost twenty years a series of American administrations had kept the Shah on a relatively short leash, but in 1972 Richard Nixon and Henry Kissinger had changed the policy and given the Shah a virtual carte blanche to the American armory. This was done not so much because anyone in the national security complex believed that Iran needed advanced weapons, but more as a means of flattering and appeasing a leader whose ambition for world position man-ifested itself, among other ways, in a voracious appetite for the newest of the Pentagon's toys. In the four years after Nixon and Kissinger had visited him, the Shah had ordered $9 billion worth of America's most sophisticated military equipment. To some high Washington officials that leap in Iran's military capacity signaled mounting problems for both Iran and the United States.

The relationship between the Shah and his principal allies, the Americans, had never been an easy one. Because the Americans had helped create him, the Shah had to go to lengths to prove that he was not a puppet; that particular challenge, to show he was his own man, seemed to fire his megalomania. The Americans had constantly pressured him to modernize and liberalize his regime, but he always seemed to disappoint them, as they disappointed him by finding too many flaws in his rule. The modernization of any Islamic country was a difficult task under the best of circumstances, but for someone who owed his original legitimacy to Westerners, it was an almost impossible one. To many Islamic fundamentalists, the Shah's ties with America, his relentless buying of arms, his modernization of many traditional aspects of Iranian life meant too much and too rapid change. "Westoxification," the Ayatollah Khomeini called it—intoxication with all things Western. On the other hand, some middle-class, educated Iranians who had found their way into the Tudeh, the Iranian Communist party, felt the Shah was changing too little too slowly. Increasingly it seemed as if he could please fewer and fewer of his subjects.

When protest began against the Shah in 1978, he seemed likely to ride it out as he had ridden out earlier periods of unrest. But it soon became clear that this time it was more serious. The true base of the protest was Islamic religious leaders, rather than radical leftists, and therefore it was harder to crush. For it was one thing to send the security police or the army against Communists; it was quite another to challenge the power of the mullahs, or holy men. That was a popularity contest of a different sort, one the Shah might well not win, for in a conflict like that there were no guarantees of the loyalty of his troops. If he moved against the mullahs, he might momentarily slow them down but create powerful martyrs. "To step on a Persian carpet or a mullah," went an old Iranian proverb, "increases its value." The Shah had plainly underestimated the strength of the resistance to his reforms among his own people; there had been little protest against him earlier in the seventies simply because the country, bulging with oil revenues, had been distracted by its immense new prosperity.

Week after week as the protests grew, the Shah seemed immobilized, unable to act, wary, he said, of constantly shedding the blood of his own people in order to hold power. The weeks turned into months. In the end what was negotiated was the terms of his departure. He had spent billions in buying America's most modern weapons, and in the end they had done him no good; not a bullet had been fired on his behalf, and his administration had collapsed of its own weight and grandiosity. On January 16, 1979, the Shah left Teheran.

2.
AMAYA SURVEYS THE OIL AGE

One Japanese civil servant watched the fall of the Shah of Iran with considerable misgivings. Naohiro Amaya, slim, graying, scholarly, a senior bureaucrat in a nation in which bureaucrats wield exceptional power and influence, had to a large degree foreseen the events now unfolding, and he thought that their consequences were likely to be profound for the United States, and thus for Japan as well. Thinking about the future was Amaya's particular responsibility. His job was to make sure that Japan, a most vulnerable nation, was not surprised by catastrophic events outside its control. This duty had made him an expert on world energy, and as such he had realized by the late sixties that his country was becoming far too dependent upon oil. The Japanese economy was like a miniaturized version of the United States economy. Like the Americans, the Japanese had shifted from coal to oil as their prime source of energy, leaving Japan exceedingly exposed, since it produced no oil of its own. Japan was highly industrialized, and at the core of its postwar economy were the traditional smokestack industries, steel and shipbuilding, auto and petrochemicals. All of them were heavily dependent upon oil, every drop of which had to be imported.

Bureaucrat but also political visionary, poet, and amateur historian, Amaya was a senior official in the Ministry of International Trade and Industry, one of the most powerful institutions in Japan. MITI helped decide in which industries Japan would concentrate its limited resources, which companies would receive vital government subsidies, and which potential imports Japan would discourage. There was no comparable agency in America, for in America, a rich country well endowed with farmland and minerals, there had never seemed much need to plan and regulate. Because Japan was poorly endowed with such things, Amaya was important in a way few American bureaucrats were. So critical to Japan were the central issues of trade that someone like Amaya, who had risen to a high level at MITI, was comparable to someone at the very highest level of America's national security complex, like someone at a decision-making level at the State or Defense Department. If Amaya or one of his fellow bureaucrats at MITI decided that a certain policy on a crucial issue contributed to the greater long-range good of Japan, and if that policy went against the wishes of a group of leading industrialists, then in the end, after much subtle negotiation, Amaya and his colleagues would quite possibly win; they spoke for Japan and its future, and the industrialists spoke for a more narrow, parochial interest—the present, at best. Planning was an urgent fact of life in Japan, a country that a generation before had fought a disastrous war in no small part to secure its sources of oil and other essential materials. Because its population was so large, 117 million people in a small and infertile land, and because its desire to be a great industrial power was so strong, Japan had to plan everything. It could not afford to let events take their own course as America had for so much of the postwar era. A rise in commodity prices of the sort that might send a ripple of discomfort through the American economy could devastate the Japanese.

Amaya was chosen from among the best products of the Japanese system. He was born in Fukui province in 1925 of farmers who managed a simple living on a small plot of land. His family, he later said, resembled the people once called yeomen in America—hardworking, uncomplaining, and proud. The first son of his grandfather was immune from the draft—his duty was to work the land—but Amaya's father, the second son, went into the army and became a lieutenant general. He was away a great deal, and eventually he and Amaya's mother divorced. The Amaya family held a counsel and decided that two-year-old Naohiro should be adopted by his oldest uncle, who had no children of his own. The arrangement was successful until his uncle's wife died and he remarried and had children of his own. Amaya, then eleven, was returned to his real father. Because his father was away most of the time, Amaya boarded at a dormitory. He had a sense in later years that his independence stemmed from his having always been set apart. His father wanted him to go to a military academy in preparation for a career in the army, but a teacher argued that he would not fit into the mold and was better suited for intellectual pursuits. His father conceded and allowed the boy to go to a good local high school and then to Tokyo University, called Todai, the most prestigious of Japan's universities.

In America the ablest students were, as now, often restless and contentious, but this was rarely true of Japan, where the most valuable students proved their worthiness by accepting rigorous discipline without challenge or complaint. Western professors teaching in Japanese colleges for the first time were often worried by the lack of response in the classroom, fearing it meant that the students had not understood or that the language barrier was too great. However, it was simply that the students had been told that questioning authority was wrong. Teaching was more about molding egos than molding minds. But Todai was important as a symbol. Acceptance there almost guaranteed a young man, even one of modest means, like Amaya, a place on the great conveyor belt. The critical part of the delivery system was getting in. From then on a bright and eager young man could hardly fail to get a job in a ministry or large company. He did not even know if he had done well as a student until upon graduation he was accepted at MITI, one of the choice places for an enterprising young man. He enthusiastically accepted the job, because he had graduated right after the war and felt it his duty to help his country extricate itself from economic ruin.

At MITI he gradually developed a reputation as a kind of one-man think tank. To many of those in authority he was an *enfant terrible*, an unlikely product of Todai, too sure of his skills and his intellect and short on the selflessness befitting a young man—a kozo, one of them told Chalmers Johnson, the Berkeley political scientist, using the Japanese word for a little squirt (although Johnson noted that it was also the word for a Buddhist monk who tells his superior a truth he does not want to hear in a less than reverential manner). At one point in the early sixties Amaya was exiled to a post in Australia for the dual sins, it appeared, of a lack of deference and an inadequate job of hiding his own intelligence. He was not especially popular among his peers at MITI either. Something of an outsider, he never rose to quite the level he should have within the ministry. It was considered a small payback for his arrogance. This did not bother Amaya. Whenever there were difficult negotiations, particularly with the Americans, his colleagues came to him. He had a good reputation with the Americans—for understanding American political realities and for being able to get Japanese support once a position was staked out. "He is the key man on their SWAT team," said one American diplomat. "Whenever they're in trouble, they go to Amaya."

In the United States, a land where so much opportunity awaits the graduates of the best schools and where the pressure for individual achievement is immense, the word "bureaucrat" is almost pejorative, implying, first, that someone who works for the government does so because he is unfit for the private sector and, second, that his duties consist largely of impeding the normal free-market efforts of his fellow citizens. But the civil service in Japan is different, more like that of the British tradition, in which distinguished officials put country above all else and are truly servants of her majesty's realm. Japan's civil servants are honored as few nations honor their officials. A businessman, no matter how much he accomplishes for the good of Japan, represents finally a selfish interest, but a top man in one of the choice ministries has pledged himself completely to the good of the nation. Nothing reveals this more than the word the Japanese have for the moment when a senior bureaucrat leaves one of the key ministries late in his career to be farmed out to a company— amakudari, which means that the bureaucrat has descended from heaven into the more plebian world of business. Although the top ministerial jobs do not pay particularly well, that in itself is an asset, for it shows that the official has no purpose other than serving the nation. Near the end of Amaya's career in the ministry, Jim Abegglen, an American consultant in Tokyo, had dinner with him at a restaurant in the Ginza and asked him what his plans were.

"I don't have any," Amaya replied.

"Why not?" Abegglen, a little worried, asked.

"Because," he said simply, "MITI will take care of me." And of course it was true; he was taken care of.

The honored place held by a senior bureaucrat in Japan, as opposed to the status of a comparable American official, reflects the tremendous differences between the forms of capitalism in the two societies. In Japan, because there are so few resources, all rewards and profits must be shared. No one may become too rich, since his opulence would come at the expense of too many ordinary citizens. To ensure a fairly equal distribution of wealth, Japan developed not just a communal capitalism but a capitalism in which the arbiter of what is good for the nation is the high-level bureaucrat. In America it is assumed that capitalism is the right system. The immense prosperity of the postwar years made the possibility of a conflict between what was good for the individual capitalist and what was good for the nation seem inconceivable. "What's good for General Motors," Engine Charley Wilson more or less said (and was certainly credited with saying and probably meant), "is good for the country." Therefore, American capitalism evolved to benefit the individual, while the Japanese variety was tailored to benefit a more complicated assortment of interests.

Amaya was someone special within the Japanese bureaucracy, a practicing intellectual who on occasion seemed more historian than bureaucrat. He was more willing than many of his colleagues to hold and pursue ideas that differed from current assumptions, and he always seemed to be thinking about either the past or the future. Characteristic of him were his remarks at a meeting of Japanese and American officials in the summer of 1983, a time when both nations were obsessed with the impact of Japan's exports on America and when protectionist feeling was increasing at an alarming rate. That was not the problem, he said. Both nations were well equipped for the economic competition ahead; the pie was large enough for both to come out with viable industrial and high-technology economies. The real problem was what Japanese-American competition and cooperation might do to Western Europe, which was lagging in the contest for supremacy in high technology. It was, thought one of his American friends, typical of Amaya to be wondering about an issue farther down the road when everyone else was still concerned about a problem he had dealt with twelve years earlier. Most of Amaya's contemporaries took their definition of Japan from that which was—the existing power structure of the nation. Amaya went beyond that. His loyalty was to a higher definition, Japan as it might be, the loftiest possible vision of the society. A colleague spoke admiringly of him as a man apart in a nation where few men were comfortable in a role that made them different. He seemed to have such faith in his own judgment as to wear his individualism with ease. As such a person, Amaya let criticism from mere politicians glance lightly off his back. When he was criticized in the Tokyo press, and he often was, harshly, he consoled himself that any truly worthy political act offended important people. Only the most conventional of decisions did not offend. The wiser the act, the more likely it was to cause displeasure. He was openly contemptuous of most politicians anyway. The stronger they were, the likelier they were to lust for power, usually, he suspected, at the expense of the national good. When he briefed members of the Diet, he seemed to take a deliberate pleasure in leaving nothing out of his briefing; it was, thought a friend, as if he were lecturing schoolchildren. He was, like all good senior servants of Japan, duly modest in public comportment, but there was about Amaya's modesty a subtle prickliness. Dealing with him, hearing his cool and unsparing comments about his own society and observing his exceptional courtesy, visitors knew it was well not to ask any foolish questions. Those who opposed him on a given issue did so with a certain trepidation; they might enjoy superior political connections, but they could rarely argue as forcefully.

Amaya was aware of this and seemed to enjoy his special position. On a flight to Washington for a summit conference, sitting in the front cabin among his minister-peers—who would be busily studying position papers for the coming meeting—Amaya almost surely would be reading instead some esoteric book on twelfth-century China. The implication was clear:

The answers were not in those briefing papers, the answers were in the distant past. On the way back from the summit—while the others were preparing their reports—Amaya would sit there writing his haiku, a treasured Japanese form of poetry, each poem exactly seventeen syllables long. His haiku would be at once delicate and by implication political, perhaps describing his sorrow in seeing the decline of some great Western city.

He loved, while relaxing, to describe the relative merits and perils of ancient Venice and modern Japan, two mercantile shipping societies surviving in a hostile world by their wits. That was Amaya being Amaya, letting the others know he was a little different. When his daughter married, he did not, as was the custom, lay on a huge wedding to which all of his colleagues were invited. Instead only close friends of the two families were asked. Some of his senior colleagues considered it a snub. When he visited MITI bureaus in foreign cities, he did not, as did most Japanese officials, bring some small gift, offered more out of ritual than friendship. If he brought anything it was likely to be an inscribed book of his own poems. Among younger MITI officials, these books were greatly valued, for to them Amaya was almost a cult figure; they appreciated the fact that when they made their presentations he paid less attention to their place in the hierarchy than to the substance of their arguments.

The Japanese economy, Amaya recognized in the late sixties, was perched on something terribly volatile, the world price of oil. What was worse, its oil came from sources that were totally alien to Japan. Only Arab sheiks, Texas oilmen, and acts of God could determine the price of oil, Amaya liked to say, and they were all beyond Japanese control. As MITI's director of planning, he was asked in the late sixties by one of his superiors to study the energy situation, and the more he studied it, the more pessimistic he became. More and more countries, he decided, were coming into what he had called "the oil culture"; that is, they were making their economies, indeed their very way of life, dependent upon oil. He believed that sooner or later the price would explode, perhaps doubling or even quadrupling, and if that happened, it would devastate the Japanese economy, virtually unique in the developed world in that it resembled a colonial economy without colonies. The Japanese imported raw materials, negotiating masterfully to minimize the price, used a skilled but (by the standards of Western and developed nations) modestly paid work force to produce at home, and then exported finished goods with a fury at cut-rate prices. Thus any significant changes in the price of oil could throw a finely tuned system completely out of kilter. What was worrisome to Amaya was that in the late sixties and early seventies Japan was taking roughly 10 percent of the free world's oil; if his country continued at its current rate of growth, Amaya believed, it might soon be taking 20 percent. Thus in order to justify its rate of growth and pay for the immense amounts of energy it was now consuming, it would have to export more and more goods. To Amaya, there was the danger that this would make the Japanese economy, already close to being overheated, genuinely frenzied.

What was more, there was political hazard in all this. Amaya realized, though most of his countrymen did not, that Japan's success with its exports did not endear it to its Western trading partners, all of which seemed to be undergoing considerable stress in their industrial sectors and most of which were frustrated by their own inability to penetrate the Japanese market. If Japan pushed even harder with exports, then it was likely to cross the line between what was healthy for Japan economically and what was dangerous for Japan politically.

In short, Amaya concluded, Japan was becoming a hostage to oil. He believed that this was as perilous as a military miscalculation might have been in another age. Since there was only a limited supply of oil in the world, the price was bound to go up dramatically one day. It might happen overnight, he thought, a kind of oil shock. Amaya himself did not know the form of the shock, or what would trigger it, but he knew where the epicenter would be. The Muslim states of Iran, Saudi Arabia, Iraq, and Libya, in his view, either were hostile in culture and politics or, if friendly, had fragile governments. It was frightening to be dependent for one's industrial lifeblood on nations such as these. Therefore, in the late sixties, at just about the same time that Japan had arrived as a true member of the oil culture, Amaya resolved that it must start shifting its economy from the traditional heavy industries, which demanded so much oil, into the new high-technology industries, which used far less.

There was an additional reason for Amaya to propose this shift. The great surge in the Japanese economy had come during the fifties and sixties, when a considerable part of its competitive advantage was due to highly disciplined, inexpensive labor. That era was ending, however, as Japan became middle-class. The same dynamic that had functioned in the West was at work in Japan, no matter how hard the nation's fathers tried to control the economy and master inflation. The more successful it became, the more the standard of living went up and the more prosperous and better paid its workers became. That meant that there was a serious possibility that the very thing the Japanese had done to the West might now in turn be done to them by their neighbors, countries like Korea or Singapore, where the work force was even more disciplined, hungrier, and willing to labor for a good deal less. Much earlier, Amaya had handled the textile negotiations with the Americans. He had done that well, but he had learned a profound lesson by the time the session ended: Not only did America need protection from the Japanese, but the Japanese also needed protection from Taiwan and Singapore. He was a disciple of the English historian Arnold Toynbee, and this experience had strengthened Toynbee's influence on him. In the world of challenge and response, Japan could easily become vulnerable at the more primitive end of its economy to a nation like Korea.

By the seventies there were in fact considerable signs that the much-despised Koreans (for the Japanese, having colonized the Koreans, still regarded them as inferior) were about to make a major challenge in steel and shipbuilding. It would not be hard, Amaya thought, for the Koreans to mount a successful assault upon the Japanese in many of these smoke-stack industries. The true strength of Japan, faced with such a challenge from leaner, poorer neighbors, was in the educational level of its people, which was dramatically higher than that of its rivals' populations. The only abundant Japanese natural resource, in his own phrase, was the human brain. Japan's educational level—all the millions of dollars the nation had poured into its universities in order to mount a scientific and technological challenge to the West—translated directly into the difference between the old economy, a smokestack economy, and the new high-technology economy. The Koreans and others might be able to compete quite readily in steel and shipping and perhaps one day even in autos, but they would be far behind in the new world of computers and related industries. They simply lacked sufficient numbers of skilled scientists. Japan with its communal, state-guided capitalism would be able to funnel its most talented people into precisely the kind of education and jobs where they might do the nation the most good. That would be Amaya's mission.

Thus as early as 1969, Amaya started working on a report recommending that Japan switch emphasis from the old economy to the new one. He found it frightening that Japan, with its vulnerable economy, was emulating the far better supplied American one. America had the luxury of making economic mistakes; it could survive if critical sections of its economy became less and less productive. Japan lacked that luxury. In the late sixties Amaya did not think that the future oil shock would hit until some time in the early 1980s, but he wanted Japan to start making the transition as soon as possible. His report was finished in 1970 and published in 1971, some two years before the Yom Kippur War. He believed as he worked on it that the United States would be immune to the vagaries of the Middle East and the Arab changes in oil pricing that could so easily bring Japan to its knees. He regarded America as rich in domestic oil, and it did not occur to him that the economy that had been the very symbol of the oil culture could be hurt. What others had called the American century he believed was the oil century, and it had begun in America.

The nineteenth century, which Amaya thought of as the coal century, had created a highly stratified economic and social system. In the coal culture a few owners were rich, the multitudes of workers were poor, and there was little in the way of a middle class. Workers were not consumers; at best they were survivors. The goods they produced were heavy ones like steam engines, for example, that served industry, not—as in the oil culture—mass-produced goods that directly benefited and were used by consumers. What distinguished the oil age, in Amaya's opinion, was that the worker was also the consumer. The better he was paid, the more he consumed, and he gradually became a genuine participant in the economy, both economically and politically. The coal century was British, he believed, and it was better suited to the nature of British and European cultures with their sharp class divisions than it was to America's more meritocratic society. The oil culture was far better suited to America because it was designed for a society that considered itself free of class restraints. If Karl Marx had written his basic works after the age of Henry Ford, Amaya believed, he would have been forced to revise much of his thinking, for he had not conceived of an industrial system so rich and powerful that it generated affluence not just for the owners but for the workers as well. That was one of the things that distinguished the oil culture, the sheer richness of what that energy let loose. It simply created vastly more wealth, a wealth so great that it could be shared by ordinary people.

The first great figure of the oil culture, Amaya felt, was the original Henry Ford. Ford had not just designed the first mass car, but he had also pioneered in mass industrial production, and he had paid workers enough to permit them to enjoy the fruits of an economy they had once only served. Suddenly, thanks to oil, there was an explosion in the means of production. Factories now had the capacity to turn out goods on a mass scale, but these goods could not be sold unless the masses had the capacity to buy them. Amaya was always amused by the way other capitalists had turned on Henry Ford when he had decided to pay his workers the unheard-of sum of $5 a day. Yet, by so doing, Henry Ford begat his own consumers. That was revolutionary. For a long time, Amaya believed, the United States was alone in the oil culture. America's native richness had allowed it, for example, to bring the advantages of oil to agriculture while the rest of the world still plowed with draft animals. Now Americans not only had their vast and abundant plains, but they were able to mechanize the farming of those plains. The rest of the world was still working on tiny plots that could be handled by one man while America with its mechanized implements was creating larger and larger farms and greater and greater harvests. By the 1920s, 90 percent of the world's oil production and consumption was in the United States; the United States was leaping ahead of other nations, almost unaware of its newfound sources of power.

World War I, Amaya believed, brought a great increase in American world power because a war-ravaged Europe, still essentially mired in the coal age, had needed vast stores of American food and materiel. One reason for the Great Depression in America, Amaya decided, was that the oil culture had come so quickly that, in the beginning, production had vastly outstripped the capacity for consumption. A new middle class was gradually evolving in America, but it was still embryonic; its limited purchasing power was unable to keep pace with the relentless surge in productivity. Part of that surge had been taken care of during the war, when the Europeans had needed American goods, but in the postwar era, when production outpaced demand, prices collapsed and the Depression took place. That led, in turn, to Keynesian economics in America and to the New Deal. To Amaya, the rise of Franklin Roosevelt was the first substantial political result of the oil culture, the first evidence that a new mass economy had created a political system to represent itself. For Franklin Roosevelt was the candidate of the new forces. Elected largely by the working class, he became the mediator between traditional, narrower, more rigid American capitalism and the Keynesian capitalism of the oil culture. He was an old-fashioned Brahmin capitalist responding to changed political and economic realities, a man of an outmoded economic class making a deft lateral movement to embrace an ascendant class.

Until World War II, Amaya thought, no one, least of all the Americans, had truly realized the awesome extent of American mechanical and technological power, or how far it had left other nations behind. But with the war the Japanese, more than any other people, came to appreciate the full force of American might, what the oil culture unleashing its full technological fury could do. There had been those in Japan who even at the start of the war had warned their leaders against it. A group of bright young men from the aviation industry went to see Japan's powerful new warlords and asked not that they not go to war but that they wait twenty years or so, until Japan was better prepared. The Americans were caught asleep at Pearl Harbor, but within thirteen months, at the Battle of Midway, they were able to demonstrate their absolute superiority as an industrial society. No one could match their ability to mass-produce planes and ships. From then on the war, in Japanese eyes, was a tale of superior

American technology simply crushing the individual valor of the Japanese soldier. Like almost every Japanese of his generation, Amaya had a memory of the magnitude of American power, of the sky filled with planes, of endless tanks rolling across beaches, of ships in such numbers assaulting a Japanese shore that the ocean itself was obscured to those poor men awaiting their dismal fate.

He was a young second private at the end of the war, in his words the lowest of the low, stationed at a small city until then relatively untouched by American bombing, Hiroshima. It was a major military staging area for the South Pacific, and Amaya was among the thousands of troops preparing to defend against the American invasion of Okinawa. Though the propaganda ministries endlessly issued bulletins of brilliant Japanese victories, there was, of course, a more cynical version of the war's progress among returning veterans, and Amaya, like other Japanese, had not only heard the more pessimistic stories but had seen the swarms of American bombers that periodically darkened the sky over Japan. By 1945 the Americans flew at their pleasure, in daylight or darkness, virtually unopposed by defending Japanese aircraft. Just as he was about to be sent to Okinawa, which was one of the bloodiest battlegrounds of the war, the island fell. With that his regiment was moved out of Hiroshima, which, he later realized, almost surely saved his life. He was in the artillery, and the cannon that his crew serviced had been made in 1905, for the Russo-Japanese War. Although it doubtless had been of great value during those hostilities, the ensuing forty years had made it entirely obsolete. For one thing, it had to be pulled by six horses.

A few months later, when the war ended at last, the Americans finally began to land in Japan in full force, and for the Japanese, who had endured the physical hardships of the last few years, their arrival was a staggering sight. By the time the war was over there were very few cars and trucks in Japan, and those few that existed often got around by burning wood. Here now were the victors, a new and separate species of man with trucks and jeeps and boats as far as the eye could see. It was astonishing, young Amaya thought, that a nation could go through a war and still have so many jeeps and trucks. What, after all, about the ones that they had lost? Had Japan and Germany made no dent at all? It was not just that the Americans retained such military force, nor was it that they had so much food in a country where no one, not even the rich, had food. It was the aura about them that struck Amaya, their absolute confidence in themselves and what they were doing, even the way they walked, as if born to rule the world. In Japan the world had collapsed, not just the war effort but something critical and basic to the essence of Japanese existence, a belief in the worthiness of Japan's purpose. The Americans seemed to have everything and to know everything; by contrast everything that the Japanese had once believed in had been proved false. The Americans therefore were like gods to the Japanese, and Amaya, like most Japanese of his generation, was eager to lean as much as possible from this superior species. He wanted to learn their secrets, for surely a nation this powerful and this rich above all else had secrets.

That had led him to study America and to form his vision of the oil century, which others thought of as the American century. Many historians of technology, he thought, misunderstood the nature of what often happened with a given invention. The invention was important, but it had to take root in the right society, a society with an affinity for it. The automobile was a good example. The original inventions were mostly European (the early vocabulary—*automobile, garage, chauffeur*—was French), but America, unlike France, for example, had a seemingly unlimited source of cheap energy and a large population that needed automobiles. It was a huge land, with great distances to traverse; it had an immensely vital entrepreneurial class that was accustomed to trying to invent new machines and methods; it had ready capital to finance new inventions; and it had a labor force with a naturally egalitarian spirit that matched the more egalitarian nature of the new order. Given its size and the size of its market, America was well suited to become the first mass-production culture. Amaya privately believed that in the postwar world the new culture of oil would demand social and political systems with considerable flex. A totalitarian society like the Soviet Union would not be able to adapt as well, but America, far more pragmatic in both political and economic systems, would be able to adjust its society quite readily to the coming new riches.

For Amaya, America in the postwar years was like a nation living out the dreams of other, poorer nations. Everyone wanted to be like America, and it was not surprising that so many countries, Japan included, modeled their economies on the American one. The fifties and sixties, he observed, now from his vantage point at MITI, were the great flowering of the oil culture. In those years there was a flood of machines and inventions for the average American home—dishwashers, washing and drying machines for clothes, air conditioners. The Americans were even electrifying, he was astonished to learn, all sorts of unlikely kitchen tools, including can openers and knives, and, for their bathrooms, toothbrushes. Middle-class American families had two or three cars when wealthy Japanese had none. America in that moment seemed to be getting richer and richer, with more people buying more things, which meant that more people were making these things. It was, he thought, like a sun from which light and heat emanated all over the world. If there was any danger in this, Amaya decided, it was that the sources of energy were certain to diminish, the price bound to go up, even for the Americans. More than that, the Americans seemed to him to have reached the outer limits of inventing devices of use to the average citizen. Machines that opened cans and machines that polished shoes were different from heavy domestic machines like washers and dryers, they were less basic, less necessary. He began to believe that the oil culture might be entering its twilight. Still, Amaya did not ponder too long. By the early seventies he was too busy trying to get Japanese firms to shift their industrial force from energy-consuming industries to newer, less energy-dependent ones. It was not an easy process and it caused great dislocation, but gradually Japan began to pull back from aluminum and petrochemicals and to deemphasize shipping.

That America, the land inhabited by those men who had seemed like gods, might become vulnerable did not occur to him until, in the late seventies, the second oil shock hit. With that the Japanese suddenly made far more serious inroads into the American auto market than anyone had anticipated. More than anyone realized at the time, the American economy had been floating on cheap oil, and now the era of cheap oil was over. Amaya had been surprised by the collapse of the American auto industry. He knew that the Americans were exposed in the low end of the market because the Japanese had a basic price advantage. But this was something graver. He had heard from friends of his in the auto business that the once mighty American auto industry had become sloppy about quality. At first he had not believed it. Eventually he concluded that the Americans had become too successful for their own good. Almost as soon as the second oil shock struck, in 1979, the Japanese captured an incredibly large portion of the American auto market—some 25 percent. Soon after, it became the melancholy duty of Naohiro Amaya to negotiate with the Americans an agreement limiting the export of Japanese cars to America.

During the seventies, Amaya had come to feel that if Japanese auto imports to America stayed at 10 percent, things would be all right, but that if they went to 20 percent, there would be a major political reaction in America. Now they were at 30 percent, and America was in the grip of an industrial crisis. Clearly, though restrictions might anger the triumphant barons of Japan's auto industry, its success now threatened its cherished political relationship with its greatest trading partner and principal military protector. Amaya believed that Japan's economic success had outstripped its foreign policy. In one of his essays he had described how Japan after World War II had chosen to be a merchant rather than a samurai society by forfeiting a national defense. This idea enraged many of his contemporaries, who still liked to think of themselves as members of a samurai society and for whom the word "merchant" was still tainted. It could, wrote Amaya, remain a merchant society, "a rabbit in the jungle," protected completely by the United States, but in that case it had to be extremely sensitive to its defender's political moods. The alternative was to become a samurai nation again, which would entail a huge defense bill that could threaten much of its prosperity. He acknowledged that this was a tough decision, but Japan could not have it both ways. Restrictions were necessary.

He did not particularly look forward to the auto negotiations. He did not mind dealing with the Americans; there was a certain fascination in that kind of challenge. But if limits were to be set, persuading the leaders of Japan's auto industry to restrain their exports at the very moment of their greatest triumph was not going to be easy or pleasant. He was right about that; before the negotiations were over, Japanese journals and Japanese auto men were regularly calling him a whore for the Americans. Preparing for the meetings, he thought again of America. It had always been a blessed society, but, he decided somewhat ruefully, there was a danger in being too blessed. The Americans had adapted brilliantly to the new possibilities of the oil culture and to their new wealth, but he was not at all confident that they would do as well as their possibilities gradually began to diminish. The oil culture, with its easy affluence, was like an addiction. Americans had been rich for some sixty years, and several generations had become accustomed to prosperity. Affluence was ingrained in them, and their expectations were very high. They were not a people, Amaya reflected, who would readily respond to calls for new levels of personal sacrifice.

3.
DETROIT'S
BLEAK WINTER
OF 1982

It was the third bleak winter in a row. For many years prosperity had been viewed as a kind of birthright by most Americans, particularly those who were the beneficiaries of the auto industry. But now, in the cold early months of 1982, prosperity seemed a distant memory in Detroit and the state of Michigan, something come and then gone, perhaps irretrievably. It was now nearly three years since the day when, in the words of Lee Iacocca, Detroit's principal phrasemaker, the Shah left town.

The rest of the country was suffering from what was usually called a recession, but Detroit and most of the old industrial heartland of the Midwest were caught in an all-out depression. More than a quarter of a million autoworkers were unemployed, and the ripple effect of that throughout the region, in steel mills and glass and rubber factories, was immense. In thousands of Midwestern towns there was only one small factory making one tiny part for an automobile company; times were now hard for those factories and thus for those towns. In countless homes, male blue-collar workers, out of a job, watched in frustration as their wives went to work—for a quarter of what they themselves had once made at the factory—at a McDonald's or some other adjunct of the new American service economy. Steadily the grim distress spread out from Michigan, into Ohio and Illinois and Wisconsin.

The forecasts for auto production in the coming year steadily diminished. No one had expected 1982 to be a really good year, not like the great ones when ten or eleven million cars were built, the factories ran at capacity, two and three shifts, the union men complained about too much overtime, and the top executives of the companies drew their handsome salaries and then three times as much as their salaries in bonuses. But at the beginning of the year the auto men had hoped for a mild recovery. Possibly, they said, the figure might go back up to eight million. There was a lot of confident talk about things getting better. "Listen, girlie," said one of the executives of Cadillac, a particularly troubled company, to Maryann Keller, an astute and skeptical financial analyst on Wall Street, "it's ready to turn around, and it's going to be bigger than ever." He and others were privy to demographic studies which showed a lot of loyal Americans out there driving old models, very old models, which they were soon going to have to turn in. Soon it would swing around. It was the American way to turn in a four- or five-year-old car.

That boomer spirit, the creed of a boomer's city, where everything was going to get better because everything had in fact always gotten better, was needed more than ever because times were so mean. The huge Good-year sign on I-94 on the way in from Metro Airport, which announced how many cars had been built that year, was flashing anemic numbers. The sign had symbolized the city's power, energy, and immodesty, for the numbers increased even as the visitor drove by. It proclaimed the city's strength and vitality, hundreds and thousands and millions of cars rolling down huge assembly lines, the sign saying, in effect, "Look at us, look at our muscle, look at what we are building even as you sit on your tail riding in a car." It was easy to do the multiples: If the sign showed two million by the end of February, then a ten-million or eleven-million year was possible. But now the sign was a painful reproof. The numbers lagged farther and farther behind, reflecting the industry's hard times, a symbol not of strength but of shame. Perhaps 1982 would not even be a six-million year. Each week the local newspapers told of a decision to close, at least temporarily, some Ford or GM plant. By the end of February the Detroit papers, reporting on one of the city's most significant indexes, announced that the industry had a 107-day selling supply of new cars, twice the normal inventory. No one was buying. In many a town and small city, Ford, GM, and Chrysler dealers, normally pillars of their communities, were on the verge of closing down.

The entire American economy seemed out of whack. Interests rates were too high, fluctuating between 15 and 20 percent. Even the ordinary person now knew about interest rates and about money funds, and rather than pay 16 percent on an $8000 car, he was holding on to his car, patching here and there, and placing his money in an account where he could earn 12 percent. The difference between getting the interest instead of paying it might mean thousands of dollars a year for a family. What was truly worrying about Detroit's plight was that many previously steadfast customers now believed that there had been a breach of faith. The early Japanese inroads into the American market had come because Japan had made smaller, cheaper cars, but the industry's recent surveys were showing that many Americans now believed that the Japanese made better cars.

The Japanese, aided by the jump in the price of oil, had come in during the worst of times and captured 30 percent of the American market. That had stung not just the city's economy but its pride, for the men of Detroit believed not only that their own cars were the best in the world but also that the Japanese made shoddy, tinny ones. Japanese goods rattled and fell apart. Scratch the bodies of their cars, went the standing Detroit joke (even when the Japanese had been producing the best steel in the world for more than ten years), and you could still see the Budweiser labels.

Because at first the Japanese success was attributed to the fact that Japan made smaller, less expensive cars that consumed less gas, Detroit had been sure that when it offered its own small, energy-efficient cars, its customers would return. But that had not proved to be true; the Japanese had generated a surprising degree of loyalty among their American customers, and they were proving a good deal more difficult to dislodge than anyone expected. Indeed, the Japanese were doing so well that in the spring of 1981, fearing a strong protectionist reaction, they had reluctantly but voluntarily imposed a ceiling on their exports to the United States— 1.68 million cars a year. But even this restriction had not rescued Detroit. Americans had simply gone out and bought cars imported from other countries, most dispiriting of all, often favoring Volvos, Audis and BMWs to the traditional top-of-the-line American models.

Detroit was mortified that large numbers of Americans believed Japanese cars were of higher quality, so suddenly quality became a hot topic. American universities offered seminars that explained the Japanese method of manufacturing and management. Books about the apparently harmonious state of worker-management relations in Japan became best-sellers. In Japan countless international symposia were held at which Japanese managers and workers dutifully explained to their now shaken Western colleagues how they had achieved such a high level of quality. (The Japanese pride in this, that the industrial world was coming their way, was evident; it prompted a number of jokes. In one, a Frenchman, an American, and a Japanese are captured by a hostile tribe. All three are to be killed but are granted one last wish. The Frenchman asks to sing the "Marseillaise," and the Japanese asks to give his lecture on quality control one last time. It is the American's turn. His request is to be shot before the Japanese, so he will not have to listen to any more Japanese lectures on quality.)

Madison Avenue responded, devoting millions of dollars to commercials extolling the rising quality of American cars. Almost all of Ford's new advertising stressed quality—it was "Job One"—and for Chrysler there was Lee Iacocca himself saying that, well, yes, perhaps American cars might have slipped in quality in the past, but Detroit was rededicating itself to craftsmanship. Iacocca, heading Chrysler, now emerged into national prominence as both symbol and spokesman of the new Detroit, and thus of American's industrial regeneration. He was a gifted sloganeer. If you can buy a better car than his new Chrysler, he said, then buy it.

Chrysler nonetheless was hovering near bankruptcy. Iacocca said repeatedly that interest rates would have to come down to 12 percent for the company to survive. Only a huge government bailout had saved Chrysler two years earlier. That had been painful enough for Detroit purists, who not only believed in free enterprise but even saw themselves as the very embodiment of it. The idea that one of their own, one of the Big Three, had been forced to go to the government for a glorified welfare dole had shaken them mightily. Nor was Ford much more secure than Chrysler. By 1982 it had lost more than $1 billion in each of two consecutive years, and the forecasts for 1982 were still grim. There were those who thought that the very act of bailing out Chrysler might seriously weaken Ford, since Chrysler now would enjoy financial and labor benefits unavailable to Ford, and since potentially every Chrysler purchased was a Ford unpurchased. Not even the mighty GM was free from the profound malaise that had settled over a once omnipotent industry.

The terms from the feds had been very tough on Chrysler. The government had even demanded that Iacocca give up his company jet. That hurt. In the upper stratum of American business, particularly in Detroit, the company jet was the mark of executive power. The feds had argued that it was unbecoming for Iacocca to fly around the country in his private jet while Chrysler was being subsidized by the tax dollars of ordinary Americans. Iacocca, who loved the perks of the office even more than most Detroit executives, the private plane above all, had grudgingly sold the Chrysler plane, but shortly thereafter he managed to work out a complicated lease deal, the net result of which was that there was always a chartered jet on hand for Chrysler's top executives. Lee Iacocca was once again airborne. When a high Treasury official complained, saying that this was contrary to the spirit of the agreement and pointing out that the Secretary of the Treasury of the United States of America himself traveled by commercial jet, an Iacocca subordinate told the press that yes, it was all right for the Secretary to travel this way because he was not particularly well known, but Iacocca could not, since he had become such a public figure, a far greater public figure than the Secretary, certainly, and, given his fame, his security now demanded that he travel in a private plane. The jet stayed.

To the rage of most of the city's auto executives, the most successful industrialist in Detroit that season was a young man named William Agee, who headed Bendix, one of the great old-line parts suppliers. Agee was at heart a finance man, not an industrialist in the traditional sense, and he had made Bendix prosper in a down industrial economy by shrewdly selling off certain of its ancillary companies and by playing the market right. He had taken the proceeds, put them into the most conservative of financial accounts, and, benefiting from the stagnant industrial climate, made some $900 million. Bill Agee, said an angry Lee Iacocca, struggling to keep Chrysler alive, was not a manufacturer but a portfolio manager. Iacocca's anger at Agee was easy to understand. Chrysler remained afloat in 1980 and 1981, often meeting its payrolls by the barest of margins, in no small degree thanks to the force of Iacocca's personality and his sheer professional strength. The ledgers began to look a little better, but the company, a true industrial giant, was still living a hand-to-mouth existence. Iacocca had gone on national television and remarked to Tom Brokaw of NBC on the irony of his position, that it was more profitable for him as the head of a great manufacturing company to make money off money—to have Chrysler become, in effect, a financial house—than it was for him to actually to produce something.

That seemed to sum up the dilemma of industrial America in the early 1980s. In the first half of this century America had been the most dynamic and productive society in the world. Now, in the latter part of the century, its strengths were diminished. Manufacturing something, actually producing something, had become costly and difficult. The definition of quality had eroded badly. Except in the world of high technology, where national scientific excellence and American venture-capital skills could be translated into small, highly successful companies (which often used foreign plants for a good deal of the manufacturing), the actual making of goods had become a burden. Labor costs were high. Management had become bloated. Few of the men running industrial companies had spent very much time in the pit, working in factories, learning the process of manufacturing. The industrial base itself—America's machines and productive facilities—had gotten older. Nations just emerging into the industrial sphere, particularly those in Asia, were proving fierce and unrelenting competitors. Nor did American capitalism show its own much mercy. Profit margins in what were called mature companies were now predictably slim, when they existed at all, so Wall Street, wanting faster and bigger returns, sought them elsewhere, in new, more exciting companies—anywhere but in the old core American economy, the foundry that had once made America strong. Money could still be made there, but it was harder and harder to make it being productive in the classic sense. Rather, money shrewdly applied, money leveraged, could be used to beget money. Money could be put into money funds where it sat, making more money than could be earned if put into the blue-chip industrial stocks of yore.

The most successful people on Wall Street now were those called the arbs, from "arbitrage," the rapid-fire buying and selling of stocks in order to profit from price differences. A smart arb, working just ahead of a big merger, making the right call on who would be the winner, could in a matter of minutes make millions of dollars in an economy like this one, where production was less and less valuable. In a 1981 merger battle, DuPont took over Conoco, and roughly $7 billion changed hands among arbs, stockholders, lawyers, and security men. It was the famous instance, but there were a thousand smaller ones. Billions had been passed back and forth, the stock had gone up, millionaires had been made, but not a single extra barrel of oil had been produced. Soon the market became so volatile, the profits generated by raiders and merger hunters so great, that the tail on Wall Street was wagging the dog, and instead of arbs responding to mergers, some were actually initiating them, suggesting likely targets of opportunity to would-be raiders.

As a general rule, the people now making a lot of money were not producing things, and the people who were producing things were not making a lot of money. It was a dismaying equation for a nation once colossally productive, and a bitter pill for many companies, cut off from their past and unsure of their future. Some executives of big companies talked with excitement of America as the leader in the new service economy; others, from the industrial companies, were warier, and talked of the danger of an America that did laundry for the rest of the world, and where the main industry was the sale of franchised hamburgers. In Detroit that prophecy seemed real enough, for one measure of economic power was the ownership of sports teams—the Tigers had been owned by the Briggses, an old manufacturing family for whom the baseball park had been named, and the football team by William Clay Ford, Henry's brother—and in the early eighties the two newest owners, of the Tigers and the hockey Redwings, were pizza franchisers.

The men at the top of the Ford Motor Company were grimly aware of the seriousness of the company's position. The fall from grace had come so quickly and been so drastic they could have hardly have ignored it. In the late seventies, Ford, as in the past, had been the second most powerful industrial company in the country. Then, in the treacherous new world economy, the Ford leadership had bet wrong, it had made some terrible decisions. On the eve of the second oil crisis, for example, it had chosen to make big cars instead of small ones, and thus had been caught going the wrong way in a market that was reversing itself. Finally, under the most difficult conditions, it had been forced to spend billions to retool itself for new, small, not particularly profitable cars in an absurdly inflated economy.

It was a terrible time. Ford lost money not only if the inexpensive little cars did not sell but even when they did sell; by its own financial analyses, Ford lost perhaps as much as $400 a car for its Escorts. The cost of redoing nearly its entire line had hurt the company's financial position, contributing enormously to those two successive $1 billion annual losses. The Ford stock, which had averaged around 32 on the Dow Jones in 1978, had begun to fall with the crisis in Iran. In 1981 it had dropped to 16. At the same time the company's bank rating with both Moody's and Standard & Poor's declined. With Standard & Poor's it fell from AAA to AA in April 1980; in October of 1980 it fell again, to an A; and then in March 1982, in another humiliation for so proud and powerful a company, it was reduced to BBB. The company, in the words of one executive, was hemorrhaging badly. It might have gone bankrupt, or perhaps have been forced to merge with a foreign auto company or a domestic energy company, except for its highly profitable operations overseas, which in both years had helped offset the losses in North America. "We are actually a very healthy company," went the joke at Ford. "Most of our operations are doing quite well. We have only one little problem—North America." In belated response to the crisis, Ford had cut back its executive rolls, closed factories, spent billions tooling up to make better, more energy-efficient smaller cars. Now it was waiting.

There were hopes that the market might begin to turn around for Ford in 1982, and whenever there was a slight blip on the radar—perhaps an upturn after a program of rebates—it was seized on as the sign that the big turnaround was finally taking place, that the hundreds of thousands of good Americans, Ford buyers in the past, sons and daughters of Ford buyers, were finally turning in the tired, overaged cars that everyone knew they were driving, and coming home. But it didn't seem to be happening in 1982, and now the Ford people were talking about 1983 and some about 1984; those were the years when the company simply had to turn around, when the customers would reward Ford for the fortune it had spent on its new lines. The very survival of the Ford Motor Company was now at stake.

Keith Crain, publisher of an automotive trade journal, liked to say that in 1945, Henry Ford II, at the age of twenty-eight, had taken over the company in order to save it. It was then losing $1 million a day. Save it he had, said Crain, and now, thirty-seven years later, it was losing $3 million a day. Henry Ford II was in partial retirement, by the end of 1979 no longer chief executive officer and by 1980 no longer chairman of the board, but still active in the company. It seemed a reflection of the modern era that he now spent a good deal of his time in real estate deals. He was downsizing there, too. Unable to sell his immense home in Grosse Pointe for the $2 million he wanted, he was busy getting a variance from the city council so that he could raze the famous house and build one-family cluster houses on the land. The seventy-six-room house had been built in 1927 by Roy Chapin, the president of Hudson Motors, and Ford had bought it in 1956 for $400,000. He had lived there through two marriages (Cristina, by the terms of the divorce, had been allotted one hundred days in which to vacate it), but his third wife, Kathy, was underwhelmed and spoke of it as a "place that gave you the feeling you had to dress up for breakfast." The Grosse Pointe Farms council gave Ford its approval to build eighteen small houses on the eight acres, each to sell at about $300,000, a deal that might bring Ford some $3 million. At the same time he was also in the process of buying a house in Florida, because, he told friends, "I can't afford to die in Michigan—the taxes are too high."

He was still linked to the glory days by dint of his name and the fact that he owned his company and was not an employee. But he was worn out. He had been troubled by bad health, a messy divorce, and a bitter internal struggle with Iacocca, and was preparing to step aside. In 1982, *Forbes* magazine published a list of the country's four hundred richest men. Seven from Michigan were listed, and although his brother, William Clay Ford, made the list (a richer wife, no expensive divorces), Henry Ford did not. His personal worth was valued at only $80 million, *Forbes* pointed out, mostly in badly depressed Ford stock, worth only $23 a share. Had the survey been done in 1973, before the energy crisis changed the economy and when the stock was worth $66 a share, he would have made the list handily. Just recently at a party in Grosse Pointe, Henry Ford had run into a man named Norman Krandall, an unusually blunt Ford executive who was highly critical of recent company policies. He was particularly incensed at Ford's failure to reinvest in new products in the late seventies as the Japanese challenge had intensified. Krandall had recently done a paper entitled "The Decline of Ford's Market Share," a serious, pessimistic warning that he had reason to believe had never reached Henry Ford. So Krandall, who was thinking of retiring anyway, seized this opportunity to confront a boss he rather liked. The Ford Company, he told Ford, was not equipped to deal with the Japanese challenge. Not only was it doing poorly, he said, but it might not be able to hold its existing share in the future.

Krandall had suspected a short, testy answer, but instead Ford looked at him and agreed. "It may not be long," he said, "before we're selling not just cars but apples."

So much for industrial giants. Collapsing economies are hard even on the titans. Henry Ford was still a king in Detroit, though—Hank the Deuce, as he was popularly known—and the city's media still chronicled him as they might royalty. He bore the city's most famous name, he was a man of the present who was linked to the past, he always had something colorful to say, and his marital escapades, curricular and extracurricular, had brought a little excitement to the world of heavy industry, something that the gray men of GM rarely provided. Still, he was clearly phasing himself out. Fortunately for the city, there was a new media star, Iacocca, by then the sworn enemy of Henry Ford. Iacocca had always displayed a particular genius for focusing attention on himself. Now he appeared on the verge of becoming something of a national hero while standing in the ashes of a dying company. The worse Detroit's condition became, the more quotable he became, phrases issuing from his lips, as David E. Davis put it, as if a Xerox machine were always at the ready.

But it was a city in decline, and cities in decline do not easily create heroes. Where once Detroit had spawned hard men of brute strength and unlimited confidence both in themselves and in the industry, now it produced a more pallid generation of leaders, men who began not as tinkerers in converted garages but as calculators in accounting offices, disciples of the bottom line. They gave off no feel for product. It was hard to imagine them fooling with an engine or even changing a tire. They gave off little sense of power, either. They had made it up the executive ladder by playing it safe, and once they had arrived at the top that caution was palpable in their personalities.

The old Detroit had had a certain swagger to it. Its leaders thought of themselves as big men doing a big job, and they dealt on a scale that dwarfed all other enterprise in America. When, in the immediate postwar era, someone at Chrysler had designed a smaller, low-slung car, K. T. Keller, the company's top executive, had mocked it. "Chrysler builds cars to sit in," he said, "not to piss over." It had been a city filled with men whose strength was that they could always hear the truth in their own voices. They were passionate men, who loved what they did, loved the process of making things. "There is in manufacturing," Walter Chrysler, one of the city's great industrialists, once wrote, "a creative job that only poets are supposed to know. Someday I'd like to show a poet how it feels to design and build a railroad locomotive."

They were a product of a singularly successful era. They looked down not only on the government and on foreign companies but on other American businesses as well. They believed that if other businessmen were as true to their calling as the auto men were to theirs, then they would be just as prosperous. They had the special confidence of men who had been successful for so long, whose success was measured in such large sums, and whose product was so important that beside them all else paled. In the years after World War II, as America became the world's first great middle-class society, the auto became the litmus test of middle-class status. These men saw this success not as something larger than themselves, something societal of which they had been among the principal beneficiaries, but rather as something they themselves had wrought. Once, in the early Eisenhower years, C. D. Jackson, the former publisher of *Fortune* then on loan to the Eisenhower circle, had returned to New York to lunch with his former colleagues. One editor asked him about Charles Wilson—"Engine Charley"—the General Motors president who had become the administration's Defense Secretary and who was thought to have said that what was good for GM was good for the country. What he really said was that what was good for the country was good for GM, and vice versa.

C. D. Jackson replied, "There is a certain special stupidity and narrowness that exists in many of the more successful businessmen in this country, more so in the Midwest than other places, and nowhere else so much as in Detroit, and Charley Wilson is a perfect example. He knows one thing, and that one thing has worked quite well for him, and because it has worked he thinks he knows everything else, and then you meet him and he knows so little about anything else that you begin to wonder whether in fact he knows anything at all about the one subject he's supposed to know so much about."

That arrogance and confidence was long gone from Detroit. The city, now on hard times, felt betrayed, as if fellow Americans, instead of appreciating its labors and sympathizing with it for the overnight failure of its truths, were now blaming it for everything that had gone wrong in the economy. Detroit dinner parties at the highest level were no longer what they used to be. Before, when the very powerful had congregated, these parties had been performances where rich, egocentric men, enjoying their might, had regally patronized those around them. In those days men like GM's Ed Cole would hold forth for an entire evening on their favorite topic—in Cole's case an invention called the flying wing, an airplane he was designing, which would move an entire combat division to a battle station. Who, at the end of one of Ed Cole's loving descriptions of his coming military breakthrough, would dare disagree and say that it would never see battle?

Henry Ford II had dominated many a dinner, although he was more sedate and careful in Detroit than he was in New York. Other guests would watch him, sometimes made uneasy by how quiet he seemed, in contrast to his reputation, though he could, late in the evening, restless and finally ready to assert his presence, turn to some intruder who had drawn his anger and say, "You're full of shit," ending all argument. There was also Lynn Townsend of Chrysler, perhaps having had one drink more than prescribed, going around the table and taking pleasure in describing in detail the deficiencies of his guests, both physical and mental. All of this was done in great good humor, of course, so that no matter what Lynn said, everyone laughed, and no one got up to describe Lynn's physical or intellectual limitations.

Slowly, as the industry had changed, the social atmosphere had changed too. The new titans were men who could read a complicated financial statement, deal with government, and handle the company's lawyers. Men like that did not swagger. Dinner parties in the early eighties were still done the old way, highly stratified according to level and company, with little cross-pollination; Ford ate with Ford, Chrysler with Chrysler, GM with GM. A dinner party would still include at least one person from a level above the host and one from the level below, a requirement of Detroit's special caste system. (Experts believed they could read the pecking order of the men without knowing their titles, just by gauging the level of supplication at which the wives operated; they were as involved in the caste system as the men.) Those dinner parties had never been about food or social mixing in the old-fashioned sense; they had always been about career, about stroking and being stroked.

But now they were less fun. The men from the peripheral businesses, the suppliers, for example, whose presence at the parties had barely been tolerated, no longer were so eager to attend, for there was less pleasure in going. There was a growing anger, and the evenings were more likely than not to go sour. The car men intoned a lament: They had been forsaken by their customers, who had no sense of loyalty; betrayed by their government, from which they felt alienated; undercut by the Japanese, whose skills few of them still would accept, claiming that the Japanese were good only at fit-and-finish (tight doors and good paint jobs). The lament swelled: the Arabs, the workers, Ralph Nader. They were like men of true faith whose god had suddenly failed them.

Despite the defiant talk, arrogance was harder to carry off. In 1982 a man named Arvid Jouppi, a leading analyst in Detroit, a man who tried to explain Wall Street to auto men and auto men to Wall Street, went to the Country Club of Detroit in Grosse Pointe where he spotted one of the top advertising executives in town, a man who dealt almost exclusively with the auto industry. Jouppi asked him how things were going.

"Never better, Arvid," the executive had answered, "never better."

"That's amazing," Jouppi said. "It's so hard on everyone else."

"Oh, it's hard on me too. Economically, very hard," the man had answered. "But it's wonderful too. Wonderful psychologically, I'd say. For the first time in my life, I go in to meet with these car people, and they don't treat me like crap."

Throughout the city were men who had been staggered by so abrupt an end to so successful an era. Some in the upper and middle managerial levels had held on to their jobs but for the moment at least had lost something almost as precious, their bonuses, which had often been twice the size of their regular salaries and upon which they had counted for the lavish style of living to which they had become accustomed. Others, however, had lost their jobs, something that would have been almost unthinkable in the Detroit of the past. They had been fired in one of the drastic house-cleanings that all of the companies now had to go through. The term for what was happening was "cutting back fixed costs." At Ford, for example, $4 billion a year was cut from fixed costs, most of it from closing plants and laying off workers, some of it in management salaries. These executives, soon departed, became statistics that other executives would point to with pride during labor negotiations as proof that they were being tough not only with labor but with their very own, with white-collar workers.

For a time those who had been severed went to their usual haunts, the Dearborn Country Club, the Birmingham Country Club. They accepted dinner invitations from old friends just as they had in the past. But it was awkward now at social gatherings, as if they embarrassed everyone by their presence. They soon sensed it would be better if they simply disappeared. They stopped going to the country clubs. They began to turn down dinner invitations, which was not hard, because there were fewer and fewer invitations anyway. They tried putting their houses up for sale, but the market, they promptly learned, was very soft. The houses did not move. There were not a lot of middle-level executives moving to Detroit and buying expensive houses.

It was now a city of men, whether fired or not, who had lost their confidence. Their world had once been founded on certitudes. The ethic had been simple and straightforward enough: All they had to do was wait their turn, as those before them had waited theirs, succeed as those before them had succeeded, and they too would be duly rewarded. Sometimes when they talked among themselves now, they acknowledged that during the good times, those wonderful, bountiful years from the early fifties to the first oil embargo, they had never really known how good they had had it. In those days, for example, Ford had faced only two problems—labor and GM. Labor had not been that hard. After an ugly strike or two, the postwar managements of the different companies had evolved a policy of bringing labor in, making it in effect a junior partner, granting much of its wage demands and passing on the additional labor costs to the customer.

Ford's General Motors problem had seemed more difficult. In an industry where scale of operation was ever more important, where bigger meant cheaper, which in turn meant greater profits, GM was the new American industrial colossus. If it decided to keep prices down, even though this meant minimizing profits, then Ford and Chrysler were immediately in jeopardy. GM had cast a huge shadow over its competitors. One of Ralph Nader's young staff people had once asked Henry Ford II what it was like competing against General Motors, and Ford had answered, "Like trying to screw an elephant." But even the power of GM was limited; the Justice Department had always been there, hovering off to the side, making sure that GM did not put Ford or Chrysler out of business. GM certainly could have cut its prices in those years, and the burden would not have been on itself but rather on Ford and Chrysler, but it did not, and so it grew ever more prosperous, and Ford and Chrysler survived.

That was the era now viewed as a golden time. America was rich, the first truly middle-class society in the world, and the rest of the world was still poor. Everyone seemed hungry for cars. There was virtually no foreign competition. The auto industry had been in effect an American industry, a protected industry (too expensive for would-be domestic competitors to enter), in the wealthiest country in the world. There had been warnings about the danger of monopoly, mostly from liberal academics, but one of the more telling had come from the head of the smallest competitor, George Romney, the president of American Motors. Romney was a maverick in American business. Because of the shakiness of his own company, Romney had an early glimpse of what GM's power was doing to the rest of the industry. Because it was so large and so strong, it could afford to sign handsome contracts with the United Auto Workers, contracts that seemed good for both GM and the union. Perhaps GM's margin of profit would go down a little, but it was still doing so much volume that the new labor contracts, in the short run at least, were worth it. The real burden of these contracts fell not on GM but on the weaker companies, which were eventually forced to accept the same terms and were soon working on ever narrower margins.

Clearly, Romney at American Motors was the most vulnerable, but he visualized a day when Chrysler and perhaps even mighty Ford would have problems as their margin of profit continued to decline. The entire industry, he believed, was unconsciously becoming more monopolistic and, as such, less competitive and innovative, for in a monopoly there is no pressure to innovate.

In the late fifties Romney had been a forceful advocate of breaking up GM. That, he believed, would make everyone leaner and more competitive. In 1957 he went before the Kefauver Senate committee on monopolies. Before he testified he was summoned to the Ford headquarters by Henry Ford and Ernie Breech, the chairman of the company, who were nervous about what he was going to say and wanted to get some idea of his thrust. Romney explained what he wanted: the breaking up of GM and perhaps even Ford.

"But that would just make the competition tougher," Ford had said. "If you broke up GM the rest of us would suffer."

"That's exactly what I mean," Romney had said.

"Listen, I think it's tough enough the way it is—it's a damn hard dollar," Ford had answered.

From there Romney had gone to see Harlow Curtice, the head of GM.

"Why don't you split up GM?" Romney had suggested.

"Who the hell would that help?" Curtice had asked.

"Everyone but you, Harlow," Romney had said, "but you'd be one hell of a hero."

Curtice declined the chance to be a hero of that particular order. Romney soon became a pariah among his peers, and GM became bigger than ever. But in those days of the fifties and sixties no one complained very much, because everyone seemed to be benefiting. The weaknesses of the system, the inherent dangers of being a part of a domestic monopoly in an industry open to other countries, had not yet revealed themselves. So, while other areas of the American economy remained competitive, no one challenged the auto industry until the full-scale assault of the Japanese in the seventies. When it finally came, the extent of American vulnerability surprised even those who had been critical. Years later, Hal Sperlich, possibly the most talented product man of his generation in Detroit, said that the earlier era was marked by what was virtually an illusion of competition and hard work but in truth was a competition within a protected zone, finally more about the changing of hemlines than anything else. He compared the old days to being the best tennis players in a pleasant suburban country club, aware that everyone else in the club watched their fast, smooth Sunday game. "And then one day," he said, speaking of the arrival of the Japanese, "Bjorn Borg and John McEnroe walked on the court."

Soon it became clear that a basic theorem held true: The larger the American industry (steel, auto), the less prepared it was for economic rivalry. American workers had not realized that as the highest-paid workers in the world, they might be at a disadvantage in competing with workers in other nations who were hungrier, more grateful for their jobs, more willing to accept authority and to work longer hours for much lower pay. To American labor, Japanese unions often seemed to be extensions of management. What Japanese working people expected and considered themselves entitled to as a life-style—a term that had only recently entered the American vocabulary—was strikingly limited, resembling more closely the expectations of American workers in the thirties than those of present-day Americans. Of the simplicity of the Japanese worker's life, of his willingness to work hard and save much of what he made, Paul McCracken, the University of Michigan economist, had said, "If John Calvin came back to earth, the nation he would feel most comfortable in would be Japan, that is where his real children would be."

That was what was most ominous about the Japanese challenge in autos. To some it was more than just a growing imbalance in auto sales and a mounting trade deficit. They feared it might reflect an imbalance of values between the two societies, one poor but careful with its resources, the other rich and blessed and increasingly careless with its vast resources—the conflict, in sum, between the culture of adversity and the culture of affluence.

Thus the bad news on the Goodyear sign in Detroit, which continued to proclaim disastrous auto production figures for 1982, might be even worse than it seemed. It might mean not only that the Japanese made better autos, that they had newer plants, that the relationship between workers and managers was better, but that Japanese society, with its greater harmony, its greater belief and discipline in basic education, its more limited personal freedoms, was better prepared for the coming century. That was the real crisis, the grimmer one that hung over America.

By 1982 the sheer magnitude of this crisis had become evident to many. This was not some minor cyclical downturn but in fact might mark the beginning of the end of a historical era. Since the war, any difficulties in Detroit had been mercifully short-lived. A company might have brought out the wrong car in the wrong year and seen sales dive. Or the American consumer for a variety of economic and political reasons might have held back awhile on buying cars. People still talked about how terrible a year 1958 had been, because of Sputnik; Ford sales had dropped from 1.88 million units to 1.21. Just a bad year, everyone agreed, the first truly bad one in the postwar era. A hot car the next year, it was always said, would bring you right back. Sure enough, in 1959 sales had climbed all the way up again. But this crisis was different. There was a permanence about what was happening. It reflected basic changes in the nature of work and in the nature of the world economy. The time when the Big Three had something close to a global monopoly was over. No longer could Ford and Chrysler simply wait for GM to set the price so that they could set theirs, all under the attentive eye of a benign Justice Department that wanted no one to go out of business. In the new world economy the Americans were pursued by the Japanese who were pursued by the Koreans who were pursued by Hong Kong and Singapore.

There were other, less visible signs of this fundamental change. That Japanese cars were flooding the American market was bad enough. But now Detroit was putting more and more Japanese and foreign *parts* under American hoods, which meant that hundreds of thousands of other jobs were quietly departing the country, part of an invisible erosion of the core economy. In some places manual workers on traditional assembly lines were being replaced by what Harley Shaiken, a knowledgeable professor at MIT and himself a former worker on the GM line, called "superautomation." Superautomation, as he defined it, meant the coming of robots run by highly computerized control systems. Throughout this century, he pointed out, one of the most firmly held tenets of America's broad-based and wildly successful capitalism was that high profitability was tied to broad employment. Workers eventually became consumers. But the coming of superautomation, Shaiken believed, was likely to sever that link.

America was in transition from the old economy, which was focused on heavy industry, to the new economy, which was pointed toward high technology. The old American economy created jobs and wealth; the wealth was broadly based, shared among workers who were the best-paid in the world and the owners. The new economy was more brilliant, more stimulating for those who bet on themselves and won. It was filled with opportunities for talented, restless scientists to break away from their present companies, work night and day for three or four years on a certain small aspect of technology, and, if successful, to reap immense rewards, as would those venture capitalists who had been shrewd enough to back them. Both the scientists and the venture capitalists were likely to become rich overnight, but the inventions rarely created much in the way of jobs, or at least well-paying jobs. If there was a factory at all, it was likely to be small, nonunion, and, more often than not, overseas.

By 1982, Shaiken had concluded that the auto executives no longer believed that they could compete with the Japanese in the old way. What they were trying to do, he believed, was create a different kind of auto industry, one that attained the same level of profitability through far lower levels of employment. Shaiken thought that the companies would make rising numbers of joint-production deals with the Japanese and the Koreans in the small-car lines, and that even with the larger cars an ever-growing percentage of parts would be made overseas. The portion of the manufacturing process that remained in America would be increasingly robotized. There was a danger, he and others felt, that the auto companies, almost without realizing it, were on their way to becoming marketing rather than manufacturing companies. A year later Shaiken went to a conference on productivity. There he heard an executive from RCA get up and say that RCA was proud to announce that it could now manufacture a television tube which was better and cheaper than anything Sony could produce. Shaiken was sitting in the audience half asleep when he heard the statement, and it brought him alive—that was really news. But even as he came alert, he realized that the executive was talking about RCA *Taiwan*, not RCA Indiana. To RCA it might be the same, but to the communities served by the company it was not. The effect of all this intrinsic change, Shaiken believed, was crushing to the general Middle Atlantic region. He saw a once-prosperous and vibrant heartland slowly turning into a vast new Appalachia, a tired region with a shrinking tax base, a withering school system, and diminishing hopes.

Nowhere was the impact of these changes more obvious than in Michigan. In 1982 the official federal unemployment statistics placed the rate at about 16 percent compared to the national average of 9 percent. But in Detroit most people thought the rate was closer to 20 percent and in some communities as high as 25 percent. The reason was that the federal statisticians did not count the unemployed once their benefit checks ran out. They disappeared from the statistics. Sometimes they disappeared from Michigan itself, although the pain and humiliation of being jobless did not disappear.

One of the great migratory movements in American history had brought rural Appalachian whites and poor Southern blacks to Detroit in hopes of industrial jobs. They had come to Detroit City, as it was known to them, from the hamlets of the South, lured by the promise of regular work and by paychecks that seemed the bounty of rich men. During boom periods, employers had gone through small Southern towns handing out just enough money to buy a one-way bus or train ticket to Detroit or some other Midwestern industrial city. After World War II, as Southern plantation owners mechanized (with the aid of federal subsidies) and forced the now unwanted blacks off their spreads, the jobless had come in even greater numbers.

Now, in the erosion of the great American industrial core, the workers if not the managers had an intuitive sense that there was something indelible about the decline, and that the region would never again be what it had been, so by 1982 a new migration was well underway. It was sending hundreds of thousands of Americans, white and black, from the Great Lakes region to the booming, energy-dominated economy of the Southwest. For although the skyrocketing of energy prices had helped undermine the industrial base of America, it had made the business of oil and all its by-product industries suddenly much more successful than ever. In 1982 the out-of-town papers that sold best in Detroit were the two Houston papers, the *Post* and the *Chronicle*, bought eagerly by men desperate to study the help-wanted columns. One unemployed auto executive, seeking to keep himself afloat financially, started driving to Houston each weekend; there, on Saturday night, he loaded up his small truck with copies of the Sunday papers and then drove all night back to Detroit in order to get there first and sell his papers at highly inflated rates. The two Detroit newspapers, both of which were losing millions of dollars, took a certain malicious pleasure in featuring articles about rising crime and unemployment in Houston. A Detroit magazine ran an article listing all the things wrong with the quality of life in Houston. It made no difference. Houston and the Southwest, surging on a brief energy boom, held out a hope that the Great Lakes region no longer did.

The new migratory pattern reversed the old. One member of a family would go to Texas looking for a job on a rig. If he found one, he took the simplest housing available, sometimes sharing a trailer home with another worker. Soon he called back to Detroit, and another male member of the extended family arrived. If things worked out, women and children followed. Robert Teeter, a Michigan-based pollster for Republican candidates, was advising a group of Texas politicians about a forthcoming election. The one thing that puzzled him was the constant references to the "black-tag vote." Which way, the politicians kept asking, would the black-tag people vote? Who, Teeter wondered, were the black-tag people? Were they blacks? Were they Vietnamese immigrants? Were they some right-wing faction? Finally he asked one of the Texans. "Oh, them," the Texan answered, "they're your people from Detroit—you know, they come down here with those black Michigan license plates on their cars, and their pro-labor ways, and we don't have any fix at all on how they're going to affect our politics."

Back in Michigan, the harsh, ugly signs of a depression were everywhere. Both the city and the state had nearly gone bankrupt. Perched precariously on the precipice of fiscal collapse, almost unable to keep its universities open, the state had been rescued by, of all people, the Japanese. It was the ultimate humiliation. A consortium of five Japanese banks had loaned Michigan $500 million to get through the fiscal crisis. Since the new Michigan public relations motto, designed to inject hope into a depressed population, was "Say yes to Michigan" (it was used in television commercials showing fresh-faced young people eager to go to work), an assistant to the assistant governor, George Weeks, said that the new motto should be "Say yen to Michigan." In countless homes, once-solid wage earners were desperate for jobs. One small company, looking for a glorified messenger boy, decided to put an ad in the local paper. It never got around to it: word of mouth spread through town, and on a Monday morning some two hundred men had shown up at the office applying for a job as yet unlisted. When a department store needing two hundred workers was ready to open, it too never had to advertise. Somehow the word got out that the company was ready to process applications, and eighteen hundred people showed up. There was pain in daily existence as the lives of thousands of citizens collapsed. There were more broken homes, households where the men could no longer face the fact that they had failed as providers and simply left. Social welfare offices reported a dramatic climb in cases of wife and child beating. There was a major increase in suicides. The school system printed up small guide books for students whose parents were unemployed, telling them how to handle certain situations, warning them their fathers were likely to be shorter of temper.

In many areas of the Midwest the pawnshops were doing a brisk business, but oddly enough this was not true in Detroit. One reason, a pawnshop owner said, was that by this time almost everything that could be pawned in working-class houses had already been turned in. What was particularly ominous in a city of industrial craftsmen, he added, was the number of skilled craftsmen who were pawning their most precious professional possession, their tool kits. These kits, worth as much as $2000 each, were the key to the livelihood of each man pawning one, so turning one in was the ultimate act of despair. In normal times, said one large pawnbroker, he might get two or three kits a month; now he was getting twenty or more. It was a sign, he added, of how mean the times were. A craftsman who pawned his tool kit was a man beyond hope.

Everywhere one saw signs of decay in a city that once prided itself on its grandeur. Its early citizens had envisioned Detroit on a majestic scale. The thoroughfares would reflect nothing less than Paris, handsome boulevards radiating from the center of the city like giant spokes. Along them huge ornate buildings were constructed, some residential, some elegantly overwrought factories, monuments as much to the men who made them as to the products being manufactured. For fifty years some of them had stood, symbols of the city and the industry's permanence. Now many were empty, the windows smashed, the parking lots deserted or used as centers for late-night drug action. The great thoroughfares were now pitted with massive potholes the city was too poor to repair, and frustrated people penned angry letters to the local papers. The auto industry, wrote one irate soul, would begin to pick up soon if enough Detroit citizens broke their cars in the potholes of the city's streets. Wrote another: "Were we bombed on the east side? Did I miss a shelling on East Seven Mile Road between VanDyke and Kelly? Those aren't potholes. They're more like shell craters." The streets were not safe, for the crime in Detroit was as great as or greater than that of any major city, and citizens driving short distances within the city locked their car doors and rolled up their windows in transit. The great downtown department store, Hudson's, now part of a large national chain, announced that it would close. The downtown Hudson's had embodied the city's splendid past; the best people had come in from Grosse Pointe and bought the best goods there rather than go to New York for them, a reflection of stubborn Midwestern pride. Shopping at Hudson's on Saturday had been a tradition, not just in Detroit but in all the surrounding Michigan cities. For there were no branch stores then, no suburban malls, to lure business away from center cities. A trip to Hudson's was an event: Everyone in the family dressed up; there would be lunch in the store's fine restaurant. In 1953, at the beginning of the

Eisenhower era and the glory years of the auto industry, Hudson's had done $153 million in retail sales; in 1981 the downtown Hudson's had done only $44 million—a figure, if adjusted for inflation, about 6 percent of the 1953 total. Much of the merchandise was chained to the counters, and the better-quality goods offered by the store were now in the plusher, safer suburban branches. The announcement that it would close seemed to mark the end of an era. For after the race riots of 1967, the city had changed with a finality. The whites had accelerated their flight to the suburbs, taking stores, restaurants, law offices, and banks with them. The downtown had become a crater, a place entered warily by workers every morning and left in the evening as quickly as possible. Unsuspecting visitors were warned against staying at hotels bearing once-proud names, for reasons of security.

Nothing seemed to go right for the city's fathers. Their attempts to boost Detroit often went sour. The Super Bowl, an athletic extravaganza of considerable national importance, was secured for the new domed stadium in nearby Pontiac, in no small part because the car advertisers had considerable leverage in the world of television, which was of course the world of advertising. Having the Super Bowl in Detroit was considered a coup, a sign that the city was not yet defeated, that it would rise again. But the assembled sporting press, accustomed to having lush expense-account midwinter trips to New Orleans or Miami, arrived in Detroit in a foul mood. In print and on the air they complained about the city, the weather, the restaurants, the crime, the lack of easy access to the pleasures of flesh. One writer wrote that the first thing that Detroiters did for a good time, when they were able to afford it, was leave town. Others unkindly pointed out that much of the advertising done during the Super Bowl telecasts was for Japanese cars. Perhaps the unkindest cut of all came from Herb Caen, a nationally known columnist from San Francisco, who said that the city's futuristic Renaissance Center, the personal pride of Henry Ford II, emblematic of the city's coming spiritual renewal, in fact looked like the world's largest cappuccino machine.

It was, of course, not just Detroit that was mortal. The entire industrial heartland was in trouble. Throughout the Midwest once-great companies like International Harvester were on the brink of bankruptcy. The steel industry was in dreadful shape. Driving along the Monongahela River in Pittsburgh, a visitor could see once-mighty steel mills now cold and silent. On the roofs of their buildings were painted huge for-rent signs with phone numbers on them, in case anyone wanted to rent a steel mill. The steel business, even more than the auto business, was suffering dreadfully, unable to compete with new, more modern foreign companies which were always subsidized by the parent government. U.S. Steel, once one of the most powerful and arrogant of American companies, now hoping to become less of a steel company, hoping in fact simply to survive, had moved to merge with Marathon Oil. Only a partnership with a rich oil company, its executives believed, would offer it any kind of future. Who otherwise would buy stock in U.S. Steel, an ailing company in a moribund industry that could no longer compete?

For the foundry of the nation was sick. The factories were old. The cost of building new plants and adding new technology had, by inflation, grown so great that few companies in mature industries dared take the risk. It was easier to merge with existing companies than actually invest money and build something to compete in the difficult new world order. Management was topheavy and soft. Managers groused about the work force (privately but not publicly, since management was trying to win concessions from labor in delicate negotiations that would reverse the gains of the last forty-five years); labor today, said management, was less diligent, less committed to the idea of work than the old work force, the children of the great waves of the European immigration. The workers in turn complained bitterly about executive salaries, bonuses, and perks. There was widespread agreement that something terrible had happened to the old-fashioned American work ethic, although everyone seemed to blame everyone else.

Everyone had his own scapegoat—the Japanese, the government, the Arabs, Wall Street. No one seemed to accept any responsibility for any actions that might have sapped the country's industrial strength. It was as if the country's affluence had come so easily and stayed so long that no one was prepared for an era of diminishing possibilities. Now, it seemed to management, the government, in contrast to the governments of other industrial nations, was committed not to helping basic industries but to monitoring and hectoring them. That in itself was a sure sign of a nation's reaching middle-class status; a poorer nation was grateful for any jobs that would help its people to achieve a minimally acceptable standard of living, while a society like America's, with its governmental regulatory agencies, its innumerable citizens' groups, took its material success for granted.

"What we never understood about that era," said Irving Shapiro, the head of DuPont and one of the most respected businessmen in the country, "because we were all busy working so hard and proud of ourselves for how well we were doing, was how easy it was to make money then." The postwar years, the immense material strength and physical might, two generations of unrivaled prosperity—it all had lulled America into thinking it had attained an economic utopia, a kind of guaranteed national prosperity, like a concession won in some marathon bargaining session with God, a guaranteed annual increase in the standard of living. In those few postwar decades, America had taken a temporary historical accident and construed it as a permanent condition. Then, as if overnight, it had all started unraveling. "In just twenty-five years," said Felix Rohatyn, the financier and social critic, "we have gone from the American century to the American crisis. That is an astonishing turnaround—perhaps the shortest parabola in history."

PART
TWO

PART
TWO

4.
THE FOUNDER

Late in the life of the first Henry Ford a boy named John Dahlinger, who more than likely was Ford's illegitimate son, had a discussion with the old man about education and found himself frustrated by Ford's very narrow view of what schooling should be. "But sir," Dahlinger told Ford, "these are different times— this is the modern age, and—" Ford cut him off. "Young man," he said, "I invented the modern age."

The American century had indeed begun in Detroit, created by a man of simple agrarian principles. His father, an Irish immigrant, had arrived in America almost penniless, bringing with him only his hand tools. To William Ford the greatest opportunity that America offered was the chance for an ordinary man of ordinary means to buy and own land, and he was appalled when his own son proved to be restless with such good fortune and unwilling to work the family soil. Like his father, Ford started with scarcely a dollar in his pocket. When he was working on his first car, he held two jobs, one to support his family, the other to earn enough money to buy the metal and parts he needed for his prototype. When he died in 1946 his worth was placed at $600 million. Of his most famous car, the Model T, he sold 15,456,868. Mass production, he once said, was "the new messiah," and indeed it was almost God to him. When he began producing the Model T, it took twelve and a half hours to make one car. His dream was to make one car every minute. It took him only twelve years to achieve that goal, and five years after that, in 1925, he was making one every ten seconds. His name was attached not just to cars but to a way of life, and it became a verb—"to fordize" meant to standardize a product and manufacture it by mass means at a price so low that the common man could afford to buy it. Though his name is primarily associated with the world of the auto, his true genius lay in mass production. He came to love his factory more than his car; he would spare no expense to modernize his plant, but he resisted virtually every attempt to change the Model T until he—and the car—were overtaken by younger, more entrepreneurial competitors making better autos. Only then, slightly embittered toward the customers who were deserting him for General Motors, did he change.

When he began production, automobiles had been for the rich. Woodrow Wilson had even complained about them as symbols of the upper class flaunting its money. The best chauffeurs, observed the local weekly *Detroit Saturday Night* in 1909, came from "the servant class." They could be counted on, the paper said, to know "exactly what is expected of them by their masters." Henry Ford wanted none of that; from the start he had been determined to make a people's car. He was interested in transportation for men like himself, especially farmers. The secret to that lay in mass production. "Every time I reduce the price of the car by one dollar," he said early in the production of the T, "I get one thousand new buyers," and he ruthlessly brought the price down every year, seeking—as the Japanese would some sixty years later—size of market rather than maximum profit per piece. He also knew in a shrewd, intuitive way what few others did in that era, that as a manufacturer and employer he was part of a critical cycle that expanded the buying power of the common man. One year his advertising people brought him a new slogan that read, "Buy a Ford—save the difference," and he quickly changed it to "Buy a Ford —spend the difference," for though he was innately thrifty himself, he believed that the key to prosperity lay not in saving but in spending and turning money over. Money in banks was idle money, and he did not like that. When one of the children of his friend Harvey Firestone boasted that he had some savings in the bank, Ford lectured the child. That money was idle. What the child should do, Ford said, was spend the money on tools. "Make something," he admonished. "Create something."

For better or worse, his values were absolutely the values of the common man of his day. That allowed him to be perfectly in touch with the average worker and average farmer. Out of his own restlessness with farm work he understood how farmers, burdened by premechanized agricultural life, felt about the loneliness, monotony, and hardship of the farm. Yet though he shared the principles, yearnings, and prejudices of his countrymen, he vastly altered their world. What he wrought reconstituted the nature of work and began a profound change in the relationship of man to his job. By the end of the century it was clear that he had played a major part in creating a new kind of society in which man thought as much about leisure time as about his work. Ironically, the idea of leisure itself, or even worse, a leisure culture, was anathema to him. He once told the writer William Richards, "Energy should be spent on something useful." Children, he continued, should be allowed to learn to swim because that was useful, since they might one day be in a boat that tipped over. "They ought to play games so they will be strong enough to protect themselves. But golf . . ." His voice, Richards said, broke off into contempt and disparagement. He was never entirely comfortable with the fruits of his success, even though he lived in a magnificent fifty-six-room house. "I still like boiled potatoes with the skins on," he said, "and I do not want a man standing in back of my chair, laughing up his sleeve at me while I am taking the potatoes' jackets off." Of pleasure and material things he was wary. "I have never known what to do with money after my expenses were paid. I can't squander it on myself without hurting myself," he said, "and nobody wants to do that."

Only work gave purpose: "Thinking men know that work is the salvation of the race, morally, physically, socially. Work does more than get us our living. It gets us our life. I do not," he once said, "think that man can ever leave his business. You think of it by day and dream of it by night." Work was not just the critical part of life to him, it was life.

Born poor, he became at one point the richest man in the United States. How does it feel, a magazine reporter once asked him, to be the nation's first billionaire? "Oh shit," he answered. As a good farmboy should, he hated alcohol and tobacco, and he once said that alcohol was the real cause of World War I—the beer-drinking German taking after the wine-drinking Frenchman. His strength in his early years—which were also his good years—was in the purity of his technical instincts. "We go forward without facts, and we learn the facts as we go along," he once said. Having helped create an urbanized world where millions of God-fearing young men left the farm and went to the cities, he was profoundly uneasy with his own handiwork, preferring the simpler, slower America he had aided in diminishing. For all his romanticizing of farm life, however, the truth was that he had always been bored by farm work and could not wait to leave the farm and play with machines. They were his real love.

When Ford was born in 1863 on a farm in Dearborn, Michigan, the Civil War was still on. His mother died at the age of thirty-seven delivering her eighth child. He had idolized her, and her death was a bitter blow. "I thought a great wrong had been done to me," he said. Later in his life he not only built a house which was an almost exact replica of his earlier home, including the Ford family's very own stove, whose serial number he had memorized, but had a cousin who resembled his mother dress up in an exact imitation of the way she dressed and wear her hair in the same style.

His father's people were new Americans. When the great potato blight had struck Ireland in 1846, ruining the most important crop, the country had been devastated. Of a population of eight million, one million had died, and one million had emigrated to America. That migration included William Ford, who had set off to the magic land with two borrowed pounds and his set of tools. He was a skilled carpenter, and when he arrived, he moved quickly to Michigan, where some of his brothers had already settled.

A century before, Michigan had been virgin wilderness. The first white settlers were French-speaking trappers, many of whom became rich in the fur trade. They were followed by the New England merchants; harder of eye and less joyous in their pursuit of pleasure than their French predecessors, many soon made fortunes organizing the fur trade and the wondrous new timber business.

A major westward migration started, however, in the second quarter of the nineteenth century. New York and New England farmers, exhausted from working small, rocky, infertile plots, were drawn by word of this rich new frontier. They were the first agricultural settlers of what was to prove one of the great granaries of the world.

What had so recently been frontier was linked almost overnight to the centers of American commerce. In 1825 the Erie Canal, all 263 miles of it, was completed. It connected the East with what Americans rather innocently thought was the West and caused shipping rates to drop dramatically. Before the canal it had cost almost 20 cents a mile to ship a ton of freight overland from Buffalo to New York; with the new waterway it was soon less than a penny a mile. The Midwestern farm now served the Eastern consumer; the Michigan mine supplied the Eastern manufacturer. The effect on Detroit was stunning. It became the hub of a region selling tobacco and flour and salted fish to people some seven hundred miles away. The effect on New York City, joined to the canal by the Hudson River, was equally important. It soon surpassed Boston as a center of commerce.

The arrival of people like the Fords was part of the first massive immigration to America. It was encouraged by America's business elite, who thought the cost of native labor too high and wanted to bring in desperate Europeans who would work for much less. In the 1830s, there were 599,000 new immigrants, in the 1840s 1.7 million, and in the 1850s 2.6 million. Detroit was one focus of the influx. Its population, 9000 in 1820, would be well over 200,000 by the end of the century. It was well placed to benefit from the continuing westward expansion. Was there a demand for wood to build wooden carriages and wooden railroad cars and wooden ties for the expanding network of track? The surrounding area was rich in timber. Was iron needed for the building of a variety of machines? The mines to the north (manned by Cornish workers who were making $64 a month, five times what they made back in England) produced iron and copper as well. Soon Detroit workers were making 150,000 iron stoves a year, as the members of the new middle class of America gratefully replaced open hearths with stoves.

Its early industries, those that developed in the middle of the nineteenth century, drew men with particular skills that evolved into the skills required in the early twentieth century. The carriage makers, for example, became the auto makers; the stove makers became the metalworkers in the automotive body and engine shops; the leatherworkers who did the upholstery for carriages eventually made seat covers for cars. (David Buick, founder of the Buick company, was a plumbing manufacturer before turning to cars.) Soon the railroad boom made Detroit even more of an industrial center: Workers turned out thousands of railroad cars for the rapidly expanding nation.

What had been a wood and leather and iron town in the middle of the century was by 1900 using steel too. America as an industrial nation was beginning to take off, and new cities like Detroit were providing the base for that explosion. Much of the start-up money invested in the early auto companies came from Detroit's older successful businesses; for example, some of the early money invested in Ford and Cadillac came from the barons of iron, copper, and lumber.

It was a raw, angry, dynamic city of the unassimilated; there was simply no time to assimilate. The city was growing beyond its capacity to absorb people, a phenomenon central to the angry and antagonistic relationship that developed between labor and management. Soon the city was an uneasy aggregation of ethnic islands—Corktown (Irish), Polacktown, Dutchtown, Sauerkraut Row (German), and Kentucky (blacks). Each group was ready to hate the newest arrivals. The conditions in which they lived were dreadful; pestilence and a fearsome rate of infant death were commonplace. But there was also, whatever else, the promise of a better future.

William Ford promptly found work making railroad ties. With his savings he bought some land and built a house, in awe of an America that had so readily allowed him to do so. To him Ireland was a place where a man was a tenant on the land, and America was a place where he owned it.

Henry Ford started school when he was seven. His first teacher was a seventeen-year-old girl. Most of the teaching was done by women, because the men were out farming. The earlier grades had more students, because the older children were out working the fields along with their fathers. The basic book was the *McGuffey Eclectic Reader*, which Ford loved. It stressed moral values, but it included sections from Dickens, Washington Irving, and other major writers, which enticed many children into a genuine appreciation of literature. Although Ford loved *McGuffey*, he did not like books in general or the alien ideas they sometimes transmitted. History, he once said, coining a famous phrase, "is the bunk." On another occasion, he said, "We read to escape thinking. Reading can become a dope habit. . . . Book sickness is a modern ailment." By that, he meant reading that was neither technical nor functional, reading as an end in itself, as a pleasure without a practical purpose. But he was wary even of practical volumes. "If it is in a book, it is at least four years old, and I don't have any use for it," he told one of his designers.

What he truly loved was machinery. He had a gift for looking at a machine and quickly understanding it, not only repairing it but making it work better. The timing of his career could not have been more perfect for a man of his gifts, for he came to manhood at precisely the beginning of the modern machine age. Men like him were beginning to invent devices to mechanize work beyond the comprehension of their elders, and other men were discovering huge sources of oil that would permit those machines to run. Coal had produced steam, which had powered gigantic engines, albeit expensively; oil would allow both small and large engines to run cheaply.

In this dawn of the oil age, a man with an inventive bent could use his own shed as a factory. That was perfect for the young Henry Ford. He had always played with machines, ignoring all else around him. Even as a little boy he was an obsessive tinkerer. Once, when he was a grown man, someone asked him what toys he had loved as a boy. "My toys were all tools," he answered. "They still are." He stayed in school only as long as he had to, and even then his mind was elsewhere. During class, he would hide behind a geography book and fiddle with some gadget. In his early teens he designed a mechanism that allowed his father to close the farm gate without leaving his wagon. Watches fascinated him. When he was given a watch at thirteen, he immediately took it apart and put it back together. He soon started repairing watches for his friends. His father complained that he should get paid for this, but he never listened, for it was a labor of love. That same year he saw a steam engine, a threshing machine which could also move. It was the first time he had seen a thresher that was not drawn by horses. Ford jumped out of his wagon and talked to the engineer. Twenty years later he could repeat in exact detail every word the engineer had uttered, including the fact that the engine was making two hundred turns a minute.

His father wanted him to become a farmer, but it was a vain hope. He hated the drudgery of the farm. "What a waste it is," he once said, "for human beings to spend hours and days behind a slowly moving team of horses when in the same time a tractor could do six times as much work." To William Ford, on his own land at last, free of the old country, the farm was liberating; to Henry Ford, bored and restless, it was like a prison. (Cows came to symbolize his hatred of the farm. They were lazy, and they lay around all the time. He spent an entire lifetime railing against them. "The cow is the crudest machine in the world," he once said. On another occasion he said that if people would destroy all the cows in the world, they would eliminate the sources of war. When his company became large, he had his labs working constantly to find substitutes for dairy products.)

In 1879 Henry Ford entered his seventeenth year, which in those days was considered maturity. On the first day of December of that year, he left for Detroit, a most consequential departure. He walked to the city, half a day's journey. The Detroit of 1879 was a city of 116,000, a place of foundries and machine shops and carriage makers. There were some nine hundred manufacturing and mechanical businesses, many of them one-room operations but some of them large. It was an industrial city in the making. Ten railroads ran through it. As New York City, later in the century, was a mecca for young Americans interested in the arts, Detroit was just becoming a city with a pull for young men who wanted to work with machines. The surge in small industries was beginning, and a young man who was good with his hands could always find a job.

Henry Ford found a job repairing machines at the Michigan Car Company. He was paid $1.10 a day and worked six days a week. But he was too talented for the job. He left very soon, and there are two theories as to why. One is that he had repaired some machinery that older workers could not fix, thus earning their enmity. The other is that he had accomplished in half an hour what other workers did in six. For whatever reason, and it was neither lack of talent nor lack of ambition, he was fired. He then went to work at James Flowers and Brothers, a machine shop with an exceptional reputation for quality and diversity of product. The Flowers brothers were, like many ambitious young entrepreneurs of Detroit, immigrant craftsmen who had taken their tools and left Europe for the new world, and they were men of skill and imagination. As an apprentice there, Ford was immersed in the world of machinery, working among men who, like himself, thought only of the future applications of machines. He made

$2.50 a week, boarded at a house which charged him $3.50 a week, and walked to work. His salary left him $1 a week short, and as a good, enterprising young man he set out to make up the difference. He heard that the McGill jewelry shop had just gotten a large supply of clocks from another store. Ford offered to clean and repair the clocks for 50 cents a night. He did so well that he was soon repairing watches, although the owner insisted that he do the watch repair in the back room, since his youthfulness would not instill confidence in customers. That job added another $2 to his weekly salary, so he was now $1 a week ahead.

His fascination with watches led him to what he was sure was a brilliant idea. He would invent a watch so elementary in design that it could be mass-produced. Two thousand of them a day would come off a simple assembly line and they would cost only 30 cents each to produce. He was absolutely certain he could design and produce the watch; the only problem, he decided, was in marketing 600,000 watches a year. It was not a challenge that appealed to him, so he dropped the project, but the basic idea of simplifying a product in order to mass-produce it stayed with him.

He went from Flowers and Brothers to a company called Detroit Dry Docks, which built new vessels and repaired steamboats, barges, tugs, and ferries. His job was to work on the engines, and he gloried in it, staying there two years. There was, he later said, nothing to do every day but learn. In 1886, however, at the age of twenty-three, he returned to the farm, lured by an offer from his father of forty acres of timberland. William Ford made the offer because he wanted to rescue his wayward son from the city and his damnable machines; Henry Ford took it because he momentarily needed security—he was about to marry Clara Bryant. Nothing convinced him more of his love of machines than the drudgery of being back on the farm. Again he spent every spare minute tinkering and trying to invent and reading every technical magazine he could. He experimented with the sawmill on the farm; he tried to invent a steam engine for a plow. Crude stationary gasoline engines had been developed, and Ford was sure a new world of efficient gasoline-powered machines was about to arrive. He wanted to be part of it. Five years later, with all the timber on the farm cut, he was bored to death. Positive that important new inventions were just around the corner, he told Clara they were going back to Detroit. His father continued to worry about him. "He just doesn't seem to settle down," William Ford told friends. "I don't know what will become of him."

The last thing Henry Ford was interested in was settling down. He intended, he told his wife, to invent a horseless carriage. But first he needed to know a good deal more about electricity. So he took a job with

Detroit Edison at $45 a month. Thomas Edison was one of his heroes, and Ford thought he could learn more about the electrical system for the internal-combustion engine, which a number of young inventors were toying with at the time. He did well at Edison. He was soon the company's most skilled engineer, making the grand salary of $100 a month. But that wasn't enough. He needed extra money to pay for the materials for his inventing, so he worked at night teaching would-be machinists at the Detroit YMCA.

In the few years since he had first arrived, Detroit had grown considerably; its population was now over 205,000. The railroads had begun to open the country up, and no other city in America had grown as quickly, save Chicago. Detroit now had streetlights. There were more machine shops than ever before. The newest arrivals were mainly immigrants, Germans, Scandinavians, Irishmen, Poles, and some Englishmen. In this city the age of coal and steam was about to end.

Though America's sources of liquid fuel were still somewhat limited, the dreams of her young inventors were not; it seemed almost every young inventor in the country, and in Europe as well, thought himself destined to invent a practical horseless carriage. Detroit was the perfect center for these inventors. It had specialized in making bicycles, and a number of inventors were experimenting with putting a gas engine on a bicycle in some form or another. (In fact, Ford referred to his first car as a quadricycle.)

In 1891 Ford was using the kitchen of his and Clara's apartment as a lab; he fastened a primitive gas engine he had made to the kitchen sink. Eventually, no doubt to Clara's considerable relief, he moved his shop into a nearby shed. By 1896, at the age of thirty-three, he finally had his first car on the street. Because the handful of cars in those days—for other inventors had gotten to the road-test stage too—were so much resented for scaring horses and making noise, he needed a special permit to drive it in the streets. Ford was so excited before his first ride that he had barely slept for forty-eight hours. He had been so obsessed and preoccupied during the creation of the car that he had overlooked the fact that the door of the garage was too small for the car to exit. So he simply took an ax and knocked down some of the brick wall to let the car out. His friend James Bishop rode ahead on a bike to warn off pedestrians. A spring in the car broke during the ride, but they fixed it quickly. Then Henry Ford went home so he could sleep for a few hours before going to work. Later he drove the car out to his father's farm, but William Ford refused to ride in it. Why, he asked, should he risk his life for such a brief thrill?

Ford's early years trying to build a good car were not easy. Detroit was filled with scores of talented machinists chasing exactly the same dream. By the turn of the century about fifty companies *a year*, most of them in Detroit, were entering the auto business. Many of them did not even last the year. Some men lacked entrepreneurial abilities. Others lacked the toughness to survive in what was to be a business of hard men. Some lacked the money to sustain their dreams, and many lacked the passion to continue after their first attempts did not entirely succeed.

Henry Ford sold his first car for $200 and used the money to start work immediately on his next. He had been encouraged by his great hero, Thomas Edison, whom he met at a convention. Edison had asked the young Ford a series of pointed questions. Then, after Ford had sketched out his ideas, Edison told him, "Young man, that's the thing! You have it—the self-contained unit carrying its own fuel with it! Keep at it!" That was all the encouragement he needed, particularly since it came from the great Edison.

Ford's next model was considerably heavier than the first, more of a car and less of a quadricycle. He persuaded a lumber merchant named William Murphy to invest in the project by giving him a ride around town. "Well," said Murphy when he reached home safely, "now we will organize a company." In August 1899, Murphy brought together a consortium of men who put up $15,000 to finance Ford's Detroit Automobile Company. Ford thereupon left Detroit Edison so he could work full-time on his car. Alexander Dow, his boss at Edison, who thought him immensely talented, tried to dissuade him. "Electricity, yes," Dow told Ford. "That's the coming thing. But gas—no."

In February 1900, at the threshold of the twentieth century, Ford was ready to take a reporter from the *Detroit News Tribune* for a ride. The car, he said, would go twenty-five miles an hour. The reporter sensed that he was witness to the dawn of a new era. Steam, he later wrote, had "been the compelling power of civilization," but now the shriek of the steam whistle was about to yield to a new noise, the noise of the auto. "What kind of noise is it?" the reporter asked. "That is difficult to set down on paper. It is not like any other sound ever heard in this world. It is not like the puff! puff! of the exhaust of gasoline in a river launch; neither is it like the cry! cry! of a working steam engine; but a long quick mellow gurgling sound, not harsh, not unmusical, not distressing; a note that falls with pleasure on the ear. It must be heard to be appreciated. And the sooner you hear its newest chuck! chuck! the sooner you will be in touch with civilization's latest lisp, its newest voice." On the trip Ford and the reporter passed a harness shop. "His trade is doomed," Ford said.

Ford was not satisfied with the cars he was making at the Detroit

Automobile Company. They were not far behind the quality of the cars being made by Duryea or Olds, but they remained too expensive for his vision. Ford desperately wanted to make a cheaper car, but his stockholders were unenthusiastic. By November 1900, the company had died. But Ford was as determined as ever to make his basic car, and he decided that the way to call attention to himself and pull ahead of the dozens of competing automakers was to go into racing. In 1901 he entered a race to be held in Grosse Pointe. It was to be a major event, twenty-five miles (it had to be cut to ten because other races earlier in the day had taken so long to run). The morning of the race more than a hundred cars had driven through the city's streets, an awesome spectacle, wrote the reporter for the *Detroit Evening Press*, who noted, "and not a horse in sight." Ford won the race and became, in that small, new mechanical world, something of a celebrity. That propelled him ahead of his competitors.

Two years later, in 1903, he set out to start the Ford Motor Company. He was forty years old and had, he felt, been apprenticing long enough. There were eight hundred cars in the city at that time, and some owners even had what were called motor houses to keep them in. Ford soon worked up his plan for his ideal, inexpensive new car, but he needed money. He thought he would need $3000 for the supplies for the prototype (instead the cost was $4000). He got the money from a man named Alexander Malcolmson, who supplied coal by wagon to houses and companies; his slogan was "Hotter Than Sunshine." Ford and Malcolmson capitalized their company for $150,000, with fifteen thousand shares. Though the early investors were to do very well indeed, some did not have a great deal of confidence in the company. John Gray, Malcolmson's uncle, who was also the company's biggest stockholder, made a 500 percent return on his early investment but went around saying that he could not really ask his friends to buy into the company. "This business cannot last," he said. James Couzens, Malcolmson's bookkeeper, debated at great length with his sister, a schoolteacher, on how much of her savings of $250 she should risk in this fledgling company. They decided on $100. From that she made roughly $262,000. Couzens himself managed to put together $2500 to invest, and from that, when he finally sold out to Ford in 1919, he made $29 million.

This time Ford was ready. He was experienced, he hired good men, and he knew the car he would build. From the start there was no doubt in his mind what he wanted—a car that could be mass-produced by a manufacturing process that was as standardized as possible. "The way to make automobiles," he told John Anderson, one of his financial backers in 1903, "is to make one automobile like another automobile; just as one pin is like another pin, or one match is like another match when it comes from a match factory." He wanted to make many cars at a low price. "Better and cheaper," he would say. "More of them, better and cheaper." That was his complete vision of manufacturing. "Shoemakers," he once said, "ought to settle on one shoe, stove makers on one stove. Me, I like specialists."

But he and Malcolmson soon split over the direction of the company: Malcolmson argued that fancy cars costing $2200 to $4700 were what would sell. At the time half of the cars being made in America fell into this category; a decade later, largely because of Ford, those cars would represent only 2 percent of the market. Malcolmson wanted a car for the rich, Ford one for the multitude. Even Ford's father was wary of his move to a popular car; he warned his son that the market would be glutted if he went to more than thirty-five cars a day. Though the early models were successful—the company sold an amazing total of fifteen hundred cars in its first fifteen months—it was the coming of the Model T in 1908 that sent Ford's career rocketing. With the Model T the modern industrial age—the industrial age that benefited rather than exploited the common man—began.

It was the car that Henry Ford had always wanted to build because it was the car that he had always wanted to drive—simple, durable, absolutely without frills, one that the farmer could use and, more important, afford. Nor did Henry Ford like the idea of making cars for the rich. He was an agrarian populist, and his own people were farmers, simple people; if he could make their lives easier, it would give him pleasure. He planned to have a car whose engine was detachable so the farmer could also use it to saw wood, pump water, and run farm machinery. The Model T, said his first sales manager, was "practically a farmer's car." Ford's great success in making a car that the average man could enjoy launched the cycle of mass production and mass consumption in America. Mass-producing the cars would provide jobs and a decent wage for more and more people, and as the cost of the car came down with mass production, the workers could soon afford to buy one themselves.

The Model T was tough, compact, and light, and in its creation Ford was helped by breakthroughs in steel technology. The first vanadium steel, a lighter, stronger form developed in Britain, had been poured in the United States a year before the planning of the Model T. It had a tensile strength three times that of the steel then available in America and could be machined much more readily. That was major progress. Ford instantly understood what the new steel signified. He turned to one of his top men,

Charles Sorensen, and told him it permitted them to have a lighter and cheaper car.

The T was a brilliantly simple machine; when something went wrong the average owner could get out and fix it. Unimproved dirt tracks built for horses, which made up most of the nation's roads and which defeated fancier cars, posed no problem for it. Its chassis was high, and it could ride right over serious bumps. It was, wrote Keith Sward, a biographer of Ford, all bone and muscle with no fat. Soon the Ford company's biggest difficulty was keeping up with orders. Fortunately for Ford, the teachings of Frederick Winslow Taylor, the first authority on scientific industrial management, had just come into vogue. Taylor, armed always with a watch and an abiding disbelief in the enthusiasm of the average worker for his chores, had brought the new technique of time-and-motion studies to the steel industry and others. Taylor had, for example, measured how much a worker with a shovel could do on a given day; he had found the worker most efficient when instead of scooping up the maximum shovelful, thirty-eight pounds, he scooped up twenty-one pounds, since it allowed him to shovel more loads. Taylor became important because the times demanded it. As machines began to dominate men in factories, allowing one production breakthrough after another, the study of efficiency took on greater meaning. Ford, fascinated by efficiency of production, absorbed Taylor's principles and began to use them in his plant, eventually developing and applying them to an almost mythic degree.

Because the Model T was so successful—it was in such demand that dealers were sometimes commanded to stop taking orders—Ford's attention now turned to manufacturing. The factory and, even more, the process of manufacturing became his real passions. The process, he told everyone, was the fun in his world, for he could see such dramatic changes in production possibilities and accomplishments every day that working in the factory had become like working in the future. Even before the T's success he had been concerned about the production process. In 1908 he had hired an industrial efficiency expert named Walter Flanders and offered him a whopping bonus of $20,000 if he could make the plant produce ten thousand cars in twelve months. Flanders completely reorganized the factory and made the deadline by two days. He also helped convince Ford that they needed a larger space. Flanders understood that the increasing mechanization of the line meant that the days of the garage-shop car maker were over. There was a process now, a *line*, and the process was going to demand more and more money and employees. Flanders understood that every small success on the line, each increment that permitted greater speed of production and cut the cost of the car, mandated as well an inevitable increase in the size of the company. "Henceforth the history of the industry will be the history of the conflict of giants," he told a Detroit reporter.

Ford thereupon bought his Highland Park grounds. Here he intended to employ the most modern ideas about production, particularly those of Frederick Winslow Taylor. These would bring, as Taylor had prophesied, an absolute rationality to the industrial process. The idea was to break each function down into much smaller units so that each could be mechanized and speeded up and eventually flow into a straight-line production of little pieces becoming steadily larger. Continuity above all. What he wanted, and what he soon got, in the words of Keith Sward, was a mechanized process that was "like a river and its tributaries," with the subassembly tributaries merging to produce an ever more assembled car. The process began to change in the spring of 1913. The first piece on the modern assembly line was the magneto coil assembly. In the past a worker—and he had to be a skilled worker—had made a flywheel magneto from start to finish. A good employee could make thirty-five or forty a day. Now, however, there was an assembly line for magnetos. It was divided into twenty-nine different operations performed by twenty-nine different men. In the old system it took twenty minutes to make a magneto; now it took thirteen.

Ford and his men soon moved to bring the same rationality to the rest of the factory. Quickly they imposed a comparable system for the assembly of motors and transmissions. Then, in the summer of 1913, they took on the final assembly, which, as the rest of the process had speeded up, had become the great bottleneck. The workers moved as quickly as they could around a stationary metal object, the car they were putting together. If the men could remain stationary as the semifinished car moved up the line through them, less of the workers' time—Ford's time—would be wasted.

Charles Sorensen, who had become one of Ford's top production people, had a Model T chassis pulled slowly by a windlass across 250 feet of factory floor, timing the process all the while. Behind him walked six workers, picking up parts from carefully spaced piles on the floor and fitting them to the chassis. That was the birth of the assembly line, the very essence of what would become America's industrial revolution. Before, it had taken some thirteen hours to make a car; now they had cut the time of assembly in half, to five hours and fifty minutes. Not satisfied, they pushed even harder, lengthening the line and bringing in more specialized workers for the final assembly. Within weeks they could complete a car in only two hours and thirty-eight minutes. Now the breakthroughs came even more rapidly. In January 1914, Ford installed the first automatic conveyor belt. It was, he said, the first moving line ever used in an industrial plant, and it was fashioned after the overhead trolley that the Chicago meat-packers employed to move beef. Within two months of that innovation, Ford could assemble a car in an hour and a half. It was a stunning accomplishment, but it merely whetted their zeal. Everything now had to be timed, rationalized, broken down into smaller pieces, and speeded up. Just a few years before, in the days of stationary chassis assembly, the best record for putting a car together had been 728 hours of one man's work; with the new moving line it required only ninety-three minutes. Ford's top executives celebrated their victory with a dinner at Detroit's Pontchartrain Hotel. Fittingly, they rigged a simple conveyor belt to a five-horsepower engine with a bicycle chain and used the conveyor to serve the food around the table. It typified the spirit, camaraderie, and confidence of the early days.

The new age beckoned. Henry Ford could now mass-produce his cars, and as he did so, he cut prices dramatically. In 1909 the average profit on a car had been $220.11; by 1913, with the coming of the new, speeded-up line, it was only $99.34. But the total profits to the company were ascending rapidly because he was selling so many more. When the company began making the Model T, its cash balance was slightly over $2 million. Nineteen years and more than fifteen million cars later, when Ford reluctantly came to the conclusion that he had to stop making the T, the company balance was $673 million. And this was not merely a company's success; it was the beginning of a social revolution. Ford himself knew exactly what he had achieved—a breakthrough for the common man. "Mass production," he wrote later, "precedes mass consumption, and makes it possible by reducing costs and thus permitting both greater use-convenience and price-convenience."

The price of the Model T continued to come down, from $780 in the fiscal year 1910–11 to $690 the following year, then to $600, to $550, and, on the eve of World War I, to $360. At that price Ford sold 730,041 cars. He was outproducing everyone in the world. In 1914 the Ford Motor Company with 13,000 employees produced 267,720 cars; the other 299 American auto companies, with 66,350 employees, produced only 286,770. Cutting his price as his production soared, he saw his share of the market surge—9.4 percent in 1908, 20.3 in 1911, 39.6 in 1913, and with the full benefits of his mechanization, 48 percent in 1914. By 1915 the company was making $100 million in annual sales; by 1920 the average monthly earning after taxes was $6 million. The world had never seen anything remotely like it. The cars simply poured off the line. An early illuminated sign in Cadillac Square showed a woman with a scarf around her neck. It said: "Watch the Fords Go By." Ford's dreams, in a startlingly brief time, had all come true. He had lived his own prophecy.

There was a moment, however, in 1909 when Ford almost sold the entire company. William C. Durant, the entrepreneur who put General Motors together from several fledgling companies, felt him out about selling the company. An earlier offer of $3 million had fallen through because Ford wanted cash and Durant wanted to pay in stock. This time, his company more successful, Ford demanded $8 million. But again he wanted cash, or in his phrase to Durant, "gold on the table."

"How do you mean that?" Durant asked.

"I mean cash," Ford answered.

The GM board thought the price too high and again pulled back.

Ford's timing in holding on to his company, it turned out, was exquisite. The coming of Ford was almost perfectly synchronized with the discovery in the American Southwest of vast new reserves of oil. America became, with those discoveries, the one industrialized nation in the world with cheap sources of energy. Now every man could afford to drive an Everyman's Car.

If, as Naohiro Amaya of Japan's Ministry of International Trade believed, the American century and the oil century were one and the same thing, then that century began on January 10, 1901, in a field just outside Beaumont, Texas. The field was named Spindletop, because of the scrubby pines that grew there, which looked like spindles. For years local children had liked to go out to Spindletop and toss lighted matches into the field; as the matches hit the strong petroleum vapors seeping up through the soil, a handsome flame would be ignited. But anyone who believed that there was real oil beneath the ground was thought an eccentric. Oil was not found in Texas; it was found in places like Pennsylvania, West Virginia, and Ohio. Those states were all Standard Oil territory, and the Rockefeller people had no interest in the Southwest. "I will drink any drop of oil west of the Mississippi," boasted John D. Archbold of Standard.

But Patillo Higgins, a Beaumont man, insisted that there was oil underneath Spindletop, and for several years he tried to prove it. It had cost him $30,000 of his own money, and he owed friends an additional $17,000. As each attempt failed and he was forced to go to others for financial help in order to continue drilling, his own share of the operation shrank. Higgins's faith never flagged, but he became more and more a figure of ridicule in his hometown. His neighbors nicknamed him "Millionaire." The drilling got harder and harder; just before New Year's Day they had gone through 140 feet of solid rock, to a level of 1020 feet. On January 10 it happened. A geyser of oil roared out of the ground and shot a hundred feet above the derrick. No one had ever seen anything like it before; with it, the word "gusher" came into use.

At first no one could figure out how much oil the field was producing. Some said 30,000 barrels a day, some said 40,000. Captain Anthony Lucas, who had become a partner of Higgins, said 6000, because he had never heard of a larger hole in America. In fact, that one gusher was producing 100,000 barrels a day, roughly 60 percent of the total American production. One new well at Spindletop produced as much as the total from all the 37,000 wells back East in the Rockefeller territory did. Within a short time there were five more hits. Eventually analysts found that the oil from the first six holes, some 136 million barrels annually, more than twice surpassed what Russia, then the world's leading petroleum producer, could generate. Indeed, before Spindletop, the total for American production had been 58 million barrels a year, 48 million of them controlled by Standard Oil.

Beaumont, Texas, immediately became the first of the Southwestern oil-boom towns that erupted into colossal affluence. Almost overnight it swelled from a tiny town to a raw, instant city of fifty thousand. It was a world of men eager to make their fortunes—oil boomers. "Hi, boomer," strangers said to each other in greeting. Men looked at each other and wondered who would become a millionaire by nightfall. A commissary clerk in town had bought four acres for $60 and sold them for $100,000. A woman who was a pig farmer and garbage collector, named Mrs. Sullivan but known as Mrs. Slop, sold a lease on some of her acreage for $35,000 and went back the next day to collecting garbage. In the middle of the boom a man stood on the porch at the Crosby House waving a hundred $1000 bills and asking for a single acre in the proven territory. All deals were cash. The local barber, who had twenty chairs in his shop, always filled, had a terrible time changing $1000 bills. There was always a water shortage, and at the height of the boom water sold for $6 a barrel while oil was bringing 3 cents a barrel. Because there were not enough toilets, enterprising young boys could make $10 a day by standing in line for the toilets and then selling their places to impatient men. Where there were boomers, there were also hookers, and the hookers brazenly went right into the fields to find the men. Thus did the new age dawn.

Within a year, five hundred corporations were in the oil business in

Texas. Printers in Galveston, Houston, and New Orleans were kept busy printing stock certificates. There were dollar stock certificates and even penny certificates. Spindletop alone had changed the nature of the American economy and, indeed, the American future. Before the strike, oil was used for illumination, not for energy. (Until 1911 the sales of kerosene were greater than the sales of gasoline.) Spindletop inaugurated the liquid-fuel age in America. If the energy of the new age was to be oil, then America suddenly was rich in it. John W. "Bet-a-Million" Gates, an adventurer-gambler of the era, said prophetically that this new find would bring all Americans together as neighbors, once they built a good road system.

Oil was a much more desirable fuel than coal. Because it could flow, it was more easily transportable. It was cleaner, and, at least in the beginning, it was cheaper. Three barrels of oil had the heating capacity of one ton of coal, and the oil cost only half as much. Because of oil, the number of men tending the furnaces on a steamship could be reduced from a hundred to four. Loading a ship with coal had taken a hundred men several days; now one man in one day could load a ship with oil. The industrial as well as the consumer possibilities were endless; oil meant that the machine age could arrive, that small machines, consumer machines such as the ones being invented by Henry Ford, could have practical and inexpensive daily application. Within a year after Spindletop, oil was being put to all kinds of new industrial and consumer purposes, and the economy began switching from coal and to oil. An entire society was in the process of being modernized, industrialized, mechanized, and electrified.

In geopolitical terms, the oil discoveries made America the most powerful nation in the world, though America did not yet realize it. Everywhere the balance of power changed. World War I was the first oil war. Marshal Joffre won the Battle of the Marne by commandeering every taxi in Paris and driving his troops to the front. The Allies, Lord Curzon said later, "floated to victory on a wave of oil." The chief of the German general staff, Erich Ludendorff, later blamed Germany's defeat on its lack of oil, and the French foreign minister, Aristide Briand, noted, "In our day, petroleum makes foreign policy."

As the sources of energy in America changed, the sources of power changed as well. In the late nineteenth century, in the coal age, the great scandals had involved the railroads, as tycoons carved up the land, deciding where the cities would be and who would be rich and who would be poor. The coming of oil instigated the century-long decline of railroad power. The first great scandal of this century, Teapot Dome, was about oil rights. At the 1920 Republican convention an oilman offered fifty-two delegates to General Leonard Wood, the heir of Teddy Roosevelt, for, among other benefits, the right to name the next Secretary of the Interior, jobs of the first importance to the oil industry. ("I'm an American soldier, and I'll be damned if I'll betray my country," said General Wood. "Get the hell out of here.")

By the thirties, as more and more new fields were discovered, no other country in the world was as rich in oil and gas or as successful in taking wealth out of the ground as America. Inevitably the small boomers were soon replaced by bigger, better-financed operators, and they in turn were often replaced by giant corporations. Standard Oil, to no one's surprise, moved swiftly into the new oil territories. The problem in the twenties and thirties seemed not supply but distribution. Huge pipelines were being laid throughout the country at a cost of about $9000 a mile.

Oil was the new currency of the industrialized world, and America was rich and the other industrialized nations relatively poor. Though the French had pioneered even more than the Americans in the early development of cars, they lacked both the market and the sources of oil to match the Americans' surge into the oil age. The scope of all those finds had kept the price of oil low. So much wealth was being generated that not only did the oilmen create a standard of wealth all their own, but the masses profited as well. If there were a handful of men who made countless millions off the oil strikes, most Americans seemed not to care, for they too had become beneficiaries of the windfalls, and their lives were rapidly improving. Though Americans seemed at that moment blessed, they soon began to take their subterranean wealth for granted, as they did many of their other blessings. Few Americans realized that their country in those years was different or particularly fortunate. Those whose lives were eased by cheap oil soon forgot that they had lived in any other manner.

People in other industrialized nations were more aware of America's blessing. Being less sure of their sources of energy, they were warier about its dispensation. America hastily turned its industrial plant and its electrical grid over to oil; Europeans waited until after World War II, and then only under the joint pressure of striking left-wing coal miners and American political policy did they begin to convert from coal to oil. As oil was a potential source of vulnerability for those who lacked it, European nations pegged the price of gasoline high; consequently in Europe the car did not become a middle-class vehicle until twenty or thirty years after it became one in America, and European cars, were smaller and more fuel-efficient. As America moved rapidly to mechanized agriculture, its farming flourished. Modern farms became bigger, and small, old-fashioned farms began to die. In many parts of Europe, by contrast, farmers continued even into the fifties and sixties to cultivate small plots with horse-drawn implements.

The availability of cheap energy and an inexpensive mass car soon transformed the American landscape. Suddenly there were roads everywhere, paid for, naturally enough, by a gas tax. Towns that had been too small for the railroads were reached now by roads, and farmers could get to once-unattainable markets. Country stores that sat on old rural crossroads and sold every conceivable kind of merchandise were soon replaced by specialized stores, for people could now drive off and shop where they wanted to. Families that had necessarily been close and inwardly focused in part because there was nowhere else to go at night became somewhat weaker as family members got in their cars and took off to do whatever they wanted to do. The car stimulated the expansiveness of the American psyche and the rootlessness of the American people; a generation of Americans felt freer than ever to forsake the region and the habits of their parents and strike out on their own.

If America differed from Europe even before the coming of the auto in that its people were cut off from the past and felt they had a right to determine their own lives, then the auto added profoundly to that difference. In Europe young men and women felt themselves prisoners of the past; they had grown up in a certain class in a certain village, and they would stay in that village, and they would go as far in their education as their parents had, and they would do what their parents had done for a living. But the car abetted the new physical and social mobility of America. One need not live where one's father or grandfather had lived; one need not do what they had done for a living. If a small town seemed confining, all the modern American had to do was get in a car and drive somewhere else. In the breaking down of class barriers and the further separation of America from its European origins, the car was yet another formidable instrument.

The extraordinary expansion of the oil industry greatly increased Henry Ford's importance and success. He was providing the cars, Texas was providing the gas. The only limits on him were those imposed by production, and he continued to be obsessed by manufacturing. He wanted to put as much of his money as he could back into the factory. He hated bankers and financial people anyway, and he did not want to waste the company's money on stockholders. They were, to his mind, parasites, men who lived off other men's labor. In 1917 the Dodge brothers, who had manufactured many of the early components for Ford and who had been rewarded with sizable amounts of stock, sued him for withholding stock dividends and pouring too much money into his factory. The suit was a famous one, and some $40 million was at stake. During the trial, Ford testified that putting money back into the plant was the real fun he got from being in business. Fun, the opposing attorney retorted, "at Ford Motor Company expense."

"There wouldn't be any fun if we didn't try things people said we can't do," Ford answered.

That was the trial in which he referred to the profits he was making as "awful," and when questioned about that by attorneys for the other side, he had replied, with absolute sincerity, "We don't seem to be able to keep the profits down." Ford lost the suit, and the court ordered him to pay $19 million in dividends, $11 million of which went to Ford himself. The decision probably influenced him, as much as anything else did, to take as complete control of the company's stock as he could, so that as little money would be wasted as possible. Money to stockholders was a waste, money gone idle; money for the factory was not.

Out of that suit came both the means and the determination to build the Rouge, his great industrial masterpiece, a totally independent industrial city-state. Nothing in the period that followed was too good for the Rouge; it had the best blast furnaces, the best machine tools, the best metal labs, the best electrical systems, the most efficient efficiency experts. At its maturity in the mid-twenties, the Rouge dwarfed all other industrial complexes. It was a mile and a half long and three quarters of a mile wide. Its eleven hundred acres contained ninety-three buildings, twenty-three of them major. There were ninety-three miles of railroad track on it and twenty-seven miles of conveyor belts. Some seventy-five thousand men worked there, five thousand of them doing nothing but keeping it clean, using eighty-six tons of soap and wearing out five thousand mops each month. By the standards of the day the Rouge was, in fact, clean and quiet. Little was wasted. A British historian of the time, J. A. Spender, wrote of its systems: "If absolute completeness and perfect adaptation of means to end justify the word, they are in their own way works of art." Dissatisfied with the supply and quality of the steel he was getting from the steel companies, Ford asked how much it would cost to build a steel plant within the Rouge. About $35 million, Sorensen told him. "What are you waiting for?" said Ford. Equally dissatisfied with both the availability and the quality of glass, he built a glass factory at the Rouge as well. The price of glass had been roughly 30 cents a square foot early in the life of the T; soon it had soared to $1.50 a foot. With the glass plant at the Rouge, the price of glass came down to 20 cents a foot. Barges carrying iron ore would steam into the inland docks, and even as they were tying up, huge cranes would be swinging out to start the unloading. The process was revolutionary. On Monday morning a barge bearing ore would arrive in a slip, and the ore would go to the blast furnace. By Tuesday it would be poured into a foundry mold and later that day would become an engine. John DeVenter, a business historian, wrote in awe: "Here is the conversion of raw material to cash in approximately thirty-three hours." Some sixty years later Toyota would be credited for its just-in-time theory of manufacturing, in which parts arrived from suppliers just in time to be part of the final assembly. But in any real sense that process began at the Rouge. Toasting Philip Caldwell, the head of Ford who in 1982 was visiting Japan, Eiji Toyoda, of the Toyota company, said, "There is no secret to how we learned to do what we do, Mr. Caldwell. We learned it at the Rouge."

All of this, the creation of the Rouge as the ultimate modern plant, speeded up production even more. The Rouge had opened in increments, first building Eagle Boats in 1918, then making pig iron in 1920, then by 1925 making tractors and auto engines. It was only in 1928, as Ford switched from the Model T to the A, that it became the most awesomely integrated plant in industrial history. The production of a complete car from raw material to finished item dropped from twenty-one days to only four.

The Rouge was Henry Ford's greatest triumph, and with its completion he stood alone as the dominant figure in America and the entire developed world. He had brought the process of manufacture to its ultimate moment, and what he did at the Rouge would be copied in smaller scale by countless others. He had given the world the first people's car and had accumulated riches far beyond his ability or desire to spend. He had become an immensely popular man as well, the man who had lived the American dream. But even then, forces he had helped set in motion would begin to summon the darkness in his character.

Some fifty-eight years later, in 1983, a high member of the American embassy in Tokyo ran into a senior executive of Nippon Kokan, one of the great Japanese steelmakers. At that moment Nippon Kokan was thinking of buying the old Rouge steel plant, which several decades earlier had been considered the most modern in the world.

"How does the plant look?" the American diplomat asked.

"Very good by American standards," the Japanese executive answered.

"Will you have to make any modifications?" the American asked.

"Yes," said the Japanese. "The first thing we will have to do is bring in a continuous casting process." That, the American knew, had since become the guts of any truly modern steel plant.

"Anything else?" he asked.

"A new rolling line," he said, mentioning a process that brought steel to the exact grade. "And a new annealing line." That was a tempering process.

All he is talking about, thought the American, is an entirely new plant.

The deal in the end did not go through. There was a conflict between the Japanese owners and the American workers, and the Japanese, hardly eager in the first place, backed off. It was left to the Ford Motor Company to modernize the Rouge. Three hundred million dollars was to be spent trying to make what was once the world's most modern steel plant competitive with those of Japans and Korea.

5.
THE DESTROYER

Although Henry Ford seemed to dominate every aspect of industrial achievement, his strengths eventually became his weaknesses. One notorious example was staying with his basic car far too long, ignoring technological change in the cars themselves while obsessively pursuing technological change in their manufacture. From the very start he fought off every attempt to perfect the Model T. In 1912, while he was off on a trip to Europe, his top engineers made a few small changes intended to improve the car. Their version of the T was lower and some twelve inches longer. It was a better, smoother-riding vehicle, and his associates hoped to surprise and please him. When he returned, they showed it to him. He walked around it several times. Finally he approached the left-hand door and ripped it off. Then he ripped off the other door. Then he smashed the windshield. Then he threw out the backseat and bashed in the roof of the car with his shoe. During all this he said nothing. There was no doubt whose car the T was and no doubt who was the only man permitted to change it.

When Frank Kulick, an old buddy from Ford's racing days, wanted more power in the engine and suggested making bigger valves, Ford created a special engine with valves reduced from 1¼ inches to 1 inch. He said nothing of this reduction to Kulick and then asked him innocently if the new engine had more power. Kulick, believing that the new engine was larger, said that it did. "Let's tear it down and find out what made it go," Ford said. With pleasure he watched humiliation come over Kulick's face as he saw that the valves were smaller. The lesson was clear: Do not suggest improvements on my car. For the next thirty years, anyone wanting to improve a Ford car ran into a stone wall.

What had been another Ford strength, his use of manpower, also turned sour. The early workers at Ford had been skilled artisans, tinkering with designs as they worked. A job at Ford's, as it was known, had been desirable because Henry Ford was at the cutting edge of technology, always trying to do things better, and men who cared about quality wanted to be a part of his operation. In the early days he had his pick of the best men in Detroit. But the mechanized line changed the workplace. These new jobs demanded much less skill and offered much less satisfaction. The pressure to maximize production was relentless. Men who had prided themselves on their skills and had loved working with machines found themselves slaves to those machines, their skills unsummoned. The machines, they discovered to their rage, were more important than they were. The company seemed to care more about the equipment than it did about them. The more the plant was mechanized, the more the work force began to unravel. Men began walking out of the Ford plant. Ford himself was derided among workers as "the speed-up king." Detroit was known as a company town with weak unions. Now the IWW, the Industrial Workers of the World, one of the country's more radical labor movements, was begining to talk about an all-out assault on Ford.

The turnover in the labor force in 1913, the year of the great mechanization, was 380 percent. It soon became even worse. In order to keep a hundred men working, Ford had to hire nearly a thousand. Ford and his principal business partner, James Couzens, realized they had to stabilize the work force. So they came up with the idea of the $5 day—that is, of doubling the existing pay. There were some who thought it was Couzens's idea, though Ford later took credit for it. Perceived by most observers as an act of generosity, it was in fact an act of desperation. Ford calculated that a $5 day would attract the best workers, diminish labor unrest, and thus bring him even greater profits. Besides, he believed, it was a mistake to spend money on the finest machinery and then put those precious machines into the hands of disgruntled, unreliable, perhaps incompetent men.

Nonetheless, other capitalists roundly attacked Ford as a traitor to his class—though in fact Ford had never thought of himself as being one of them; he saw himself as part of the productive class. Speaking of the allegedly exorbitant wage, one Michigan journal wrote that any man whose wife wanted more than two calico dresses was married to "an indecent woman." The *Wall Street Journal* said that the wage was an "economic crime," the *New York Times* called it "distinctly utopian," and another publication said it would make the lower class unhappy forever. Ford's instincts, however, were right. Not only did the decision solidify the work force; it was so successful a public-relations gesture that it allowed Ford to cut back sharply on his advertising. He liked to refer to it as one of the smartest cost-cutting moves he had ever made and insisted that he had no philanthropic intent. This denial of altruism, a young Detroit theologian named Reinhold Niebuhr said later, was "like the assurance of an old spinster that her reputation as a flirt has been grossly exaggerated." Indeed in 1914, 1915, and 1916, the first three years of the $5 wage, the Ford Motor Company's profits after taxes were $30 million, $20 million, and $60 million. To working men, the $5 day was electrifying. The day after his announcement of the new wage, more than ten thousand men stormed the gates of the Ford plant looking for work. Ford had wanted the pick of workers; the pick he now had. For days the crowds grew, and policemen were needed to keep them under control.

It was probably the first time that the fruits of the oil-fueled industrial age had reached down to the average worker. Formally a worker had a grim and thankless job that rarely let him get ahead. He would end his life as he began it, and his children were doomed to the same existence. Now, however, with cheap oil and mass production, the industrial cycle was different. It was more dynamic; it generated much more profit and many more goods, which required customers with money to buy them. The worker became the consumer in an ever-widening circle of affluence. More than a decade later, when Ford's personal fortune was estimated at nearly $1 billion, a writer asked him to compare his wealth and privilege with that of the pharaohs. Ford replied that there was a better article to be written comparing the life of a Ford worker, whose wage had by then risen to $7 a day, "with a fellow on the pyramids who worked for ten cents a day."

Henry Ford was an odd, shrewd, somewhat cantankerous Michigan farmer whose mechanical skills had catapulted him far above the place in society where he felt comfortable. He was also perhaps the greatest celebrity of his time. Reporters hung out at his office, and his every word was quoted. That both helped and hurt him, because although he was a genius in manufacturing and perhaps a near-genius for a long time in business, much of what he said was nonsense, if highly quotable nonsense. On cigarettes: "Study the history of almost any criminal, and you will find an inveterate cigarette smoker." On Jews: "When there is something wrong in this country, you'll find Jews." The Jews, he thought, were particularly unproductive people, and he once vowed to pay $1000 to anyone who would bring him a Jewish farmer, dead or alive. He hated the diet of Americans of his generation—"Most people dig their graves with their teeth," he once said. He was prophetic about the nutritional uses of the soybean and intuitive about the value of whole-wheat bread. He felt that people who wore glasses were making a serious mistake; they should throw away their glasses and exercise their eyes. For almost all of his adult life, he used unadulterated kerosene as a hair cream. He did this because he had observed, he said, that men who worked in the oil fields always had good heads of hair. "They get their hands filled with the oil, and they are always rubbing their hands through their hair," he said, "and that is the reason they have good hair." One of the jobs of E. G. Liebold, his private secretary, was to keep a gallon of No. 10 light kerosene on hand for Ford's hair, and constantly to watch that it did not become contaminated.

His feistiness did not make him any less a folk figure. Indeed, there was a deliberate attempt to exploit his folksiness and to maximize the myth of Henry Ford for the benefit of the company. In his later years, if he injured his ankle at work, it was announced that he had hurt it playing football with his grandchildren. When he went to Atlantic City for the issuance of a stamp commemorating the life of his friend Edison, he did not, it appeared, have any money with him, and so there was a photograph sent around the world of the head of the Ford Motor Company, perhaps the richest man in the country, borrowing two cents from the mayor of Atlantic City in order to buy a stamp. Photographers who missed that shot could have one of him shooting craps with the porters on his private train. On one occasion someone noticed that his shoes did not match; he replied that every year on his birthday he put on one old shoe to remind himself that he had once been poor and might be poor again. At the height of his power and wealth, he visited Edward Stokesbury, a Morgan partner whose house had 145 rooms and 45 bathrooms. Reporters stopped him as he was leaving Stokesbury's residence and captured the perfect quote: "It is a great experience to see how the rich live."

He was in some ways a shy man. In the old Ford factory his office had a window through which he used to crawl in order to escape visitors. Nonetheless, he was acutely aware that his name was the company name and that his personal publicity generally helped the company. All news from the Ford Motor Company was about him. At a time when few public figures got much mail, Henry Ford received as many as eight thousand letters a week. He was also a hard man, and he became harder as he became older. He distrusted friendship and thought it made him vulnerable—friends might want something from him. He used a company group called the Ford Sociology Department to check up on employees and find out whether they drank at home or had union sympathies. If they were guilty of either, they were fired. While allegedly started to help workers with personal problems in finances or health, the department became a sinister means of spying on workers. For all of his populism, he always took a dim view of the average employee. Men worked for two reasons, he said: "One is for wages, and one is for fear of losing their jobs." He thought of labor in the simplest terms—discipline. He once told a journalist named William Richards, "I have a thousand men who if I say 'Be at the northeast corner of the building at four A.M.' will be there at four A.M. That's what we want—obedience."

Even in the days before he became isolated and eccentric, he liked playing cruel tricks on his top people. He loved pitting them against each other. One of his favorite ploys was to give the identical title to two men without telling either about the other. He enjoyed watching the ensuing struggle. The weaker man, he said, would always back down. His basic management style, said Frank Hadas, an employee in the Lincoln plant, was " 'Let's you and him have a fight and see how we come out.' If you decided to drop it, well, you were the weaker one." He liked the idea of keeping even his highest aides anxious about their jobs. It was good for them, he said. His idea of harmony, his colleague Charles Sorensen wrote, "was constant turmoil." Firings were often cruel and brutal. When Ford decided that he had had enough of Frank Kulick, the man who had favored larger valves and was humiliated for it, he turned the job of firing him over to Harry Bennett, his chief of security. Bennett led Kulick over to a car and asked him to listen to the magneto; something, said Bennett, appeared to be wrong. Kulick climbed onto the fender to listen. Bennett then raced the car out of the factory into the yard, and turned sharply so that Kulick was thrown to the ground. Bennett raced the car back into the factory and then locked the gates. Kulick was never allowed inside again. The same sort of thing was going on in the factories. The foremen, the men who ruled the factory floor, had once been chosen for their ability; now, increasingly, they were chosen for physical strength. If a worker seemed to be loitering, a foreman simply knocked him down. The rules against workers talking to each other on the job were strict. Making a worker insecure was of the essence. "A great business is really too big to be human," Ford himself once told the historian Allan Nevins.

Throughout the twenties, Henry Ford steadily lost touch. He had played a critical role in breeding new attitudes in both workers and customers. But as they changed, he did not, and he became more and more a caricature of himself. "The isolation of Henry Ford's mind is about as near perfect as it is possible to make it," said Samuel Marquis, a Detroit minister who had headed the Ford Sociology Department when its purpose had been to help the employees and who later became its harshest critic. If Ford was still known outside Detroit as a benefactor of the common man, that reputation had diminished in Detroit itself. There he was known as an owner who pushed men to the extremes of their endurance in order to serve his machines. His labor practices turned harsh and ugly, and he became bitterly antilabor. As the working population of the entire country became increasingly restless and sophisticated, he turned to the fist and the club to maintain his power. His treatment of the workingman, once so widely praised, now became the very symbol of oppression.

Ford was a giant company run more and more by the whim of an aging, mean-spirited, often irrational eccentric. It was no longer a creative company focused on an exciting new idea and headed by an ingenious leader. Now, the more modern the idea the more likely Henry Ford was to oppose it. On occasion he would talk about trying something new, and there would be a flurry of activity, and then he would completely forget what he had started, and the idea would slowly die. For its engineers and designers, the Ford Motor Company, only a decade earlier the most exciting place to work in America, was professionally a backwater. Sycophants rose, and men of integrity were harassed. Rival companies were pushing ahead with technological developments, and Ford was standing pat with the Tin Lizzie. His own best people became restless under his narrow, frequently arbitrary, even ignorant policies. He cut off anyone who disagreed with him. Anyone who might be a threat within the company, because of superior leadership ability, was scorned as often and as publicly as possible.

Eventually he drove out Big Bill Knudsen, the Danish immigrant who was largely responsible for gearing up the Ford plants during World War I and was widely considered the ablest man in the company. Knudsen was a formidable production man who had been in charge of organizing and outfitting the Model T assembly plants; he had set up fourteen of them in two years. An admired man in the emerging society of industrial Detroit, he was immensely capable and hardworking, and he employed none of the tactics of intimidation used by so many of the other top Ford people. He cajoled and inspired rather than threatened; in an era of such primitive management, that set him apart, not entirely to his own good. Similarly, his prodigious work during World War I made him a target of perverse attacks by Henry Ford. Knudsen was a big, burly man, six-foot-three and 230 pounds, and he drank, smoked, and cursed, all of which annoyed the puritanical Ford. Worse, Knudsen was clearly becoming something of an independent figure within the company. He was also drawing closer to Ford's son, Edsel, believing him a young man of talent, vision, and most remarkable of all, sanity. Together they talked of trying to improve the Model T. They were sure that the ability to change gears—which meant that the gears would operate with different ratios—was the coming thing, and they talked of amenities such as two front doors, not just one. All of this merely infuriated the senior Ford and convinced him that Knudsen was an intriguer and becoming too big for his place.

Ford took his revenge by making a great show of constantly counter-
manding Knudsen's production decisions. Knudsen became frustrated with
these public humiliations and with the company's failure to move ahead
technologically. He finally told his wife that he did not think he could
work there any longer. He was sure he was going to have a major confrontation with Henry Ford.

"I can't avoid it if I stay," he said, "and I can't stay and keep my self-
respect. I just can't stand the jealousy of the place anymore."

"Then get out," she said.

"But I'm making fifty thousand a year. That's more money than we can
make anywhere else."

"We'll get along," she said. "We did before you went to work there."

In 1921 he quit, virtually forced out. "I let him go not because he wasn't
good, but because he was too good—for me," Ford later said.

Knudsen went to General Motors, where he was almost immediately
put in charge of the company's sluggish Chevrolet division. It was the
perfect time to join GM. What Ford had once done better than anyone
else, others now did as well or better; what he had never learned about
business and marketing—there had been no need to learn because he
could dictate style and taste—others now did with exceptional skill. Alfred
P. Sloan of GM was putting together a modern automotive giant, building
on Ford's advances in simplifying the means of production and bringing
to that manufacturing success the best of modern business practices. Within
three years of Knudsen's arrival, GM became a serious challenger to Ford.

As good men left in ever greater numbers and GM became an ever
more formidable competitor, Henry Ford responded by turning in on
himself and surrounding himself with thugs. His dealers, watching the
rise of Chevy and sensing that Chevy was listening to its dealers and
customers as Ford was not, pleaded with him to change. He turned a deaf
ear. By the early twenties the rumblings from the dealers were mounting.
In particular they wanted changes in the ignition system. Some of them
were invited to Detroit to meet with Henry Ford.

"You can have them [the changes] over my dead body," Ford said.
"That magneto stays on as long as I'm alive." Later that same day Bill
Klann, one of Ford's principal engine men, ran into Edsel Ford.

"Don't you think your dad made a mistake?" he asked.

"Yes," said Edsel, "but he's the boss, Bill."

At almost the same time some of the dealers asked Ford if he would
vary the color of the Model T. "You can have them any color you want
boys, as long as they're black," Ford answered.

A year later, in 1922, he listened to a group of Ford salesmen warn about the challenge from Chevy and then abruptly dismissed it. "Well, gentlemen," he said, "as far as I can see, the only trouble with the Ford car is—that we can't make them fast enough."

He had become so egocentric that criticism of the Model T struck him as criticism of himself. Soon Chevrolet began to surge. Ford defiantly stayed with the Model T. Perhaps 1922 can be considered the high-water mark of Ford's domination of the market. Sales were never higher, and with an average profit of $50 a car, the company netted more than $100 million. From then on it was downhill. As Chevy made its challenge, the traditional Ford response, simply cutting back on the price, no longer worked. The success of that maneuver had been based on volume sales, and the volume was peaking. From 1920 to 1924, Ford cut the price eight times, but the thinner margins were beginning to undermine Ford's success. The signs got worse and worse. For the calendar year ending February 1924, the Ford company's net profit was $82 million; of that, $29 million came from the sales of spare parts. If anything reflected the stagnation of the company, it was that figure.

In 1926 Ford's sales dropped from 1.87 million to 1.67 million. At the same time, Chevy nearly doubled its sales, from 280,000 to 400,000. America's roads were getting better, and people wanted speed and comfort. Chevy, unlike Ford, was responding. In the face of GM's continuing challenge, Henry Ford's only response was once again to cut prices— twice in that year. The Model T was beginning to die. Finally, in May of 1927, on the eve of the manufacture of the fifteen-millionth Model T, Henry Ford announced that his company would build a new car. The T was dead. His domination over a market that he himself had created was over. With that he closed his factories for retooling, laying off his workers (many of them permanently).

The new car was the Model A. It had shock absorbers, a standard gearshift, a gas gauge, and a speedometer, all things that Chevy had been moving ahead on and that Ford himself had resisted installing. In all ways it seemed better than its predecessor—more comfortable, twice as powerful, and faster. At first the nation seemed to hunger for the long-awaited new car from Ford. When it was finally ready to be revealed, huge crowds thronged around every showplace. In New York, 100,000 people turned up at the dealership to see the unveiling. In order to accommodate the mob, the manager moved the car to Madison Square Garden. Newspapers ranked the arrival of the Model A along with Lindbergh's solo transatlantic flight as the top news story of the decade. The car was an immense success. Even before it was available there were 727,000 orders on hand.

Yet the Model A's success was relatively short-lived, for once again

Henry Ford froze his technology. Even the brief triumph of the Model A did not halt the downward spiral of the company. Henry Ford remained locked into the past. He grew more erratic and finally senile. At the end of his life he believed that World War II did not exist, that it was simply a ploy made up by the newspapers to help the munitions industry. No one could reach the old man anymore. It was a spectacular self-destruction, one that would never again be matched in a giant American corporation. It was as if the old man, having made the company, felt he had a right to destroy it.

With Knudsen's departure the burden of trying to deal with Ford fell on his son, Edsel. Gentle and intelligent, Edsel Ford reflected the contradictions in his father's life. He had been born while the Fords were still poor. (As a little boy Edsel had written Santa Claus a letter complaining: "I haven't had a Christmas tree in four years and I have broken all my trimmings and I want some more.") By the time he entered manhood, his father was the richest man in the country, unsettled by the material part of his success and ambivalent about the more privileged life to which his son was being introduced. Henry Ford wanted to bestow on his son all possible advantages and to spare him all hardship, but, having done that, he became convinced that Edsel was too soft to deal with the harsh, brutal world of industry, symbolized by nothing better than the Ford Motor Company.

Edsel Ford was not a mechanical tinkerer himself, but he had spent his life apprenticing in the auto business, and he knew who in the company was good and who was not; he was comfortable with the engineers and the designers. Edsel knew that times were changing and that the Ford Motor Company was dying. During his father's worst years, he became a magnet for the most talented men in the company, who came to regard his defeats as their defeats. He was a capable and confident executive, and an exceptionally well-trained one. His apprenticeship was a full and thorough one—it lasted thirty years. Absolutely confident in his own judgment, about both people and cars, Edsel Ford was beloved by his friends and yet respected in the automobile business for his obvious good sense. "Henry," John Dodge, Henry Ford's early partner and later his rival, once said, "I don't envy you a damn thing except that boy of yours."

Edsel Ford was the first scion of the automotive world. He married Eleanor Clay, a member of the Hudson family, which ran Detroit's most famous department store. They were society, and the marriage was a great event, the two worlds of Detroit merging, the old and the new, a Ford and a Clay. When the engagement was first announced, reporters flocked to Eleanor's home to interview her. "We are going to live very simply," she told them. They lived simply in Grosse Pointe (a thirty-room house), in Hobe Sound, Florida, and in Seal Island, Maine (where the house was so grand and the security against kidnappers so complete that Edsel's son, Henry Ford II, later said that while growing up there during the summers he never saw anyone outside of his immediate family and the servants).

Henry Ford hated the fact that Edsel had married into the Clay family, of the Detroit elite, and had moved to Grosse Pointe. He knew that Edsel went to parties and on occasion took a drink with his friends, not all of whom were manufacturing people and some of whom were upper-class— worse, upper-class citified people—and was sure all this had corrupted him. It was as if Edsel, by marrying Eleanor, had confuted one of Henry Ford's favorite sayings: "A Ford will take you everywhere except into society."

On top of all his other burdens, it was Edsel's unfortunate duty to represent the future to a father now absolutely locked in a dying past. Genuinely loyal to his father, Edsel patiently and lovingly tried to talk Henry Ford into modernizing the company, but the old man regarded his son's loyalty as weakness and spurned him and his advice, preferring instead the sycophancy first of Charlie Sorensen and then of Harry Bennett. Edsel, recognizing the growing force of the GM challenge and the professionalism of the management group that Alfred P. Sloan had put together, argued constantly for a new, professional managerial staff at Ford; the old man snapped back that if he wanted a job done correctly, he would always pick a man who knew nothing about it. Sometimes he would give Edsel permission to start a project and then, without Edsel's knowing it, gleefully have the project stopped. On occasion he would give Edsel a chance, but even then it would turn out to be more of a half chance than a full one. Edsel, for example, pushed for hydraulic brakes, but his father hated them. He had tried them when he was young, he said, and a hose had come loose and the brakes had failed. Finally Edsel persuaded his father to drive one of several cars he had equipped with hydraulic brakes. Henry Ford got in, sat down, and started the car. It went a half mile and then stopped. That was it for hydraulic brakes as far as Henry Ford was concerned.

When everyone else in the company agreed that a particular issue had to be brought before the old man, Edsel became the designated spokes- man. With Knudsen now gone, he usually stood alone. He was probably the only person who told the truth to his father. It was Edsel's job to tell his father that sales were down, Edsel's job to represent the six-cylinder engine, which the company desperately needed, Edsel's job to speak for better suspension systems. Others, such as Sorensen, were supposed to come to Edsel's defense during these meetings, but they never did. Sorensen, brutal with everyone else in the company, was the complete toady with the founder, and always turned tail in the face of Henry Ford's opposition. Once when Edsel was to make the case for hydraulic brakes still again, he checked with Sorensen and Ed Martin, one of the top plant men, before the meeting, and they both promised Edsel they would support him. When Edsel started to make his pitch, Ford stood up and shouted, "Edsel, you shut up!" There was not a word from Sorensen or Martin.

All the while the competition was getting better faster. Alfred Sloan was a formidable administrator, and Knudsen was perhaps the ablest all-around manufacturing man of the twenties and thirties. Chevy was introducing styling, and offering different colors, thermostats for heaters, and improved brakes. Ford stood still. Gadgets and knickknacks, Henry Ford called them. He knew his customers, knew that they were simple, God-fearing people who would not want these corrupting luxuries and would not desert him. But it proved that he no longer knew his customers so well, and Sloan and his bright young managerial people knew them better. Chevy had hydraulic brakes in 1924; Ford added them fourteen years later. When Chevy went to a six-cylinder car in 1929, Edsel pleaded even more passionately with his father to modernize the Ford engine. A six, his father retorted, could never be a balanced car. "I've no use for an engine that has more spark plugs than a cow has teats," he said. After all, he had built one back in 1909, and he had not liked it. The six-cylinder engine stood between the two Fords. The quintessential story about Henry Ford and the six-cylinder engine—for it reflects not just his hatred of the new but his contempt for his son as well—concerns a project that Edsel and Laurence Sheldrick, the company's chief engineer, had been working on. It was a new engine, a six, and Edsel believed he had gotten paternal permission to start experimenting with it. He and Sheldrick labored for about six months, and they were delighted with the prototype. One day when they were just about ready to test it, Sheldrick got a call from Henry Ford.

"Sheldrick," he said, "I've got a new scrap conveyor that I'm very proud of. It goes right to the cupola at the top of the plant. I'd like you to come and take a look at it. I'm really proud of it."

Sheldrick joined Ford at the top of the cupola, where they could watch the conveyor work. To Sheldrick's surprise, Edsel was there too. Soon the conveyor started. The first thing riding up in it, on its way to becoming junk, was Edsel Ford and Larry Sheldrick's engine.

"Now," said the old man, "don't you try anything like that again. Don't you ever, do you hear?"

In 1936, his company under mounting pressure, Henry Ford reluctantly built a six-cylinder engine. It went into production a year later. But moves like this were too late.

Those who had once been fervent admirers watched now in horror as he destroyed his own company. "The world's worst salesman," *Fortune* called him. He became more and more distant from the reality of his own company. As he became more senile and more threatened by growing pressure from a restive labor force, he began to cut back on the power of Charlie Sorensen and to grant it instead to Harry Bennett. Sorensen had been a brutal man, hated by many, capable of great cruelty, eager to settle most disputes with his fists, but at least he knew something about production. Bennett, head of the company's security forces, was worse. He was an ex-sailor who had boxed professionally under the name Sailor Reese, and he had come to power in the days after World War I, when his assignment was to hire bullies and ex-cons and wrestlers and boxers to help control the plant and keep the union out. Bennett was well suited for that role. He kept a pistol in his office and often took target practice while talking with visitors. Those he could not crush he sought to co-opt. He might offer someone, as he did John Davis, a senior sales executive, a farm, or a house, or he might simply give someone a better car than the one he had. The first time John Bugas, a local FBI man, came to see Bennett, he found when he returned to the parking lot that his Ford had been replaced by a Lincoln, the Ford company's luxury car. But Bennett greatly favored the stick over the carrot. For his was an empire within an empire, and that inner empire was built on fear. He padded his pockets with Ford money—the finances of the company were in chaos, and there was no coherent bookkeeping. He built at least four houses with his appropriated wealth. His rise exactly paralleled the decline of the old man, and he played on all the fears the old man had, especially fear of labor and fear of kidnapping, Ford had faith that Bennett, with his connections in the underworld, could stop any attempt to kidnap his son or grandchildren. Ford loved Bennett's use of force to intimidate people. "Harry gets things done in a hurry," he liked to say.

Bennett's power over Ford grew almost without check in the 1930s, when Ford was in his seventies. His hold on the founder was almost complete, to the distress of Ford's family. Board meetings were a travesty. Often Ford did not show up. Or he would walk in at the last minute with Bennett and after a few minutes say, "Come on, Harry, let's get the hell out of here. We'll probably change everything they do anyway." Once the magazine writer William Richards was in a car with Ford and Bennett, and he asked Ford who was the greatest man he had ever known—after all, in so rich and varied a career he had known quite a few exceptional people. Ford simply pointed at Bennett and said: "Him."

At the very end he used Bennett as his principal weapon against his son. The last years were truly ugly. Sure that he was protected by Ford, Bennett harassed Edsel mercilessly, to the old man's obvious pleasure. Already emotionally beaten down by his father, Edsel had become a sick man. He had remained loyal to his father and endured his humiliations while healthy. Now, battling stomach cancer, he had less and less to fight back with. In 1942 Edsel got undulant fever from drinking milk from his father's dairy; Ford disapproved of pasteurization. The old man blamed his illness on Edsel's bad habits. Edsel's last years were hard, as he struggled to expedite the war-production work his father hated while at the same time resisting his ailments. In 1943 Edsel died. He was only forty-nine. Almost everyone who knew both Henry and Edsel Ford thought the son had really died of a broken heart. Four days after Edsel's death the old man came to work, turned to Ernest Liebold, his secretary, and said, "I am going to fire everyone around here who worried Edsel."

It was the final malevolent chapter in Henry Ford's own life. Not only had he destroyed his son and all but ruined a once-great industrial empire, but also as World War II approached, he was treating the government of the United States as if it were an enemy. When Bill Knudsen, by then the head of war production, came out in 1940 to talk to him about building Rolls-Royce airplane engines at Ford for the British Spitfires, Ford turned him down.

"You're all right, William," he said, "but you're in with a bad bunch down there."

By the middle of the war, the Ford Motor Company was in such poor shape, teetering on collapse, that high government officials pondered whether to take it over, for the government had to keep the giant going. Without the stimulus of the war and the work it eventually brought the company, it is possible that Ford might have failed completely. As the government debated, two women stepped forward. Clara Bryant Ford and Eleanor Clay Ford, one Henry Ford's wife and the other Edsel's widow, had watched it all with dismay—the old man's senility, the crushing of Edsel, the rise of Bennett—but with a certain helplessness. "Who is this man Bennett who has such power over my husband and my son?" Clara Ford once asked. She had hated it when Bennett and Sorensen had spoken for Henry against Edsel and had participated in and encouraged his destruction. Now both women feared that the same forces might prevent young Henry, Edsel's son, from ascending and assuming power.

Henry Ford II had been serving in the navy during the war, enjoying a taste of personal freedom. But in August 1943, thanks to intervention by his mother and grandmother, he got orders sending him back to Detroit; the nation's highest officials feared that after Edsel's death, Harry Bennett might actually take over the company. He returned reluctantly, but he was the firstborn of Edsel Ford, and familial obligation demanded it. He had no illusions about the challenge ahead. He knew that the struggle would be difficult, and that except for a very few men the Ford Motor Company was a corrupt and corrupting place.

Bennett and Sorensen immediately began belittling him, Bennett by undoing what young Henry was attempting to do each day and Sorensen by demeaning him in front of other people and by always calling him "young man." "He might just as well have called me Sonny," Henry later told friends. Henry Ford II might have titular power—he was named vice-president in December 1943—and the power of blood, but unless his grandfather moved aside and Bennett left the company, he would never be able to take control. Even as he returned, Bennett was in the process of destroying Sorensen, and young Henry seemed very vulnerable. Again Eleanor Clay Ford put her foot down and forced an issue. Widowhood had stirred in her the kind of indignation her husband had always lacked. He had been too loyal to challenge his father, but now Edsel's company stock was hers to vote, and she felt a great deal less loyalty. She threatened to sell her stock unless old Henry moved aside in favor of his grandson. Her son would not be destroyed as her husband had been. Clara Bryant Ford backed her completely. They fought off the old man's excuses and his delaying ploys. With that threat, and a sense that these women were intensely serious, Henry Ford finally, furiously, gave up, and Henry Ford II took control.

Henry Ford had outlived his era and his usefulness. Once a popular figure with the average man, he had become known as one of the nation's leading labor baiters. He had helped usher in a new era of economic dignity for the common man, but he could not deal with the consequences. His public statements during the Depression, while millions suffered—including thousands upon thousands of his own workers—were perhaps the most pitiless ever uttered by any capitalist. He repeatedly said that the Depression was good for the country and the only problem was that it might not last long enough, in which case people might not learn enough from it.

"If there is unemployment in America," he said, "it is because the un-employed do not want to work." His workers, embittered by his labor policies, marched against him in the thirties, and were put down by Bennett's truncheons and guns. His security people were so vicious that when Ford's workers marched, they wore masks over their faces to hide their identity—something rare in America.

In business he was overtaken by General Motors, which relentlessly modernized its design, its production, and its marketing. GM fed the appetites Henry Ford had helped create. In addition, GM inaugurated a dynamic that haunted the Ford company for the next fifty years; buyers started out driving Fords when they were young and had little money and slowly, as their earnings rose, graduated to more expensive GM cars. As a workingman's hero, he was replaced by Franklin Roosevelt. What had once been charming about his eccentricity now became contemptible.

His legacy was a complicated one. Forty years after his death few re-membered the ugliness of his final years. The harshness of his actions had been softened by time. He became again the classic symbol of what a simple man with the right idea could do. He was also, in casual recollec-tion, still the personification of the modern industrial era, in which the common man was paid well enough to consume as well as produce. That, along with his role in accelerating mass production, was his most vital contribution to the world. But within Detroit and the Ford Motor Com-pany, his legacy remained in many ways much darker. In his first decade and a half he had been brilliant—charmed, really, his every move the right one—but what he had done to the company in his next thirty years still sorely burdened it.

Nothing reflected his failures more tellingly than the fate of the River Rouge manufacturing complex. It was an industrial masterpiece, and it should have stood long after his death as a beacon to the genius of its founder. But the treatment of human beings there had been so mean and violent, the reputation of the Rouge so scurrilous, that in the postwar era it stood as an embarrassment to the new men running Ford, a reputation that had to be undone.

The bequest had other unfortunate aspects. By fighting the unions so intransigently, Ford and the other Detroit industrialists had ensured that when the unions finally won power they would be as strong as the com-panies themselves, and that there would be a carryover of distrust and hatred which would make them—even in the postwar years when the unions became a junior partner—an adversarial, distrustful junior partner. There were other, more concrete, burdens as well. Because he had been locked in the past and had frozen his technology, the company was on the verge of bankruptcy. Worse, he had done something that was truly cruel and, in a family company, professionally ruinous—he had destroyed his own heir, one who was, in Detroit's phrase, a damn good car man. There was no doubt in the minds of the ablest Ford men of that day, and of their competitors at GM, that if the old man had stepped aside, Edsel Ford would have improved the company tremendously. But he never got the chance. He was crushed, and a whole generation of good men were forced out, which put a heavy weight on the succeeding generation.

When the passage of family leadership took place, it was to Edsel's son. The second Henry Ford was twenty-eight years old when he took over in September 1945, and he had had only the scantest apprenticeship in this vast and complicated world. No one who knew the young Henry Ford over the next thirty-five years ever doubted his shrewdness, or his toughness, or his single-minded purpose—to save, secure, and strengthen the Ford Motor Company. Nor did they doubt that, having taken over the company very young, he had handled himself well, choosing able, older executives, putting his ego aside and deferring to them. But in the years that followed, the fifties and the sixties, the top car people in that company sensed in Henry Ford a doubt about his own automotive instincts. It was a lack of feel, and it was expressed in his caution and conservatism. He was a good, serious businessman, but he had no natural touch. He had never served a real apprenticeship.

Probably no major industrial company in America's history was ever run so poorly for so long. Only its sheer size saved it, that and, in the war, the government's dependence upon it for military production. A smaller company managed so badly would surely have closed. By the beginning of 1946, it was estimated, Ford was losing $10 million a month. The chaos was remarkable, but some of it, at least, was deliberate. The old Henry Ford hated the government and in particular the federal income tax, and by creating utter clerical confusion he hoped to baffle the IRS. He also hated bookkeepers and accountants. As far as he was concerned, they were parasitical, and from time to time he enjoyed arbitrarily getting rid of them. There was almost a ritual to it.

"What do these people do?" he would ask his aide as he strode into a room filled with white-collar workers.

"They're accountants, Mr. Ford," the aide would say.

"I want them all fired," he would say. "They're not productive, they don't do any real work. Get them out of here today."

Fired they would be, though some of them might later slip back into the company. The result was a bookkeeping nightmare.

When Arjay Miller, who later became president of the company, joined

Ford in 1946, he was given an assignment by Ernie Breech, then the executive vice-president. Breech, who had just come over from Bendix, was both an accountant and an industrialist, and the first thing he wanted was the profit forecast for the next month. So he sent Miller to get it. Miller went down to the office building, where the financial operations were kept. There he found a long table with a lot of older men, who looked to him like stereotypes of the old-fashioned bookkeeper. These men were confronted by bills, thousands of bills, and they were dividing them into categories, A, B, C, D. The piles were immense, some several feet high. To Miller's amazement the bookkeepers were actually estimating how many million dollars there were per foot of paper. That was the system, if it could be called a system.

Twenty years earlier it had been worse. Bothered by their inability to keep up with the bills, they had broken them down into two categories, those under $10 an item and those over. Serious investigation had shown that the average figure for bills under $10 was $2.43, and so they used that figure to multiply against the gross weight of the paper.

Miller, on his mission, asked what the estimates for the following month's profits were. Charles Martindale, one of the men working there, looked at him and asked, "What do you want them to be?"

"What?" asked Miller.

"I can make them anything you want," said Martindale.

He meant it, Miller decided. It was truly a never-never land.

Harry Bennett's last stand took place on the farms that Henry Ford had established in Dearborn to remind him of his origins. There a man named Ray Dahlinger, a surviving warlord from the Bennett years, was ensconced, and he ran the farm as if it were his empire. He had several hundred people on his payroll, which came to about $500,000 each year. Though Dahlinger had been a Bennett deputy, he had stayed on long after the others had been fired. He was, it seemed, a close friend of Henry Ford's widow. Indeed, Dahlinger's wife, it was said by many, including her son, who later wrote a book on the subject, had been Henry Ford's mistress. Clara Ford had in time taken her revenge on Henry in an odd, indirect fashion—by being exceptionally protective of Dahlinger, the mistress's husband. Thus secure, Dahlinger treated everyone, including the new regime of Henry Ford II, with a special imperiousness, and indulged himself freely. He was the last vestige of the days when Bennett and his people, as their whim directed, siphoned off company money for their own personal use. He had his own valet and his own barber and a legion of gardeners. The gardeners did not work in vain, for the terraces that they tended were wonderful. The grapes in the greenhouse were huge, each bunch hand-tied to give it more sun. It was a lovely life for Ray Dahlinger—gargantuan grapes, beautiful roses, breathtaking terraces, a striking waterfall; a luxurious, unmolested existence, all of it paid for by the Ford Motor Company.

Young Henry Ford wanted to end this dukedom. So in 1947 he called in Arjay Miller, by then an assistant treasurer.

"Arjay," said Ford, "you'll be pleased to know that Dahlinger now works for you."

"Does he know this?" Miller asked.

"No," said Henry Ford. So it was decided that Ford would write a letter advising Dahlinger that he worked for Miller. That was done, and although Miller was a man clearly on the rise, Dahlinger treated him with contempt.

"Young man," he said, "you may not remember a time when another financial officer, a fellow named Burt Craig, came and told me we were losing more than five million a year, and I told him if he didn't like it he could stick his nose up my ass."

That might be, Miller said, and then tried to suggest that things were going to be done a little differently from then on, that all expenditures would be countersigned in the treasurer's office, and if that Dahlinger had any questions he could call Henry Ford. Dahlinger grumbled but accepted the new system.

About three years later, Clara Bryant Ford died. Henry Ford was in New York at the time, and he picked up the phone and called Arjay Miller in Detroit.

"Arjay," he said, "I have just one message for you—fire Dahlinger."

Miller did that, finding the mighty Dahlinger unexpectedly meek. Miller told him he had twenty-four hours to get off the property. With that the old era finally ended.

Henry Ford had hated accountants so much that he left his grandson a company in absolute financial disrepair. It was not surprising, then, that the young Henry Ford, seeking to bring sense to the madness he found all around him, turned to an entirely new breed of executive, the professional managers, the bright young financial experts who knew, if not automobiles and manufacturing plants, at least systems and bottom lines. To them Henry Ford II gave nearly unlimited power. Thus again did the past influence the future. For the past was always present. If the old order had been more sensible, perhaps the new order would have been more sensible as well.

PART
THREE

6.
THE VICTOR

The first American vision of Japan in the postwar years was a liberal one. It came, ironically, from a deeply conservative man, Douglas MacArthur, the Supreme Commander for the Allied Powers. His was the first and last American raj. He had a powerful sense of both his nation's destiny and his own; like Charles de Gaulle, whom as a leader he greatly resembled, he saw no difference between the two. Difficult, egocentric, vainglorious, he demanded complete loyalty from those beneath him but did not always bestow comparable loyalty on those above him. He saw himself without living peers; the only men, he thought, from whom he might learn were Lincoln and Washington. His belief in his own vision and fate was so strong that few other men dared challenge it. Politically that made him something akin to a live hand grenade. "Douglas," Franklin Roosevelt once told him in a moment of insight, "I think you may be our best general, but I believe you could be our worst politician." He was almost incapable of saying anything respectful of any general who had fought in the European theater, most particularly Dwight Eisenhower, his former aide, whose strengths were precisely MacArthur's weaknesses. For Eisenhower was gifted at restraining his own ego and blending the talents of diverse, headstrong people for a common purpose.

No civilian who ever dealt with MacArthur relished the assignment, and during the Korean War, Secretary of State Dean Acheson (who called him "the Oracle") said of him, "While General MacArthur had many of the attributes of a foreign sovereign . . . and was quite as difficult as any, it did not seem wise to recognize him as one." Harry Truman, angered by MacArthur's challenge to civilian authority, once pointed to a portrait of him and told Carlos Romulo of the Philippines, "You know who that is? That's God."

"Mr. President," Romulo answered, "there are millions of Filipinos who think he is just that."

He was alternately capable of nobility and of remarkable pettiness. Obeyed and revered, he grew in stature; disputed, he became mean and petulant, given to sulks. In some ways Japan, then, was the perfect stage for him; it was a country where authority was respected and his word would be law. There, as was not the case in America, the head of government and the legislature would not lightly confront him; there they would rubber-stamp his wishes. There he would go unchallenged, at least directly, by either Americans or Japanese. (If an American journalist wrote something that displeased him, he would not censor that correspondent, but, since he controlled entry to Japan, he would make sure that the offending reporter did not reenter his domain.) It was the perfect situation for him, and it evoked at the end of a distinguished but often contentious military career his best qualities.

He knew his was a historic role, and his vision for the Japanese was generous. He intended to take this militaristic, authoritarian society, many of whose practices were still feudal, and bring it into the modern age. It was his finest hour, and certainly one of his country's. His country behaved generously in no small part because he forced it to.

He was, like de Gaulle, the complete thespian. His every move was studied; he was always aware of his position and the symbolism of his deeds. Vain about his appearance, he worked endlessly to cover his baldness with his remaining wisps of hair. Although he almost always wore glasses, he refused to be photographed wearing them. (De Gaulle, facing the same problem late in his career, held presidential press conferences before which questions had been handed out to friendly reporters. That allowed him to memorize the answers so that—in those days before TelePrompTers—he would not have to squint at cue cards or stumble through impromptu answers.) Everything MacArthur did was about impact and about the theater of being a general. "If MacArthur had ever gone on stage, you never would have heard of John Barrymore," said Rear Admiral James Doyle, who had watched MacArthur persuade the reluctant navy to undertake the amphibious landing at Inchon. "I seem to have more confidence in the navy than the navy has in itself," MacArthur had said at the meeting. "The navy has never let me down in the past, and it will not let me down this time." The star of the show would always be Douglas MacArthur. "He does not intend that any other actor shall walk on the stage and receive any applause if he can help it," said General Robert Eichelberger, one of the officers who knew him best. For him to play his own role to the fullest, others would have to see their roles diminished. That quality made him endless enemies.

His years in Japan reflected his skilled use of theatrics. Not by chance did he arrive for the first time at Atsugi airport in Japan unarmed. It was immediately after the Japanese surrender; only a handful of American troops were in the country, and his aides still worried about the possibility of a right-wing rebellion. But MacArthur was serene. Years of service in Asia, he explained later, "had taught the Far East that I was its friend." Nor was it by chance that he then bided his time and let the Emperor come to him, so that the lesson would be clear to all, most notably the Emperor, that Douglas MacArthur was now the ruler of this country. Lest there be any doubt that the torch had been passed, he permitted publication of the photograph of their meeting. Nothing could be more telling—the Emperor, small, ill-at-ease, in top hat and striped pants; MaArthur, patrician and yet quintessentially the informal American, wearing his khakis without battle ribbons, shirt open at the collar, towering over the Emperor. There could be no doubt who was the conqueror and who was the conquered.

Though a conqueror, he held no contempt for the conquered and even sympathized with their plight. That made him very much the exception among his associates both in Tokyo and in Washington, where the feeling, after so cruel a four-year campaign against a foe perceived as an oppressor, was rancorous. For many of the senior Allied officers the memories of the Pacific war and what the Japanese had done to their prisoners were vivid. Few generals and admirals could forget the cadaverous figure of Lieutenant General Jonathan Wainwright, finally released from the hell of a Japanese prison camp, joining them at the surrender ceremonies. Some wanted vengeance in various forms; Admiral William Halsey spoke of riding the Emperor's white horse down the main streets of Tokyo. But from the start MacArthur saw beyond that. His job was not to punish but to create a society which would never again follow that path. He knew his enemy was ravaged; he then would be the most magnanimous of victors. This was the great chance not only to bring Japan into the modern era but also to fashion a democracy. From the beginning, at the ceremonies aboard the battleship *Missouri*, he stressed the theme of the generous victor. He had decided on that long before the war was over (although after the outcome was no longer in doubt). In March 1945 he told the writer Robert Sherwood that victory over Japan would make America the most powerful nation in Asia. "If we exert that influence in an imperialistic manner," he said, "or for the sole purpose of commercial advantage, then we shall lose our golden opportunity; but if our influence and strength are expressed in terms of essential liberalism we shall have the friendship and the cooperation of the Asiatic peoples far into the future."

That was his goal. He let the Japanese disarm themselves, thus saving them the humiliation of being disarmed by their conqueror. Knowing that Japan was desperately short of food, he ordered his troops to subsist on their rations and not plunder the local supplies. He canceled Eichelberger's early orders setting a curfew and creating martial law. When Admiral Halsey, fearing sabotage, prohibited fishermen from crossing Tokyo Bay on their way to their fishing grounds, MacArthur, aware that this was a critical source of food for the country as well as the fishermen's livelihood, rescinded the order. Sensitive to the importance of the Emperor to the Japanese people, sure that he could use him for his own purposes, he had Hirohito's name crossed off a list of those to be charged as war criminals. In the early days, when many in Washington would have been content to watch Japan starve, he fought hard for food. "Give me bread or give me bullets," he cabled home. At that same time he fought against those in the United States and among the Allies who intended to strip Japan of what little industrial capacity it had left. He intended, as a counterbalance to the forces that had brought Japan into World War II, to democratize the society, and to push it, in his words, "left of center." John Gunther, the liberal journalist, was staggered by the completeness of MacArthur's vision for Japan. Occupied Japan reminded him of Republican Spain before the Communists moved in. The programs, Gunther wrote, were remarkably similar, "an attempt to end feudalism, drastic curtailment of ancient privilege, land reform, liberation of women, extremely advanced labor legislation, education for the mass, 'bookmobiles' out in the villages, abolition of the nobility, wide extension of social service, birth control, public health, steep taxation of the unconverted rich, discredit of the military, and embracing almost everything in every field, reform, *reform*, RE-FORM."

In those years after the war, perhaps nothing was more important than his will, especially his determination to reform Japanese society to his specifications. For postwar Japan was a place of immense turbulence, a society waiting to be redefined. The country was devastated. There was very little housing or food. The essential functioning economy was the black market. Members of aristocratic families, once rich and grand, now fallen on hard times, bartered their heirlooms for a day's nourishment. Treasured family kimonos were traded for enough rice for two people. Japan became almost overnight a society without form, its traditional hierarchical order turned upside down. Those who had once ruled, both in government and in industry, were contaminated by their wartime experiences. The higher someone had been in the old order, the more likely he was to have been tainted by participation in the war effort; only those at the bottom who had been critical of that effort were legitimized, and many of these, as it happened, were Communists. MacArthur had no use for the special privilege that the prewar Japan had afforded the zaibatsu, the huge, interconnected industrial complexes that had dominated the nation and were believed to have helped push Japan into the war. He said that the zaibatsu, in which government and giant industries were intertwined, represented "private socialism." He believed that the society had to be changed and that political democratization by itself was not sufficient. Without introducing economic change as well, the Americans would be creating a fertile field for a radical new order. Political change had to be accompanied by economic change—especially the redistribution of land from the large landowners to poor tenant farmers. (Under the orders of the American occupiers, reluctant Japanese landlords finally had to do the unthinkable: sell their land to those who tilled it—a historic step.) He also wanted to limit the power of the zaibatsu and give greater economic power to the average worker.

The attitude of Washington to all this, in those early years, seemed somewhat ambivalent. In Europe it was clear fairly soon after the war that the Americans intended to rebuild not just their allies but their adversaries as well; in Japan, American intentions were not nearly so benevolent. The amount of American aid to Japan, for example, even in terms of the most basic kind of food, was extremely limited. MacArthur had a considerable respect for the quality of men he had just fought and for their willingness to bear terrible burdens. He was, in fact, among the first of the conquerors to recognize the Japanese work ethic. In 1950, during the Korean War, he told Averell Harriman that the Japanese were remarkable in the way they venerated work. "He spoke," Harriman noted, "of the great quality of the Japanese; his desire to work, the satisfaction of the Japanese in work, his respect for the dignity of work. He compared it favorably to the desire in the United States for more luxury and less work."

It was by no means certain whether Americans other than MacArthur wanted Japan to rise again as an industrial force: Clearly it would not be allowed to rise as a military force. An antagonism which was at least partly racial affected the average American's view of the average Japanese as it did not affect an American's perception of the average German. In addition, almost from the moment the war in Europe ended there was a sense of the Soviet Union as a serious adversary; thus there was a need in Europe to bolster the defeated enemy as part of the bulwark against a newer enemy. That same need did not seem to extend to Japan. At the end of the war, China, not yet Communist, was still perceived as a U.S. ally. The Cold War came to Asia some two years after it arrived in Europe.

MacArthur was seen by his fellow citizens as an archconservative, and so his plan to liberalize Japan was astonishing not just to his critics back in the States but to old-time members of the general's staff. His head-quarters staff often seemed divided between the traditionalists, some of whom were very conservative, who had been with him a long time, and who greatly preferred to deal with Japan's existing business order, and the bright young New Dealers, bent on redoing the old imperial order, who were determined to loosen the power of the zaibatsu and purge some of the prewar business figures. His headquarters was filled with intrigue as both sides struggled for his ear. Much of the tension within the offices of the Supreme Commander for the Allied Powers (SCAP) centered around the Occupation's attitude toward labor unions and the rather radical labor leaders who were just beginning to emerge. Among the new freedoms given the Japanese was the right to organize. The Americans viewed this as being not only right and proper, the sort of thing that an egalitarian society should bestow, but also a means of checking the power of the zaibatsu. MacArthur made union membership legal and actively encour-aged the unions. Where there had been only 400,000 union members before the war, by May 1946 there were 2.7 million and, by the end of that year, more than 4.5 million. This postwar American idealism did not come without its problems. For one thing, Japan had almost no history of moderate trade unionism. Most of the top labor leaders in that era were in fact Communists.

There were two quite separate political phases to the MacArthur Oc-cupation. The first, which lasted from 1945 through part of 1947, was the idealistic one, of which the general himself was the primary architect. In that period the Americans, bent on rescuing a physically prostrated Japan and trying to create some basis for a new democratic order, were tolerant of radical political forces they often privately detested. Japanese busi-nessmen who had been leaders in the zaibatsu were purged. Excesses on the part of the unions were condoned. The second phase began in 1949. The policy changed not so much because of events in Japan but because of events in the world. The Cold War had intensified in Europe, the Communists were about to win in China, and Washington, which was already in the process of strengthening and reindustrializing West Ger-many, suddenly began to see Japan differently: It should become a free-world bastion in Asia. It should be industrialized. Its traditional business structure should be strengthened, not undermined. Assaults upon the zaibatsu were to stop. There was to be pressure against the left, particularly against radical trade unions. All of this had a profound effect on the even-tual formation of Japanese unions and their role in their companies. Thus the relationships between Japanese workers and managers that American businessmen in the seventies and eighties found so frustrating were engineered in the late forties and early fifties under the auspices of the American Occupation.

In that first period MacArthur's job was doubly difficult, for not only did he have limited support back home, but he was also dealing with a series of governments in Japan that were distinctly unsympathetic to the idea of any kind of reform. The Americans needed a government through which to operate, but their choices were quite limited. The most experienced public figures were from the old order and wanted little change; those who were sympathetic to change either had too little experience or might want not just change but revolution. Faced with this dilemma, the Americans chose to work through surviving politicians of the old order, who were inevitably far more conservative in their vision of the future than MacArthur was. There simply was no alternative as far as SCAP was concerned. It might have wanted a Japanese version of the New Deal, a nice, moderately liberal administration with strong connections to labor and to the masses, but no such group existed. So it happened that the dominant politician of those years was a man that the American officials never particularly liked.

Shigeru Yoshida headed five cabinets between 1946 and 1954, and that time was known, properly enough, as the Yoshida era. His first priority, the restoration of the old order in Japan, from the beginning brought him in constant conflict with MacArthur and his headquarters. To the Americans, Japan's militarism had stemmed from significant structural weaknesses that now had to be addressed by American reforms. The Americans were appalled by Japan's feudal attributes and by the gulf that separated the few who were privileged from the millions who were not. To Allied theorists, Japanese soldiers had behaved brutally in victory as a "transfer of oppression," a result of the harshness with which they themselves had been treated. A more balanced and more democratic society, the Americans believed, would not so readily have been pulled by its jingoists into so tragic a war.

Yoshida disagreed fervently. What the Americans were criticizing was what he represented. He was the perfect embodiment of the best of the old order—aristocratic, intelligent, snobbish, politically unreconstructed. Unlike the militarists who came to power in the thirties, who were anti-Western, he was pro-Western (but more Anglophile than pro-American). He had opposed the Pacific war (but not Japanese imperialism in China, which he supported and which he had seen as something that could be conducted in the British colonial tradition, possibly even with British approval). He had regarded Pearl Harbor and the war that ensued as a disaster for Japan. To him the rise of the Japanese military was an aberration. During the war he had been part of a secret group maneuvering for peace; he did this because he knew Japan was losing the war, and he feared not just the inevitable defeat but, even more frightening, the left-wing apocalypse he was convinced would follow if the war dragged on. Because of these activities he had been arrested by the Kempeitai, the secret police, near the end of the war and held for forty days. To a considerable degree that helped validate him in the eyes of the occupiers as a certified antiwar figure. Yet from the start of the American Occupation he accepted on the part of his class no blame for what had happened before and during the war. To Yoshida there was nothing unjust or parasitic about the prewar ruling class. Rather it was paternalistic and high-minded. Japan, in his eyes, should be run by the right people, an old-boy network of men from the right social class who had gone to the right schools. He hated the purge of the zaibatsu carried on by SCAP in the early postwar years, for by and large these were his friends and colleagues who were being eliminated from public life. At one press conference he defended the zaibatsu. Many of them, he said, had worked for the militarists not at a profit but at a loss during the war. The true profiteers were the new rich, whose fortunes had soared because of the war. The old rich, he said, had welcomed the end of the war.

He was a crusty, abrasive, egocentric, sharp-tongued man who had come from a privileged background. His blood father was descended from the samurai, his mother was probably a geisha. (In his later years he spent a lot of time with geishas himself, and questioned about this, he answered, "Geishas' sons like geishas.") His father was in prison for his political activities at the time of his birth, and it was decided that he should be adopted by a friend of his father, Kenzo Yoshida. With that he had gone from being the fifth son of a moderately successful family to the only son in a very rich one. His new father, the operator of a successful shipping agency, had become remarkably wealthy in a very short time; when he died in 1887, he left his adopted nine-year-old son some $6 million. The boy was raised by his mother to be, as he later put it, "proud and egotistical." "The child," she liked to say of him, "doesn't make mistakes." He was reared as a proper young gentleman of post-Meiji Japan. He was liberal for the society from which he had sprung, not so much in his view of Japanese domestic politics but in his acceptance of the idea of a world beyond Japan itself. He was from the start brilliantly connected; when he married it was to Yukiko Makino, the eldest daughter of Nobuaki Makino, who later became foreign minister and privy seal and one of the Emperor's closest advisers. As a young and wealthy foreign service officer he had been noted for his arrogance; later he liked to tell of the time when he was consul general in Tientsin, China, and a member of the Diet came by the official residence: " 'I wish to see the consul general.' 'The consul general is out,' I said. 'Really?' he asked in disbelief, whereupon I replied: 'If the consul general himself says he is absent, then he is really absent.' "

Yoshida and his wife were probably the closest Japanese friends of Ambassador and Mrs. Joseph Grew in the tense times just before the start of the war. In 1941, when Mrs. Yoshida was dying of cancer, it was the Grews who provided Ovaltine, which was the only nourishment she could take at the time, and gave Yoshida a car so that he could visit his wife in the hospital. When his group lost their struggle with the militarists, Yoshida sat out most of the war until he was arrested. When the war was over, Yoshida, fresh out of political prison, was an attractive figure for the Americans trying to compose a government. He was antimilitarist, pro-Western, and experienced in international affairs. In 1945, when Yoshida was made foreign minister in the Shidehara cabinet, Prince Fumimaro Konoe, the prewar prime minister, said of him: "I am not behind others in my admiration for Yoshida, but Yoshida's consciousness is the consciousness of the era of Imperial Japan, and I wonder if that can go well in a defeated Japan."

True enough, Yoshida's relationship with the Americans was never easy. MacArthur once spoke of him as "monumentally lazy and politically inept," a significant misreading of Yoshida, who was neither lazy nor inept, but who did not want the same things as MacArthur and thus became exceptionally skilled at not hearing what he chose not to hear and dragging his feet when the Americans wanted him to move ahead. He saw his job as preserving Japan, not changing it, and to the degree that he could slow down the reformers, he intended to do it. Often he seemed to taunt the conquerors in small subtle ways, deliberately going to Shinto shrines in the postwar years although the Americans felt that Shintoism was part of the reason for Japanese militarism, on other occasions signing letters to the Emperor "your loyal servant Shigeru" when he knew the Americans wanted those in government to be *public* servants, not servants—as in the past—of the Emperor. Comfortable with the prewar British and their colonialist realpolitik, he found the postwar American policymakers too innocent. He hated the idealists in SCAP ("quite peculiar types," he said), who seemed to promote what he termed "revolution for revolution's sake."

Yoshida's strategy was canny. Rather than confront the Americans on everything, he conducted a delaying action, slowing them down if at all possible, hoping to roll back some of their reforms once they had departed. Among the few reforms he did not oppose was the land reform, although he told Hiroo Wada, who was in charge of carrying it out, "As a conservative I am opposed to this on principle." Typically, when the Americans wanted to change the names of some of the zaibatsu, which might have cost businessmen millions and millions of yen, Yoshida fought the reform and won. What the Americans saw as legitimate grievances on the part of large segments of the Japanese population, whether workers or farmers, he never accepted. He thought the people with grievances were those leaders of the business and financial community whom the Americans were busy purging. To him purging was guilt by association, a practice, he said, in which civilized nations no longer indulged. In early 1947, when his own minister of finance, Tanzan Ishibashi, was purged, Yoshida consoled him by saying, "Just imagine that you have been bitten by a mad dog."

Of all SCAP's reforms he most hated the liberalization of laws permitting the formation of labor unions. The Communists had always been a part of his nightmare, and he had feared the power they might gain once the war effort collapsed. Now here were his old enemies, the leftists, coming back, gathering strength within the union movement, tolerated by the Americans, trying to undermine his efforts to re-create the right Japan. Even worse, they were attacking him personally. His opposition was not just to the radical unions; in his heart he hated moderate ones as well. His view of what labor should do was relatively simple: Its job was to work hard, to raise productivity, and not to challenge management on rights and wages.

Yoshida regarded Douglas MacArthur with considerable suspicion. In that first phase of the Occupation, MacArthur's command was trying to do something fairly delicate: Under the most difficult conditions of hunger and poverty, it was trying to nurture a non-Communist, democratic union movement against the opposition of a conservative Japanese government while tolerating what it considered abuses of democratic freedoms on the part of a particularly skillful Communist leadership. It was doing this, rather than arbitrarily cracking down on the Communists, because it was eager to teach the Japanese lessons in democracy, and it would not be fitting, no matter how suspicious MacArthur and his aides were of the Communists, to begin its lessons in democracy by squashing a newly legalized opposition party, particularly an opposition party whose rhetoric sounded much like that of SCAP. Besides, SCAP was confident of its own power and its ability to crush the Communists if need be.

The conservative Yoshida government was furious with the early American tolerance of the far left, in no small part because Yoshida himself was a choice target of the Communists. He complained constantly to Mac-

Arthur's headquarters about its encouragement of what he believed were subversive elements in the unions, and he repeatedly criticized MacArthur's own staff, claiming that it was riddled with Communists. Yoshida even told MacArthur that Theodore Cohen, his liberal labor staff man, was a Communist. (Cohen retaliated by asking Yoshida at one gathering whether the prime minister had ever had a single friend who was a working man. Yoshida said nothing, but quickly walked off.) Not only was MacArthur convinced that labor unions had to be part of the new Japan, a balancing force to the powerful ingrained business interests, but he also had serious political ambitions in America and had no desire to return as a candidate who had just crushed Japanese labor. Yoshida kept pushing MacArthur to move against the Communists, but in 1945 and 1946 the general held back. (Yoshida also disliked the Socialists, whom he compared to mermaids: "Their faces suggest they are beautiful maidens, but their bodies are like fish. Yes, they smell of fish.") He and others, principally the country's industrialists, were insisting to the American authorities that the Communists in the unions could not be controlled.

Though the Communist party in Japan was rather small (it had been made legal in the fall of 1945), its hold on certain unions was almost complete; the Communist labor leaders liked to boast that a handful of party members controlled the teamsters, the printers, and the newspaper unions. There was little reason to doubt this. The most influential labor leaders in many of the unions were Communists, and the most powerful figure on the left in the country was Kyuichi Tokuda, the head of the Communist party, who had just been released after some eighteen years in jail as a political prisoner. He was a fiery speaker, a talented organizer, and a true revolutionary. He believed that Japan, because of disillusion over the war and because of hunger and poverty, was ripe for revolution. He saw the labor unions as the means to that revolution. Tokuda was somewhat surprised by the legitimacy the Americans permitted him and surprised even more by their tolerance of his mounting protest movement. Few though they were, the Communists were extremely well organized, and they had considerable prestige, since no other group had suffered nearly as much at the hands of the militarists. That MacArthur's headquarters had not acted against them added to their popularity among many Japanese; if the Americans did not crush them, it was reasoned, then they must be supporting them.

The radicalism of the unions seemed to grow in 1946, as the economic situation worsened. Inflation was out of control, government expenditures exceeded receipts by some 67 percent that year, and the only thing the government could do was keep printing money. The harvest was bad, and at one point there was only four days' supply of rice in government hands. Some of the growing rebelliousness was the product of genuine grievance, some of it the result of manipulation on the part of the Communists. In the fall of 1946, Tokuda decided that this was the perfect moment to press the Communist case. He organized a series of mass meetings at which the left demanded food and listed other complaints. The great moment for the radicals came in early 1947. Mass meetings held outside the Imperial Palace drew huge crowds. It was as if a tide were carrying the left forward.

In those heady weeks, the Communists seemed to be surging toward power without opposition. Indeed, one high Communist leader used American naval craft to meet with dock workers; to the Japanese that represented not merely American tolerance but American support. The government seemed immobilized. The radicals suddenly looked like winners, and in Japan that was a powerful asset. Tokuda intended to bring the business of the nation to a halt; if he did, he believed, he could seize power in the chaos. He skillfully brought the more moderate unions under his control, at least momentarily. In this he was aided by Yoshida's stubbornness. Yoshida and his government were unable to make any accommodation with the moderate unions and thus isolate the more radical ones. A general strike was called for February 1, 1947. Slowly and steadily, support for the strike appeared to grow. Much of the Japanese press seemed to favor it. Early reports at MacArthur's headquarters estimated that two million Japanese workers would take part. But Tokuda continued to gain strength. SCAP changed its estimate: Four million Japanese would take part. Then a Communist leader was found stabbed to death in his home, a victim of right-wing zealots in an assassination that was painfully reminiscent of the prewar assassinations. That too fed the radical movement. After the stabbing the Socialists joined with Tokuda. That meant six million workers might go out on strike.

Until the very eve of the strike, MacArthur held back. His view of himself mandated that he stay above the fray, that the Japanese deal only with his underlings and that they divine his intentions, which were that this strike should not take place. But he was loath to give them orders, preferring instead that they find that his way was their way. Through his subordinates he had already sent out very clear messages to Tokuda and his allies that he would not permit a strike like this to cripple an already fragile society with so ravaged an economy. The Communists had not seemed to take the warnings seriously. They mistook MacArthur's Olympian distance as a sign of weakness. It was a mistake. Finally, only nine and a half hours before the strike deadline, MacArthur moved. There was only a three-day supply of food and gas in the country, and he would not accept a strike that was virtually life-threatening. "I will not permit," his statement declared, "the use of so deadly a social weapon in the present impoverished and emaciated condition of Japan." He also censored the Communist paper, and his headquarters began to crack down in other ways on Communist activity, for example by limiting contact between labor officials and representatives of Communist nations.

For a moment Tokuda and his people considered defying MacArthur. But their strength was only at the top of the unions; they had little organization and standing among the rank-and-file, and ordinary Japanese workers were not about to challenge Douglas MacArthur at that moment. The Communists had mistaken influence for power. They had overplayed their hand, and when they backed down in front of MacArthur, they immediately lost face. They had hoped to gain some fifteen seats in the Diet in the April elections; instead they lost one. Tokuda himself was purged by MacArthur in 1950, right after the Korean War began. He slipped out of Japan and made his way to China, where he died in the mid-fifties.

After that incident, MacArthur continued to move against the far left. Within his headquarters the conservatives gained power over the New Dealers. (Part of the reason, it was always believed by those who knew the general well, was that back home in America, the conservatives had done exceptionally well in the 1946 elections, which in turn affected MacArthur's attitude toward Japanese unions.) Soon, with American help, the Japanese began to strip their unions of Communists. In 1949, with MacArthur's support, there was an all-out assault upon Communist leadership in the unions which became known as "the Red Purge." In union after union the Communists and some of their colleagues were simply arrested and removed from their jobs. As many as ten thousand workers were fired during these purges, and hundreds of thousands were pulled back from union membership. The American army sent its counterintelligence people, many of them Nisei, to go through the country looking for Communist leaders.

These events in Japan reflected the larger changes taking place in international politics. American policy in Japan was about to shift because American foreign policy throughout the world was very quickly changing. The Cold War was intensifying. The wartime alliances were over. Old allies were the new adversaries, and old adversaries were about to be the new allies. Not only was American involvement in the Cold War deepening but also, as it deepened, it affected domestic American politics, and thus

Washington's attitudes, as well. By 1948 it was obvious that Chiang Kai-shek's power was diminishing and that America could not count on a stable anti-Communist China. Instead, China was likely to go Communist. That brought a profound change in Washington's attitude toward Japan. In the past MacArthur had had to fight for every scrap of aid, be it food or financial. A weak Japan did not bother many high-level Americans in those days. But when the Cold War extended to the Pacific, Washington's attitude changed. Suddenly there was a need for a Pacific bastion. Washington, which had been slightly amused by (and only marginally supportive of) MacArthur's on-the-job attempt to teach the Japanese democracy by permitting them to stumble ahead themselves and make their own mistakes, suddenly became nervous about a nation so economically vulnerable. It was no longer the quality of Japanese domestic life which was at stake but, instead, American geopolitics.

Where the tilt in MacArthur's headquarters had been somewhat to the left and against the old industrialists, Washington now wanted to favor the Japanese business community. There was increasing pressure on MacArthur from American conservatives to bring some coherence and stability to the Japanese economy and to stop what some people in Washington regarded as his persecution of the zaibatsu. As far as Washington was concerned, MacArthur was permissive toward the left and too tolerant of incompetent governmental machinery; his headquarters was sponsoring an inflated, undisciplined economy. The problem could not be MacArthur himself; everyone in Washington knew how conservative he was. Therefore, it had to be the New Dealers around him. George Kennan, then the national security establishment's leading authority on Communism, had repeatedly warned against occupation policies that weakened the power of business and against a general drift toward socialism, which might eventually turn the country Communist. Others, like James Forrestal, warned against the power of leftist New Dealers in MacArthur's headquarters. It was time to shape up the Japanese economy and, by so doing, stiffen the country against the Communists.

The first move against MacArthur's control of the economy was a visit in the fall of 1947 by William Draper, a former general and Dillon Read banker who was then undersecretary of the army. Draper's visit was an important one. He had already played a pivotal role in West Germany, where, as an aide to General Lucius Clay, MacArthur's counterpart in Europe, he had in effect ended one program, that of denazification of West German politics and the breaking up of the old German cartels, and started a new one, that of strengthening German industry. When Draper left Germany, America was no longer looking for Nazis; it was, under the pressure of a growing confrontation with the Soviet Union, looking for allies. Now, in Japan, his role was to be strikingly similar. In Tokyo Draper announced that he wanted to reduce the expense of American support for Japan. "Tremendous costs have accrued to the victor," Draper noted. But what he really wanted to do was change the direction of the policy. Draper lobbied forcefully with MacArthur against SCAP's reforms. America needed to strengthen the Japanese business community, not hobble it with trust-busting and decentralization, he argued. The purges of businessmen must stop, he insisted. In 1948 Draper returned to Tokyo to press his case again with MacArthur. It was clearer now than ever before that Washington wanted to change its policies in Tokyo. Still frustrated by what he considered the lack of urgency at MacArthur's headquarters, Draper asked MacArthur if he would accept a man named Joseph Dodge on temporary assignment to his staff. Dodge's job would be to tighten up the Japanese economy by enforcing earlier Washington directives. MacArthur said he had no objection as long as Dodge was under his command.

Joseph Dodge arrived in Tokyo on February, 1, 1949. His stay was to last only three months. He was a small, somewhat self-important, pugnacious man who even in Japan, where men were generally short, wore lifts in his shoes. He had graduated from high school in Detroit and instead of going to college had immediately set to work as a clerk in a bank. In Japan he was sent on the most complicated of modern international missions, but he remained the ultimate conservative small-town banker (although later in his career he headed a large bank in Detroit.) No relation to the automobile family, Dodge was the product of grinding, suspicious, and unsentimental times in America. As far as he was concerned, the banker's job was to say no—with few exceptions. Banks succeeded not by being visionary and anticipating the changes in society but by lending only small amounts to the surest candidates under the strictest conditions. He was, said one friend, a nickel-and-dime man.

He liked to boast that when he served as a bank examiner for the state of Michigan, he enjoyed his work immensely. The other examiners, he said, would take the word of the local banker about how much cash was in the vault. Not Joseph Dodge. He liked to gather the bank's staff and, with them, go into the vault, whereupon the evening would be spent counting every dollar.

He had taken over what was to become the Detroit Bank in 1933, one of the worst moments of the Depression, when that city's banks were probably hit harder than any in the country. By dint of the toughness of his approach—the relentless manner with which he scrutinized every loan and rejected all he possibly could—he held that bank together during the bad times, so that afterward, during the war, it became very successful. No one, he liked to point out, had ever given anything away to him, and he had no intention of giving anything away to anyone else. He liked to boast that he had dealt with the possibility of his bank's giving out bad loans during the Depression by the simplest of all methods—depriving all bank officers, including himself, of the authority to lend money. He hated an economy that was loose, where money moved around too easily, where the standards of lending were too flexible.

He knew of nothing but work. Other bankers, the Grosse Pointe men who were connected to GM and Ford, might have had a certain panache that allowed them to mix in the upper-class social milieu of the city, but Joe Dodge was always edgy there. He thought a lot of those fancier bankers were soft, men who depended on social connections instead of hard work. His lack of education hung heavily on him, and there was nothing he could talk about but the bank. He was comfortable when he was working and uncomfortable when he was not. To the day he retired he was at his desk both Saturdays and Sundays. He was a man for mean times, not good times; parsimonious during the Depression, he had difficulty adjusting to the lusher postwar American economy. The boom—easy money, too many people buying too many things—made him nervous. In those years he deliberately took his bank out of one of the most profitable of all areas, lending construction money both to individuals and to institutions. The building boom was something he neither liked nor understood. He believed there were simply too many people buying and building houses for the first time in their lives, people to whom in the past he never would have lent money. When he was young, people of this class did not own their own houses, and he could not conceive of them doing so now. To him life was simple—no one should ever spend more than he made—and the bank was the enforcer of that Puritan credo. A simple, conservative man of the American Midwest, he believed in the verities—a balanced budget, the free market, and as little government interference in business as possible. "The imperial accountant," Ted Cohen, one of the SCAP liberals, called him.

Dodge had already worked for Bill Draper in Germany, where he had created a new currency, the deutsche mark. Wary of taking on the Japanese society, he had been talked into the assignment by Harry Truman, who said, first, that he desperately needed him, and second, that he would back him up completely. The condition of the Japanese economy simply staggered Dodge. To his eye, everything that possibly could be wrong with an economy was wrong with Japan's. There was runaway inflation. Fiscal discipline had completely broken down. Most odiously, two thirds of the Japanese gross national product passed through the hands of the government. If the budget did not work out as planned, the government simply printed more money. What more could be wrong? Japan's economy was like a man on stilts, he said; one stilt was American aid, and the other stilt was government subsidies to industry. He intended to kick away the stilts.

He had no illusions that he knew anything about Japan. For the first few weeks he did nothing but interview top Japanese officials, preferably bankers, preferably conservative, listening to what they thought their needs were. (He was immediately impressed by one aspect of their planning, he later told his friends in Detroit; from the start they had decided to have a weak yen so that it would be easy to export, and at the same time hard to import—there would be less temptation for them to buy the West's goods if they were priced exorbitantly. To Dodge, unhappy with the drift of American consumerism, that made a great deal of sense.) Then he was ready. He recommended Draconian measures to control what he thought was fiscal madness. More than anything else he intended to end inflation. The Japanese, he said, were going to have to learn to live within their means. The entire nation would have to tighten its belt. So the belts were tightened. Thousands of small and medium-sized companies, too deeply in debt already, with work forces too large for their relatively low levels of production, were forced into bankruptcy. Dodge chilled the economy almost immediately. "A textbook example of how a budget can stop an inflation cold," he later said of it.

His relationship with MacArthur was guarded; MacArthur had not particularly wanted Dodge out there, and almost anything Dodge recommended was implicitly a challenge to the way MacArthur's own trusted staff had operated. When Dodge finally made his recommendations to MacArthur, emphasizing a brutal cutting back of the existing budget, he was sure that the general would be enraged, for it implied that the military had been wasteful. As Dodge spoke for the new, more stringent budget, he watched MacArthur's face cloud up and become cold and angry. This is it, thought Dodge, he's really going to come down on me. For what seemed an uncommonly long time, the general said nothing. He simply stared out the window. Then he came over pointed his finger into Dodge's chest ("so hard that I thought he had pierced me," he later recalled) and said, "You're right—let's get on with it."

During Dodge's first year, revenues went to 108.7 percent of expenditures, and there was a governmental surplus of $1 billion. But the price was terrible for the many Japanese who, almost overnight, were told that they were no longer needed. This was particularly painful in a country where people were coming to expect that a job, once granted, was permanent. But the tide had turned. Once MacArthur's headquarters had been perceived as filled with liberal do-gooders carrying on experiments in Japan that they hadn't been able to get away with back in America. Now it was the turn of the conservatives. Dodge had been frustrated by the domestic policies of the New Deal. Now he was finally able to install in this distant Asian country the tough financial mechanisms that the New Dealers in the United States would never accept. Japan for him was an American ideologue's paradise, a miniature would-be America where a man of clear vision could play with the political and economic systems without having to deal with any domestic American opponents. Bankers, after all, might be rich and successful and even respected back in the United States, but in those years, at least, they were politically impotent. Here was a country worthy of their talents. Here was a country where people had to listen. Dodge's word was like the gospel. Fifteen years after Dodge left Tokyo, one of his deputies, Orville MacDiarmid, returned to Japan as a representative of the World Bank and urged the vice-minister of finance to issue domestic bonds to finance much-needed public works. The vice-minister was properly shocked. "But Mr. Dodge told us not to do that," he said. It was as if Dodge had been there only the day before.

The Yoshida government was delighted with Dodge's arrival. Yoshida might dissent from Dodge on minor points, but, after dealing with the New Dealers in MacArthur headquarters, here at last was the representative of conservative fiscal America that Yoshida had been looking for. Dodge was ordering Yoshida to do exactly what he had always wanted to do. Business-as-usual America was linking up with business-as-usual Japan. The assault upon the zaibatsu soon stopped. The yen was pegged to a fixed rate. If the Dodge policy was hard on lesser firms, which, lacking connections to banks, could not so readily ride out a hard time, it strengthened the position of the larger companies. "It can't be helped if one or two businessmen commit suicide," Hayato Ikeda, Yoshida's economic chief and liaison with Dodge, told the press. Equally important now, because of Dodge and the Americans, powerful Japanese businessmen had a mandate to become tougher with their workers than they had dared in the past two years.

Ikeda, who later became prime minister, grew quite close to Dodge. One day Ikeda came to their regular meeting and announced that the worst of the inflation was over and, with it, the worst of the black-marketeering. The recovery, Ikeda said, had finally begun.

"How do you know?" asked a suspicious Dodge.

"Because the police chief of Tokyo told me so today."

"And how does the police chief of Tokyo know?"

"Oh, he said he was sure that the recovery had begun because for the first time in years, Tokyo's thieves have started stealing money from people again. Until now, the money was not worth enough to steal."

Some friends thought that Dodge was more comfortable socially in Toyko than Detroit. He had been taken up by the upper crust of the Japanese business world. Yoshida connected him to the members of the royal family, and he soon joined with them in duck-netting, a sport of the nobility. (Ducks were funneled into small canals with high walls; they had to fly straight up, often into the net of the waiting duck-netter.) He came to like Japan immensely, particularly its puritanism. "This is the only country in the world," he told an aide named Ralph Reid, "where you can go out for dinner, have a good time, and still be home in bed by nine o'clock."

In America, outside of Detroit, the name of Joseph Dodge is barely known; in Japan, particularly in business circles, his name is an especially famous one. For his coming was an important moment in the postwar history of Japan. Dodge took the full authority of the American occupiers, which was still awesome at that time, and placed it completely behind the most conservative men in Japan. The old order, somewhat revitalized and slimmer and more modern, would be restored. Business would be strong, domestic competition more intense than before the war, labor unions by comparison weak, currency tight. Dodge had helped give the postwar ruling class what it had longed for but been too impotent and discredited to achieve on its own.

From then on in Japan it was called the Dodge Line. It brought a harsh new austerity to the country. Hundreds of thousands of men were fired. Fierce battles took place between labor and management over the issue of letting workers go; in many cases more than a third of the work force was dispensed with. There were strikes all over the country. Until then the labor unions had seemed to have the blessing of the Americans. Now the Americans seemed to be tilting the other way, deliberately placing their influence on the other side. At Toyota, Keiichi Toyoda, the head of the company and a member of the founding family (the family is spelled Toyoda, the car is spelled Toyota), tried desperately to honor the family tradition and not let go of his employees; he kept his workers on, and Toyota came so near bankruptcy that Toyoda himself had to leave the company—the bank chose his successor. What was at stake in these struggles, industry by industry, was the future definition of Japanese capitalism, though few realized it at the time. Eventually the ability to control its labor force proved to be critical in Japan's challenge to other Western nations, but no one was thinking that far ahead. No thought could have been more distant than the idea of challenging the United States. Everyone was preoccupied with survival. The question for most Japanese industrialists then was how to allot the nation's meager resources. Dodge and these men concurred: Japan had to use what little it had for machinery, not for pay raises.

It was, then, a period fraught with ironies. Business interests in America were enthusiastically on the side of the American mission as it cracked down on leftists in the labor unions. That, of course, vastly strengthened the capitalists in Japan, but in the long run it also created a relationship between labor and capital in Japan that greatly assisted production. As one radical union after another fell, the Japanese industrialists replaced them with unions that to Americans seemed company-sponsored. What was emerging were management-union (or, some would say, management-management) relations that Americans could not match, an advantage that American industrialists did not themselves enjoy.

The name Dodge became an honored one in both Tokyo and Detroit, but there was a painful awareness in the early eighties among some of the financial men of Detroit, as they surveyed that city's financial ruins, that their old mentor Joseph Dodge was in good part responsible. He had taught the challenger how to be so tough.

7.
THE BANKER

What happened at Nissan was a microcosm of the struggles going on throughout the country. In the early 1950s Japan's industrial class was still shaken and groggy from the war. Against it, an energetic working class was rising, often led by militant radicals. A confrontation was inevitable. When it occurred, at Nissan, it helped define the future of Japan and had profound implications for America.

The militants tended to mount their main challenge against the leading company in each industry, and in autos this meant either Toyota or Nissan. Because Toyota was in Toyota City, a classic company town near Nagoya, it was a less attractive target than Nissan, headquartered in Tokyo. They believed that if they could crack a company as strong as Nissan, then the lesser auto companies would readily fall in line. The businessmen, not just the other auto men but other industrialists throughout Japan, agreed with that reasoning. They were worried about Nissan, because its union was powerful and well led. By contrast, its management was weak, badly thinned out by the American purges. Yoshisuke Ayukawa, the founder, had been purged. He had put together the Nissan-Hitachi combine, which had rivaled Mitsui and Mitsubishi as a zaibatsu and which, backed by the Japanese army, had played a major role in the Japanese colonization of Manchuria; for that the Americans purged him. With him and several of his top aides gone there was a considerable vacuum in Nissan's leadership. As for the Nissan union, though many of the Communists had been driven out during the Red Purge, it had remained left-of-center. Its leader, Tetsuo Masuda, was considered brilliant and charismatic. His rhetoric was sometimes anti-American, which was ironic, because what he wanted to do— and what the industrialists feared he would do—was to create an American-style, industry-wide union modeled along the lines of the United Auto Workers.

In the postwar years Japan was different from the Western nations that had gone through comparable periods of industrialization. It had a pro-

letariat, but it did not see itself as having a proletariat. Rather it had a
hierarchy, into which everyone fit. (Even today, when Japan is one of the
two or three most industrialized nations in the world and when the class
distinctions, to Americans at least, seem distinct, the Japanese themselves
insist that they are a classless society. If that is true, then it is a classless
society in which everyone knows his place.) There was little tradition of
trade unions, and the prewar union movement had been pitifully weak.
In the past, most attempts to form a strong union movement had foundered
on the nation's powerful Confucian value system, in which a boss was to
be a good paternalist and the employee a loyal worker. The American
occupation somewhat changed that. New, alien ideas, based on Western
tradition of class conflict, had suddenly been imported. That gave a great
boost to the Japanese labor leaders, heretofore struggling with the Confucian order. Until the occupation, a labor leader who challenged the boss
was virtually challenging the order of the nation, and in Japan, the order
was the nation.

Yet if there was ever a time in Japan for rebellion, this was it. The old
regime had failed. It had lost most of its legitimacy because of its association
with a war that no one wanted to be connected to anymore. Furthermore,
the times were terrible. Years later the average Japanese worker or small
businessman, remembering those days, would recall first and foremost
two things: the constant, pervasive hunger and the feeling of always being
cold. The immediate postwar years for most Japanese had been given over
to an almost constant daily search for food. The day began with thoughts
of food and it ended with thoughts of food. In larger families in the cities,
usually one member was detailed to do nothing each day but get on a
train and go out into the countryside and try to negotiate with a farmer
for rice, if the family could afford it. Rice had once been the staple of the
diet, but it was too scarce and too expensive for most Japanese, and
anything available—wheat or cornmeal or anything procured from the
Americans—would do.

Sometimes if a family was lucky there was not only rice but an egg or
two as well, a genuine feast. No one ate very much chicken, for no one
was killing chickens in those days—they were a source of eggs. (Yoichi
Funabashi, later a major journalist on the *Asahi Shimbun*, remembered
that when he was a boy his family's two chickens were named Hansel and
Gretel—that is, they were not to be eaten.) Anyone who had a family
member who worked for the Americans was considered unusually fortunate, because the Americans, so carelessly rich, were a wondrous source
of foodstuffs and could upon occasion even supply tinned meats and canned
milk to the desperate Japanese. The tinned meat was judged to have a

somewhat unpleasant taste, and there were Japanese who even as they were eating it and grateful to be doing so wondered why a people so affluent would consume such a thing. The shrewd traders among the Japanese, and it was a time when shrewdness was critical to survival, took the goods from the Americans and bartered them with other Japanese for rice.

The cold was just as bad. Housing was extremely scarce. The endless bombings had left Tokyo with many buildings that were just shells. What American bombs had torn asunder, people now patched as best they could to keep out the cold. Families clustered in unfinished and unheatable rooms. Often several families would live in what had ostensibly been one house, though in fact very little of the house remained. Tokyo winters are hard anyway, not cold in the Russian sense, with heavy snow and very low temperatures, but cold with a relentless, penetrating dampness that enters the bones early in the winter and does not depart until long after spring arrives. Everyone seemed to have one suit of clothes and one overcoat, and no one took his coat off indoors. Whenever anyone entered a room from outdoors, he did it as quickly as possible, sliding in through a barely opened passage, so that whatever heat there was—most of it from other human bodies—would not escape. Years later, when Japan was a successful capitalist society, Westerners riding in taxis in the winter or entering offices would find them flagrantly overheated. Yes, their Japanese friends would confide, it *was* overheated, but this was because they had such clear memories of so many cold days and nights. It was if their bodies were still trying to catch up for warmth long ago missed.

What little resources the nation had just after the war had gone into the most basic of industries, railroads, steel, and shipping. For a time it was unclear whether or not Toyota and Nissan would be allowed to produce passenger cars. Trucks, certainly. But even trucks were hard to make, so meager were the resources. An American named Robert Alexander, a captain of an ordnance battalion at the end of the war and later a high Ford executive, happened to be at the Nissan factory in early 1946 when the first postwar truck was produced. It was a festive occasion, one of the few Alexander had seen in the devastated country. The Emperor had shown up, and Alexander was impressed by that, by the regenerative spirit it represented. When the first truck came down the line, Alexander was startled by how naked it looked. It had neither cab nor fenders. It was a box on wheels. There was some modest applause. Someone got in and tried to start the truck. It would not start. Alexander left, pessimistic about the prospects for a Japanese truck and auto industry.

The nation needed trucks, and so trucks they were willing to build. But passenger cars were the symbol of a frivolous society, too expensive for the average Japanese, a waste of precious metal. Where would the fuel come from? Besides, there was a feeling that it was a mistake to enter auto production because the Americans were simply too powerful there; if Japan needed cars for its most successful citizens, it could import a few of them from America. Most senior officials of the Japanese industrial establishment were opposed to an auto industry. These, after all, were prosperous men in their sixties and seventies, and they did not drive cars, their friends did not drive cars, and they saw no need for cars. But the younger men carried the day, the labor unions helped lobby for the loans, and an embryonic auto industry started in 1949.

The early postwar years at Nissan were very difficult. The union seemed stronger than management and dominated the decisions about wages. Until the Dodge Line the company had largely accommodated to the union; it believed that it was supposed to, that that was what the Americans wanted. Beyond this, there was a lack of will to draw the line. Those who normally would have been running the company had been purged by the Americans. Those who were running the company were still in shock, doubting their own legitimacy. Nissan was not part of the industrial-financial houses that were extensions of a family-bound ruling class, one of the old and time-honored zaibatsu, whose histories were bound up with the nation's history. Rather Nissan (the name was an abbreviation for Nippon Sangyo, or Japan Industries) was a new, almost instant zaibatsu, and Yoshisuke Ayukawa, the founder, was an arriviste among the old boys of the great family empires, Sumitomo, Mitsui, and Mitsubishi. Where they, at the start of the automotive age in Japan, had been cautious and wary, Ayukawa was enterprising and adventurous. His rise as an industrial leader in the 1930s had coincided with the rise of the militarists, and he became, inevitably, their partner, particularly in the Manchurian adventure. In the militarists' view, which was essentially fascistic, the zaibatsu reflected the old, gray, decadent Japan, a Japan that was too subservient to the West, and on occasion they assassinated zaibatsu leaders just as they murdered political rivals. But Ayukawa was closer in age to their own generation, a go-getter, a builder, someone they could deal with. So his company rose faster in the thirties and early forties than most of its competitors. After the war, however, by which time Nissan had grown into a complex of seventy-four different firms, it was considered tainted, more than most big companies, because of its cooperation with the militarists; its activities in Manchuria were considered especially damning. As a result, it was devastated psychologically—more than physically—by the demise of the Japan that had created it.

Before the war Ayukawa had been a wunderkind of the new Japan, a brilliant entrepreneur and dealmaker who had an unerring talent for making the right connections. He was born to a good family of the samurai class. His mother was a niece of a man named Kaoru Inoue, a powerful politician and adviser to the Mitsui family. The young Ayukawa always had access to power, and to money. He had graduated from Tokyo University with a degree in engineering, worked in the Mitsui machine-tool shop, and in 1905, as a young man of twenty-five, had gone to America. There, for two years, he had worked in American companies in New York and Pennsylvania, studying new techniques in iron casting. He had returned and formed his first company, Tobata Casting, which prospered during World War I. Between the wars he embarked upon a truly remarkable program of growth, using different members of his family to push into related industries such as mining and electrical supplies, constantly expanding. Unlike the older zaibatsu, which were family-held companies and in which the lines between the banking and industry were almost impossible to draw, Nissan was listed on the stock exchange, and Ayukawa sought public funds to finance its growth. Because he was so well grounded technically, he understood the changing nature of the industrial economy as the older men, heading rival zaibatsu, did not, and his touch was almost perfect. Part Henry Ford, part Alfred P. Sloan, he was connected, talented, and alert to the possibilities of the moment. He was a better dealmaker than those who knew more about technology, and he knew more about technology than those who were better dealers. As his reputation grew, so did his legend, and so did the value of the stock, making his expansions easier and easier.

He had long wanted to go into the area of auto and truck manufacture, and in the early thirties he put together what became Nissan Motors. He was encouraged by the fact that the older zaibatsu were too nervous and would not invest in the automotive business, so it was an area in which he could dominate. Almost all his advisers warned him against entering the world of auto; Ford and GM, which shipped knocked-down units to Japan, were too powerful, they argued. No Japanese firm could make it. That, as far as he was concerned, was all the more reason to try. He spent only $4 million to launch Nissan Motors, using money gathered from the sale of stock from his other companies. He intended to start small: five thousand cars a year at first and perhaps, if he was lucky, fifteen thousand in five years. But the war soon ended the production of civilian cars.

As Japan readied for war, Ayukawa became more closely involved than ever with the Japanese military. He was a major manufacturer of the trucks used by the imperial army to invade Manchuria, and he soon became a principal partner of its new colonial government, Manchukuo, transferring his holding company there (for tax reasons, it was said). He had become a symbol of what many considered the new Japan. When that new Japan crashed in August 1945, he was sent to prison for twenty-one months. Finally released, he was purged, which meant that he could hold neither corporate nor public office, a ban that lasted until 1951. Until his death he was frustrated because he was not allowed to return to his old company. He was not alone. Others, who would have been his natural successors, were also tainted. Shoji Yamamato, an able, aggressive man, ran the company from 1945 until 1947, when he too was purged, and Genshichi Asahara, the company's most talented scientist, who was a favorite of Ayukawa's, was purged for a time as well. Those who thought they should be running Nissan seemed to be finished, and those who were put in charge of running it felt ill prepared for their new roles and very much on the moral defensive about the company's major role in the Manchurian affair. As the prewar alliance with the militarists and the war itself had strengthened the company, now it weakened it.

The president after Yamamoto was removed in 1947 was Taichi Minoura. New to the company, uncomfortable with technology, uncomfortable grappling with a mutinous labor union, uncomfortable with finance, he was overwhelmed by his problems. During one set of difficult labor negotiations he collapsed—as much out of fear of the union leaders, it was said, as out of exhaustion. In the summer of 1947, four months after his arrival, he asked the Industrial Bank of Japan to send him a financial man.

It was at this point that the banker came on stage. The banker was a forty-two-year-old man named Katsuji Kawamata, and he knew nothing about cars, not even, it was said, how to drive one. He knew even less about production and manufacturing. But he knew about money; he was a man of the bank.

The IBJ—the Industrial Bank of Japan—was a powerful force in the reindustrialization of Japan. A very conservative institution, it was in charge of deciding (with, of course, the guidance of the Ministry of International Trade, MITI) how to divvy up Japan's limited capital among the nation's struggling companies. It was not unusual for the banks, because they held such immense power, to dispatch one of their people to help run a company. It was seen as a way of keeping a stern hand on the company's business practices (which the bank inevitably regarded as poor) and at the same time of farming out some of the bank's excess executives, the ones who were probably not going to make it there. Even so, the men from the IBJ were considered very good. If there was a shortage of good managers in most Japanese companies, there were more at the IBJ than elsewhere. Banking was a respected profession in Japan, there being little in the way of a stock market to drain off the financial talent. Yet in contrast to industry, banking had not been hit very hard by the purges. The Americans had decided that the act of banking was a passive one, while being a manager of a company engaged in wartime industrial production was an active one. Few institutions in the postwar years were as consequential as the IBJ; it held the power of life and death over major companies. A certain arrogance inevitably went with that power, for the IBJ and other banks. Twenty-five years later, when Japan's economy was successful beyond everyone's dreams and the balance had changed because the companies did not need the banks as badly—Toyota was so cash-rich that it was known as the Bank of Toyota—there were industrialists who had not forgotten and did not forgive. They deliberately used the banks as little as possible. It was not so much that the banks had set hard terms. It was more the manner in which they had treated their clients in those years when they had held total control.

Kawamata, the banker from the IBJ, was an immensely ambitious man, but few of his contemporaries at the IBJ had perceived the full measure of that ambition. On the surface he had not seemed that driven. By the standards of Tokyo's bankers, some of whom were exceedingly sophisticated and polished, men who either were from the upper class or were imitating it, he was a bit primitive—almost, it sometimes seemed, deliberately so. He had appeared a little too rough, too blunt, for a successful career at the bank, and in 1947 he had been shunted off to Nissan, so urgently in need of financial help. The news of his transfer had not pleased Kawamata either. He was somewhat angered by the rebuff implicit in his being moved around. Indeed there were old colleagues of Kawamata's who thought that he had been somewhat lazy at the IBJ, and that it was only when the bank scorned him and placed him outside that he became ambitious, as if to prove that the IBJ had been wrong.

Immediately after the war, fresh out of the army, Kawamata had returned to the bank as assistant manager in the loans department in Tokyo. He was resentful and irascible, his attention rarely focused. Like many Japanese at that time, he was overwhelmed by a psychic exhaustion. The defeat of the nation was absorbed as a personal defeat as well. The Japan he had been a part of had failed completely; lost in that collapse were all his own hopes. He was not sure how much point there was to postwar life. ("Not just the cities but the hearts of the people have been burned out," Edwin Reischauer wrote of that period.) At the office he tried all day to edge nearer a small electric stove, with an old army overcoat over his head as a kind of cape to keep him warm. Some superiors urged him to work harder, but he did as little as he could. All he wanted to do was to stay warm, and read newspapers and magazines, and keep his mind as far from the bank as possible. His superiors, less than pleased by his performance, transferred him to Hiroshima as the manager there.

The order to Hiroshima appalled him. Hiroshima was a regional office, and a relatively unimportant one at that, hardly the sort of post that would go to a rising star. He wanted no part of that tragic, devastated city, and for a time he thought of tearing up his assignment order. Years later he could remember every detail of his arrival in Hiroshima. It was at five o'clock in the morning. The only people there to greet him were the city's numerous black marketeers, gathered around little fires that they had lit to keep warm. Kawamata was wearing his army overcoat and long boots and carrying his army mess tin. Had ever, he wondered, a banker made a less imposing arrival in a less imposing city? He walked from the station along burned-out streets until he reached the street where the bank was. The gods had not been any gentler with the bank building than they had with anything else in the center of Hiroshima. It was a cavern of burned bricks; it looked as if it had been crushed by some enormous hand. He looked around and found a few sticks of wood and started a fire to cook his rice. There were still a few rooms left, all of them in shambles. He wanted to sit in the manager's office, but the janitor would not let him in; that was where the main fire was kept to heat the soup served to the employees each day. The place, he soon decided, was more a soup kitchen than a bank.

There was no place to live. For a time he stayed in a bare dormitory and commuted to work. He badly wanted his family with him, but there was no housing. Finally, after six months, he rented half of a farmer's house and brought his family down. He was, he realized, luckier than almost anyone else in Hiroshima. It was a painful time in a ravaged place. The city was filled with ghosts, its memories unfailingly sad. The sense of defeat was pervasive. In 1947, when he received the news from the home office to go to Nissan, the one thing about it that he liked was that he could now return to Tokyo. Other than that he was not really very happy about the move. That night he told his wife what happened. Nissan, after all, was not a very important firm. "What kind of company is Nissan?" she asked.

His first day at Nissan, Kawamata was stunned by the chaos of the operation. That morning he expected to attend a board meeting. Where are the other executives? he asked. Oh, he was told, they are all holding wage negotiations with the union. Later that day he was told that the workers were excited by his arrival. The fact that a powerful new man had come from the IBJ was good news. To them it meant the company would be able to borrow money more readily and they would therefore be able to get even bigger raises. That was not exactly the way Kawamata saw it. His instructions were quite different—to take a company that was out of control and bring some order to it and, above all, to end the labor troubles.

There were strikes almost all the time. The union was stronger than the management, and management feared it. It was all the company could do to make a small number of trucks; it was constantly in the red, and yet its workers were always demanding raises. Kawamata had had almost no experience with unions. Once when he had been with the IBJ in Hiroshima his employees, who had formed what they thought of as a union, had handed him a seven-point petition complaining about his personal behavior, including the fact that he on occasion put his feet on his desk and smoked. This was deemed arrogant, and he was asked to stop. He pondered this request for a time and decided that it was the sign of employees who had no earthly idea what a union was supposed to do. Clearly, someone had told the workers that he, Kawamata, worked for the ruling class, and they, the workers, were supposed to rein in his power. Kawamata with his feet brazenly placed on the desk was a symbol of the excesses of the ruling class. He had taken his feet off the desk, and his union problems had disappeared. His experiences at Hiroshima had in no way prepared him for the force and the fury of the Nissan union. He expected to run a poor company in difficult times and compete with other companies for funds. The last thing he had expected was to play the villain to his own workers. He was also alarmed by how weak the existing management was and how readily it yielded to the workers' demands. As far as he was concerned, that was going to end, and end soon. But it did not. Years of constant confrontation awaited him.

During most of that period the most important man in management was Genshichi Asahara, a protégé of Ayukawa, the founder of the company. Asahara, who had returned from being purged to serve as president, was a mild, almost sweet man. He was a chemist by profession and had neither the taste nor the talent for dealing with the crisis now in front of him. He much preferred trying to invent—eventually with some success—artificial sake. When labor crises exploded, Asahara's first reaction was to hide, which he often did. Failing that, he acquiesced. He was both overwhelmed and charmed by Tetsuo Masuda, the formidable union leader. Asahara's own son, Hideo, then still in college, often argued with his father about what was happening. The son was appalled to find that Asahara was writing plaintive letters to the union that said things like "We must work together. I am not your enemy. I am not a capitalist. These things don't exist in Japan."

That, said the son to his father, would not go over well with the Nik-keiren (an antiunion organization of businessmen).

"Don't you think so?" said the senior Asahara. "Well, you probably know more about labor relations than I do. But you must remember that Masuda-san is a very capable man, one of the ablest I have seen. We should pay a great deal of attention to him."

Kawamata, roused from his own lethargy, was aghast at the management approach. Everyone at Nissan, he told friends back at the bank, was afraid of the union. The union was always demanding more rights, while the workers never worked. What had happened to Japanese respect for work? It was one thing to lose a war, he believed, but another to lose a sense of all things Japanese. The problem, he decided, was not the Americans, it was the Japanese people themselves. Something precious in the Japanese spirit had been lost. Slowly, it seemed, jarred by this experience, Kawamata began coming up out of his own postwar death.

In the late 1940s small strikes kept breaking out like brushfires. They were over pay increases, and they were over the question of whether management or the union would control promotions. The first strike that Kawamata had to deal with came in 1949, after the Dodge Line. That summer Kawamata had been forced once again to borrow from the IBJ. He had gone to the Hiroshima branch because he had better contacts there, and he had successfully negotiated a discounted bill. But he had been wearied by the process and by the knowledge that when the bank people gave him a cool and skeptical eye, barely disguising their contempt, they were right—his house was not in order. Nissan was a poorly run company. The production was low, the payroll was high. It was time to get tougher. He knew he was going to have to let people go in order to save the company. Otherwise he would hit the limit of the bank's tolerance. He could detect from his talks with the IBJ in Hiroshima and Tokyo its growing impatience. He knew some of the people there thought Nissan was going to fail, and he sensed that some of them would not be unhappy to see that happen. But Nissan was now his company, and he did not want to fail. He welcomed the Dodge Line, because it gave him the direction he needed. He left Hiroshima and went back to Tokyo and told his colleagues at Nissan of his decision to cut back the work force, the first austerity measure for a company so loosely controlled. Everyone in the room was silent. No one, he realized, wanted to challenge the union.

There were about eighty-five hundred employes at Nissan at the time of the Dodge Line, and Kawamata decided to let go of about two thousand. He knew nothing of the procedures on how to do this. There had to be some termination pay and the company was broke, but he went secretly to the IBJ and to two local banks and got 80 million yen (or about $220,000) extra for this. He got it by promising that this was the beginning of a new and harder line on the part of management. In September, Kawamata announced that the company was going to fire some 1760 employees. To the degree that it could distinguish between radical workers and regular, less politicized workers, the company fired the radicals. The union immediately called a strike. The strike went on for forty days, and in the end management won. The dismissals stood. But the lines were drawn and the union had become more radical than ever.

Tetsuo Masuda, the leader of the union, seemed to welcome the challenge from Kawamata. This was the enemy he had longed to meet. He had been deeply alienated by the war and thoroughly radicalized by the poverty and desperation of postwar Japan. He talked constantly about democracy, and in his definition of democracy, workers made as much as the owners and, even more important, had political control of their workplace. Confident of his cause and even more certain of his tactical abilities, Masuda enjoyed nothing more than finding some unsuspecting member of management and embroiling him in debate, baiting him and then cutting him up, in front of as many workers as possible. In these impromptu little debates he never lost. The workers loved it. They would watch him as he walked through a plant, spotted a manager, and took him on. They immediately clustered around. No one had ever argued for them before, not here, not in school, not in the army; now, finally, someone was doing it, someone quicker and smarter than the bosses, someone who always won. This was a victory for their Japan over the old Japan.

What distinguished Masuda, besides his intelligence, was his independence. He toadied to no one, not to the existing hierarchy nor, as many of the radical labor leaders did, to the Communist party. There was nothing tentative about him, no area in which he showed any doubt. Where the men in the ranks, in confrontation with their superiors, felt nervous and uncertain, Masuda brought his absolute confidence. "We had our fears of where we were going and what we were doing," one of his friends said later, "and he always had answers, he was always so sure of himself." Because Masuda spoke for the workers and because management was afraid of him, the friend said, "he seemed to make our lives bigger. And our lives had never been very big before."

To many of his contemporaries in management, some of whom had been at Tokyo University with him, he remained a puzzle, a man who had

betrayed his origins. There were, after all, any number of men from Tokyo
University—or Todai, as it is known—in the CP, good theoretical Marx-
ists, but there were few sons of Todai in the unions. Once, during heated
labor negotiations, one of these managers had complained about the union's
intractability, and Masuda had answered, "The problem is not the anger
of workers who cannot get enough to eat. The problem is you. Why are
you always on the wrong side of an issue—is it that you do not know
better and are wrong in your mind, or that you know better and are wrong
in your soul?" To the men around him, such moments were memorable.
In America, on the Richter scale of union-management confrontation this
would have seemed relatively mild, but in Japan an assault like that on
existing authority was staggering. He was by far the most forceful man in
the entire union, not just at Nissan, but throughout the entire auto industry. One of the things that terrified the nation's industrialists was that
he was spending more and more of his energy organizing not just Nissan
but other auto companies. That constituted a true challenge to Japanese
tradition; it meant that the workers would be allied on a class basis instead
of a company basis—a Western rather than a Japanese concept of
organization—and thus could potentially be very dangerous. The Americans had said that the Japanese could have unions; thus what the workers
were doing was legal. But this was still Japan, and from the lowliest peasant
to the Emperor himself it was a hierarchical society. There was a hierarchy
in the home, a hierarchy in the school, a hierarchy in the village, and a
hierarchy at work. The question of whether the union truly had the right,
once established, to challenge those above it in the hierarchy might be
established by American law, but it was not yet accepted by Japanese
custom. Masuda was trying hard to make the new law as powerful as the
old tradition.

He was not from the working class himself. That did not seem to bother
anybody. Most of the labor leaders of that era, like many of the Communists, came from the middle or upper middle class. Masuda was privileged by Japanese standards, certainly as much a product of the new
ruling class as Kawamata. He had been born in 1914 on the island of
Tokunoshima, off Kagoshima in the south. Later one of his critics, trying
to understand why someone with so normal a background could be so
completely alienated, blamed it on the region. Those island people, he
said, because they had been so badly treated by the government in Kagoshima, were always difficult and rebellious, although they were not as
bad as the Okinawans. Of the region, Masuda himself had said that it was
so poor that even the most fortunate people there ate one meal a day
instead of three. Only in that way could they save the money to send their

children to the universities in Tokyo. His father had run a small shipping company. But the company had gone bankrupt when Masuda was young, and the family moved from the island to Kagoshima. His father died just as Masuda was about to enter high school. To start earning the money to go to a university, he began to tutor the son of a wealthy local doctor while attending high school himself. He lived in the doctor's house, and eventually a marriage was arranged between him and his student's younger sister. To an American his childhood might have seemed hard, but by Japanese standards of that era it was not particularly difficult. If anything he was luckier than most. He had, after all, gone to Todai, the greatest of Japan's universities.

Todai is the Japanese equivalent of Havard or Yale, with West Point's sense of duty. The competition to get in is fierce. In a way that Harvard and Yale do not, Todai serves not so much the entering student as the nation. It is not concerned with brilliance and originality but rather with discipline and obligation. It is accepted in Japan that though a young man may not be from the governing class when he enters Todai, he is when he graduates. In that way it is more like Oxford or Cambridge than Harvard. Upon graduation he will do not so much what is good for himself as what is good for the nation. At that time, if he is outstanding, he will enter one of the most important parts of the bureaucracy, MITI, or the ministries of finance or foreign affairs, or he will go to work for one of the top companies. He will not challenge the existing order, because as a man of Todai he is now a part of that order. He will wait his turn, and in time the right to rule will be his. If he is patient and virtuous, the society will reward him. It is a formidable system, for the nation's talent is always funneled into those key sectors where it is most needed.

Masuda had gone to work for Nissan in 1938, in the days before Japan was fully embroiled in the Pacific war but when every Japanese knew that a major war was approaching. For a Todai graduate he was something of a hick. "You could take one look at him and know he wasn't from Tokyo," said Michio Hatada, then a young Nissan employee from the same department and his closest friend. "Everything about him said country boy—his face, his haircut, his clothes, the way he walked. I think he decided I should be his friend because I was from the country too and I felt just as alien in Tokyo. We both felt the snobbery of Tokyo around us all the time."

Masuda was smart, there was no doubt of that; he had done his college work at Todai in only three years and he had spent the last year doing nothing but playing baseball, which was his real passion in those days. It was a time, Hatada recalled of their early days at Nissan, when many of the young men of Japan were without dreams and ambitions; everyone in their age group knew that the war was coming and that they did not control their own destinies. There was an odd aimlessness to life. They did not sit around talking about their future in the company, their ambitions for high position, the women they might marry. Rather they talked of the war. Hatada and Masuda and a few others took a night course once a week in the Malay language, in the mistaken belief that the war would take them to Malaya. It was a small, almost pitiful attempt to have some control over their lives. "Other than that, we were all going to be good Japanese," Hatada said. "We were going to go to war and many of us were going to die, and we did not argue with that fate. To argue would have been cowardly."

Essentially apolitical when he had gone off to war, Masuda had returned a different man, completely politicized. He himself had not had a particularly difficult time in the war. He had served as a medic with the Japanese forces in China and had contracted malaria there. He had been sent home suffering from a high fever, had gone back to work for Nissan briefly, and then had gone back into the service. His mother and his sister had been killed when Kagoshima had been bombed. There was a new bitterness to his voice. Sometimes he would talk about the men who had run the country in the prewar days and had taken the country to war, and he would say, "They ruined us, they ruined our lives. They left us with nothing." Back in Tokyo he found the results of the war all around him. Japan was not like America, said Hideya Nakamura, one of his friends in the union; veterans did not come back and tell war stories about what they had been through. In Japan there was no need to do that, for the destruction was a completely shared experience. No family had been spared. Those who had made it back from Okinawa or Iwo did not have to tell those from Hiroshima about the devastation, nor did anyone from Hiroshima have to tell anyone from Tokyo lucky enough to survive the fire-bombing what a terrible war it had been.

Masuda's friend Nakamura had not been in the army but had worked instead at an office that Nissan had set up outside of Yokohama. The main Nissan plant was in Yokohama itself, but the American bombings had become so intense that company officials decided to keep much of the clerical staff—and the company's papers—at a small primary school in the countryside. The factories would be vulnerable, they thought, but the paperwork would not be. It was very Japanese of them, Nakamura later decided, to think at a moment like that of preserving all that paperwork for the future. One terrible day in April 1945, Nakamura arrived at work to see that the bombers had preceded him. The school was destroyed and the bodies of little schoolchildren were mixed among the rubble. He had worked alongside the mothers sifting through the debris, trying to find the bodies and not knowing which was worse, finding them or not finding them, for they were like mangled little dolls when found. It was something he never forgot, the violence visited upon the innocent. He changed politically in that moment, from an accepting, law-abiding man to an alienated one who did not accept authority. He was not angry at the Americans for having done what they did; he was angry at the Japanese, who had decided to start the war and who now had to suffer the consequences.

On rare occasions Nakamura and Masuda would speak about the war; Nakamura would say a few words and Masuda would add something, both talking in a kind of shorthand, communicating things without having to say them because most of it was unsayable. Once, however, after they had talked, Masuda had said: "We must never be at war again. None of this must happen again. Ever!" His anger was tangible. Nakamura felt that Masuda was not so much politicized as almost completely alienated from the Japan of the past. The war had done that to many. It had torn apart one generation of Japanese, those who had been young men when it started and had believed in all the accepted values of the nation and who, when it ended, had lost not just everything they owned but, more important, everything they believed in.

Working in Nissan's Yoshiwara factory, Masuda got involved with the union. His talents were soon evident: a powerful intellect, absolute fearlessness, an unwavering sense of purpose, and exceptional skill as a speaker. Soon Nakamura, who headed the union in those days, arranged for Masuda's transfer to Yokohama, where he was much needed. Nakamura had grown worried about Nissan's opposition to the union, and worried that he himself might not be strong enough to stand up to management. He thought that Masuda would be a more courageous leader. Later, as the struggle between the union and the company escalated, Nakamura had a premonition about Masuda's vulnerability, of Masuda's standing alone against an increasingly powerful business class once again determined to exert its will.

"They are going to get you," he told Masuda.

"Don't worry, Nakamura-san," Masuda said. "You will always be around to pick up my bones."

Nakamura believed that for Masuda the union was a means of checking the power of the old zaibatsu and thus of preventing any resurgence of Japanese militarism. Nissan, after all, had been a part of a zaibatsu, and it had been a major beneficiary of the Japanese invasion of Manchuria.

The animosity he felt for management was in reality his rage against the war and the warmakers. *They* had done it once, he told Nakamura, and they could do it again.

For some of Masuda's old prewar friends his increasing radicalization was disturbing. Here after all was a young man with a good chance of becoming a senior officer of the company, and instead of helping his career he was risking it by challenging the very order to which he by right belonged. "You, a man of Todai, you should be ashamed of what you're doing," a member of management who had known him at college had said during one battle over salaries. "Look at who your friends and supporters are."

"Todai," Masuda replied, "should be ashamed of itself for having so few like me, and so many like you. You went there and learned nothing."

Most Japanese accepted the hierarchy; Masuda was contemptuous of it. The order, he said, should be revised. "Good is bad," he would say. "Up should be down, and down should be up." At first some of his people were confused when he talked like this, but gradually they understood. His adversaries in management thought him a Communist, but none of the men who worked closely with him believed that. What made him distinctive was his independence; he belonged to no one except his own workers. Most of the real Communists had been weeded out of the union during the Red Purge. Certainly he was left-wing, and surely some of his views often coincided with those of the far-left Socialists or the Communists. "He wanted the union to be strong, to be on the left," said Tokuichi Kumagai, a good friend, "but he did not want it to be Communist." That would have meant that it was answerable to someone other than the workers themselves. The orders might have come from Moscow.

Once Kyuichi Tokuda, the secretary of the Communist party, had debated with Masuda over the role of unions and the left. Masuda's friends had been surprised not just that Masuda had turned out to be a better debater than Tokuda, who was a legendary speaker, but by the vehemence with which he challenged Tokuda's position. The Communists, he said, wanted to use the workers and the union for their own purposes, which were first and foremost political. He wanted to keep the union the way it was, serving the workers. On occasion their purposes might intersect, but the union was for the workers, not for some larger political cause, he said. "Masuda wanted to be the first Japanese man of the French Revolution," said Kumagaya, "of the new liberty and equality and fraternity— all that was supposed to happen here and, of course, never did."

Masuda became furious with friends when they were active in politics outside the union; he wanted no mixing of their interests. He could see no purpose save his own. When Nissan officials argued that wage increases would hurt the company, that it was not yet strong enough for them, that it desperately needed what limited resources it had for capital reinvestment, he scoffed. It was not possible, he believed, for something to be good for the union and bad for the company. The company did not really matter. The union did.

Up until the Dodge Line, Masuda won almost every battle with the company. There was no doubt that he had intimidated the management, and no doubt that he had enjoyed this. He deliberately sought confrontation. In retrospect, some of his colleagues thought that the early years had spoiled him and made him arrogant. He alone exerted power within the union, and while he seemed to listen to others, it became clear that his idea of a democratic union was one where people spoke when he let them. When they were finished, he did exactly what he had intended to do in the first place. He talked of democracy and was authoritarian. "This is a democratic dictatorship, Tanaka-san," he often told his deputy, Akinori Tanaka, after there had been a meeting in which he had stifled dissent, "and as long as they understand that, we'll be all right." No one was supposed to challenge him. Once during a general union meeting, when Masuda was out drinking with delegates from other companies, a Toyota union man had turned to him and said, "You've gone rather quickly from Keynes to Marx." Masuda, enraged, picked up his plate and started hitting the Toyota man. The Emperor Masuda, some of the people in middle management called him.

In 1951 it became time to choose a new president of Nissan auto. There were those who thought that Katsuji Kawamata, the banker, wanted the job. But he was simply too new. The purge of tainted executives had just ended, which meant that both Genshichi Asahara and Shoji Yamamoto were candidates. Both had been purged, and both were anxious to get back to the company. Now Kawamata gave the first evidence of how skilled an infighter he was. He saw that the ambitions of the gentle, diffident Asahara were quite modulated—he was interested only in cars. Yamamoto, by contrast, he saw as quite capable of running the company, eager to do it, and not very eager to share power with anyone else, particularly a man of finance. Kawamata realized that under Asahara there would be plenty of room for him to continue to deal with the labor people to whom Asahara had been so deferential and to keep control over the company bureaucracy, whereas under Yamamoto, there would be very little room to maneuver. So Kawamata threw his and the IBJ's support to Asahara. Ironically, so did Masuda and his union. Asahara got the job.

Because of his early victories, Masuda was becoming confident to the point of arrogance, some of his friends thought, and that was dangerous. Management had changed: Asahara was the head of the company, but Kawamata was clearly the more dominant figure, and anyone who watched Kawamata sensed for the first time that the union had a true adversary. Kawamata was ruthless and determined. Masuda did not perceive the threat, nor did he realize that Kawamata was readying himself for a showdown. For Kawamata's own career was now on the line. His ambition did not extend merely to limiting the power of the union; he might have come over to Nissan on temporary loan, but he liked it there, and he intended to stay on and make it his own company. From the time he arrived, Kawamata let everyone know that he was the bank and the bank had power over the company. What was gradually taking place, an Asahara associate realized, was nothing less than a takeover. "Why," Kawamata asked an executive who worked in Asahara's office, "did you take that matter to Asahara instead of to me? Didn't you want a decision made?" Soon Kawamata was reaching out to recruit his own people. Young management men had the distinct impression that very quietly a Kawamata team was being formed. Furthermore, he started going around the factory giving out small sums of money to workers who might be working exceptionally late. Here, he would tell them, go to a bar and have a few drinks. This was an executive letting the workers know that he was the main man. It had never been done that way before.

Many of the Asahara people, who fancied themselves old-style car and product men, came to dislike Kawamata. He was a man from the wrong world, meddling in their company, and they called him "the banker" with special disdain, though not to his face. "The banker would like a car that will sell more but cost less," one might say sarcastically. "Can you please design such a car for the banker?" One of them even sketched a car to take a banker to and from the bank. It was specially designed so an unusually heavy man (Kawamata was not that heavy, but in their caricature they made him so) could get in and out as easily as possible. There was room for only one person in it. The rest of the space was filled with huge baskets in which he could put all the money he took to the bank. For Japanese working in a company like Nissan this was an unusually irreverent act, and though the sketch was passed around and enjoyed, the artist made sure he destroyed it that night. But laugh though they might at Kawamata, there was no doubt that he was taking over Nissan. What was worse for

Asahara, the longer the labor crisis seemed to go, the more it strengthened Kawamata—who took a harder line against the union—and weakened Asahara.

Kawamata liked letting everyone at Nissan know that he was tough. He was almost deliberately crude in his manner. Bankers, even in the days right after the war, were comparatively well dressed. Kawamata, however, never dressed well. He wore suits, to be sure, but they were badly cut, and they never seemed to fit him. His shirt was always wrinkled, and his tie, one associate noticed, never was tied quite right and was always off to the side. His language was coarser than that of most of his colleagues. He seemed to take pleasure in the fact that the other men around him were more polished. "I know you're fancier than I am," he would tell the others. "I'm from the country, I don't move in the world you move in. All of you grew up a lot richer than me—we were very poor." But that, they soon decided as they found out more about him, was odd, since he came from Mito, which was fairly near, not really country, and since his family had moved to Tokyo when he was still young. Besides, his father had been a perfectly respectable middle-level functionary, and Kawamata himself had gone to quite a good college. For his own reasons, however, it seemed important to him to cast himself this way. If he was bored at meetings—and most high-level meetings were boring—he would take a little nap; his arms and head would hit the table, and he would promptly be asleep—indeed, snoring quite loudly. Asahara did not know how to handle these scenes and, being genteel, would let him sleep on. Soon it became clear what engaged Kawamata—money—and what did not—technology. If the subject was technology, his eyes soon closed; when it came back to money he was wide awake and very much in charge.

At first some of the others thought it was merely rudeness, and wondered whether Kawamata knew how much he shocked and offended his colleagues; only later did some of them realize that that was precisely what he had intended to do. It was, they realized belatedly, a power play. "What he was telling us—and we did not realize it at first—was that what interested us did not have to interest him," one of them said years later, "but what interested him had to interest us."

The dismissal of nearly two thousand men at Nissan at the time of the Dodge Line changed all the relationships there. Kawamata stood almost alone among management on that issue in the beginning.

"Are you sure that you are not being too hard?" one of his colleagues asked him.

"I am not sure that I am being hard enough," he answered.

"Why?" the colleague persisted.

"Because I am not sure what kind of jobs any of us will be able to get when we tell people we came from an auto company that just closed."

The union conducted constant negotiations trying to head off the dismissals, but Nissan, like every other company in Japan, was feeling the crunch of the Dodge Line. The bank was being squeezed by the government, and it in turn was squeezing Nissan. Day after day Tetsuo Masuda shuttled back and forth between meetings of his union and meetings with management. After each meeting with management he would go back to the Yokohama factory and speak to the massed workers, and his words would be picked up and broadcast to the Yoshiwara plant. As a speaker he was at his best. He had a rich, powerful voice and an almost perfect sense for the mood of his audience. There was a hypnotic quality to these speeches. "He was, and I hate to say this," said Hatada, "almost like Hitler. I would stand there transfixed listening to him, and I would wonder, 'Is this my old friend the baseball player?'" In the end Masuda lost. The cutbacks were not just what management and the conservative leaders of the Nikkeiren, the industrialists' labor-policy board, wanted; they were what the Americans under the Dodge Line were insisting on.

Masuda became more bitter after this. It was as if management and especially Kawamata were his personal enemies now. He spoke of them in a new, more hostile way. For Kawamata, it was a victory. The fact that he had pulled it off increased his power within management immeasurably.

All the heroic battles between 1946 and 1950 were waged over precious little, for there was in fact not much to Nissan Motors. It was an antiquated place with two worn-out factories producing very little. In 1950, for example, Nissan built a grand total of 11,072 prewar-type trucks and 865 cars. It lost a great deal of money. Wrangles between labor and management were almost like a fight for possession of a carcass. Suddenly, this all changed. The reason was simple: the Korean War. The Americans urgently needed Japan's industrial facilities, they needed trucks and jeeps and repair shops, and they poured money into Japan. "A gift from the gods," Prime Minister Yoshida called the Korean War, in that it fixed American policy into a permanent position of anti-Communism and at the same time boosted the Japanese economy at a critical moment. It was a shot of plasma for an anemic economy. Six months before the Korean War, Toyota was in the red, and six months after it started, Toyota was in the black. Much the same happened at Nissan. It made trucks and jeeps. It

made casings for napalm shells as well, though that was something of a
secret at the time; the union might have been radical and its leadership
somewhat anti-American, but the union needed the work so desperately
that it put its politics aside and worked for the Americans. Even with the
benefits from the war, however, feelings were bitter. Workers who had
once complained about a lack of work now complained about the primitive
work conditions and having to work overtime without any choice. Overtime was a particular sticking point. The workers were poorly paid, and
they needed the small sums that the overtime brought, but they came to
believe that management had deliberately set the base wage so low that
only with overtime could they make enough. It was, the workers believed,
a management gimmick for expanding the basic work day.

By late 1952, as the Korean War slowed down, the artificial boom in
the Japanese auto industry began to end. But the inflation caused by the
war did not. The workers were making more than they ever had, management argued. Yes, the union replied, but the wage increases were
being wiped out by inflation. Masuda wanted a market-basket formula;
the workers would have the right to earn enough to fill a market basket
to a certain level. Management resisted. It felt that if the company was
to have any kind of future, it had to have some control over its finances
and simply had to have new machinery. It had succeeded in making
vehicles using possibly the most ramshackle, outmoded equipment in the
industrialized world. Only the sheer doggedness of the work force had
allowed Nissan to overcome what were immense technological handicaps.
The Americans and the Europeans, the Japanese knew, had modern factories which by comparison were wondrously automated. In America there
were fine new machines, some of which did the work of thirty men; the
American plants were dazzling. The facilities the Japanese were using in
the mid-fifties were probably more primitive than what America had in
the mid-thirties. To the men who ran Japan, the need to modernize placed
an inpenetrable ceiling on wage raises. To the articulate and forceful men
running the union, workers came before machines. This meant that there
was a division of the most fundamental sort in a capitalist society: How
would the money be used—to whose benefit?

In the spring of 1953, then, as the Korean War drew toward a truce,
Masuda was more eager than ever for confrontation with management.
His wife, however, who came from a good family, was uneasy about his
plans. She kept asking him to pull back. Some of his close advisers in the
union were uneasy as well. They detected what seemed to be a real change
in the mood of management that spring; it was less accommodating, even
less willing to negotiate. Something was happening. Japan had just signed

a peace treaty with the United States, which meant that whatever restraints the American presence had brought to labor relations had ended. There were reports of secret meetings involving Nissan management and executives from other companies. There were rumors that Kawamata had obtained secret loans from the banks in order to finance a strike. There were still other rumors that the IBJ had decided that this time it wanted Nissan to take the strike, and to crush the union once and for all. Masuda's longtime friend Michio Hatada was terrified by the path Masuda was on. He believed that Masuda had placed himself on a collision course with management, that he lacked flexibility, and that he was now surrounded largely by people who played to his vanity. Hatada gathered a group of Masuda's old friends together—the Malayan Language Study Group, he called it—so that they could try to make him see his situation. "You have to slow down," Hatada told him. "This whole thing is out of control and they are not going to let you get away with it. You are asking for too much. They are not going to stand for it, and they have too many allies, too many weapons. They are going to destroy you."

The more Hatada and the others warned Masuda, the less impact they had. His contempt for them was obvious. It was as if he were laughing at them, a lone man of religion scoffing at the apostates. When one of them mentioned the fragility of the company's finances, he brushed the point aside. "If the company collapses," he declared, "the union survives." It had all gone to his head, Hatada believed. Masuda did not deal with mortals anymore. Certainly he did not listen to them. He did not listen when some people whose sources of information were quite good warned him that the company had started to hire toughs in preparation for the showdown. Nor did he listen to Miyoji Ochiai, one of his principal assistants. "The nail that sticks out gets hammered in," Ochiai said, citing a Japanese proverb. "You," he added, "are the nail."

8.
THE TURNING POINT

It was a heady time for Tetsuo Masuda. He was at the height of his popularity. The more management challenged him, the stronger he became in the eyes of the workers. His ability to reach them seemed almost perfect that spring, as if each was perfectly tuned to the other. He could address five thousand workers and, no matter what doubts they might have harbored when he started speaking, they were once again in his hands. Everything he had said sounded so simple and so right. Part of it was that for the first time in their lives a man of Todai—Tokyo University—had taken on the world of Todai in their behalf. In so doing, he had touched something latent and deep within them, more psychological than political. All their lives, from the time they were born, they had been confronted with total hierarchy, total authority. It was the essential obligation of Japanese society that each person accept the authority of those above him. The lowly were not to have secret grievances over their lowliness. Indeed, they were not to think of their resentments as resentments but to accept them as life itself. All their lives the system, the fact of being Japanese, had forced them to bury whatever grudges they had had—against parents, teachers, bosses—if they were to be good Japanese. But Masuda's appeal was unique. They had a right to listen to him because he was a leader—a labor leader, a figure of authority. Yet Masuda, a leader, a figure of authority, was telling them they were justified in having these hidden complaints, that the secret self was real, the hardships and indignities not imagined. Thus they did not blindly have to accept life as it was. It was a powerful appeal. The crowds Masuda drew that spring were remarkable. Thirty years later his colleagues could still remember him addressing an outdoor rally on a wet day. At first the heavy drizzle subdued the meeting. The workers stood stolidly, spread out over a considerable area, separated from each other and from the rostrum by their umbrellas. Then Masuda started to speak.

"Put away your umbrellas," he called out to them. "Come nearer. I want to hear you, and I want you to hear me. How can we be close to each other when our umbrellas are in the way, keeping us from being with each other?"

The umbrellas came down.

"Now come close," he said, "so I can see you and you can see me." They gathered around the rostrum. The rain no longer mattered. Once again he had them.

It was an unruly time. Workers deliberately arrived late to work and went to the cafeteria early. Near the close of the day, before the end of the shift, they played chess or mah-jongg. They held frequent shop-steward meetings, one almost every day, and they demanded to be paid for the hours they spent at these meetings. The production process fell into chaos. How anything got manufactured at all, let alone anything as complicated as a car, mystified anyone who visited the plants. The company countered with the most basic policy of all: no pay for no work. At the same time it tried to split the ranks of the union. It declared that the kachos, or section chiefs, were no longer part of the union but were now part of top management. That was an ingenious move. The kachos were not only important in the shops but respected personally, and their membership in the union had given it additional legitimacy. Now suddenly, instead of being allies, they were enemies. Now they shunned the workers, refused their demands, and in any confrontation repeated the company line. That enraged Masuda, and in retaliation he decided to use physical intimidation. He reasoned that although management might have its titles and privileges and higher pay, if the factory floor belonged to the workers—if the managers were too frightened of the workers to venture onto the floor—then the union would control the company. The tactic he chose was a kind of kangaroo court held on the factory floor itself. The proceeding was known as suribachi, which meant mortar and pestle, implements used to grind something down. The something was the kachos, the section chiefs, now the highest level of management actually working on the floor.

Each day the workers marched down the aisles and surrounded a kacho. They avoided assaulting the particular kacho they worked for, for this would be deemed impolite; they chose some other section's kacho. Japanese amenities, after all, had to be observed. (Besides, by going after an alien kacho the workers were protecting themselves; the victim was unable to punish his tormentors the next day.) They would tightly surround their victim's desk—some would actually sit on it. Others would pack in closely from all sides, and still others would stand on the neighboring desks. All of them were prosecutors. The kacho was the accused, cut off from everyone else in the factory by the wall of bodies. No one could get through to help him, and for those who tried, the penalty was to be accused and tried themselves the next day. They started with the strongest kachos first, on the theory that if they broke them, the weaker ones would fall more readily into line. They would demand that a kacho repudiate the company position on no-work-no-pay. If he did not, they went at him. At first they vilified him: You murdering dog of the capitalist class, you useless bastard, you killer of little children. Then they would interrogate him. The prosecutors were kept fresh. Each would interrogate for twenty or thirty minutes, pour his full fury into it, and then go off to lunch or to rest while another would take up the cudgel. The accused felt totally alone. At first he would try to defend himself, but there was no defense. No matter what he said, they would simply come at him with more charges. He might be able to withstand the pressure for three or four hours, but eventually they wore him down. Even the strong ones stopped resisting after five hours and simply remained silent. That, however, did not stop the harassment. It was like an endless wave of punishment, always someone fresh leading it, the cast of characters changing as the workers replaced each other and some went home for the night. If his accusers were lenient, the accused might be allowed to go to the bathroom.

The ordeal was exhausting and terrifying. "I sat there," one kacho said years later, "and by the fourth hour I thought to myself that this had been going on for all of my life, that nothing had ever existed before it, and worse, that it was going to go on for the rest of my life. It seemed my destiny." The trials would last for twenty or thirty hours. The company could not protect its own people on its own factory floor. Yet as the kangaroo courts continued, the kachos, who had at first been turned against the union by company decree, now turned against it in their hearts as well.

Asahara seemed stunned by that growing confrontation. He was caught between forces far too strong for him. When some of the union leaders went to see him to talk about the next year's wage levels, he seemed pessimistic and depressed. One of the union people asked what was wrong. "I don't think Nissan wages are that much higher than those of other companies," he answered, "but all I hear from the Nikkeiren is how soft we are. They make me feel like a failure—whatever I do, it won't be enough." That, thought Nakamura, when he and his fellow labor leaders left Asahara's office, is a scared man. Not scared of us, but scared of his own side.

Such fears did not afflict Kawamata. He was, ironically enough, the beneficiary of Masuda's challenge. The more turbulent the company's labor relations the more he became the company's most powerful figure and chief decision-maker. If he had ever had a doubt that he had to move against the union, the suribachi technique ended it. The union, he later told friends, was abusing his people. So it was that he decided to support a second union, one much more sympathetic to the company, because, according to his wish, it would be formed not by labor but by middle management. The theory behind Kawamata's plan was wonderfully simple. The Americans had decreed in the new constitution that workers had the right to organize and have collective bargaining. The Americans had promoted the idea of unions because they wanted a more egalitarian society, but they had not decreed what kind of unions they had to be, or to what aims and ideals the unions had to be true. Thus there was nothing to keep companies from creating their own more loyal, more compliant unions, unions sharing the objectives of the company itself. If there was competition between two unions within a company, one hostile and one friendly, then it would be the most natural thing to help the friendly one.

This strategy was not unique to Nissan; it was embraced by firms all over Japan in the early fifties. It was the policy of the Nikkeiren, and it became the critical device by which the traditional Japanese order reasserted itself against what business leadership felt was the anti-Japanese nature of some of MacArthur's reforms. The Nikkeiren even sent out organizers to teach companies how to do it. It made sure that extra funds were available to shaky companies so they could, if necessary, outlast a union during a strike. Soon almost every major company troubled by unions began to create its own. At Nissan what made the conflict different was the level of bitterness. At many companies—Toyota, for example— the first union collapsed quite easily and very quickly became a company union. But at Nissan the Masuda union was very strong, and any union that sought to crush it had to be equally strong and tough.

Even as Kawamata was looking for a second union, one had been forming at Nissan under a man named Masaru Miyake. In a way Kawamata had been looking for Miyake, and Miyake had been looking for Kawamata. They found each other in the spring of 1953. Miyake was a young man who had served as a fighter pilot during the war, flying the famed Zero, which gave him added prestige with many of the workers. He had flirted briefly with the radical left after his return to Japan, and then, after joining Nissan, he had moved steadily to the right. He had begun to rise in the company up through the lower management levels in the accounting department, and in 1949, during the Dodge Line crisis, he began to emerge as a visible dissenter from the radical union. When the union had challenged the company's right to fire the 1760 workers, Miyake had quite vocally backed the company's right, indeed its need, to tighten its belt. Soon he became an outspoken critic of Masuda—and a target of the radicals.

In Japanese companies young aspiring management men were able to belong to the unions; it seemed perfectly natural that men running the unions had white-collar backgrounds. Among some of the other middle-level people, Miyake's willingness to fight back against the union further enhanced his status; it had taken considerable courage in those days to challenge Masuda. Miyake began meeting regularly with other men like himself in the company, men in their late twenties and early thirties who were just edging up into middle management. There was a bar they went to almost every night near the Shimbashi station, and there they talked endlessly about reforming the union. Masuda, they agreed, had to be stopped. The union had to be less confrontational. It had to help support the company, they agreed, not destroy it. These young men were all college graduates, and they were all from the middle class. (Eventually some ten members from Miyake's group served on the Nissan board of directors.) The more Miyake and his group spoke among themselves, the more concerned they became that the company might go bankrupt. Soon they began to talk about starting a new and loyal union.

Miyake and the others in his group regarded Kawamata as the only hope of the company. Kawamata was the only one in management, they agreed, who was strong enough to fight back. Asahara was too soft, in their view, a man afraid of Masuda and his own shadow. Miyake managed to talk to Kawamata. The subject of the second union came up. Kawamata seemed to encourage the idea of a second union. Something, he told Miyake, had to be done. That was just the way Miyake felt. Management and workers had to be friendly, Kawamata said; they had a common goal. Second unions were being formed at other companies, and they were proving successful in case after case. Kawamata would help all he could. Miyake and Kawamata soon discovered that they had a connection. They had gone to the same university, Hitotsubashi (almost but not quite as good as Todai as a means of entry into Japan's elite). That nourished their friendship. Miyake even knew people in the International Bank of Japan.

The last thing that Miyake had wanted to do when he first went to work at Nissan was became a union leader. He thought of himself as a son of the middle class; his father had been a small businessman. Miyake had wanted to go into a large company and be a part of management. It would have been nice to end up on the board. As a pilot during the war he had loved flying, and when the war was over he had wanted more than anything to work in the aircraft industry. But nations that lose wars, he learned somewhat ruefully, are not allowed to keep their aircraft industries. So he had gone to work in autos, at Nissan, which he judged the next best thing. He considered himself lucky anyway, simply in that he was alive. He had been in a squadron stationed in the South Pacific, and most of the pilots he had flown with, once so bright and eager and proud, were dead.

At first the Japanese pilots had been better than the Americans, and the Zeroes had been faster and more maneuverable than the American planes. Then, all too quickly for the Japanese, the American pilots had gotten better and their planes were swifter, reached higher altitudes, and dove faster. There were also a great many more of them. The Zero of which they had once been so proud suddenly seemed quite backward. It did not even have a self-starter; it had to be started by flipping the propeller. The pilots also, in contrast to the Americans, had very little protection inside the plane. Zero lighters, some of the pilots called them, because they would simply burst into flame. Men in squadrons like Miyake's knew far ahead of most Japanese that the tide had turned in the war. By 1943 there was a sad new ritual at his air base; at the mess table each day there were fewer and fewer seats needed for the pilots, because fewer and fewer were returning from the air battles, so from time to time the mess officer would simply remove an entire mess table.

He was based in Borneo. One day in 1944 the Americans came in full force—the day of the Americans, he later called it. On that particular day he did not fly, because since they had lost even more planes than pilots, there were now more pilots than planes, and so they took turns; this was Miyake's day without a plane. That, he always realized, was why he had lived. There had been heavy raids before, but Miyake had never seen anything like this one. They came and came and came—about four hundred B-24s and P-38s, all based on Guadalcanal (where his brother, a naval doctor, had already died). The Japanese had about 120 aircraft, and they managed to get most of them up, and there were dogfights all over the sky. The Americans left, but soon they were back. All afternoon the battle continued. For the second raid the Japanese had managed to get up about sixty aircraft, and then to everyone's horror the Americans returned again, as if untouched and undamaged by all that action, with as many planes as on the first raid. Possibly thirty Japanese went up to meet them. It was not that the Americans were winning the individual dogfights; if anything, thought Miyake, standing and watching the terrifying action in the sky, the human circus above him, they were probably evenly matched in terms of individual skill and bravery. It was simply the numbers. If one American was shot down, there were always more of them. By the end of the day the Japanese had been reduced to five operative planes. Almost everyone on the ground knew then that the war was over, but still there were naval-academy traditionalists who wanted to kill every American they could, even though it was hopeless. To Miyake, it was a great lesson in the power of technology and the strength of a truly industrialized nation.

The war left Miyake with a certain melancholia. Years later he visited the Philippines and placed some flowers on a monument there to kamikaze pilots who had given their lives. The Filipinos had been very impressed by the spirit of the kamikazes. Men of suicide, they called them. Many of the Filipinos wanted to talk to Miyake about how wonderful his comrades had been. Miyake had thought it stupid and wasteful and was immensely saddened by the day. But the one thing that the war had done, he realized later, was to make him outspoken. He had never been outspoken before—that was not his way or the Japanese way—but he had fought in the war and seen so much death that when he returned to Japan he believed he had the right to speak out, that this above all he had earned. There was going to be a new Japan, and in the new Japan, which was going to be much like America, people would be encouraged to say what they thought. He belonged to a generation that had sacrificed their lives and were now entitled to some measure of freedom. No one was going to push him around.

When he took the job at Nissan, he soon came to hate the union. Workers were being paid for twelve months of work, but what with all the stoppages and wildcat strikes they actually worked more like nine months. He came to think that Masuda was a bully. Furthermore, Masuda was a leftist. Miyake thought that America was a very strange occupying power: It was a capitalist country, and yet it was allowing labor unions as radical as this to form. General MacArthur, he thought, was a particularly strange American. All the Americans, including the general himself, said he was politically very conservative. But he went around Japan creating left-wing labor unions. Just what did he want from the Japanese?

What finally turned Miyake around was a congress of labor officials at a resort near the town of Ito in the middle of 1952. Miyake was hardly an important figure at the conference, simply a minor delegate from the Nissan accounting department. Masuda got up and started an assault on management, and finally Miyake challenged him and asked him who would pay for all the raises he wanted, and the two started to argue. The argument went on long into the night. Masuda brought in his support troops, officials from the Isuzu and Toyota unions, and they started browbeating Miyake. It seemed to go on forever. The assault was designed to prove to him not

just that he was wrong, but even more important, that he was alone.
During that evening he felt very much alone. It was very personal: Why
was he with the capitalists? Why was he against the working men? What
was his real relationship with Kawamata? Which side was he on? It was,
he thought, just short of physical intimidation, but there was no doubt
that every word carried some kind of warning with it. Those who go against
us will pay a price, Masuda had said; we will remember our enemies.
Miyake had no reason to doubt him, none at all. When he returned, he
decided that something had to be done, that it was not just jobs the workers
were in danger of losing but freedoms as well. These union men were not
interested in making cars, he realized; the cars were a means to an end.

Back at Nissan, Miyake began to meet more often with his Shimbashi-
station colleagues about the problem of the union. Later they became
known to some as the Secret Group, not only because they met secretly
but also because what they were planning was in effect a coup d'état, an
attempt to wrest power from the union with covert management support.
They were able to keep in close touch with Kawamata because one of their
members was Kuniyuki Tanabe, a bright young engineer who was also a
cousin of Kawamata's—all angles had been covered. What Kawamata allegedly communicated to the Secret Group was that if it came to a strike,
then the company would be ready; it would borrow the money from the
banks to fund the people who were on its side. Thus the new union was
financially solid. It had powerful friends who wanted the radical union
crushed. With commitments from the banks, the company was better
prepared to last out a long strike than the Masuda union. A strike might
not be such a bad thing this time. Perhaps the company needed it.

There was about Katsuji Kawamata a quality of self-importance and brus-
queness that other Japanese, those below him and even those above him,
disliked. He did not, they felt, pay nearly enough attention to the time-
honored amenities of the society. He was arrogant, and while other bankers
and heads of companies were also arrogant, they put more effort into
concealing it. Kawamata did not mind their disapproval. That he could be
arrogant and get away with it was a sign of his strength.

One of the things Kawamata liked to recall about his childhood was that
it was so much harder than that of modern youth. In his later years, looking
at Japan's young, he was astonished by how many presents Japanese children received, how filled the stores were with toys. They got toys at ten
o'clock in the morning and an hour later they were bored with them, he
once told a reporter. They expected that pleasure could be bought in a

store and handed to them. His generation had been different, he recalled. "We were poor without knowing that we were poor. We did not have toys, and so we went outside and played all day, climbing trees and playing ball and fishing. We had a simpler life, and we were connected to each other through the way we played, not through toys." Today's Japanese children, he added, beneficiaries of so much better a diet, were tall, "like electric light poles," whereas his generation had been shorter and stockier but "stronger and more muscled."

He often felt nostalgic about his boyhood in the town of Mito, and, like many Japanese of his generation, he believed in his heart that the Japan of the early twentieth century was a much healthier place than the modern country. It was a more austere life, but that austerity was good. When he was a boy, there were no expensive pastries to eat every day, he remarked, and no fruit. A bunch of sweet potatoes was considered a great delicacy. He could remember pounding rice cakes, something he had not enjoyed at the time but regarded with pleasure in retrospect. His boyhood had been lived without central heating and without air conditioning, and he was not sure that those who would someday inherit a great nation should be raised with either. The family's house was cold, but because everyone shared the same hardship, Kawamata had not thought he was cold; that was the way people lived, that was the temperature that the whole world lived at. "Who knows what is cold until you are warm?" he once told a reporter.

As a boy he wore a kimono; not until he was in high school did he wear Western-style clothes. There was no radio in the town of Mito, and the main means of transportation was a small trolley, which ran back and forth through the town. There was a little fire engine that had been built in the United States and was pulled by four horses. He did not see his first car until he was eighteen. It was right after the great earthquake of 1923. The car was a huge black box that seemed to move on its own, and he was fascinated by it. Some thirty years later, when he was almost fifty and just about to take over one of the leading auto companies in Japan, he came to own his first car.

Mito is about sixty miles from Tokyo, a four-hour train ride then, a suburban commute today. Neither of his parents had come from particularly well-off families, and neither had been a Kawamata. The Kawamatas were a relatively successful family in Mito, but they had no children. As is still the custom in Japan, a moneyed but childless family might adopt the child of poorer neighbors who had extra children. So it was that Kawamata's father, who was a Tange, and his mother, who was a Tanabe, both were adopted into the Kawamata family. That way the name lived

on: The successful had access to children, and the less successful had
access to the resources and connections of the wealthy. Kawamata's now
father had been a minor official in the state tobacco monopoly ("a very
ordinary, salaried man, nothing unusual about him," Kawamata would
describe him later). When Kawamata was about eight years old, the family
moved to Tokyo so that the children could go to good high schools and
thus have a chance at college education. Kawamata became the first member of his family to go to a real university. He had thought of becoming
an engineer, but he had terrible handwriting, and he was not capable, he
decided, of making good drafts. Many of the young men in school with
him were going into the bureaucracy, but Kawamata was not enthusiastic
about that idea. He had watched his father's life, and it had seemed a
rather limited one. Instead he wanted to work for a trading company,
because it meant he could travel. In 1929, when he graduated, he applied
to one of the leading trading companies, Mitsubishi, and was turned down.
Times were hard and it was not easy to get jobs. But Kawamata's father
had a friend at the Industrial Bank, and he made a call, and a job was
offered. Kawamata rather reluctantly accepted it, largely because it was
the only one available. He led a fairly typical, insular Japanese life. When
he was twenty-eight his mother told him it was time to marry the daughter
of a friend of hers in Mito. Kawamata himself would have much preferred
to marry a Tokyo girl, for Tokyo women were more sophisticated, but he
bowed to his mother's wishes (just as earlier, wanting to take dancing
lessons, he had asked for his mother's approval, not wanting to upset her).
His mother had been rather insistent about his marrying a small-town
girl. It was, she had pointed out, much harder to check the bloodline of
a Tokyo person. (That meant that there could be a secret "buraku"—an
untouchable—in there somewhere.) A "miai," or match, was arranged and
Kawamata thought she was all right, and so they got married.

He went into the army in 1941 and spent the war on the home front,
a relatively easy war. When it was over, he went back to the IBJ; other
men in his age group seemed to be ahead of him. While the posting to
Nissan came as a shock and he resented it at first, it was not long before
he understood the challenge in it and even more the possibilities of it.
This was a troubled small company, but it might become both untroubled
and large. There was talk of mounting a major highway program in Japan
and rumors that MITI, once steel and shipping were secured as powerful
competitive industries, might move to the auto industry, encouraging it
as an obvious adjunct of the steel industry. There might be more future
than others realized. It was at this moment that Kawamata suddenly became very ambitious. If Nissan became a powerful company, it would be,

in the most personal way imaginable, his success. By 1953 his only real impediment was Tetsuo Masuda.

It was precisely at this time that one of the key figures in the drama, a man who was to be a most important figure in the history of Nissan, joined the company. His name was Ichiro Shioji, and he came to work at Nissan in the personnel department. He was twenty-six years old when he was hired, and in his own immodest way he decided he wanted to be president of the company and nothing less. He had almost not been hired. He had come highly recommended by his superiors at Nippon Oil and Soap, which was part of the Nissan group. He had helped fight a radical union there, and he had proved energetic and physically tough. But he had been to what Nissan officials judged a second-rate school, Meiji University, much of the time in night school, and he had not done well on the written examination administered by Nissan. However, the Nissan men who had overseen his interview, including Kawamata, had been impressed by his manner, his eagerness and confidence. That day they had looked at several other prospective employees, all of whom had been to better schools and who got better scores on the exam, but when the day was over, the man who stood out was Shioji. (The leaders of the Masuda union were convinced years later that the fix had been on, that the people at Nippon Oil had recommended him not so much as an energetic young worker, but rather as a strikebreaker.) Kawamata in particular had been impressed. "He is a tough one," he had told the personnel director, "the kind we need."

About Ichiro Shioji, there was always controversy. He was prototypical of the men of the new Japan, the men partially released from the restraints of the past. The turmoil of the postwar years had allowed a certain number of men who under normal circumstances would never have reached a position of power in Japan to push above their normal hierarchical level, and Shioji was one of them. In a nation where men hid their egos, Shioji was openly egocentric; in a nation where men were willing to reach for power as long as no one realized that they were reaching, Shioji coveted it unabashedly. He was the rare classless man in the new allegedly classless society. As a labor leader, which he was to become at Nissan, he was attacked by the left for being too close to management, yet he was watched warily by management in his own and other companies, for the managers were worried by his hunger for power. Many of his heroes, like Walter Reuther, were American, and he often seemed in manner more American than Japanese. Watching him enjoy the perquisites of power, watching the cocky way he bustled about and gave orders, watching the phalanx of men who seemed to precede him everywhere he went, opening doors and running small errands, a visitor might think he was seeing a Japanese version of Mayor Richard Daley of Chicago, the last of the American political bosses. In a land of self-conscious modesty, much of it on the part of men who were hardly modest at all, there was something refreshing about Shioji's fierce ego. Like Kawamata's, his clothes conveyed a message. Somehow he had escaped from the requisite dark blue suit of the Japanese executive, which bespoke seriousness and caution and thus, in Japan, worthiness. As a senior labor official he dominated every meeting, and the men around him remained on all occasions silent. Later in his career, when one of Shioji's deputies broke with him, analysts trying to estimate what the younger man was like had no idea. They had seen him at perhaps twenty meetings, but they had never heard him say a word.

His impact was immediate. One day soon after he was hired, Kisaburo Tsubura, an official of Masuda's union, went to one of the executive offices. It was just before the second union was formed, and there he saw Miyake, the man who was founding it. There was also a young man Tsubura had never met before. Tsubura had with him six demands which Masuda had told him to present to the company. Tsubura outlined the first demand.

"This is stupid," the young man next to Miyake said.

Tsubura outlined another labor proposal, this one for larger bonuses.

"That's even more stupid," the young man said.

Tsubura started to outline a third.

"You're stupid too," the young man said. "Why don't you get out of here before we become as stupid as you?"

Tsubura tried to finish the list. Then he left the personnel department as quickly as he could. "Who was that young man making all that noise?" he asked the first person who might know.

"Someone named Shioji—Miyake's new bag carrier," he was told.

Others in the new union were never entirely comfortable with their roles. Miyake, for example, had always longed for a position in management. But from the start Shioji was in his element. He was in effect Miyake's bodyguard at first, and he loved best what the majority of the others feared most about those days—physical confrontation, muscle against muscle. He loved wheeling and dealing and marshaling his forces. He was a natural politician and a born street fighter, and he had apprenticed for that in the turmoil of postwar Tokyo.

Shioji had been born in the Kanda section of Tokyo in 1927. His father and uncle ran a small milk-processing company. He was destined to become a good son of the middle class, but the war tore everything apart. He was just a little too young for it, not quite fifteen at the time of Pearl

Harbor, and he hurried through his education and attended the naval academy, graduating just as Japan surrendered. He returned to a Tokyo obliterated by bombing. His father died at the end of the war, and he became responsible for taking care of the rest of his family. The death of his father was particularly painful. His father had been the most successful member of the family, the man who guaranteed loans for his in-laws and got them jobs, and while he was alive, young Ichiro had basked in the reflected glow of his father's position. Whenever there had been family gatherings, certain uncles had flattered him and told him that he ought to go to the University of Kyoto, where they lived, and, of course, stay with them. At his father's funeral the very same people turned from him coldly and told him that they would not be able to help him go to college. In fact, they said, it was quite presumptuous for him even to think of college. He had wanted to become an engineer, but now he had to quit school to feed his family.

For him as for many others that was a desperate time. Tokyo was filled with men who had been perfectly good wage earners before the war and now, no longer able to provide for their families, were permanently crushed. Shioji decided instantly, not even consciously, that he would be a survivor, and that somehow he would end up on top.

Food was rationed, and there was never enough. Bullies would go into a neighborhood, corner the market on what little food there was, buy it, go into the next neighborhood, and sell it for twice as much. Wealthy families were as desperate as poor ones, and Shioji remembered seeing an old women from a good family sell several antique kimonos, which were priceless and must have been in the family for generations, for enough money to buy five kilos of rice. If black marketeering was what it took for survival, Shioji decided, then he would do it. Periodically he would go out into the countryside on what were called buying trains—the earliest trains leaving Tokyo each morning. The people of Tokyo crowded aboard them with sacks and bags and suitcases to prepare to do battle with the farmers. They would wander around the countryside, trying to pick up rumors about which farmers had food; they would buy whatever food there was, grab the last train back to Tokyo, and then sell the produce in the city. There was nothing pleasant about the buying trains; they were filled with terrified, selfish people, each suspicious of the other, each hoping to find some sort of deal and wary that someone else might cut him out of it. Only the farmers had food, which meant that only the farmers were wealthy. The farmers were bastards, Shioji thought. They could control the price of food, and they did, turning the screw as hard as they could. These were Japanese sticking it to other Japanese. It was a time that made people hard. No one could afford to be generous. That was a lesson for Shioji.

Shioji had been a good engineering student at the naval academy, and he had always liked working with wireless sets. After the war it struck him that he had a talent for this, and he announced that he was an electrician whose specialty was repairing radios or making them from scratch. There was no such thing as television yet, and radio was a prime means of communication, but there were no radios for sale. So someone bright and hardworking who could repair a radio and had access to spare parts —which Shioji always managed to have—was a valuable man. There were Japanese who wanted radios and American soldiers who wanted them, and Shioji kept busy and managed to survive. He did it for a few years and managed to make it through the worst of the postwar period.

The Nissan strike was like a small war. It began on May 25. The company wanted it. The union wanted it. Masuda was on a high. The crowds he was drawing were immense, five thousand and six thousand to each meeting. The workers were totally committed. Almost every Nissan worker was a member of the union, and almost everyone was at the meetings. For Masuda, it was as if the resolution of five years of struggle was finally at hand.

His strategy, a colleague said later, was win or die. There would be nothing in the middle. His oldest and closest associates continued to warn him that management had changed, that there was something new in the air, and that he'd better be more cautious. Yet the more they exhorted him, the more excited he became, and the more eager for conflict. "Look at my people," he said after one of the meetings. "Have you ever seen such enthusiasm? Do you doubt who is going to win?" The men of management, he said, were old men from the past, who knew nothing of what was going to happen in the Japan now forming. They were the same men who had killed Japan. Men of death, he said. His people were the new Japan, and they were finally taking control. The new Japan was Masuda and his workers running the factories and insisting on their rights, and the old Japan was the zaibatsu, it was the bank sending Kawamata over to crush a union. Anyone who opposed him was the old Japan. He had never seemed so sure of himself. There was irony in that, his friend Nakamura realized years later. For in reality they knew nothing. They were children. None of them had ever been part of a labor union. None of them had ever been overseas or had ever observed a full-fledged union or talked with an international union leader. None had any real sense of the ebb and flow of a union's relationship with management, or of the resources a company can summon that a union cannot. Above all, none of them knew how much pressure an average Japanese worker would take when confronted by conflicting definitions of authority. "We were all too innocent," Nakamura said.

Kawamata chose a hard-line policy. He decided to exhaust the union through its own strike. If the union struck, fine; there would be no pay. The company had secured its position for the near future. It might be able to last six months or a year in a strike, particularly if the work force was divided. It had special loans from the IBJ, which eased some of the financial pressure. It intended to lend some of that money to its key parts suppliers. Their financial position was even more precarious than that of the main company, and it was important that they survive the strike. The suppliers in turn would lend a considerable amount back to the second union, once it was formed. It would have been illegal for Nissan itself to lend to the second union, but this way the loan was permissible.

The Nikkeiren was also ready to aid the company by helping its suppliers, arranging for them to get temporary work from other manufacturers. Because it feared the strong-arm tactics of the union, the company hired its own thugs, several hundred young men, many of whom were either unemployed longshoremen or yakuza—toughs who modeled themselves on what they perceived to be the style and manner of American gangsters. They flaunted their tattoo marks, and some were using drugs. Older Nissan executives were stunned to go to the men's room and find their new allies, needles out, getting high for a day's head-banging with the radical union. The thugs were there to protect the second union when it entered combat with the old one. After all, at the start the second union was going to be composed largely of kachos and buchos, men of the middle level. They would need protection, and they would have it.

Management now sat back and played it cool. For the first time it began to cut the union off. When Masuda wanted to talk, management did not return his phone calls. When he wanted to hold meetings, there was always a reason why the meetings could not be held. Key management people who were supposed to deal with the union were told not to come to work. Many executives went fishing or simply hid out in rural inns. A skeleton managerial staff showed up at work, just enough to manage the office. When executives did meet among themselves, they chose a different site every time; they wanted complete secrecy. The union, increasingly frustrated, tried to find out where the executives were meeting, so it could gather, picket, and harass them. What was clear, some of the union people realized much later, was that management had a very carefully orchestrated plan, and it involved baiting and provoking the union.

Inevitably the union moved closer to violence. Though a strike was going on, the union people felt free to enter the factory, and they held suribachi courts on the factory floor, more brutal than in the past. Masuda's people carried their battle into the workers' dormitories. The dorms became the center of the worst kind of civil war, conducted within the larger one. There the union people assaulted anyone they thought was against them. They harassed entire families, blocking some from using the toilets or the kitchens. Sometimes they set their wives upon the wife of a wavering worker; the wives would taunt the woman for several days, cutting her off, making fun of her, making it impossible for her to cook for her family. One worker years later could remember coming home and finding a huge sign outside the door of his room. It said, "The spy for the company lives here." Inside were five men. He had seen only one of them before. "We know what you are up to," one said. "Do not think you can fool us." Then they remained silent. For four hours they just sat there, not saying anything. No one spoke to him. When his children tried to move around, they were told to be quiet, as if they were intruders in the house. The only noise was the occasional sound of weeping from one of the children. Finally one of the men turned to the others and said, "Do you think he gets the idea?" Then they got up and left. For days afterward the worker wondered what he had done to bring them to his apartment. He had been a member of the union, he had believed in Masuda. He had, it was true, been a little uneasy about the conduct of the union, and in his heart he believed that a man should be paid only if he worked. But he could not remember having revealed any of these seditious thoughts to anyone, not even his wife.

For nine weeks Kawamata waited. He was in absolutely uncharted waters. It was the hardest period of his life. All the other businessmen in the Nikkeiren were pushing him and encouraging him, and his own instincts told him this was the right way. Moreover, knowing he faced a protracted strike, he had received a critical bit of additional support from the Nikkeiren people; they had arranged with his two top competitors, Toyota and Isuzu, not to exploit the long strike by taking some of Nissan's market share. It was a reflection of a far more controlled society than America's, and one in which antitrust laws were quite different. It freed Kawamata from the kind of fear that had long plagued and divided the American companies and that the United Auto Workers, the UAW, had so skillfully exploited—the fear of loss, perhaps permanent, of market share to a competitor during a strike. (When International Harvester took on the UAW in a long, complicated, bitterly fought strike in 1979, Arch McCardell, the head of Harvester, who had once been a Ford finance man, was at a business council meeting, where he ran into Philip Caldwell, the head of Ford. Caldwell praised his heroism in standing up to the UAW. "Somebody has to stand up and do this, Archie," Caldwell said, as quoted by Barbara Marsh in her excellent book on Harvester, *A Corporate Tragedy*. "You just stick in there." McCardell's pleasure was somewhat diminished by the knowledge that Ford sales people were already quite systematically going after Harvester's truck customers.) That alone strengthened Kawamata's hand considerably. It meant that he was fighting on only one front, not two, and it meant that time was on his side and working against the union. His strategy now was to use time to wear the workers down with the absence of paychecks. He wanted their wives to start working on them. He did not want his countermoves to come too quickly. The strikers' ideological passion must be tempered by hunger and fear. In June and July the union and the company struggled with each other. Then, on August 5, Kawamata finally made his move. He locked out the Masuda union. On August 7 the second union surfaced at a mass meeting, and on August 10 came the crucial confrontation.

For Kawamata the lockout was the most difficult move imaginable. It was, he said later, the act of a desperate man. It caught the union completely by surprise. The management put up barricades, and the union, perplexed, responded with force. Its people crashed through the barricades and, led by Masuda, poured onto the factory floor. There were fist fights everywhere between Masuda's people and the yakuza, and the police were called. The struggle went on day after day. The first barricade had been flimsy; the next barricade was stronger, and again Masuda's people charged it. Masuda was arrested.

Now the initiative passed to management. For the first time Kawamata was setting the rules. He was well financed as the union was not, with an estimated $1.5 million in special loans from the IBJ and the Fuji Bank to support him as he took on this radical force. That was a sum nearly equal to what the company made in a year. He had blocked the union out, worn down its people by cutting off salaries, and now was creating an alternative outlet for most of the workers. Once the second union was formed, its people were allowed to come to work, and they were paid immediately, even though the company was barely able to function. Most of those in the second union were white-collar people who had been appalled by the suribachi trials and the hostile tactics of the union. Some were there on the direct orders of management to strengthen the handful of loyalists in the new group. Some were former members of the Masuda union who had been thrown out for opposing the strike. In the beginning there were almost no working men in it. "Those who love the company love the union," went one of Miyake's slogans. Miyake thought it a frightening time. He knew he was backed by Kawamata, but some of the Asahara people were warning him that he had chosen a risky course. At the time the second union was formed there were about seven thousand workers, and they were all in the Masuda union. In the first meetings of the new union there had been perhaps forty members at the most. They knew they had to form a new core out of the white-collar class. Each person was told to bring in ten recruits.

Miyake decided to have an open rally. He hoped that five hundred workers would come. All of Tokyo was watching. The meeting was broadcast on Tokyo radio and there were journalists everywhere. Some four hundred people showed up to listen to Miyake. That was a little disappointing, but not bad, he felt. Outside the hall were throngs of Masuda's men, about two thousand of them, and they looked very tough and angry. Many of them had clubs. Miyake and Shioji had assigned their own young toughs to guard the doors, but Miyake was not sure they could hold the line. There were scuffles each time someone tried to enter the hall. Miyake wondered if the guards he had appointed were formidable enough. The night before they had looked strong. "Can anyone do judo?" he had asked, and then appointed those who had said yes to guard the door. The police made the critical difference. The government wanted this meeting to take place. That decision, Miyake knew, had been made at a high level.

Just before he walked out to talk to the crowd, he was hit with a terrible wave of fear. He knew that he could not allow himself to show it. The audience, he could tell, was already terrified. Most of them were sitting in their seats nervously, looking straight ahead. The hall was curiously silent. For the last two days Miyake had been receiving calls from friends who had once been filled with brave talk about the role they would play in the new union and who now, without explanation, were begging off coming to the meeting. Later he realized how scared the two thousand Masuda people outside must have been, and how frightened even the cops were, but he did not think about it at the time. Miyake had been so busy planning the meeting that he had not thought very much about what he was going to say. In the end he tried to make it simple: "If you break the law in this country you go to prison for that crime," he said, "and you can never get out. But although this first union is like a prison, you have the chance to get out. You can determine it yourself. But you have to fight for it. You have to join us, and you have to bring a friend, just one friend to the next meeting. Then we will have a thousand members. Then they will bring a friend. But unless we fight back, we will all have to leave, because we will have no place in this company, we will not be able to control who we are and how we work and what hours we work. We will lose our livelihood. We are already close to it. Therefore we have to fight back." When the meeting was over, a police captain came up to Miyake and said quietly, "You are supposed to come with me, sir," and escorted him quickly out the back way. Otherwise, Miyake was sure, he never would have been able to escape from the building.

Now the second union began to take over. It had been legitimized by that meeting. Almost immediately it took the struggle into the dorms. It had jobs to offer; it was paying workers who joined it roughly 60 percent of their salaries, while the other striking workers were getting nothing. It had carefully drawn lists of which workers were reportedly anti-Masuda, which were on the fence, which were moderately pro-union, and which were intensely pro-union. Miyake and Shioji and their men liked going into the dorms, in groups of five or six. They came armed with both carrot and stick. There might be a few workers sitting around in a room. "You've been good in this, Watanabe-san," Miyake would say to one of them. "You are a loyal son of Nissan. Kawamata-san was told of you yesterday, and he was very pleased by the good things that were said. Kawamata-san said that men like you should be rewarded. We are going to promote you, and we are going to give you a raise tomorrow." Then he might turn to Shioji, who, naming another man in the room, would say, "It is a shame about Ikeda-san. He listens to all the wrong people. What will he do when he leaves Nissan? I do not think we have a place for men like this, men who are against a strong Japan. But Ikeda-san seems to want to listen to foreigners instead of his fellow Japanese."

What pleased Miyake and Shioji about their meetings in the dorms was that the wives were often there. The country was poor, money for food was scarce, the company was hardly a success, and the wives were all too aware of the possible consequences of what was happening. They were uneasy with Masuda's course, frightened by the confrontation and the rising level of violence, and, of course, the end of the paycheck. After Miyake and Shioji had left the dorms, the wives, they believed, would continue to press their arguments. What Masuda had been doing, Miyake and his men continually emphasized, was alien. It was anti-Japanese. It was as if some foreign force were at hand. Japanese people were not like this; Japanese people, they stressed, believed in work and in settling their differences peacefully. The one thing they had in common above all else was that they were Japanese. Who was behind this union? The answer, he said, was the Communists. That meant the Russians.

Which way the workers went was critical now. Masuda was confident that they were his. The rallies had been bigger than ever. It never occurred to him, filled with passion as he was, that the workers were no longer with him as he was with them. Some of the men around him saw signs of slippage, signs of doubt among the workers; he did not. Some of his friends tried to tell him that this was a time to reconsider and to pull back, that he was overextended and playing into the hands of the company. But Masuda, challenged, seemed if anything more anxious for confrontation. He was confident of the workers and their commitment to the union. But certain advisers had the feeling that he did not know the workers as well as he thought he did. He might be their leader, they might in fact love him and believe they were loyal to him, but he was not *of* them. Their lives, unlike his, were not about speeches and ideas and polemics; their lives were about getting through one more day.

9.
THE CRUSHING
OF MASUDA

The struggle was largely beyond the workers. They were at once exhilarated and fearful. Wary by nature, they grew warier the longer the strike went on.

That spring Sanosuke Tanaka, a worker at the Nissan plant at Yoshiwara, was thirty-eight years old. That made him one of the older workers in the company. He had worked for Nissan before the war; most of the men at the plant had been hired after the war as the company had slowly expanded. He had joined Nissan in 1937 after a series of lesser jobs. There had been a small ad in a newspaper saying that Nissan was going to hire a few people for its assembly plant. Nissan, to a peasant like Tanaka, had seemed a great company, and he had immediately wanted to go to work there. More than three hundred people had applied, and he had been one of twenty-four selected. He had considered himself very fortunate. He had been paid 40 yen a month, small by the standards of the Tokyo middle class in those days but princely by the standards that Tanaka had been accustomed to. Only a few years earlier he had been paid 50 yen for an entire year for working in a store. But it was more than just the paycheck, it was that he was now a man of Nissan. He belonged to an important company. Only very good people could work there. He was not just choosing a place to work and a means to earn a salary but, in a larger sense, he was joining a community. "In Japan work is a ceremony . . ." the Japanese writer Ichiro Kawasaki had written. "To the Western worker, the job is an instrument for the enrichment and satisfaction of the real part of his life, which exists outside the place of work. For the Japanese worker, life and job are so closely interwoven that it cannot be said where one ends and the other begins." So it was with Tanaka. Nissan was a big company, perhaps not as big as the steel companies, but trucks were important. Nissan was his new family, and it defined him in the most positive sense. He gained prestige among the people he knew by the fact that he worked for Nissan. His family was proud of his success, and in the little village from which he had so recently come, it now was said of him by those who had once looked down on him that they had always known he would make good. Soon almost all his friends were fellow Nissan workers. This was his community now, almost his family. He intended to work there for the rest of his life.

He was a country man, and he could barely believe that he had one of the best jobs in Japan. With his first paycheck he paid 10 yen to his sister in Yokohama, with whom he was living, and then he went to a movie theater and saw a movie. A few days later on his day off, still euphoric, he took some money and went with a friend to climb Mount Fuji. Then, summoning his courage, he went to a small store that sold Western-style clothing—there were more and more of them now in Yokohama—and bought himself a Western suit. The suit was gray, and it cost him 10 yen. All the rest of his life he would remember that moment, standing in the back of the store, wearing his new suit, and looking in the mirror and seeing a person he had never seen before. This is a real person, completely independent, he thought, this is a man of the city. When he walked out of that store he was prouder than he had ever been before, because for the first time in his life he truly felt released from his poverty. I am wearing a suit, he thought the rest of the day, I am wearing a suit just like anyone else.

Tanaka and men like him had traded an old, severe rural life for a new, difficult but dramatically more bearable urban and industrialized life, a life that promised something better for their children. Tanaka was born on a tiny farm outside of Tokyo, in Kanagawa prefecture, in 1915. His memory was that Japan was poor, his village was poorer, and his family was poorer still. His father, Hanshichi Tanaka, was a tenant farmer working for a rich landlord on a tiny spit of land. His father, aided by the older boys in the family, could grow about 850 pounds of rice a year, and of this he was allowed to keep about 150 pounds for his own family. The rest went to the landowner. His father did not quarrel with this arrangement, though looking back later Tanaka himself was struck by the injustice of it. It was the way people were supposed to live, and the proof of that was that it was the way they had always lived. You were poor, you had always been poor, and you would remain poor. A tenant farmer might have enough to eat, but rarely would he have enough rice so that he might actually get ahead. The system was designed so that those who began the year poor ended it poor. His father, Tanaka said, never thought of rebelling because he could not conceive of a better situation. It was his responsibility to accept what he had.

There were about five hundred people in the village. A tiny handful of them owned almost all the land. As a boy you could walk and walk and never seem to leave the property of these rich men, Tanaka remembered. A few people had small plots of land themselves, but most were like Tanaka's father, tenant farmers. The majority of the children were those of tenant farmers; they lived in thatch-roofed huts like Tanaka and his family, all five or six sleeping, as his family of seven did, in one tiny room. In those days it was easy to tell the children of the landowners from the other children; they wore clean kimonos every day at school. Sometimes they wore oshimas, a classier form of kimono. All the others had raggedy old kimonos. Shoes were particularly precious; they were very expensive. Tanaka had no memory of new shoes, only of hand-me-downs from his brothers. Whenever it rained he would go around barefoot, because he did not want to get his shoes wet and ruin them. At graduation the landowners' children would always have brand-new shoes, whereas the tenants' children had worn shoes, meticulously cleaned for the occasion, and handed down inevitably through several siblings.

The Tanaka family knew nothing but hardship. There was always enough food but never any luxury. The basis of the diet when the harvest was good was rice. More often than not, however, things were hard, and the rice was mixed with millet. Tanaka loved rice but he hated millet, and when he would look at his plate and see that his dinner was mostly millet, he would carefully, as little boys do, separate the rice he loved from the millet he hated. Once in a while, when they were very lucky, there were some vegetables. On still rarer occasions there was fish. There was never meat. As a boy Tanaka helped his parents with every chore and worked in the fields. Sometimes he had one of the easier chores, like working in the mulberry fields, picking cocoons to sell to the silk dealers. Years later a friend asked him what he had done for leisure as a boy, and he had looked puzzled; he simply did not understand the question, for there had never been any leisure.

Tanaka often wondered, when he was a grown man, who had had the harder life, his father or mother. They were both people who had suffered without even knowing they were suffering. His father would get up in the morning and work the harsh paddy all day long. It was backbreaking labor. If he had any pleasure in life, it was his sake. Sometimes, Tanaka knew, he drank too much sake and beat his wife. Even as a little boy Tanaka had known that there were terrible fights between his parents. He remembered that when his older brother was in the army and he had once written asking for a little money; his mother had gotten the letter and tried to hide it from the father, for fear of the anger it would create. It was very easy for his father to go from exhaustion into rage. As a boy he had understood in some elemental way that the drinking and the anger were always connected, but he had never decided whether the anger caused the drinking or the drinking caused the anger. Some of those nights were hard on everyone in the little hut.

Tanaka thought his mother had an even harder life than his father. She got up earlier than anyone else and prepared the simple peasant breakfast for the entire family—bean-paste soup, boiled barley, and pickles. That finished, she would pack a lunch for her husband and join him in the field, working side by side, until she came home a little before him to fix dinner. That was her day. She had borne five children and had worked in the field until an hour or so before she delivered them. Her life, he realized later, had been merciless; she died when he was eight, of jaundice, he thought. When she died, he, the youngest, became responsible for most of the housework. His kimonos—it was a mild source of shame—were always a little more ragged than those of his schoolmates because there was no one at home to repair them.

The village was self-contained, almost completely cut off from the outside world. There was no television or radio to keep the peasants informed of news from Tokyo, nor were there cars hurtling down the highway, bringing people in contact with one another. When he was eight years old Tanaka saw his first gas-driven vehicle; the date was September 1, 1923 (he remembered it because it was the day of the great Tokyo earthquake, and he later realized that his own tiny home had survived the earthquake only because it was so small that it shifted with the earth and thus was not destroyed). He had been walking along the road when a huge metal contraption rolled by. It was, he later realized, a bus. It seemed the grandest thing he had ever seen in his life. He stood there transfixed, and then he noticed that it seemed to be leaking something. He knelt down after it had passed, touched the spot on the road, and for the first time in his life smelled the scent of gasoline. He thought the smell was wonderful, and he stayed there for a long time, a little boy by the roadside sniffing this wondrous odor left behind by the bus, hypnotized by the smell and the idea of such a powerful machine. The idea of movement by machine was nearly unthinkable. Tanaka himself walked to and from every place he visited. There was a rich landowning family nearby, and the daughters of the family rode bicycles to school. Tanaka would watch them come and go, and sixty years later he could still remember the intensity of his envy, how much he wanted what they had, how much freer they were than he was.

The principal pleasure in Tanaka's life was school. He loved school, and he was good at it. Sixty years later a reporter could walk through the tiny village, now a distant suburban extension of Tokyo, and talk with the assistant principal of the elementary school, who had been a classmate of Tanaka's, and hear him explain how everyone in the entire village had always known that Tanaka was the brightest boy in the village and would succeed. For in this meager society, school was the only equalizer. Tanaka might not be able to buy books at the little bookstore in the village, which he passed every day and longed to enter, but school was different. Poor and rich children were treated the same by the teachers. Studying for him was everything. He took his pleasure from those moments when he alone was able to answer a question from the teacher.

His teacher was named Rennosuke Takeda, and he had from an early time encouraged Tanaka to continue his studies. Tanaka was clearly the best student in the class, and Takeda told the young boy that he could, by dint of hard work, become a teacher himself. He was that gifted. That seemed a dream almost beyond Tanaka's comprehension; teachers were men of learning and power. Hearing his teacher talk like that, he thought that teaching would lead him to the most wonderful of worlds. Japanese compulsory education ended, however, with the sixth grade, and poor children like Tanaka usually dropped out then and went to work in the fields. His three older brothers had finished their education with the sixth grade. At that point if a child still wanted education, his parents had to pay. Tanaka's father did not want his fourth son to continue with his education. A sixth-grade education had been good enough for all the other children; it would be good enough for this son.

But in a rare gesture of a teacher on behalf of a student, Takeda himself went to the house and pleaded with Hanshichi Tanaka to allow the boy to go on. Just two more years, he had argued. He is my best student. He loves to study, and he can be a fine teacher. He will certainly do well at the teachers college. There is a future for him beyond this village. That last argument did not enchant the elder Tanaka, for whom the village had been quite good enough, but in the end, Takeda prevailed—he was a teacher and a man of authority, and his authority held that day in the house. So the boy was allowed to continue with his schooling. The school fees in those days were 20 sen a month. It was not a great deal of money, just about enough for three packs of cigarettes, but for a very poor family it was difficult to raise. Tanaka, because he was the best student in the

class, was assigned the task of collecting the school fees each month. Often
he was unable to bring his own payment. Takeda would ask him at the
end of the collection, "Do you have it all?" No, Tanaka would answer, we
don't have it all, but we're close. Tanaka, of course, was the one person
who had not brought the money, and he would manage to delay the
payment until there was a little money at home. It was quite possible, he
realized later, that Takeda had arranged it in this way, knowing how hard
it was on him and wanting to give him a bit of grace.

When Tanaka was finished with the eighth grade, Takeda began preparing to push Tanaka for the next level of education. There was a normal
school he would be able to attend without paying anything; he would,
however, be obligated to teach for many years afterward. Takeda wanted
to come to the house to make the argument in favor of continuing, but it
could not be done. Tanaka's father was tired of this foolishness. The
boy had to accept his fate. He had already, without consulting the boy,
sold his services for five years. His father had broken the news to him
without any emotion; Tanaka sensed that his father was very sad when he
had to do it, but that he had learned long ago how to control his emotions
in such scenes. After all, Tanaka reasoned, he had done it three times
before.

Tanaka was sharply disappointed. The idea of becoming a teacher was
a powerful one, and, encouraged by his teacher, he had believed he would
be able to do it. And then he found out he had been sold. In later generations, he thought, there might have been some recourse. At the very
least he might have been able to run away. But in those days one accepted
it. His father had indentured him to a family in a neighboring village. His
father had done this because he was poor and needed the money; therefore,
it was his obligation to serve his father. If he did not accept the terms he
would bring shame to his family. If he had fled, he might have been able
to find a job somewhere, but people would have laughed at his family,
and the shame would have hung over them and him for the rest of his
life. There was simply no alternative to accepting; a young boy from the
country did not simply pack up and leave his village without parental
permission. If he had violated the earliest level of authority, that of the
family, then anyone thinking of hiring him would assume he would violate
the next level of authority, that of commerce. The terms were simple: He
would work for five years for this family. He would receive room and
board—the plainest imaginable. The money he earned would be sent to
his father. For the first year he was paid 50 yen; for the second, 70; for
the third, 90; for the fourth, 110; and for the last year, 130.

His job was to carry coal from the local coal merchant to the families in the village. The woman who ran the coal store was a widow, and part of his job was to tutor her ten-year-old son, who became almost like a brother to him. He never forgot for a day that he might have become a teacher. When his five years were up, his life was finally his own, and he left the village immediately and headed for Yokohama. The eldest son was supposed to stay and help the father work the land, and the younger sons were supposed to go to the city. Tanaka's sister Taka, his favorite in all the family, was living in Yokohama with her family. She had been able to attend even less school than the boys, because at a very young age she had been sent off to work for wealthy families as a maid or a baby-sitter. Then an uncle had decided that a bachelor in his family should marry her. Tanaka's sister did not want to marry him, but there was no choice. She subsequently had nine children; Tanaka did not think she was very happy in her marriage.

He went to Yokohama when he was just twenty, and for a time he worked for a delivery service. Then he saw the ad for jobs at Nissan, applied, and was accepted. He proudly sent money home. He had made good, and he was a good son. He worked in the axle-assembly section for two years, then in the chassis section, and then was drafted. He spent a year in China and served in the South Pacific. In 1946 he returned to Nissan. He remembered those postwar years as the hardest period in his life. He had gotten married during the war, and in 1946 he and his wife had started having children. They had been luckier than most couples, because their little house in Yokohama had not been burned down by the American incendiary bombs. But it was a desperate time as far as food was concerned. One child had just been born and now another was on the way, and Tanaka thought of himself a failure; he had a job, but he was unable to provide enough food for his wife and child. Whatever money he made at work he brought home, and it was used for food. He was paid only once a month, and prices went up almost daily. Every month there was only one thought on his mind: Will this paycheck last even close to the arrival of the next one?

On Saturday when he was through work at the factory, he would go out into the country and forage for food. Only the black marketeers had rice, and they were hard men, they demanded cash; they would not take a poor man's promise, or his barter. On Sunday, his day off, he hung around the area where the Americans were based, hoping to get work as a day laborer. At the very least, if he did not get work, he sometimes could bring home scraps of food. The American soldiers were very rich, and their army cooks would take the loaves of bread and cut off the end crusts, what the Japanese called the ears of the bread. This, if nothing else was available, became his family's food. Somehow he always managed to find enough to eat.

His second child was born healthy, and then a third. Gradually things got better. He remembered precisely when it was he had realized the postwar period was truly over. Rice had begun to appear in the markets. The black marketeers no longer controlled the rice market. Soon they began to disappear. When the black marketeers no longer had power over him, no longer made him feel a failure, he knew that the war was finally over, and that the real peace had begun.

He joined the union after the war, and he liked the idea of belonging to it; workers, he was told, were supposed to have rights and dignity, and the union would help them in this. He accepted the idea of that, although he also believed that work itself was dignity and that if you worked hard you did not have to assert any additional dignity. He became the union representative from an assembly section. But he was bothered by the growing turbulence at Nissan as the tensions mounted between management and the union. There were now so many authorized and unauthorized strikes and slowdowns that it was almost impossible to work. Work would start, and there would be a strike, and it would stop, and it would start again and stop again. That dismayed Tanaka more than anything else: He had a powerful belief that it was a shame not to work, that you were put on earth to work, not so much for yourself and your family, but because that was the right thing to do and because it improved the condition of everyone. The purpose of life, he believed, was work.

The union began to make him nervous. He did not like the work stoppages, and he thought that the company, not the union, had the right to decide which worker held which job. He wanted to challenge the leadership of the union, but he was afraid to. Other men spoke up and there was quick retaliation against them, the suribachi trials. Sometimes he wanted to help the men who were on trial, but he was afraid to. Was he a coward? he wondered. He was a peasant, and peasants, he knew, were not supposed to speak up. They were supposed to be quiet and listen and do what they were told. So he was left each day with his thoughts; at night he would think of all the things he had wanted to say, about how they had to work harder and save the company, and then in the daytime he would not say them. He was afraid all the time. He became suspicious of Masuda. Masuda was from Todai, he was from the elite—what did he really know about working men? Had his wife and children ever starved? Did Masuda forage for food? The people who got ahead in his union were the ones who were the most left-wing, not the ones who were the best workers. Was that right? "Masuda was the son of a rich man, and I was the son of a peasant," Tanaka later said. "He was the moon and I was the turtle."

When the 1953 strike began he was very unhappy. He hated going to the factory every day when there was no work. Nothing in his life had ever seemed so wrong. Other men began to talk about splitting the union and forming a new one, but that seemed wrong to him too. However, when the second union was finally formed, on August 30, he joined almost immediately, on September 13. When the second union went back to work, Tanaka did too, with a great feeling of relief. Something treasured, his sense of purpose, had been taken away, and now it was being returned.

Masuda stayed in jail about two weeks, and when he came back the second union was becoming stronger by the day. Oddly, Masuda seemed exhilarated. He had loved being in jail. He could not wait to tell his union colleagues about what it had been like. He had been with common criminals, and they had been amazed that a graduate of Todai, so well educated, had been in the same cell. He had given political instruction to them, he said, explaining to them why they were in prison and why they were victims of Japan's class system. He seemed almost oblivious to the rise of the new union. It had no legitimacy with the workers, he said. Its leaders were agents of management. The workers would see that. When some of the men around him tried to argue that the struggle had changed, that the second union was picking up strength very quickly, Masuda stopped them short. "The men are loyal," he would say. "All you have to do is walk across the floor or go to a rally." His rallies were greater than ever, and far more emotional. That was so, the others replied, there was no doubt that he was winning the war of the rallies, and he would win a plebiscite, but the management and the second union were winning the war in the dormitories. Masuda, his friend Ochiai thought, had been too sure for too long of his own victory, and then when it became clear that the victory was slipping away, too proud to negotiate. He was, said Ochiai, like the Japanese commanders in the Pacific whom Masuda despised because they had held on too long after it was hopeless for them.

Kawamata was slowly squeezing Masuda's union. There were some loans to workers, and they were given with the understanding that they would not have to be paid back. Sometimes Miyake's men would take a wavering worker to a bar, spend the evening filling him with drink and praise, and at the end of the evening some money might change hands, a bonus it was called. Sometimes a handful of them would visit a worker in the dorm, preferably in front of his wife, and talk to him about the job he might have. It was constant pressure now, and one side had the money and the jobs to offer, and the other did not. It could offer only dying hopes.

Now the section chiefs, who had been beaten up so badly during the suribachi trials, were getting their revenge. They gave those workers who came back not just their regular salaries but bonuses. They warned those who remained with the Masuda union that there might never be another chance. There were going to be dismissals. For those who hesitated there would certainly never be any promotions. Promotions would go to those who had tried to save the company. The company would remember. The company already remembered. We have lists of those who caused all the trouble, Miyake's people said. Right now your name is not on it. But we can add it to the list in a day or two. It is very easy to add a name to the list, and it is impossible to get it off once it has been added. Very quickly the tide turned. The second union concentrated on those workers, like Tanaka, who were the least political, and on those who seemed to be wavering. It simply ignored those who were committed to Masuda. The union, Miyake's people kept repeating, is Communist. Look, they said, even its flag is red. If a worker spoke of loyalty to Masuda, the Miyake people would laugh: Masuda, they said, Masuda is from Todai, Masuda is not going to starve—and you, are you going to enter Todai when you lose your job?

There were constant scuffles and fights as marauding groups encountered each other, the ugliness of it intensifying because it was a family feud and both sides knew each other so well. Shioji was in charge of the youth group from the second union. His assignment was to keep an eye on the first union and to match its force with his own. He loved it; he was always on the move, the head of Action Central, checking out trouble spots, sending his own people in. He seemed almost joyous, his friends thought, the one person who seemed to revel in the confrontation and who was always able to rise to it. Miyake was the head of the second union, but a great deal of the energy and strategy was coming from Shioji. He was already a power. By the end of September the new union had more than three thousand workers among its members. Finally Masuda understood what had happened. "They have us now," he told his friends. "The only thing to do is save as many of our people as we can." He never spoke to others about any miscalculations he had made: As far as he was concerned, he had done everything right until one day it had suddenly all gone wrong. Since the confrontation in August, when his union was locked out, his people had become broken and tired. He was fighting against a well-organized and well-financed foe—indeed, against the full force of postwar Japanese capitalism. He had underestimated his opponent. Having no alternative, he accepted the company offer, ended the strike, and sent his people back to work.

They went back, of course, at the mercy of the company. Those who had been strong Masuda people were given the worst jobs, and some of those were eventually pressured into leaving the company. Masuda himself and about seven of his leaders soon received letters saying that they were fired. A few weeks later the second tier of his leadership was fired as well. The letters were very simple: They said that the recipient had broken the rules of the company and would no longer be needed. Some, like Masuda, decided to challenge the firing in the courts, but most did not. For them, they knew, it was over. By the end of 1953 the new union had complete control of the factory floor.

Masuda was finished. His first mistake had been underestimating his opponents, and his second and perhaps even greater mistake had been overestimating his own men, thinking that they believed everything he believed and that they would stay the course. He had thought that Japan had truly changed after the war, and that a new order, of which he was an important part, had taken power. Instead, there had been a change not so much in the society but within the old order. Newer men had been allowed to come to the fore, and some of the older men had been forced into retirement because of their association with the old war-making machine. The old order had been democratized, modernized, slimmed down, and energized; the banking system was simplified, the companies made less cumbersome. But the old order had not changed. The strike at Nissan was the final proof. Limits on political and economic freedom were subtly being imposed.

Nissan promptly expelled its old enemies and put loyalists in key jobs. Over the next few years nearly two thousand workers were fired. Now, the radical union broken and a new one sympathetic to management installed, Nissan stabilized itself. Basic wages for workers were cut 16 percent in the first year. Production schedules were tightened. Workers no longer challenged their superiors; instead, foremen watched their workers carefully for any murmur of dissent.

Most significant was the death of Masuda's dream—of an industry-wide union strong enough to stand up not just to one company but to the entire industry and indeed the state. From now on, each company would have its own union, which would be totally loyal to its parent company and dependent upon the marketplace success of the company for its own success. Management had won; it could not go back to the pre-MacArthur days, when there were no unions at all, but it had defined labor on its own terms, incorporated labor into the company itself, and ended any possibility of labor as an adversarial force within. Years later, when Japan finally challenged Western industries, it was clear that one of the most critical factors in its success was the creation of the second unions and the elimination of radical ones.

Masuda's world had collapsed. Nearly all his old union associates reestablished themselves. Some made lateral moves to jobs in supplier companies or joined left-wing groups. But Masuda just drifted. His friends always thought his plight was proof that he had never been a member of the Communist party, because the party, which normally took care of its own, did nothing for him. The other members of his union felt themselves bound to each other and stayed in touch; they went to the same bars to drink and reminisce and try to understand what had happened. Indeed, in the true style of Japan, where there is a group for almost everything —be it the company group or the fifth-grade group or a group for the wounded in an army hospital—they formed an association of those who had been forced out of Nissan. They even had a name for themselves, the Association of the Bad Guys, and they got together for annual reunions. But Masuda never showed up. He avoided his old friends. When an auto journalist named Hideo Numasaki tried to interview him, Masuda answered, "All of that is past. All of it is done."

He had a difficult time supporting himself. For a long time he did not work, and then, using money borrowed from his mother-in-law, he set himself up as a small supplier, running an auto-body-stamping shop. Before long he had serious labor troubles. He struggled with his workers, there were dismissals, and the workers, who did not have a union, thought of bringing charges against him in the labor council. Friends intervened, and the charges were not brought, but the company, which had never been very strong, went bankrupt. When friends tried to help him find other jobs, he pulled back; he was a proud man, and he did not want to be helped. By the early sixties he was unemployed and living as a single man, his life disorderly and lonely.

One day in the early sixties one of his sons came to see Michio Hatada, Masuda's oldest friend. The son seemed quite desperate; he wanted to quit college and go to work in an auto company, but even more, he needed advice about his father. Masuda, the son reported, did not live at home, but was not yet divorced from his mother. On occasion he came over to visit his family. If no one was home, he always took something—a radio, a lamp, an heirloom, a kimono—and went to the pawnshop for money. Hatada went by the house, talked with Mrs. Masuda, heard the story, and urged her to divorce her husband. It was her only protection, he said.

Masuda dropped even further out of sight. No one heard from him until in 1964 an employee of a small manufacturing company in Tokyo called Masuda's family and said he had died of a heart attack. He had worked for the company as some sort of manager. One day while he was handing out the summer bonuses he keeled over. He was fifty years old. In his wallet someone found a photograph of his family and his old address. The family arranged the funeral. The only one of his old friends who was contacted was Hatada. He got a postcard notifying him of the funeral on the day it was taking place, and he went. It turned out to be just him, the ex-wife, her mother, and Masuda's three sons. The family wanted no one from the union. Hatada found the day almost unbearable. He kept remembering the young man with so much promise and ambition, and then the glory years of the strike and his passion for the new Japan. Hatada found it hard to understand how a life so promising could end in such loneliness and failure. He was the Japanese Don Quixote, Hatada thought, a dreamer in a nation not much given to dreams.

Thirty years later Katsuji Kawamata was asked by a journalist about Masuda. "Masuda?" he said. "I don't really remember him. Besides, he is dead, so why even talk about him?"

Kawamata was the big winner of the strike. He now had a union that was sympathetic to management. His labor troubles were over. He had increased his prestige greatly in the world of Japanese finance and industry, for he was the man who had broken the toughest union of all. He was seen, and he now saw himself, not just as the banker who had gone to Nissan but as an industrialist, the man who went into the pit with formidable labor leaders and held his own. He was a tough man now, a man to be reckoned with.

Until the strike he had been a somewhat solitary figure at Nissan, the outsider sent over by the bank, never entirely trusted by the old hands. The contempt of the Asahara people for him, because he knew nothing about cars, was as great as his contempt for them, for being afraid of the union. But Kawamata, as it turned out, had both crushed a union and at the same time performed something of a coup: He had taken over the whole company. His power base was the Miyake union. For union leaders they might be, but their loyalties were much more complicated. In America being a union leader meant one thing, a responsibility to the working men and to the union itself; the company, it was assumed, could take care of itself. But in Japan there was another meaning. Yes, they were union leaders, but they were white-collar men of middle management, and their ambitions were managerial. They were an extension of management.

In terms of loyalties, they were very much Kawamata's men. Some had been encouraged to go into the union by him, others had turned to him as the only man capable of standing up to Masuda. Now Kawamata began to place them in important jobs throughout the company. They formed a cadre loyal first and foremost to him. They could, for example, pressure Asahara and his men if, as seemed inevitable, there was a conflict between Kawamata and Asahara. The Miyake union virtually took over the personnel department of the company. Anybody who got ahead, not just at the lower levels but in middle management, now had to have the union's approval. Middle managers who belonged to neither union and had breathed a sigh of relief when the strike was over were now stunned by the power of the new union and the personalization of the company. Executives found themselves on the outside, judged on political rather than professional grounds, often by men who knew nothing about cars. They began to find out about significant personnel shifts not from their superiors but from the union; the union always seemed to know about these changes first. The implication was clear, that Miyake and Shioji had played a key role in effecting them. The ancillary message was equally clear: Play ball with Miyake and Shioji and Kawamata, and you will get ahead. Stay outside the reach of this powerful new network, and your future is uncertain at best. Anyone who challenged this new team was going to be squeezed and squeezed hard.

Twenty years later, when Japan was becoming an industrial giant, Leonard Woodcock, then the head of the UAW, went to the founding convention of the Japan Auto Workers. He went at the special invitation of Ichiro Shioji. By then the head of the Nissan union, Shioji was something of a protégé of the UAW leaders. The union had sponsored his tour at Harvard Business School, and he had often visited its offices at Solidarity House in Detroit. Indeed, at this convention Woodcock was struck by the degree to which Shioji's union imitated the UAW: It was the JAW, the Japan Auto Workers; the pin that its members wore was similar to the UAW's; the banner behind the rostrum seemed a very close imitation of the UAW banner. The difference, of course, and it was critical to the way the two industries had developed, was that Shioji's own union, like the unions at

Toyota and Mazda, was a company-wide union and the UAW was an industry-wide union.

Woodcock was an honored guest at the JAW convention. The translations of the speeches into English, though imperfect, began to fascinate him. Speaker after speaker was getting up and talking about something terrible which had happened in 1953 and pledging that it must never happen again.

"What are they all talking about?" he asked Shioji.

"A strike we had here in 1953," Shioji said, "a long and difficult one."

Woodcock had never heard of this event, one that had and was to continue to have the most profound impact on his own union and industry. "What happened?" he said.

"It was very bitter," Shioji replied. "It went on four months, and in the end the Communists were crushed, and our union came into being."

"Why did you never tell me this before?"

"You never asked me," said Shioji.

PART
FOUR

10.
TOUGH LITTLE RICH BOY

Henry Ford II was a man trying to perpetuate privilege in an age unsympathetic to it. That was not easily done, for it demanded that he comport himself as the modern egalitarian industrial leader while at the same time living the kingly private and corporate life in which he was always served. This split in his role produced contradictions in behavior. Single-minded in his desire to preserve the family industry, a man of intelligence and toughness and social grace, he sometimes seemed determined to conceal his abilities and play the boisterous sophomore. As such, he was an easy man to underestimate.

He had always been an industrial prince. With the possible exception of Nelson and David Rockefeller and Averell Harriman, no public figure was raised in such splendor. In 1920, when he was almost three years old, he held the torch that lit the blast furnace for the mighty Rouge, the greatest factory ever created. He grew up in a sixty-room house in Grosse Pointe, son of a refined mother and a father who was a passionate art lover. As a little boy he rode on his own child-sized railroad, authentic in all but dimensions, with a coal-burning locomotive. Each December he took friends by sleigh to a place on his grandfather's property known as Santa's Workshop; there the children would be given toys by Santa and could pet his specially imported live reindeer. Before he was ten he had a small British sports car and could drive it around the ninety-acre estate. He spent the summers at his parents' stone house in Seal Harbor, Maine, surrounded by security men, and in the winter he sailed out of Hobe Sound in Florida on his father's 125-foot yacht, the *Onika*, with its Chippendale living room. There were always servants, ready to do for him what was not done for very many of his fellow countrymen. Even as a child, his future was omnipresent. The boys who played with him, all of them from Grosse Pointe, their parents friends of his parents, were always aware that he was little Henry and that he would inherit a huge industrial firm. One of them, Philip Stearns, said years later that in that magical house, on the largest piece of property any of them had ever seen, filled with things to play with, they always did what Henry wanted to do.

The Grosse Pointe that he was raised in was an isolated place of provincial splendor. It is unlikely that in pre–World War II America there was another community quite so sheltered and quite so rich. There was neither economic nor social diversity. Catholics were viewed with suspicion and, on occasion, hatred. (When Henry as a young man married a Catholic and converted, it sent shivers throughout the community; his oldest friends regarded it as at least partly a declaration of independence from his past.) Jews too were unwelcome, and there was a great deal of dinner-party discussion as to whether Walter Chrysler was actually, despite what he claimed, Jewish. Neither World War II nor the coming of modern communications and transportation, which so changed and expanded people's lives, had yet occurred. It was a secure, comfortable, insular place, largely untouched by the modern world. If Grosse Pointers traveled to New York, they traveled by train, on The Detroiter, where they knew the porter and he knew them; if they traveled to Europe they traveled with each other. The assumption was that Grosse Pointe was the center of the universe; once, announcing the engagement of a Grosse Pointe girl to a young man from Cincinnati, the *Detroit Free Press* used the headline "Local Girl to Marry Eastern Man."

The social life was built around the country club and home entertaining. The entertaining was serious. The same families tended to be at the main dinner parties—the Fords, the Chapins, the Stearnses, the Bonbrights, the Andersons. At the parties the ladies quietly competed in showing off their new dresses and wore the maximum amount of jewels. The men wore black tie and drank in earnest, starting early and ending late. Mostly it was hard liquor, not wine. A favorite was called a gin toddy, which was gin on ice. (It was also called the throwaway martini, because you took the vermouth and threw it away.) A *New Yorker* cartoon of that era shows a hostess greeting an outsider while, behind her, everyone at the party seems to be falling-down drunk. "I bet you didn't know we were so sophisticated here in Grosse Pointe," she says. Many of the local fortunes had been made directly or indirectly through the auto industry, and the men talked business all the time. "The problem with all these people," said Frederick Stearns, the father of Philip, whose money came from a pharmaceutical company and who was the resident skeptic, "is that if you opened the tops of their heads, instead of brains you'd find carburetors."

When the men weren't talking business, they were cursing Roosevelt and labor. The women did not so much talk as, in the words of one visitor, palaver. They did not say how they really felt or what they really thought. They said how nice, how sad, how attractive, how unfortunate. No one disagreed because there was nothing to disagree about. It was a world dominated by servants. The parents, in most of the families, were distant, formal figures who showed up long enough to explain the rules and obligations. If there was any intimacy, any nurturing in the homes, it likely came from a servant who had taken pity on a lonely youngster and bestowed kindness along with service. It was a society governed by rituals. Coming-out parties were big events, for they marked both the coming of age of a young person and the status of the parents, and couples decorously competed to give the grandest party. (That tradition continued through the next generation. In 1959 when Henry Ford's daughter Charlotte had her coming-out party, it was recognized as the fanciest one of the year, not just in Detroit but in the country; some $150,000 was spent, a figure exceeded a year and a half later when her sister, Anne, had her coming-out party, at a cost estimated at $250,000.)

The people who lived in Grosse Pointe were not bored with it, for they knew of nothing else and wanted nothing else. They could not conceive of life being different or better. Billy Chapin—grandson of Roy, the first sales manager of the pioneer Old Motor Company, and son of Roy, president of American Motors—said that the trouble with the awful creamed spinach at the Grosse Pointe's club was that just about the moment you became influential enough to have it taken off the menu, you found that you liked it. In that world everyone was rich, and each child was privileged, but Edsel and Ellie Ford were by far the richest, and young Henry was the most privileged because everyone always knew he was going to run the Ford Motor Company.

That someone who came from this kind of background would grow up strong defied the assumptions of American life. By all rights he should have been ruined by the affluence and succumbed to self-indulgence. Instead he turned out to be a shrewd, industrious executive capable of the coldest scrutiny of those around him. He was an odd combination, a man both spoiled and hard. Within the company he was almost impossible to con. It was almost genetic with him; he had grown up assuming that most of the people he met on a given day wanted something from him, and he had therefore developed, as the most basic of his reflexes, the ability to judge motives.

Part of the reason for his toughness stemmed from the special circumstances of his childhood. For Henry Ford might have been raised in one of the two or three grandest homes in America, but a dark shadow hung over it nevertheless. He had been just a boy during the years in which his grandfather systematically crushed his father, destroying first Edsel's emotional and then his physical health, and he was shielded from as much of the tragedy as possible. But the residual impact was always there, a father ruined by a grandfather, a mother determined never to let this happen to her own children. For what had happened in his home was evidently evil; it was very close to filicide.

From his boyhood, when it was clear that his father's health was failing, Henry Ford became the heir apparent; he would assume the family obligations. His mother, whose elegance hid much of her fortitude, raised him that way. He would have to be strong enough to resist the forces that had overwhelmed her husband. Edsel Ford had been too gentle. That would not be true of her son. As her husband had been destroyed, so now would her son triumph. She was for many years the secret force and strength of the Ford Motor Company. Women did not hold jobs in industrial companies like Ford then (nor later—Henry Ford II completely shielded his two daughters from his business; even though he praised the business acumen of the elder, Charlotte, neither she nor Anne was ever put on the Ford board). Still, Eleanor Clay Ford held the power. She had played a crucial role in forcing the old man, reluctant though he was, to turn control over to his grandson, and she had pushed her son to make the right moves. Very much the elegant, genteel Grosse Pointe lady, she never appeared in the offices, yet she knew the company inside and out. No one was promoted to a high office without her approval.

One Saturday morning in 1961, Gene Bordinat, a talented young man in the design shop, had gone shopping at the downtown Hudson's with his wife. As they came out of the store a handsomely tailored chauffeur walked up, asked them if they were Mr. and Mrs. Bordinat, and, when they said yes, said, "Mrs. Edsel Ford would like to talk to you." He took them to a wonderful old touring car, in the backseat of which sat a patrician lady. For twenty minutes (later Bordinat said it seemed more like two hours) she deftly and gracefully passed the time with small talk. It was obviously an inspection, however deftly done. A few days later Bordinat was named vice-president of design at Ford. How, he always wondered, had Mrs. Ford known that he would be shopping at Hudson's that morning?

On the outside, few knew of her power; within the family, no one questioned it. Every Sunday after young Henry became head of the company, the Fords gathered for a family meeting at Eleanor Ford's house. There was a ritual to it. For two hours or so before dinner they did nothing but talk business in the most elemental way. When dinner was served, all business talk ceased for that day; they were a family, not a business. The symbolism of where the meetings were held was unmistakable. They were not at young Henry's house, they were at his mother's. He might be the head of the company, but she was still the head of the family. Her particular gift to her oldest son was to free him from all family responsibilities so that he could concentrate his energies on the company. She was zestful and positive, and she tried to pass those qualities on to others. In 1975, when she was seventy-nine years old, she spent a day with her oldest son because Lord Snowdon was taking family pictures. The session was being shot at her house, and as it was ending she turned to Henry and said that she wanted him to come to dinner that night. "I want to talk about these paintings," she said, gesturing at the treasures on the walls, "who gets what, because I'm getting old and I want to be ready."

"Oh, Mother," said the chairman of the Ford Motor Company, "why are you always talking about death?"

"I'm not, Henry," she said, "but I think death is going to be a wonderful experience, and I'm really looking forward to it, and I want to be ready."

Henry was, of course, the favored son. If there was always some distance between him and his two brothers, Benson and William Clay, it was because it had been made so clear so early that the company would be his; he was the oldest and they would have to be satisfied with ancillary roles. For a time this was hard on Bill Ford, who had a genuine love of cars and probably a more natural affinity for the product side than his older brother. He spent much of a lifetime in jobs that had titles but rarely had power, and on more than one occasion he saw his pet projects dismantled. Finally he bought the Detroit Lions professional football team to give himself an interest outside the Ford Motor Company.

If in later years Henry could go so suddenly from the workaholic at the office to the buffoonish, almost crude playboy, his closest friends thought they understood why. It was, they believed, his one way of escaping the responsibility that had been imposed upon him so early in life and having some fun. In the role of Henry Ford II, he was awesomely burdened and severely constrained. Only in the role of carouser could he let go, become another person. He could be the head of the Ford Motor Company during the day and a roisterer at night. He became somewhat famous for going off on ferocious late-night drinking bouts and, the next day, boasting to the poor men who had suffered through those long hours with him that he had never had a hangover in his life. Often when he was younger there were dives fully clothed into swimming pools. That became something of a rite, and there was a time when he was younger that a party was not deemed a success, be it at Southampton, Grosse Pointe, or Palm Beach, until Henry Ford II went into the swimming pool in his suit.

"What was wrong with the party last night?" Charlotte Ford once asked at breakfast.

"Why?" asked Anne Ford.

"Well," she said, "Daddy didn't end up in the pool."

During one particularly joyous party in the late forties, he found occasion to apply lipstick to the portrait of Newell Tilton, the president of the Southampton Beach Club, behavior which Mr. Tilton did not find amusing. "I made the fatal mistake," said Kay Meehan, wife of his friend Joe Meehan, who was dancing with him at the time, "of saying, 'Henry, don't.' If I had said, 'Oh, Henry, go ahead,' the entire incident might have been avoided."

The contrast between his exceptional diligence inside the office and his erratic behavior outside it diminished his reputation in some circles and puzzled many.

"Tell me about Henry Ford," the Israeli foreign minister Abba Eban once asked his friend Richard Clurman, the New York journalist.

"Well, he's like Jekyll and Hyde," Clurman answered.

"Yes," Eban said, "but I understand that the Jekyll is just as bad as the Hyde."

A succession of high executives at the Ford Motor Company, men who believed that they had been anointed by Ford and that he truly liked them, found to their surprise one day that they had gotten too close or taken too much for granted. Either they had presumed on what they thought was their relationship, or, worst of all, they had begun to bore him, and he, as arbitrarily as his grandfather, had decided he was no longer interested in them. Often they were soon gone. He had no doubts about whose company it really was. When the Glass House was being completed, there was some discussion about the fact that it was to be called World Headquarters. "Ford World Headquarters," Henry Ford told his aides, "is where I am on any given day." He did not like to be crowded and he did not like to be bored. He was particularly sensitive to anyone who pushed too hard or seemed to want to take too much. When his close friend Joseph Meehan died of a heart attack, Henry Ford was offended by the demanding way Meehan's lawyer seemed to be handling Kay in the days right after the death. Ford approved one document drafted by the lawyer, but as he did, he peered over his little half-glasses and said, his voice uncommonly frosty, "Do not make the mistake of thinking this means you will be the lawyer for the estate."

He was terribly spoiled, not only by power but by an extraordinary standard of living and by people whose sole purpose in life was to please him. ("You were smart, Henry," Walter Reuther once told him. "You chose the right grandfather.") He always indulged himself freely in whatever his taste demanded. David E. Davis, the Detroit auto writer, was once buying a new suit at Anderson & Sheppard, the Savile Row tailor, when he heard the tailor talk about Henry Ford's particular affection for smoking jackets.

"He likes velvet smoking jackets," the tailor said. Davis shrugged.

"Yes," continued the man, "I once did seventeen velvet smoking jackets for Mr. Ford. He's a very good customer."

"Can you imagine that?" Davis said to his wife as they left the shop. "Seventeen copies of the same jacket."

"I'm sure it's because he has so many residences in so many different parts of the world," Jeannie Davis explained to him, "and he likes to travel light."

By chance not long after that, when the Davises were on their way back to Detroit, Henry Ford was on the same plane. Davis waited at the baggage area in order to learn how much luggage Henry Ford traveled with. "There," he said triumphantly to his wife. "Traveling light—thirty-five suitcases."

Henry Ford's life had always been like that. On the day he was married, Edsel Ford had given him (in addition to a house in Grosse Pointe) twenty-five thousand shares of Ford Motor Company stock, then valued at $135 a share—a wedding present worth well over $3 million. When he was a boy, there had always been servants; as a grown man he had houses full of servants, and he raised his family through the proxy of his servants. At Christmas, when it was time to decorate his family tree, employees from the Ford Motor Company art department dutifully arrived and did the tree and the wreath, just as they also on occasion handled the decorations for the Ford parties. The children of Henry Ford did not answer the phone in their house; servants did. Nor did they make their own beds.

They were, however, under severe pressure to keep their rooms tidy, for Henry Ford II was meticulous. That was a legacy from his mother. Ellie Ford, concerned about the privileges enjoyed by her children, tried hard to inculcate in each a sense of responsibility for his or her personal behavior. Neatness was *very* important. When the young Fords went off to school each fall, they had to go to the cellar, get their trunks, and pack them properly, and when they returned home for the summer, they had to unpack them, put things away, and return the trunks to their place. In later years, if someone moved Henry's notebook or datebook, he immediately noticed it, and he did not like it. "Who has moved my things?" he would ask. He was accustomed to having his own way. He had, said one longtime aide unhappily, a brilliant eye for picking out what did not please him. His whim was always served. If it was not, the offender was likely to be dismissed. He once told Calvin Beauregard, the man in charge of the New York office and whose specialty was taking care of VIP requests, "Cal, if the answer to one of my requests is no, then I don't need you." In his mind, after the President he was the nation's leading VIP. Among the perks that he offered Lyndon and Lady Bird Johnson when Johnson was President was the use of the Ford company limo when Lady Bird came to New York (license plate FM-9), an amenity she readily accepted. Once when Henry Ford came to the city and attended a benefit at the Metropolitan Opera, he noticed the car ahead of him had the license plate GM-1. Out stepped Mrs. Johnson.

"How come she's not in this car?" he asked his chauffeur.

"Because you're using it, Mr. Ford," the chauffeur said.

"That's the right answer," he said.

If he was in a car, then it was black. It was never red. He hated red cars. It never had snow tires. He hated snow tires. Once at a board meeting in Philadelphia it began to snow heavily. "Are there snow tires on the car, or do I have to take the train back?" he asked an aide. The aide, who had made sure that the despised snow tires were not on the car, looked at him and said, "Your car is ready, Mr. Ford." Again, it was the right answer.

One of his favorite foods was hamburger, and it was typical of him that he constantly complained, when he ate hamburger on the road, that it was never as good as it was at his dining room in the Ford building, which was not a surprise for those who knew the Ford kitchen well; few res- tuarants, no matter how fine their kitchens, ground up filet mignon to make their hamburger. As he had come to expect the rights of the seigneur, so too did his children. The Ford limousines based in New York were for company use and for VIPs, but for a long time they were used by the children for daily errands—picking up the grandchildren, shuttling nan- nies back and forth, and having servants pick up packages at stores.

In the modern world of the self-made man, Henry Ford was easy to underestimate. The beginnings of his career were hardly impressive. At Yale he had been a somewhat unhappy, overweight young man, nicknamed Lard Ass. He had been expelled for having someone else write a paper for him. That he had departed Yale before graduation was first seen by his peers as tangible proof that he was not very smart; later, as evidence of his shrewdness and ability mounted, it was seen differently, particularly by serious students of upper-class behavior—it was a sign that the man- datory tests of ability that the American establishment inflicts upon most young men as part of their rites of passage did not apply to him. Yale soon confirmed that interpretation; the Yale Political Union invited him back to speak. He confirmed it himself by standing before the assembled Yalies on that day, holding up his speech, and saying somewhat proudly, "And I didn't write this one either."

When he first took over the company, he handled himself with skill. He had been duly modest in the beginning. "I'm all alone here," he told John Bugas, his first ally as he wrested power away from Harry Bennett. "It's supposed to be my company, but I'm the outsider. No one in the company wants to be seen with me." Anyone interested in how tough he was likely to be when the family interest was at issue had only to remember the time when he finally had to confront Harry Bennett and tell him he was finished at the company. Since Bennett was considered a dangerous figure—he always carried a gun—the question of who was going to face him down was a serious one. Bugas, the former FBI agent, asked if he could handle Bennett. But young Henry Ford turned him down. This was a family matter. Confronting Bennett was necessary, he pointed out, if the company was to be returned to family hands, from which it had slipped because of the senility of his grandfather. Therefore, it was his obligation. Besides, he sensed that historians would judge this act. "If I don't do it," he told Bugas, "people will always know that at a critical moment when it was my responsibility, I let someone do my dirty work for me."

To understand him it was important to understand that sense of duty. He had not just taken a job at Ford; it was as if he had taken an oath of office, had sworn his allegiance to strengthen and protect the Ford Motor Company from all outside forces and to perpetuate it as a family trust. He never lost sight of that mission. Ford was not just a company, it was a family company. He had not even wanted to come back to it during the war, when his father died; he wanted to serve overseas in the navy. He wanted to be like all the other young men of his generation, but, of course, he could never be that. He did not want to fight the battle of Detroit, a battle that had just helped kill his father; he wanted to live his own life and make his own mistakes. Not for the first time was he to find that his was, on anything important, a life without choice. But he had come back dutifully—it was what his mother and his grandmother wanted, and they were the family.

When learning the business, he was quite content to defer. He knew he needed help. In 1946 he knew he was lucky to get Ernest Breech and his team to come over from Bendix and GM to run the company. (The manner in which he sweetened the pot for Breech and his colleagues was quite ingenious. Ford was not yet a public company, so Ford stock was

not the answer, since no value had as yet been set on the stock; and taxes
on executive salaries were extremely high in those days. So Henry Ford
gave Breech and the others sizable amounts of shares in Dearborn Tractor,
a company owned by Ford. Breech got 20 percent of Dearborn's stock,
the others 10 percent. The company, until then a low-priority Ford satellite, suddenly began getting first-rate employees and much more attention in general. Ten years later, Breech's share was said to be worth $6
million.) He was modest with Breech and genuinely acquiescent for more
than a decade. It might be Henry Ford's company, but there was no doubt
in those first postwar years that Ernie Breech was in control.

Then, slowly, Henry Ford began to gain in confidence. Very subtly the
balance began to change in meetings where both men were present, Henry
Ford asserting himself more. Others noticed it before Breech did, the
quiet self-assertion of the founder's grandson. Henry knew it would never
really be his company as long as Breech was there. Soon he was looking
for a way to get rid of him. What had once been a valued participation
had become an intrusion into Henry Ford's domain, without Breech's
realizing it until, of course, it was too late. Finally Breech picked up on
it. "Henry doesn't need me anymore," he told friends. Breech had hoped
to retire in 1962 when he was sixty-five; instead he left in 1961. It was
another sign that the young heir was capable of being as callous as his
grandfather.

Soon, because his personnel policies were so arbitrary, because some
people would be favored and then just as quickly unfavored, the company
was, as it had been in his grandfather's day, faction-ridden. It made Ford
a more interesting and more exciting place to work than GM, for there
was far greater chance of quick advancement, and also far greater chance
of quick decapitation. It was a very political company. "You had to be
careful not to be hit by one of those giant steel balls coming down the
corridor at you at Ford," said Donald Frey, one of Ford's senior executives
in the sixties. "You never knew who aimed it, all you knew was you'd
better take cover fast." Of Henry Ford II, it was soon said that he had
not so much a hiring policy as a firing policy. The most trusted of old
friends could be forced out of it suited him. There was nothing sentimental,
he once told John Bugas, about running an industrial company, and he
later proved it to Bugas by ousting him. The young man who had ascended
to the Ford throne was surprisingly obdurate, veteran Ford executives
decided, more like his grandfather than his father. He trusted almost no
one and confided in almost no one. If he had deferred at first, in due
course he developed an imperial style. Those who were smart understood
how to read it, knew when not to crowd him. They learned that his self-

deprecating manner was just that, a manner. They learned that the true code on any critical issue—never spoken but as real as it could be—was *Don't cross me on this.*

Henry Ford II was an anomaly in the modern industrial era. He was of the blood. Even after the company went public, his control never wavered, and he liked to demonstrate this by the audacity of his personal behavior. In the modern era of management, that made him stand apart. For so many companies had been sold or gone public that a new, professional managerial class had emerged, composed of careful, serious men who ran these old companies as antiseptically as they could for five or six years, usually leaving little trace of themselves, going on eventually to other things, retirements that were described as well deserved but that they did not really want, or directorships of large philanthropic institutions or memberships on the boards of other companies. These modern men generally led upright, proscribed lives. Within the accepted boundaries of executive competition they might be savage combatants, but their personal lives were supposed to be above reproach and more often than not were. There were to be few displays—on the way up the ladder, at least—of weakness of the flesh. It was advisable—well into the 1960s, at least—to remain married to the first wife, if at all possible, and it was advisable that the wife be a good sport, that is, good with other wives, knowing her place at all times, which wives were above her and which below her, never confusing the two. If the corporate balance sheet was sufficiently above reproach, then on occasion personal behavior could be marginally below reproach and a second wife was permissible. The chief executive was beholden to the board, and the board was always careful.

At the Ford Motor Company, where blood still worked, the reverse was true. There was a board of directors, including outsider directors, but the board did not lightly interfere with actions Henry Ford wanted to take. If anything, it was beholden to him. The Ford finance staff would prepare brilliant briefings for the board, the best *son et lumière* shows a company could offer, but in the end his real attitude toward the board, oft expressed, was "Wine 'em, dine 'em, and screw 'em." When there was an important issue before the board, Henry Ford would smile and say, "Well, of course, I have only one vote on this, but my answer to it is no." That was his way of giving the board its marching orders; the vote of the board was, of course, no.

In any company save his own, Henry Ford's personal conduct—the instinct at certain moments in his life, when his marriages were not going well, to womanize; his drinking (he was often surprisingly sloppy about it for so public a figure) and ensuing vulgarity—might have worked against him. But his behavior was never a problem at the Ford Motor Company. He was perceived as a throwback to another era, when men were men and ran their own companies the way they wanted, did what they damn well pleased in their own hours, and said whatever crossed their minds. That freedom, in so gray a corporate world, humanized him and made him a popular figure. Other major corporate leaders were careful and used management-speak, a deliberately neutered language devoid of feeling, humanity, and viewpoint, a language that left as little record as possible. Beyond constraint, with no board looking over his shoulder, Ford took pleasure in saying what he felt. That became part of his style, and he gloried in it. Told at a meeting that one of his executives had put Michelin tires on a Mustang, he said, "I don't like frog tires." Told that he could use foreign steel more cheaply than domestic, he said simply, "I don't want any goddam foreign steel in my cars." Asked at a shareholders' meeting about a particular policy which had turned out badly, he did not say he had made a mistake but said, "I screwed up." Caught by a California state trooper drunk-driving with a lady most definitely not his wife, he said only, "Never explain, never complain." (In fact, he was not loath to complain; whenever a newspaper or a magazine printed something about him that he did not like, he and his people were capable of raising a great deal of fuss.)

Other men might have fallen, if not from their jobs then at least from grace, on that last one, but not Henry Ford II. A few days later he walked into a meeting of the Detroit Economic Club, a center for the Detroit establishment, and received a standing ovation. Nor was it just other executives who took pleasure in his style. His blunt, pseudo-candid style, Henry Ford as the common man, appealed to workers on the line as well. To them he was independent and free, a man who could tell the other big guys off and sometimes did. At the height of tensions between labor and management, he could walk down a Ford line and still be hailed, worker after worker rushing over to shake his hand. He said the things they would have liked to say, and even more important, lived the life they would have liked to lead.

The greatest mistake that anyone could make was to confuse the rowdy Henry Ford of the night before—the Henry Ford who in the very same sentence introduced himself to a young lady and suggested that they spend the night together—with the hard-eyed man at his desk the next morning. For the carousing buccaneer was in no small part a device, a way of disguising the fact that he had been born to his position, that he was the head of the Ford Motor Company by right of primogeniture. He had chosen a style that said, I'm one of the boys, I could have made it from the bottom, and I'm just as rough and tough as anyone on the line. In fact he was an aristrocrat born and an aristocrat raised. He was very much his mother's son, and his mother believed fervently in good manners and good behavior. When he summoned his manners, they were, indeed, very good. As a boy he was told to write thank-you notes for gifts, and as a grown man he still sent graceful handwritten notes to people thanking them for favors. As a boy he was told to keep his room neat, and as a man he could not stand personal messiness. For all his bluster and crude language he spoke excellent French, and he had an exceptional eye for art and perhaps an even better one for English country antiques. He might be good at trooping the line among the workers at a Ford plant in the Midwest, and he might deal well with his peers in the world of business (in truth he thought he had no peers; most companies were too small, and the ones that were big were run by colorless managers who did not own them), but his real pleasure was spending time first among the American gentry and later among the beautiful people of Europe.

The swashbuckler comportment, then, was more style than substance. It was true that in his personal life there was a considerable amount of audacity and bravado, that he loved to live high, and that he enjoyed breaking conventions. But at the same time his professional manner was very careful, and he became steadily more conservative. Under the mounting pressure upon the modern American industrialist (increased labor costs, increased governmental regulation, increased consumer sensitivity, increased competition), he was ever more cautious. Much of his energy went into not making mistakes. The longer he ran it, the more conservative the Ford Motor Company became.

11.
THE WHIZ KIDS

Charles Bates Thornton was a striking new kind of American success story, a man with a childhood worthy of Horatio Alger but also with the most modern vision for postwar American management that one could imagine. He was born in Haskell, Texas. His father had made fortunes and lost fortunes running a fire-fighting service for oil-well owners. He had abandoned his family when his son was an infant. His wife took over the raising of the family. She instilled in her son a strong sense of enterprise; he was to have odd jobs, she decreed, and to save money from them, not squander it. So he did, starting to save at the age of twelve and buying forty acres of land by the time he was fourteen. That set a pattern. He was running a service station by the time he was in Texas Tech. He then moved to Washington, so he could work at the Department of the Interior during the day and go to George Washington University at night. When he graduated he stayed at Interior. There, in the late thirties, he happened to do a report on low-cost federal housing. It was seen by Robert Lovett, then assistant secretary of war for air, who was eager to bring modern management techniques to the pathetically understaffed prewar Army Air Corps. Lovett, a prime architect of American preparedness, immediately understood that Thornton had a new and special talent—he knew how to draw information from seemingly aimless and unconnected statistics. He quickly signed up Thornton as an air corps lieutenant. At the start of World War II, Thornton, at Lovett's request, put together a team of brilliant young statisticians whose assignment was to bring order and direction to what was becoming in effect one of the world's largest corporations.

For his staff, Tex Thornton wanted only the best. Selections were made in the simplest way: The brightest graduates of the nation's business schools were sent to Officer Candidate School. Then the two top people in every OCS class were sent to Harvard Business School for a special two-month course in the use of statistics, and the two brightest people in each class at the business school were plucked out and sent to work for Thornton. Arjay Miller, who later headed the Ford Motor Company, thought it the fastest possible way to select the most talented people for a powerful new professional discipline. The premise behind it all was that this vast, new, mechanized war was as much about production and allocation of resources as it was about combat bravery, and the best brains should be applied to that challenge. Thornton's group of talented young management executives developed a system of statistical control to bring rationality to decisions about military production. By their control of numbers they could decide what was needed where and how best to get it there.

When the European war was ending, for example, Thornton's team studied whether or not it made sense to move the B-17 bombers from Germany to the Pacific. To the surprise of the military their studies showed that it was more cost-effective to leave the B-17s in Germany and build more B-29s for the Pacific. Moving the B-17s from Europe, they found, would be more expensive than anyone had imagined, and the planes lacked the flying range needed for the great distances in the Pacific theater of war. Most senior officers regarded this recommendation as sacrilege: These costly planes, which had proved so valuable, would now sit on airfields and go to waste. But on the estimates of these very junior, very confident young men, this and many other such critical decisions were made, decisions that often placed the young statisticians against experienced and venerated combat veterans.

The Whiz Kids formed an odd little group inside the Pentagon, and some of the regulars had a hard time with them. They were young, after all; none of them had ever heard a shot fired in anger, and yet their word seemed like law. Once one of the youngsters, Arjay Miller, walked into a general's office with his jacket off. The general, who was probably twenty years older than Miller, did not see his insignia and immediately snapped to attention. "It's all right, general," Miller said. "I'm only a second lieutenant."

Those years made all of them see that a powerful new professional discipline was being born—that there were great possibilities for the use of statistical control systems in peacetime production. Peacetime application might prove even more effective, for then they would not be hindered by the enormous bureaucracy of the U.S. military. To many young men the war had been filled with lessons in doubt; to this group it had been one great lesson in truths. It had taught them that a business enterprise could be made to operate rationally on an immense scale. As the war drew toward an end, they talked endlessly among themselves about their future. Encouraged by their success in the Pentagon, sensing as few in America did the possibilities in their skills, Tex Thornton and his team decided that when peace came they would sell themselves as a group. They would seek some needy company; it did not seem to matter too much which one, although the weaker the company the better the chance to exploit en masse their teamwork and expertise. Their connection was to each other and to their particular skill, not to any one industry.

They thought briefly of forming their own company to do the most modern kind of market research, along the lines of A. C. Nielsen. But that required some $3 million in start-up money, and none of them had any money. For a time they centered their interest on Alleghany, a seriously troubled holding company, and they almost went there. Indeed, Alleghany made them an offer and gave them a week to decide. On a whim, and because one of them knew an executive at Ford through family connections, they decided to try Ford as well. They were convinced that no company in America needed them more than Ford did. In many ways it was a wreck after fifteen years of the old man's madness. So they sent Henry Ford II a cable, which in retrospect some of them thought quite impudent. In effect it said: TERRIFIC YOUNG MANAGERIAL TEAM READY TO MODERNIZE AND SAVE YOUR COMPANY. They were young and talented and sure of themselves. Thornton, their grand old man, was all of thirty-two.

Henry Ford was immediately interested. The inheritor of the shell of a once-great industrial enterprise, he desperately needed not just talent but allies. He invited them to Detroit and had John Bugas, the former FBI man who was his only trusted aide, meet them and look them over. Later, at a meeting they had with both Bugas and Ford, Bugas turned to his boss and said, "Well, Mr. Ford, if you want to hire these people—" Ford cut him off. It was clear that he had already made up his mind to hire them.

"What do you think of them?" Ford asked Bugas when they were alone.

"They're all smart, almost too smart," Bugas replied. "They want about twelve thousand each, but I think we can get them for ten."

"Pay them the twelve thousand," Henry Ford said, and the Thornton team was hired. Secretly Henry Ford had hedged his bets. Unbeknownst to the young men, he was also bringing in a complete management team from General Motors under Ernest Breech. There were, in fact, people at GM who believed that Ford was getting a brighter executive group in the one headed by Breech than the one that was taking over GM.

The coming of the Whiz Kids, as they came to be known, was an important moment, for it reflected a major change about to take place in many American companies. These eager, able young men were not car men. They were not, like those who had gone before them, rooted in the business itself, lured to it by love of mechanical devices or by the excitement of making something. Nothing, indeed, could have been more alien to them. The Whiz Kids were the forerunner of the new class in American business. Their knowledge was not concrete, about a product, but abstract, about systems—systems that could, if used properly, govern any company. Their approach was largely theoretical, their language closer to that of the business school than the auto assembly line. Some of them, in fact, like Robert McNamara and J. Edward Lundy, had taught at universities before the war and had planned to return to them after the war.

Ordered to punch time clocks like hundreds of thousands of Ford employees before them, they rebelled. They made very clear to their superiors that they were eager to go to work, they were in pursuit of dazzling careers, they would labor twelve and fourteen hours a day, but they would not punch a time clock to justify their actions or certify their whereabouts. They were beyond that, for they were the new class. To them their not punching a time clock was a statement of purpose; to others, who knew the company better, it seemed more a statement of class.

Within the company they were feared and resented from the start. They went everywhere and pried into everything, asking endless questions. (Their earlier nickname was not the Whiz Kids but the Quiz Kids.) They perplexed old-timers with their combination of innocence and intelligence. A little more than a year after they had arrived, Jack Reith, one of the group, turned to an assistant and, obviously irritated by some decision, said, "In all my thirteen months I've been in this business I've never seen anything like this."

Tex Thornton, upset about the hiring of Breech, soon left the company to work for Hughes Aircraft. "He wanted his bite out of the apple too soon," Lewis Crusoe, one of his rivals from the Breech group, said later. As befitting a true son of Horatio Alger, Thornton left Hughes in 1953 and, after borrowing $1.5 million, founded Litton Industries, one of the nation's first conglomerates. A little more than a decade later it made $1 billion in sales. Tex Thornton was not a man to look back.

From the moment of Thornton's departure it was clear that Robert McNamara was the driving force of the group, the Whiz Kid most likely to succeed. It was not just ability, though his ability was immense; it was his relentless ambition. Even among the Whiz Kids he stood out as wanting success much more than the others. At first no one was exactly sure why he wanted it, for he seemed indifferent not just to cars but to money. But he wanted it, and his ambition was manifest.

No one in the Ford Motor Company had ever seen anything like Bob McNamara before. He was at once a man who very soon knew everything quantifiable about the business and who had absolutely no feel for it. Gradually it became clear what drove him, an almost missionary belief in the rightness of what he was doing. He was pioneering a new kind of economic and managerial philosophy that would make Ford a better company and, by setting that noble example, make America a better country and the world a better planet. But it subtly became apparent that this was not all that drove him. There was also power. Power would elevate not just his vision but himself. He sought truth, but in searching for truth he sought power as well.

In the world of Ford he quickly and deliberately marked himself as a man apart. Where others were extroverted back-slappers, he was cold and distant. He shunned small talk. Small talk wasted time and encouraged intimacies. Intimacies were unwanted; they involved emotion and thus made rational decisions harder. The people above him, Breech, Crusoe, Del Harder, the manufacturing man, were always *Mr.* Breech, *Mr.* Crusoe, and *Mr.* Harder. He was always eager to please them, always ready not just with an answer but with a *factual* answer, because he knew they'd like that. "You know that son of a bitch always has an answer," Lee Iacocca once told Don Frey, a Ford executive, "and it always sounds so good— but you know, I checked some of it out after a meeting, and some of it is really bullshit. Stuff he just made up. But he always sounds good." Overly respectful, almost obsequious with his superiors, he was often brusque, almost rude, with his subordinates unless they were his protégés—themselves scions of the business school, young men who shared his vision. Those who could articulate the issues as he would have them articulated rose in the company. Those who could not speak to him in his language felt his contempt. Those who crossed him instantly regretted it.

His style at work was different from his manner after hours; off duty he could be congenial and even outgoing. It was his way of saying that friendship and old-boy connections meant nothing; only facts were important, and their truth must be served. He seemed particularly distrustful of those who, in their presentations, cited their experience, their many years in the auto business, and who talked of the way things had always been done. Experience to him was not just expertise, it was more than likely to be bias as well. McNamara sought rationality in an irrational world, and if he had had his way he would have manufactured and sold only rational cars. If other men in the company took their pleasure from designing cars, or from making a better, more sophisticated part, or from turning a paper design into a metal reality, he took his pleasure in his numbers. Numbers were not just a belief but more like a theology to him. Cars themselves were almost secondary. During his ascent to power, when he was general manager of the Ford Division—the section that made the cars called Fords, not Lincolns or Mercurys—he had come in one morning and given Don Frey, who was then one of his top product men, a piece of paper. It was a church leaflet with penciling on the back; McNamara, Frey gathered, had been daydreaming in church. The penciling described a car. But it was not a sketch of what the car should look like, or a statement about how it should handle, or a notion about what group of customers it should appeal to. It was a series of statistics—what the car should weigh and cost.

"Bob," Frey finally said, "you've got everything down except what kind of car you want."

"What do you mean?" McNamara asked.

"Well, do you want a soft car, a hot, sexy car, a comfortable car, a car for the young, or a car for the middle class? Whose car is it, what does it feel like?"

"That's very interesting," McNamara said. "Write down what you think is right."

Deviations from the truth of numbers bothered him. Numbers should be true. In 1959, when Ford was in the final stages of producing a car called the Falcon, a man named Jack Hooven had a terrible time with McNamara. Hooven was in charge of testing the prototypes on the tracks, and the numbers he was giving McNamara for gasoline mileage varied from test to test. This enraged McNamara. They had designed the Falcon to give a certain mileage, and the mileage should be exactly that figure, every time. Hooven tried to explain to McNamara that there were always variations, in the wind conditions, among the drivers, and among the cars themselves. But McNamara was insistent; they had graphs and charts, and the numbers should come out right. Logic and math demanded it. Hooven tried to reply that cars were not entirely logic and math, cars were cars, but McNamara brushed him aside, and Hooven returned to his shop thoroughly beaten. He could not really fight back, because he had no weapon, no equal truth with which to counter this onslaught. What saved him was a bright young man working for him named Jerry Greenwald. Greenwald had a background in finance, and he knew what was happening. He suggested to Hooven, "Why don't you do the testing, and then, when it's done, I'll go in a corner and smooth over the numbers a little? That should bring it near what he wants." Greenwald smoothed over the numbers, and Hooven brought them to McNamara, who beamed. The Falcon was performing as he would have it perform—true to him, true to his numbers.

The coming of McNamara to the Ford Motor Company, his protégé

Lee Iacocca once said, was one of the best things that ever happened to the company, and his leaving it, Iacocca added, was also one of the best things that ever happened. McNamara seemed to embody the strengths and weaknesses of the new class. He was clearly the ablest of his group and the most ambitious as well, and certainly the most politicized, the first to turn his power with numbers into power within the company. He brought discipline to the accounting system—if old Henry's intentional chaos could be called a system—and throughout Ford he imposed order on the most disorderly processes imaginable. He and his colleagues, in short, harnessed the worst-run large company in America. Before the Whiz Kids arrived, waste and petty profiteering were a way of life at Ford. McNamara did more than cleanse the company, he purified it, although whether or not purification is good for an automobile company became a question that haunted it some twenty years later.

No company in the country needed discipline as the Ford Motor Company did, or benefited from it more. Under McNamara, for the first time in more than twenty-five years, the company always knew where it was, how much it was spending and how much it was making, and it could project both costs and earnings. Soon it could readily tell where its faults were. In the past the men at Ford who used numbers were the accountants, and a few of them might have been powerful, but accounting had been an essentially passive trade. McNamara was different. He was the forerunner of a revolution. He was a manager who was also a genius with numbers. He could see their meaning, indeed their truth, long before others around him; he could see the relationships between numbers where others saw nothing. At his best he was dazzling, and the rigors of meeting his standards forced a generation of his subordinates to be far more exacting in their own use of numbers, to become experts who could scan a sheet and pick out the one number that was wrong. For those who could understand him and how his mind worked and who could phrase themselves in words he found acceptable, working for McNamara was exciting. For others as knowledgeable about cars or more so but clumsier in their presentations, dealing with him was nothing less than a nightmare.

Inevitably he was too strong and too forceful to use figures in a passive way; he used them aggressively. He soon went beyond the limits of his knowledge, his critics thought, and intruded where numbers and figures were no longer applicable. For beyond the fact that he did not know about cars and did not pretend to know about cars, there was a suspicion among those who worked with him every day that McNamara regarded the auto business as a little unsavory—all those dealers skinning the customers, the company pressuring the dealers to sell as many options as they could.

Yet this disdain, they felt, and his immunity to the pleasures that motivated other men in the industry, the love of turning steel into marvelous machines, made McNamara a more formidable figure in the relentless drive for profit. Because he prefered smaller and more utilitarian cars than those his company was making, he was under an even greater self-imposed pressure to prove that he could turn an ever greater profit.

The Whiz Kids did not make the instant climb to total executive power that they had envisioned. The coming of the Breech team delayed their ascendancy some six or seven years. Still, their arrival soon transformed the internal norms of the company. The older car men who had looked down on them found out to their discomfort that if the Whiz Kids did not know cars, they most certainly knew a lot of answers. More unsettling to the old-timers, it became clear they were not just a financial force but a political force as well, and a dominating one. What the car men were offering was risk and the uncertainty that went with risk; what the financial people were offering was certitude. The Whiz Kids, it promptly turned out, despite their academic backgrounds and their high-mindedness, were extremely skilled in-house manipulators, and none more so than McNamara. At first it was hard to imagine McNamara as an adept politician at Ford; he seemed so cold, so devoid of charm. For Detroit's charm was boisterous, it featured a certain self-conscious locker-room masculinity, and McNamara was almost austere. Detroit's role models went out on the golf course and shot a good game and joked about their handicaps, and they hunted birds, and they fished at distant camps where they went unattended by women. McNamara's contempt for those rituals was complete. He did not play golf, he did not tell Sammy Davis, Jr., jokes in the locker room, and he went mountain climbing on his vacations. He did not want to be buddies with the men around him. In fact, he did not want to ease the tension of a confrontation. The more tension, the more rigid the relationship, the better it seemed to serve him. His loyalty was not to cronies but to efficiency. Once when he was lecturing some of the men around him about the need for precision and exactitude, Charley Beacham, an old-time marketing man who was the polar opposite of McNamara in temperament, turned and said, "It's too bad, isn't it, Bob, that the place has to be run with people—they have so many flaws."

MacNamara was a symbol of the rootless, educated American of the postwar era. He worked in Detroit and did very well there, but he was not a man of Detroit: He had been born on the West Coast and gone to school there and on the East Coast, and now he was working in the Midwest. He chose to live in Ann Arbor, to enjoy the state university's intellectual climate and escape a social life where people talked nothing but shop. He and his men were a new breed, the forerunners of the Yuppies, young upwardly mobile professionals. They had far greater freedoms and possibilities than their parents, and thus they were far less tied, in the traditional sense, to locale and to job. Many of those who followed the Whiz Kids to Ford went not so much to make a career there as to use it as a springboard to another company. McNamara was aware of this and, in an interview in January 1960 with the staff of the historian Allan Nevins, who was writing an authorized history of Ford, bemoaned the lack of loyalty among these talented newcomers, whom he considered far more able than the old-timers (for whom he otherwise generally felt contempt but who, he noted, seemed to have a greater feel for the company). He spoke prophetically. Within the calendar year he would be made president of the Ford Motor Company, and within a few weeks of that most cherished appointment he would leave Ford to take the job of Secretary of Defense.

For he embodied much of the new era's strengths as well as its weaknesses. He was far better educated than men he replaced, higher of purpose, more aware of a larger social responsibility. But he was also a driving new executive who had served no apprenticeship, and as such he represented knowledge without experience. His ultimate goals were different from those of the men around him, and different from those of the industry; in that sense he was always a partially compromised man. When Henry Ford looked at him, it was said by one man who knew them both, he saw Volkswagen.

At Ford it was clear very early on that McNamara was not just a brilliant man but a formidable one as well. His special ability was using numbers to tilt a decision in the direction he wanted, which was almost surely the direction his superior wanted. McNamara was devastating in intramural arguments, so sure of his own facts that he seemed without bias, the ultimate rational man wanting only the rational decision. The arguments were often with the product men, who usually wanted to spend money that McNamara wanted to save. Anytime he and his disciples wanted to, they could make a product man feel inadequate, make him feel he had failed. With this gift, McNamara was precisely what young Henry Ford needed in those days; his command of numbers made him strongest where Ford, who had not finished college, was weakest. When Ford watched McNamara hold forth at a meeting, coldly analytical, he was seeing not only the first incarnation of the modern professional manager, but his very own business-school dean performing. In those years McNamara always seemed to be saying that yes, there were not merely answers to every question, but *right* answers to every question. This was not just a business but a science, he implied.

During an attempt to build a new transmission for the 1958 cars it was discovered that the cost was $5 more than anyone had expected. That was a lot of money, and McNamara, annoyed, let the engineers in the room know that they had failed him. He assigned Sev Vass, one of his deputies, to find out what had gone wrong. Vass made his reconnaissance and at the next meeting announced that the increase in the cost had not, after all, been caused by a more expensive design, but rather by the finance people's reallocation of overhead; more of it had fallen on the new transmission than had originally been calculated. It was a change not in production but in bookkeeping. "Well, Bob," said Fred Hooven, one of the company's most talented engineers, "I'm glad to see that accounting is no more an exact science than you accuse engineering of being." McNamara, the precision of his order challenged, flashed red with anger, but let it pass.

Such moments notwithstanding, in most conflicts between the product people and their counterparts in finance, the advantage lay with the finance men. For the product men were arguing taste and instinct, and the finance people were arguing certitudes. It was an unfair match. McNamara not only had the numbers and thus the truth but was saving money as well, and the money he was saving was Henry Ford's. To a young man unsure of himself, taking over the family firm that was also a great industrial company, wary of the excesses of the past and edgy about the future, there was comfort in the clinical new skills of these men. They were his support system, his guarantee that no one would slip something by him.

Out of that need grew the immense power of the finance people. A powerful, confident, modern bureaucracy was being installed at the Ford Motor Company, sure of its skills, sure of its goals. It knew how to take care of itself, to help its own, and above all to replenish itself. For there was no easy way to replenish real car men, no graduate school readily turning out designers who were both creative and professional or manufacturing men who could run a happy, efficient factory. People of instinct and creativity, really talented ones, came along only rarely. The great business schools of America could not produce genius or intuition, but they could and did turn out every year a large number of able, ambitious young men and women who were good at management, who knew numbers and systems, and who knew first and foremost how to minimize costs and maximize profits.

Inevitably the company's hiring policies in the postwar years reflected this. Authentic car men were hard to identify young and took a long time to prove themselves. By contrast, smart financial people were easy to hire; it was relatively simple to tell how good they were from their records and recommendations. Theirs, after all, was a *provable* discipline. The Ford Motor Company was rich, and in those days it could offer earlier success and larger salaries than other companies. It also placed a high priority on recruiting; in the fifties it was getting the cream of the nation's business-school graduates.

In the words of one critic, the financial people were cloning themselves. They were brilliant networkers. They were connected through professors they had had at Harvard or Wharton; having been sent on to Ford by a particular professor, they naturally fell in with the professor's other protégés at Ford. As they themselves became senior, they too became mentors. They took good care of their younger men, placing them in critical slots throughout the company, a practice that inevitably helped both protégé and sponsor. The sponsor got credit for having bright young assistants, and the assistants, in the new dynamic of the company, were sucked upward by the success of their sponsors. Starting in the late forties with the Whiz Kids, the financial people built up the single most powerful faction of the Ford Motor Company. In fact, it was so strong, so finely tuned to its own values and to its own leadership at every level, that it was not really a faction but a cadre. As that cadre sought and accumulated power and redefined the company by its norms, winning battle after battle, it inevitably transformed both the company and its purpose.

Its first great victory was over the manufacturing people. In the past, manufacturing had dominated the company, for manufacturing was the great love of the old man, the thing he cared about the most. In the plants reposed the culture of Ford Motor Company, and it was a culture in which uneducated men held power by dint of physical force. After the war, Ford had to change. Henry Ford and Ernie Breech wanted no brutality in their workplace, and there was a union now to protect the workers. The governance of the company changed. It was natural, then, that the manufacturing men became the first targets of the finance men. The finance people saw the factories as the worst of the legacy of the old man—crude but also wasteful and inefficient. Faced by this challenge from the new political clique in the head office, the manufacturing men, predictably, fought back in a stubborn and primitive way. They intended to do things as they always had. They knew cars, and they knew production, and their plants were their fiefdoms. No one was going to tell them what to do, certainly no shiny-ass Harvard bookkeepers, as the newcomers were called at first. ("Bean-counters," or just "beanies," came later.)

There was an old-timer named Bill Singleton who ran the Chester,

Pennsylvania, plant, and his hatred of the new business-school recruits was fairly typical. At bonus time he would go through the list of his people, and he would say, "This guy is a real manufacturing guy—give him a real bonus. . . . This is a shiny-ass bookkeeper—cut his bonus. . . . This is a goddam crew-cut clerk—cut his bonus. . . . Here's a car guy—give him a good one." The plant men fought to keep these bright young men off their staffs, which turned out to be easy enough to do; the reputation of the plants was so appalling that few of the new finance men wanted any part of them. The plants were not just backwaters but likely to be hostile backwaters. When Dearborn nevertheless sent one of the young men to a plant, the plant men made him feel as alien and misplaced as they could.

Between the factory men and the Whiz Kids lay a chasm of class. The factory men typically were blue-collar men who had risen by dint of energy, zeal, and shrewdness. They were elemental men, physical in any confrontation, often heavy drinkers after hours. They knew what they knew but seldom could articulate it except in the crudest way, with the aid of anger and obscenity. Few of them had finished high school. The Whiz Kids had been to college, had received graduate degrees, and might even have taught at great universities. They were the vanguard of the new meritocratic American middle class that, in America's postwar affluence, was ascending to become the upper middle class. Their world could not have been more different from that of the manufacturing men. In 1956 a top manufacturing man named Ward Folsom went to New York for a meeting along with McNamara and Jim Wright, a Whiz Kid who was somewhat of a McNamara protégé. McNamara and Wright and their wives had gone out to dinner and then to see *Long Day's Journey into Night*. They had not asked Folsom to accompany them either to dinner or to the theater. When he returned to Detroit, Folsom was bitter. "Those sons of bitches—I never wanted to see their goddam play, and I didn't want to have dinner with them, but the least they could have done was ask me. That's all, just ask me."

The idea that in order to defend their terrain they would have to adapt and blend some of these bright young men into the service of manufacturing came to the factory men far too late. In the brief time during which they might have made some accommodation, they were too arrogant to try; by the time they realized what had happened, it was too late. Power had been taken away from them and centralized in Detroit. Their response was resentment. If they could, they tried to keep the finance men out of their plants; they were not above making someone like McNamara, so obviously a rising power, cool his heels for several hours when he came to visit.

If there was resentment on one side, there was snobbery on the other. The finance people did indeed look down on the manufacturing men. They were contemptuous of the old order of which these men had been part, and they believed in their hearts that many of them had gotten rich by exploiting the company, a practice they intended to halt. They knew which way the company was going, they could see their own superiors ascending, and they did not think the manufacturing people representative of the new Ford Motor Company of which they themselves intended to be an important part.

It was evident by the early fifties that the finance people were seizing power, and that the decisions would be made in Detroit more and more, and made to finance's specification, not the specifications of the plants. Enraged by an edict from Detroit which limited to $5000 the amount a plant manager could spend without authorization, Emil "Duke" Duquette, who ran the Somerville, Massachusetts, plant, decided to find a way around them. The Massachusetts winter was hard, and Duquette had no paved storage space. That meant that a lot of his material was covered with ice in the winter and mud in the spring. Frustrated by Detroit's deaf ear to this problem, he approved $250,000 worth of $5000 vouchers to pave the yard. The finance people back in Detroit were not amused. Duquette was soon gone from the company. He was not alone. Systematically the old-timers were taken out, their fiefdoms annexed. Only a few were smart enough to adjust.

In 1952 a young finance officer named Don Lennox walked into the Chester, Pennsylvania, assembly plant and immediately found himself caught in a war between the home office and the men around him in the plant. Lennox had joined Ford after college and business school, and he was proud to be one of the bright young men on the financial staff. Every-one in Detroit had told him when he first arrived in Detroit how lucky he was, that he was a part of the right team at the right time. Then he had been called in by Ted Rickard, who was in the controller's office and was one of the key deputies to Ed Lundy, an original Whiz Kid himself and a rising power in finance. Rickard offered him a job in the Omaha parts depot. That had not been the kind of assignment a bright young man with a brilliant future like Lennox had in mind. The doubt must have showed in his face, because Rickard immediately said that he would give Lennox a substantial raise and, even more important, guaranteed a major bonus, one far larger than anything Lennox had dared consider. "Can you really *guarantee* it?" Lennox asked. Rickard nodded and picked up the phone and called Ed Lundy. "Ed, I've got Lennox here," he said, "and I told him I wanted him to go to the Omaha depot. I've told him we would guarantee his bonus." He then named both the salary and the bonus. "Thanks a lot, Ed," Rickard said and hung up. He turned to Lennox. "It's all taken care of," he said. It was the first example Lennox saw of the financial side at work. They really have it down, he thought admiringly. Thus initiated, he was delighted to go to Omaha as part of this elite group which took such good care of its people and had such an impressive capacity to deliver instantly.

Lennox did well there, and in 1955 he was assigned to be the controller at the Chester plant, one of the oldest of the company's assembly factories. Lennox had already been made aware that the bright young men of finance were not welcome in the factories. One of his first assignments after joining Ford had taken him to the Buffalo assembly plant for an early-morning appointment with Sam Simmons, who ran the plant. About fifteen minutes after Lennox arrived, Simmons came in, walked by him, and then shouted out from the inner office to his secretary as loudly as he could, "Who's that stupid-looking son of a bitch sitting out there?" Welcome to Buffalo, Don, Lennox had thought. So when he arrived in Chester he was prepared for the likelihood that George Vincent, the plant manager, would be equally happy to see him. In that expectation Vincent and the men around him did not disappoint Lennox. "The college boy" was what the top men called him, and not in a flattering way. For as controller, he represented the central finance office, and he was outside Vincent's authority. A plant manager could control everything in his territory except the controller; he could fire anyone on the premises except the people in the controller's office. The controller's loyalty was to Detroit and to the now dangerous financial staff, so in the mind of the plant manager, the controller was nothing less than a spy, the one man who might see through all the little tricks that a plant manager used to protect himself from Detroit's mounting surveillance and pressures.

Vincent was the quintessential old-timer. He had just replaced Big Bill Singleton. That in itself, Lennox soon found out, was an improvement, for Singleton had ruled by fear. A big, rough man, he was said to have risen in the company simply by punching out anyone who disagreed with him. His legend still hung over the factory. One of the things Lennox found as soon as he started working as the controller at Chester was that the ratio between indirect labor and direct labor in the export section for the KD, or knocked-down, cars seemed out of line. Knocked-down cars were those manufactured at Chester and then exported and assembled in another country. According to the ledgers, virtually all the costs went into direct labor—that is, the work for the KD cars that took place directly on the line—and almost nothing into indirect, which was the labor that went into the support system. That puzzled Lennox, and he went and found John McKenna, who was in charge of the export section. "I know, I know," said McKenna. "It's the weirdest labor clasification I've ever seen." McKenna explained that Singleton had once gotten a letter from the home office saying there was too much labor in the indirect section, and so the next day Singleton stormed over to McKenna and said, "Starting tomorrow, everything in all the indirect labor groups now gets listed as direct labor." McKenna started to protest. "McKenna, shut the hell up," Singleton said. "Tomorrow you don't even known how to spell indirect labor."

By contrast with Singleton, George Vincent was not an intimidating man physically. He did, however, share the same outlook. He had an eighth-grade education and was openly suspicious of anyone who had more. He came from an era in which only the fittest survived. He had started as an hourly worker and had become a foreman when his own foreman had gone on vacation for two weeks. Their mutual boss had turned to Vincent and told him that he had been trying to reduce the number of men in his section by two for the last two months but that the present foreman had fought him, saying it could not be done. "If you can do it," the boss told Vincent, "the job is yours. Permanently." Vincent got rid of the two men and thus became a foreman. Like all manufacturing men from the old days, he always wore a hat indoors. It was a sign of his trade and his status. When Lennox arrived at the plant his first day, Vincent interviewed him, but it was not a real interview, since both men knew that Vincent was powerless in this matter. He could not stop Lennox from coming to work. He could only isolate him within the plant, which he promptly proceeded to do. Vincent let Lennox know from the start that he wanted no part of him. Lennox realized that he was on trial, caught between loyalty to Detroit and loyalty to Vincent. He would be judged at both ends and possibly fail at both ends. The factory was filled with all kinds of secrets that Detroit was not to know. Vincent and the others were watching to see if Lennox could find them out and, if he did, whether he would betray them to Detroit. They were also watching to see if he talked down to them.

Shortly after he arrived, the company started using some thin trim on car panels. The trim was made of anodized aluminum. At a meeting Vincent talked about them and called them "oxidized aluminum panels." Later, when they were by themselves, Lennox took Vincent aside and said, "Mr. Vincent, that is anodized aluminum."

"Lennox," said Vincent, "in my goddam plant when I say it's oxidized aluminum, it's oxidized aluminum, and it stays that way."

Lennox worked for Detroit, but to all the men around him, Detroit was the enemy. This was not the normal disdain of one office in a company for another, not the usual feeling that the home office lacked sympathy for the problems in the field. This was lethal. The men of this plant had disliked Detroit in the past; now in the new era they hated it. The new Detroit for them was a place that made arbitrary rules, raised the production quotas, and then denied them the means to meet those requirements. Detroit, under McNamara, had no understanding at all of what the Chester plant did, they felt; in fact, it seemed to disrespect what they did. Detroit was pushing numbers at Chester, and there was no way that Chester could respond. The managers lived and died by the weekly rating wires, which graded the different factories on basic costs. These were like weekly report cards. Enough bad ones, and a manager was out. Lennox, aware that Vincent was in trouble on his reports, made some suggestions on how to improve them, but Vincent turned him down coldly. Lennox was the intruder, and the suggestions of an intruder were not welcome.

Eventually he won acceptance, but it came only after he changed sides. For midway through his tour at Chester, Lennox did something unusual for a financial man of that generation. He decided to switch from finance to manufacturing. It was something he had thought about for a long time, and he was prompted by several factors. For one thing he simply liked manufacturing, enjoyed *making* something more than dealing with numbers and paper. It was something that he had only gradually found out about himself. His father had been a sheet-metal worker who had his own business until he went broke in 1931 during the Depression and then worked as an hourly man for Westinghouse. Don Lennox had grown up working for his father on weekends, doing sheet-metal work on commercial kitchens, and he had liked the work more than he then realized. Though he went on to business school after college, he later came to feel that at heart he was a frustrated engineer. The work of the controller had not been very much fun, and he had felt drawn to the factory floor. There was an excitement about it, particularly at the time of the changeover from one year's models to next year's. For Lennox, manufacturing seemed more comfortable, more positive than finance. The promise of a hot career in finance did not seize him as it did so many of his contemporaries. If anything, their mass desire negatively affected his choice. Looking around, he could tell that finance was loaded up with talent, and he foresaw that the competition for the best jobs would be savage. Simply because manufacturing was such a backwater and because none of the better people wanted to move into it, he stood a very good chance of a major career at Ford if he switched over.

Slowly, in his years at Chester, Lennox came to admire George Vincent.

That was not always easy. Vincent's suspicion had put Lennox off, and Vincent's skills were not at first visible to an ambitious young college graduate. But Lennox developed a regard for Vincent's ability to survive the harsh earlier years at Ford, and then an even greater regard for the suppleness with which he handled all the demands of a potentially brutalizing institution. Vincent, he decided somewhat to his surprise, was very *good* at his job. He made wise choices in promoting people. He had a delicate sense of how much the people around him could take and when the burden would become too great. He knew when to praise people and when to come down hard on them. He also had a genuine pride in what he did; he hated careless work.

Even as Lennox was beginning to think of changing over, he noticed a turn in Vincent's attitude toward him. Vincent seemed to be accepting the fact that despite Lennox's connection to Detroit, he was able to serve two masters. Vincent now understood that he needed this kind of person to protect him from Detroit. Lennox, Vincent noted, had not squealed on him, and in fact on several occasions had saved him from embarrassment. Lennox talked about his plan with Vincent, and Vincent encouraged him. He also tried, in vain, to get him to wear a hat indoors. "You won't really be accepted by the other guys until you do," he said. So it was that in 1957 Don Lennox, business-school graduate and finance man, switched over to manufacturing.

Still, complete acceptance came grudgingly. A few months later, when it was time for the model changeover, Lennox tried drawing up plans for it. In the past, he thought, the changeover had been spirited but wasteful, an example of semiorganized chaos. This time, he decided, it would be *planned*, each step done with the utmost rationality. He promptly scheduled a series of meetings. But an old German named George Schaup looked at the schedule and shook his head. "Meetings, always meetings," he said. "That's the trouble with you college boys, you love to have meetings. You have your meetings, and at the meetings you schedule more meetings, and you spend all your time writing down what you're going to do. We're different. We go out and do it, and we do it right, and we do it quickly, and then we have our meetings to talk about how we did it."

When Lennox switched, he was admitted for the first time into the inner world of the plant managers. It was filled with secrets, and the name of the game was Screw Detroit. He was impressed by the natural canniness of it all, and he knew that what he was seeing in Chester was taking place at Ford factories around the country. The managers felt themselves buffeted by the ever more frequent directives from Detroit. That was bad enough. But unlike their predecessors they had to achieve Detroit's requirements in a new unionized age, and it was harder now to turn the screws on workers. So they had learned to cheat Detroit as best they could in order to preserve the integrity of their own operation. They did this with admirable cunning. Were the windows of the cars supposed to be subjected to a water test that simulated a terrible storm? Vincent's men were skilled at producing wonderfully realistic deluges while jiggling the water gauges so that they read maximum pressure, while the water was actually at a much lower pressure. Were there too many parts left over at the end of a model's life? Detroit hated that, so each year the plant people faithfully reported to the home office that they had only sixty-one of one part remaining and only forty-eight of another. Detroit, they were telling the home office, had been every bit as efficient as it hoped. Meanwhile they dumped thousands and thousands of useless parts into the nearby Delaware River. Detroit loved how little waste there was, how well the numbers had matched out, and the people in Chester joked that you didn't have to swim the Delaware, you could walk across on the rusted parts of 1950 and 1951 Fords. It was the most critical part of the code: Tell Detroit what it wanted to hear and then do the best you could with the limited time and resources available to you.

Did Detroit want extra production? Vincent could not speed up the line. There were strict union rules against that. But he could manipulate the line. For example, on the conveyor there was a wooden stick which separated each auto frame from the next. The stick was supposed to be forty-eight inches long. Vincent simply had his people surreptitiously take all the wooden sticks and trim three inches off them, not enough to be noticed. Shorter sticks between the frames meant more frames on the conveyor. The gambit allowed roughly a 6 percent increase in production, and 6 percent over a day and then a week and then a month was an enormous difference. The union people knew that something was wrong, but they could not pick up on it. They kept timing the line, and the line was moving at the agreed speed. All this extra production was kept secret, not only from the union but from Detroit. It was for a rainy day when Detroit came down with some impossible production quota that they could not otherwise handle. The name for this covert reserve was "the kitty," and only a handful of people in the plant knew about it. Job One was the first job on a car, but Vincent generally liked to run his own excess production first; thus Job One, instead of being the first car down the line, might well be the fifty-first. Fifty cars went into the kitty before the production actually started. The controller knew nothing about it, but the plant manager and his top people knew. The day at Chester that someone knew what the real Job One was, instead of the paper Job One, was the day he had been let into the inner circle by Vincent. A month after he switched, Lennox was let in on it.

The more Lennox studied the operation, the more ingenious it all seemed. Detroit had a system for demanding quality, and it periodically sent out inspectors to check the plants. But Chester could always rig the system, delivering to the visiting auditors precisely the cars it intended, cars of higher than normal quality. Vincent was like a great card shark dealing off the bottom of the deck. Every time Detroit managed to figure out how to stop the newest abuse, Chester would come out with an even more sophisticated one. It was, thought Lennox, like watching a battle between the IRS and a master tax lawyer; every time the IRS came up with some new tax, the tax lawyer found a new loophole. Chester's rationale for this cheating was simple. In the minds of the plant men, Detroit and the financial people were the real cheats. They spoke of McNamara bitterly as a man who did not want to know the truth. McNamara and his people in Detroit were the ones who kept making liberal agreements with the unions and at the same time setting higher and higher levels of production while always demanding increased quality. They talked about quality, but they did not give the plant managers the means for quality; what they really wanted was production. So the plant managers were giving them what they wanted, numbers, while paying lip service to quality. Years later in Vietnam some American officers, knowing McNamara's love of numbers, cleverly juggled the numbers and played games with body counts in order to make a stalemated war look more successful than it was. They did this not because they were dishonest, but because they thought if Washington really wanted the truth it would have sought the truth in an honest way. In doing so they were the spiritual descendants of the Ford factory managers of the fifties.

When Don Lennox decided to go over to manufacturing, he knew that in career terms it was risky in several respects. In manufacturing there was no clique, no old-boy network, as there was in finance. Each plant was autonomous, and the men who ran them had scant opportunity to push or shield protégés; by the fifties it was all they could do to hunker down and protect themselves. Lennox was choosing a career without sponsorship in a company in which everyone else he knew was in some way sponsored. Those who went to finance and made it would be watched over and would, of course, in due time watch over others. By contrast almost everyone else in the company was vulnerable. In manufacturing, he knew, it would be easy to make enemies, and the enemies might remain permanent as the friendships might not. He talked about his decision to Ted Rickard, who by then was controller of the Ford division, and to Ed Lundy, who, next to McNamara, was the most important man in the financial cadre. "I wish you were being smarter," Rickard said. "You're going to the wrong side. That side is in the past." In a way Lennox understood this, but he had come not only to love the manufacturing side but to believe in it. When he arrived, it was a jungle, and the law of the jungle still held; it would be his job, he decided, to try to change the factory, bring it into the modern era, make it more efficient and, equally important, more humane. There would be ample opportunity, he knew, to find things to change.

He was right about that. In 1958, soon after he became planning and engineering manager at Chester, there was a crisis. The line was down. It was down because the parts could not get up to the main line quickly enough. That meant the body bucks (that is, the frames that were used for body assembly) were down. In an assembly plant, that was a cardinal sin. Lennox and Clarence Oldenburg, the production-control manager, rushed to the offending area. There they found a foremen filled with misery, stalled machinery in front of him, overwhelmed by circumstances beyond his control. Oldenburg went up to him. "What did I tell you would happen if I ever found this place fucked up again?" Oldenburg said.

"You'd fire me," the foreman said.

"Is it fucked up?" Oldenburg asked.

"Yes," said the foreman.

"You're fired," said Oldenburg.

That, thought Lennox, is precisely what I have to stop, and so a few days later he quietly, without forcing Oldenburg to lose face, brought the foreman back.

Every day in manufacturing, Lennox had the same thought: This is where things are *made*. The great pleasure for him was the challenge of it, of creating something in metal on a mass scale, of taking ideas which had been sketched on paper and turning them into cars. The best time each year was when they had to change the assembly line over for the new car models. They had two weeks to do it, to go from an easy high-volume run to complete shambles and then, with luck, to smooth high volume again. As the last car from the old model came down the line, the crews of maintenance men and engineers were poised like vultures, ready to tear the line apart. Everyone cooperated, mechanical engineers, design engineers, electricians. All the normal friction was gone. In those two weeks, amid all the pressure and the tension, Don Lennox never loved the Ford Motor Company or his job more. This, he was sure, was why he had chosen the lonelier role of manufacturing man.

12.
FORD GOES PUBLIC

The Ford family in the days after World War II was both rich and impoverished. It was caught in a dilemma caused by the original Henry Ford's will. The old man had hated the government, hated taxes, hated banks. He wanted very much to keep the company in the family. If he had left the stock to his grandchildren, it would have effectively terminated family ownership, for the young Fords would have had to sell so much stock to pay their inheritance taxes that their hold on the company would have been shaky. In order to beat inheritance taxes the old man had created a foundation, the Ford Foundation, and had given it most of the stock; the family got a much smaller percentage—only 5 percent of the equity in the company. The family, however, held the voting stock; the Foundation had none. Thus the family could retain control of the company without paying devastating inheritance taxes.

There were two problems with this scheme, as it went into effect after Ford's death. The first was that since the old man had not in any sense been a charitable person, he had created a foundation with a lot of stock and virtually no function. Little about its actual operation suggested generosity. This bothered congressional authorities, who saw the foundation for what it was, a shameless tax dodge. The other problem was the family itself. The various Ford heirs and heiresses had not been amused to find, upon the death of the founder, that they owned only 5 percent of their own company. The surprise was particularly unpleasant because in the postwar years the family had come on what, for it, seemed like hard times. Fords were accustomed to a very grand style. In the new egalitarian and meritocratic America, few families lived like the Grosse Pointe Fords. Some of the households had as many as sixteen servants. Unfortunately, the company was not generating nearly enough money for them to continue this lavish existence. Ernie Breech was certainly bringing the company back to life, and it might again become very successful, but the overhead required for the company's regeneration was heavy, and in the meantime there was little in the way of dividends for the family. Henry, Bill, and Benson all had jobs at the company and drew salaries that were considerable but not so large that, by themselves, they were sufficient to cover their families' colossal expenditures. At every family financial meeting there was urgent talk about doing something to relieve the dividends crisis. There was a lot of elegant poor-mouthing at these sessions, as the servants moved among the family members and their advisers, serving drinks and coffee. What the family wanted was cash. What they had instead was an extraordinarily valuable piece of property from which very little in the way of money was coming.

The obvious solution was to take the company public—to sell its stock on the open market. Not only did the family's needs mandate this; the needs of the company itself, the enormous expenses involved in building new factories and keeping the existing operation healthy, meant that it could not be run as it had been in the founder's day, like a small grocery store, out of its own cashbox. There had to be additional sources of revenue, and the best one was the booming new equity market. Taking Ford public, however, was easier said than done. Its size and prestige demanded that it be listed on the New York Stock Exchange. Anything less would be embarrassing. But the NYSE would not list a nonvoting stock. That was just one of the difficulties. Somehow there would have to be a plan that would satisfy not only the New York Stock Exchange but also the Ford family, the Ford Foundation, and the ever watchful IRS. Secrecy was critical, for this was the touchiest deal imaginable, and if word slipped out, there might be considerable opposition to what the Ford family was trying to do.

The offering was three years in preparation, and all that time, security was extremely tight. During the long, delicate discussions, Sidney Weinberg, the senior partner at the New York investment banking firm of Goldman Sachs, who put the deal together, was careful not to maintain a file in his office with accumulated Ford data. To make sure no briefcase with Ford papers in it could be misplaced or stolen, he gave up carrying a briefcase. After all, he knew what no other banker and no ordinary citizen had ever known before, the intimate details of the Ford family's finances. Most of it he kept in his head. The rest, the essential numbers, was written on several pages that he kept with him at all times, in an old brown envelope. Once he almost blew the whole thing. Upon his arrival at the Detroit airport on a trip to meet with the Ford family, he stopped at a newsstand to buy a local paper. He put down the brown envelope containing the Ford family's intimate financial information, bought the paper, and walked away, leaving the envelope behind him. Thirty minutes later, approaching Eleanor Ford's home, he realized what he had done, had his driver turn around, and raced desperately back to the airport. The envelope was still there, in the hands of the man who ran the newsstand. The Ford secrets were still secret; Weinberg had not betrayed his trust. When Henry Ford II went to Europe during a crucial stage, he and Weinberg used a homemade code to keep in touch. Young Henry Ford was Alice, his brothers were Ann and Audrey, the company was Agnes, the family lawyer was Meg, the Ford Foundation was Grace, Weinberg was Edith, Gloria was the new limited common stock, and Florence was the market value. Someone reading the cables, the writer E. J. Kahn later noted, would have thought he was reading passages from *Little Women*.

Weinberg's efforts with the New York Stock Exchange were helped by the fact that the head of the exchange, Keith Funston, was a protégé of Weinberg's and that Weinberg had pushed him for the stock-exchange job. Satisfying the other parties was a little harder, but Weinberg kept plugging away, and at last, after three years of convoluted negotiations, of endless meetings, of stalemates, of monkey wrenches thrown and retrieved, of moments when the whole thing seemed impossible, a deal was done. The company would be recapitalized. The family share would rise from 5 to 12.1 percent. The family would retain 40 percent of the vote for its class of stock, regardless of what percentage of the shares it owned. (The original figure had been 30 percent, which the Ford family and Weinberg had decided would permit the family to retain working control. On the day the final arrangements were being worked out, however, Bill Ford had walked into his older brother's office and said, "I don't know about you, Henry, but I like owning this company. Let's be a little more on the safe side and make it forty." Forty, then, it was.) The Ford Foundation would get some votes to go with its stock; the family would give up some of its voting shares but would gain back a larger share in the equity of the company. As for the company, it would now be free to offer its stock to the public in future issues. The New York Stock Exchange agreed to list the stock, and the IRS gave its approval.

The announcement that Ford was going public, which came in November 1955, was stunning news. Ford was the last of the great American companies still privately owned, and the Ford name was at once mighty and universally recognizable. Average citizens who had always thought of Wall Street as a distant and alien place belonging to the very rich felt they could participate, and they did. Later John Whitehead of Goldman Sachs, who helped midwife the public issue, talked of it as not only a landmark deal but one that launched the era of what came to be called people's capitalism. It made ordinary citizens believe that buying stock—owning part of a giant company—was a real possibility in their lives. By purchasing this stock they became participants in American capitalism, *owners* as well as workers, junior partners of Henry Ford II. In an era when the market was still based on blue-chip stocks with no hot new high-technology companies to rival them, the magnetism of the Ford name, Whitehead thought, was strong. It was as if in a different era, some thirty years later, IBM had been a private company and announced it was going public.

The news generated excitement rarely seen on Wall Street. Everyone wanted in on the issue. Weinberg was besieged by people, both famous and not so famous, who claimed to know him and demanded that they be allowed to buy a hundred shares of Ford stock. There simply was not enough to go around. Early in the negotiations the principals had agreed that $50 per share would be satisfactory. But the fever kept building. The actual price turned out to be $64.50. Some ten million shares were sold, and it took 722 underwriters to handle them. At a time when $100 million was considered a handsome result from a public offering, this one brought $640 million—the sheer scale of it was staggering. The fever continued, greatly inflating the stock, but though it briefly surged up near $70 it soon hit a plateau near $50. The Ford family had been joined by some 300,000 new co-owners of their company. It was, said Keith Funston of the New York Stock Exchange, "a landmark in the history of public ownership." It was a landmark in tax avoidance too; estimates were that Eleanor Clay Ford and her four children saved some $300 million in taxes while keeping control of the company.

It also marked the beginning of a historic shift in American capitalism, a major increase in the influence of Wall Street in companies like Ford. The Street was a partner of the family now, and the family had to respond to its norms. In the old days, the Street did not demand too much of the companies whose stock it sold. But the stock market was changing now. Before the war only a small number of Americans held stocks, and they were to a large degree of the same class as the owners of the old-line companies. The market was a kind of gentleman's club, virtually off limits to the rest of the society. People owned stocks because their families had *always* owned stocks. They invested not so much to gain but to protect. The one exception to this was the period from 1926 to 1929, when the market turned speculative; then, instead of one million Americans owning stocks—the usual number—the number swelled to four or five million. Even then, though there were speculators, they were the exception; they did not set the market's values. There was no real pressure on the part of those who invested money to make the owners of the companies produce anything more than a healthy long-term gain. Those who were in the market were generally rich and were in for the long haul. The men who went to work on Wall Street were from what were called good families. They were not pushy, and they patiently waited to rise to the top in the good investment-banking houses. Breeding was often more important than talent. Certain of the old-line firms were very Waspy indeed, and some were German Jewish—"Our Crowd," as they spoke of themselves—and in manner they were sometimes even Waspier than the Wasps.

World War II altered all that. Affluence spread, and merit came to count for more. The great elite universities of America, under the pressure of the war and the GI Bill, had opened their doors to people who never would have been permitted to attend a decade before. The merit standard invaded Wall Street too. The old families were squeezed by inheritance taxes, and their wealth and their position began to diminish. The invest-ment houses could less readily support themselves in their accustomed handsome style by simply doing the bidding of the old families, who were, of course, connected to the old companies. The investment houses saw that they were going to have to become more aggressive.

The old order of American capitalism was beginning to give way. At the same time a new order was appearing. Millions and millions of people who had never owned stock before were now buying in, and in many ways that was healthy for the country; the economy was more democratic, more broadly based, and more balanced. There was more scrutiny and more pressure to perform, and generally that too was a good thing. The New Deal had made the labor unions rich and powerful, and those unions had pension-fund money to invest; other groups began to emerge as potentially powerful institutional investors. New industries were on the horizon, and a new breed of stockbroker was taking his place on Wall Street. While the old breed had been born to it, heirs to a class and a culture, comfortable and protected and with no burning need to conquer, the new breed was different. The typical new stockbroker had made it on his own to one of the better Eastern schools and then had gone to Harvard Business School or Wharton. He was young and ambitious and did not share the values or observe the restraints of those who had once dominated the Street. Above all he was not about to wait around for seniority to grant its slow reward. He was looking for hot stocks that would provide an immediate reward. He was not interested in protecting an existing investment in an established world; he wanted to be a winner, and he wanted action.

The new capitalism was not only more intense, it was explosive. Sud-denly millions of Americans whose parents had never been in the stock market but had put their limited savings in banks for the nice little 4 percent interest they earned (and whose closest acquaintanceship with a bond had been their careful and dutiful buying of war bonds—$18.75 for a bond worth $25 after ten years) were buying stocks. Keith Funston began to talk about his plan to make every American a shareholder. Middle-class Americans began to read in their newspapers of brilliant young men in their twenties and thirties who took a small amount of money, perhaps no more than $2000 or so, and in one year doubled or tripled it through a magical device called a mutual fund. The mutual fund hedged the bet, for the brilliant young broker was investing in enough different and terrific companies to offset the effect of the failure of one. Most of the companies seemed to have sexy names like Tritex or Ultratonix. Almost overnight, mutual funds, which had been a completely neglected field of action, became the vogue.

By the early sixties the market was taking off, as if the Street, once so staid and prim, had a fever. There was even a name for it, the go-go market, which implied not merely action but a break with the past. One did not think, after all, of the older generation, the men from Louis Auchincloss's novels, as go-go investors. Theirs had been a world of deliberate decorum. Now decorum was out the window. For the new investors it was a time when all the old unwritten rules were being broken, when everyone was becoming rich and doing it quickly, and no one was a loser (although there seemed to be winners and superwinners). Wall Street, which in the past had produced men whose culture was distilled in a Bachrach photograph emphasizing quiet distinction, was now producing something quite different, stars. The stars were the portfolio managers, and they were the darlings of the Street and the media. They could pick the hot stocks before they were hot and get rid of them just as they began to cool. They loved the new at the expense of the old. Of these stars, the exemplar was a man named Gerry Tsai.

Nothing reflected the madness of the market so much as the fascination with Tsai. He was the first of the high rollers created by the postwar changes. In those days everyone wanted to know what Tsai, or the Chinaman, as he became known on the Street, was doing. Rumors about what he was buying and selling seemed to dominate the shop talk of the Street. The Chinaman had a hot hand. Born in Shanghai, where his father, a graduate of the University of Michigan, was a Ford district manager ("Everyone there wanted to buy a Ford," Tsai once said. "It was a great sign of status"), he had come to America at nineteen as the Chiang government was falling. He later said that one of the advantages he had had was that he brought with him no connections, no family ties. He was not locked into the preconception that the world consisted of blue-chip stocks.

Not tied to the past, he was free to delve into the future, to concentrate on what might happen next. The best thing about the new era, Tsai liked to say, was that there was no penalty for being a foreigner. All you had to do was perform. "If you buy General Motors at forty and it goes to fifty," he said, "whether you are an Oriental or a Buddhist or an Italian doesn't make a difference."

Tsai got his big break in Boston in 1952 when he went to work for a man named Edward Johnson, who headed the Fidelity Fund. Johnson himself was something of a maverick. When he had taken over the fund, nine years before, he decided not just to sit there quietly and politely and let things accrue on their own. He intended to speculate. He did not, he explained, feel married to a stock. Rather, he said, it was more like a "companionate marriage" and occasionally a mere liaison. The misnamed Fidelity Fund was the perfect place for Tsai. He had a boss who encouraged him, he was bright, a mathematical whiz, and he intuitively understood the changing economy.

At first he worked as an analyst for Johnson, and he was good from the start. Because it was a small firm, he had to cover thirteen different industries, including auto, textile, steel, and machine tools. Working much as a reporter would, he visited the companies, listening to their best young people. He soon had a sense of foreboding about the traditional smokestack industries. They were mature, beset by high labor costs and the beginnings of serious foreign competition. Looking at them, all he could see was problems. They might or might not be able to continue their essential industrial success in the next twenty-five years, he thought, but there was no way, given their burdens, that they would be growth stocks. What he was looking for and what he soon discovered was the vital new companies, many of which were founded on recent technology and employed few workers. He heard that a company named AMF had developed a way to automate the process of setting up pins in bowling alleys. Though installing them might be expensive for the alley owners, soon their only cost would be the electricity involved. Tsai called on AMF, was impressed by the pin-setting machines, did a rough calculation of how many bowling alleys there were in the United States, figured that almost all of them would buy the equipment, and decided to buy the stock. It was a big winner.

After several years of working for Johnson, he decided to follow his intuition in a major way. He had observed that because of postwar afflu-ence, all sorts of new investors were coming into the market. The average amount invested was ranging between $2000 and $3000. No self-respecting portfolio manager wanted to handle sums as small as that, and so these investors had to go without good professional advice. Tsai saw an answer for them—mutual funds, in which the risks were spread and the small investor could benefit from the investment wisdom of the fund's managers. Tsai wrote Johnson a two-page memo asking for permission to start his own growth fund. Johnson called him in.

"How much will it take to start it?" he asked.

"Two hundred and fifty thousand dollars," Tsai answered.

"Go ahead," said Johnson. "Here's your rope." He would give Tsai what he needed to hang himself with. Tsai did not hang himself. He knew exactly what he wanted—stocks in the high-technology field or the service industry. The stocks he chose for his first list in 1958 later came to be blue-chips, but at the time almost all of them were speculative: Polaroid, Xerox, Texas Instruments, Avon, IBM. His touch, colleagues soon realized, was awesome. It was as if he had a sixth sense about where the market was going to go. "What grace, what timing—glorious," Johnson told writer John Brooks of *The New Yorker*.

His timing was indeed exquisite. For one thing, he entered the field just as the old blue-chip stocks had ceased to dominate, and as investment money became available for companies no one had ever heard of. Suddenly the offbeat was what people wanted. If the Ford Motor Company had gone public five years later, it would never have created so great a stir, for by then blue-chips were no longer so important. For another thing, Tsai happened to start his fund just as the first generation of postwar entrepreneurs were surfacing. Tsai understood these new companies and what they represented for the future, and he understood that with the country undergoing unparalleled prosperity, the money would be there to invest in them. Starting with the $250,000 from Johnson, he reached $200 million three years later. When he began, there was only $78 million invested in mutual funds; within thirty years, in no small degree because of Tsai's stimulus and example, it had risen to $24 *billion*.

In those days he was like a man on a roll at a gambling table. He loved speculating. He bought in huge blocks, ten thousand shares at a time, and the turnover of his portfolio was incredible. Where in the past a stockbroker might have turned over a family's portfolio some 5 or, at the most, 10 percent in a year, Tsai was turning over his portfolio more than 100 percent annually. Everyone wanted to know what he was buying. Tipsters used his name to push their pet stock: "Tsai is buying it." In some ways there was an advantage to his fame, he mused, because the moment it came out that he had bought, others jumped in and the stock surged. But it was hard to keep his purchases a secret long enough to make his entire buy at the original price, because so many followers had their eye on him and would try to buy in. He was the action. In 1965 he attained a growth of 50 percent on a turnover of 120 percent. On February 9, 1966, the Dow hit 1000 for the first time, just as Tsai had predicted, and that made him all the more a prophet.

In late 1965, aware that Johnson intended his own son as his successor, Tsai left Boston for New York, where he started the Manhattan Fund, a hedge fund (a private mutual fund restricted to the rich; a customer could not buy in with less than $100,000). Tsai hoped to sell about $25 million in shares, but his reputation was so extraordinary that he immediately sold $247 million. He eventually sold the company to CNA for $30 million.

In the midst of the sixties, Gerry Tsai was the symbol of the new Wall Street. He was smart and charming, and he was hungry. He had no special respect for the past. In the past people had wanted financial gain but had been afraid to admit it. The fear of admitting it, of appearing to be greedy, had limited their success. Tsai was different. His driving motive was an ever-escalating profit, and so was that of his friends. They were the new conglomerateurs, like Harold Geneen, Charles Bluhdorn, and Saul Steinberg, men who were creating corporate kingdoms largely by astute use of accountants. They were making the Street an exciting place. To them the stock market was an end in itself, not a means of financing enterprise. In the old days there had been a loyalty between stockholder and company; these new stockholders, and particularly the new institutional investors, barely knew the company. All they knew was three or four facts—numbers, really. They were not there for the long haul; they were there to hit the right stock on the rise, and then get rid of it when it leveled out. Loyalty and emotion were encumbrances. By the mid-sixties the market became in effect a caricature of what many thought was its purpose and a nightmare for the managers of old-line companies. No one talked about safe buys; there was too much action for that. Companies like Xerox and Polaroid replaced U.S. Steel and Ford as smart buys, and they in turn were replaced by fried-chicken companies and nursing-home syndicates. That the effect of these transactions, the sudden surge and the equally sudden descent of the stock, might be dangerous to the companies themselves, and potentially damaging to the long-range health of the American economy, did not seem to matter. A basic assumption of the American system—that was good for the market was good for American capitalism, and therefore good for the country—had been challenged. For the moment what was good for the market was good for the market.

With less loyalty, there was less stability for the companies involved. Also significant for anyone involved in business—whether the investors, the managers of the companies, or the bright young men coming out of business schools—was the effect on the talent flow. One could make far more money by playing the market on Wall Street—where cleverness was rewarded immediately—than by joining a company and getting in line to do something as mundane as producing something. The effect of this drain of ability away from the companies themselves was incalculable.

Few who were watching were particularly upset. Some of the older men were wary of the consequences, and some were shrewd enough to know that it could not and would not last, that the ascending spiral was too steep to sustain, that no country was that rich or could afford to offer that much profit to that many people for so long. To some it was clear that people were taking too much out of the companies and, worse, taking out more than was being put in. Some of the new conglomerates were put together not so much because their subsidiary companies had any connection to each other but because it gave accountants a creative run at the country's tax policies and offered a chance to improve the looks of a given stock without necessarily improving the company's basic productivity. The conglomerateurs displayed skill in the leveraging of money. One of the early ones, Meshulin Riklis, head of a conglomerate called Rapid American, once said, "I am a conglomerate. Me, personally," and confessed that he was successful "because of the effective nonuse of cash." This was creative bookkeeping at its most adroit. A company that had what was known as a high multiple bought a company that had what was known as a low multiple, and the merged company came out looking better and hotter than either of the originals. Paper, rather than reality, was emerging from an economy like this, and illusion rather than production preoccupied the successful new manager.

There was a certain madness to all this, a frenzy. The old stock market, which was still alive and which was for fuddy-duddies, was perhaps turning over at 10 or 12 percent. The new market was for the dazzling young men, and it was turning over at 40 and 50 percent. Soon it was not just the hotshots who were embracing it. In 1969 the prestigious and conservative Ford Foundation, whose very name reflected the legitimacy of the old companies, issued a report saying in effect that institutional investors such as universities should not just sit there clipping coupons but should become more hip and more speculative with their portfolios.

Over the years this view profoundly influenced bedrock American capitalism. While the go-go market rewarded those shrewd enough to skim it quickly, exploiting the first surge of the postwar economy, it was the industrial core, ironically, that it most threatened. The immediate problem was a difficulty in competing for talent. Who, after all, by the early sixties wanted to go from Harvard Business School to U.S. Steel or Ford or some small-parts manufacturer in Ohio when Xerox or Donaldson Lufkin & Jenrette or other comparably exciting companies beckoned? Why go to an already carved-up and probably diminishing world when there were brand-new worlds opening up right in front of you? And of those whom the older companies were able to woo from the great business schools, who wanted to go out and work in the assembly plants? The traditional companies, already having difficulty recruiting able young people, had to offer as much incentive as they could now. In those older companies there was a fast track and a slow track. The fast track, with quicker advancement and bigger pay and bonuses, was in management, which now meant the financial end, and the slow track, for the second-class citizens, was in the factories.

But the long-range impact was even more serious. What was happening, slowly, unconsciously, insidiously, was that the industrial companies were adapting to the norms being set by the hot new companies, the darlings of the Street. In the most difficult of atmospheres, they had to drive their stock up, and over two decades that effort systematically gave power to the finance people. It was the need to compete with young companies on the ascent that in many ways was changing the internal balance of these old-line companies, deeding power not to manufacturing and product men but to finance men. The finance men, after all, were the ones who could at least try to make the stock competitive. What was happening at the Ford Motor Company was a good example. Not only were the top people there mainly from finance, but the bias of the market invisibly but critically bore on the company's decisions. Arjay Miller, who was for a time president of Ford during this period, later denied that he was affected by the market, and it was probably true that Ford was less dependent on the market for its financing than many other companies; it had to raise less money from the equity market than others did. But in all kinds of subliminal and not so subliminal ways, Miller and men like him were responding to pressures that had become so much a part of the equation that no one was even aware of responding to them anymore. There was a great deal of talk about the effect of production decisions on the stock. Henry Ford II was always aware of the value of the stock, everyone in the company knew that; it was an aspect of his stewardship of the company, a family company the value of whose stock was the true indicator of the family's current wealth.

A good example of the insidious pressure came in the early seventies, when the trustees of the Ford Foundation decided it was time to diversify the portfolio. That meant selling Ford stock, and the higher the stock, of course, the better for the foundation. Within the company there developed an all-out need to get the price of the stock up. If it was low, then the Ford Foundation's resources were smaller. If the Ford Foundation was smaller, Henry Ford was unhappy. He did not, in those years of flamboyant American affluence, like coming to New York and hearing that the stock was low.

13.
THE QUIET MAN

Finance was soon a power of its own. Its principal driving force was Bob McNamara, and its basic philosophy was: Whatever the product men and the manufacturing men want, deny it. Make them sweat and then make them present it again, and once again delay it as long as possible. If in the end it has to be granted, cut it in half. Always make them fight the balance sheet, and always put the burden of truth on them. That way they will always be on the defensive and will think twice about asking for anything.

By the early fifties there was growing tension between McNamara and Lewis Crusoe. Crusoe had become general manager of the Ford division, one of the two or three most important jobs in the company, in 1949. He was a man who could bridge both sides in a company in transition. A former finance man whose roots were in accounting, he had come from the Fisher Body division of General Motors, where he had been divisional controller, and he had also served as assistant treasurer of GM. He was a money man, then, meticulous, always careful about spending money. But he was also a man steeped in the car industry, with a genuine love of cars, and the product men at Ford enjoyed working for him. He knew all the tricks of the finance people, and he protected product. The original two-seat Ford Thunderbird, one of the loveliest automobiles of the postwar era, was completely his. Since finance did not think a two-seat sports car practical, he had virtually had it designed in secret and sneaked into production.

Starting in 1949 he engaged in a full-blown battle with McNamara and Ted Yntema, who had succeeded Crusoe in finance, over the condition of the manufacturing plants. The factories, Crusoe complained, were in desperate condition. They were antiquated and run-down; they limited production, and they made it impossible for the manufacturing people to provide quality. They were really leftover Model T factories. The plant people could not even get a forklift into them to move materials back and forth, because the aisles were too narrow. They could barely get the cars through the paint ovens and could not generate enough heat in the ovens to get modern paints to dry properly.

What became an almost three-year struggle over the condition of the factories started innocently enough. Crusoe, frustrated and increasingly angry over what the run-down plants were doing to the quality of his cars, asked for the modernization of the Louisville plant. That job would cost several million dollars. McNamara, then controller of the company, immediately said no, they needed a comprehensive study of *all* the plants. That sounded logical enough to Crusoe, and he agreed, thinking the study would take six months. But it dragged on and on. Three years passed. The more information Crusoe and his people produced, the more McNamara wanted. Crusoe knew exactly what McNamara was doing, he was stalling and stalling—later the phrase for it, among the product people, was slow walking—delaying the massive expenditure as long as he could. Meanwhile the 1952 Ford was a winner, selling very well, but the factories simply weren't able to turn them out quickly enough to meet the demand. Crusoe was not a man who used expletives lightly, but in private he would rage about McNamara, what the son of a bitch was doing, did he think he was fooling anyone. My people, he said, are damn well dying out there because they can't get the cars built. There were more and more meetings, more and more documents. (The finance people were clever at using documents, piling them up, making every presentation seem more impressive by the height of the stacks; so one of Crusoe's men filled a number of briefing books with cut-up *Wall Street Journals*, which the manufacturing men wheeled into the meetings to make their own case look weightier, as if the briefing books were full of information that could be summoned to support their arguments.)

In early 1953 they held the meeting that would decide the plant renovation issue. The total cost of building new plants and modernizing the existing ones, Crusoe told the meeting, was $1 billion. ("Why, that's more money than the entire net worth of Chrysler," a stunned Ed Lundy, one of McNamara's principal aides, said later.) Not all of the money would be spent at once, Crusoe noted; some of the bad plants would be closed, and there was a schedule for renovating the remaining ones. Again McNamara began to argue against the expansion. Max Wiesmyer, who was in charge of the assembly plants, started to argue back. Crusoe patted him on the hand. "I'll take care of this, Max," he said. So again he spoke: What they were talking about, he said, was not so much spending money on factories but a larger question, whether Ford had an expanding future and whether it would ever be able to compete with General Motors and, as he had always dreamed of doing, overtake Chevrolet. It could not compete with a dying physical plant. Did in anyone in that room, he asked, believe for a minute that GM's plants were like this? Did anyone believe that GM in this boom economy was not going to pour more and more money into its plants? "We will never catch GM unless we decide to go ahead today," he said.

When Crusoe finished, there was a dramatic silence. Finally Henry Ford said, "Isn't anybody going to say anything?" McNamara got up and said that the finance people had been in close touch with the people in charge of the study, that they essentially agreed with the findings of Crusoe and his staff, but that considering the size of the project, the amount of money involved, the fact that Ford would surely have to go to the bank and borrow the money (that was still the special raw nerve, touching as it did on the traditional Ford fear of banks, which had survived long after the old man had died), perhaps it would be a good idea if they studied this a little longer.

Crusoe, listening to him, began to shake with anger. "We have to go now," he said. "We can't wait anymore. The quality is bad, the paint is bad. We can't even get our cars dried out. We can't meet our own stand-ards." Although he did not say so, he privately believed that it would be a good idea if Ford borrowed from the banks, that the discipline of owing money would be beneficial for the company, that one of the problems in the past had been that Ford had too much cash and that the cash had bred a great many bad habits.

The decision hung in the balance. Henry Ford started going around the room. First he turned to his brother Benson. "Benson, what do you think?" he asked.

"Come on, Henry," the younger brother said, "you know I'm no big brain. What do you expect from me?" No one else volunteered. This seemed to be a decision so important that it had to be made by the family. That meant Henry. Finally he spoke. "Bob," he said, "the problem with you is you always want to study things. You never want to do anything." With that he gave the go-ahead to a compromise that would commit some $500 million to the modernization of the Ford division alone. It was less than half of what Crusoe felt was needed if Ford was to be strong and competitive, but it was a victory of sorts.

In those years Crusoe was still convinced that he could handle Mc-Namara. Like McNamara, he knew numbers, but unlike McNamara and his staff, he knew cars, and that gave him an advantage. He believed that McNamara was a major asset to the company. The problem, he always said, was in controlling the controller. Crusoe was sure he could do it.

Shortly after the modernization battle, McNamara went to work for Crusoe as his assistant in the Ford division. When colleagues questioned Crusoe, he told them not to worry. McNamara, he said, was extremely able—brilliant, really—possibly the smartest man who had ever entered the company. The trick was to keep him in check; without firm direction he became too strong, but with it he accomplished great things. Crusoe was confident he would be able to stay in effective charge of McNamara for a long time.

Crusoe was wrong. In January 1955 he was promoted at Ford, made executive vice-president of the car and truck division, assigned to strengthen Lincoln and Mercury and help with the secret new car they were working on, the Edsel—all as part of a long-awaited challenge to GM in the upper range, where the profits were far greater. At the same time, McNamara got Crusoe's old job, becoming general manager and vice-president of the Ford division. It was ten years after the war, and with McNamara's appointment the old order had clearly changed at the company; this was highest operational job attained by one of the Whiz Kids. Almost the first thing McNamara did when he took over at Ford was to call in Sanford Kaplan, who had been Crusoe's man in charge of much of the manufacturing-plant study. He told Kaplan to produce a brief report showing that delaying the modernization of the plants, rather than going ahead right away, had been more profitable for the company.

"But Bob," said Kaplan, "that's just not true." He was well aware that Crusoe was extremely bitter over lost sales and production on the '52 Ford and blamed McNamara and his resistance to the study for the loss.

"I want you to do it," McNamara said, pressing on. "I think it would be very helpful." Suddenly Kaplan realized that a loyalty test of sorts was being administered and that his career hinged on what he did. Kaplan thought about that a long time, and he thought of his wife and two children, and he wrote a report which with some hedging and softening seemed to make McNamara's point. As he wrote it he was sure for the first time that he would one day leave the Ford Motor Company.

Observers who watched what happened next thought that it was not that Bob McNamara deliberately set out to break the once mighty and unquestioned power of the manufacturing and assembly division. But it offended him; he was modern and rational, and it, as it stood, was old-fashioned, often corrupt, and run by its own secret systems which to him were irrational. If nothing else, it was in his way. He was contemptuous of the plant managers and their backgrounds and what they represented, and he believed that they were wasteful, either deliberately so, out of avarice, or unintentionally, out of incompetence. Even the best of them had little chance with him; none of them could ever explain to his satisfaction or in his language why they did certain things. He set out instead to convert them, but to the men in the plants his idea of conversion was their idea of destruction. What in fact took place was a political act that would have an immense effect on the future of the company. At the time, of course, no one had any idea that something of such magnitude was taking place.

In the beginning he rolled over Max Wiesmyer, the head of manufacturing. Wiesmyer was the central figure: He was the plant managers' man in Detroit. When they really needed something, they called Max, and he would break through the red tape and get it for them. On one occasion, when one of his plant managers sent in an appropriations request, Wiesmyer gave it to one of his assistants, who examined it and told Wiesmyer that it was as phony as a three-dollar bill. "Max, we have to send this one back," the assistant said. "It just isn't any good."

"Listen," Wiesmyer answered, "when one of my plant managers requests an appropriation, it's not your job to examine it and find out what's wrong—it's your job to take it and fix it up so McNamara won't bounce it."

No one else in this new age reflected the old era so faithfully as Wiesmyer. He knew all the sins of the past, and had managed, by governing his ambition, to avoid getting caught up in the endless power struggles under the original Henry Ford. Once when one of the bright young finance men assigned to him was asking a lot of questions, Wiesmyer said, "Young man, this is a company where you do not always want to know all the answers. What you don't know may be better for you than what you do know." He was born in Whitemore Lake, Michigan, in 1899, the son of a carpenter and small-time contractor. When he was eighteen, he thought about being a carpenter too, but the work those days was erratic, so Wiesmyer told his father he was going to try to land a position at Ford's. He was worried that the anti-German feeling of the time might keep him from being hired, but he quickly got a job working in the machine-tool shop at 47 cents an hour. To him that was astonishing, making almost $5 a day for indoor work. He kept boasting to his friends that he had this miraculous job which kept him out of the cold. Over the next thirty years he worked at almost every job there was at Ford. In that career he had seen it all. He had laid out plants throughout America, and Europe as well. He had been in Holland when the first Henry Ford arrived to dedicate a new plant at Rotterdam.

"Mr. Ford, here is our new plant," Lord Perry, who was the head of Ford in Europe, said proudly.

"Where is the water?" the old man asked.

"There isn't any water," Lord Perry replied.

"Well, let's get out of here," Ford said. "I don't even want to look at it." That had ended the ceremony. Ford had driven off, and they had torn down the plant and moved it to a deep-water site.

Wiesmyer stayed as far as he could from the power struggles between Sorensen and Bennett that marked the thirties at Ford. A Whiz Kid once asked him how he had survived the Sorensen-Bennett era, and Wiesmyer replied: "I was very good at being no one's enemy and no one's favorite." Sorensen once bawled out Wiesmyer for the way he had laid out a plant in Richmond, California. "Why did you do it this badly?" Sorensen had screamed at him.

"Mr. Sorensen, I thought . . ." Wiesmyer began.

A dark look came over Sorensen's face. "Who in the hell ever told you that you were supposed to think?" he said. And Sorensen, in Wiesmyer's view, was better than Bennett. At least Sorensen was a good factory man. Bennett was just a bully. All he knew was how to beat up people.

That someone so essentially decent as Wiesmyer had survived in so difficult an environment was no small badge of honor. That alone won him respect, for Max had kept his integrity when integrity had not been fashionable. His strength was that he was good with the men under him, and they, in turn, working under difficult conditions, would do things for him that they would not do for another boss. As long as Crusoe was the head of the Ford division, Wiesmyer was protected, for Crusoe understood this and knew his value. Wiesmyer had been offered the job of head of the Ford division before Crusoe had, but he had turned it down, thinking himself not properly prepared. Though they were very different men— Crusoe fastidious and college-educated, Wiesmyer rough-hewn—they became friends, taking vacations together in Palm Springs, and speaking, it seemed, their own private language as they puzzled out how to sustain a company so shaky that had needs so huge. Above all, Crusoe thoroughly understood and appreciated that Wiesmyer was holding together a once great but now ramshackle operation, and that he was doing it by virtue of the personal loyalties he generated. The assembly plants, Crusoe knew, were critical. In his words, they were the court of last resort, where things either were done the right way or they would be irretrievably wrong. Wiesmyer was the representative of the men who ran those assembly plants. He knew that there was waste built into the system, that all kinds of games were being played, but he had decided long ago that they were his men, they were running their factories under terrible conditions, and if they were playing games, these were merely games of survival, not games of greed. Thus his job was to protect them from finance and McNamara.

With Crusoe elevated and McNamara at the head of the Ford division, Wiesmyer never had a chance. What he did best, his greatest skill, the handling of people, McNamara never gave him credit for; in fact, he distrusted him for it—to him it smacked of cronyism. Wiesmyer's greatest weakness, the quantifying of what was happening in his factories, the turning of this clumsy, haphazard mechanical process into one yielding constant numerical truths, was McNamara's strength—and his weapon. Wiesmyer hated McNamara's numbers; he knew that each represented a loss of autonomy, and he could not cope with them. He was old-fashioned, he relied on personal trust, but McNamara seemed to brush all that aside. He pushed Wiesmyer relentlessly with numbers: Quantify this, meet these figures. He even demanded, for a time, that quality be quantified—points subtracted for things that were wrong. The effort came apart when it became clear that the men in the plants had learned to rig the system by having a few high-quality cars on hand for inspection and by taking the inspectors from Detroit out for drinks on the night they arrived. Don Bastion, one of the top manufacturing people, finally pleaded with Detroit to change the system. "You're turning all my plant guys into drunks," he said.

Wiesmyer knew what was happening, that McNamara was moving on him, centralizing power, taking things that had once been under the jurisdiction of the plants and turning them over to Detroit, where the finance people could dominate them. The realities of manufacturing meant less and less; what those realities *should* be, according to Detroit's numbers, meant more and more. McNamara wanted not only budgets, which was legitimate; he wanted more and more control over the plant managers. For example, he ordered a salary freeze, so that no one new could be hired at the plants without Detroit's approval. Every month there were more rules, more controls, all of them alien. From a world of instinct, the plants became a world of authorizations. Now there were constant directives coming from this alien capital, usually about production numbers, seldom about quality. Wiesmyer was furious. "If he wants to run the goddam factories," Wiesmyer once said of McNamara, "why doesn't he go out there and take one over and run it for a year? But not do it on paper."

Nothing reflected the new split personality of the Ford Motor Company, the clash between modern efficiency and old-time flawed reality, more than the battle of the paint ovens. Because the plants were in bad shape, inadequate to produce cars for the hungry postwar customers, there was soon a violent collision between McNamara and the manufacturing men over these facilities. The plant men wanted newer and better factories. McNamara wanted greater speed from the existing plants. The bottleneck, it quickly became clear, was the paint ovens. They were old, technologically outdated, and too small for contemporary cars. A manufacturing man, Neil Waud, told McNamara at one meeting of senior officials that there was no way that the painting could be expedited. Waud was stunned when McNamara then suggested that the chassis be built in two main parts, painted, and then welded together into one piece. Waud quickly explained why it was impractical, that the welding could not come after the painting and that even if it could, the car thus produced would be significantly weakened and vulnerable to all kinds of stress. But McNamara was insistent; there had to be a way to do this to speed up production. The more insistent he was, the blunter Waud became. "The problem with you," Waud shouted, "is you don't known a goddam thing about how our cars are actually made." After the meeting broke up, McNamara turned to Sanford Kaplan, one of Waud's superiors, and said, "I don't want that man at any more meetings."

Wiesmyer, hearing the story, was both comforted and discomforted. It assured him that he himself was not crazy; it also made clear that there was no relief in sight.

For McNamara was like a drill, relentlessly boring in on the assembly plants. No one worked as hard as he did, no one was as single-minded. Every day there was some new regulation, some new instrument of control. "I can't deal with him," Wiesmyer would tell friends. "This guy is crazy. It's not about cars—I can deal with cars. It's about numbers. Do you know what this guy does for a vacation? He climbs mountains. How can you deal with a guy who on his time off flies to some God-forsaken place and then climbs a mountain? You know, he pays good money to do that."

Wiesmyer began to change. He came to hate McNamara, and he would talk about him as "the son of a bitch." "I know what he's up to," he would say. "He wants to get me, and he wants to get my people. They'll be nothing left of us when he's done." First he fought actively, and when that failed, he fought McNamara with a kind of passive resistance. Once ebullient and extroverted, he began to retreat within himself. He became sullen and morose. Even McNamara was aware that something was happening. "What's wrong with Max?" he would ask, and Wiesmyer's friends would explain that Max was terrified of McNamara, that he could no longer defend himself, that he was sure that each meeting was going to expose some failure on his part. McNamara seemed to listen, but his approach

never changed. Wiesmyer's hands began to tremble. His speech sometimes became incoherent. At the end he became almost catatonic. After
a little more than a year without Crusoe's protection he had a complete
breakdown. He was given shock treatment and had somewhat of a recovery, and in March 1956 he was given a job as a consultant, which demanded
far less of him. In 1962 he retired, still shaken by his experience.

With the elimination of Max Wiesmyer, the power of Ford manufacturing was effectively destroyed. The decisions on production—decisions
the plants had to live with each day—were made in Detroit now, and
made by men who had never worked in the plants. The old-timers and
the men who could not keep up with the new style just faded away. They
were not fired, except in rare circumstances. Many left the company of
their own accord. Others, men in their late forties and their fifties, stayed
but melted into the background, assigned to meaningless jobs. They were
sinking and everyone knew it, and no one wanted to look at them. They
existed but they did not exist. No wonder then that, with exceptions like
Don Lennox, the bright young men at Ford did not want to go into the
factories. The factories were a no-man's-land, a limbo at best.

So manufacturing, weakened, continued to weaken for lack of new blood.
Politically, its power began to contract. There was one brief period, between 1961 and 1963, when John Dykstra, one of the GM people who
had been brought over by Ernie Breech, served as president. But that
was almost a fluke, and not a very happy one; it helped convince Henry
Ford that he needed the new breed rather than the old at the top. Their
decline accelerated from then on. The younger men were on a slower
track. The senior manufacturing men rarely served on the board or reached
the inner circle of Glass House power. Falling short of real power themselves, they could not reward their protégés. The company's new elite,
coming as it did from the nation's best schools, looked down on these men
who had usually been to middling state schools and whose clothes and
way of speaking reflected it. The finance people begot strength; the manufacturing men's weakness begot weakness. There was not only a diminished respect for them personally but also a corresponding disdain for what
they did. They were no longer in the company's most important division.
They were now in its backwater.

The Big Three in the auto industry stood virtually alone, possessors of
what was in effect a shared monopoly, for the price of entry was too great
for any start-up company. In an environment like that, power moved
steadily from the product men, who took risks but were normally the
creators of market share, to finance, whose agents knew how to maximize
the profits of an existing share in a static industry. Since competition within

the auto industry was mild, there was no impulse to innovate; to the finance people, innovation not only was expensive but seemed unnecessary. When engineers, especially foreigners, made breakthroughs like disk brakes and radial tires and fuel injection, it would be years, sometimes many years, before Detroit finally went ahead and added them either as standard equipment or as options. Why bother, after all? In America's rush to become a middle-class society, there was an almost insatiable demand for cars. It was impossible not to make money, and there was a conviction that no matter what the sales were this year, they would be even greater the next. So there was little stress on improving the cars. From 1949, when the automatic transmission was introduced, to the late seventies, the cars remained remarkably the same. What innovation there was came almost reluctantly.

Indeed, change, in the later part of that era, was contrived not to improve but in the most subtle way to weaken each car model, year by year. The company, in its drive for greater profit, would take the essential auto structure of the year before and figure out ways to increase the profits by reducing the cost of some of the parts. Not a lot was subtracted. From the outside the car might seem much the same as its forerunner, but Detroit had saved $1 million here and $2 million there by cutting tiny corners.

The Ford Motor Company was becoming a stagnant place at which to work. The impulse of product, to make the best and most modern cars possible, was giving way to the impulse of profit, to maximize the margins and drive both the profit and the stock up. It did not happen overnight. It had begun with McNamara and his systems. Those systems, brought in originally because the company was in such desperate shape and needed discipline, became a force unto themselves. Men like Charley Beacham —the old-time boomer and salesman, Lee Iacocca's great tutor—began to complain that men like Arjay Miller and Ed Lundy, both of them original Whiz Kids, both of them rising stars, didn't really like cars, didn't like dealers, and didn't really like the business. Beacham was constantly urging Miller and Lundy to go to the dealers' conventions, which were the real communal rites of the auto business; you had to attend if you wanted to find out what was happening out there in America, for the dealers were the people who actually sold the cars. More often than not they refused. On the rare occasions that they did go, Beacham was struck by how uncomfortable they were, how difficult it was for them to talk to people whose passion in life was not so much even cars as the *selling* of cars. They could only, he claimed, talk to people just like themselves. When they did go to a convention, he would observe them ruefully. "Watch, now," he would tell Iacocca. "Watch Arjay and Ed. They've been here as long as they can stand it. Now watch them start moving for the back door so they can get the hell out." And sure enough, soon they would disappear.

But it was as if the lack of feel for cars was beside the point. The finance people were rising to power because the company needed them and their skills. The decisions facing these huge postwar companies were novel and complicated, and no one with the average manufacturing man's background could hope to run such a company or even play an important role. The government was now more involved in business, there were more lawyers and more pressure groups, the cost of doing everything was greater. It was, in short, becoming a far more difficult time in which to do business, and that helped the finance people, because they were trained to deal with the difficulties. They understood the complex new business world, and how to survive in it, as the old-timers did not.

Because business was so profitable, the one thing that no one in management wanted was a strike. The result of this was that the settlements with the UAW became handsomer every year. After all, the industry was highly profitable, and no one knew that better than Walter Reuther. While Nissan was crushing its troublesome unions, Ford and the other American auto makers were granting settlements so generous that doing business was becoming more expensive every year. That further helped the finance people, because it was their job to make a profit in spite of the rising costs.

Besides, there were now fewer good product men coming along, fewer men who grew up experimenting with cars and loving the feel of machinery. The poor America of the Depression had generated a lot of tinkerers. Much of the tinkering had been involuntary, done on the farms because there was no access to a repair shop and the farmer had to fix things himself. But in the new America the small farms were dying, and there were not as many farmboys to watch their fathers hand-tool parts for a tractor or a car. There were fewer self-taught engineers in America now, men who could fix things in their garages. In the more affluent America of the postwar years, the people who as boys had played with engines did not go to college; the people who did go to college came from homes where when something wore out you went to a store and bought a replacement. Men were still showing up in Detroit with engineering degrees, but their hands were clean now. Rare was the new engineer who had ever actually built something. The nation's technical knowledge was becoming more and more abstract. The brightest young men went to law school and business school; the best engineers wanted to work in the space program or in defense.

So there were more people than ever from the business schools, and where they had once had only slide rules for their calculations, now they had computers, which greatly increased their capacity to quantify any concept and to put those numbers to use. Computers were a powerful new weapon for the finance people. Every year now they had greater access to financial detail and greater skill in using that detail within the company. With the coming of computers, the financial people were like prophets armed.

The changing role of Wall Street was also having an impact on the Ford Motor Company, as on many other companies. The traditional blue-chip companies were no longer very interesting, because they had completed their principal growth; they were already big and rich. The trick now was to find a company that was just about to make it and catch it before everyone else got in on it, to ride it while it was hot and then get off just before it reached its plateau. That was the key to the go-go market. It was a far more speculative arena than the old Street. Profit was no longer enough now; superprofit was of the essence. This trend placed an exceptional burden on traditional companies, companies whose profits, no matter how considerable, had leveled out. For they were competing with all the sexy new industries in the country.

Gradually the companies began to respond to what the Street wanted and tried to become hotter themselves in order to compete for capital. Some of those companies were like middle-aged women fighting to keep their husbands by putting on too much makeup and wearing clothes more appropriate for a twenty-year-old. As the companies changed their style, so too did they—almost imperceptibly at first—change their purpose. It was no longer enough simply to make a good product and a solid profit; now more and more the object was to drive the stock up. The stock was the point of it all, not the product. Gene Bordinat, the Ford designer, remembered being with Chrysler executive Lynn Townsend (who was credited by many within Chrysler with driving Chrysler to artificially high production in order to make the company's numbers look better) and telling Townsend that he was worried about the declining level of quality in the entire industry, and Townsend said, "Hell, Gene, all the public wants is its splits [stock splits]. That's all you have to give them." The new American public to him was not the people who bought the car, the public was the people who bought the stock. Inevitably that preoccupation with the stock forced old-line companies to make short-range moves designed to make the present look good at the expense of the future. Research and development were chopped back because they were expensive and cut into profits and hurt the way the company looked on its books. So the pressure to slash expenses became intense. Since labor costs were constantly rising, the reductions were always accomplished by subtracting from innovation and product and factory maintenance. That approach, which was particularly hard on a mature industrial company like Ford, seeped through the entire economy. Without anyone's realizing it, the maneuvering room within American capitalism was becoming more and more restricted.

The change in the purpose of companies produced a change, sometimes hidden, in the disposition of power. Some thought, for example, that during the next two decades, the sixties and seventies, Ford belonged to Lee Iacocca—so visible was he, such a dominating force. Others assumed it was Henry Ford's company simply because he bore the family name and could make the ultimate decisions. But others, who knew how things worked there, believed it was really J. Edward Lundy's company.

Ed Lundy was the quiet man of the Ford Motor Company. As treasurer, then controller, and in 1962 vice-president of finance, he was heir to the power that McNamara had accumulated. Outside of Ford, except for his fellow chief financial officers almost no one knew his name. Within Ford his name was not only known, it was *the* name. (In the upper echelons of the company at that time there might have been hundreds of Edwards, but there was only one Ed. When someone said "Ed wants to know . . ." or "Ed thinks . . ." he meant *the* Ed, Ed Lundy.) He specialized in collecting the brightest young men from the nation's business-school campuses and turning them into a professional cadre, and if Ed Lundy said that a particular young man had the right stuff, then the young man was home free.

He never married, and he lived a monastic life. The Ford Motor Company was his real family, and those fine young men whose careers he guided were his sons. Sometimes he would even try to be one of the boys with them, might refer affectionately to one of them with light profanity —"Bob, you little turd," or, "Steve, you little bastard, you"—remarks that sounded odd and stilted from this formal, old-fashioned man but were treasured nonetheless by the young men themselves not just as proof that Ed Lundy knew their names but as a sign that he liked them and they had been in some way anointed. Those he liked became part of his extended family, and he was uncommonly generous to them and their families. The basement room in his handsome condo in Dearborn was like a well-organized gift shop, from which he sent out hundreds of presents every year. There, neatly laid out on a huge table, were the wrapping paper and the ribbon with the legend "A gift of J. Edward Lundy" repeatedly printed on it, and, in a drawer, that new plastic bubble-filled material designed to keep glassware from breaking. In cabinets were the gifts themselves, leather datebooks, gold cufflinks, Steuben glass. The gifts went out not only at Christmas but in a constant stream, and children of former Ford employees, long after their fathers had left the company, might receive something from him at a graduation or on a birthday.

Ford was his life, that and the Roman Catholic Church, of which he was a devout member. When his men were to get a statistical report to him over the weekend, often they were told to leave it at St. Joseph's Catholic Church in Dearborn, where he spent much time. When he moved into his apartment at the Fairlane complex near the company headquarters, he even had a special chute installed, like the depositories outside banks, for nighttime deliveries. That way the bright young men in finance could drop off their late-night reports, which he in turn could read before going to bed. He was at work before anyone else in the company each morning, eating a Ford breakfast. Ambitious young financial officers learned that one of the best times to talk with Ed Lundy was at breakfast at six-thirty, and they scheduled their breakfast time to match his.

In a city where success usually involved a certain amount of ostentation, Lundy lived a rare ascetic life—St. Thomas Aquinas in Motor City, thought one Ford colleague, Don Frey. Most of his colleagues loved the gratifications provided by the company; Lundy did not. The fact that Ford had its own airline (the seventeenth largest airline in the world, they called it) meant a certain amount of free travel was available to the deserving. Ed Lundy hated to travel, hated going to meetings on foreign soil. Work for him was being in Detroit, playing with the numbers, making them come out right.

His apartment was not really a home. Elizabeth Bourke and her husband, Bill, a high-level Ford man, lived nearby during the seventies, and one day she came over to give Lundy—who had a sweet tooth—some small tinned cakes from Nieman Marcus. The cakes needed to be heated. Elizabeth Bourke put them in Lundy's oven and nothing happened. The oven didn't work. A repairman from the company was called and was astonished: The oven was four years old, and this was the first time it had ever been used. Stories like that added to his legend among Lundy aficionados; they seemed to complete the portrait of the ascetic, totally selfless man. But there were others, men outside the clubby world of finance and wary of both Lundy and his legion, who believed that his life-style was a calculated aspect of his legend, as if he was proving again and again that he was someone for whom there was no existence save Ford, for whom hours off duty were the same as hours on.

If he was an ascetic, he nevertheless loved good clothes and spent a

considerable amount of money on them. He was not much given to modern
fashions—well into the seventies he still sported the same brush haircut
that he had brought to the Ford Motor Company as a young army major
fresh from the war—and his clothes were conservative, the suits almost
invariably from Brooks Brothers. Indeed his look, traditional Ivy League,
became almost the uniform of the finance people and thus the upper class
of the Ford Motor Company. He dressed in a very careful, precise way.
A certain suit was always worn with a certain shirt and a certain tie. A
certain pair of shoes went with dark suits; another pair went with lighter
suits. None of the combinations was venturesome; everything blended.
His dress was virtually his signature. Invited by friends one summer
Sunday to come to their patio for a cookout and told the guests were
dressing informally, he showed up in one of his suits—but without a tie;
that was informality.

In sharp contrast to Iacocca, who found personal publicity irresistible,
Lundy hated all publicity. He never gave interviews, and he avoided any
public role. He was shy, but it was more than that; he knew it was not
considered a good idea to draw too much attention to oneself at Ford. It
inevitably backfired, and it could only make you a target for critics. In a
company known for powerful men of robust egos—Ford, Breech, Thornton, McNamara, Iacocca, Frey, Caldwell, and Bourke—Lundy seemed
curiously mild and modest. He wanted only what was good for the Ford
Motor Company. He wanted nothing for himself. He had no taste for self-
aggrandizement. In his earlier years he had pushed not his own career
but that of his closest friend, Arjay Miller. Lundy was too diffident to be
out front, but Miller, he believed, was perfect for the top job—good with
people, the perfect manager, skilled in numbers. What could be better
than Miller as the top man and Lundy quietly in the background lending
his support? Lundy became a sort of adopted member of the Miller family,
an extra uncle for the Miller children. The Millers and Lundy took their
vacations together, and as deftly as he could in the critical years when
they were all going up the ladder, Lundy talked up Miller and made sure
that his own people made Arjay look good. When Miller was made president in 1963, Lundy was delighted. But a few years later, in one of those
frequent power shifts that made Ford such an interesting and terrifying
place to work, Henry Ford surprised everyone and replaced Miller. Miller
himself took the news with some equanimity, but Lundy was devastated,
and some friends worried about his health. Eventually he reconciled himself to what had happened and stayed on.

When the Whiz Kids first arrived in Detroit, Arjay Miller had decided
that Ed Lundy was the one who would probably stay the shortest time,

that the automotive world was too harsh and crude a place for him. Ed, thought Miller, was more likely to end up in academia or one of the foundations, slightly sheltered from the more predatory qualities of American business. He was, Miller thought, the brightest of them all, though McNamara from the start was clearly the most ambitious. When they all first arrived at Ford, they had undergone three days of extremely difficult tests. It had been hard on all of them; the tension and stress had been evident. Only Lundy had seemed immune to the pressure; he would finish his exams long before the others and then calmly leave the room while everyone else still struggled.

Born in Clarion, Iowa, and a graduate of Iowa University, he had taught at Princeton before the war, a popular professor there. During the war, as he and the others did statistical control for the air force, there had always been the feeling that he was intellectually the most superior of the group. Lundy's first job was to brief General H. H. Arnold, chief of the Army Air Forces, every morning at four-thirty. The young statisticians were aware that in having Hap Arnold as their boss they were blessed, for he listened to them carefully and trusted them and did not make fun of them, as he might have, for being a bunch of green kids who had never flown a fighter or a bomber. When Tex Thornton decided to take his team and sell it to industry, Lundy went along, somewhat to the surprise of the others, who assumed that he would return to Princeton. Arjay Miller was sure Lundy had merely come as a favor to the rest and would quickly tire of Detroit. What the others had not yet understood, and perhaps not even Lundy, was that at Ford he had found a home.

He emerged over the years as the secret power in the Ford Motor Company. No one knew that it was happening, that he was accruing that much power, until it had happened. One reason he was so successful at what he did was that there was an absolute ceiling on his ambition. He never longed to be president of the company. Being chief financial officer was enough. He never professed to know public taste or anything about styling. He had his beloved numbers and that was enough. He knew how to use them. But the main reason, the basis of his empire, was his control over the company's hiring and personnel policies. Year after year Ed Lundy and his deputies went out and hired the top graduates of the nation's best business schools and brought them to Ford. Then, if they passed his own tests, if they were the right type, he worked to guide their careers, moving them into better jobs in the most critical areas.

He liked to test his new men very early. If he called one on an interoffice squawk box, that man had sixty seconds to be in Lundy's office. When a young man joined the company, Ed Lundy looked him over very carefully.

It was one thing to examine the scores and recommendations from his old friends at the business schools, but it was another thing to see for himself what the young man was like, whether there was the proper mix of both ambition and self-control. Would he be confident but not cocky? Would he believe in the company and readily accept its systems, or was there too much ego there? Would his wife be an acceptable adjunct member of the team? So it was that, early on, a new man was informed by Lundy's secretary that it was considered incumbent upon him and his wife to invite Lundy to dinner. There was, the secretary explained, a certain regimen to this. Mr. Lundy would arrive at a specified time. He would have one drink. Then he would sit down to dinner. He would leave, she explained, at a certain time. Those evenings would be filled with small talk which was not really small talk at all, but chatter of the most consequential sort. For Ed Lundy was testing out the young families, trying to find out what he had gotten for the Ford Motor Company. The highest compliment of all was if Lundy, a few days after a newcomer and his family had endured the dinner test, told the employee's superior, "I like the cut of that young man. I'm going to keep my eye on him."

He did indeed keep his eye on those who had impressed him. If he liked something that someone had done, he would take a three-by-five card and on it inscribe a short message of praise, each word carefully chosen. These cards were cherished. The Lundy eye was also quick to discern an offender. He was a somewhat stern chaplain, a kind of farm-belt Catholic moralist, as one friend put it. When one of his young finance men started an affair with a woman in the office, Lundy was furious. He called the young man's boss and said very evenly, "Get him out of here," and the man was sent to a distant place. That Lundy was passing on a morality to those below him not necessarily observed by the man he worked for did not seem to matter. To him, Henry Ford's occasionally erratic behavior was a practical problem. If one of Lundy's protégés was going to take a job with Ford overseas, he would take the man aside and impart the most sacred and secret of warnings. This was difficult for Lundy, because it involved a conflict of loyalties; in order to protect his progeny he had to be critical of his superior. Before he gave the warning, his eyes would go to the door to be sure that no one could hear. Then he would speak, almost sadly. "Mr. Ford likes to come and visit the foreign offices," he would say, "and Mr. Ford, as you know, is a very fine man. A very fine man. But the moment he lifts his first glass with liquor in it is a very good time for you to disappear as quickly as you can."

The young MBAs just starting out knew that the best jobs were those that brought them in daily contact with Ed Lundy. One of the most coveted positions was handling Ed Lundy's personal clipping service. The job required that the young man be at work by six-thirty each morning so that a complete digest of that morning's press was on Lundy's desk by seven-thirty. The task was prized not because the work itself was interesting—it was just clip-and-paste—but because it offered daily access to Lundy. The privilege was passed on annually to another bright acolyte, and when a young man was so anointed, his envious and stricken contemporaries had to be assured by their superiors that their failure to get this job did not mean that their careers were damaged; there was still hope for them.

An equally prized job was that of the young man who ran the projector. He would be at all the critical meetings, he would see how the top executives dealt with each other, he might easily make powerful connections. "He who runs the projector runs the company," went the saying at Ford, and finance always ran the projector. The down side of that job was that Lundy was, of course, a taskmaster, and he demanded perfection in a presentation. A typo in a slide or a flub during a presentation was unacceptable. Thus the night before a major presentation was a nerve-shattering time, as the projectionist sweated to make sure there would be no slip-ups. Once one of them put a slide in upside down, and the fallout lasted for weeks. It was spoken of not as a mistake but as a potentially ruined career.

He had elaborate rules for financial presentations. Some of them were his, and some had been handed down by his predecessor, Ted Yntema, and embellished by him. The word "employee," for example, must always be written with only one "e" at the end. Ford must always be referred to in a presentation as "The Company." No infinitives could be split. As long as Ed Lundy was with the Ford Motor Company, it was never "under these circumstances," it was always "in these circumstances." Something would be "compared with," not "compared to." The phrase "due to" was not to be used, since "due," he liked to say, was a word used in connection with library books; similarly the word "current" as a synonym for "present" was barred, for a current was a river. Sentences were not to start with the word "however." He kept a Webster's dictionary on his desk, the classic Second Edition, not the Third, for he thought the editors had corrupted the Third. Once during a critical meeting to consider an expenditure of more than $100 million, a young staff member was startled to find that the principal issue between Lundy and one of his top deputies, Will Caldwell, also a grammarian, was not the topic at hand but the proper use of "which" and "that."

Lundy was a great blue-penciler, working on other people's copy, correcting them both on paper and in person. Marvin Runyon, then a young manufacturing man, once went in to see him. "Mr. Lundy," he said, "we have this problem, and we have three alternatives to it." "No, you don't," Lundy answered. "You have two alternatives or three choices." A book for presentation was to be ready forty-eight, not forty-nine, hours before the presentation. It would be bound in black, and it would have three rings. Over the top and bottom ring hole on each sheet (but not the middle hole), paper reinforcing doughnuts must be pasted, and the brightest young men out of the nation's business schools had all done their tours sticking the doughnuts on the pages. When anything was taped into a backup book, the tape had to extend along the entire length of the piece of paper; it was not enough to put tape on the corners. The tabs that were used as dividers were also important; dividers themselves could not be used, because Lundy did not like them. A red tab was for a major section, pink was for an important subtopic, and clear tabs were for backup items. That allowed him to flip through his book quickly during a meeting. To Lundy, this was no idle drill. Presentations were a source of power. Those who presented well dominated meetings. "Manage by presentation," he told his young men, and by that he meant that the way in which they laid out their figures and graphs should lead an audience to the right and inevitable conclusion.

Not only the graphs but the young men themselves should look right for a meeting. Their clothes were always to be a little better than the clothes of men from other departments—that was important to Lundy. If one of his junior men was going to make a presentation, Lundy checked out his attire. If a man's tie was a little flashy—inappropriate, he would say—Lundy reached into his own desk drawer, where he kept a small supply of ties, and selected one that was appropriate. Thus, uniform in attitude, the Lundy men became uniform in appearance. In a company where clothes had once meant nothing—whose founder wore a dark suit and a stiff collar, so that he and all those who dressed like him looked as if they were equally ready to go to work or a funeral—clothes now became important. They were a statement of background and purpose and finesse and especially class—softer of cloth, narrower of lapel, quieter of pattern. Time and money and thought went into them, for they were an advertisement; they said that the wearer had been to the right schools, was well connected in the company, and had a promising future. The Lundy Look, some of the nonfinance people called it; one of them, Ben Bidwell, had his own word for these men—"suits," he called them. Years later, after he had left Ford to go to Chrysler, he scanned a list of rising Chrysler executives and picked them out: "This guy's a suit. . . . This one's okay. . . . He's a suit. . . . He's good. . . . He's a suit. . . ."

For over twenty-five years Lundy filled the company with his people, highly intelligent and highly motivated men who knew systems and understood how to apply them in the most forceful way. His was by far the best-organized and most disciplined group within the company. That discipline came from Lundy himself; he was able to instill his principles in the younger men, to minimize rivalries among them. Thus his wing was never faction-ridden. He made sure that earlier generations of Lundy protégés took care of succeeding ones. The older Lundy protégés were happy to annex the younger ones, for it was a sign of a rising star that he could get good people to work for him. They formed a company within a company. They knew both their place and their status, and those who were successful mastered the art of moving swiftly but cautiously up the company's rungs, careful not to get ahead of themselves and become threatening to their superiors. It was said of one ambitious young finance man that on the day he received word of his vice-presidency, he drove out of the Glass House parking lot and headed straight for a real estate office where he put his house up for sale and inquired about prices of what would surely be an even grander house in Bloomfield Hills.

Their loyalties were not to cars but to careers, their own and those of the men they served. They had all been to the same schools—if not to one of the best Eastern schools, then at least to a very good business school. (Harvard Business School was the desired one, and a Baker Scholar from Harvard was better than a non–Baker Scholar, just as a Sloan Scholar from MIT was better than a non–Sloan Scholar. Fred Secrest, one of Lundy's deputies, kept a small card in his pocket with the number of Harvard Business School graduates in the company tallied on it. "Freddy," Iacocca once chided him, "why don't you keep a card with the sales figures on it?") They had the same connections both within and outside the company, they had their own channels of communication, their own codewords. Within the company they were known as part of the Lundy School of Economics, or, for short, the Lundy School. "It's a fraternity, Lee," Charley Beacham, Lee Iacocca's sponsor, once told him, "a closed Greek fraternity, and there's no place for people like you or me in it." The members were Ed's boys; they served, and in turn they would be served.

Year after year he consolidated his power, pushing his people into increasingly meaningful slots. He sulked if someone criticized the performance of one of them, and even Henry Ford tried to be tactful. If he had to pass a message to Lundy through another executive which somehow reflected poorly on a finance man, he would take the executive aside and say, "Now for God's sake, be gentle with Lundy—I don't want him upset. You know he's so damn sensitive about things like this." If any of his people had to be disciplined, then the problem was taken to him, so he could do the disciplining.

The company's personnel charts were marked with green tape to designate employees who were outstanding. An exceptional number of Lundy's people, because they were smart but also because they were doing each other's personnel reports, were graded outstanding and had strips of green by their names on their charts. There was noticably less green in the charts from the other departments, which irritated some. When Iacocca or one of the others challenged Lundy about the green awarded one of his boys, he grew immediately defensive. "Of course he's green, he's one of my best people," he would answer. (Later, after Iacocca and his team of ex-Ford men went to Chrysler, all of them in their minds victims of the finance people, they would on occasion talk about a young man at Chrysler, and one of them would say, "He's a green-tape guy." It was not a compliment. It was their shorthand for a man seriously overrated.)

If Lundy thought an area of the Ford company was undermanned by finance people, he would move some of his better people in there. He kept a close score of how many of his troops had gone on to other divisions and other companies, and each Lundy man who went on and did well was a feather in his cap, one more acknowledgment that he turned out the best people in the country. The nation's headhunters, always searching for an able, restless young man to run some company, loved Lundy, for his reports on the men he had employed were detailed and unbiased, and the discipline they had had was a given. Lundy was intensely proud of his people, and he did not mind sharing them with other divisions and even other companies, particularly the men who were not on his absolute A list. But he did not like poaching; the movement of talent had to be done on his terms. In the late sixties, Xerox, a rising company looking for talent, took what Lundy considered too many Ford people. Lundy refused to forgive either Xerox or the men who left. Though the amount of paperwork generated by the finance people was prodigious and required endless copying, he refused to let his staff use a Xerox machine. Instead they had to use a much more primitive device called an Ozalid, which was less efficient and, among other shortcomings, did not collate the papers it copied.

To Lundy the growth of his cadre meant that the company was more

disciplined than ever before, that its processes were more rational, and
that therefore it would make fewer mistakes. He and his people regarded
it as their mission to slow down the creative people and make them think
twice. Others in the company took a different view. Lundy had built his
power base too well, they thought. Where there had once been a system
of checks and balances, now, because of the growth of finance, there were
too many checks.

Lundy's growing power was a reflection of Henry Ford's conservatism.
More and more, Ford feared the risks and wanted to preserve what he
already had, for himself and for his family. That made Lundy's the welcome
voice; he was the one who was always talking about preserving the company, while the product men like Iacocca and Frey always seemed to be
talking about risking it. He had still another strength: He could speak with
authority on what Wall Street would think of a particular course of action.
That was the ultimate power. If there was a meeting and the product
people were pushing for a sizable expenditure, Ed Lundy would often say
what the impact would be on Wall Street. Invariably, it seemed, the Street
preferred the Ford Motor Company to save rather than spend its resources. "If we do that, Mr. Ford," he would say, "the market won't like
it," or merely, "The stock will go down." For the product men, it was the
unanswerable pronouncement, what they privately called the doomsday
argument.

It was Lundy who defined the postwar culture of the Ford Motor Company. The newcomers were conventional in their thinking, ambitions, and
behavior, but they were also quick and verbal. They were especially good
at sensing the mood of the company. They could tell whose star was on
the rise, and whose descending. They knew the various tracks within the
company, which ones were fast and which ones were slow, and whose
bandwagon they should hitch on to. The one thing you should never do,
they warned each other, was go to the plants or into the hinterland. It
was as if a key part of their code was that in order to succeed it was
important to stay as far away as possible from the reality of the company.
To the top men in finance, talent was its own reward, and there could
never be enough bright young brains. Lundy and his colleagues seemed
to hire two MBAs where one was enough. If nothing else, that heightened
the competition among them. To someone like Lundy, so sure of what he
was doing for the Ford Motor Company, the more gifted young finance
disciples the company had, the better. But to those from other divisions
who crossed paths with them, something was amiss. Too much manpower
was being applied too far from the real business at hand. They were putting

too much effort into gamesmanship, into making themselves and finance look good at the expense of other divisions, and at the possible expense of Ford.

For their loyalty was channeled not so much to Ford as to finance. In the early sixties, Iacocca took Paul Lorenz, a smart young man from finance, under his wing in the parts-and-services division. It was a particularly difficult and important part of the company's operation, and Lorenz did well there and showed an aptitude for the job. When his tour was up, Iacocca suggested that he might want to stay around and work there some more. "I'd like to," Lorenz answered, "but I can't." Why not? Iacocca had pushed him. "If I do," Lorenz replied, "I'll lose my union card." It was important for an ambitious executive to get back to headquarters and rejoin the finance people and be seen again. Visibility was crucial. The boondocks might be where the cars were made, but they were death on careers. When Steve Miller, a comer in finance, thought he might like to work for Ford in Mexico for a few years, because it would be more exciting and there would be more to learn, his superior frowned on the idea, for it would remove him—at least momentarily—from the pecking order. The best I can promise you, he told Miller, is that when you come back you can have your old job back. "Sometimes," said Phil Caldwell, eventually Ford's president and himself very much a product of that system, "I think that the problem with the Ford Motor Company is that we are growing too many sunflowers, flowers with big heads who rise too high seeking the sun at the expense of all else."

They were the right men for the era. Starting in the late fifties and then more rapidly in the sixties and the seventies, Ford and companies like it promoted men who would conserve what existed, rather than men who would risk what they had for an increasingly expensive shot at gaining even more. The growing power of the finance people made the creative people more vulnerable than ever. For the creative people always, no matter how good they were, made mistakes. No product man was perfect; for every model that was a success, there were others best forgotten. By contrast, the finance men were careful. They were never identified with a particular product. They never had to create anything. In meetings they attacked but never had to defend, while the product people defended and could never attack. Once Iacocca told Lundy, "Ed, the great thing about being in finance is, you don't have to worry about ten-day reports, you don't have to worry about sales, you don't have to worry about design, you don't have to worry about manufacturing breakdowns—just what is it you guys do for a living?" But Iacocca made sure when he chided Lundy like this that there was no one else around. Criticism of finance or of Lundy, even light joking, was permissible, but never in front of anyone else.

He came to be a man apart. He even had his own chair in the Ford executive dining room. Everyone else, even Henry Ford, took a chair at random as he filed in. Not J. Edward Lundy. Over the years he had managed, without anyone's realizing it, to do what no one else had done—he had staked out his own chair. (A few of the older, more senior people knew why—Lundy had trouble with his eyes and liked to sit with his back to the glare from the window—but most did not know and simply accepted it.) No one dared to walk in and occupy that chair. If he hadn't arrived, the others left his seat vacant. If it was positively known Lundy was out of town, someone might eventually take the seat, but timorously. It was only a chair in an executive lunchroom, a small thing, but it was also an extraordinary manifestation of power.

Lundy was the one Whiz Kid who stayed the whole course. Of the original group, both McNamara and Arjay Miller had made president, but McNamara served for only a few weeks, and Miller's term was comparatively brief and uneventful. Lundy made it all the way through, and, more than either of them, he put his stamp on the Ford Motor Company. That he could hold so much power for so long surprised men who had in the earlier years underestimated him. In the end it was a reflection of the age of the company, the need to preserve and conserve rather than to create, and the fact that he represented, in the most personal way, the Ford family interest. That was critical. For Henry Ford was not just the head of the Ford Motor Company but the head of the Ford family and the conservator of its interests. Ed Lundy was his life-support system. Lundy's job was to protect Ford. He knew the company, he had no other loyalty, he had none of the raging ambition of an Iacocca or the troublesome talent of a Don Frey, and he would spend as little Ford money as possible. Lundy and Ford were on the phone all the time, and Henry Ford checked out everything with Ed Lundy. Everything. They were not close socially, and Lundy avoided social occasions in Detroit and the foreign trips as much as he could, fearing, his friends suspected, what would happen when Henry Ford started to drink, and the sudden cruelty of Ford's tongue. But most in the company knew how much Henry Ford trusted Lundy, and for those who did not there were constant indications. It was clear, for example, that before every important meeting Lundy and Ford had caucused, that to a large degree the decisions had been made by these two men even before the meeting started. Once it convened, Henry Ford would turn to Lundy and say, "Well, Ed, as we were just saying . . ." or Lundy would turn to Ford and say, "Of course, Mr. Ford, you know my position on this . . ." No one else in the company had that access and that trust, and thus no one else in the company had that much power.

Even his opponents respected Lundy. He was a man of goodwill. Product men who thought that the power of the finance people was pernicious nevertheless believed that in contrast to McNamara, he was a fair man. He did not bully those who disagreed with him. He did not, as McNamara did, load the questions so that there was only one answer. (There were, it was believed, few honest answers given at Ford during McNamara's years because there were few honest questions.) He had none of McNamara's overwhelming ambition. McNamara had ruled by the force of his personality, often intimidating the people beneath him; Lundy ruled by kindness—almost, one critic thought, by love. That he was pledged to the greater good of the company there was no doubt. He was decent and fair, but the system he created was not.

PART
FIVE

PART
FIVE

14.
THE
GAIJIN TEACHERS

The Japanese had always been good students. The Japanese way was to find the foreign expert, listen to him, learn everything they could, and then adapt the information to Japanese needs and dimensions. The earliest teachers at Nissan had been Americans, most particularly an extraordinary man named William R. Gorham. In terms of technology, Gorham was the founder of the Nissan motor company. In 1983, sixty-five years after he first arrived in Tokyo and thirty-five years after his death, young Nissan engineers who had never met him spoke of him as if he were a god and could describe in detail his years at the company and his many inventions.

Gorham was an American original, the inventor and mechanical engineer as missionary. He was a man who loved to tinker in an age when tinkering with mechanical devices was at the center of an exciting and expanding new industrial order. As a boy of fourteen, in 1902, he took a simple engine from a lawnmower and grafted it to a child's wagon, thus creating his own self-propelled, motorized wagon. Coming to his maturity at the time of World War I, he judged that as an inventor he was too late for the auto industry, and he concentrated on airplanes instead. He developed a water-cooled aircraft engine that he considered a breakthrough, and he was disappointed when American industrialists took little notice of it or him.

His father, a traveling salesmen, had worked the Orient, selling the Chinese rubber for their bikes and oil for their lamps. He loved to boast that he had sold them two million pounds of rubber erasers before they even had pencils. He had taken his young son William with him on a sales visit to Japan, and the country had made a strong impression on the boy, one that had lasted into adulthood. Frustrated by lack of recognition in the United States, he decided that Japan would be more receptive to his work. He answered an ad run by the Japanese government for engineers to design fighter planes, and in 1918 he took his wife, Hazel, and his two infant sons and moved to Japan. By the time he arrived in Tokyo, the war was over, and the Japanese no longer wanted fighter planes. But, he would later claim, since he didn't have the money for the voyage home, he and his family stayed on. He liked the society immediately, the civility and subtle courtesies of daily Japanese existence, and he liked being treated as a great American mechanical guru. A Christian Scientist, he approved of Japanese personal qualities: They were industrious, careful, not wasteful, and serious about their work. They were also good at obeying, and Gorham was a man who liked to be obeyed and obeyed quickly.

Gorham's airplane engine did not turn out to be a success, and the Japanese aircraft industry was too weak to support him, so Gorham looked for other challenges. He saw the streets filled with rickshaws and decided they were not an acceptable way to travel in the modern age, so he invented the Gorham Motorized Rickshaw, a three-wheeler with a simple engine. It was an immediate success not only in Japan but throughout Southeast Asia. At one point he moved his family to Kyushu, the southernmost of the four main islands, where they lived very simply. At first the local school officials refused to admit the Gorham children, claiming they had no capacity for educating foreigners. But Hazel Gorham was made of stern stuff, and she stared them down, and the school had its first gaijin (foreign) students. On the Gorham boys' first day of school, it was snowing and bitter cold. When the two little boys arrived, wearing their leather shoes, the principal met them at the door and told them if they were going to attend a Japanese school they would dress like Japanese, and he sent them home to get the wooden getas that all the Japanese children wore. That was their welcome; it was to be an austere, disciplined childhood, both in school and at home.

Their father, having invented the mechanized rickshaw, then built a diesel engine for Japanese fishing boats. His legend grew. There was nothing, it was said, that this American could not do, and more important, no one that he would turn away. He was a new kind of god, an American mechanical god who had come to help the Japanese. About that time, Yoshisuke Ayukawa, eager to start a Japanese auto industry, got in touch with him. Gorham immediately liked Ayukawa, and as it happened Gorham had already produced his own car, the Gorham-Shiki (or Gorham-style) automobile. It was, said one friend, like two bicycles stapled together with a small motorcycle engine between them. That car was a small success, selling about sixty units, enough to convince Gorham that he had the talent to design a very good workable car. He knew, however, that he lacked the patience and interest to market and sell his car. As early as 1921 he had begun working as a consultant for Ayukawa, and in the mid-twenties he was designing gas engines for boats and farm equipment for him. In the late twenties he started working with Ayukawa to design a small, inexpensive car. At that time the few cars being made in Japan were elaborate and expensive, for the very rich, but Ayukawa had long dreamed of a car like the Model T, which the average citizen of Japan could afford. Gorham responded enthusiastically, for he revered Henry Ford. Gorham's son later remembered countless family dinner conversations about Ford. No one dared praise a GM car around Gorham; people who bought GM cars were fools. "Too many cooks spoiling that soup," he would say disdainfully of GM. When Ford was about to unveil the Model A, it was as if Gorham himself were having a baby.

Gorham and Ayukawa needed a considerable amount of professional help in their venture—Gorham was talented but he could not run an entire automobile factory—and they needed to build a manufacturing line. So Gorham took off for America in 1932, hired Americans to come out and to help and teach the Japanese at every level. Not only would his countrymen be well paid, he emphasized, but their work would be appreciated, and they would be listened to as they had never been before. There was George Motherwell, a specialist in forging, and Harry Marshall, a Ford man, and others. Gorham also wandered around looking for manufacturing equipment. In Detroit in those days companies opened and closed regularly, and Gorham visited the recently defunct Graham-Paige plant, looked it over, and with Ayukawa's consent purchased its manufacturing line and machinery. Everything was broken down, then packed up and sent to Japan. It all was reassembled in Japan, and Japan had its first auto assembly line. A year later, in 1933, the first Datsun, a car almost completely designed by an American, William Gorham, came off that line, the forerunner of millions of others.

Of the American car men only Gorham stayed on. He and his family led a Japanese life and ate Japanese food, even though he never learned to speak very much Japanese; the Gorham sons spoke Japanese and played with Japanese kids, particularly the Ayukawa children, to whom Hazel Gorham taught English. Gorham was fond of Ayukawa, a man who understood not just engineering but how to be creative and entrepreneurial within something as clumsy and conservative as a zaibatsu. Ayukawa, in turn, loved Gorham, a man who was afraid of no challenge, tried to do everything perfectly, and wanted remarkably little for himself.

Gorham went on to invent hundreds of things, many of which were widely used in Japan, but he never made very much money off his inventions, because he was not interested in money. Instead he loved the doing of it, and the value that the Japanese placed on what he did. He took pleasure in being around men who were so passionate about engineering and who wanted to learn everything. He loved the way the Japanese paid attention to everything he said, but he often despaired of them because their manufacturing capability constantly fell short of what he felt they should be able to do. Time after time he would think they were finally ready to do something on their own, and then they would come apart at the critical moment. There was, he often told his sons, an almost fatal lack of confidence on the part of the Japanese. They had at once so much skill and ability and so little confidence that he wondered if they would ever make it into the modern industrial century.

In the mid-thirties, as the Japanese military rose to power, things changed, and Japan began to pull back inside itself. The military, it became obvious, did not want Nissan building a Japanese people's car, it wanted trucks instead, and so auto assembly came to a halt. Ayukawa went to Manchuria and played an important role in the development of the heavy industrial projects that the new imperial Japan wanted there. He asked Gorham to work with him, and for the first time Gorham turned down his friend. (Ayukawa was judged after the war to be a Class A war criminal; he was purged from Nissan, but later, as the governmental policy changed, he managed to spend some time in the Japanese Diet.) The late thirties were a hard time for Gorham; he saw that war was coming, and that he was going to be caught between his two countries. On one of his buying trips back in America he argued Japan's case with American businessmen. He was opposed to the rise of the Japanese military, but he believed that American pressures on Japan, the trade restrictions, were simply playing into the hands of the jingoists, with nationalism in one country begetting nationalism in the other. It was a sad time.

In 1940 his older son, William, was studying at Cal Tech, but his younger son, Don, was still in Japan, just finishing Tokyo Imperial University. Gorham took him aside. "Your mother and I," he said, "have thought about this a lot. We think there's going to be a war with the United States. Our lives are here. Our friends are here. We would like to live here and die here. This is our choice. We have thought about it a great deal. I am going to take out citizenship soon, but I will wait until you are safely back in America." Just before Don Gorham returned to the United States, he went to say goodbye to Ayukawa. "As long as Ayukawa's eyes remain black," said the older man, meaning that as long as he was alive, "I give you my personal guarantee that nothing will happen to your father." Young

Gorham burst into tears, left Japan, and, like his brother, served with naval intelligence during the war.

His father did become a Japanese citizen and took a Japanese name, Katsundo Goahamu. (Katsundo meant conqueror, and Donald Gorham thought the name meant William Gorham the conqueror.) He and his wife were put under house arrest after Pearl Harbor, but the gentlest house arrest imaginable; they were allowed maximum privileges, there was no harassment, and they were given double the normal food rations. Though Gorham technically did not work for Nissan anymore, Ayukawa continued to pay his salary throughout the war. There were also constant conferences at the Gorham house between William Gorham and Ayukawa and his younger engineers about how to make better machine tools for Japanese industry—which was, of course, the Japanese military machine. He started by helping design machine tools, and then having taken that first step, he was pulled along in tiny increments. Soon he was designing planes. He rationalized it by stressing to himself that they were only training planes, but the requests for more and more participation never abated. It was all done very skillfully; Ayukawa was under pressure from his superiors, and from time to time he would let Gorham know that unless Gorham did a little more, Ayukawa would be the one who would suffer. It always worked, of course.

As soon as the war was over, Gorham turned himself in to American authorities and reported very accurately what he had done during the war. He told his son Don that he had been caught up in circumstances beyond his control. He also volunteered to help the Americans should they need technical help in the rebuilding of Japan's industry. The American authorities decided not to charge him with being a traitor; he had, after all, been a Japanese citizen. Indeed, they were unusually understanding. Within a few months he was working in liaison with MacArthur headquarters on industrial problems. He died in Tokyo in 1949. At the end of his life he was helping old friends at Canon on their new cameras, as part of the preparation for Japan's first major industrial conquest of America.

If Gorham had found the Japanese willing students in the prewar days, then his lineal descendants, those Americans who came to Tokyo after the war, found them even more attentive. The defeat at the hands of the Americans, and in particular the obvious superiority of American technology, had proved to the Japanese that they knew nothing and that they had everything to learn. That was their greatest asset, that and the traditional belief that it was quite proper to go to the foreigners, be they Chinese or Westerners, and find out whatever it was that they did better, bring it back, and Japanize it. Starting in the fifties, Nissan, like so many other Japanese companies, began importing experts to Tokyo and exporting teams to America to study what the Americans did and how they did it. America was the land where everything worked. The Americans thus would be the teachers, and the Japanese would be the students. Japan's only resource was its people, dutiful, obedient, disciplined, educated, eager to restore their nation to greatness. The key to modern greatness was industrial strength. There was no arrogance to the Japanese in those days. If anything they were too humble, too ready to seize on any American and credit him with omniscience. All Americans were experts.

In 1955 when Donald Stone, a retired engineer from Willys-Overland, was brought to Nissan to lecture on engines, all the Nissan engineers were very excited. Nissan had scouted around carefully and checked Stone out, and there was no doubt that he had excellent credentials, that he was one of the most knowledgeable men on the subject. The Japanese engineers were even more pleased when Stone showed up. Though he was small for an American, almost Japanese in size, he looked the part, rather tweedy and professorial, which was appropriate, because the engineers expected him to run the equivalent of a small university for them. That way they would know all the American secrets.

They were soon disappointed in Stone. They had expected fifteen lectures in fifteen categories—a lecture on the carburetor, a lecture on the crankshaft, a lecture on the ignition system, and so on. But it became clear that Stone, professorial though he might look, had almost no interest in lecturing them. He appeared bored with his lectures, delivering them in a weary monotone, rushing through them. What he really wanted to do was to go to their factory floor and discover their problems. The Nissan people were about to get a critical lesson in American engineering: The Americans were not very theoretical. Stone, it turned out, was a brilliant teacher, but not of the sort the Japanese expected. He was not a man of theory but a man of practice, and he believed that the best place to learn and to teach was not the classroom but the workplace.

The Japanese had always heard about American pragmatism, and now they were witnessing it. Every day after he had raced through his lecture Stone called the Japanese around him informally and asked them what their problems were. At first they were shy about speaking up, but then gradually they became less so. They were, after all, engineers speaking to engineers, and Stone was easy to talk to. There was no superiority in his manner. What are your problems? he would ask. Well, a Japanese engineer would say hesitantly, the crankshaft keeps bending. So they would go off to the Yokohama factory where the crankshafts were made, and they would inspect it, and Stone would make them explain what had gone wrong, and then, patiently, he would prod them into coming up with ideas for correcting the problem. He was teaching them that engineering advanced by small degrees, always based upon performance. He was also teaching them that they were better at their jobs than they thought, that all they lacked was confidence. He repeated to them again and again his basic approach: Find out what was wrong, try to understand why it had gone wrong, and then break down the corrective process into modest steps.

At the time Stone arrived, Nissan was preparing to develop a brand-new engine for a smaller car. The smaller car would be used for domestic consumption and possibly for export, though at the time that prospect seemed distant. The dream of a new Nissan-designed engine was an old one. After the war, as Nissan began to resurrect itself, it had reluctantly concluded that its technology was too limited, its engineers too inexperienced, to design its own engine, and that it would have to find one overseas. Genshichi Asahara, who was both president of Nissan and its senior science executive, had thought first of the Americans, who had been so generous to other struggling Japanese industries, such as steel. But an automotive marriage with the Americans was difficult; their cars were too big, and their engines burned too much gas. Volkswagen was interested in a deal, but Asahara was not. The VW had an air-cooled engine, he pointed out, and Japanese engineers would be more familiar with a water-cooled engine. Some thought his reasons were more complicated, that he was reluctant to make another German-Japanese tie-up so soon after the war. Shortly thereafter he chose Austin. In 1952 he went to England to sign the licensing deal. In those days Austin was doing well, and British engineering and manufacturing were admired throughout the world. Asahara took a Nissan executive named Kanichi Tanaka with him. "It will be a little unpleasant going there," Asahara told Tanaka. "There may be some rudeness. It is not personal. It's just the British being British." Tanaka was awed by the size and splendor of the Austin plant. It was grander and more modern than anything he could have imagined. He also was aware of the hatred on the faces of the workers every time he walked through the plant. Looking at those faces, he knew the war was not yet over. But the men from Nissan came away with the rights to the Austin engine, and it was the right one—a 1.5-liter engine, good, solid, and dependable. "Now we have our start," Asahara told Tanaka on the way home.

But now Nissan wanted a smaller engine for a smaller car. Yet, only two years after the great strike, the company was still short of funds and short of technological resource. The Nissan engineers asked Stone for his help. "You don't need a new engine," Stone said, to their surprise. "You've already got the perfect engine for what you want." Which engine was that? one of the Japanese engineers asked. "The engine you've already got," he answered. "The Austin. All you have to do is to adjust the size. You can use the same basic engine and the same manufacturing line and save yourselves a lot of money. As I understand it, you don't have a lot of money to throw around."

No one believed him, so he began to explain. They had a good basic engine. They need only to change it a little. Stone studied the engine for a few days and recommended that since they wanted to go from a 1500cc engine to a 1000cc, the way to do it would be to shorten the stroke—the distance the piston traveled from one end of its motion to the other. Since the stroke was currently 89mm long, it should be shortened by one third to 59mm. The shorter stroke would create a less powerful engine for a lighter car. It would save them manufacturing costs just as it would save the consumers gas. Stone was adamant about this solution, but no one believed him, because it seemed unlikely that the company could get so much for so little. Stone insisted on a demonstration. They worked on it, cutting the engine down as he suggested, and to their amazement, he was absolutely right. It did everything he said it would, and it allowed them to go into production much sooner than they had anticipated. It saved them a great deal of money. It was named, in his honor, the Stone Engine. It allowed Nissan to compete in the market for smaller cars. It also let Nissan enter America with an engine that could expand, in increments, as the American requirements demanded a larger and larger engine. Having shrunk their basic engine from 1500cc to 1000cc, the Japanese, who had become as practical as Stone had taught them to be, simply took that basic engine and built it back up again.

So it was that Nissan was finally ready to join in Japan's challenge to the West. Japan was ready for that challenge well before most Westerners could imagine. What looked to most Westerners like a poor, ravaged, helpless society was becoming, by the early fifties, a disciplined one with a singular sense of national purpose. Its leaders' vision had been surprisingly consistent. Even as World War II was ending, they were planning the nation's future. The dream of Japanese greatness through military power had proved a false and destructive one. The ashes of that dream were all around them. There had to be another path. Quickly a consensus evolved: Japan was so limited in size and natural resources, so vulnerable—as seen at Hiroshima and Nagasaki—to modern weaponry, that it could become strong only if it focused all of its energies on commerce and completely avoided military solutions.

In the dark days of the end of the war, Saburo Okita, who was to become one of the principal architects of the postwar Japanese economic miracle, remembered an old Japanese legend. It was about a man who wanted to become a great warrior. He spent all of his money on arms and shields instead of food; more and more burdened by the weight of his armament and ever weaker from lack of food, he was easily slain in combat. The moral was clear: Little Japan in a world of superpowers like the United States and the Soviet Union must conserve its energies and derive its power solely from its human and commercial strengths. It could waste nothing, and for any nation, particularly one so devoid of resources, military expenditures were a waste. Because he used an economist, Okita had known since 1941 that Japan's industrial production was declining every year, and thus had understood long before almost anyone else in the country that defeat was inevitable. As the war wound down, Okita and others, mostly young economists, had held clandestine meetings, slipping past the military police of a dying empire to plan the new Japan. Among the lessons of the immediate past, they realized, was the fact that the American victory had been based not on greater valor, though the Americans had fought bravely, but on technological supremacy. The new Japan must be highly modernized and mechanized. There might be some blessing in all the tragedy of defeat that was around them, Okita thought, for a new, highly industrialized, far more pragmatic society, one less burdened by ancient vainglorious myths, might rise in its place.

Most of the parts—at least the nonphysical parts—were already there. Japan was not like most other Asian nations, trying to escape a colonial past; it was fiercely independent, likelier to colonize than be colonized. It was well on its way to becoming an urban rather than an agricultural society. Its people adapted well to modern times; there was no problem, for example, in adjusting the birthrate to urban conditions. In addition, Japan had a highly developed public educational system, as good as those of the leading industrialized nations, and it would be easy enough to add on an additional element, a far greater engineering component for university students. The religion, unlike religions in some parts of the underdeveloped world, was not a hindrance to a society trying to enter a modern scientific world; the basic religion, Confucianism, was almost an educational system itself. It strengthened the role of teachers and helped confirm the power of the hierarchy in all aspects of daily life. The idea of *nation*, albeit badly shaken by the experiences of World War II, was still powerful, almost a religion itself, for Japan was innately cohesive; it was in truth a nation that, because of language, history, and geographical separation, thought of itself as a race. Thus all Japanese were apart from everyone else, and connected to each other and dependent on each other. In Japan, foreigners were not Russians or Americans or Frenchmen; they were first and foremost gaijin, *not one of us*. Though Japan might look ravaged to the Westerner, the essential tissue of the nation remained largely undamaged. If anything, postwar Japan was more cohesive, for the reforms imposed by the Americans made it more egalitarian, heightened the sense of economic and political justice, and diminished the often suffocating power of the old order. By the early fifties it was clear that the postwar Japan was a more equitable one. Men like Honda, with his own auto company, were unlikely to have emerged as major entrepreneurial industrialists in the prewar era.

The essential cohesiveness—the shared condition which bound all Japanese together—allowed economic architects like Okita, planning for the next ten years, to assume considerable sacrifices on the part of ordinary people, sacrifices that they unfailingly made. Certainly Japan was a country that at that moment lent itself to serious economic planning. But this was not just because the Japanese were dutiful and obedient. Rather it was because what Okita was planning—a kind of shared economic growth, good for the state, good for the citizen—was what the average Japanese wanted. Japan as a nation needed to be made strong and viable again, yet on the same agenda was a desire to let people lead better lives. That life for ordinary people soon improved in many small increments helped Okita and men like him immeasurably. Yet Japan often seemed perplexing to Westerners. By Western standards, it did not feel like a democracy. The Japanese seemed more cautious in their exercise of personal freedom than Westerners. Was this then a mock democracy, an essentially authoritarian country? How much free will was involved in all this?

The answer was not that the government of Japan was authoritarian, for it was not, but that the *condition* of Japan was authoritarian, harsh, unsparing. There were too many people on too small and unsympathetic a piece of land, there was too little to go around if individuals became too selfish. Given the contradiction between its physical condition and its intense ambitions, Japan would have to be either a carefully controlled communal society or a bitterly divided and selfish one. The only way the society could achieve greatness was if the average Japanese accepted considerable limits on his own possibilities. He had to give as much as he could and not ask for too much in return. What really restricted personal freedom in Japan was not so much the written laws as the unwritten covenants. For many talented Japanese these convenants were not always easy; one of them compared it to having a racing car but spending your life in a forty-five-mile-per-hour speed zone.

Japan was evolving its own unique form of state-guided communal capitalism. It was not the American variety; its roots were in Japanese communal traditions, and the obligation of the individual to the larger group. It reflected the belief that a largely uncontrolled capitalism such as existed in America might be ruinous for Japan, that without sufficient controls too few men would become too rich in too poor a nation. That would create intolerable tensions and divisions, so the state and the capitalists themselves had to regulate it. It was the job of the key government ministries to concentrate the nation's limited resource in areas where it could best serve Japan. Japan would be an industrialized capitalist society, but the capitalism must fit the needs and specifications of Japan.

In the postwar years, the leaders of Japan relied on this tradition, the communal nature of the nation, to build an extraordinary industrial base. The economic good of the nation was deftly balanced with the economic good of the individual. The good of the state would not deprive the individual of all personal expectations.

In Eastern Europe, as the state bureaucrats reinvested relentlessly in their own heavy industries, the workers felt that they were the servants, not the beneficiaries of the state, and the Communist economies, shorn of any true community on the part of the workers, began to stall of their own sluggishness.

By contrast, the men running Japan knew that consumer goods must eventually be available, there must be some material rewards and some incentives. The workers must also become good consumers. So it was that, starting in the early fifties, there was a sense of Japan's slowly entering into the middle class. The early postwar years, however, were ones of industrial rebuilding and of immense human sacrifice. The smokestack industries came first. All material comforts and pleasures had to wait while the railroad system and the steel, shipbuilding, and petrochemical industries were rebuilt.

The Japanese, like the Americans upon whose society they intended to model their own, wanted to belong to the oil age. That was a considerable challenge for a nation so poor that it could in the beginning barely afford to buy its first postwar barrels of oil. There was a time right after the war when Japan seemed caught in a vicious circle: To make steel the Japanese needed coal, and they were capable of mining just so much coal. The economy was barely able to sustain itself. Okita thought of Japan as a sick man with just enough food to stay alive but not enough to get well. Finally Yoshida, the prime minister, asked Okita to draft a letter to MacArthur asking for the right to buy twenty thousand tons of heavy oil to make steel. That would allow them to break out of the vicious circle. For several months they heard nothing from MacArthur's office. Then the word came back: Yes, the oil was available, and they could have it for the steel industry. It was, thought Okita, the first Allied decision on behalf of the new Japan. Until then there were fears that the Americans might require Japan to be a backward agrarian society and nothing more. This decision on the oil was the first signal that the Americans might allow Japan to industrialize.

In the beginning the state put its efforts into steel. Steel was essential to a developed industrial society. In 1853, Commodore Perry had sailed into Tokyo Harbor aboard what the Japanese forever after called "the black ships," and the era of Japan's isolation had ended. The black ships were made of steel, and they symbolized the gap between the mighty, advanced West and the backward, feudal Japan. For Japan was a shipping nation, and yet it lacked these powerful steel vessels, which were both carriers of trade goods and awesome new weapons of war. Perry's arrival meant to the Japanese that they had lost their most precious thing, their shipping rights. From then on the power of the steel men in Japan was unquestioned. Steel is the nation, went a Japanese saying. If the nation had a strong steel industry, then it would have a strong shipbuilding industry, and it would be a powerful, respectable nation again. Thus the efforts in the postwar years centered first and foremost on steel. The recovery did not come easily. At the end of the war only three of the nation's thirty-five blast furnaces were in operation, the others closed down as much from lack of raw material as from American bombs. The nation was poor, hard currency was limited, but the government poured much of its treasure into steel. By 1949 Japan had reached its prewar steel-production figures. But the steel was not yet of a particularly high grade, nor was it inexpensive; the postwar inflation kept the cost high. Yet the Japanese steel executives, supported by both government and banks, continued to put money into new plants; the result was an extraordinary modernization of an entire industry, gradual lowering of the price, and raising of quality, all of which would serve the Japanese well in international competition.

The key to this was something American executives, in competition with the Japanese, would come to hate. The great dependence of the Japanese companies on their banks, the high debt-to-earnings ratio that became a mark of Japanese business. As far back as 1949 some of the steel men had built new plants ahead of what the director of the Bank of Japan wanted; that of itself was remarkable, for defiance of the bank was rare indeed. But the steel men were different. It was as if they had even in those terrible years retained absolute belief in themselves and the future of their industry. Later that very same confidence was often perceived as arrogance, but at that perilous moment it was judged to be courage.

The huge debt assumed by the steel industry placed it under great stress, but by the middle of the decade the investment began to pay off. In the five years beginning in 1949, when Japanese steel regained its prewar volume, production doubled, and the plants were so modern that the steel was of very high quality. As productivity increased, the price went down. The Japanese, who always took a long-term view of their markets—selling at low prices in order to seize a maximum share—pushed ahead. For the first time the Western giants going against them realized what relentless competitors the Japanese could be. Given an advantage, they did not slow down but poured money back in and pressed even harder. By 1957, a mere eleven years after its devastation, Japan not only had the most modern steel mills in the world but was the foremost steel producer in the world. But that was just the beginning: In the decade following 1957, Japanese steel production grew by 170 percent—while the American steel industry grew only 20 percent. The American steel industry, believing itself invulnerable, was headed by a complacent and insular management which was slow to bring in modern technology and which, even as the challenger grew more proficient, locked the industry into ever costlier labor agreements. By 1964, 28 percent of Japan's steel exports was going to America. In Japan, a thrust in shipbuilding followed closely upon the success in steel; by 1956 Japan had replaced Britain as the world's leading shipbuilding nation.

A decade after the end of the war, Japan had created the base for the strongest and most modern core economy in history. The force of that economy was not yet obvious to ordinary Americans purchasing consumer goods, but anyone attuned to trends in heavy industry saw the surge as enormous. To the Japanese, the sacrifices seemed worth it.

From the start, even as the decisions had been made that steel and shipping must take precedence over all other industrial needs, the Japanese establishment had also decided to funnel its best young people into careers in engineering. The future, as World War II had proved, belonged not to a nation of artisans but to a nation that could mechanize its production. So men like Okita decided to create a great new university system with special emphasis on graduating engineers. Someone who wanted to study the liberal arts needed wealthy parents; someone who wanted to study science needed little help from his parents, for he had the friendship of the state. The basic educational system was already there, and Okita and his colleagues simply added the final dimension, a great new engineering complex which offered thousands and thousands of Japanese a chance to become the first college-educated members of their families, and to serve the nation at the same time. The nation's educational system, said the historian Frank Gibney, describing the rise of industrial Japan, was "the key that winds the watch."

The war had made the Japanese more eager than ever to accept outside ideas. What class restrictions there had been, subtle and powerful, had been somewhat loosened both by the loss of the war and by the egalitarian emphasis of the Americans. Perry Miller, the distinguished Harvard professor of English who taught a course on the Puritan past, went to Japan as a visiting professor in the summer of 1952 and was impressed by the degree to which the American occupation experience had intensified a puritan instinct already powerful among the Japanese. The Occupation policy, he wrote, "was an effort to make of Japan, a new Middle West— not, of course, the Middle West as it is, or in fact ever was, but as it perpetually dreams of being." The Japanese respected work, respected their elders and their superiors, were thrifty, and wanted desperately to get ahead. Education was the primary channel for that ambition. Since the Meiji era, beginning in 1844, there had been a strong tradition of poorer families using the educational system to climb in status. Where upper-class elites in other societies were wary of giving lesser classes access to education, Japan was different. In modern Japan the good of the nation was more important than the good of the class. A poor but talented and diligent boy had a chance to rise as high as he could. The status of an elementary-school teacher in a village was, in the postwar years, far greater than that of a teacher in a comparable American small town. The educational system was critical to the rise of modern Japan: It crystallized, legitimized, and modernized values already existing. It removed a great deal of potential class resentment on the part of the poor, and it provided Japan with an extraordinarily well-qualified, proud, amenable, and ambitious working class. If the modern postwar Japan was perhaps the world's most efficient distillation system, in which remarkably little was wasted, in human, material, or capital terms, then a vital part of it was the educational system: It supplied the nation with the right number of workers, the right number of engineers, and the right number of managers for every need of a modern society, but, equally important, it brought to the poorest homes the sense that there were better possibilities for the children.

Not only did these new workers have very good basic schooling, particularly in mathematics, on a level well above their counterparts in American industry, but they were much more driven by social ambition. George DeVos, a Berkeley anthropologist who did psychological testing of workers throughout the world, was impressed by the results of his tests on the Japanese and other East Asian workers. They were astonishingly like the immigrants particularly the Jews, who had been successful in America; they were strivers, their children reflected the immense hopes and ambitions of their less privileged parents, they sought achievement in a society where achievement was honored, and they had been taught in their homes from a very early age that education was the key to their success. They were exceptionally well prepared for an industrial society that had become increasingly, if somewhat involuntarily, meritocratic. The values of these Japanese workers in the fifties and sixties were like the values which had been passed on to the children of American immigrants, values that these Americans, in their affluence, were no longer so successfully passing on to their own offspring.

In the postwar years the emphasis was on producing engineers—Okita and the men around him believed that was of the essence. The world in which Japan would compete was increasingly a technological one; it could compete only by capitalizing on the mathematical and scientific skills of its talented young and getting more and more of them into engineering schools. If the West produced scientists who were more original, the Japan would counter by producing more good competent engineers, proportionately to the size of its population, than any other industrialized country in the world. To encourage entry into engineering, all kinds of scholarships and other incentives were offered to promising young students. In the ten years after the war, Okita estimated, he doubled the number of engineering graduates.

Some thought of Okita as a barbarian for that, for downplaying the liberal arts, and he was on occasion cruelly caricatured in the press as a man who was corrupting Japan's traditional love of learning for commercial goals. His critics bitterly accused him of distorting the purpose of education, rather than serve the larger good of the nation, they said, he had changed it to serve the economy. He was creating a new functional state of functional people. Okita did not really dissent, for to his mind the economy at this moment in Japanese history was the nation. The kind of education his critics favored belonged to a languid, more privileged past, where the children of the rich could study French literature. The luxury of the liberal arts education could come later. It was better, he argued, to have a surplus in engineering students than a surplus in law graduates. It might be cheaper for the state to produce a law graduate, for providing an engineering degree to a peasant boy was an expensive matter. But the rewards were immense. Creating that many engineers, he said, meant that Japan could afford to keep its engineers right on the factory floor. They might work on something tiny, perhaps a task a good deal smaller than what they had dreamed of while they were students, but the cumulative effect of so many talented engineers working on so many small things would be incalculable. What he planned, of course, soon happened.

15.
THE ENGINEER

When he was a boy, he loved playing with model airplanes. It was the only pure thing of his life. All around him the world was collapsing, and the Japanese planes were disappearing from the sky, but his model planes were perfect and flew beautifully. Forty years later, telling a visitor about his childhood obsession, he would go to a cabinet in his living room and pull out his collection of model-airplane magazines of those years, carefully preserved, and show pictures of each plane he had so lovingly made. Going through his boyhood possessions, he also came across a notebook he had used in junior high school; on it was his name, and next to it he had written "engineer." There had never been any doubt in his mind that someday he would be an engineer.

Minoru Tanaka came from an ordinary background. His parents were relatively simple people of the middle class. They lived in a village outside Yokohama. His father had been the chauffeur of a member of the Diet, driving him around in one of Japan's early cars, and when the Diet member had died, his widow had given the car to Tanaka's father, who had driven it as a taxi and used the money he saved to buy other cars, first a Citroën, then a Ford, then a Plymouth, then a Chevrolet. He had gotten one of the early telephones and had run one of the country's first telephone taxi services. The only real expense was the cars; the drivers did not want a salary and refused to work for Tanaka's father if he insisted on paying them one. If they received a salary, the customers would know it and would not tip them, and they would end up making less money. By the start of the war the family was prosperous, Tanaka realized later; there was always money to spend on his model planes.

The drive for education had been implanted so early that he could not remember a time when it had not been important for him to excel. His mother, he said, was what the Japanese called an "education mama," one who ceaselessly pushed her child through school, her own ambition becoming the son's ambition. In the fourth grade he had been lucky to have

Takuzo Hiki as his teacher. Hiki, who was then twenty-three and a bachelor, had only two passions—baseball and mathematics. Of the seventy-two children in his class, the most talented was Minoru Tanaka. Hiki himself was gifted both in mathematics and as a teacher, but he was the second son of a farmer, and in his generation there was never going to be enough money to send him to college. His only chance was to become a teacher, and so he attended Kanagawa Teachers College. He longed to teach in a junior high school, where he could concentrate on math, but because of his limited background he was assigned to an elementary school, where he had to teach everything, including music. He even had to play the piano, a difficult assignment, since he played quite poorly. Undaunted, Hiki kept studying mathematics so that someday he could take the examination that would allow him to teach in a junior high. He conveyed his passion for mathematics to his better students, including Tanaka.

One day Tanaka, the fourth-grader, fascinated by numbers, went to downtown Tokyo to buy a slide rule. The store refused to sell him one because he was so young. Only junior high students could have them, the owner said. So he had to go back to Hiki and get a letter saying that although he was only nine years old, he was a smart little boy and would they please sell him a slide rule. Soon, caught up in the world of math, Tanaka began visiting Hiki regularly to study math with him, often staying so late that he spent the night. Hiki gave him increasingly difficult assignments, and the harder they became, the more excited Tanaka grew. Even after he left the fourth grade Tanaka studied with Hiki, and by the time Tanaka was in the sixth grade Hiki had nothing left to teach him. Tanaka could solve problems that were difficult for students four and five years older. He then became an assistant to the teacher in both science and math. The other boys did not seem to resent this; Tanaka had done well simply because it was so natural for him to do well.

The model planes he loved to build were to him an extension of the numbers he also loved. He soon learned that in order to make the models fly well, he constantly had to adjust their weight and trim—his earliest training as mathematician-engineer. When he was twelve he was finally allowed to buy an engine for one of his planes. It was a day that remained clear in his memory. On previous occasions he had carefully reconnoitered the shop—the Tenshodo Store, in the Ginza—before actually making the purchase. The engine he wanted was the Ishizue (or Cornerstone) model. It cost 60 yen, a great deal of money at a time when many families were living on almost that much a month, but his mother had systematically taken the money out of his father's earnings for him. Building the engine into one of his planes was the most thrilling moment of his childhood.

The pleasure of it all—that he could build these planes to the specifications shown in the kits and magazines, and that they would indeed fly, just as they were supposed to—was overwhelming.

When Tanaka was in the fifth grade, Hiki encouraged him to take the exam for Yokohama Number One Junior High, which was one of the best schools in the country and very difficult to get into. By the rules, Tanaka should not have taken the exam for another year, but pushed by Hiki he went ahead. The assistant principal of Yokohama Number One called Hiki and said the boy had done startlingly well and that if he took the exam again in a year and did that well again, they would admit him. A year later he took the exam and did even better. He was only the second boy from his village to get into Yokohama Number One. That was the critical hurdle. It meant that he would probably be able to go to Yokohama High School and a good college and become an engineer. At first Yokohama Number One was very hard on him. He was an unsophisticated country boy among city kids who went out of their way to make him feel inadequate. Tanaka complained to his mother, but she was unsympathetic. "I didn't ask you to go to this school," she told him. "You and Hiki-san picked it out. If you don't like it, you can always quit." She knew, of course, that he would never quit. With that he stopped complaining. To make it easier on Tanaka, the family moved to the Yokohama suburbs.

Tanaka was just a little too young for World War II. When he finished junior high, he did not go on to high school, as he might have in peacetime, but instead became a naval officer cadet. He spent the last months of the war waiting for it to end, hoping to survive, depressed about Japan's collapse. He did survive, and his family was all right. To avoid the bombing of Yokohama, his father had moved the family back to the village where Tanaka had grown up.

The next step for him was to try to get into a senior high school—the avenue to college. Difficult under the best of circumstances, that task had suddenly become even harder. For in addition to the normal number of applicants of his own age, there were many thousands of young men who had gone off to the army and navy instead of going to school, and now they were returning, eager to resume their education. That meant that the competition would be extraordinary. Tanaka was sure it would be too hard to get into the schools he dreamed of, Tokyo Number One or Tokyo Number Two. He decided to try for Seijo High School in Tokyo, which, although not quite as good as those other two, was one of the best in the country. The authorities at Seijo announced that there were so many applicants for the class entering in 1946 that only one out of twenty-three applicants would be admitted. It was the same, Tanaka knew, all over the country. One out of twenty-three. If he was not that one, if he were among the twenty-two, he would not be able to become an engineer.

To cram for the exam he set up a schedule calling for twenty hours of study a day. He saw none of his friends and barely saw his family. Even that schedule, however, did not allow time to study English, and there was an exam in English as well. He knew he must somehow study English during the four hours allotted to sleep. To maximize his privacy—something almost nonexistent in Japanese homes—he created a bedroom for himself in what had been a corridor in the house. He built a bunk bed there, and his father got some straw to put on it for him to sleep on. Several times a day his mother passed food through the sliding door on a tray so that he need not interrupt his studies. He soon lost all sense of time, and he could not tell whether it was day or night. It was the worst six months of his life. His greatest problem was not the confinement or even the lack of sleep but fear of the odds against him. To ease the fear, he developed a rationale: Half of the twenty-three he was competing against, he decided, were not really serious, so that cut the ratio to one in twelve. Then he decided that he was smarter than at least half of the people remaining, so that cut the odds down to one in six. Then he decided that he was working harder than many of the others, and that further shaved the odds. When he sat down at his desk in the exam room, he looked on both sides of him and thought to himself: All I have to do is get better marks than these two guys, and I'm home free. Buoyed by this drastic reduction in the odds, he scored high and was accepted at Seijo.

He did well at Seijo, his talents in math and science carrying him well above the norm even of so competitive a school, and getting into Tokyo University became almost easy. Just before he entered Todai, he went to see Hiki, his old elementary-school teacher. Hiki went into another room and came out with his most treasured possession, a book called *An Introduction to Analysis*, a classic on higher mathematics by a professor named Teiji Takagi. Hiki had bought it for himself, but it had proved too difficult. Now he gave it to his prize student for Todai. The torch had been passed. There was an entrance ceremony for Todai, but neither of his parents was able to attend, his father too busy working, his mother, he suspected, too shy. That night, however, his mother cooked a dish, rice with red beans, which was prepared only on celebratory occasions. Todai, Todai, his father sometimes complained, the boys of Todai were a bunch of snobs who no longer spoke to the ordinary people they knew when they were growing up; the more he talked like that, his friends knew, the prouder he was.

Tanaka remembered Todai happily. He never had to work too hard there. He quickly became a protégé of Tsuyoshi Hayashi, one of Japan's great aeronautical experts. Hayashi was considered one of the most distinguished men on the Todai faculty, even though he was young. He had gone to Todai himself and graduated in 1935, one of the few aeronautical engineers of his generation. During the war he worked on the Zero fighter plane, which was exceptionally well designed. After the war he went back to Todai to teach aircraft engineering, though it was called applied mathematics because the American authorities would not allow Japan to have aeronautical-engineering departments in its universities. Hayashi in those days was known as the Wall, because he never seemed to be looking at his students but instead was always facing the blackboard, writing out his own formulas. Though there was no possibility of constructing aircraft, Hayashi was fascinated by the main challenge of aeronautical engineering, building with lighter but stronger materials. To make things lighter *and* stronger—that was the direction in which the professor pushed his students. Tanaka took several courses from him, and by his senior year he was one of only two undergraduate students in Hayashi's graduate seminar on light structural theory.

Tanaka, however, in the tradition of Todai students, who worked and competed ruthlessly to get in and then took it easy for a few years, had become somewhat self-indulgent—he had taken up sailing, belonged to the sailing club, and gave his weekends over to sailing—and he was often late for his Monday seminar. Whenever Tanaka came in, no matter how late, Professor Hayashi would say sarcastically, "Oh, here's Tanaka-san. Let's start from the beginning for his sake." In general, Hayashi was tolerant of Tanaka's youthful excesses, but as Tanaka's senior year started and Hayashi found out how little work he had done on his dissertation, he became furious with him. "If you had read one book a day for the last year," he said in reproach, "you would have three hundred and sixty-five books read, and you would be ready. Instead you have done almost nothing." With that he made a huge list of books, and Tanaka read every one. A few months later, pleased with Tanaka's work, Hayashi turned to the other students and said, "Well, it looks like our sportsman here can do anything he wants if he puts his mind to it."

But getting a job after graduation was something of a problem, since few employers knew what applied mathematics was; it sounded too rarefied for them. Hayashi in those days often made telephone calls to potential employers on behalf of his students only to find a cool response. "Why are you trying to send us a mathematician," the employer would say, "when what we want is an engineer?" There was nothing in the way of airplane designing, for there was no aircraft industry, and nothing that interested him. A friend who had been a year ahead of him at school had gone to work repairing American jet fighters, and there was a possibility of getting Tanaka that kind of job, but it held no interest for the young graduate. That was repair—the work of a mechanic, not an engineer. So Professor Hayashi arranged a job for Tanaka at the Niigata Ironworks, designing ships. For Tanaka, anything that Hayashi suggested, no matter how gently, was the same as an order, and he quickly and gladly accepted the job. Hayashi was the venerated figure of his life, the great teacher who had been merciful enough to take some interest in Tanaka. Tanaka dared not have any other idea of how he would spend his life; Hayashi in this system could make of his prize student what he wished, and could send him where he wanted.

At first the job seemed exciting: Japan was just becoming a major ship-building nation, and Tanaka was designing ships. But some of the larger companies were building ten-thousand-ton ships, and Tanaka was working on ships much smaller than that. By the fourth year he was bored. Part of it was the work, which was not as challenging as he hoped, and part of it was in being in Niigata, far from the high life of Tokyo. Tanaka later suspected that Professor Hayashi heard of his restlessness; in any case, at this point he got a call from Hayashi saying that Nissan was looking for an expert in structural engineering, someone quite brilliant, because it wanted to make cars with unitary, or frameless, body structure.

Hayashi was becoming well connected at Nissan. (By 1985 he could note that seventeen former students of his had served on the Nissan board of directors.) A number of his best graduates had gone to work for the company in the past several years. He was also doing some consulting for it, and he was well aware of what was going on there. In those days, however, he was just cementing his relationship with this new and still somewhat shaky company, where both the technology and, even worse, the attitude toward technology were so primitive. When Tanaka had been looking for work, Hayashi was still dubious about the auto industry, because it all but spurned the use of science and math in its design shops. In those days the companies did virtually no analysis of weight, strength, and structure. There was no theoretical component in the design, only practical. The practical, he thought, had its value, but the auto industry's disdain for the theoretical possibilities was hard on any skilled engineer working there. The men at the top did things as they had done them before the war, and they were not eager to learn new methods. But this attitude was rapidly changing. By 1956 Hayashi had come to believe that Nissan was serious about wanting first-class technical specialists. Hearing that there was a spot for a true structural engineer, he called and said that Tanaka was the best of the new generation of body-frame people.

Tanaka knew nothing of automobiles and had had no interest in them until that moment, but he would have done whatever Professor Hayashi wanted anyway, and the fact that the job was in Tokyo clinched it. He came to Tokyo and was interviewed by four Nissan executives, including Takashi Ishihara, the future president of the company. Are you interested in the auto business? one of them asked. Oh, yes, said Tanaka, it is something I care about a great deal. Can you drive a car? the man continued. No, said Tanaka, but I can learn. He thereupon enrolled in a driving school and some two weeks later emerged with his license. He also went to work for Nissan. The men who interviewed him had warned him that they had plenty of able men and that advancement would probably be slow. But he did not mind. He was doing what his professor had told him to do. Hayashi was much more pleased with this assignment for Tanaka than he was with the one at Niigata. There was going to be more chance for the young engineer to experiment, he was sure. Besides, he thought, automobiles were a more appropriate challenge for the true Japanese engineer. Japan was small, and much of its landmass was not really usable. Thus the Japanese engineer must be skilled at dealing with the limits of space. Almost everything that was built in Japan had to be smaller and to use less space than would be required anywhere else. Autos were much smaller than ships, so Nissan was a much better place than Niigata for so talented a protégé as Tanaka.

As he placed men like Tanaka at companies like Nissan, Professor Hayashi was also aware that something very important was happening. Because Japan had no defense industry, he knew, and not even an airplane industry, the best engineers of a generation were being funneled into other, seemingly more prosaic sectors, like automobiles, for example, and steel. These industries, which in America were having increasingly difficulty competing for top engineers, were getting the absolute cream in Japan. This advantage in talent was already making a considerable difference, Hayashi believed, as Japan's heavy industries began to compete in the world's markets.

16.
THE FIRST VICTORY

At the time of the Nissan strike, Yutaka Katayama was a rising young executive in the company. He was a conservative young man of upper-class origins. His grandfather had been a rich landowner in Saitama prefecture, a man with some seventy acres of land, an immense plot in Japan, and some thirty tenant farmers. The grandfather had been an exuberant and enlightened man. Whatever was new, whether it was a bicycle, a car, or some device for the kitchen, he had to have it. He insisted that his sons go to college, even his first son, which was unusual in Japan, where the duty of the first son was to stay behind and work the land and learn nothing that would make him restless with his destiny. Yutaka Katayama's father went to Keio, one of the country's elite colleges, and then, instead of returning home as his father wished, pleaded for one year in business first. He loved business and the world of the city and never returned. That was somewhat shocking, a minor footnote to the steady urbanization and modernization of Japan.

The family name was not Katayama but Asoh. When it came time for young Yutaka Asoh to marry—he wed the daughter of a man who worked for the Bank of Tokyo, a good marriage—he took his wife's family name, Katayama, since there were no sons in that family. The Katayama family was Christian, so in the process he became a Christian too, though not a very religious one. His friends later thought it might have made him broader, less insular. He himself suspected it made him a good deal more aggressive, less accepting of fate, than most Japanese. Certainly travel had broadened him. His father had been posted to many different places, and wherever he went, the entire family went too, along with two or three maids. Later, as the head of Nissan in the American West, Katayama liked to check into Denver's Brown Palace, a wondrous old-fashioned hotel with a huge central atrium. Standing in the lobby, one could look up and see ring after ring of balconies all the way to the top. Asked why he loved the Brown Palace, he explained that when he was young, his father had sent him to China to further his education, both intellectual and social. The Brown Palace reminded him of happy youthful days at an old Chinese whorehouse; you simply went in, clapped your hands, and girls would come running out of the rooms onto the balconies to greet you.

Most Japanese in the years after the war wanted to forget the past, but Katayama, who had been excused from military service because of weak eyesight, still savored it. He was in no way burdened by the war. Unlike most Japanese, who came to regard the changes wrought in their society by Douglas MacArthur and the bright liberal young New Dealers around him as a major force for good, Katayama in many ways longed for the old order. MacArthur, he sometimes thought, was responsible not so much for Japan's rise but for its decline. The three things that MacArthur had perpetrated from which Japan would never recover, he claimed, were women's suffrage, the coming of management consultants, and the legalization of labor unions. Katayama's family had lost almost all of its valuable land under MacArthur's land reform. They had been able to keep two acres and the farmhouse. All else was gone. He never complained about this; he knew that this was right and humane, and that his family's good fortune in the prewar years had been at the expense of many poorer people.

Katayama's privileged childhood had made him somewhat different from other Japanese. For one thing, it had given him a desire for a higher level of independence. For another, it had made him an absolute car nut. He had grown up with classic cars in his family. His father had owned two very sporty cars, an Erskine and a Star Durant. In the postwar years when everyone else was preoccupied with finding a place to live and something to eat, Katayama was obsessed with finding a vintage car to drive and a place where the roads were not so bad that they would destroy it. He organized the first postwar auto sports club in Japan. Its members were Japanese with fond memories of other days and a handful of American officers; their cars were a few treasured MGs and some prewar roadsters lovingly reconstructed. It was his love of cars that had brought him to Nissan. His fellow workers saw Nissan as a big company likely to expand. Katayama chose Nissan because it was about cars, and he was about cars, and he not only wanted to build them, he wanted to drive them. At one point in the early fifties, frustrated with the politics of Nissan, he tried to start his own company. He and a friend tried to design their own car, an ultralight car for people in a poor country where gas was expensive. The Flying Feather, Katayama named it. They built the prototype in the second story of a Tokyo building, then found they could not get the car out the door. Finally it was taken out through the window. He was, he decided, an insufficiently practical man to run his own company.

That did not diminish his love of cars. When he was not working at Nissan, he was out driving a car as fast as he could. In a nation filled with laws and restrictions and inhibitions, racing around in a sports car was to him the highest form of personal freedom. Years later when he became the head of Nissan on the American West Coast and purchased a house in Palos Verdes, California, he continued to speed. It was said of Katayama that he had more speeding tickets than anyone else in town. At first he passed himself off to the local traffic cops as a simple Japanese businessman who knew no English, but the cops soon caught on. One of them would chase after him, catch up with his car, and say, "Good morning, how are you today, Mr. Katayama? And by the way, here is your ticket." By the end of his tour he had a chauffeur, since if he had gotten another ticket he would have lost his license.

At Nissan he was always anti-union. During the worst of the 1953 strikes, when the Masuda union had surrounded the plant and sealed off a few lonely management people inside the building, Katayama had taken great pleasure in slipping through the lines, bringing the semihostages not only food but movies. In his perfect world, there would be no unions. Managers would deal with their workers in a traditional, honorable Japanese manner that reflected well on both labor and management and that accorded both sides dignity and honor; in a slightly less perfect world where there had to be unions, management would make decisions, and labor could go through the motions of pretending that it had fought valiantly to improve things. That kind of relationship he could understand. Masuda was anathema to him. But his troubles did not end with the fall of Masuda. He soon ran into trouble with the second, or Miyake, union and with the idea of labor as an extension of management. It was something he could not understand, and he resisted the new union stubbornly, with considerable detriment to his career. He resented the fact that people with union connections were getting the plum assignments within management, whether they deserved them or not. His friends warned him to keep his mouth shut, pointing out that the deed was done, that the right side had won, and that even if the union was abusing its victory, he ought to at least play it smart. Do not, one of his more senior friends warned, worry about what is good for the company; worry for once about what is best for Katayama. He never listened. When almost everyone else in middle management was joining the Miyake union, Katayama stood on the sidelines. "I was a conscientious objector during the war," he said later. For that he was not forgiven. He eventually (belatedly, it was decided) joined, but he was never considered a loyal member. For one thing he turned down repeated requests from Miyake to run for union office. Each time he turned

Miyake down, he knew he was cutting another part of his career off and throwing it away. "We have our friends," Miyake once said to him, "and we have our enemies." There were constant pressures and threats like this. Miyake had expanded his power greatly and was quite ruthless in keeping people in line. The Emperor Miyake, others in the company had begun to call him. Early on, Katayama had made another critical mistake. He had complained bitterly to members of the board that the union knew of important board decisions long before most people in management. This, he said, was unacceptable in a real business.

He and a handful of others like him felt they were in a no-man's-land in the company. Clearly the power of the union as a force within management, and as an agent of Kawamata's personal control, was becoming stronger every year. The union and the personnel section of the company were virtually one and the same thing. Those who had challenged the new union—the management people who were uneasy with its new powerful role—were quickly pushed aside. Some quietly left the company. Subsidiary companies such as Nissan Diesel, which made trucks, became a refuge for these irreconcilables. Others were pushed out of the mainstream and told to take jobs as Nissan dealers, a demotion of the first order. Katayama himself was desperate. His attempt to develop his own car had failed. He began to think seriously of leaving the company. He was not alone in his unhappiness. Good young executives were now leaving the company, not because they were afraid of being fired but because they did not want to work in a company that was run upside down.

In those days Katayama was already a serious reader of all auto magazines; he did not speak English well, but he read it, and he read it to keep up with his beloved world of sports-car racing. That world, he realized, was a fantasy world, and his job at Nissan the grim reality. He had just about decided to leave Nissan when in early 1958 he read about an upcoming rally in Australia, a grueling nineteen-day run of ten thousand miles over rugged terrain. The Japanese, he thought, might just win a race like this. Their cars were not very good—in fact, they were graceless cars of questionable performance. But the one thing they were—and had to be, given how bad the roads were in Japan—was durable. The Australian rally would be over rough, rocky, often muddy roads; that was the only kind of road the Japanese knew. Nissan auto bodies were strong, and they had, whatever else, endurance. Japanese auto construction, Katayama knew, was not very sophisticated, not very original, but it was very solid. It was quite possible that Nissan could enter the competition and do well. It might not win, but it could surprise some people.

On his own Katayama took the rules, painstakingly translated them into

Japanese, and brought them to the board of directors. Almost no one else in the company was interested. There was, he thought, a pervasive inferiority complex to the Japanese in those days, and it extended to almost everything they did. His superiors, he believed, were afraid of entering. If they entered they might lose, and if they lost they would bring dishonor on their country, their company, and their careers. One of the most powerful forces in Japan, Katayama believed, was the fear of failure. When his superiors argued against it, Katayama always responded that if they were ever to enter any kind of competition, now was the time, because they had so much to gain and so little to lose. If they entered and lost, no one would blame them, and they would lose no prestige. After all, they had no prestige to start with. They were like invisible men, he said. That seemed a compelling argument, and eventually he won his case. He was a little old for the rally himself, because it was so arduous. Besides, someone had to be in charge of the team. But he knew some good drivers at Nissan, and he assumed that he would be able to put together his own team.

He was soon disabused of this idea. There would be two sedans and four drivers, and the drivers would be picked by Miyake and the union. Katayama was appalled when the four union men showed up. They knew nothing about sports-car driving. They had been chosen for their political loyalty rather than for their driving ability. For a brief moment he considered bailing out of the project, and then he realized he had one great advantage. It was not that he was the head of the team or that he had a higher rank; these young men knew that they were better connected within the company than he was. It was that he, however primitively, could handle English, and they could not. They would be Japanese in a foreign land without any preparation for it. The moment they reached Australia they would be completely dependent upon him. He found that thought wonderfully comforting.

He plunged ahead in preparation. It was not always easy. There were no test tracks to work out on, and the speed limit in Japan was sixty kilometers or roughly forty miles an hour. He and his drivers were often stopped by the police for speeding. They tried to explain that they were preparing for a race in Australia. Japanese racing in Australia? the police would ask in disbelief, barely able to hold back their laughter. Katayama would try to explain, but by then the police would simply wave them on. The police had no desire to arrest madmen.

It went as Katayama expected. When the drivers, who had been hostile, arrived in Australia, they soon became terrified. It was a world without Japanese, where no one spoke Japanese. They pulled back inside themselves, clung to him, and listened to his every word as they had not back in Japan. Katayama was also right about the little Datsun car. It was rugged—built really like a small truck with a truck's suspension. It was a poor man's car from a poor man's country. It lacked acceleration, it lacked comfort, its brakes left something to be desired, its steel was too thick because the Japanese steel industry was not yet sophisticated enough to deliver what the auto industry wanted. But it was perfect for this competition. It was a small tank disguised as a car. (Two of the drivers were, fillingly enough, former tank drivers.) It was supposed, once built, to last forever, and this rally was a challenge to durability rather than grace.

Australia turned out to be a pleasant experience. Everyone was very nice to the Japanese. We are seen as the poor little gentlemen of Japan, Katayama realized; we have lost the war, rather badly, and everyone feels sorry for us and wants to help us. He was amused by that, and wondered how long it would last. The Volkswagen people were particularly friendly, and he was in awe of them, even more than he was of the Americans. The Americans were rich and powerful, but here was VW, fewer than ten years after the war, thousands of miles from home, and it was doing everything right. Its logistic base—the ability to repair what it sold— seemed especially strong, and the Volkswagen name was all over Australia.

At the same time he tried to prepare for an upset. Every night Katayama took his own drivers out for beer. At these sessions he played on their nationalism, the Japaneseness of them all; they were all in this together, in the land of the gaijin driving against all these gaijin. Gradually they became a team, and gradually he took command of it. Then the race began, and he was surprised. He had thought the Datsun would do well, but not this well. The rugged Datsun held up; the one Katayama had named Fuji won, and the other finished well up in its field. In Japan, desperate in the postwar years for any kind of cheer, Katayama overnight became a national hero. He had given Japan a major victory. Upon his return, Kawamata, the president of Nissan for a year now, and most of the board of directors came out to Haneda airport to greet his plane. There was a huge procession into town, and thousands of people lined the way to hail him.

For a year Katayama was a celebrity. He was also a man without a job. While he had been off in Australia his old post as advertising manager had been taken. By whom? he had asked, somewhat puzzled by this odd reward. "By a very active union member," a friend told him. His disloyalty had not been forgotten, but for the moment his heroics were more important, and he spent the year going all over the country talking as modestly as he could about the triumph of Japan in Australia. He was intrigued by the response within Nissan. No longer denigrating their product, his superiors had now decided they were among the world's best auto producers. He was amused by that. The Japanese had certain strengths, but only in manufacturing. What they knew about cars, and what they cared about cars, was almost nothing.

Katayama enjoyed his celebrity for a while, but he soon became bored. He was also aware that it did not solve his real problem, which was whether or not he had a future with Nissan. Indeed, he realized, it might have added to his problem: In the past there had been powerful people who had disliked him; now that he had become something of a national figure, it was likely that those same people hated him. Now, more than ever, he was a marked man.

So it was, after the triumph in Australia, that the people at Nissan began to think seriously about exporting cars. They had always known that they would have to export. They had delayed the decision for as long as they could, because theirs was so fragile and primitive a company. But if they were to win and dominate in the domestic market, then they would have to export cars as well, for the ability to export would greatly expand their volume and cut their costs. That would be crucial in securing a healthy share of the domestic market, which was what really mattered to them. Every car that they sold overseas would cut their costs at home. They knew that their workers were as good as those in America and Western Europe, perhaps even better, and they were paid less. Still, they were nervous about exporting to America. They had done some limited exporting, mostly trucks and buses, into Southeast Asia. But it was one thing to sell buses or trucks to the Thais and another thing to sell cars to Americans. Whoever made the decision to export into the United States would be blamed if the venture did not work. Careers were at stake.

Actually—and it was not something that the people at Nissan liked to recall in later years—they had had to be pushed to export their cars to America. The first push had already come, a year before the Australian rally, from a man named Nobe Wakatsuki, who worked for a major trading company called Marubeni. (In the company's own history of its experience in America, Wakatsuki makes only the smallest appearance, without even the mention of his first name.) The role of the trading companies was vital in the world of Japanese commerce. Because Japan was so isolated, physically, psychologically, and linguistically, dealing with foreigners was inordinately painful for most senior Japanese businessmen. They lacked not just the language but, more important, the ability to deal with people who were not Japanese. Thus the Japanese, since they were totally dependent on exports and imports, had created the shosha, or trading company, to act as a middleman between Japanese firms and the great world beyond.

Wakatsuki was a genuine Japanese aristocrat; his grandfather had served as prime minister twice in the prewar period and had been one of the handful of influential civilians who had tried to oppose the rise of Japanese militarism. He had been pushed aside by the military but had remained an adviser to the Emperor during the war. The young Nobe had been close to his grandfather after the war, had taken care of him as he was dying, and had listened to his stories about the rest of the world. Because of that he had grown up less suspicious of foreign ways than the average Japanese. He was a cross-cultural person, extroverted for a Japanese, ebullient and confident, almost, it seemed, incautious. If he was a good and loyal son of Japan, he was also a rather skeptical one. In 1954 the Marubeni trading company had picked him to be its man in Los Angeles. He had already been unusually successful in the United States, arranging, among other things, for the export of American nuclear reactors to Japan, a deal that had surprised the Japanese, who had not expected the Americans to part so readily with such technology. In Los Angeles, looking for new deals to make, Wakatsuki became aware for the first time of the importance of the car in American life. Americans, he decided, began conversations by asking each other first where they lived, and then what kind of car they drove. They seemed quite surprised on meeting him to find out that he did not own a car. A car, he soon learned, was essential not only to getting around in Los Angeles but to a person's identity as well. Wakatsuki was always looking for a Japanese export product that the Americans would need, something basic but that would occasionally need to be replaced. In Japan such an item was the geta, the Japanese sandal; in Japan everyone needed getas, and eventually they had to be replaced. In America, he realized, the perfect item was the car; everyone had to have a car, and, because it was a rich country, people turned cars in after only three or four years.

On his own he investigated the requirements for importing a car into America. He was surprised to learn how easy it was. In Japan, he knew, the regulations were as thick as a phone book, designed to keep intruders out. The American market, by contrast, appeared blithely open. The only regulation seemed to be that that the cars must have sealed-beam headlights from General Electric. He visited the California Chamber of Commerce and asked about the possibility of bringing Japanese cars to America. "I didn't know the Japanese made cars," the man there said. "I thought they got their cars from Jimmy." Jimmy? Wakatsuki asked. Jimmy who? Jimmy, it turned out, was GM. As he gathered information, he kept

feeding it to his Marubeni colleagues back in Tokyo, urging them to get
something going. They in turn went to Nissan, and Nissan somewhat
suspiciously examined Wakatsuki's reports.

In the fall of 1957 there was to be an auto show in Los Angeles, and
Wakatsuki exhorted Nissan to send some cars. Marubeni was dubious,
and so were the Nissan people. A friend of Wakatsuki's told him, "They
are saying, 'There goes that crazy Nobe again. He's always too quick.' "
But eventually Nissan decided to send two cars and a pickup truck. When
Wakatsuki went to the dock to see them come off the ship from Japan,
he could not believe his eyes. The car was the ugliest he had ever seen.
Is that a car or a black box that moves? he wondered. He turned to a
friend of his who had come along, a Nisei Japanese who had once worked
for Lincoln, and asked how they would ever be able to sell it. "Nobe,"
said his friend, "this is America. The first thing you have to understand
is that everyone has the right to try anything. They will always let you
try. The other thing you have to understand is that one percent of all
Americans are crazy. They like to do something crazy, and so perhaps a
few of these will do something very crazy like buying a Japanese car."
The car was displayed at the Los Angeles auto show, and people were
fascinated.

"What is a Datsun?" a customer would ask Wakatsuki.

"It's a Japanese car," he would answer.

"I didn't know the Japanese made cars." Then the customer would open
the hood. "That's an Austin engine," he would say.

"Yes," Wakatsuki would answer, "but it's an Austin engine made in
Japan." Wakatsuki decided to price it the same as the VW bug, but people
were resistant. If it was Japanese, they insisted, it had to be cheaply made,
and therefore it should not cost as much. Because the styling was old-
fashioned, the Nissan people eventually made a virtue out of necessity
and sold the Datsun as a classic car. In a way that was what it was. More
than even they realized, it was a car from another time. Japanese auto
manufacturing had been primitive even before the war; it had just been
getting started when the military converted the nascent industry to truck
manufacturing. Then American bombs leveled most of the plants. In the
postwar years the factories still had dirt floors, and there were apprentices
whose job it was to spray down the floors every day to keep down the
dust. The manufacturing process was very similar to that of an American
factory in the twenties. In the rest of the world, highly automated machines
were starting to be introduced, but buying them was out of the question
for the Nissan. However, Nissan's labor was cheap. The company now
had absolute control over the workplace, and thus not only a skilled work

force but a hungry one. Nissan could use this advantage to keep itself competitive while it earned the hard currency to invest in modern machinery.

In 1958 the Japanese began their assault upon the strongest of American markets. They approached that decision cautiously. They would send a car and a pickup truck to America to be tested under American conditions. The car that Nissan intended to experiment with was a closer relative of the first Gorham car, mechanically, than anyone wanted to admit. It was supposed to be a passenger car, but it was more like a taxi, and indeed in Japan its main customers were not ordinary consumers, who could not afford cars, but taxi companies. It was for function, not pleasure. The car was not built for the highway, with acceleration, speed, and comfort; in Japan highways barely existed. It was built for survival in the city, to be driven on some of the worst streets in the world by drivers who drove with such ferocity that their fellow citizens called them kamikazes, after the suicide pilots who had crashed their planes into American ships during the war. It was designed for short hauls on bad roads. Its brakes were not very good, because no one ever got going fast enough to need truly strong brakes. It lasted forever.

With the car and the pickup Nissan also sent the first of what were to be hundreds of teams of engineers to study American cars and the American market. It was the beginning of a major invasion. The job for the four men on that first team was to study the Datsun as it performed not under simulated conditions but under real American driving conditions and to see if Nissan could make enough minor adjustments to produce a viable car for export. The four were among Nissan's best young engineers. One member, Kuniyuki Tanabe, was not only a smart, up-and-coming engineer but related by marriage to Kawamata, Nissan's president. That gave the team extra leverage; it was a powerful connection never discussed but always felt.

The four men were acutely aware of their car's weaknesses. It was not really a car, thought Tanabe, but a truck. It had an exceedingly heavy frame, and the steel of the body was too thick. The Japanese steel industry might be improving, but it was not yet sophisticated, and it lacked the ability to bring steel down to the desired thinness, six or seven tenths of a millimeter; the Datsun's was a full millimeter, which made the car heavy. It was also awkward and slow.

They soon realized how poor they and their country were, and by contrast, how rich America was. Each man had $15 a day for expenses. That had to cover everything. Even in the pre-inflation days of 1958, $15 was very little money, and each of them kept a chart showing how much

money he had spent and how much he had left. For the first few nights
they stayed at what seemed to them a good hotel in downtown Los Angeles,
the Biltmore, but then to their dismay they found it cost a great deal of
money, so they had to move to a fleabag that cost only $6 and seemed to
be inhabited largely by pickpockets. They might have been absolutely
terrified, four Japanese who spoke barely a word of English, but they had
each other. Each would help and protect and comfort the others. Each
would lift the others up. Whatever the hardships, they were always shared.
It was a theme that was critical to the success of the emerging Japan,
people sharing both their strengths and weaknesses. None of the four was
to use the trip to America to get ahead of the others; the career of each
would succeed only to the degree that the group succeeded.

The language was a constant problem. They had all taken English lessons, but it had been too hard. Tanabe had taken his at the end of his
regular twelve-hour day at Nissan, and he had never managed to stay
awake. Now, in America, he, like his colleagues, always got things wrong.
Once Tanabe was doing some test driving in Nevada and a state trooper
signaled him to pull over. It was just what Tanabe had feared, a confrontation with American authorities, and so he began patiently in his broken
English to prove to this awesome symbol of American law that he was a
good Japanese. He started to explain every single thing he had done in
America since his arrival, until finally the trooper, impatient with all this
incomprehensible blather, yelled, "For God's sake, go on and get going,"
and waved him on. Ordering meals was an ordeal. Whenever Tanabe
wanted a small orange juice at breakfast, a large tomato juice would arrive.
They never knew what they were going to get to eat, and they were often
bothered by the richness of the food and the sheer size of American meals.
Once Tanabe and his colleague Shin Maki stopped at a roadside grill,
looked at the menu, and decided to order the day's special, ham steak.
They were appalled when an immense slab of meat arrived. They knew
immediately that they had been cheated. In Japan, ham, which was expensive, was very thinly sliced. "Excuse me," Tanabe said irately to the
waitress, "but we ordered ham." A short, heated discussion ensued. Soon
the two Japanese were ushered back into the kitchen and shown a huge
ham. It was where the steak had come from. They had simply never seen
meat sliced that thick.

It was the first time that any of the four had ever felt poor. That was
the oddest sensation of all; they lived in what was manifestly a poor country, yet the poverty was so evenly distributed that it seemed not a judgment on them as individuals but, instead, a larger social condition. But
in America, how little they actually owned and possessed came home to

them, in endless ways, whether it was in the daily rationing of their meager allowance or professionally in the constant sense of America's industrial opulence and their own pathetic accomplishments.

They were always aware of that gap between their poverty and America's richness. Teiichi Hara, the senior member of the group, sometimes felt overwhelmed by the scope of the world of automobiles in America. Here he was, trying to test his two little Japanese vehicles, and around him was nothing but cars, thousands of them, all bigger and faster than any he had ever seen, all roaring past him on the grandest highways he had ever seen. The Americans driving those cars would honk their horns angrily when his little Japanese car could not accelerate from the ramp onto the freeway fast enough. Hara was stunned by the impossibility of his task. Even as he and his friends were fumbling to improve their little car, the Americans, he was sure, were out there learning even more on their brilliant test tracks in Detroit.

Tanabe, who was younger, felt differently. It was like coming to America with a toy car, he knew, but rather than being intimidated by American automotive muscle he was thrilled by how much there was to learn. Tanabe was an auto engineer, and for a man of that profession this was Mecca. It was the country of Gorham, and he was a disciple of Gorham. He had never met him, but he knew the date and place of Gorham's birth, he knew Gorham's middle name and the inventions he had brought to Nissan, even the names of his sons, whom he had never, of course, met. Tanabe knew that when Gorham had designed the first Datsun, he had drawn up the parts himself and sent the designs off to be machine-tooled, and that when the parts had arrived they had—it was almost miraculous—fitted together perfectly. But it was more than Gorham, it was that this was America, and America was the land of machinery, all machinery, but principally automobiles. He wanted to make cars like the American cars and the only way to do that was to come and study them. Visiting America, he decided, was like going to the greatest auto university in the world. It was there every day in front of you, the size and the strength and the love of cars. There was so much room, and so much power. He felt intoxicated by the sight and noise of cars. But there was so little time to take it all in. The four had only one month in America. They needed more time, they knew, but time cost money, hard currency, and there was almost none of that. What little they had had been earned from the sale of those buses to Thailand.

Since there were no test tracks in Japan, they had to do their testing on the American highways. Their problems, they soon realized, were how to stabilize the car, how to cut down on the vibration at higher speeds, and how to improve the brakes. They were engineers, not mechanics, and they desperately needed a mechanic, because they had to fiddle with the engine every day. But there hadn't been enough money to send over a mechanic. Wakatsuki had found them a small garage, but they had a terrible time trying to explain their very precise technical requirements in English. Their manuals were not in English, and finally they began to do everything themselves. Day after day they would run the car and then come back and tinker with the differential gear, trying to keep the engine from revving too fast. They found themselves taking the differential gear apart and then putting it back together. They had been away from that kind of work a very long time, and it was a little humiliating, Tanabe thought, that men who thought themselves skilled as engineers could be so incompetent as mechanics. An American mechanic who worked with them taught them how to improve the adhesion on the brakes, how to regrind them and make them apply evenly so that the car would not swerve. At times Tanabe felt sure the American mechanic was wrong, and he realized later that he had automatically condescended to the American, reacting against the idea of receiving technical lessons from so uneducated a man. But somehow the mechanic was always right, and Tanabe was surprised that a man with so little technical training could know so much. Slowly their car got better, its acceleration improved, and it began to handle the American highways.

The day that Tanabe knew that somehow there would be a chance for them in America came right at the end of that hectic and often frightening month. It was the day they went up against the Volkswagen. They were test driving every day on the California highway system. There was one stretch on the San Diego Freeway outside of Bakersfield that they particularly liked because it was a God-given test track, a long climb up a hill and thus a prolonged challenge to the power of the engine, and very hard on the gears. On this particular day, as they were approaching that stretch, a Volkswagen with two Americans in it pulled alongside the Datsun with the two Japanese inside. The Americans stared at the Datsun. Tanabe, who was driving, did not like their looks, or their expression, which seemed to say that the Datsun was unworthy. The two cars drove alongside each other for a few moments, the Americans still staring, and then, as happens at a moment like this, Tanabe, angry and frustrated, made it a race. Eventually, he thought, you have to make a try. Back and forth they went, one car taking a little lead and then the other, until they came to the big slope, not a steep hill but steady and punishing for a small car. Tanabe decided to go to third gear and give it all the power he had. Gradually the Datsun began to pull away from the VW. At first it was a small edge and then the length of the car, and then the VW began to slip back. Tanabe did not wave out the window, but he did not take his eye off the rearview mirror until the VW disappeared. We can beat the Volkswagen, he kept thinking, we can beat the Volkswagen. What a good engine, what a tough little engine. Then it dawned on him: If we can beat the Volkswagen in a country where people are still lined up to buy it, we will be all right in America, we poor little Japanese.

They were all getting ready to return to Tokyo for their final report, which would recommend that with some upgrading the Datsun had a chance in America, when the accident took place. Hara was driving with Maki in the Datsun, and Tanabe was right behind them in a borrowed VW. Suddenly a big American car in front of Hara hit its brakes. The Datsun smashed into the American car, and the VW smashed into the Datsun. Maki's head went through the windshield, and he lost two teeth. One snapped off at the gumline, and one broke in half. A California highway patrolman showed up and seemed a bit irritated when he found that Hara did not have a driving license. But someone telephoned Nobe Wakatsuki, and Wakatsuki, who seemed to have an absolute genius for fixing things that went wrong in America, made a few phone calls, and Hara did not have to go to prison. The patrolman suggested, however, that Hara never drive on California roads again. Hara, the shiest of the group, was very embarrassed about what had happened and thought it an occasion of considerable shame. He had dishonored Nissan. So chagrined was he that it was decided that they would make no mention of it when they returned to Tokyo.

When they arrived at the Tokyo airport, they found that Kawamata, the president of Nissan, had decided to bring the entire board of directors to the airport to meet them. The four of them would then make their report. It was to be a properly dramatic moment in Nissan's history. Maki started making his report—and then clamped his hand over his mouth. To hide the fact that two of his teeth were missing, he had tried to stick them back on with chewing gum. As he was reading his report to the president and the board, the teeth had come loose. He tried to stick them on again. Again they came loose. Again he tried to fix them. "What the hell are you doing?" Kawamata asked. So finally Maki admitted that there had been an accident, and Hara, the bearer now of double shame, had to apologize for the accident and also for having tried to keep it secret. Then they made their report. They were all nervous; the sight of the entire board at the airport was a reminder of how grave a decision it was.

Kawamata was very direct. "Okay," he said after the report. "You say the pickup is all right for American conditions. Then go ahead with it. On the passenger car, what you can't change, you can't change. But on what you can, go ahead and do it as quickly as possible."

It had been fun in America, but Tanabe suddenly realized how serious their mission had been. With a feeling that bordered on terror, Nissan had decided to export to the United States. The Japanese were going to try to sell their strong but sad little car in the land of Gorham.

17.
DEMING FINDS AN AUDIENCE

The first postwar decade was hard on the Japanese. The little capital all their labor produced was poured back into the industrial rebuilding of Japan. But the sacrifice at least was communal, the hardships shared. People made do with very little. Food and clothes remained dear. Most businessmen seemed to have two suits, a good one and bad one. The bad suit they wore around home; the good suit they wore to the office. It somehow always looked freshly pressed. On the train between Osaka and Tokyo, Japanese businessmen sometimes sat in their undershorts so that they would not wrinkle the pants of that good suit. Most had only two shirts, too. Yet the astonishing thing, one Westerner who lived there at the time remembered, was how clean everyone was, and how clean their clothes were. The Westerner, a German businessman named Eric Klestadt, often wondered how they did it. He knew how poor they were, how hard it was to feed a family, and how much of a family's energy went into finding enough food to survive; he knew as well how few clothes they had and under what difficult conditions they were living at home. Yet on a crowded subway, he noticed, no one seemed to smell bad. Thinking of the effort that they must be putting into personal hygiene, he remarked to himself on the stoicism with which the Japanese accepted and bore their burdens.

It was the promise that things might get better that sustained them in those days. For Tokyo residents it was the subway system that embodied hope and represented the future. Before the war the city had had only one subway line. In Tokyo in the early fifties there were three different lines, and there always seemed to be a new station opening up, to the delight and pride of all. The subway stations were theirs in a way that the new smokestacks over steel plants were not, and they seemed to guarantee that life was not static and that just as they could now get from their homes to work more and more quickly, so other aspects of life would also change and become easier. Their industriousness would be rewarded.

The first modest sign of postwar prosperity had come in 1950, when rice could be bought without having to go through the black market. The inflation was still severe, and even those with good jobs felt that they were spending more than they were earning; it was one of the main reasons for the labor troubles of the late forties and early fifties. But there were stirrings of a vigorous consumer society. By 1953, coffee houses had begun to appear, and they almost immediately became crowded. Part of it was the need to get out of the tiny little homes, for housing was still desperately tight, and the coffee houses, crowded and noisy and filled with cigarette smoke, were at the least warm and comforting. The coming of coffee houses, as some Japanese remembered it, marked the beginning of the return of pleasure.

Soon there were things other than essentials to buy. The first two successful consumer appliances were radios and sewing machines, both of them inexpensive. Television had not yet arrived, and radio offered a form of larger community and free entertainment. Sewing machines were treasures; clothes were still expensive, and the machines allowed Japanese women to make their own and to repair them cheaply. But disposable income was still extremely limited; what little money people made seemed targeted for food. Real consumerism had to wait until the steel industry had been rebuilt. After radios and sewing machines came cameras, and then soon there were motorbikes. The motorbikes heralded a consumer revolution. It was as if one day no one had them and a few weeks later the entire population had them. Then clothes began to get better. Flush toilets began to appear in homes. Sometimes they were not yet connected to sewer lines, but they were there nonetheless, and the neighbors made pilgrimages to see them. As more and more people had flush plumbing, the honey pots began to disappear, and the streets at last began to lose some of their primal aroma.

Yet the sacrifices were still enormous. In the late fifties the left, which had been somewhat quiescent for much of the decade, became more attractive again, this time not so much with workers but with Japan's most priceless resource, its young college students. Where the Americans had once been gods to the Japanese, now there was an almost inevitable stirring of serious anti-Americanism, mostly among the young. In 1960 the government, aware of political restlessness in the population, more confident of its own economic underpinnings, moved to share some of the fruit from all that labor with the workers themselves. Prime Minister Hayato Ikeda, the man who had once worked so closely with Joseph Dodge as his counterpart, announced a double-your-income program for the coming decade: All good Japanese would work hard, expenses would be held down, inflation would be controlled, and over the decade incomes would double. He projected an annual growth rate of 7.2 percent for the decade; in fact, it was 11 percent, and the climb was steady. To critics, Ikeda's program was a pacifier, a means of buying off the workers. That it might well have been, but the average Japanese, after some thirty years of hardship and sacrifice, was hardly interested in arguing. The Japanese gratefully accepted their first fruits in a long time.

Thus by 1960 both the highest officials in the bureaucracy and their peers in industry were almost simultaneously coming to the conclusion that it was time to relax the economy and make it more flexible. No longer would the economy serve so exclusively the purposes of the state; it was time now to broaden it to serve the less serious but keenly felt needs of the people themselves. There were ample signs that the population was restless and needed some rewards; in addition, the core economy had reached the point in its growth where it was strengthened not only when it produced major industrial items but when it produced consumer goods as well.

The planners in MITI believed that cars were a perfect product to mark this relaxation. They were a cherished consumer goal while at the same time their production gave new work to the steel industry. By 1960, Taizo Ishida, the president of Toyota, was talking of a new "yen revolution." There had already been the 50,000-yen revolution, which meant that the average Japanese could afford to buy home electrical appliances in the $150 price range. Now, Ishida said, the 500,000-yen revolution was approaching, and it would apply to cars: If someone could produce a car that could be priced at that level—about $1500—his company might get in on the ground floor with young Japanese consumers. That was what Toyota proceeded to do, with the Toyopet.

Nissan had not yet produced an economy car, because its president, Katsuji Kawamata, was too cautious; if the customers wanted cheap cars, he said, they could buy used ones. His default, which enraged Nissan's product people, gave Toyota an early domestic lead over Nissan. Nevertheless, Nissan, like Toyota, was gearing up for real mass production. At last it was modernizing, or at least making a start on it. Until 1960 Nissan had been completely dependent on manual labor. Now, for the first time, it bought some automatic welding machines. The pace within the factories was beginning to pick up quite dramatically. More and more orders were coming in, pushing the work force to its limits. In 1959 Nissan had made only 33,000 passenger cars; in 1960 production jumped to 66,000. (By 1964 it would be 213,000.) The ever-increasing increments indicated that Nissan was getting its base structure in place and was now ready to make its assault. Its costs were about to go down and its quality up.

A handful of American consultants had started working in Japan in the late fifties, helping bring American technical expertise to Japanese firms. They were among the first Americans to warn their countrymen of the rising force and excellence of Japanese industry. No one paid very much attention to them in the beginning, or for that matter, even near the end. One of them, James Abegglen, was one of the first to write about how effectively the Japanese had adapted their traditional cultural and social forms to the modern factory, and how formidable they had become once that had happened. It was important, he said early on, not to underestimate the Japanese. At the beginning of an industrial effort they might seem slow and awkward around machines, their products shabby, but Americans should not be deceived. This was a society that had made a powerful commitment to industrial excellence. Their own domestic competition was fierce, there always seemed to be too many companies, and out of that domestic competition, in no matter what field, several very skilled, tough, and finally quite formidable companies would emerge. They learned quickly, and once they learned, their expertise improved at a dramatic rate, far beyond the expectations of most of their nominal Western teachers. They poured money into their plants, and they kept abreast of modern technology, imitating ruthlessly, often without giving very much credit to those from whom they had learned. Their engineers swiftly became first-rate, and as they did, the companies ceased to be the shaky imitators they had been and became dynamic and confident. All of this expedited the movement into mass production, and as the Japanese moved into mass production, their costs fell remarkably. Nor was this a leisurely game conducted by gentlemen under gentlemen's rules. The intensity of domestic competitition in Japan ensured that it would be brutal and relentless, a true survival of the fittest. All efforts were geared toward market share.

It was important for American auto manufacturers not to underestimate their Japanese competition, Abegglen felt. Having watched the process in other businesses, he knew that once the Japanese edged toward mass production and a growing market, they did battle domestically with a single-mindedness that went well beyond American levels of competition. Abegglen felt that the auto competition would be especially bitter. First, because of the very cost of a car, the stakes were unusually large. Second, the auto industry had been protected by MITI since the war, and it had been impossible for foreigners to penetrate the Japanese market. But now, as the Japanese exported, they would lose much of that protection, and so the pressure on the Japanese auto companies to lock up their own domestic market, keeping out the Americans and the Europeans, would be vicious.

In 1960, as the auto companies readied themselves for the assault, Abegglen had a sense of déjà vu; he had seen the same thing happen in steel and shipping and motorbikes. He knew how the Japanese would do it. First they would study the Americans and the Europeans, adopting what suited them. Next they would go all over the world buying the most modern technology available for their factories, or buying single machines which they would then copy and make themselves. At this juncture, profit would not be important. Abegglen realized, long before other Americans, that in the beginning, when a market was opening up, the Japanese would base their critical decisions not on profit but on share of market. They would sacrifice everything for market share. Profits, paying back their bank loans, would all come later, after they got their share. Market share was essential; if a company gained it, all else would follow. If it failed at securing an acceptable piece of the market, then the company would fail.

The fury with which Japan unleashed itself upon international trade, the kind of economic Darwinism that was at the center of its impulse, originally came not just from each company's desire to conquer the world but from its desire to take market share away from domestic competitors. In Japan there was always someone ready to undersell someone else, and there was always someone on the edge of bankruptcy. The intensity of that competition was a powerful force in pushing the Japanese to export; the greater the exports, the greater the mass volume, and the more they could cut their costs at home. The more they could cut their costs at home, the stronger their hold on the domestic market. That, Abegglen knew, had made them particularly tough competitors for the unsuspecting Americans and Europeans. For any Japanese company venturing overseas had first survived and then triumphed in the most rigorous competition imaginable. By the time a Japanese company entered the international scene, all the baby fat was off. In that kind of competition, victory often depended on the tiniest of advantages. In the early sixties, Abegglen realized, the auto industry was just opening up. He had seen Japanese companies in other fields go after one another at comparable moments, clashing horrendously, and he knew that whoever was strong enough to win the predatory conflict in the domestic Japanese auto game would be a powerful player in the American market.

The classic lesson for all Japanese industrial companies, he was aware, one that was all but branded on the forehead of every aspiring Japanese industrialist, was the occasion in the mid-fifties when Honda simply took the motorbike market away from what had been a much bigger, richer company named Tohatsu. As the competition began, Tohatsu held a large share of the market, 22 percent, with Honda just behind at 20 percent. Honda was heavily in debt, and Tohatsu was not. Tohatsu's after-tax profits were 8 percent of sales, Honda's only 3.4 percent. It seemed a complete mismatch. But Soichiro Honda was an authentic genius, a man who loved to create and to experiment, the closest thing that modern Japan had produced to the first Henry Ford. His timing was impeccable. In the late fifties the motorbike had allowed Japan to motorize itself. Cars were scarce, gas was expensive, and the motorbike had become the vehicle of the rising middle manager. In 1955 the market started growing at about 40 percent a year. Honda had a better bike and better marketing, and his company simply took command of the new middle-class segment. Tohatsu responded to a growing market with great complacency. So when the five explosive years of growth were done, Honda had destroyed Tohatsu. It had eleven times Tohatsu's share of the Japanese market, 44 percent to 4. In 1964, Tohatsu declared bankruptcy. There were comparable stories in other businesses.

Because of that dynamic, Abegglen thought that while the social and cultural forces behind the Japanese industrial surge were important, they were on occasion overemphasized. A crucial part of Japan's success came from the fact that the country was both coming into its industrial prime and achieving a middle-class life-style. The Japanese were accomplishing in a period of ten or fifteen years something that earlier in the century had taken the United States forty or fifty years. Abegglen and other consultants had studied the statistics, and they had concluded that in no other country in the world did the market for a coveted consumer item go so quickly to saturation as in Japan. In a period of just three years the market could grow from perhaps less than 15 percent of its potential to more than 75 percent. In Western Europe, by contrast, it took eight years or more for a market to become saturated.

There were several reasons for this. To start with, Japanese salaries were remarkably even; no one segment of the population seemed to be either dramatically richer or poorer than another. Everyone seemed to arrive at the ability to buy a hot new item at roughly the same time. In addition, the Japanese were natural consumers, and status was closely allied with consumption. If someone had the first television set or motorbike or piano on the block, or had taken a trip to Hawaii, then everyone on the block wanted the same thing, and not to have it brought a certain shame. Finally, the population was physically concentrated as the populations of most Western countries, with the possible exception of England, were not. This meant that it was an unusually easy audience to reach by advertising in both print and broadcast.

Very few Americans, Abegglen believed, ever realized how big the Japanese market was; there was somehow a vague Western assumption that since Japan was a small country, it was a small market. Yet it was in the postwar years a country of some hundred million people, twice the size of West Germany. Still, the American automotive industry was unwilling to make right-side-drive cars in order to sell in that market. Japan was potentially one of the great markets in the developed world, albeit a highly protected one, and a market that could explode. There had been rare examples of consumption explosion in America—the race to buy television sets, first black-and-white and then color, had been extraordinary. But in Japan everything was explosive. An industrialist had to hit the expanding market or die. It was a hothouse economy, all of this consumer energy whipped to a high pitch by modern advertising and marketing.

The pressure on the industrialists was particularly intense. Abegglen felt for Nissan's president, Katsuji Kawamata, in the early sixties. Everyone would be coming to him and demanding money—money for plants, for steel, for shipping facilities, expenditures that anticipated the battle still to come—and Kawamata would have to make a decision on every request. Even if he made them right, there was still a long period before any return would be visible; if he made the wrong ones he would be dead. There was what the consultant groups liked to call a learning curve in an industry. In its most elemental phrasing it went like this: The more cars you manufactured, the better you became; your engineers got better and your processes got better. Thus as you produced more and better cars, the cost of each car not only went down but went down sharply. In a way this was what had happened to the Ford Motor Company in its early years, when Henry Ford had systematically upgraded his assembly line without really changing his car. Now this was happening in Japan, with one major difference: Again and again Henry Ford had had to wait for technology to catch up with his dreams, but the Japanese were going through their growing period when the technology, often foreign-developed, was already available and was fifty years more advanced than in Ford's day. That meant the race was even faster and the speed of the learning curve was even quicker. The Boston Consulting Group, of which Abegglen was a founder, had figured out that in Japan, for each doubling in the learning curve, or in accumulated experience (the accumulated experience was the total number of cars manufactured), the cost in real terms dropped somewhere between 20 and 30 percent. Since in the days of explosive growth a company might go through a doubling every year, that meant that its costs were coming down at an astonishing rate. The stress in a period like this was immense, for the only way to win was to pour money back in, expand some plants, build others, and keep them running two or three shifts. Abegglen, who had watched Japan come into industry after industry, doubted that the American auto companies had any idea of what this might mean to them, and of how good the Japanese would quickly become. The Japanese might make an appalling number of mistakes in the beginning, but they would not make mistakes very long, and their quality would soon be very high.

A decade later, a study done by two of Abegglen's colleagues in the Boston Consulting Group, Thomas Hout and William Rapp, showed how right he had been. The study compared the prices of similar Japanese and American cars. In 1952 the American car had cost $1500, the Japanese car $2950; by 1959 the gap had begun to close, roughly $1900 for the American car, $2100 for the Japanese. By 1961 the Japanese car was slightly cheaper, $1750, as opposed to $1850 for the American. By 1964 the economies of scale had had a clear effect; a Japanese car cost $1400, an American $1900. By 1970 the difference was dramatic, $1210 for the Japanese, $2215 for the American.

The stress of those years, as Nissan went from a crude, weak company to a major auto maker was enormous. At every level of the operation but particularly for the engineers, it was a revolution rather than an evolution. For the company that Minoru Tanaka, the engineer, had joined in 1956 struck him as primitive, compared to the Niigata Ironworks. The ironworks was not a particularly rich company, even by Japanese standards, but it had an electric calculator for line drawing, while the engineers at Nissan were forced to use a wooden one, hand wound and hand driven. Tanaka's early meetings with the then engineering staff at Nissan shocked him. Tanaka had just emerged from a world where there was great emphasis on structural analysis and where plans were done scientifically, with numbers always containing the truth. Nissan did not do any structural analysis. Its engineers simply took four wheels and put a box on them and fastened the box to the wheels. Soon there was a major split between the old guard and the new breed, men like himself, who wanted to apply the mathematical skills they had learned for aircraft construction. One thing Tanaka realized early on was that Nissan was becoming the beneficiary of the prohibition against an airplane industry. He saw that an exceptional number of highly sophisticated young engineers were now entering the company.

Very quickly the engineers were divided over what was the best way of building a body. The old-timers wanted to build simple, heavy frames and put the rest of the auto assembly upon them. The new men, with their aircraft construction training, favored the unitary, or monocoque, construction used in aircraft—no heavy metal frame on which everything sat but the weight distributed over a light network of connected supports. Almost as soon as Tanaka went to Nissan, he went to work on the A49X, a unitary version of the Volkswagen Beetle. Tanaka and his fellow engineers were crushed when Kawamata finally vetoed it. The 210 had just won the Australian rally and had thus achieved instant fame. The top officials were afraid the A49X would siphon sales from the 210. As far as Tanaka was concerned, an excellent car had been killed in favor of an ordinary car.

In 1963, a rising star in the engineering section, Tanaka was asked to design the Nissan President, which was to be the company's prestige car. In the beginning it was a lonely task. The only person working with him was a young secretary. After the first day she failed to show up. Tanaka had to go to her house to find her; she had not showed up because she was a modest Japanese girl and afraid to be alone with just one man. There was a delicacy to the unitary design, Tanaka thought, which was more demanding than the frame design. In the frame design there was always room for adjustment; the frame itself was the support system and the pieces fit together somewhat naturally. But with the unitary design, each component had to fit in perfectly. Tanaka was designing the car so that the engine would be slipped into the car from underneath. He had a recurring nightmare: The car was finished, production had started, the engines were placed in the bodies, and then all the engines fell out.

Tanaka's orders had been simple. He was to bring home a luxurious car that the chairman's friends would want to be driven in. Price was not the issue. He was pleased with his prototype, which he thought was proof than the unitary construction worked with big cars as well. But he had come in 440 pounds over the projected weight. Desperate, he went around Tokyo demanding that the suppliers take weight out of the component parts. Even then the President came in some 220 pounds heavier than it was supposed to. No one above him seemed to mind. It cost three times what a car in Japan normally cost, but the high price seemed to add to its prestige. From then on, Tanaka was the head of the Nissan design center, and the debate over unitary versus frame bodies was over.

If adequate production and engineering were important problems for Nissan, then quality of product was another. Above all the Japanese knew they had to gain a reputation for quality. Autos, more than any other item, would test whether the Japanese could overcome their prewar reputation for shoddy goods. For most Americans in the early sixties, that reputation still existed; the Japanese had already excelled in areas like steel and shipping, but those were products that the average American consumer did not encounter, and so they were unaware of the change. Even the men in Detroit were still joking about Japanese quality—that you had to close the doors gently in order not to bend them. Meanwhile, hundreds of Japanese productivity teams were landing in America, endlessly touring American factories. They came in groups, and to the Americans watching them they often seemed comical little men. They were all the same height, and they wore the same blue suit, and they carried the same camera. They measured, they photographed, they sketched, and they tape-recorded everything they could. Their questions were precise. They were surprised how open the Americans were—open as they might not have been for, say, English or West German visitors. The truth was, there was a certain condescension in all this; the Americans were open because they never took these odd little Asians seriously. They were both prejudiced and generous.

The Japanese exploited this prejudice skillfully, playing the role to the hilt. It was, said Masami Muramatsu, an interpreter who accompanied many of these teams, almost embarrassing the way they poor-mouthed, becoming ever more humble as they dealt with Americans. We are the poor little Japanese, they would say, we have been devastated, you are very rich and generous, and we have come to learn everything we can. The Americans, he suspected, had obviously liked their complementary role of bountiful benefector. Their lectures were a commercial extension of the American missionary spirit. In the beginning the Japanese were staggered by America, the ease, indeed eagerness, with which Americans talked to strangers, about professional matters but also about personal things. Why, the travelers would tell their friends upon their return, the Americans wanted to show visiting Japanese not just their houses, but their bedrooms!

The Americans were proud and confident in those days, and somehow innocent. Their own world was so complete that they did not really need to think of any world outside it. The American market was quite sufficient for most American managers. The visiting Japanese productivity teams were potential customers as well as students, but the major American companies never seemed very interested in talking to them about exporting—neither about selling them a main product line nor about customizing a particular product to make it suitable for Japan. There was an unusual pride to the Americans then, Muramatsu thought, a pride that was attractive in its generosity of spirit but flawed by self-satisfaction. The Americans were powerful, they were rich, they were helping their former adversaries; but they did not need to look beyond their own coasts, and they did not need to learn. There was one incident that seemed trivial at the time but that stayed with Muramatsu for long afterward. A Japanese team had been at Cincinnati Milacron, and they were about to leave on their chartered bus, and everyone was either bowing or shaking hands, when one of the company's PR men, who had been in Japan at the end of the war and who fancied that he spoke some Japanese, told them, "*Anata mata sugu kitene.*" He thought he was merely inviting them to return, a friendly parting remark. But to the Japanese it was offensive, for it was bar talk: "Honey, come back soon." The Japanese all laughed in a muffled, uncomfortable way, and got on the bus. It had been wounding, more than any of them wanted to admit. A quarter century later Muramatsu pondered why it had seemed so significant to him. In the end he decided that it was the unconscious arrogance: Americans did not need to know the languages of others; they could always do business on their terms.

There was one other thing that bothered the Japanese visitors: Americans' shameful ignorance of W. Edwards Deming. Deming was an American expert on quality control, and by the late fifties he had become something of a god in Japan. With the possible exception of Douglas MacArthur he was the most famous and most revered American in Japan during the postwar years. Beginning in 1951, the Japanese annually awarded a medal named in his honor to those companies that attained the highest level of quality. (Fittingly enough and typical of Deming, he himself supplied the prize money, from the royalties on his books, which, virtually unknown in the United States, were best-sellers in Japan.) Only an award from the Emperor was more prestigious. But when Japanese productivity teams visiting America mentioned Deming to their hosts, the Americans rarely knew his name. The few who did seemed to regard him as some kind of crank. To the Japanese that was particularly puzzling, for when a Japanese team came to America and made the rounds, city after city, factory after factory, the one American all its members wanted to see was Edwards Deming. It was like a pilgrimmage. When they did come to see him at his home in Washington, Deming knew many of them by name, because he had visited them in Japan, and he was always able to ask about their colleagues back home. As was their custom, the Japanese always came with presents, small ones lest Deming be embarrassed, and Muramatsu, the interpreter, who made countless visits to Deming's home, once decided that Dr. Deming must have more small Japanese dolls than any other person in the world.

Among the many things the Japanese liked about Deming was that he lived so modestly. The productivity teams had visited many American cities, and they were often entertained at the rather grand homes of American businessmen. Yet here was, to them, the most important man in America living in an ordinary house. The furniture was simple and the rooms were rather poorly lit, with a certain mustiness to them. That impressed them all the more. Deming's passion was for making better products, or more accurately for creating a system that could make better products. It was not for making money. He clearly had little interest in material things. He was the kind of American they had always heard about, a spiritual man, not a materialistic one. The Japanese who trekked to see him were aware that he could have profited immensely in those days, selling himself and his services to Japanese companies. The subject just never seemed to come up. There was another way in which he differed from the other Americans they were visiting. The others would lecture them, and the lectures were, however unconsciously, an exercise in power. Deming listened as much as he talked.

If Edwards Deming was gentle and courteous with the Japanese, understanding the extreme touchiness resulting from their postwar poverty, then he was often brusque with his fellow countrymen and scornful of them. He hated waste, and he felt that America had become a wasteful country, not only of its abundant natural resources but also of its human talents. It was a nation, he believed, about to squander its exceptional blessings. He mocked American management, finding it responsible for most of the nation's woes, and he liked to tell audiences that the one thing this country must never do is export its managerial class—at least to friendly nations. He had little tolerance for fools (and he thought most American managers fools), especially those who pretended to care about his principles but had no intention of changing their ways. He was for most of his career virtually unknown in America, a prophet without honor in his own land, but he was one of the most important figures of the second industrial revolution, that is, the challenge of East Asia to the West. As much as any man he gave the Japanese the system that allowed them to maximize their greatest natural strength, their manpower. His system, for quality control provided them with a series of industrial disciplines mathematically defined, and with a manner of group participation that fitted well with the traditions of their culture. It was in essence a mathematical means of controlling the level of quality on an industrial line by seeking ever finer manufacturing tolerances.

What Deming and the other leading American authority on quality control, Joseph Juran, were telling the Japanese was that quality was not some minor function that could be accomplished by having some of the workers at the lowest levels attend a class or two, or by appointing a certain number of inspectors to keep an eye on things. True quality demanded a totality of commitment that began at the very top; if top management was committed to the idea of quality and if executive promotions were tied to quality, then the priority would seep down into the middle and lower levels of management, and thus inevitably to the workers. It could not, as so many American companies seemed to expect, be imposed at the bottom. American companies could not appoint some medium-level executive, usually one whom no division of the company particularly wanted, and, for lack of something better to do with him, put him in charge of something called quality. The first thing that an executive like that would do, Deming said, and quite possibly the only thing, was to come up with slogans and display them on banners. If the company treated quality as a gimmick or an afterthought, then true quality would never result. Above all, he was saying, quality had to be central to the purpose of a company.

The America of the fifties and sixties had scorned Deming and his teaching and in effect driven him abroad to find his students. America in those years was rich and unchallenged, the customers seemed satisfied, and in most important fields there were few competing foreign products against which a buyer might judge the quality of an American product and find it wanting. The theory of management then asserting itself in American business was a new one: Managers should no longer be *of* the plant. They should come from the managerial class, as it arrived from the best colleges and business schools, and they should view management as a modern science. Their experience should not be practical, as it had been in previous generations, but abstract. Practical experience was, if anything, a handicap. They were not men who knew the factory floor, nor did the people on their boards of directors know it either. Later, after Japan became immensely successful, too much was made, Deming thought, of the fact that an ordinary Japanese worker had a lifetime contract with his company; too little was made of the fact that the Japanese manager had a comparable contract—he would stay the course, remain absolutely loyal to the company and thus to the product, and his restraint on his ambition might be its own reward. Too little was also made, Deming believed, of that fact that the Japanese manager's roots were typically in science and engineering, as were those of the men on the board of directors that judged him, while the American manager came from a business or law school, as did the board that judged *him*.

Nothing appalled Deming more than the idea of the interchangeable manager. "What is the motivation and purpose of men like this?" he would say with contempt. "Do they even know what they do anymore? What do they produce?" All they knew about was numbers, not product. All they thought about was maximum profit, not excellence of product. The numbers, of course, he added, always lied. "They know all the visible numbers, but the visible numbers tell them so little. They know nothing of the invisible numbers. Who can put a price on a satisfied customer, and who can figure out the cost of a dissatisfied customer?" One of Deming's American disciples, Ron Moen, said it was as if Deming saw work as a kind of zen experience. "What he is really asking," Moen pointed out, "is 'What is the purpose of life, and what is the purpose of work? Why are you doing this? Who truly benefits from what you do other than yourself?' Those are not questions that many people in American business want to answer anymore."

It was that belief in the value of work and in the excellence of products as ends in themselves that made him so compatible with the Japanese. The Japanese had been aware of the low level of their quality, both before the war, when Japanese goods were mocked for their shabbiness, an international joke, and even more by the middle of the war, when Japanese engineers saw American military machinery consistently outperform their own. Japan's engineers had understood long before its military the vast American superiority in engineering and manufacturing, and above all in mass production. When an American plane was captured, it would be brought back to Japanese engineers to study, and by 1942 those engineers knew the vastness of the technological gap. As they examined captured material they were sickeningly aware that the Americans were turning out better-made machines—yet machines that were obviously mass-produced—and that Japanese pilots were being sent into the skies hopelessly mismatched. Even in the immediate postwar years the Japanese were embarrassed by the shoddiness of their goods. If it rained in Tokyo, ten thousand phones might be out of order.

At the same time that the Japanese were becoming exasperated with the quality of their manufacturing, Edwards Deming was becoming frustrated with American industry. His quest, to improve the quality of industrial products by applying statistical controls, evoked no interest in the booming postwar American economy, a time of frantic and uncritical demand. Deming had been influenced by Walter Shewhart, an American physicist who at Bell Laboratories in the twenties and thirties had pioneered in the use of statistics to assure industrial quality. The Americans had used Shewhart's techniques during World War II. Indeed, the War

Department had created a small think tank at Stanford to teach and propagate those ideas, and Deming had been a part of it. So pleased was the War Department with the work of the Stanford group that it demanded that many of its defense contractors apply Shewhart's standards. Deming became expert in that application and came to love the work, for it concerned itself not just with mathematical excellence but with social value as well, helping people to make their products better and thus to make lives better. But in the mushrooming affluence of the postwar years, there was suddenly no more interest in statistical quality control, at least on the part of the new generation of managers. They felt there was no need for it, no time for it, because no company seemed able to produce fast enough for the hungry new American consumers. Instead of the use of controls to improve quality, the use of systems to expand *production* became the hot new managerial ticket in America. The result, Deming was absolutely confident, was going to be production without quality.

Deming sensed considerable sympathy for his ideas among the working engineers but none among their superiors. He liked to tell about one engineer who had worked for Western Electric during the war, when it had been a center for quality control and when the *Western Electric Control Book* was a kind of quality-control bible; the man left Western Electric in the late forties and returned eight years later to find that all the control charts had simply disappeared. For a time Deming had fought that trend, continuing to lecture and to try to inspire young engineers, but he had soon tired of the indifference of the companies themselves. "I was lighting a lot of fires," he said later of that period, "but they were all going out." When he met these new managers and tried to convince them of the importance of what he was talking about, he was acutely aware of their disdain. They did not care, he realized, and for Deming that was a serious matter, because it meant the country did not care. Blocked in his main effort, he took refuge as a statistician at the U.S. Bureau of the Census.

In 1946 and again in 1948, the bureau sent him to Japan to help the Japanese improve their census capability so that they could subsequently improve their ability to feed and house their population. But his real interest was not census-taking but quality control. While in Tokyo he met some Japanese engineers who knew of Shewhart's work and that Deming was a Shewhart man. He was impressed to find that these Japanese engineers had actually translated Shewhart's book themselves and copied it by hand. They were very unsure of themselves, he knew, but they had a surprisingly good grasp of what Shewhart was trying to say, and they sensed that it might be applicable to Japan. They were the early founders of the Japanese Union of Engineers. (They were technically not a union, but since MacArthur had said that the country could have unions, they had decided that calling themselves one was the easiest way to gain official recognition.) They would eat and drink together, which was very hard in those days, since there was so little food, but one of them worked for a company producing electric light bulbs, which were even scarcer than food, and so they traded light bulbs for their meals.

In 1950 Deming was asked by his new Japanese friends to give some lectures on quality control in Japan. He agreed to, though with some misgivings; once again, he suspected, he was going to be wasting his time. He had a terrible vision of the same cycle repeating itself in Japan. So he told one of his sponsors, Ichiro Ichikawa, that it would be worthless if he talked only to working engineers and that there was no sense in lecturing unless the highest executives of the industrial complex attended as well. Deming had no idea how Japan worked at that time, or how important Ichikawa was (he turned out to have been a former professor of most of the foremost industrialists and was exceptionally influential, being among other things the head of the Keidanren, the most prestigious of Japan's business organizations). There was no signal from Ichikawa, and Deming, who was already worn out by the language problem, believed that the lectures would be pointless. But Ichikawa *had* understood, and he cabled the top forty-five Japanese industrialists telling them to come to a meeting to hear a lecture on quality control by a famous American. Given his standing as a beloved teacher, his cable was close to an order. All forty-five came, and Deming knew that he was in business.

These people had their backs to the wall, and they had no place to turn except to him. To keep their hopes up he told them that if they listened to him they would be competitive with the West in five years. That would be 1955 and seemed an impossible goal. One Japanese executive wrote in his diary: "Here was this tall, strange American telling us that we would be an important force in five years if we did what he said. We really didn't believe him, but in order not to lose face, we did what we were told and it worked." A few months after Deming's first lecture, a wire company whose president had attended it reported a 30 percent increase in productivity, and within months other companies were reporting comparable improvements. Deming's reputation as an oracle was secured. From then on the quality-control movement had its own dynamic. The top people came to Deming with a desire to learn that bordered on obssession. Watching them, listening to their intense, often awkward questions, Deming knew that he was taking on an odd kind of permanence, that every single thing he said was being not so much memorized as codified.

Deming, who was accustomed to being ignored, realized he had touched something formidable. It was like watching some raw, powerful human force trying to assert itself. They were going to succeed, he realized. He could tell that. No one was going to stop these people, because they so earnestly wanted to succeed. They had no other priority. They would make any sacrifice. They might make a great many errors in the beginning, but they would learn to do it right, and then there would be no stopping them. Their unity of purpose—the fact that everyone in the country, from top to bottom, had the same goal—was staggering to him. The Japanese workers were clearly a manager's dream—worthy, durable, industrious, unspoiled—and they were perfect for a system like Deming's, which required mathematical skill. Even ordinary workers were amazingly adept at basic mathematics. (Indeed, the Japanese, Deming believed, possibly because of the rigors involved in mastering their own language, had what he later called the best natural statistical ability in the world.) Their managers were almost pathetically eager to do the right thing. When he told them that if they were careful and operated correctly, they could have the Americans demanding protection within five years, the Japanese could not believe him. But Deming was in fact very serious. So far as he was concerned, all the requisite elements were there. Most particularly, the Japanese were willing to work at basics while his own countrymen were moving away from them.

Edwards Deming became not just a consultant but a guru for the Japanese. It was as if this one rather professorial man could explain the inner mystery of how America had won the war. In Deming's view he was merely describing industrial systems and techniques; in their view he was giving out precious secrets. He returned almost every year to give seminars, and admittance to those seminars took on incredible status. To the Japanese privileged to hear him, he was the best kind of teacher, low-key, comfortable with himself. His lessons were simple: The company's engineers should not be separated from the manufacturing line in some nice sanitary office but should be out on the factory floor as much as possible, as much a part of the line as the workers themselves. Arriving at a difficult time for the Japanese, Deming never condescended to them. He looked at them, and, unlike so many of his fellow citizens, he saw not their poverty but their purpose. At a moment when Americans were powerful and rich and the Japanese weak and vulnerable, he, unlike many Americans, never made them feel inferior. On the contrary, he genuinely reassured them. If this brilliant American expert believed in them, they could begin to believe in themselves.

Soon they came to realize that he preferred dealing with them to dealing

with his own countrymen. It was puzzling. Here was this genius who was
becoming so famous in Japan, whose every word was so important, and
whose words actually turned into deeds—there was tangible evidence that
what he said was true, that statistical controls could bring higher quality.
Yet he was not famous at all in his own country and seemed excluded
from the main business circles. They did not bring this up with him for
fear it might embarrass him. Occasionally he made reference to it himself.
It was not that it seemed to bother him. It was as if he was apologizing
for his fellow countrymen—he was sorry they did not pay very much
attention to quality control. On occasion he would scoff at American companies that thought that managers were interchangeable. On that subject
he was an angry man. He acknowledged that many important American
business educators thought men like him were old-fashioned, but he was
sure he was right and equally sure there would eventually be a severe
punishment for companies that failed to stress quality.

Even as he was spurned by American manufacturers, his standards and
teachings were being picked up by Japanese companies, including Nissan.
The process reflected the old-boy network still operative in Japan. Deming's first sponsor had been Ichiro Ichikawa, then the head of the Keidanren business group. As quality control became a subject of compelling
importance in Japan, Ichikawa's son Kaoru became one of the top authorities on it. Kaoru Ichikawa was a professor of engineering at Todai,
and he was wired into Nissan. Soon his former students were pushing
Nissan to use Deming's techniques, and in 1953 the first quality-control
efforts were organized. In 1960, at a time when American auto companies
were paying no attention to quality at all, Nissan won the Deming prize.

PART
SIX

eight cylinders. It was a golden age for auto makers. (Indeed, in a p
ularly ostentatious celebration of GM's fifty-millionth car, in 1955, Har
Curtice, GM's president, ordered the car sprayed with a special gold
glint paint, its parts gold-plated, and its seat covers made of gold viny
The auto industry alone represented almost 20 percent of the America
GNP in those years. Not only was the industry rich but it was on the
threshold of becoming richer, for one of the most powerful lobbies ever
assembled, consisting of steel men, auto manufacturers, construction companies, real estate men, and labor unions, among others, had been pushing
for a national highway bill, and in the following year, 1956, Congress
passed it, committing the nation to $25 billion for a giant highway network,
90 percent funded by the federal government. As dinky little two-lane
roads became six-lane superhighways, cars could become even bigger and
more powerful.

The enabler of all this was curiously uncomfortable with what he wrought.
Charles Kettering of General Motors, who liked to say, "I am a wrench-
and-pliers man," invented what became known as the high-compression
engine—one that generated a great deal more power than its predecessors.
With more powerful engines, cars could become vastly bigger and carry
more of the weighty and often power-consuming optional equipment
Americans had come to crave. That was the result of Kettering's invention,
but it had not been his intention. He prized efficiency above all else. He
had seen the high-compression engine as a means of bringing far greater
efficiency to fuel consumption, but this, the last of his many great inventions, was co-opted almost from the start. Instead of bringing an era of
greater efficiency, the engine opened the door to an era of unparalleled
excess. The age of the gas guzzler had arrived.

Kettering was the exceptional man, a true American genius. He was
born on a farm in Ohio in 1876, and his early years were not easy. Getting
an education was hard enough because of his family's scant income—to
earn money he had to teach school at the same time he went to it—but
it was made much harder by his poor eyesight; it was so bad that he
needed someone to read all his textbooks to him, and so it took him six
years to graduate from Ohio State. As a brand-new chemical engineer he
got a job with the National Cash Register Company in Dayton, where he
invented a small motor that allowed cash registers to be operated electrically. The Cadillac people approached him with the suggestion that he
adapt the motor to automobiles, to serve as a self-starter, replacing the
handcrank. The idea appealed to Kettering; both uses required an engine
that could deliver a brief but strong burst of power. Working in the hayloft
of a barn with moonlighting fellow engineers from National Cash

18.
HENRY KAISER
TRIES DETROIT

Ⅰt was an age of excess. The country
was richer than ever before, and its wealth was spread more widely
Instead of a small market of the rich and a large but impotent market o
the poor, there was now a huge new middle class, for there had been
quantum leap in the disposable income of ordinary citizens. In a perceptiv
series in *Fortune* in 1953, Gilbert Burck and Sanford Parker describe
the explosion of the middle class. In 1929, they pointed out, there ha
been one million family units that were truly rich; this 3 percent of th
population received 22 percent of the total income. The lower class wa
huge—twenty-nine million families, or 80 percent of the population—bı
it received only 46 percent of the nation's income. By 1953, the percen
ages had altered dramatically. The great change had been in families wi
disposable incomes of between $4000 and $7500 (with the 1929 figur
adjusted for 1952 dollars). Once negligible as a potential market—it h
been a mere 15 percent of the 1929 population—this group, the very cc
of the middle class, suddenly represented 35 percent of the national to
and had 42 percent of the total consumer cash income. This group h
grown 44 percent in just five and a half years.

These figures both chronicled the past and foretold the future. A decı
of almost uninterrupted prosperity was ahead, most of it to be enjoyed
this new middle class and much of it to be manifested in an irresistible u
to buy larger cars. In the decade beginning in 1950, as the gross natic
product rose 37 percent, the number of registered vehicles jumped fı
49.3 million to 73.8 million, and though the rate of inflation was relati'
low, the cost of the average car went from $1270 to $1822. The cars v
getting bigger every year. In the mid-fifties, Chevrolet, struck by
trend to ever-larger Fords, decided to junk its six-cylinder cars and g

Register—"the barn gang," they called themselves—he invented a starter motor that took the need for muscle out of starting cars, enabling women and older people to drive. The innovation, introduced in the 1912 Cadillacs, boosted Cadillac's sales from ten thousand to fourteen thousand. The name of the company Kettering set up was Dayton Engineering Laboratories Company, which became known as Delco; in 1916 Delco became part of General Motors, and Kettering soon became GM's head of research.

"Most people," he once said, "think of research as either highbrow or impractical." That was wrong, he insisted. "Research is an organized method of finding out what you are going to do when you can't keep on doing what you are doing now." Immensely practical, he was someone the Japanese would have understood, for he was not so much a creator as a man of application. His other inventions included heaters for cars, chrome plating, all-purpose Duco paint (which sped the time required for car paint to dry from seventeen days to three hours), antiknock fuel, freon for refrigerators, and improved diesel engines. His greatest frustration had been his failure to create an efficient air-cooled engine. Angered because GM would no longer support his research, he resigned from the company and had to be cajoled back by Alfred Sloan, the head of GM, himself. ("Accounting always kills research," Kettering said at the time.) All of those inventions put him, at the height of his career, in fourteenth place on *Fortune*'s list of America's one hundred richest men. But none of his inventions was as important as that which led to the high-compression engine.

The larger engine Kettering was thinking about required a different kind of gasoline, one whose vapor could be more tightly confined in the cylinders before exploding and driving back the pistons. The greater that compression, the greater the power the engine would generate. For years he pushed the oil companies to develop gas of the higher octane levels needed for high compression. "When Mother Nature formed petroleum in the earth," he said, "she did not have the automobile in mind any more than the hog intended his bristles for toothbrushes, and it is foolish to expect the best molecules in gasoline to be found in crude oil." But the oil companies resisted. If he raised the compression, they told him, his cars would run poorly and the ignition systems would be damaged. In 1946, three years after retiring from GM, he began his own experiments in his lab in Detroit; he produced a high-octane gasoline and tried it out in a Chevy with a high-compression engine. The performance was far better than that of a normal Chevy, and despite the warnings of people in the petroleum industry, the gas did no damage to the engine. In 1947, at the age of seventy-one, some thirty years after his first important invention, Kettering presented a technical paper explaining his approach. He proposed a V-8 engine with overhead valves and a compression ratio virtually double the existing level of 6.5:1. It would use Kettering's new gasoline, which was easy to produce. The way was now open for much bigger cars.

The Kettering engine was installed for the first time in the 1949 Cadillac. Although the car was large, it still got twenty miles to the gallon. That pleased him. What followed did not. Soon there were huge new cars with giant engines and loaded with accessories like air conditioners, power brakes, and power steering. American cars had surged not just in power but in size; they grew two feet wider and two feet longer than they used to be, and as they grew they needed still more power. The size of automobile engines in postwar America climbed at an amazing rate, from 90 to 100 cubic inches, to 160, to 250, and finally Chevies with 325- and 400-cubic-inch engines. An ad for the 400-horsepower model said that driving it was "cheaper than psychiatry." The gas mileage, of course, went steadily down. A *New Yorker* cartoon of that era showed a Cadillac in a gas station, its engine idling as the attendant was filling it up; the attendant yelled to the driver: "Turn off the motor. You're gaining on me." As Hal Sperlich, first of Ford and then of Chrysler, pointed out, auto engineers no longer sought maximum efficiency but deliberate waste.

Extravagant waste was now feasible because of the discovery of immense new oil reserves—not, this time, in the American Southwest but in the Middle East. World War II had taught America the importance of oil. The new machines of war were fueled by oil. Etched in the minds of American planners were scenes such as the seaborne and airborne U.S. Navy systematically destroying the oil-starved Japanese in the South Pacific, and of combat engineers in France and Germany laying fifty miles of pipeline a day as they raced to keep up with George Patton's tanks. It was not, some experts said, the American bombing of the German war machine that had crushed the Third Reich; it was the failure of the Germans to find sufficient oil to keep that war machine running. During the war the Allies had had access to 86 percent of the world's oil. The significance of that statistic was not lost on the American national security establishment. Even as the war was ending, the Americans, the ascending Western power, aware that their own domestic oil production was somewhat stagnant, moved to strengthen their position in the Middle East. From 1939 to 1946, a time when geologists were finally understanding how rich the deposits in Saudi Arabia were, the American reserves increased only 6 percent, whereas the world reserves, mostly in the Middle

East, increased 60 percent. The new world of American and Western oil was in the Arab fields—"our reserves," as Harold Ickes, Franklin Roosevelt's Secretary of the Interior, called them.

Even during the war the Western nations were busy flattering the Saudis. The Americans, somewhat to the surprise of the Saudis, had offered them Lend-Lease aid, and when the Saudis had asked for very little, the Americans had not let that stand in their way. They gave the Saudis so much that, historian Herbert Feis wrote, "They have gone fishing for a carp and caught a whale." Roosevelt, on his way back from the Teheran conference, stopped off to meet with King Ibn Saud, and, courting him, promised him an airplane; a few days later Winston Churchill, not to be outdone, promised him a Rolls-Royce. At the meeting with Roosevelt Ibn Saud raised the question of what would happen to the Jews; Roosevelt promised that he would not change his position on Palestine without consulting the Arabs.

Quietly, without anyone's completely understanding what was happening, the foundation for eventual crisis was being laid. The aspects of it were these: America's energy resources were proving static, but the Middle East's were richer than ever. Those reserves were so bountiful that the idea of an oil shortage seemed ludicrous; there seemed to be an overabundance of oil. This glut weakened the leverage of the proprietor states. In addition they were weak, many of them just emerging from colonialism, unsure of themselves and their power, and attributing awesome power to the Westerners who had dealt with them so knowingly in the past. Thus was their negotiating power severely limited in the beginning. Futhermore, they did business not so much with the Western governments as with the Western oil companies, which were virtually nations unto themselves. The companies inevitably became their political allies, while, in the United States, the State Department became the ally of the new state of Israel. The issue of American support for Israel had been raised but not resolved. But no one worried very much then about the contradiction; the Arabs were weak and divided, the West was strong, and the oil was so plentiful that a shortage was almost beyond comprehension.

Experts were only then beginning to realize how valuable the Saudi reserves were. Some explorers for SoCal had stumbled on the Saudi deposits in 1932 while working in Bahrain, a small island off the Saudi coast. They found oil in Bahrain, but some domelike structures on the nearby mainland looked even more promising. SoCal immediately set about trying to get the concession for the fields. They made their approaches through Harry Philby, a British Arabist (and father of the famed Soviet agent Kim

Philby) who was advising the Saudi royal family and by chance also advising British Petroleum. King Abdul Aziz's finance minister, Abdullah Suleyman, demanded 50,000 pounds sterling in gold for the concessions. (It all seemed like a scene from a bad 1930s movie about dealing with the Arabs.) SoCal offered 50,000 pounds, and the British, who were hardly interested in the field, treated the Saudis with exceptional disdain and made only a token offer. Aided by Philby, who had become a Muslim and served all parties, the Americans won. In 1945 SoCal joined Texaco in a company called Aramco, to develop the field. At the start the Americans were quite casual about the field, and they did not, to the irritation of the Saudis, get it operating very quickly. There was pressure from the Saudi government to get greater production, and Esso and Mobil were let in to speed the process.

SoCal had at first thought the field unrewarding; it was only near the end of World War II that its full dimensions were revealed. The key was the giant Ghawar deposit; it was to other oil deposits, Christopher Rand wrote in his book *Making Democracy Safe for Oil*, what Everest was to other mountains. Some of the giant deposits in the Middle East were as long as 20 miles; Ghawar stretched for 140 miles and was up to 20 miles wide. Every time geologists tried to estimate how much oil was beneath the surface they seemed more staggered than before; it all but defied their calculations. This was truly the jewel of the Middle East. The Texas gushers had dwarfed all previous oil finds; now the Ghawar field seemed to mock those gushers too. The oil was close to the surface and close to the sea, and production in the postwar years soon became a fully automated process. In Texas it cost about $1 to produce a barrel of oil; in the Ghawar it cost 5 cents. The political problems of dealing with the Saudis were relatively minor; the companies had only to talk to one man, the king, and the government was conservative and feudal. One authority on the Saudis said it was not so much a government but a country run by one thousand people all of whom were cousins.

If geopolitics in the Middle East were fraught with danger, no one seemed to worry about it at the time. Yet a good political-scientist-cum-statistician, starting in the fifties, could probably have charted two curves predicting a crisis of considerable import. The first would have been the growing number of countries entering the oil culture and basing their economies on it. They were mainly Western European nations like France and West Germany, which, pushed by the Americans, who were financing and midwifing their recovery, were switching from coal to oil. That change-over was expedited by political considerations: The Americans and some of the European governments were wary of renewing their dependency upon coal, since the coal-mining unions were left-wing; oil, by contrast, seemed a labor-free energy. The second curve was that of rising, potentially anti-Western nationalism in the Middle East. But the intersection of those curves was still in the future; in the meantime the oil coming out of the Arab world was cheap and plentiful, a perfect support system for a nation splurging on bigger and heavier cars with more and more options. That binge shaped the decade of the fifties, years in America of a constantly expanding market. The car became the emblem of this rich new society and of its remarkable fluidity.

No organization was better suited to exploiting this dynamic than GM with its different stalls in the marketplace, a car for each stage of the upward social journey. In 1955 GM became the first American corporation to make $1 billion after taxes, on revenues of $12 billion. In that same year Harlow Curtice, the president of GM, received $750,000 in salary, bonuses, and stock options, which was both a reflection of the corporation's success and a signal to the workers to be sure to get their share too. Big was becoming bigger as the smaller independent auto makers fell by the wayside, crushed by these giants who enjoyed economy of scale. Crosley died, Hudson and Nash joined to become American Motors, Packard merged with a frail Studebaker. The pattern was very clear. When Curtice took over in 1952, GM's market share was 42 percent; three years later it was 50.9 percent. The joke at GM went: "The boss says we're still losing five out of ten sales."

The trends continued through the rest of the fifties, and the decade ended with the Big Three seemingly healthier than ever, confident that as there had been no limits in the past, there would be no limits in the future and that there would always be more people buying larger cars with more options. The scale became larger, the companies became wealthier, the industry became tighter and more controlled. Colossal GM dominated and determined pricing. Ford watched it like a hawk, and Chrysler watched Ford and tried to survive. The games within games that this monopoly occasioned were intriguing, a parody of competition. In 1956, for example, Ford brought out a brand-new model to go against a Chevy that was in the last year of that model's three-year cycle. That move seemed to favor Ford in the market. But because GM was so powerful, Ford was quite cautious about putting a higher price on its new car; the price it chose was only 2.9 percent more than that of the previous year's model. Undaunted, GM charged ahead; it gave its old Chevy a minor cosmetic change and raised its prices between $50 and $166. Ford then dared to reach for a little more; a week later it put its price up another $50. Ted Yntema of Ford later told Senator Estes Kefauver's Senate Monopoly subcommittee that this pricing episode was "like a boxing game where you try to guess what your opponent is going to do. . . . We made a very bad guess." In response to another Kefauver question he admitted that yes, if Ford had cut the price it might have sold more cars; what he did not say was that Ford was afraid to cut the price, for fear of getting into a price war with GM that it would most assuredly have lost. Because of GM's ability to raise prices without fear of being undercut by the competition, hundreds of thousands of people had to pay more for their cars, and neither Ford nor GM was under much competitive pressure to produce a better machine. Only a few observers of the industry seemed to see that in a situation like this, all companies were bound to develop bad habits.

What had happened, of course, without anyone realizing it, was that the industry had become monopolistic—what Patrick Wright called a shared monopoly—and monopolies, free of fresh challenges and new ideas, inevitably become cautious and staid. At the time, George Romney of American Motors, which was struggling along, warned of what was happening. While the Big Three, he pointed out, were musclebound and mindless in the domestic market—increasingly locked into practices that their best people knew were destructive but unable to break out of so profitable a syndrome—their European subsidiaries were often innovative, because on the Continent they encountered genuine competition. Romney realized that he was different from the other auto men, that his insights were an involuntary result of the precariousness of his position, but he was also sure that he was right, that, in his words, "there is nothing more vulnerable than entrenched success."

In the postwar years, not only did the number of automobile companies decline but the cost of doing business went up—because of large labor settlements and the inflated salaries and bonuses for management. Yet the very scale made it harder and harder to create a new company. "I thought then, and I know I was right, that something terrible was happening," Romney said years later. "A healthy sector of an economy needs births as well as deaths." The one significant postwar challenge to Detroit had come in 1945, when Henry Kaiser had tried to enter the auto business. If anyone had the ability and the resources to make it as an outsider in the closed world of autos, then it was Henry Kaiser. "No industrialist since Henry Ford has achieved so much in so short a time," *Fortune* once said of him. Henry Kaiser was not a small-time operator.

He had started as a road-paving man on the West Coast. By the time he took on Detroit he had succeeded in gravel, aluminum, and steel. He had been a principal builder of the Bonneville, Grand Coulee, and Shasta dams, as well as the San Francisco–Oakland Bridge, and during the war his factories made vast numbers of planes and military vehicles, while his shipyards turned out fleets of standardized vessels by assembly-line methods. He had long coveted a place in Detroit, and during the war, even while he was commanding prodigious war-related enterprises, Kaiser had a team of some of his best engineers tear down all kinds of cars and study them. He wanted his own people, not Detroit engineers, doing this, because he did not want to be a prisoner of Detroit's techniques. He saw himself as the rightful heir of the first Henry Ford: He dreamed of building a small, $400 car for Everyman; he would be the common man's industrialist. Right up until 1945 he went back and forth on the decision to try Detroit. In the spring of 1945 he decided to pull back. "We didn't, any of us, want to live in the East," said his son Edgar. (His offices were in Oakland, California.) But when it became clear that Henry Ford did not plan to use his Willow Run facilities after the war, Kaiser became interested. UAW officials, fearing postwar unemployment, encouraged him.

He soon decided to become partners with Joe Frazer, a maverick figure in Detroit, a supreme salesman, an Iacocca before Iacocca, who had been successful in earlier incarnations at Chrysler and Willys-Overland, among other companies, and who had decided to produce his own car. (Frazer as a Detroit insider in 1942, hearing that Kaiser was planning to build a car, had called his ideas half-baked.) Kaiser, a man of limitless confidence and optimism, was one of the great risk-takers of his era. He had dazzled most Americans with his shipbuilding successes during the war and was primed for even greater success in the postwar era. Golden years were just ahead of America, he liked to say. Look, he would tell doubters, at the $43 billion accumulated by Americans during the war in savings bonds. That was just waiting to be taken by the right entrepreneur. "That's not debt," he said. "That forty-three billion is pure venture capital."

He was constantly expanding his operations, delving into new areas. He liked to boast that every time he went to see Fred Feroggiaro, his man at the Bank of America, the banker would caution him in the same way.

"Henry, your cash position is weak."

"Fred," he would answer, "why don't you get a record of that so you won't have to waste your time telling me the same thing again and again?"

He and Frazer were able to rent the Willow Run plant from the government for very little. Everything seemed to be in place. Yet everyone who had any experience with the automobile industry warned against his entry. The stakes were too high, the costs too great, and the existing companies too strong. If anything, with young Henry Ford about to rejuvenate Ford, the competition was likely to become more formidable than ever before. Those doubts never moved Kaiser. "They tell me I'm going out on a limb," he said. "Well, that's where I like to be—way out on a limb. We're going to service the nation, the whole world. We're going to produce thirteen million cars." Besides, getting into something like autos was part of a dream to him. The problem with most of what he did, he often said, was that you built a bridge or a dam and, no matter how great a job it was, when you were finished, it was done. "I want to get into a business that will know no end," he added, "where you build something and then keep on building it."

Kaiser and Frazer made two public stock offerings. The Kaiser name was an extraordinary draw, and the results were remarkable. Wall Street was stunned. The first offering went at $24 a share, the next one at $20. After the first issue, which raised $16 million, Henry Kaiser called in Clay Bedford, who was in charge of manufacturing.

"What do you think, Clay?" he asked.

"Not bad, Henry," said Bedford. "The only thing wrong is you should have moved.the decimal point over, made it a hundred and sixty million, and then multiplied by two. With three hundred and twenty million we might have a chance."

The two offerings raised some $53 million. The sum pleased Frazer, who, unlike the Kaiser men, was confident they had enough money. In January 1946, Frazer gave a dinner in honor of Henry Kaiser at the Detroit Club. That night many of the city's auto potentates turned out to meet the new gun in town. There was a certain edginess, for this was a society that did not freely admit newcomers. Many top General Motors executives were there, and K. T. Keller, the head of Chrysler, showed up. The Ford people were noticeably absent. Kaiser, who became quite expansive that night, kept referring to Keller as "my good friend J.T.," which did not exactly ease the suspicion of him. He and Joe Frazer, he told the gathering, were not taking this step lightly. This was serious business. Why, he said, they had raised more than $50 million, and they intended to spend all of it right here in Detroit. "Give that man one white chip," said a voice from the back of the room, referring to the smallest chip in a poker game. That was it, one white chip, for in truth, on the scale of what it took to make autos now—production facilities, supplies, dealerships, labor—that was all the two of them had, one chip in the poker game.

That evening seemed to symbolize Detroit's attitude toward these interlopers, who had made ships, not autos. When the spare tire of one of the early Kaiser cars was mounted on the left side of the car, there was soon a joke going around the Detroit Club: Said a Kaiser manufacturing men to the designer, "You've got it all wrong—you've got the life preserver on the port instead of the starboard." Yet if anyone had a chance of cracking what was virtually a closed industry, it was Kaiser. There was a certain frontier fearlessness to him; he had spent his life conquering the unconquerable, achieving the impossible. He and his men had performed brilliantly as manufacturers during the war; Bedford, his manufacturing chief, had once built thirty-seven ships in one month. Their timing was good, too. During the war the number of cars on the American road had dropped from twenty-nine to twenty-two million, and the country was starved for cars.

In a way Henry Kaiser surprised his critics. He had to put aside his dreams of an aluminum car and a front-wheel-drive car, but he and Frazer were in production by the fall of 1946, within a year of their first handshake. That was astounding. The quality of the engineering in their cars impressed Detroit old-timers. The compression in the engines, Clay Bedford thought, might have been better, but in general their cars won high marks for beginners. The problem was always money. There was simply never enough. The company was always undercapitalized. It would have taken ten years, some members of the company realized later, to build up a reputation and a small tradition and a good dealer network. The $53 million was start-up money, nothing more. It cost $15 million just for a line to produce the engine blocks; it cost $10 million more for a line to build bumpers. The expenditures were so immense that the Kaiser people were overwhelmed. "Henry never understood the scale," Bedford said later. "He knew how to deal with challenge—he could build Grand Coulee Dam. He knew cement and sand and steel. But he didn't understand the complexity of scale in auto. I'm not sure anyone does. At one point I tried to explain it to him. 'Henry,' I said, 'they've got an entire engineering room over at General Motors where the only thing they do is try to figure out how to take one tenth of one cent off of each floor mat.'"

Completely unprepared for what he had taken on, Kaiser soon discovered that his partner, Joe Frazer, who was supposed to know the business, was primarily a salesman—he knew less about what really took place in a factory than the Kaiser people did. "We hit the bottom of the pot so quickly," said Clay Bedford. The company could afford to buy only those tools that would pay for themselves within sixty days. It was always a company on short rations. In 1947 Kaiser-Frazer had to borrow $12 million from the Bank of America. Soon Kaiser and Frazer decided to float a third common-stock issue. But the underwriting company backed out even as the stock was supposed to be sold. Nothing could have been more damaging. That killed a new line of cars scheduled for 1949. Meanwhile the other auto companies, slowly returning to production after the war, were bringing out full lines and squeezing Kaiser's territory. In 1949, Frazer broke with the Kaisers and became only a sales adviser. The strings on the company were getting shorter. The financial pressure kept mounting; the hurdles were getting higher and there were shorter intervals between them. The 1949 model did not sell. Desperate, Kaiser's son Edgar went to the Bank of America for more money. "I'll lend you money on anything," Fred Feroggiaro replied, "except Kaiser-Frazer."

The end was nearing. For the first five years of its life, Kaiser-Frazer had a net loss of $34 million, and its creditors had a larger share in the company than its stockholders. In 1949 it made 58,000 cars and lost $39 million on its operation. The next year was better, but even then, when it sold 151,000 cars, it lost $13 million. That year Packard made $5 million on sales of 72,000. In 1951, with the Korean War at its height, Henry Kaiser remained ebullient, despite his automotive problems. Willow Run was producing planes for defense again. "Do you think I'm worried?" he said. "How could I be when I see well over five hundred million dollars in defense backlogs? As for earnings, I can't be bothered to worry about accounting mechanics—pushing figures back and forth. Why, after this trouble [the Korean War], I see ribbons of cargo planes in the sky." In 1953, Kaiser-Frazer merged its remnants into Willys-Overland, its brief history a case study of how hard it was to get into the auto industry with only one white chip. "I knew it would be hard and I knew we might not make it," Henry Kaiser said later on, "but I never thought we'd put so much in and it would disappear without a ripple."

There was no better industrialist in America, and he had failed in Detroit, and failed during an auto boom. The fact of that failure closed off the auto industry from normal capitalism, made it immune to challenge from new competitors. Prospective industrialists, pondering the possibility of going into the auto business, always had the case of Henry Kaiser to consider. The ideal circumstance for capitalism in America in the late seventies, a knowledgeable venture capitalist named Bill Hambrecht once said, came when the price of entry was between $5 million and $20 million. In that area the new high-technology companies would flourish; a talented man with a good scientific background and the right idea could raise that kind of money, and it would be enough money to start his company the right way. Below $5 million, he said, too many people tended to enter the field. It was what he called a hotdog-stand price: Soon there would be too many hotdog stands. At the other extreme was heavy industry— wildly expensive. There the ticket was so high that most would-be entrepreneurs were scared off. Thus the existing companies went unchallenged and a de facto monopoly was created.

If the price in the auto industry was $300 million in 1945, then it was infinitely higher three decades later. Certainly by the late seventies, said one Detroit expert, $2 billion was conservative.

In 1950, as the handwriting on the wall became ever more legible to him, Henry Kaiser asked his manufacturing boss, Clay Bedford, and Bedford's wife, along with Edgar Kaiser, to dinner at the Book Cadillac, one of the best hotels in Detroit. Bedford had been the one who had told Kaiser the hard news that the $32 million gained from the first stock sale was a mere fraction of what was needed. "Clay was right and I was absolutely wrong," Kaiser said to Mrs. Bedford. "We were always completely undercapitalized. Everything that went wrong was my mistake."

19.
THE ORGANIZER

In the midst of one of the periodic struggles in the fifties between Ford and GM in which Ford, seeing GM raise its price, immediately raised its own, Walter Reuther, head of the United Auto Workers, had scoffed at the Ford people. "This is the first time in the history of free enterprise," he said, "where a company raised the price of its products in order to be competitive." No one had a better sense of the weaknesses of the auto companies than Reuther; no one could tweak them better, and anticipate and counter their moves even before they knew they were going to make them. He towered over other labor leaders of his generation, idealistic and pragmatic, visionary and shrewd, the only man in America, Murray Kempton once wrote, who could reminisce about the future.

He was not much afflicted by self-doubt, and it never occurred to him that the men running the companies might be his spiritual or intellectual equals. Once Charles E. "Engine Charley" Wilson, the head of General Motors, turned to Peter Drucker, the business historian, and told him that Walter Reuther was a remarkable man, perhaps the ablest man in the entire auto business, and that if he had only been able to finish college, why he might be sitting right where Wilson was, as the head of GM. Drucker, mistakenly thinking the story flattering, repeated it to Reuther, who was terribly offended by Wilson's suggestion. "It would *never* have taken me that long to become head of General Motors," he said.

He was a man of considerable social conscience, who railed against the power of the Big Three but who would not admit that the union might have gotten too powerful as well. When his friend George Romney would argue with him about this, suggesting that the union had in effect joined the companies as part of the monopoly, Reuther would answer that there was no problem, since the union's power would be well and positively used, and he, Walter Reuther, was the guarantor of that. Romney, fond as he was of Walter Reuther, was not so sure. He was not at all convinced that even the most benevolent of men could handle unchecked power. Reuther was stung to the heart that he could be accused of even potentially abusing power. As far as he was concerned, his life was about restraining power, not abusing it.

He came from a German immigrant family in which the only thing rivaling the Lutheran religion in importance was socialist politics. It was not surprising that he was the ultimate puritan. He was legendary in the world of union leaders for his lack of personal indulgence. Other labor leaders wore expensively tailored suits and large, flashy rings; Reuther wore suits off the rack and no jewelry. Other labor leaders flaunted the elegance of their vices, drinking only the best brands of liquor and smoking the finest cigars; Reuther did not smoke and barely drank. The puritanism was natural to him, but it was also an extension of his idealism. He hated the annual AFL-CIO conventions, which always seemed to be held in Florida; to him the conspicuous consumption that took place at them mimicked the least attractive habits of management, men fattening themselves on the labor of ordinary workers. He went, but he went under a kind of personal protest; he brought along his own orange-juice squeezer and bought his own oranges so that he would not have to pay exorbitant hotel prices for fresh orange juice. When the other labor leaders went on union-sponsored trips to the racetrack, Walter and May Reuther went along, but only to tour the stables and look at the horses; they never went to the races. When he and the other UAW leaders went out to dinner, they did not, as most other comparable officials in America did, simply sign for the check. Reuther made them all pay from their own pockets, and each person paid exactly according to what he had eaten.

He deliberately paid himself a low salary in order to keep down the style of living of the other UAW executives. In 1945 his salary was $7000 a year, and Charley Wilson's was $459,000, a disparity that seemed to comfort Reuther, for it justified his cause. During the Eisenhower years, there was a congressional investigation of the union's finances. "Do you really mean to tell me," one of the investigators, who had just checked Reuther's hotel bills, asked a union official, "that Walter Reuther pays for his own dry cleaning when he stays in a hotel?" Yes, said the official; in fact Reuther had once handed in an expense account that included a charge for $1.50 for dry cleaning, and Earl Maizey, another union official, had bounced it. Reuther was as careful with his own money as he was with the union's. His personal investments were not exactly daring. In 1948 he put $1000 into Nash Kelvinator stock, and some eight years later sold it for $1001.26. When that transaction was made public at a congressional hearing, one Detroit reporter at the press table sent a note to another: "Reuther—the fox of Wall Street."

His life was not about material things. The constant success of the union was reward enough. In his lifetime and under his leadership he had watched the United Auto Workers grow from a small, badly fragmented group of scared, disenfranchised workers to one of the most powerful and proudest social-industrial organizations in the world. Even men who were critical of most unions spoke of the UAW as special, a union that was about somehting more than just annual raises, a union with a larger purpose. Indeed, some of the auto executives paid it the highest compliment of all. They sometimes wished, they said, that they were dealing with the Teamsters, which was a corrupt and undemocratic union, rather than the UAW, because with the Teamsters you could cut a deal and bypass the rank-and-file.

If there was a certain nobility of purpose—a vision of a better and more just society—that drove the union, then much of that came from Walter Reuther. Certainly part of the reason as well was the era; he had been the right man at the right time, coming along at the beginning of the New Deal when Detroit's huge, beleaguered, angry work force, embittered by the Depression and full of nascent energy, was not only willing to stand up to management but, for the first time in the century, receiving some governmental protection. Reuther believed in the union, believed in what he had done. Some thought there was an innocence to his conviction about the attainability of a better society, but he had already seen it happen.

Some found him single-minded, and they were right. He had almost no other interests, the union was his life, and he was unable to relax and become involved in anything else. Everything to him was serious. Even the annual Christmas-carol sing at Walter Reuther's house, one friend noted, was a *serious* Christmas-carol sing. In all things other than work, one close friend noted, he was something of a bore, possibly the only native-born, working-class, adult male in all Detroit, a great blue-collar city, who had no interest in the Detroit Tigers. Small talk around him was virtually impossible. If his buddies persuaded him to go out with them for an evening and have some fun, suddenly, in the middle of dinner, there would be Reuther, pushing the others back to business. "We aren't getting any workers organized sitting here and talking," he would say. It was said that if you asked Walter Reuther what time it was, he would tell you not only how to make a watch but how much to pay the workers. His speeches were always long; often they went on for two or three hours and were delivered in an oddly strident voice. To people not in the union they could seem dull and interminable. To the workers they were spellbinding. His passion always showed through, and it profoundly affected them.

He was never really one of the boys. That was the first obstacle he overcame. Many of the best of the labor leaders of his generation had a certain earthiness to them; they were good natural politicians, gifted story-tellers who had worked their way up through the ranks by dint of shrewd-ness and gab, friends of everyone, fixers of problems, men more of charm than of vision. Reuther, fairly humorless and, thanks to his mother, the product of a stern Lutheran upbringing, was different. He went to meet-ings to achieve goals, not to pal around. The essential rites of a labor union eluded him. Valentine Reuther, his father, once boasted, "I can drink more than all four of my sons put together."

The other obstacle was that in the earlier years, at least, he was much farther to the left than the average worker. He was a true socialist, his real aims reaching well beyond the primal needs of the membership. But his devotion to their cause was so complete, he was so clean and straight and unbuyable, that workers who might not be at ease with him personally gave him their absolute professional trust. His beliefs were the product of an almost unique kind of upbringing. As the sons of Joseph Kennedy had been raised to run for public office, preferably the presidency, so the sons of Val Reuther had been raised to bring social justice to an indus-trialized world that most demonstrably lacked it. Theirs was a home im-mersed in socialist principles. Jacob Reuther, Walter's grandfather, was a socialist and a pacifist who, fearing the rising tide of Prussian militarism, came to the United States in 1892 rather than have his sons conscripted into the German army. The family lived a spare, harsh existence; years later Walter Reuther's younger brother Victor remembered the starkness of his grandfather's house in Effingham, Illinois, a log cabin whose only heat was from the kitchen stove, and whose only light, well into this century, came from lanterns. Jacob Reuther was a religious dissident, and as a young man he had often complained about the kind of clergymen who neglected the human needs of the ordinary members of his flock while ministering only to the whims of the wealthy. In Jacob Reuther's house the children were not entertained with folklore and myth; he did not want his children to believe in the righteousness of kings, who, as far as he was concerned, were simply highwaymen who had used force to attain power. Life, he lectured his children, was filled with economic injustice. He liked to tell them the story of an election in his hometown in Germany, how a man named Dr. Gross, a major employer and public official, had run for reelection with a banner that said, "He who does not vote for Dr. Gross will find himself, on the day after, out of work." He was a pious man who refused for religious reasons to slaughter animals; his wife, knowing the family needed meat and poultry, finally did it. Frustrated by the bland preaching in the local Lutheran church, he decided to hold his own services at home.

Valentine Reuther was very much his father's son. He had remained a good Lutheran in the new world, but as a young man when he heard his pastor attack labor unions, he stood up in front of the congregation, denounced the pastor, and left the church for good. He was a part of the wave of immigration, he told his sons, of men who made 15 cents an hour in America instead of 25 cents a day in the old country. That made things only a little bit better, but there was more hope in America, more promise of change. He was an early American socialist, and Eugene Debs, the great socialist leader in the early part of the century, was his idol. Val Reuther organized West Virginia three times for Debs, in 1904, 1908, and 1912. He even ran for Congress once on the Socialist ticket. The one time that Victor Reuther ever saw his father cry was after they had visited Debs in a federal prison in West Virginia, where he was serving time for pacifist activities during World War I. "How can they put a man so good in prison?" the father said to his son.

Val Reuther drove a brewery wagon, was paid $1.50 a day, and spent his years trying to organize his fellow workers in the brewery. His was a completely politicized home, finely tuned to any sort of public injustice. When Victor Reuther, as a young boy who loved comic strips, by chance brought home a copy of a Hearst newspaper, he was beaten by his father for his sin. It was also a home filled with raw immigrant idealism and with the passion to achieve in this new, freer world what had been denied in the old one. When Andrew Carnegie, in the process of bestowing libraries upon thousands of towns in America, made the mistake of trying to give one to Wheeling, he ran into Val Reuther. Earlier there had been a strike of local steelworkers which Carnegie and his men had put down by force. Val Reuther led a successful fight to reject the gift and to have the city build its own library. He had opinions on *everything*. (In 1946, at the convention that elected Walter Reuther head of the UAW, Walter had brought his parents up to the rostrum and introduced them to the delegates and had called his father "an old soap boxer, an old rabble rouser . . . I advise you not to yell for a speech when I introduce this fellow because he may make one.")

Anna Stocker Reuther, also born in Germany (she and Val had met at a workingmen's tavern in Wheeling, where he delivered the beer and she worked in the kitchen), was a strong woman, an earnest member of the Lutheran Church. Val Reuther put his energy into the politicization of his children, but his wife was equally determined that their moral fiber be worthy of their political idealism. After her husband left the church, Anna Reuther continued to take her five children to services. Val, in order not to lose political control of his boys, began to question them about what the minister had said. Soon these informal sessions grew into a Sunday debating society. Brother was pitted against brother. Their father assigned the topics—women's suffrage, pacifism, socialism, military spending— and the boys went off to the library and prepared all week for the coming disputation. Their father was timekeeper, moderator, judge. It was serious business, in effect a Reuther family town hall. Years later, as they debated opponents during the industrial struggles in Detroit, they were well trained in the art of thinking on their feet.

It was a home with very little in the way of material things. Flour sacks, bleached out, became pillowcases, sugar sacks became underclothes. The soap was made at home out of fat drippings and lye. When young Walter used a new umbrella as a parachute and ruined it, Anna Reuther promptly turned it into a black waterproof shirt. There were prayers before every meal, and there was music after dinner. Later as the family prospered a bit, the boys wanted an indoor toilet. Val protested. Finally a compromise was reached; the toilet was located indoors but just off the back porch. Val did well as a representative of a brewery, but during Prohibition West Virginia voted dry, and he lost his job. The family for a time took in boarders. At one point Walter and his brother Roy raised chickens in order to sell eggs and thus augment the family income. Since big eggs were in far greater demand than small eggs, the boys—with what was to be typical Reuther thoroughness—wrote to the West Virginia farm extension service asking about feed that would create bigger eggs. Back came sound advice. Soon the Reuther chickens began to produce bigger eggs; thus encouraged, the boys continued to experiment with feed. The eggs got bigger and bigger until finally the chickens started to die because they could not lay their own giant eggs.

Walter Reuther was a child of the modern industrial century. He was born in 1907, one year before the invention of the Model T. It was a time when the average workingman was utterly powerless, when the political and judicial structure of the society was largely the instrument of the proprietary class. It was harder to break out of class in those days. For people as poor as the Reuthers, sending one's children to college was almost unthinkable, and Walter was virtually self-educated. (Almost all his contemporaries in the UAW leadership were men who had never been to college but were voracious readers.) Young Walter Reuther dropped out of high school in his junior year and went to work for Wheeling Steel as an apprentice tool-and-die maker. He earned 11 cents an hour. Eventually he was fired for leading a protest movement. His career, he realized, as befit a son of Valentine Reuther, was more likely to be as an organizer of workers than as a worker himself. Organizing was his passion and his talent. In 1927, as was probably inevitable, he migrated to Detroit. He was nineteen and a skilled tool-and-die maker, and if any city was a magnet for a bright ambitious young organizer, it was the Detroit of the mid-twenties.

There the storm was gathering. Detroit had been an industrial center for some twenty years, and the owners, mainly through the use of spies and bully boys, had successfully resisted any intrusion by labor; there were perhaps 500,000 men working in some way or another for the auto industry, and none of them belonged to a union. It was the classic company town. The pay, once deemed good, was now poor, and the working conditions were horrible. Workers were deprived of the most elemental kind of dignity. It was an owner-worker relationship of contempt on the one hand and fear and hatred on the other. The companies and the judges and the police were all on the same side; if workers attempted to picket and company thugs attacked them, the police stood idly by and watched. But the times were changing. The New Deal had not yet arrived, but the forces that were to energize it were already coming together. The anger and the frustration and the bitterness were there. Too much money was being made off too much labor under too harsh conditions with too little going to the workers themselves. The exploitation had not dimmed the hopes of the workers, it had simply raised their consciousness. The companies themselves were growing more and more repressive; some executives sensed that the protest feeling was becoming stronger all the time.

Given the strength of the companies, the task of the union organizer seemed impossible. The companies were all-powerful, they had vast resources, spies, complete control of the government matrix. But the sheer numbers of the workers had a force of their own, and their resentment was manifest. This was not some small company town where, despite the absence of modern labor relations, there was at least a measure of paternalism on the part of the owner. This was the cruelest kind of modern industrial setting, of speeded-up production lines, of brutal foremen, and not even a glimmer of protection for workers in hard times. Just as a harsh right-wing dictatorship often begets a harsh left-wing successor, the sheer strength of the big companies, their truculence, their determination to fight off all union incursions, meant that they would undoubtedly create —as if in their reverse image—a powerful, adversarial, industry-wide union.

Walter Reuther worked briefly at the Briggs body shop, where working conditions were so bad that it was known as the Slaughterhouse, and then left to work at Ford. As an able and experienced diemaker, he was earning as much as $1.40 an hour at a time when unskilled production-line workers were making $4 a day (in a company that had once prided itself on its $5-a-day wage). While he worked he finished high school and started Detroit City College (later Wayne State). In an application for membership in a high school civics club he wrote: "I realize that to do something constructive in life, one must have an education. I seek knowledge that I may serve mankind." He was working at Ford when the Depression struck. No city in the country was harder hit by the utter collapse of the economy. Jobs disappeared overnight by the tens of thousands, nor was there the frailest kind of social mechanism to ease the workers' fierce plight. To Walter Reuther, joined now by his younger brother Victor, what had happened was a confirmation of everything he had always heard in his home. Like many in that era, he became radicalized by the experience. In the 1932 election he spoke actively for Norman Thomas, who was running on the Socialist ticket. He joined the radical autoworkers' union. He was soon fired from Ford and was always convinced that the reason for his firing was his political activity both inside and outside the plant.

Rather than wait around Detroit cursing the darkness, Walter and Victor Reuther took their savings, $900, and set off on a trip around the world, which took them through Nazi Germany and then to an auto factory in Gorki, in the Soviet Union, where they worked under desperately primitive conditions with Russian workers for a year. They felt immense sympathy for the Russian workers and had few illusions about the grim Soviet system. Eventually, in 1935, they returned to Detroit, no longer just young militants but men of the world. The time was ripe. The Detroit they returned to was much the same, and times were if anything harder. But Franklin Roosevelt had been elected President, the New Deal was under way, and for the first time the power of the government was at least neutral in industrial disputes. Roosevelt said that if he were a workingman, he would join a union; that had an electrifying effect upon union organizers, and the workers were emboldened. National sentiment was with them. In the previous year, 1934, GM had made a profit of $94.9 million while the average worker had earned only $1100. The raw human energy that had been accumulating in industrial cities like Detroit for some twenty years was finally emerging as a political force. Not only was the President of the United States sympathetic to workers, as his predecessor had not been, the new governor of Michigan, Frank Murphy, elected in 1936, was also more sympathetic than his predecessor. Union activities that in earlier days would have been crushed were now condoned. At the same time the Reuthers and their colleagues devised new techniques, such as the sit-down strike, in which the workers would, on a signal, take over a plant and barricade themselves in, while management, afraid of having its expensive machinery smashed in a battle of force, tried to figure out what to do. It was a heady moment suddenly filled with new possibilities. For the first time union organizers perceived genuine vulnerability on the part of these huge, rich companies. Walter Reuther was perfectly positioned. He had returned to Detroit absolutely determined to organize the production workers. His mission was a family affair, for Victor soon joined him, and another brother, Roy, a gifted organizer, was already in Flint.

In the fall of 1936, Reuther became the head of Local 174, a small unit on the west side of Detroit. His members worked at several companies, of which, he decided, Kelsey-Hayes was the most vulnerable. It supplied wheels and brake drums for Ford. He had Victor take a job at Kelsey-Hayes as a punch-press operator. The Reuthers, with a few colleagues, worked out their plan. On December 10, 1936, with Victor inside the plant to manage things, the strike began. A woman worker pretended to faint. Victor Reuther then pulled the switch stopping the line. The sit-down strike had begun. Paul Danzig, the company's personnel director, demanded that the workers return to their jobs. Only Walter Reuther can make them do that, replied Victor Reuther. Danzig phoned Walter Reuther demanding that he end the strike. At Reuther's suggestion, Danzig sent a car for him, and Reuther soon arrived in it, got up on a platform, and immediately started to make an organizing speech.

"What the hell is this?" Danzig asked. "You're supposed to tell them to go back to work."

"I can't tell them to do anything," Reuther answered, "until I get them organized."

In the end Kelsey-Hayes turned into a considerable victory for the UAW and for the Reuthers. Grudgingly, management came around; it accepted the union and granted an hourly wage of 75 cents an hour, double what men had been getting and more than triple what women had received. Reuther's Local 174, which had entered the Kelsey-Hayes strike as a fledgling unit of under a hundred members, grew immediately to three thousand; within a year, with the skills of all three Reuthers behind it, its membership was over thirty-five thousand. Walter Reuther was thirty years old at the time. He had proved himself an effective leader, a man with both a larger vision and the small, bureaucratic, tactical skills needed to realize it. He had taken a minor local on the west side of Detroit and turned it into a power base.

An even bigger struggle was shaping up at virtually the same time in Flint, a GM company town, where 80 percent of the families were dependent on that firm. There the union leadership planned a major attempt to organize one of the mightiest companies in the world. Reuther's part in the Flint strike was small, although both of his brothers were actively involved. The strike was supposed to take place sometime in 1937, but when Frank Murphy was elected governor, the leaders could no longer control the workers, and the workers themselves, their rage no longer bearable, went out on December 30, 1936. The company, with numerous spies on the payroll, was ready. Wyndham Mortimer, a high UAW official, had barely checked into his hotel when the phone rang and a voice said, "You'd better go back where you came from, you son of a bitch, or we'll take you out in a box." The showdown had begun. A local judge, friendly to GM, issued an injunction demanding that the workers vacate the premises. The UAW's lawyers checked and found that the judge, in a relationship that was not untypical of the period, owned some $220,000 worth of GM stock. That ended the injunction. Governor Murphy refused to permit the use of force to crush the workers. The company seemed paralyzed.

The workers and their leaders, accustomed to maneuvering against the odds and around heavy police opposition, now proved to be supple tacticians. Roy Reuther and one of his colleagues, knowing which working men were company spies, leaked to them that their target was Chevrolet Plant Number 9. In fact their target was Chevy Number 4, which manufactured all Chevy engines. They created a distraction at Number 9, faked GM management out, took over Number 4, barricaded themselves in, and thus shut down Chevrolet production. Governor Murphy refused to send in the state troopers. ("I will not go down in history as 'Bloody Murphy,' " he said.) Roosevelt pressured both sides to make a settlement. "Why can't these fellows in General Motors meet with the committee of workers?" he asked his Secretary of Labor, Frances Perkins. "Talk it all out. They would get a settlement. It wouldn't be so terrible." Finally, in early February 1937, GM capitulated. The UAW had won. The union was recognized. An era had ended.

It was now a time for organizing and, for Walter Reuther, building up influence within the union. The Reuthers were now a force. Smarter than many of their colleagues, more sure of their mission, they—particularly Walter—were rising stars. No one inside the union worked harder, and there were three of them. His brothers tripled Walter's possibilities. They constituted a wonderful intelligence system and gave him a remarkable capacity to stay in touch with the members. The brothers were great networkers; if a local leader had not been in contact with Walter, then he had surely just talked to either Roy or Victor. It was a faction-ridden union, as success began to come, and the principal danger to the UAW was that it would split apart. But the Reuther brothers systematically strengthened their position. Their ambition and their talent were self-evident, and it was clear to anyone else in the union with ambition that Walter Reuther would not be content for long as the leader merely of a local.

The Reuthers were attacked from both the right and the left; to the powerful and well-organized Communist faction they were anathema. But they were canny politicians, and no one could cast doubt on their fierce commitment to the union or the purity of their belief. At the 1946 convention their forces outmaneuvered those of R. J. Thomas and won the union presidency for Walter Reuther. Late one night during the convention one of Thomas's workers grabbed Brendan Sexton, one of Reuther's men, and pointed to Thomas, who was sitting at the bar with his cronies having a few nightcaps. "Look at that S.O.B.," the Thomas man said. "Right now Reuther's upstairs sleeping—but he'll be on the floor organizing people at six-thirty in the morning when Thomas is still sleeping it off."

If there had been any doubt of his position within the union, of his charismatic hold on the average workers, it was ended by two primitive assassination attempts upon him and one against his brother Victor. In the second of the two attempts thugs nearly killed him with a shotgun blast, and when Victor was attacked he lost an eye. The Detroit police did almost nothing, and the UAW officials believed that they were virtually co-conspirators. Joe Rauh, the influential liberal Washington lawyer, asked Attorney General Tom Clark to bring J. Edgar Hoover and the FBI in. Hoover, it turned out, had little sympathy for wounded labor leaders. "He says he's not going to send the FBI in every time some nigger woman gets raped," Clark reported back to Rauh. The UAW finally conducted its own investigation: There was no doubt that the assassinations had been carried out by Detroit underworld characters put up to it by anti-union company owners. From then on Reuther had his own security. His mother begged him to give up his union activities. "No, I must do what I'm doing," he answered. "It's bigger than I am and we can't run away from it."

He was messianic about the union. For him it was a dream that had been born in Valentine Reuther's home, an instrument of justice with which to temper an unjust world. It was not just about getting better wages; it was about leading lives of greater dignity. The UAW was not just a union, it was a community, and its job was to make the larger community of which it was a part a more decent, more tolerant place. He believed—as only someone of that generation, who had seen hard times and then the surge of that great, shared, American mass prosperity, could believe—in the attainability of a better society. He was also wary of any competing vision that might be dangled in front of his workers, and soon after taking over the leadership of the UAW he drove out his old adversaries (and only rarely, for tactical reasons, allies), the Communists.

Reuther scorned the company executives, with a few exceptions, such as Engine Charley Wilson and Big Bill Knudsen. He didn't like the politics of either of them, but he respected them for their decency and thought of them as *real*. He was aware, however, of the vast differences in their lives. "Walter," Knudsen once told him, "I had a wonderful Sunday yesterday. My children and my grandchildren were all there, and we all played by the pool, and I thought of you because it was so much like a Sunday that a worker would spend with his family." The story, as far as Reuther was concerned, reflected the innocence of even the most humane of managers. "You know, he's a nice guy and he meant well," he told friends, "but can you imagine it, him around his swimming pool thinking he was like one of our workers?" As for the other bosses, it was not that he considered them greedy; his judgment was more severe: He considered them narrow, knowing nothing and caring for nothing beyond their own insular world, accepting no larger obligation. They had power and wealth and yet thought only of themselves and others like them. The UAW, he was sure, would always be different, never like that.

In the fifties and sixties, Walter Reuther became one of the symbolic figures of American affluence, the leader of a union in an industry so wealthy that not only did its managers and stockholders become rich, but its workers were able to have lives of constantly increasing prosperity. Where other unions in their affluence became corrupt, his remained uncommonly pure. Where other unions shied away from social issues, the UAW remained committed to them, though how much of that social conscience trickled down from the top management to the workers themselves during the sixties was a matter of some question. Of the union's power there was no question. One did not readily receive a Democratic presidential nomination in those years without the approval of Walter Reuther.

He was critical of the companies, and yet in ways that he did not entirely comprehend, he was not only their opponent but also—as everyone became more prosperous, manager and worker—their partner. No one was better at playing the companies off against each other; he had the dynamics of the relationship down perfectly, and he knew how, in that flush market, to isolate one company, threaten to deprive it of its revenues, and then convert his victory over it into a victory over all three companies. He was brilliant at sensing which company least wanted a strike and moving against it. The memories of those golden days, when there was always going to be more, lingered long after the pie began to shrink, and later, when UAW officials gathered, they sometimes reminisced. They would nostalgically recall the time they had called on GM during Ed Cole's reign, and they had sat in the outer office, waiting to see one of the GM executives, and Cole had come bouncing into the room, and, not even looking at these strangers waiting there, had continued the conversation from the meeting just ended, saying, "We have got to get this goddam strike settled, and settled fast—no matter what it takes. We just can't risk the strike." They had sat there licking their chops when they heard that. Those were wonderful days. Yet in the end it was an essentially monopolistic union in an essentially monopolistic industry, in an era when American companies never seemed able to produce enough goods and when their greatest fear was of being shut down by a strike. There was a drawback, of course. Higher labor costs were inevitably passed on to the customers. Reuther had never liked that, and in 1946, while fighting for a large wage increase, he demanded that there be no price increase. But GM stonewalled him. What they did with prices was their business, they said, not his. The pass-on became a norm of the industry, and the UAW, voluntarily or no, accepted it. It was a world without illusion. The company and the union had an investment in each other. Bigness begat bigness. As the companies became increasingly centralized, so did the union. On both sides there was more and more at risk. Their relationship was about power and well-respected boundaries. At the end Walter Reuther was a man caught in the extraordinarily successful and profitable system that he had helped create.

He was aware of some of the threatening new trends, especially the coming of the small imported cars. Largely because of Volkswagen the number of small imports was beginning to rise to an appreciable figure. He had always thought Americans ought to be able to produce good, inexpensive small cars. But he knew that Detroit's heart was not in it, that the companies thought of small cars as a profitless hole. So he came up with an idea, a plan under which the three companies would be exempted from antitrust legislation for the purpose of pooling their efforts to make a high-quality small car. One company might build the body, another the transaxle, another the engine. He took the idea to Washington and called his old UAW sidekick Jack Conway, who was working in the Office of Economic Opportunity at the time. He asked Conway to set up a meeting with Lyndon Johnson. Conway did, but Johnson treated the idea unenthusiastically. The last thing he wanted to do was go to the auto manufacturers and waive the antitrust statues. Politically, he knew it was a live hand grenade. "Walter, that sounds like a very good idea to me. Makes a lot of sense," he said. "Now, I don't know the world of auto makers very well, but I've got a man working for me who does—Bob McNamara. You go over and see Bob about that, and if he thinks it's a good idea, why, we'll get right behind it." So Reuther went to see McNamara, who duly praised the idea even more generously and then said the companies would never stand for it, and the idea quickly died.

It was his way of trying to get free of the dynamic that the UAW had become part of. The union's wages and benefits had gone up constantly, and as they had risen they had become a large part of the company's rationale for producing bigger cars. The very success of the union had other implications. He saw the growing gap between what American workers and foreign workers were making, and recognized the eventual threat of that to American competitiveness. On occasion with friends he spoke eloquently about it. But he had become enmeshed in a system many aspects of which he disliked and few aspects of which he could control, a system that gave his workers a very good living. He was still caught in this dilemma at the time of his death. In May 1970, as he flew in a small private jet to the UAW's handsome new recreational center at Black Lake, Michigan—he had complained to friends about the high wages of the construction workers who built it—his plane crashed, and he and his wife were killed.

In a way the best example of Reuther's journey from radical, socialist outsider to powerful insider of the liberal establishment came during the Vietnam War, when, well into 1968, despite his own deep pacifist origins and his misgivings about this particular war, he stayed loyal to Lyndon Johnson and supported the war. All of the strains of his position and of his power and success, and of the contradictions between them, were revealed at a Passover dinner in the spring of 1968 at the home of Irving Bluestone, a top UAW official and a very close friend of all the Reuthers. The Bluestone seder was something of a tradition, for the wives of both Walter and Roy Reuther were Jewish, and there was a sense on this night of the Bluestones and the Reuthers as one extended family. Indeed, Walter Reuther loved the Passover ceremony, and when Irv Bluestone would read of the hardships suffered at the hands of the Egyptians, he would say, "There—the first speed-up in recorded history."

In 1968, however, the extended family was torn apart by the war. Barry Bluestone, son of Irv, was going out with Leslie Woodcock, daughter of Leonard Woodcock, the number-two man in the union. Barry and Leslie were both students at Ann Arbor, were serious antiwar protesters, and were embittered because Reuther, unlike Martin Luther King, was unwilling to break with Johnson on the war. They therefore refused to attend the seder. Eventually, in the good UAW tradition, after much negotiation, it was agreed that they would come and they would participate in the seder for fifteen minutes as Vietnam dissenters, Barry reading from the speeches of Martin Luther King, Leslie reading poems from World War I. When they finished, the atmosphere was emotional; both young people were in tears, and their elders were moved. Then Walter Reuther said, "You both obviously have a very good point. Let me, if I can, explain why I have not come out against the war." The UAW, he said, had debated the issue at great length, and feelings were very high. "But because we have major negotiations coming up soon—a very delicate time—there is a very strong feeling that this is not the time to break ranks with the President on this issue."

Even as he was finishing, Leslie Woodcock was shouting at him. "You've said it! You've finally said it!"

"What do you mean?" Reuther asked.

"For fifty cents an hour extra in the pay envelope," she said, "you'll let thousands of Vietnamese and Americans die in the war."

Roy Reuther, normally the gentlest of men, shouted at her, "That's not what Walter meant!"

"That's exactly what he meant," she said.

20.
THE MUSTANG

Lee Iacocca's timing could not have been better. He was rising through the Ford Motor Company in almost perfect step with the rising prosperity of postwar America. As director of marketing under Robert McNamara in the late 1950s, he was a great salesman in a salesman's paradise. There was so much to sell and so many people with so much money to buy it, and there was television, a wonderful new way to advertise. America was rich and optimistic, and it was a nation still in love with its cars. Gas remained cheap at the pump. But Iacocca was not merely selling cars; he was adapting the map of Ford to the new map of America. For those were years of great demographic change. Small towns were dying or declining. Farmland on the outskirts of countless cities was being developed into residential areas. Suburbs were appearing everywhere, a new American form of instant community: the ground was laid out, the housing subdivisions created, the highway built, the shopping centers and malls erected, all of it so quickly that the surveyors seemed barely to be gone before the moving trucks started arriving. These communities were often more affluent than the cities they were rivaling, and they could only be reached by car, which mandated that every home have one. Families with one car were buying their second. Families with two were buying a third for their children.

As much as anyone at Ford, Iacocca understood the altered American landscape, and he was doing an inspired job of making sure that everyone in this new, more affluent America could find a friendly Ford dealership nearby. The dealerships, of course, had been located in the old downtown areas, which in this rush of affluence people were leaving. It was Iacocca's job to push the old-time dealers into the new promised land, moves that many of them made reluctantly. ("You can get tired of telling your dealers," he confessed to a friend, "that if there are people in a subdivision, there will be businesses, and if there are businesses, there will one day be a Rotary or Kiwanis club there as well.")

When McNamara became president of Ford, in November 1960, Iacocca became general manager of the Ford division, a prized job at the very center of the company. Iacocca was thirty-six. Only Henry Ford II, it was said, had climbed faster in the company. There was a part of Iacocca that was grateful to McNamara, for McNamara had reached down and pulled him up and had greatly accelerated his career. But he had also chafed under McNamara's caution, his utilitarian automotive instincts, and his curious belief that auto makers had social obligations, such as in the area of safety. When McNamara went to Washington a few months later to become Secretary of Defense, Iacocca felt liberated. It was soon clear that Iacocca's regime would be more profitable than McNamara's. He created a successful truck line, and he invented the idea of a white sale in January, traditionally a terrible month for auto makers. The idea, which was to sell white cars at bargain rates, seemed almost childish at first, but it worked.

Iacocca was very careful in handling Ed Lundy and his finance people. On occasion this took every bit of his self-control. It constantly enraged him that someone so influential within the company could have so little feel for cars. Yet although Iacocca could be quite rough, single-minded to the point of insensitivity, in dealing with people whom he did not respect, he was always aware that to challenge Lundy was to challenge Henry Ford, since Lundy was Ford's life-support system. After a meeting, when he was back with his own men, he might storm about something that Lundy had said, but he was extremely polite in all encounters. Once there had been an exchange on the question of how much a certain car would cost per month. Iacocca had quickly quoted the monthly installment price, and Lundy had looked puzzled, because all he knew was the sticker price. Few of his friends and fellow executives, after all, bought cars on time. But Iacocca was the dealer's man, he still identified with the average customer, and he knew most Americans bought their cars on time. For them the critical question was how much per month. That was the real cost of the car, not the sticker price. "I don't think any of these goddam people know any real people," he told a colleague.

On another occasion he and Don Frey, his deputy, mentioned to Lundy that it was time to change the sheet metal on an aging model. Lundy asked why. Because the dealers were getting tired of it, Iacocca answered. What did that have to do with it? Lundy asked. The dealers, Iacocca explained—and Frey, knowing the explosiveness of his superior, marveled that he did not blow up—had to hype their salesmen, who in turn had to hype their customers. Thus it was important to keep the dealers excited. If the dealers became sluggish, he continued, the whole process began to unwind. In that case, said Lundy, go ahead. Afterward Iacocca turned to

Frey and shook his head. "Can you goddam imagine it?" he asked. "Can you imagine that son of a bitch trying to hawk a car?"

The finance men were a constant affront to him: They did not know cars and yet they regularly thwarted his will. He saw their power increasing at the possible expense of his own. Once when Lundy planted one of his boys in a line job, which was a little unusual, a nice pleasant man with no sense of cars and product, Iacocca fumed. It was as if the very nature of the man, so clean and upright and positive, offended him. Piffle, Iacocca nicknamed him. How's Piffle doing? he would ask. He knew immediately what Piffle's weaknesses were, and he was, in the months that followed, at once exceedingly gracious to Piffle and adept at creating situations in which Piffle's flaws were exposed. It took him only a few months to get rid of Piffle.

In the beginning he had seen Lundy's people as simply an opposing force; later he sensed the finance men, if not Lundy himself, were going after him in a way that was almost personal. Yet he never retaliated, he seldom fought back. For a man as volatile and combative as Iacocca, ready to retaliate against even the smallest slight, it was a measure of his astounding self-discipline. Yet only someone as aggressive as Lee Iacocca could have operated so effectively for so long against the numbing power of the finance people. He simply wanted success and power that much more than they did. In the smooth modern world of corporate Ford, he triumphed by the fury of his ambition, by knowing more about every aspect of the Ford Motor Company, by always being better prepared, than anyone he was dealing with. He was a man of Ford rather than of GM, for his ambition was too naked for GM, where the system was everything; he would never have lasted there. At Ford, although the system was powerful, there still was some room for idiosyncrasy. At GM ambition was supposed to manifest itself as aspiration for the system rather than for the self. Lee Iacocca's ambition was always about self. At Ford, a far more political place than GM, riddled as it was with factions (mainly because of the whimsicality of Henry Ford's leadership, his pleasure in playing people off against each other, his fear of any one executive becoming too powerful), Iacocca was the ultimate political man. In a company with so many pitfalls, he was the only man who, in fellow executive Norman Krandall's phrase, could "see around the corners."

Although he was not as mechanically gifted as the early generation of car men, he was a throwback to them in another way: He was intensely single-minded, willing to bend the rules to his needs. But Iacocca was operating in an era far less congenial to that kind of behavior. The modern era summoned a new kind of corporate ambition: Play it safe, understand the company's unwritten interior rules, bide your time, make no enemies, have no opinion save that of your superior, and in the end throw yourself upon the ultimate mercy of the corporation, for if you served the corporation, it would protect you. For most modern managers it was enough simply not to lose; for Iacocca it was of the essence that he win, and that everyone knew that he won. There was a certain barely concealed anger implicit in Iacocca's ambition that went beyond money and power. It set him apart from his generation in the industry. For Lee Iacocca there was always more to prove.

Most of the other people in the auto industry were good pleasant men from small Midwestern towns. They came from the middle class, perhaps the lower echelons of that class but at least from some part of it. Their parents might have been a little less prosperous than the town's first families, but they belonged. Most were Protestants, a few were Catholics. They were never, and this was at the crux, outsiders; unlike so many immigrants, they had never felt scorned. By going into the auto industry, which was a beacon of success throughout the Midwest, these men were opting for status and security. They were always ambitious, but it was a correct kind of ambition, mannerly, restrained, expressed according to the guidelines of class and region. They were the good, solid Americans of the heartland, confident of the essential justice America guaranteed to those who played by its rules, who served their superiors well and waited their turn.

The raw striving of the newer immigrants to America, which affected competition in certain other areas of American life, rarely touched the upper levels of the dominant industrial companies. Those immigrants, notably Jews and Italians, leery of Protestant justice, had produced sons who were fueled as much by resentment as by aspiration. They were dogged competitors, determined to avenge in one generation wrongs inflicted on their parents and grandparents. For the existing America had both welcomed and mocked the new immigrants. Edgar Guest of Detroit, then one of America's most popular writers, delighted his readers in *The Detroit Times* with a derisive ethnic ditty about a Ford worker named Giuseppe Tomassi who wore a white collar and silk hat and carried a walking stick when he took his girlfriend, Rosa, for a Sunday stroll:

> He smok' da cigar weeth da beega da band,
>   Da "three-for-da-quart" ees da kind;
> Da diamond dat flash from da back of hees hand
>   Ees da beegest Giuseppe could find. . . .
> For Giuseppe, he work at da Ford.

Most of the immigrants had shied away from the big companies. Aware of prejudice against their kind in their own hometowns, they believed the odds against them were likely to be great in the large, traditional companies. They assumed, not without good reason, that if there were two or three qualified men up for a particular job, then prejudice would inevitably weigh against them. The higher they managed to climb in the executive reaches of companies like that, the clubbier it would become, and the more important social subtleties would be in determining advancement. Unlike their parents, these young men had been able to go to college, but they still bore some of the immigrant rage within them, and they tended to choose occupations in which they would be credited as directly as possible for their own work. In terms of motives and attitudes, Iacocca was not different from the instant tycoons of Hollywood, or some of the nation's top lawyers or business entrepreneurs, but he was almost unique first in entering a place like Ford, a big, bureaucratic company, and second, once inside Ford, in staying true to his own self-definition, refusing to blend, as he so readily might have, into the company culture.

Raised in Nick Iacocca's house, an immigrant's home, he absorbed his father's odd mixture of love of America and suspicion of those who ran it, a suspicion that never left either father or son. He never voiced it except in the company of other non-Protestants who he was certain had experienced prejudice themselves. But from the beginning, Nick and Antoinette Iacocca meant to Americanize their son. Though the family was Italian and proud of it, Lee did not speak Italian because his parents did not want him to learn it. He was going to succeed in the new world, not the old one. He was exceptionally close to his father. Anyone who was Lee's friend was Nick Iacocca's friend too. When Lee was named president of Ford, Nick was at the ceremony, and it was a victory for Nick as well, a vast personal victory over prejudice. Nick believed that the world out there was controlled by Protestants, that as a matter of course they condescended to Italians, and that one could not get a fair break from them. Do not trust that world, he often counseled his son. Work for yourself, do not work for anyone else.

Nick Iacocca, from San Marco near Naples, exuberant and energetic, had largely followed his own counsel; in Allentown, Pennsylvania, he launched a series of businesses for himself. He ran hotdog restaurants, founded a car-rental company (some said it was the first of its kind in America), and branched off into real estate. He did very well in real estate, but when he was completely wiped out in the 1929 crash, he did not bemoan his luck; instead he started off again where he began—with a restaurant. Soon he was doing well enough to buy real estate, including two movie theaters and a large subdivision. He made money, and his son's childhood was privileged. Lee was the younger of two children and the only boy, and the sun in that home revolved around him. As close as he was to his father, it was his mother, Antoinette, also an immigrant, daughter of the shoemaker in Nick's hometown, whom his friends thought he truly resembled. Nick was full of energy and enthusiasm and emotion, but it was Antoinette, cooler, stronger, more controlled, always there to put the pieces back together, who watched everyone in the room warily. It was Nick's qualities, friends thought, that had gotten Lee started in the early years of Ford, but it was Antoinette's discipline that had carried him to the company's highest levels.

Lee Iacocca listened to almost everything his father told him, but he violated that first canon; he intended from the time he went to college at Lehigh to be an engineer and work for Ford. It was a choice filled with risk, for even as some prejudice were lessening in postwar America, those against Jews, for example, bias against Italians persisted. They could be singers, entertainers, and athletes (particularly baseball players), and they could be in the construction business. Or the mob. They had not been as successful as the Jews in the arts or in the media or in business. The way to true American acceptance had somehow seemed harder for the Italians. As an aspiring management trainee at Ford, Lee Iacocca knew he was in for a long, lonely struggle. He had always been aware of the prejudice around him. He believed he could trust fewer people, and that he somehow had to work harder, achieve more, and be more successful, than his fellow executive hopefuls. He was marked as different. Years later, when he had risen to the upper echelon at Ford and his relations with Henry Ford were at their best, it was still there. "I'd like you to meet my young Italian friend," Ford once said in introducing him to others. There it was, however well intentioned, *my young Italian friend.*

The loneliness and wariness persisted as long as he was at Ford. No matter how he triumphed, he was triumphing in the enemy camp. Partly as a defense mechanism he formed his own clique at Ford. Yet even among those he was close to, he would seldom let himself go and confess his true feelings. His friends were obliged to see him as he wanted to be seen, not necessarily as he was. On rare occasions his anger against the governing world, the world that set the rules, would show, and he would rage against the goddam Wasps who always took care of each other and who were never allowed to fail. Once in a meeting with some of his Ford people he mentioned hiring a particular advertising firm. One of the other executives questioned him closely, pointing out that the agency in question was a Jewish firm. Did they really want to hire a Jewish firm? the executive asked. "Listen," Iacocca snapped back, "I'd rather have one smart Jew working for me than a roomful of dumb bastards like you." But mostly his animus manifested itself in his singularity of purpose; he had come this far and would not be turned aside. He would outdo them all. He would know as much about Wall Street and banking as the financial people, as much about engineering as the engineers, as much about schedules as the manufacturing people. There would be no aspect of the business he would not master. More was always at stake with him than with others, and everything that happened was always more personalized. Each victory was sweeter because it was a victory for both himself and Nick Iacocca over a system he never trusted, and each defeat was more bitter.

But his success stemmed not from drive alone. He had almost perfect instincts for the market. That was at the core of his political strength within the company. The dealers loved him; he knew them, understood their taste, and did not look down on them as so many of the company's rising executives now did. In turn they remained remarkably loyal to him. (When he met his eventual fate at Ford, there was more than mere grumbling; there was talk of a dealer revolt.) He was, they thought, the highest-placed man in the company who still spoke their language. No one else in the upper echelons wanted to have very much to do with them, indeed even liked to acknowledge their existence. They were, after all, usually louder and brassier than the poised young Ford executives; their self-conscious good fellowship was jarring, they dressed in flashier clothes, and they wore their materialism too blatantly. The new elite of the Ford Motor Company knew how to signal its affluence discreetly; their Ivy League suits murmured success. The dealers were different. If they were successful, they wanted to shout it.

Iacocca drew strength from them, for they remained a power in the company. Most people outside the industry and a good many new Ford executives assumed that the company sold its cars to customers; in reality it sold them to dealers. The older generation of executives, the men who had run the company until the fifties, were at ease with the dealers, for these executives were rough men with few illusions about the purpose of the business. If the dealers were out there squeezing customers by selling them unnecessary options, that was just part of the game. The business-school graduates now coming to dominate the company were far less comfortable with the dealers, for the dealers were a reminder of the essential coarseness of the business itself: They were supposed to be selling something, and it often had to be done in primitive ways. The finance people didn't complain when the benefits of all that huckstering showed up on the bottom line; they just didn't want to be around it.

Bob McNamara, who had never been very much at ease in the auto business, hated doing business with the dealers. He considered them unseemly hucksters, and about the last thing he liked doing was assembling them every year to give them a pep talk about going out there and selling more for the greater glory of the Ford Motor Company. Early on, McNamara had spotted Iacocca as someone who was smart enough for him to talk to yet capable of handling the dealers for him. So McNamara expedited Iacocca's rise. Each time Iacocca dealt successfully with the dealers was one less time that McNamara had to do it. Iacocca was delighted by the early help he got from McNamara. He saw McNamara as a conflicted man, torn between his need to show an ever greater profit and his private preference for small, utilitarian cars. But if Iacocca felt sympathy for McNamara, he felt nothing but resentment toward his professional progeny, the bright young men who came after him, all those careful achievers who had been to the right colleges and then the right business schools and had had their career paths greased for them. All they really had to do, he thought, was keep their noses clean and not fail. Someone was always looking out for them. No one, Lee Iacocca was convinced, had ever been looking out for him except his family. He had gone to Ford after four years at Lehigh and graduate work at Princeton, entering the company as a $185-a-month trainee. He spent a year as a trainee, and when it was done he did not get the job in sales that he coveted. Instead he was sent to a minor plant, making automatic transmissions, in Edgewater, Pennsylvania. He wanted out immediately and tried again to get into sales. He applied for a job as a salesman in the New York office and thought he was well qualified for it, but the manager, Nelson Bowe, turned him down. Defeats of any kind rankled with Iacocca, and this one, coming at the beginning of his career, was especially painful, seen as perhaps a reflection of prejudice. More than thirty years later, when Cal Beauregard, one of his friends at Ford, mentioned casually that he had been hired by Bowe, Iacocca was stunned. Bowe had hired Beauregard but not Iacocca! How could that be? All that day Iacocca kept coming back to the subject of Bowe and of why Bowe had not hired him. Finally Beauregard said: "It was because you'd been to college. He thought you were overqualified, and he didn't want to deal with someone who had a college education— he just didn't want the problems."

Iacocca did land a low-level sales job working out of Ford's Chester, Pennsylvania, office. There he came under the aegis of Charley Beacham, the Eastern district sales manager. If McNamara and the Whiz Kids represented the company as they thought it should be, Charley Beacham represented the company as it really was. (Years later, after McNamara had gone to the Defense Department and was trying to cut back the National Guard system, Beacham was immediately doubtful. "I think Bob will lose this one," he told friends. "I don't think he knows enough about those small towns, and how they like having their parades on July Fourth, and how the governors of the states like to review the Guard like they were the damn President of the United States. No, I think I'd lay off this one—I think Bob will lose." He was of course, quite right.) The world of McNamara and his successors at Ford was a spare, ascetic place where rational people did rational things and numbers always came true, and where ambition was about achievement and not about greed. Beacham's world was a meaner place, where everyone had an angle and wanted a slice of what his neighbors had. The key to understanding human behavior was not rationality but a knowledge of human desire and snobbery. It was still a world where men bought cars because they wanted something—to impress their neighbors or a certain girl.

Charley Beacham became Lee Iacocca's foster father within the company. On the exterior Charles Rufus Beacham was a vintage good old boy, a back-slapping buddy with a cornpone style who could also, when he chose, quote Shakespeare. He always had a cigar in his mouth, but he would never smoke it; smoking cigars wasn't good for him, so he ate them instead, chewing them down to the stub. He got on with everybody, had a joke for all occasions but particularly those where there were no women present. But underneath all that Southern con there was a hard man with a hard eye. He never forgot that the good humor and the good nature were not ends in themselves but means to an end, pushing cars on customers, some of whom needed the cars and some of whom did not. The question of whether the sales benefited the customer did not arise; the only question was whether it benefited the dealer. That meant pushing the salesmen, keeping their feet to the fire, so they in turn would push the cars on the customers.

By the fifties he had become a character out of American folklore in a company filled with smooth, educated overachievers. He filled the young men around him with Beacham's rules. They did not, he said, have to answer most of their mail from Detroit. Ninety percent of it was makework, and on the rare serious query, someone from Detroit would follow up. If they were caught in a conversation from which they wanted to escape, he advised, the time to hang up was when they themselves were speaking; it was the safe way to do it—no one would believe they had hung up on themselves. *Always* go to the bathroom before any Glass

House meeting, he counseled, whether there was a need or not. "Those meetings," he said, "go on forever, and just when you do have to go, they'll slip something by you." In a meeting Beacham might scribble a note to an aide: "Notice he's talking much louder," it might say, "a sure sign his facts are weak." He maintained that little of what was called progress was in fact an improvement on man's condition. As an example, he cited the boom in outdoor home barbecuing. "When I was a boy, we went to the bathroom outdoors and cooked indoors, and now that I'm a grown man we've reversed it, and that's called progress." He bemoaned the coming of jet travel, which as far as he was concerned encouraged Detroit's ambitious young men to visit his premises and interrupt the natural conduct of business. "Your only job for the next two days," he would tell his deputy, Matt McLaughlin, of a visiting VIP, "is to make sure that he does not miss his plane leaving here."

He was a boomer from the days when American business still belonged to boomers. With the growth of television, that would change, and most of the real selling would be done on TV, and because TV was a hot medium, the selling would have to be cooler. Beacham's approach was more elemental. He knew how to excite his salesmen, for this was crucial. His counterpart at Chevy, a man named Bill Holler, had once gathered all of his regional salesmen around a brand-new model, opened the door, looked at them all long and solemnly, and then slammed the door as hard as he could. "Boys," he announced, "I've just slammed the door on the best goddam car in the world"—and a huge cheer went up. Beacham was much the same way. Once he called in his men to fire them up about what he believed was a relatively weak model, and he did it with great cunning, cajoling them until he could see the enthusiasm in their faces. He walked out of the room, turned to a friend, and said, "I don't much like my methods, but they sure as hell get results." During a bad year when the Chester office was under pressure to cut costs, he had, so the story went, formed his salesmen into two lines, one to one side of him, one on the other. "All of you here," he told the ones on the left, "are going to take a ten percent cut in pay." Their faces fell. "But don't feel too bad," he said, "because all of you here"—he pointed at the men on his right— "aren't working here anymore."

That was not out of character. He had learned that to succeed in the auto business a man had to be unsparing. He might praise his employees generally but never to their faces. He once said of Matt McLaughlin, "McLaughlin here knows more about the resale market than anyone else at Ford," realized he had gone too far, and quickly added, "Of course, no one at Ford knows a damned thing about it."

He knew the entire operation—how to squeeze the dealers and make them squeeze their salesmen so the salesmen squeezed their customers; how to withhold the hot models from the dealers who were sluggish and give them as a reward to the good dealers. Beacham's view of the auto business was primal. "Make money—screw everything else," he told the young Iacocca. He liked Iacocca because he was so smart, and because he sensed that his hunger meant he was more like Beacham's generation than the generation then taking power. He did not like the finance people, though he knew the company needed them. He would tell of a log that had frozen in the waters of a great northern river, rushing downriver with the thaw of spring, going faster and faster, with one tiny ant aboard. "That ant thinks he's steering the log," Beacham would say. "And do you know who the ant is? He's a Ford Motor Company bean-counter."

Beacham tested the young Iacocca from the start. Iacocca liked to tell of being sent to Pottstown, Pennsylvania, where a dealer had forty used trucks on his lot that he had been unable to sell. Nothing but used iron, in Iacocca's phrase, a tiny step up from junk. Iacocca went there and figured out the market and got the dealer to lower the prices so that if it was junk, it was at least heavily discounted junk. The dealer soon moved everything. Iacocca sent back word to Beacham of his great victory. The only response was a telegram from Beacham which said, "Move on to Tamaqua," another Pennsylvania town where another junk pile awaited him. The lesson he learned from those days was very basic: Get cash for junk, move it, keep nothing on the lot for more than thirty days.

In time, his career aided by Beacham, he became a star. Even more remarkable was that he was about the only one of Beacham's boys allowed to tease their leader. Once, after Iacocca had begun his ascent, he outlined his proposal for an upcoming sales campaign about which Beacham was quite dubious. There were three main reasons it would succeed, Iacocca said, and listed them. Beacham interrupted him.

"I don't know, Lee," he said. "I won't be here to help you—I'm going on vacation."

"That's reason number four," Iacocca quickly responded.

But all of his early training came from Beacham. The first law was always to push the car. The second was that the car could always be pushed. If the car had not been pushed it was the fault of the salesman, not the car. That training set Iacocca apart: In what was becoming an increasingly genteel, almost theoretical profession he was a man without illusion. He also understood right away that to succeed at Ford he needed visibility, and he was skillful in gaining it. As a very junior salesman, only one year in the company, he decided that most of the salesmen in the region were poorly prepared. So he came up with the idea of a regular evening training course to raise the level of professionalism. That promptly set him apart. Soon the idea was taken up by other regions, and his superiors were aware that Iacocca was different, more directed.

He also knew he needed self-confidence. A shy young man, he took Dale Carnegie courses and forced himself to become assertive. As success followed, he became genuinely confident. Soon he began to make a reputation within the company. The 1956 Ford was a weak car and was moving slowly, and Iacocca, by then the assistant district sales manager in Philadelphia, devised a way of speeding up sales. The cars were dull, he thought, so to make them a little racier he added some flashy side molding and repainted them two-tone. Then he cut the price. If a buyer put down 20 percent of the purchase price of a new Ford, he decreed, all he then had to pay was $56 a month for the next thirty-six months. That was the slogan, "56 for '56." It pulled Philadelphia from last place among Ford's thirty-three sales districts to first. Even better, the Iacocca slogan was picked up and used by Ford dealers throughout the country. McNamara, then general manager of the Ford division, later declared that Iacocca's idea had allowed Ford to sell an additional seventy-two thousand cars that year. It seemed typical of the new people at Ford that they might not know how to sell cars themselves, but once the cars were sold, they were able to specify exactly how many extra had been bought because of a slogan.

That was the making of Iacocca at Ford. McNamara was impressed by him. Iacocca could sell, which was fortunate, but unlike the other super-salesmen he was also smart, modern, and well educated. He knew not just when to talk but when not to talk. Where most of his colleagues were content to know all they could about their own area, Iacocca wanted to know everything about the entire company. He knew that it was the way to power. He knew especially that if he was to contend with the financial people, he had to be as smart about numbers as they were. He soon became, with the possible exception of Don Frey, the only nonfinance man knowledgeable and disciplined enough to take on the financial people on their own territory. Even as a young man in the fifties it was clear that he was different; when he walked into a meeting he was in complete control. The reason was that he had often been up the night before not just studying the subject matter but planning what he would say, readying rejoinders to points his opponents might make. What seemed so facile the next day in the meeting was hardly facile at all. It was the result of exceptional preparation.

He was absolutely driven. He constantly made lists of things he had to know. In his early years at Ford he had set goals for himself—how much money he would make by a certain age, what level of advancement he would attain by which birthday. He intended to make vice-president by the time he was thirty-five. He was very upset when he did not. A year later, however, he became vice-president and general manager of the Ford division, the best job in the company. For someone whose start in the company had been slow and difficult, it was a remarkable ascent. He had created every break for himself; he was acutely aware of that. He had been good at selling cars because it was the most natural extension of what he was best at, selling himself.

His strength came not just from his exceptional intelligence and the ability to focus that intelligence in the most practical of ways, but from his intensity of purpose. His own career was paramount. Anyone working for him who did not come up to standards was failing not only, in some vague indirect way, the Ford Motor Company; he was jeopardizing in the most direct way the career of Lee Iacocca. He never lost sight of that. In a company that was so big and so successful that it was easy for middle managers to become tolerant of ordinary work on the part of their subordinates, he was different. Other executives might be more relaxed with their subordinates because they had been produced by more comfortable circumstances, but Iacocca's zeal was fueled by the rage of the outsider. Those underneath him were allowed to disappoint him once, never twice. It was not so much a corporate matter, for the Ford Motor Company was going to prosper anyway. It was personal. In his single-minded drive he could be caustic, even scathing, to those who worked under him. For those who were part of his group, that was no problem; they were aware that the anger meant little, that as soon as the words were spoken it was over and the mood had passed, and that Iacocca's anger was as much with himself as with them. For others, not members of his inner circle, the words echoed louder and longer.

When McNamara left for Washington and Iacocca emerged as the most powerful man in the Ford division, he immediately set out to take apart what McNamara had done. He had liked McNamara as a man and respected him as a pure businessman—an efficiency expert—but he had never respected him as a car man. He had particularly disdained McNamara's last car, the Falcon. It was the ultimate utilitarian car, and it offended his sense of style, his sense of profit, and his sense of purpose. ("McNamara," said Hal Sperlich, Iacocca's deputy, referring to McNamara's deliberately austere manner, "made a car that looked like him —he had those granny glasses and he made a granny car.") Iacocca always believed that McNamara did not understand the true nature of the business. People did not just want to go from one place to another, he said; they wanted to be *seen* going from one place to another. The designs of the early models of the Falcon, which were derivative from the Thunderbird, were far sportier, and he had watched McNamara tear them up and gradually force the design into this square, functional car. "I felt like crying," he said later. He considered the Falcon an anticar. He thought it served the puritan bias of the man who made it more than the needs of the customers or the company. Now, as general manager of the Ford division, he set out to change things.

Almost the first move he made was to ask Frey if he could transform the Falcon into a convertible. Frey said he could, though the result would be one of dubious charm. They went ahead, and Frey proved right; it was an imperfect car. But Frey later realized it was Iacocca's first attempt to catch what obsessed him—the growing youth market.

At the same time a small car called the Cardinal was in an advanced stage of design at Ford in Germany, and McNamara had committed the company to it. The Cardinal was small and fuel-efficient and had front-wheel drive; $35 million had already been spent on it. Iacocca, flying over to Germany to look at it for the first time, hated it on sight. It was cramped and ugly, he thought, and it lacked a trunk. He was sure it would never sell the 300,000 pieces it was programmed for. He flew back to Detroit and told Henry Ford that it was a loser and would bring back memories of the Edsel debacle. No other curse could kill a car faster. The Cardinal was dead, the $35 million was written off. Years later Iacocca was sure he had unconsciously scored a vast number of points with Henry Ford by killing a car Ford never wanted and by being decisive enough to do it even after so much money had been committed to the project.

McNamara had taken Ford out of racing, and Iacocca wanted it back in. McNamara, somewhat ahead of his time, had tried to push safety on an unwilling Detroit and a somewhat ungrateful nation, and Iacocca hated that, too. His passion was for style and size, not really for safety at all. Safety, he said quite publicly, did not sell. His regime was going to be about selling, he made clear, and so it was. He knew the market as his predecessor did not, and it was not surprising that the company that Iacocca ran was not only flashier and gaudier than McNamara's but more profitable.

The symbol of the Iacocca years, the car that made his reputation not just at Ford but in the nation as well, was the Mustang. It came out in 1964, at what would prove to be the highwater mark of the American century, when the country was rich, the dollar strong, and inflation low. In the middle class even the young had money. It was almost twenty years since the end of World War II, and it was more than a decade since the end of the Korean War. The Vietnam War was still a guerrilla action involving relatively small numbers of American advisers. The bitter and costly part of that war, which was to take more than fifty-one thousand lives, divide the country, start a runaway inflation, and completely divert the nation's attention, was still ahead. The economy was expanding. Though many of the forces that would afflict American industry were already beginning to form, they were not yet visible, and the domestic economy had never seemed so strong.

Politically the center not only still held, it was triumphant. Lyndon Johnson, picking up John Kennedy's torch, was brilliantly using Kennedy's murder as a means of pushing social programs through the Congress. He spoke of a Great Society and of a war on the last pockets of poverty in the nation. The nation was that confident and that generous. The industrial era that Franklin Roosevelt had helped usher in some thirty years before was in full flood, and Barry Goldwater, as a conservative candidate from the Southwest, running against that industrial power, seemed oddly isolated. That year Lyndon Johnson, campaigning for the presidency, stood in Cadillac Square with Walter Reuther and Henry Ford II; it was the sign of a nation that believed it had found a common ground and was erasing class lines. There was enough for everyone; the country was enjoying unparalleled prosperity, and the pie was bigger than ever. The pie would turn out to have its limits after all, but at that halcyon moment, the future seemed unbounded. Many of the protests that were just beginning to show up that year on the political radar screen, like the Berkeley free speech movement and Ralph Nader's embryonic consumer movement, were produced by middle-class affluence as much as by underclass hardship. They were about the quality, not the quantity, of life. It was against that background that the Mustang's success—and the success of Lee Iacocca—was achieved.

Because the Mustang did so well, making so much profit on so little investment, the question of whose car it actually was, who deserved the credit for it, would be debated within the auto industry for years to come. Outside the industry, Iacocca, who controlled the publicity for the car, was always considered the father of the Mustang; from the moment he became general manager he had been looking for a youth car, something that might tap what he sensed was the growing affluence and independence among young Americans. Within Ford, however, Don Frey, the product manager, was seen as the brain behind it. It was Frey who had the specific idea for the car itself, an inexpensive sports model for the young, and did much of the original design. Iacocca took Frey's idea, made it acceptable to the reluctant finance people, and finally brought around the rest of the company, including a dubious Henry Ford II.

Iacocca and Frey were of the same generation at Ford, Frey junior in position but a year older. By Detroit's standards, Frey was more a car guy than Iacocca. Lee, said a Ford product man named Ray Geddes, who worked with both of them, would look at a car and think immediately of whether he could sell it and then what he could add on in the way of options; Don, he said, would look at a car and wonder what it felt like and how it responded to the touch and what could be done to improve its performance. For Iacocca, Geddes added, a car was a means to an end, which was big sales and the power derived therefrom; for Frey a car was an end in itself. Within Ford, Iacocca was considered the far better businessman, Frey the better car man. They were an odd couple, both ambitious, Iacocca totally political, Frey so absorbed by product that by comparison he seemed almost innocent. Iacocca, mutual friends thought, circled Frey admiringly and warily in those years, seeing him as a potential rival and never underestimating Frey's drive toward his own goals, but he also respected Frey's considerable strengths.

Frey's love of cars was famous at Ford. He was always at his desk late at night, working on some design problem. When he finished his desk work, he would go over to the test track just to drive a car. Ray Geddes, knowing that Frey loved hot cars, once took a Ford racing car, put it in the British design shop, and had a few changes made—one was the addition of a muffler—which had the effect of disguising the racer as a street car. Geddes said nothing about what he was doing. He had the car secretly shipped to Detroit. Then quite casually one night he told Frey that there was a Ford GT out in the parking lot which Frey could drive home. Frey raced out of his office to the lot, jumped into the car, and roared away. He took off in such a hurry that Geddes didn't have time to tell him how to turn on the electric fuel pump. The carburetor, of course, ran dry in about two blocks, and they had to tow Frey back. The story, Geddes thought, was typical; Frey might be a cerebral man, almost deliberately so, but around his machines he was like a kid with new toys.

At Ford he was the house egghead. His colleagues would find not only the New York papers on his desk but British ones as well, the *Manchester Guardian* and the *Economist*. There were always books there too, and he was considered to be almost as bad as McNamara in wanting to talk about a book he had just read; even more annoying, many of these books were not about business, let alone the auto industry. "The trouble with Frey is that he's too goddam smart for his own good," Henry Ford once said of him, and he did not exactly mean it as a compliment. "Maybe," Ford added, "he's a genius. Maybe not. But he's certainly a pain in the ass." Those were not things you wanted said about you by Henry Ford II.

Frey had taught at the University of Michigan before going to Ford, and he was a true sophisticate, but he was also in his heart a tinkerer of the kind that existed in America in the thirties and forties. For he had grown up in eastern Iowa, and his father farmed and worked as a tractor engineer with John Deere. In those days farmers had to be able to repair their own equipment; the nearest repairman might be forty miles away. Most farmers turned a corner of their barn into a makeshift tool shop; they could cut a needed part and grind it down a little, and it would work. Frey's father loved machinery; when Frey went off to college in the forties he found to his surprise that other kids talked about football and baseball with their fathers; he and his father had always talked about machines and the engineering sciences. To the young Frey, as to the first Henry Ford, machinery had a mystique that farming lacked. He loved the idea of taking things apart and putting them back together. When he was given his first bicycle at the age of twelve, he quickly took it apart. He couldn't get the coaster brake back together properly the first three times he tried; some forty-five years later he could still draw a diagram of the brake. Earlier, his father, who had gone to Europe on a business trip, brought home a large, old-fashioned Voightlander plate camera. He also brought back some color film, which at that time was still rare; there was no place nearby that could process it. One day young Frey photographed some of his mother's roses. Then he improvised a darkroom, and working all night, processed the film himself. The next morning he handed his mother one enlarged color photo of her own roses. She, a disciplined woman of careful emotions, looked at the photograph and then turned to him and said, "Hurry, you'll be late for school."

When he went off to college, first to Michigan State and then the University of Michigan, he loved the protected environment of academia. It was the most comfortable place he had ever been, and he stayed on to teach. In 1951, as an assistant professor of engineering doing purely theoretical work in metallurgy, he received a call from a man named Andrew Kucher who had been hired by Ernie Breech to create a scientific lab at Ford. Kucher offered him a job, and Frey turned him down. He was making $3300 at Michigan, and he was absolutely happy. But Kucher called again, and Frey eventually lunched with Breech. Breech asked what it would take to bring him to Ford. Frey thought for a moment and came up with the grandest sum he could imagine.

"Ten thousand a year," he said.

"Fine," said Breech.

So Frey went to work for Ford. He excitedly called his father to tell him the news. "That's a tough outfit, son," his father said. "You'd better leave your Ph.D. at the gate there." Gradually Frey moved from the theoretical part of the business toward the more practical engineering part. Soon he was going to high-level meetings with his superior, Hans Matthias, the chief engineer. On one occasion Matthias was questioned closely by McNamara about the status of a particular car. He seemed unable to comprehend McNamara's questions; McNamara in turn seemed equally unable to understand Matthias's engineer-speak. Finally Frey intervened. "Mr. McNamara," he said, "what Mr. Matthias is saying is that a part on the car broke in testing and we have to fix it."

"Well, for God's sake," replied McNamara, "why doesn't he just say so?"

After that occasion, McNamara, as he had reached down for Iacocca to deal with the boisterous world of dealers, now reached down to Frey to deal with the arcane world of engineers.

Frey, it turned out, liked the world of Ford even more than the world of Ann Arbor. It was, he believed, far more challenging, in large measure because cars were so complicated. A car in his view was the ultimate piece of machinery, an immensely complex series of assemblages that had to come together in perfect harmony to furnish power. Yet the car, unlike other machines, also had to be attractive, function and aesthetics serving each other. Producing a car, he believed, was even more difficult than producing an airplane, or at least more challenging for the engineers. For the auto engineer had to persuade not just a handful of large airlines but hundreds of thousands of customers to buy, and he had to do it every year. Thus he was testing himself daily, not just against some abstract standard of perfection but against the marketplace.

Iacocca and Frey talked frequently about a car that would reach the expanding youth market. They were both aware that something was happening out there, that America's demographics were changing, and that television was the perfect medium to sell a sporty car. Frey came up with the idea of a sporty little car to go up against the GM Corvette but which would cost less. It was a two-seater. But the Ford research people kept reporting that the car's appeal was too limited; too much money would be spent for a car that would capture too small a share of the market. Taking the figures from research, the finance people projected that perhaps only thirty-five thousand people would buy a two-seater. So Iacocca took the plans and reworked them, suggesting options and additions; gradually the figure for projected sales reached fifty thousand.

But the finance people were formidable foes. The McNamara years had solidified their position more than anyone had yet realized, and they were now showing their power in this struggle over the Mustang. The Mustang, they now declared, would diminish standard volume. Standard volume had become the sacrosanct figure within the company, the base sale from the previous year, in effect what Ford was already guaranteed without spending an additional penny. That choosing this figure as their base was an enormously limiting concept, locking them more and more into the past, seemed not to matter. For them it was the ideal number, for it guaranteed profit without risk. The finance people even had a label for any change that might add cost to the company's budget without necessarily guaranteeing sales. Such a change was *decremental*. Translated into English, this meant that since the company already had its share, any change might diminish it. The Mustang, then, was held to be decremental.

For a time the project seemed stymied. Then Iacocca had a brainstorm. He suggested adding jump seats in the back, making it a four-seater, a full family car. The numbers changed immediately; now it might possibly sell as many as 100,000 to 125,000 pieces. But the financial people were still tough: There was no way a bastardized little sports car was really going to work, they insisted. That it would be a relatively inexpensive car for Ford to produce—it would be able to use the platform and the engine from the Falcon and thus cost only about $75 million—did not seem to weigh in its favor with the financial people.

The key moment came when Iacocca took the decision to Henry Ford. In the past, selling Henry Ford had been something that Iacocca did particularly well. In those days, the good days, he had a sixth sense of how to handle Henry. He rarely went through channels in dealing with him, for channels were formal, and the formality, committee piled upon committee, tended to work against creativity. If he went through channels, Iacocca triggered a mechanism: The finance people immediately became the protectors of the company, and he became someone trying to take something from it. The impact of that struggle upon Henry Ford was almost always fatal to product. Iacocca's approach, instead, was to let Henry gradually become proprietarial about a model, let the car become Henry's car. He would show Henry things in stages, preparing him almost idly, with an impromptu trip through the design center, for example, or a casual look at a clay model, appealing to the part of Henry Ford that genuinely loved cars and doing it in unpressured circumstances. (The people under Iacocca worked much the same way; it was best to reach Lee outside channels, to let him smell a car on his own. If they had to force the sale on him, then they were in trouble, the designer Gene Bordinat believed, for Lee had so superb an eye for what would sell that he could always judge for himself. The sweetest satisfaction came when Iacocca took their car and sold it back to them, telling them how good it was. Then they knew they had him.) But with the Mustang, Iacocca's early attempts to interest Henry Ford did not work. Ford seemed curiously resistant to the car.

Eventually Iacocca got Henry Ford to come to the design center. He was absolutely confident that the car was irresistible. He had prepared very carefully and was fully primed for the moment. He was only a few sentences into his spiel when Henry turned on him. "I don't even want to talk about it," he said and walked out. They were all devastated. They were sure the car was a winner, and Henry had turned them down. Later they discovered that Henry Ford had come down with mononucleosis. He went straight from the design center to the hospital.

The setback with Henry Ford did not deter Iacocca. He was at his best working outside the Ford system. The system, he believed, belonged to his opponents. Within the system his strengths were minimized, because he was playing on their turf, where numbers spoke louder than impulse. Going outside the system was more dangerous; it demanded of him more audacity, more cunning, more luck. He had to have absolute knowledge of who within the company was talented and who could deliver. If he stayed within the system, that did not matter, for the system protected those who did not deliver; as it limited excellence, so it protected mediocrity. Now, with Ford apparently resisting the early bait, Iacocca set out to surround him. He did it by getting the rest of the Ford Motor Company and then the auto world intrigued about the Mustang. He began giving glimpses of the car to people inside Ford and to Detroit auto writers. Their excitement, as he knew it would, soon turned into auto-world gossip. Soon the word was out: Ford had a hot car. As outsiders heard about the Mustang, they began to question people at the upper levels of the company, and within the company, now, anticipation about the Mustang began to build.

Iacocca used the early research on the car to particularly good effect. Not only were those surveyed unusually enthusiastic about the car, but, even more remarkable, they were willing to pay a good deal more than the company had anticipated. The company's targeted showroom price was between $1800 and $1900. But most people responded that they would pay $5000 or $6000.

Eventually Iacocca's lobbying began to bear fruit. Henry Ford soon found that Iacocca had him surrounded. Both inside and outside the company people wanted to talk to him about this hot new car Ford had come up with. One day he came over to the design shop to talk to Iacocca and Frey.

"I'm tired of hearing about this goddam car," he said.

They both wondered if this was the end.

"Can you sell the goddam thing?" he asked.

Iacocca said they could.

"Well, you damn well better," said Henry Ford.

So they got the car. If it was not entirely Iacocca's car, it was certainly his victory. If that was his first great achievement, the second was the way he prepared the company for a success. Nothing else in his career at Ford so clearly reflected his confidence and his pure instinct for cars. The worst thing that could happen to a company was to have a hot car and then find its means of production too restricted to meet customer demand. The high estimates from the market research were between 75,000 and 100,000 pieces, but Iacocca was having none of that. He readied the company first for a one-plant build. That meant Ford could produce about 250,000 pieces. Having arranged that, and becoming more confident all the time, on the eve of production he moved to a two-plant build. That meant they could probably make as many as 400,000 pieces. Then, after the initial response, certain now of the success of his car, he added a third plant. He was rolling the dice very high on the Mustang. If the customers were ready, so too was Ford.

The Mustang, which came out in 1964, turned out to be the right car at the right time. The young kids just coming into the economy loved it; so did older people. Ford sold 418,812 Mustangs in the first year, which exceeded Iacocca's own goal: He wanted to sell one car more than the 417,174 pieces McNamara's Falcon had sold in the first year. More, the profitability of the Mustang, unlike that of the Falcon, was high. Iacocca had hated the bare, functional character of the Falcon. Customers might buy it, but they added little to it in the way of options. By contrast, the average Mustang buyer simply loaded his car with options. In its first year the Mustang made Ford more than $1 billion in profit. Much of that came from the options. Though the Mustang listed at $2368, the average buyer spent more than $1000 on options, where the profits were always greater. It was a triumph for Iacocca's new, lusher era over McNamara's utilitarian one.

As the car became legend, so too did Iacocca. Not did all Detroit know of his success, but he became—as few auto men ever had—a national figure. For he had chosen to identify himself as personally as he could with the Mustang. That was a risky business at the Ford company, where it was an accepted part of the ethic that there was only one person who got credit for any success, and his name was on the car. Iacocca defied that ethic. For him, everything was personalized, and that included this car; he had not come this far and gained this sweet victory to forfeit his rightful credit. So it was that with the Mustang he brilliantly publicized not just the car but his own claim to it. It was Lee Iacocca's Mustang. He thought he had a chance to get himself on the cover of either *Time* or *Newsweek*. So he began to work on Jimmy Jones, *Newsweek*'s Detroit bureau chief, and used Frey, who had gone to school with Leon Jaroff, the *Time* bureau chief, to work on *Time*. Iacocca and Frey each went to New York with photos of the Mustang to tout the car at the highest levels of both magazines. Jim Cannon, then the national editor of *Newsweek*, remembered the special magic of Iacocca at that session, his total belief both in the car and in himself, and the excitement he generated as he spoke of the car. Cannon was so impressed that he bought a car on the spot from Iacocca.

"That's car number two that we've sold in New York," Iacocca said.

"Who has car number one?" Cannon asked.

"Oh, some vice-president at *Time*," said Iacocca.

All of it worked—he hit not one cover but, in one of those rare coups, both *Time* and *Newsweek* in the same week. If you read both magazines, Don Frey thought, you'd think that Henry Ford was just a hired hand at the place. Frey believed Iacocca had for the first time crossed a line that was never supposed to be crossed. Don DeLaRossa, the designer who had done much of the work on the car, got up that morning, looked at Lee's face on both magazines, and turned to his wife and said, "That's a mistake, a serious mistake."

Still, the success was sweet for Iacocca and for Frey as well. They had beaten the odds and beaten the financial people. They had come out with the car they wanted, and they had quadrupled the projections of the finance people. The whole country wanted the Mustang. Frey later thought that if there was one moment in his entire career at Ford that justified all the long hours he spent working, it was when he watched the first completed Mustangs roll off the assembly line. He stood there transfixed as first one and then another and then hundreds of them rolled slowly by. Soon the line of gleaming new cars extended as far as Frey could see. It was the most beautiful thing he had ever witnessed. He kept telling himself that this was in no small part his car, something that he had helped sketch on paper some three years earlier, and now finally it had come into existence. He had done this. He felt like an artist who was finally satisfied with a picture he had painted. Frey was sure for the first time that he had made the right choice in his career.

Victory it might be, but there were ominous signs as well. Although Iacocca had beaten the financial people, in reality the clash over the Mustang signaled not so much his strength but the strength of his opposition. That he nearly lost on a car that was so self-evidently salable and cost so little to produce spoke volumes about whose power was on the ascent. The lesson in the Mustang was not the success of the product people but their near failure with an almost perfect, inexpensive car, at a moment when the industry was enjoying unparalleled prosperity. The Mustang prompted a curious relationship between the leaders of the two factions, Iacocca and Ed Lundy. The two men could not have been more dissimilar, Iacocca blasphemous, aggressive, egocentric, Lundy reticent, private, deeply religious. Those who knew Lundy well felt that he never entirely trusted Iacocca, that he thought Iacocca tended to cook the numbers; but Lundy was impressed by how much money Iacocca's Mustang made on so small an investment. Iacocca was the devil whom Lundy knew, and that was good enough; Lundy could estimate just how much Iacocca was bending things. During the Mustang experience they found that they could deal with each other. It was the beginning of an odd and unlikely alliance, if not a friendship; Lundy's people might be beating up on Iacocca's people every day, but at the very top the two men were surprisingly comfortable with each other.

With the birth of the Mustang, Iacocca had become a public figure. That of itself was audacious enough. There was, in the minds of some, a challenge implicit in his decision to take personal credit for the car. It meant that he saw himself as important enough, close enough to being invaluable, to break the unwritten rule. So it was that at the very pinnacle of Iacocca's success the first step was taken in the complicated process that over the next decade would drastically affect his relationship with Henry Ford. It was not so much a move for power as an assertion of ego. He did it, despite warnings from a number of friends, because he needed to. He was still respectful to Henry Ford in meetings, still careful not to surprise him. But he wanted the publicity.

Henry Ford was not unaware of this most subtle challenge. At first he said very little. Then there were low rumblings from him. At meetings Henry would throw out a mild zinger, usually about some photo of Lee in a magazine or in a newspaper. Gradually these comments became more barbed. Henry was glad, he would say, that Lee was not so overworked that he had no time to deal with reporters and photographers. The Iacocca ego was not something that Henry Ford liked very much, but in the beginning it was tolerable, part of the price of having so able an executive working for him. Later, as other things went wrong between them, the distaste for Iacocca grew. One day in the mid-seventies, Henry Ford II went on a tour of the design shop. There he encountered a young designer who was working on what he hoped would be a new car. With some excitement he showed the clay model to his ultimate boss.

"Look, Mr. Ford," he said. "We've got a really hot car here. Why, it could be another Mustang."

"Who needs that?" Henry Ford answered.

21.
THE RIVALS

Lee Iacocca's first years as general manager of the Ford division, before the Mustang, had been almost an idyll. The job liberated him. His cars always did well, and he had a genius for knowing how to make them even more profitable by adding on accessories. He was full of ideas for sales promotions. He also, in the beginning, handled Henry Ford with great skill. Lee was, after all, only the head of the Ford division, and there was a still grander position to be aspired to. Though he could be blunt and often caustic with everyone else, he was always supple and deferential with Ford, whom he unfailingly referred to as Mr. Ford. When he was with Ford, some colleagues thought, it was like watching a great lion tamer working a temperamental lion. It was all intuition, Iacocca sensing the moods of a somewhat querulous, autocratic man, adapting quickly to his every change. He knew that if Henry Ford told him that the door to his office was always open, Ford meant precisely the reverse; the door was not really open, the proper distance should always be observed, and Iacocca should not come wandering in.

Not everyone who knew both men thought they were destined for perpetual amity, for the whimsical nature of Henry Ford's friendship was well known within the company, how quickly he could grant it and how quickly he could also, for no noticeable reason, withdraw it. Nor was the danger to the friendship entirely one-sided. For some of those close to Iacocca, who knew the inner man and knew how his energy and ambition were fueled in no small part by resentments, were not sure that Lee would always be as grateful to Henry Ford for his success at Ford. Gratitude, they thought, was not necessarily a quality natural to Lee Iacocca; the inner Iacocca believed as the first article of faith that everything he had gained in this world he had not only earned himself but, even more, because he was an immigrant's son, had earned against great odds. Therefore gratitude, such as it existed, was likely to be short-lived. If anything, some of his closest friends thought, there was the possibility of a collision

between him and Henry Ford. For Lee was very much Nick Iacocca's
son, his codes were Nick's codes, and if one listened to Nick Iacocca
carefully, for all his love and praise of America and what a great country
it was, one picked up attitudes that were very different from the expressed
optimism. Nick's was the much harder, tougher theology of the newcomer
to a society dominated by a sort of aristocracy. In Nick's creed, passed on
as if by osmosis to Lee, there were certain tenets, such as Screw or Get
Screwed, and Don't Get Mad, Get Even.

Lee Iacocca, then, was grateful, but not really grateful, for his place at
Ford; confident of his skills but not of his place; aware and resentful always
that in social terms between him and Henry Ford there was not a gap but
a chasm, and that Henry Ford had no intention of closing it. Professionally
no one could have been more sensitive to Ford's moods or quicker to
remove the pressures that Henry Ford did not want to feel. He knew
never to force Henry Ford into a decision, and above all never to force a
confrontation in front of others in the company. Iacocca seemed to have
a sixth sense about the danger signals emanating from Ford, knowing
when he was ready for a new idea, knowing when Ford's light edginess
was about to flare into something more serious or was simply the normal
protective manner of a man who knew that all suggestions might in the
end cost his family money. He was smart about never showing fear; he
might be deferential, but he had learned early in his career, watching the
head of the company, that there was a trace of cruelty there. Henry Ford
could tell when a man making a presentation was nervous; he might watch
and see if a man's hands shook as he held a pointer, and if they did, he
would often bore in.

Above all, Iacocca knew when to pull back. Once Norman Krandall, a
somewhat junior colleague of Iacocca's, thought he had an agreement from
Lee to oppose Ford on naming an offshoot of the Thunderbird line the
Fiera. Henry Ford took nomenclature very seriously, particularly after
the Edsel, a great fiasco of a car that had been named after his father. On
this occasion Krandall believed he knew the game plan. He would oppose
Henry Ford on the name, fight off Ford's early resistance, and then at
the last minute Iacocca would come and tip the scales in their favor. So
Krandall had begun, and he had run into heavy resistance from the chairman, and he had pushed a little harder and the resistance had not softened.
He gave it one more shot, and Ford came back even harder. At this point
Krandall looked over to Iacocca, his reserve battalion. There was Lee,
leaning back in his chair, puffing away on his cigar, his eyes very much
on the ceiling and definitely not on Norman Krandall. There was, Krandall
thought, the smallest glimmer of a smile on Iacocca's face. Routed, Kran-

dall turned to Henry Ford. A Krandall-Ford fight would not, he knew, be a very fair one. "Well, if you feel that strongly about it, name it what you want," he said. Everyone laughed, and Krandall realized that Iacocca had read and responded to a signal that he himself had never even seen.

If McNamara had held power in no small part by intimidating Henry Ford, by assaulting him with an overwhelming array of facts and statistics and making the auto business seem more complicated than it was, then Iacocca held power at least in part by making the business seem simpler, describing choices in the most basic terms, words any car man could understand. There were no underlying tensions in these early years of Iacocca's reign at the Ford division, as there had been in the McNamara years, when McNamara covertly always wanted smaller cars; Iacocca, like his boss, wanted big, creamy, plush cars. Ford appreciated all this, and in those early days there was almost no limit to his praise of Iacocca. He was simply the smartest man he had ever seen in the car business. Lee, he said, understood the numbers as well as McNamara, but unlike McNamara he had a feel for cars and he liked to sell them. Lee, he would add, *likes* the business, and that too was a slap at McNamara, for Henry Ford had never entirely forgiven his former president for his disdain for the business.

So for a time Iacocca could do little wrong. Old friends of Henry's were made nervous by the totality of his endorsement of Lee. One of them was John Bugas, who had helped Henry take the company back from Harry Bennett and had subsequently been in and out of Ford's favor several times. "He falls in and out of love with both men and women," Bugas warned friends, when Ford became so close to Iacocca. "Usually it lasts a few years. Never more than six. For a time they can do no wrong. And then comes the time when they can do no right."

After the triumph of the Mustang, Iacocca was viewed by many in the company as the enabler, the one man in an increasingly bureaucratic operation who could make a car happen. Thus the best of the design and engineering people, even more frustrated by the bureaucracy around them, wanting to push product through the system, turned inevitably to him. That led to subtle and not so subtle divisions within the company. There were the Ford employees, and then there were Lee's people—Iacocca's Mafia, his men were called. "He's like a Medici prince," one Ford executive said. "He's created his own city-state." His demand on his staff for loyalty was implicit, but he could also be quite overt about it. "I need you, Gene," he once told Bordinat, the designer, "but don't ever forget that you need me more." A potential rival to Iacocca became not just Lee's enemy but their enemy as well. They would almost unconsciously cut him off. When one senior executive, Bill Bourke, came back after several years in Europe, Iacocca, fearing his closeness to Henry Ford, shunned him, professionally and socially, and Lee's people followed suit. Sometimes one could tell who was in and who was out with him—and who was a threat—from the way Mary Iacocca treated their wives. When the Bourkes first returned, she snubbed Elizabeth Bourke; later at an auto convention she went over to Mrs. Bourke and said, quite angrily, "I'm Mary Iacocca, and I want you to know it, so that the next time we're in a room together, you can come over and speak to me."

Through the mid-sixties Iacocca was the rising star of a prosperous industrial giant. Then, in February 1968, Henry Ford stunned the auto world in general and Lee Iacocca in particular by reaching over to General Motors to hire Semon E. Knudsen and make him president of Ford. No one, least of all Bunkie Knudsen or Lee Iacocca, was ever sure why Ford had done it. Ford had just been married for the second time, and his new wife, Cristina, a European jet-setter, most decidedly did not like Detroit. She was talking more and more about how much fun it would be to move to Washington, which, she said, unlike Detroit, was a cosmopolitan city with an international tone. Lyndon Johnson had won handily in 1964, he and Henry Ford were friends, and there was talk that Henry Ford might take an important post in Washington. At that time Iacocca was only forty-three, and apparently Ford thought him too young to run the whole company.

There had been small signs of Ford's disillusion—the jibes about personal publicity—but Ford was rarely as churlish with Iacocca as he was with others. Once, just before the Knudsen appointment, when Iacocca was pushing for a particular product, Ford snapped at him, "Oh, come on, Lee, you don't really believe that shit, do you?" It was the first time Henry Ford had ever lashed out at Iacocca, and so it had surprised everyone at the meeting. It was Lee's first public setback, and for a moment some wondered whether Lee's star might now begin to fade. But the incident passed and Ford returned to his normal manner. For most, then, the Knudsen appointment was a shocker. More than likely, some of Iacocca's friends thought, it was an almost unconscious question of class. It was all right for Iacocca to work for Ford and to make the company look good, but it was not all right for him to be the president of it, at least not yet. Iacocca dressed a bit flashier than the Ivy League style prevailing in the Ford executive suite, lapels a little wider, suits a little sharper, ties a little louder. His home, one friend noted, was decorated in a rather gaudy style, far different from the look of a Grosse Pointe home.

Iacocca was devastated by Knudsen's appointment. He had thought himself without a rival in the company. (Only Don Frey was a potential rival, an able man nearly the same age, but Frey was not a particularly good politician or bureaucrat, and his power seemed derivative of Iacocca's.) His job remained exactly the same, and it was a powerful position indeed, yet he felt something had been snatched away from him. It was as if Henry Ford had considered him and then rejected him. Worse, the post had been handed to an unsuspected rival, an executive from the almighty General Motors, a man who bore a name esteemed in Detroit. The Knudsens belonged to the city's aristocracy as the Iacoccas most decidedly did not.

Bunkie Knudsen had done well at General Motors, a division vice-president at Pontiac at forty-four, the youngest man ever to hold so high a post at GM. Pontiac had been weak, and Knudsen had turned it around. He had been shrewd and self-confident enough to sponsor the talented and ambitious young John DeLorean, instead of being threatened by him. But eventually Knudsen was passed over for the job of head of General Motors. Henry Ford, sensing that he might be disaffected, had driven over to his house (using a Chevy, not a Ford, so no one would notice) and offered him the presidency of Ford.

Almost as much as Henry Ford, Bunkie Knudsen was a scion of Detroit. His father was Big Bill Knudsen, the Danish immigrant who had been one of the most powerful figures in designing the early Ford assembly lines. Unlike most of the top men at Ford in those days, who had been hated by the workingmen, Bill Knudsen had been regarded as a figure of great strength and exceptional human decency. He had broken with Ford in 1921 and gone over to GM and asked for a job.

"How much do you want?" Alfred P. Sloan had asked him.

"Anything you like," Knudsen replied.

"How much did Mr. Ford pay you?" Sloan continued.

"Fifty thousand dollars," Knudsen said.

So it was that Alfred P. Sloan, never one to get carried away, started Big Bill Knudsen at $6000, although a few months later, when he was sent over to run Chevy, his salary was raised to $30,000. If any man other than Sloan and Charley Kettering was responsible for the boom at Chevy, it was Knudsen. He made the Chevrolet technologically superior to the Model T, and gave it a lead over the Ford that it never really relinquished. Knudsen loved cars and loved the machinery that made them. During the prolonged strike of 1937, out of which came recognition of the UAW, of all the GM executives he had been the most anxious to settle the strike. He was more sympathetic to the workers than were most of his colleagues, but it was not just that; according to Lee Pressman, a lawyer for the UAW, the idea of his machines sitting there idle, not making cars, left Knudsen in pain.

When Bunkie Knudsen was fourteen his father had given him his first car. He had simply taken all the pieces for a car and left them on a table in the garage. It was Bunkie's job to assemble the car, which he did. The father encouraged his son to buy old wrecks for $25 or $30, repair them, and sell them at a profit. The son was being taught that the most important thing he could do with his life was make something. Often Bill Knudsen took Bunkie to one construction site or another, where they could look at what was going on. These men were not just earning money, Bill Knudsen emphasized, they were creating something. Later Bill Knudsen, on a trip to the West with his family, took Bunkie to the Bay Bridge in San Francisco and talked about its builders. "There was nothing here before they did this. What these men did will be here forever," he had said with a certain awe, "and it will make people's lives better."

Bunkie Knudsen never had a chance at Ford. It was not that he lacked the skill to handle the job; indeed, that was something that almost never came up. It was that Ford was so different from GM. He was a product of the GM system, and the system worked, and it protected those who had mastered it. General Motors was a gray place and in comparison with Ford a somewhat boring place. Decisions on people's futures seemed to have been made some twenty years before they actually were announced. By contrast, Ford, reflecting the influence of the two family figures who had led the company, was a highly political place, filled with cliques and feuds and constant infighting, all under the eye, if not the actual instigation, of the two Henry Fords. Knudsen thought the organizational structure would work loyally for him because he was president, and that having the title of president was quite enough. At GM the organization was, above all else, loyal. He did not bring over many of his own people from GM. (He tried to bring DeLorean, already a star at GM, and he failed; had he succeeded his tenure at Ford might have been different.) Indeed, he brought just enough people to unsettle the Iacocca loyalists but not enough to take command of the company.

To Iacocca, Knudsen represented two things. The first was confirmation of his father's counsel that he could trust no one, that the world in which he competed was filled with men less gifted than he who were either richer or better connected. The other thing Bunkie Knudsen represented from the day he arrived at Ford was a threat. Who knew how long he would stay as president? Who knew if he might establish some other successor—like Don Frey, with whom he seemed so close? Iacocca complained to his friends from the very first day about Bunkie, that he was stupid and knew little about the business. What the hell had he ever accomplished at GM, anyway? he asked. The Mustang had been more successful than any car Bunkie had ever made. If there was a meeting and Knudsen was about to make a mistake, about to cross Henry Ford or the finance people without knowing it, the kind of mistake Iacocca knew how to avoid, he would simply sit back and remain silent, and that very small smile would cross his face. For those who knew Lee Iacocca, his temper and his shouting, the idea of a silent Lee was more disquieting than an angry one. He understood as Knudsen did not that though Henry Ford had made him president, he was only partly president, that Henry Ford had not gone to Washington and it was still his company. Henry Ford had issued the same my-door-is-always-open invitation to Knudsen, and Bunkie, not understanding how the Ford company worked, had taken it at face value, which did not displease Iacocca.

The two men fought constantly over the design center. It was the center of Lee's world, but Knudsen was equally interested in it. Each day, as he had all his life at GM, he started the day in the design center. He was there every morning at seven tinkering with what Iacocca, who liked to come to work much later, considered *his* cars. That was the most personal kind of assault on Iacocca. More, it was coming from an executive who, while not nearly as good a marketing man, had an enviable reputation as a car man. The design people were caught in the crossfire. In the morning Bunkie would go in, look at the lines of a fender, and suggest that the designers change it.

"We like it," the chief designer would say, "and Lee likes it."

"Change it," Knudsen would say.

Later that day, after it had been changed, Lee would seem puzzled. "What happened to the fender?" he would ask the designer.

"Bunkie wanted . . ." the designer would begin.

"Tell Bunkie to bag his ass," Lee would reply.

It was a civil war in which one man was on wartime footing and the other was still at peace. For others in the company it was an extremely difficult period. There was no place to hide. Don Frey remembered it as the worst time in his professional life. Because he and Knudsen were members of the same engineering association and had served on committees together, Frey had known Knudsen before he arrived at Ford. Frey's father had been an admirer of the elder Knudsen, and Bunkie decided that Frey was a natural ally. At the first reception he attended at Ford, Knudsen spotted Frey, the only familiar face in a sea of alien and rather cool Ford men, and grabbed him like a long-lost friend. Knudsen wrapped an arm around Frey and kept him next to him for a very long time. Frey later dated some of his own mounting problems with Iacocca to that moment. Bunkie's embrace was not forgotten or forgiven. From then on Frey was caught between the two men. Praise from Knudsen, of which there was a good deal ("Frey here is the only man in the shop who understands cars"), was poison. Once when Ford was finishing up a new car, Knudsen decided to add a bit of trim to it. Iacocca, who did not want the trim, accepted the order. But Frey met with Knudsen afterward and talked him out of it. Later that day Knudsen, in front of several people, announced, "Frey argued me out of that—he says it's no good and he's right, so I've changed my mind." That remark, Frey came to realize, was unfortunate, for it had shown Iacocca that Frey was close enough to Knudsen to change the latter's mind, and thus that Frey might be on Bunkie's side.

Frey knew in some ways he was failing tests, not with the company or with Henry Ford but with Iacocca. One day in the summer of 1968, Ford, Frey, and Iacocca went to the styling room to take a look at the designs for a small Lincoln. It was a car that Iacocca wanted very badly; he hoped it would help the company in the upper levels of the car market, where Ford had always been weak. Iacocca asked Frey what he thought, and Frey answered that he thought the car, which would weigh over five thousand pounds, was too heavy. Henry Ford quickly agreed. Even before the words were out of Frey's mouth he realized he had made a serious error. The only answer in this case was the one Lee wanted. Frey knew Iacocca felt Frey had forgotten his place in the pecking order, had let his ambition get out of hand. After that, Frey began to find himself isolated by Lee's people. His mistakes, mild enough, had been fatal. He was being told that as long as Lee was powerful, his own future was meager. He went to Henry Ford and told him he was tired of being the meat in the sandwich between Iacocca and Knudsen. He was getting out.

He soon learned that Iacocca did not lightly forgive those whom he judged guilty of disloyalty. First Frey was told that he would not be paid his final bonus, which was to have been approximately $90,000; Frey believed that was an Iacocca decision. Later he read something that Iacocca had said to the *Wall Street Journal*. One of the good things about working in a company as big as Ford, he'd said, was that you never had to fire anyone, you could always find them a good job somewhere else. That stung Frey, because it seemed so personal; no names were mentioned, and yet anyone who counted would know. The remark was particularly painful because Frey admired Iacocca and thought of him as by far the ablest and strongest man in the company, and they had shared a great accomplishment, the Mustang. Machiavelli lives, he decided; I can no longer do anything for him, and now he is paying me back. For some time he was puzzled as to why Lee had been so vengeful. Then he realized that he had seen Iacocca act this way with a great many other people who had gotten in his path, and that the only difference this time was that he had watched it happen to himself.

Iacocca was still resentful of the Knudsen appointment. It had interrupted his own carefully planned timetable, and, he told friends, he was sure that it had something to do with prejudice, as if somehow he were not quite elegant enough to run the Ford company. He had been depressed by it at first, but gradually, seeing the difficulties Knudsen was having in adjusting to Ford, he became confident that he could ride it out and beat Knudsen. A man named Herb Segal, who ran Chris Craft, contacted him and offered him a handsome job, a huge bonus for joining, and a chance to move into the aircraft business. Segal and Iacocca met several times over the next year. Why did they pass you over? Segal asked Iacocca, and Iacocca answered that Ford thought he was too young. "Look," said Segal, "it's a new age, they've got thirty-five-year-old kids running hundred-million-dollar companies, and if you ask them about their qualifications they tell you to go screw yourself." Segal, as he listened to Iacocca, became convinced that class was critical to Henry Ford's decision. Lee was the brilliant Italian kid who was good enough to make them a lot of money but whose manner was nonetheless a little too rough and whose clothes were a little too loud to head the company. Segal picked this up from Lee to some degree, but he got it from Mary Iacocca even more strongly. In her mind she had always been snubbed in Detroit. No matter what their contributions and successes, she felt, she and Lee would always be outsiders there. She obviously wanted her husband to get out of Ford and out of Detroit.

"Lee," said Segal, "you'll never be any hotter. You've got two hot cars [the Mustang and the Maverick], but you're the Italian kid who scares them. All these big industrial companies want someone who looks like Walter Pidgeon and who doesn't take any chances to be in charge. You're never going to look like Walter Pidgeon," he warned Iacocca.

"But that's my life—Ford, the auto industry," Iacocca said.

"Some industry," Segal answered. "One day you're the head of GM and everyone in the city kisses your ass, and the next day you're out and you can't even get a golf game at the Bloomfield Hills Country Club."

But the more they talked, the more Segal realized that though he could probably get Iacocca, Lee's heart was in Detroit. It was not the money. Segal was offering him $3 million, cash in the bank, just to come over. It was the prestige—he wanted, Segal was sure, to be the Italian kid who had beaten the system in Detroit. "You really want to wear the epaulets, don't you?" Segal said. So he advised Iacocca to use the Chris Craft offer to squeeze Knudsen out. He would have to play it to the hilt, leak word of the offer in certain circles. "You'll have to be tough about it," Segal said, "and if it backfires, I guess you go to work for me."

Shortly after that, everyone in Detroit seemed to know that Iacocca was thinking of leaving. Suddenly all sorts of people in the middle levels of Ford began to get nervous and look for jobs. Headhunters were swarming all over the place. Most of the job hunting seemed to be routed through Tex Thornton, who had once led the Whiz Kids at Ford and now headed Litton Industries, and who had little love for the Ford Motor Company. A few people actually left. The entire place was upset.

Unbeknownst to Bunkie Knudsen, he had one additional opponent within the Ford ranks. That was Ed Lundy. Most people when they thought of Knudsen's appointment thought of it in terms of what it did to Iacocca's future. Few thought of the fact that in the process Arjay Miller, who had been serving as president of Ford, had been kicked upstairs and given the title of vice-chairman. Among the very few who had been shattered by that was Ed Lundy. Miller was his best friend, and he idolized Miller. In any real sense the Miller family was his family. That the company he loved treated his closest friend so cavalierly was immensely painful to him. Lundy had seemed for a brief time almost physically affected by the news. If he had been fired himself, it could hardly have been more traumatic. Thus he never helped Bunkie Knudsen out. His attitude during the Knudsen period, Iacocca thought, was one of benign neglect, as if waiting it out. Iacocca, watching the financial people, felt they were holding back information as they had not under Miller. He also sensed that Lundy, in a subtle way, was reaching out to him more, confiding more, more willing than in the past to form an alliance.

Everyone knew something had to be done soon. The company was being torn apart. Soon it was clear that one of the two men, Bunkie or Lee, had to leave. The uncertainty was hurting the company. Those who knew Ed Lundy well believed that he cast the deciding vote. Knudsen had no support at all within the infrastructure, and Iacocca did. If Lundy did not exactly like Iacocca, he knew him and knew he could work with him. If Iacocca was forced out, the company would be ripped to pieces. If Bunkie went, it would merely damage one man's career. Insiders believed that Ed Lundy very carefully let Henry Ford know that Bunkie probably had to go. The corporate body was rejecting the new organism, not the old.

The company, Henry Ford realized, needed Iacocca. About that time an old friend ran into Ford and thought he seemed depressed. What's wrong? the friend asked. "All of my top people tell me I've got to let Bunkie go," Ford said.

On Friday of the Labor Day weekend in 1969, Henry Ford dropped by Bunkie Knudsen's office, and they talked casually about their holiday plans. Knudsen told Ford that his kids were coming in from different parts of the country. They would spend the weekend together as a family. "That sounds nice," Ford said. "Have a nice weekend."

As six-thirty on Monday morning, Labor Day itself, Knudsen got a call from Ted Mecke, who was Ford's personal public-relations man. He said he wanted to talk with Knudsen, and an hour later he showed up at his door. "I just want to tell you," he told Bunkie, "that you're no longer with the Ford Motor Company, and that tomorrow that's what you'll be told." Knudsen, puzzled, asked him why he had come to tell him that. "As a friend," Mecke said.

What does he mean, he's here as a friend? Florence Knudsen thought. She had not particularly wanted her husband to leave General Motors, where he was comfortable, for a company that was said to have so many dangerous eddies. She had never been at ease with Henry Ford; he could flick his charm switch much too easily. He played with people without any real regard for the impact of his deeds on their lives. At the funeral of Ford's old Wall Street adviser Sidney Weinberg, a month earlier, Florence Knudsen had happened to look over and catch a glimpse of Henry Ford staring at her husband. His gaze was so steely, his face so grim, that she had known something terrible was going to happen.

The day after Mecke's visit, Bunkie Knudsen, as usual, went to work at the Ford Motor Company. There Henry Ford told him that he had to leave the company. Knudsen asked Ford if there was any reason. "It just didn't work out," Ford answered. He told Knudsen to get together with Mecke to work out the details. "You can keep the [Ford] car," he said.

"I don't want the car," Knudsen replied.

Mecke promptly arrived with a statement saying that Knudsen had resigned to pursue other interests. No way, said Knudsen. He quickly typed up a release saying he had been fired and called a friend at a wire service and read it to him.

Shortly thereafter Henry Ford called a press conference and announced that he was naming Lee Iacocca as one of three unit vice-presidents. Iacocca spent the entire press conference trying, with limited success, not to seem to be gloating. When a reporter asked him how he felt about the news, he said, "I've never said 'no comment' before but I am today." Lee Iacocca, being in a rush, had taken out Semon E. Knudsen in only nineteen months. It had not been a pleasant spectacle. "There was no need for him to see me as a threat," Knudsen said of Iacocca fifteen years later. "I was twelve years older than he was, and he could have worked with me for a few years and maybe even learned a few things and then taken over the company." Thus did Bunkie Knudsen in 1984 show that he had still learned nothing about Lee Iacocca.

Lee Iacocca was the victor. A little over a year later Henry Ford named him president. It was as if the Knudsen interregnum had never existed. It often seemed now that it had not. Iacocca was delighted to get the job he had always wanted. But something in the chemistry of the two men had been permanently altered. Henry Ford might have righted what was in Iacocca's view a bad decision, but he had made a fatal mistake, he had proved he was, deep down, a snobbish Wasp. That would not be readily forgiven. In the meantime, it was Iacocca's company. He was the power within. Nothing could be pushed through the ever-tightening control system of the finance people without his support. That meant that not only the cadre of Lee's own people but anyone else in the company who wanted to do anything creative had to go through him.

In those days Iacocca was pushing bigger and flashier cars. The Mustang, once slim and sporty and relatively simple, had grown bigger and heavier, until its earlier enthusiasts could no longer recognize it. It had become, as increments of weight were added and increments of profit achieved, a big ugly car. (In his book Iacocca blamed Knudsen for doing that, but the memory of almost everyone else who worked there in those years is different. It was Lee who kept adding weight to the Mustang.) Iacocca, like Henry Ford, adopted the formula of GM, which kept producing bigger and more expensive cars for its customers as they presumably became richer and more important. For there was not much difference in the cost of making a Chevrolet and a Cadillac, but the difference in profit was immense. In the decade of the seventies, that was where Ford intended to close the gap, not just in the Ford division but in the upper levels, particularly with the Lincoln Continental. The larger profit was in the bigger cars.

Iacocca gradually became the spokesman for Detroit. The GM people were too gray; the GM organization demanded anonymity and produced few colorful characters. Chrysler was too weak. And Henry Ford seemed increasingly involved in other matters. Lee loved being the public figure of the Ford Motor Company, and he was good at it, always available, always quotable. He was the new, confident, pugnacious figure of the auto industry. The industry was healthy and going to become healthier. Cars were big and going to become bigger. He pushed racing: "Race 'em on Sunday and sell 'em on Monday." He was openly contemptuous of the earlier Ford efforts at safety. When the subject of clean air came up, he said, "We've got to pause and ask ourselves: How much clean air do we need?" When reporters mentioned something called front-wheel drive, which in the early seventies was just coming into vogue in Europe, he was again condescending. Customers, he said, couldn't see it. "I say give 'em leather. They can smell it." He disdained small cars. Though the company's own research showed with considerable finality that the people who drove small imported cars were an important new part of the market—college-educated (indeed often second-generation college-educated), upper-middle-class people who took their social definition not from expensive cars, which they could readily afford, but from other things, records, wine, travel—he resisted. Iacocca, like most of Detroit, adopted a policy of nonrecognition of this profound social change. All the warnings that this new American class was likely to get larger, and that indeed it often set taste standards for others, made no dent on Detroit. Its rules were the ones that still pertained in suburban Detroit: As you made more money, you bought a bigger car and a bigger house and joined a better country club. Status was fixed there as it had been in the past but as it was no longer fixed on either of the coasts. When Iacocca spoke of small cars, he spoke as Detroit spoke of them, as a kind of charitable obligation to the less fortunate, cars for those who could not afford the cars they truly wanted, a sort of social welfare of manufacturing.

Fifteen months after Bunkie Knudsen's departure, Iacocca was named president of the Ford Motor Company. Ten years after that, Florence Knudsen was at a supermarket in Bloomfield Hills when a woman whom she barely recognized came over to her. The woman said something, and Mrs. Knudsen continued to look puzzled. The woman, she thought seemed so fragile, so vulnerable.

"I'm Mary Iacocca, Florence," she said.

This was about a month after Lee Iacocca had been fired by Henry Ford, and Florence Knudsen, a woman of great kindness, whose own life had been changed so drastically by the whim of Henry Ford, reached out and said, "Oh, Mary, I'm so sorry."

"Now I know," said Mary Iacocca. "Now I know."

PART
SEVEN

22.
THE STATUE

As Nissan approached the year 1960, it slowly and systematically became stronger. Its tempestuous labor problems were in the past. What money it was making—and more, much more—was being spent on new machinery, and its debt had grown awesome. The strain on the entire company was enormous. Yet although it was happening in the most painful way, Nissan was evolving into a real industrial force.

Kinichi Tamura, one of the Nissan design engineers, remembered 1960 and the years just before and after as a frenzied time. New plants were being planned and old ones expanded while at the same time the company tried desperately to keep production on schedule. On the factory floor, men tried to work at their stations as all around them construction workers tore the old lines apart, while other men kept pleading for even greater production. It was a madhouse, Tamura, thought. He would visit a section to see whether the new machines that had just arrived were being installed, find that they had been, and then watch as a construction crane swept over and knocked them down. Tamura and his colleagues would spend a day marking off on the floor the exact location for the installation of new equipment, and some construction crew would come and accidentally tear the area up—and it would all have to be done over. Tamura could never remember a time like it. Normally he went home at seven in the evening, but in those years he seemed to stay at work until midnight, riding the train home for an hour and a half in the early morning, trying not to fall asleep and miss his stop. He barely saw his family. It was a strange feeling, of total exhilaration and, simultaneously, total exhaustion. For all of his problems, his excitement was almost overwhelming. For he was helping create the modern Nissan, building new wings of factories and installing new machines. He was touching the future. This was going to be a great company, and he was one of its architects. He could hardly believe his good luck.

One of Tamura's glorious moments came when he helped develop and install Nissan's first transfer machine. Transfer machines were basic to the work of Detroit, but Nissan had never had one. The transfer machine brought automation to the old process in which workers at station after station each performed one small task on a given piece such as an engine block. Some thirty yards long, the machine incorporated the work of as many as thirty stations, greatly speeding up the line and reducing manpower at the same time. Such machines could be ordered from America, but they were very expensive, perhaps several million dollars each. Do you think it would be possible, some senior Nissan executives asked their manufacturing engineers, to make our own?

At first it seemed impossible, a dream. Surely engineers and designers whose own accomplishments were so primitive could not make anything that complicated. But Tamura and his colleagues went to work on it. They took all the information brought back by from America by the traveling productivity teams, all the photos and sketches, and pieced them together into a rough design for a transfer machine. Month after month went by —precious months to a company under such ferocious pressure—and at times Tamura wondered if they had bitten off more than they could chew. There were, Tamura remembered, some thirty design meetings, and midway through them, he suddenly had a sense that he had been wrong, it *was* possible—as long as they thought of the great task in small increments. The others had come to the same insight, and it gave them confidence. When their design was complete, they took it to a local machine shop. The owner looked at it a long time. "It's the biggest thing I've ever seen," he said. The more he looked at it, the more excited he became. Yes, he said, he wanted to do it, he wanted to do it very badly. Not only was it a wondrous engineering and manufacturing challenge, but if he pulled it off, he might get many orders and become a considerably richer man. He began the job in 1960 and finished it a little less than a year later. The designers and engineers were astonished at how well he had done in creating the machine they wanted.

The installation was a great moment. Everyone in the factory wanted to see the new machine. Work throughout the plant came to a halt. Somehow a party began, and it went on for two days. Years later Tamura regarded that moment, the coming of the first transfer machine, as the dividing line between the old Nissan Motors Company and the new.

The decision to plunge Nissan into frantic expansion had been terrifying for its president, Katsuji Kawamata, the financial man who had come over from the Industrial Bank. Never had the men around him, particularly the engineers, been so frustrated by him as in the period starting in 1958 when the Japanese domestic market began to explode. This was the most important moment in the company's history, a mass market was finally opening up, and Kawamata was completely immobilized. He seemed alternately afraid to move and afraid not to move. He could see the future—he did not argue with the judgments of the professionals working for him who were suddenly so excited by the prospects of soaring sales on low-cost cars—but he was horrified by the size of the debt required for any serious growth. The top product men wanted to pour as much resource as possible into the company's overloaded production lines; they feared the consequences if Nissan did not seize the moment. Kawamata feared the consequences if it did. Those close to him in that period sometimes wondered whether he was going to come apart under the strain of conflicting pressure within the company. When the product people argued in meetings that Nissan had no choice but to expand its production capacity and expand it quickly, he would sometimes seem to agree with them, and only later would they find out that they had not moved him at all.

"How is he today?" one of the engineers asked a colleague who dealt with Kawamata daily.

"Oh, much better," said the insider. "He's much more Yes-No today than yesterday, when he was No-Yes. Of course, I cannot promise you anything for tomorrow."

That Nissan had to thrust ahead was hardly a question. Everyone knew that there was no choice, especially since Toyota was already making plans to do so. As early as 1956, Toyota had bought an old airplane factory and begun to convert it into its newest assembly plant, called Motomachi. That confirmed to everyone at Nissan that the stakes were going up quickly, and that Toyota was preparing for the day when the new market would be carved up. Toyota was finalizing its deal for Motomachi when the Nissan production engineers were only starting to look for a plant site. The problem was that Nissan was hardly the sole Japanese company getting ready for the surge of the new consumer economy. In the dense, overcrowded Tokyo-Yokohama corridor, all property, including industrial property, was expensive and becoming more so all the time. There were no bargains. The early attempts to find land around Yokohoma were all failures; no matter what Nissan's scouts came up with, Kawamata would somehow manage to turn it down—it would be too small, too distant, but mostly too expensive. That Kawamata would continue to delay even as Toyota was actually starting to build its factory increased the tension at Nissan.

There was a growing apprehension among the senior product people that the boat was going to leave without them.

Then Soichi Kawazoe, a former Nissan employee who was now working for Fuji Motors, tipped off Nissan that a huge site which once had belonged to Fuji, located at Oppama, near Yokosuka, about twelve miles south of Yokohama, was available. The price was considered surprisingly cheap, and it seemed the perfect location for Nissan. Still, Kawamata procrastinated; he began to talk about expanding the existing Yokohama plant, an idea that had long ago been discarded, or finding another location. His production people seethed. Kawazoe took the top Nissan executives around the site in the fall of 1958. The product men were thrilled. But Kawamata delayed. Ten months passed before Nissan finally made a bid to the Ministry of Finance, which was handling the sale. By then other companies were trying to buy the same land, but the ministry gave it to Nissan. Construction did not begin until February 1961, a year and a half after Toyota had *opened* its new plant. Nissan, at this crucial moment in the struggle for domestic share, was three years behind Toyota.

If that was not bad enough, a second struggle broke out, this time over the size of the factory. The failure to move quickly had already proved costly, and by 1959, with the coming of the Datsun 310, which was an immediate success, the old Nissan production lines were sorely overloaded. (In 1959, as Michael Cusamano pointed out in his excellent book on Nissan and Toyota, they ran at 94.2 percent of capacity—and by 1961 at 113.6 percent of capacity.) The men and the machines were stretched to the breaking point.

The product people were extremely confident about the future. They knew they had tapped into something formidable that was only just beginning, and they wanted a big factory. The responsibility of arguing for a large new plant fell on a young engineer named Shiro Matsuzaki, who ran the engineering section at the Yokohama plant and had a very clear idea of the degree to which Nissan's facilities were overwhelmed. Matsuzaki had studied the history of both the American and the European auto industries, and he believed that Japan was just on the edge of takeoff. He also knew how cautious Kawamata was. If only, Matsuzaki thought, Kawamata could be like Yataro Nishiyama of Kawasaki Steel. Nishiyama was a hero of Matsuzaki's, as he was of many of the young production people in Japan. For he had taken on and beaten the feared Hisato Ichimada, the very conservative head of the Bank of Japan, a man so powerful and autocratic that he was known as the Pope, a man whose instinctive response to every proposal was negative. Nishiyama, absolutely sure of the prospects of Japanese steel, had proposed a vast expansion of

Kawasaki—"ten times what we had in capital," he later told Matsuzaki. Ichimada had, of course, opposed him, and Nishiyama had gone elsewhere and obtained the financing; the result was that his firm became a leader in Japanese steel's very successful move into a highly modernized future.

Matsuzaki had visited Nishiyama at his mill and had been impressed by him and the gleaming realization of his dream. This, he thought, is a great man, one with courage. Nissan, he was certain, could do the same thing. The visit with Nishiyama encouraged him to push ahead at Nissan. He asked his superiors if he could see Kawamata personally, in order to ask him to approve his own plan for massive expansion. His superiors were perfectly happy to let him, a relatively junior figure, make the case to Kawamata. Matsuzaki and his colleagues knew what they needed: a new factory, one that could produce twenty thousand cars a month. The ability to produce twenty thousand more cars a month would carry Nissan past Toyota.

So it was that Matsuzaki went to see Kawamata. He respected Kawamata because he was a superior, and he wanted Kawamata to share Nishiyama's vision. He felt he was taking his life in his hands. He decided that if Kawamata approved the plan and the new capacity proved to be more than the company needed, he would leave Nissan. He found Kawamata unsympathetic to the idea, considering it too risky. "In order to get that much money," he said, "do you know what I would have to do?" Matsuzaki said nothing, for he knew he was not supposed to reply. "I would have to bow my head many times to the bankers. And if the project failed," Kawamata added, "I would have to enter the priesthood. Do you still want me to do it?" Matsuzaki, feeling his entire career was on the line, said yes, he thought Nissan had to push forward, that all of the company's engineers were in agreement on this. But he soon saw that Kawamata was adamant. The cost of so large a factory—perhaps $100 million—was beyond his mental capacity. He refused to budge.

Kawamata called in an American consulting team which had already done some work for Nissan, and it suggested a compromise figure for the new factory's capacity—seven thousand cars a month. Again Kawamata refused to budge. He insisted on five thousand, and five thousand it was. Thus from the start the Oppama plant was overloaded. The factory had to go on a double shift, which was hard on the workers. Even with the double shift, production was inadequate. Almost immediately Nissan's engineers had to build an additional factory at a site near Zama. From then on, many of the product people were ambivalent about Kawamata. They were aware how hard many of his decisions had been in those years; the cost of the Oppama plant, even in its scaled-down size, was greater

than the paid-up capitalization of Nissan, which was the kind of statistic
that would strike terror into the heart of any good conservative American
manager. But they thought he had been too careful and squandered a
chance to move ahead of Toyota, perhaps permanently. Years later one
of them said: "I don't know whether to be grateful to him for saving the
company or angry at him for crippling it."

Yet for all of their frustrations with him, there was no doubt as the
decade of the fifties ended that this was Kawamata's company. He had
moved aside all of his potential challengers. If he was less than confident
of his judgment on product and cautious about investing in plants, he was
vigorous in the use of his political skills to solidify his control. The basis
of his strength was the union and its leaders—Masaru Miyake, who had
formed the company-approved union at Nissan that had beat out the radical
one, and Miyake's ambitious number two, Ichiro Shioji. If executives
outside Kawamata's circle challenged or seemed to challenge Kawamata's
people, the union intervened and made their lives as difficult as possible;
suddenly there would be slowdowns on certain shifts, or supplies that had
been ordered long in advance would not show up on time. Those who
played along with Kawamata and the union looked good; those who did
not play along would always fail. Kawamata was the beneficiary—but there
was a quid pro quo. Miyake and Shioji in effect had a veto power over all
personnel changes. Some of their supporters were soon given key jobs in
middle management, pushed ahead of more senior but less trusted, less
well-connected executives. Nothing happened in the company without
their approval. Technically they were union men, but in effect they were
not only management but top management. To other employees it was as
if they ran the company.

In some ways Nissan was not that different from other Japanese companies. Though the Japanese prided themselves on the harmony of their
working environment, the truth was that most companies were beehives
of competing cliques and political factions, and there were often enormous
tensions just below the surface. The differences might not be visible to
outsiders, but they were nonetheless very real. In day-to-day workings,
much of that hostility was submerged; middle-level executives would go
out together after work and drink a good deal and complain bitterly about
their superiors, but the next morning they would be back at work, as
respectful as ever. What they had said the night before no longer existed;
it was whiskey and sake talk, and those embittered complaints might as
well have been uttered by someone else. The post-work sessions were
important; they were the one way of ventilating a system that allowed

little dissent. Since the dissent was under the influence of alcohol, it could always be disregarded later. In the end, the faction that lost out accepted the winner's mandate out of a traditional sense of obligation to authority and hierarchy, but the losers did it as well because they had absolutely no option in their lives. Thus the world of Japanese business was filled with intrigue that persisted until the very last seconds, when the contestants healed their differences and got on with the job.

Inevitably Kawamata's rise, and his use of the union leaders as his spear carriers, created resentment in the upper echelons, and resentment led to mutiny. In 1955, Kawamata's enemies decided to make one last stand against him, and therefore against the union. The leader of the dissidents was Asahara, then Nissan's president, made nervous by the growing power of his executive director and pushed as well by his peers, for he was not a confrontational man. In substance it was the old Nissan against the new Nissan. Asahara and his colleagues conferred with officials of the Industrial Bank of Japan, the IBJ. The sins of Kawamata were enumerated: He was too crude, he was too ambitious, he was too close to the union. A decision then was made to move Kawamata to a far less prestigious subsidiary, Nissan Diesel.

The coup caught Kawamata by surprise. In the early morning he found out that he had been ousted, and he immediately sent his cousin Kuniyaki Tanabe, a Nissan middle manager, to tell his closest ally, Miyake, head of the union. "They're getting rid of him," Tanabe told Miyake, "and he wants you immediately." Miyake had gone to Kawamata's house and had found him in despair. "They've trapped the bear," Kawamata told him, and he pleaded with Miyake to do something. It was the only time, Miyake told friends later, that he had seen Kawamata shorn of his arrogance and rudeness. Miyake, of course quickly agreed to help. His participation was not entirely altruistic. His power, which was considerable, derived from Kawamata. If Kawamata went, his own wings might be clipped next.

Miyake went to the IBJ that morning and spoke with Sohei Nakayama, the head of the bank, whom he had known in the past. That gave Miyake a sense of connection. In addition, he had considerable leverage of his own. Other executives might speak for the company, but Miyake, who commanded the union, spoke for the work force. In the politest manner possible he said that he thought it was a mistake for the bank to intervene in the internal affairs of the company unless someone had failed. Clearly Kawamata had not failed. "Listen," Nakayama told him, "the last thing in the world the bank wants is to get involved in something messy like this. This is your business, not ours." To remind all parties of the power of the union, Miyake ordered a strike at the Yokohama plant; it was largely a gesture. With help from a few others, Miyake won the day, and Kawamata did not go to Nissan Diesel.

From then on Asahara's own days were numbered. Two years later he decided he wanted to leave the presidency and become chairman. He was tired of the job and all the conflict it brought him, none of which he had sought. As a replacement he wanted Kyoichi Harashina, one of his oldest friends. Harashina was considered by the product people as the ablest candidate in the company, a man of technology and cars, and there was no doubt in the mind of anyone who worked there that, on merit, he was the natural successor to Asahara. He had gone to Todai, worked for Nissan before it was Nissan, back in the thirties when it was only Tobata Casting. He was a graceful and sophisticated man, popular with the product people, as Kawamata was not. The officials of the IBJ, however, favored Kawamata, and what swung its decision was the union. Miyake had made it very clear to the bank that Harashina was unacceptable. The union would accept Kawamata and no one else. Thus in 1957 Kawamata became president of Nissan, and about two years later it was Harashina who was shunted off to Nissan Diesel. Kawamata had firmed up his power, and henceforth he would owe allegiance to Miyake and Shioji.

Soon Kawamata became quite grand. Status, the place of a man in the hierarchy, was important in Japan, but it seemed particularly important to Kawamata. There had been early signs of that. At the first dealers' meeting after he had joined the company, the heads of the dealers' association had been at the head table, the company officials at the second one; the next year the company officials were at the head table, the dealers at the lesser one. These things mattered. What surprised and irritated some of Kawamata's colleagues was the aura that he began to give off as the company grew more successful, his implicit message that *he* had done it, as if he had not so much ridden the wave as created the wave, and, even more, that he was not so much a banker as an *industrialist*. That more than anything offended his colleagues, the immodesty of it. He had always been bored by anything dealing with technology. His decisions had almost always been cautious in the extreme, the minimal acceptable level of daring. He was not, they thought, an industrialist, and he had no right to pass himself off as one. Soichiro Honda was an industrialist, more a man of machines than of business, but Kawamata was not.

That quibble did not seem to bother Kawamata. He often spoke to various groups now as an expert on labor relations. His subordinates soon learned that the best way to deal with him was through flattery. They let him know how much they needed him, and they lauded his ability to handle problems, including minor ones they themselves could readily have handled on their own. Supplier company executives mastered the delicate art of managing to lose to him on the golf course, while still seeming to play a competitive game. Soon there was a statue of him—from the waist up—mounted at the new Oppama plant, the one he opposed and then severely compromised. That sort of thing was rare in Japanese companies. Perhaps in a family company a grandson might put up a statue of a grandfather or even, though it would be exceptional, of a father. But a statue to a living executive was almost unthinkable. In this case it was Miyake, who accurately understood his superior, who was responsible. "I did not want to accept," Kawamata explained in his memoirs, "but everybody in the company wanted it for me."

23.
THE BOSS

Ichiro Shioji, number two in the Nissan union, had never been a man destined to spend much of his career as anyone's deputy. It was as if some larger force carried him to the top now. This was an era in which the Japanese establishment was exercising its reclaimed mandate, bringing discipline and control to the work force, and Shioji was an instrument through which that establishment's notion of national purpose was turned into reality on the factory floor. In short, he was the muscle.

Miyake, his superior, was soon vulnerable. Having saved Kawamata from the coup and played the deciding role in assuring him the presidency, Miyake had wanted his due: He wanted to go on the Nissan board. He had asked Kawamata to put him on, and Kawamata refused—he wanted Miyake to wait a few years. Others, contemporaries of Miyake's, hearing of his demand, were scandalized. The board was an almost sacred place; it was for senior people. This was too much. Such a demand was made only by a man who lacked respect for the system. Therefore he was dangerous. A union man should know his place. Soon there was a power struggle between Miyake and Shioji. Shioji claimed that at one point Miyake even got him drunk in a restaurant, kidnapped him, and, while he was incommunicado, tried to stop the production line. The upshot of it was simple: Miyake's power was curtailed, and he eventually left the company with a job elsewhere, arranged by Kawamata. Shioji took his place, not just as the leader of the union but as the man Kawamata depended on.

It was really Shioji's union anyway. Slowly and very carefully, he had been building his authority within it. The men just below him in the union were loyal to him, not to Miyake. His ambition was more intense than that of Miyake, and it was a very different kind of ambition. Miyake had always wanted to be a member of management; he had stumbled into the union somewhat involuntarily. Even as head of the union he had coveted a high management position and a place on the board. Miyake wanted success—defined by title and affluence. Shioji, by contrast, wanted power—that was success enough. Indeed, he sought the kind of power found in America and not in Japan, power openly exercised. Shioji was a completely political man; he understood better than almost anyone of his generation that Nissan was not only a manufacturing organism but a political organism as well, with all kinds of tiny interlocking personal relationships and dependencies. Power could be exercised through those dependencies; there were always favors to trade. He loved creating the alignments that advanced his and the union's power, moving his men into the right positions, calling in the due bills when the time was right, coming down on those who stood in his way. That for him was the real satisfaction. He needed no grand management title. As head of the union he was as powerful as anyone on the executive side. Everyone had to take him seriously. He did not want to be some some gray-faced middle manager who waited thirty years for a chance to have a marginal decision-making role in company with other gray-faced middle managers. A labor leader was a man who commanded men and gave orders and whose orders were obeyed.

He was different from the men around him. In a society carefully arranged so that there would be a minimum of confrontation, Shioji loved confrontation. He was good at it. Most contemporary Japanese liked to conceal as much as they could about themselves, most particularly their ambition and ego. Shioji concealed nothing. His ambition, like his anger, was surprisingly visible. His enjoyment of the pleasures of his job was equally open; in the years to come, there would be constant complaints in the press about his life-style, the Ginza high life, and the cost of his yacht. What enraged him about the attacks was that comparable attacks were not made upon company executives who lived this way. A top executive could live the high life, own a yacht, keep a geisha somewhere, and no one said anything; an executive was *supposed* to do those things. But let someone from a labor union do them and everyone came down on him. The rule was clear; the upstart was violating an accepted pattern of behavior and, in so doing, threatening an entire system. "They always want Shioji to stay in his place," he once told a reporter. "They would like me to be unimportant and bow to the managers. But I am in my place—this is the right place for me. It is that which they cannot stand."

The people who complained bored him. As far as he was concerned, that was the old guard, the old Japan, telling him what his *limits* were, and to stay within them. Be a good boy. He was not a good boy. He liked to offend the establishment. He fulminated against the prejudice against him and against the secret snobbery of Japan as exercised through the educational system. There was supposed to be no snobbery in Japan, but in the university system there was nothing but snobbery, a snobbery he believed followed most Japanese the rest of their lives. There was Todai for those who passed the entrance exams and Keio, where the sons of the right people went, and then there was the next rank of schools, and then the third-rate schools like Meiji, where he had gone—even worse, where he had gone as a night student. No one with an education like his was ever supposed to be truly important in the society, he was convinced. It was to be his purpose to serve others. He was to accept without question decisions made by his superiors. Instead, he flaunted his independent behavior. He loved going to important meetings in a blazer instead of a suit, and he knew full well the signal he was giving: I will go on my terms, not yours, and you in fact will have to meet my terms. The fact that he wore a blazer meant that he had no superior who could disapprove of his dress and tell him to be more formal. In a world of suits, the blazer was a symbol of freedom.

He knew he had risen against the odds. Without the American presence during the Occupation the country might not have changed and he might not have been so successful. It was the Americans' arrival in Japan at the end of the war that had ended the stifling prewar society and had liberated him in the first place. It had been a rare time, he thought afterward, when the poor but strong could ascend despite their backgrounds, when one's future was less determined by one's past. A few years later, he thought, when the old order was more firmly reentrenched, he might not have done as well. He was a man of the streets, and in that postwar moment a man of the streets had a chance.

It had been a long climb. After the war, desperate to survive, he had seized on the most elemental jobs: semilegal purveyor of food, maker of homemade radios, and dance instructor. (The Americans had brought their dances with them, and almost overnight Western dancing had become a major fad in Tokyo.) He rather liked his job as a dance instructor, and it paid rather well. But his friends were highly critical of that incarnation. "Shioji," one said, "that is not a serious job. What are you doing, looking for a rich woman?" With that he quit and took a job as a worker with Nihon Paint and Oil. He also went to night school at Meiji.

In those politically charged days the radical left had been holding protest rallies outside the Imperial Palace, building up to the general strike that was scheduled for February 1, 1947. The crowds they were drawing were massive, and everyone seemed to be carrying a red flag. One day about a month before the strike was scheduled, Shioji encountered a huge demonstration outside the palace grounds, and he stopped to see what all the noise was about. So, apparently, had a uniformed American soldier who had wandered into the area. The left-wingers immediately seized the American as a spy (that was an error; the Americans generally sent Nisei Japanese in civilian clothes as their intelligence agents) and started beating and kicking him. Shioji intervened and stopped the beating. He looked at the soldier, who struck him as singularly innocent and confused. This man would not be a spy. The Americans, as far as Shioji was concerned, had acted only as friends. Shioji, with his broken English, questioned the young soldier. The American said he had seen the stage and the banners and had been under the impression that some kind of quaint Japanese theatrical production was about to take place. The artlessness of the answer matched the guilelessness in the face. With Shioji's help the American was allowed to leave.

But the incident did not die there. The next day at a union meeting the presence of the American spy at a rally was given as an added reason for going out on strike. Shioji stood and tried to explain what had happened. He had been an eyewitness to the incident, he said, and it had all been a mistake. He was shouted down as a capitalist dog. That did not deter him. He repeated what he had seen. The head of the union, at first tolerant, soon became irritated with him. "The soldier may not be a spy," the union leader said, "but the fact that you insist on saying that he is not a spy means that you are a running dog for the capitalists. You should understand that—which side you help when you speak like this."

That was the beginning of his politicization. With the Communists, he decided, the truth did not matter; only the cause mattered. The truth should serve their purpose, not its own. A few days later he had a private meeting with the head of the union, who was even more explicit. "We think you are a talented young man," the union leader said, "but we think you have much to learn. It's okay when something like this happens to use it for our cause." The unions, Shioji soon concluded, were run by the Communists. He joined a group that fought the existing union leadership at Nihon Paint. At the time of the red purge he worked to expel the Communists from their positions in the union.

But although he ended up more conservative than most workers of that era, he was not readily accepted by the managerial elite. He was working for his soap company during the day and studying at night at a not very good college. With a night degree from a lesser university he probably could not get a job with one of first-line companies. Finally in desperation he quit his job at Nihon and took and passed a difficult exam that allowed him to become a day student, thus partially legitimizing himself. Now, he thought, I am a smart Japanese because I go to school during the day; before I was a dumb Japanese because I went to school at night. Still, he was aware that he might never have been hired at Nissan if it had not been for the strike and management's needs for newcomers—tough newcomers, at that.

As he rose in power he liked to accentuate the difference between himself and his contemporaries—he was tougher. Other Japanese were somewhat afraid of foreigners, particularly Americans, and were slightly ashamed if they were too closely associated with them. They might borrow from the foreigners, especially the Americans, but only in the most superficial way. The other men, business executives all, with a few noticeable exceptions wore dark, conservative, Ivy League clothes that were modeled on those of their American colleagues, and wore the Rolex watches that they perceived to be in fashion among American executives, and favored the same Scotch, Johnny Walker Black, that they saw the Americans drink, and they patterned their industrial production lines, too, on the American lines. The Johnny Walker Japanese, Shioji privately called them; they wanted to be part of the larger world without changing at all. Spiritually Japanese, they resisted the Americanization of self to the point where they tried to spend as little time with the Americans as they could. In fact, time spent in a foreign country, they knew, worked against them; those who had spent a long while abroad were never again completely trusted by the home office, for it was believed that they might have picked up some dreaded foreign habits, and when they returned home they often began to atone for their years overseas by becoming even more chauvinistic than their colleagues. The true model was always the Japanese one.

Shioji liked to think that he had changed not just his outer self but his inner self as well. He boasted of his many American friendships, of his contacts throughout that country. Many Japanese, he knew, had made connections when they served overseas but upon return to Tokyo were careful not to be identified as friends of the gaijin. He was not like that. He often wished that Japan was more like America, more open, more meritocratic. He *liked* what he had seen in America. He had been taken up and sponsored at a relatively young age by the American labor movement. If the American business community was paying very little attention to its counterparts in Japan, the American labor movement was different. The AFL (and later the AFL-CIO) was eager to strengthen non-Communist labor movements throughout the world. To the AFL people Shioji was a promising young Japanese labor leader who was also earnestly anti-Communist. In the fifties that was the perfect combination. The Americans paid attention to him when few others in his own country had; they courted him and educated him, and he in turn gloried in that attention. In 1961, as a relatively unknown young man, with the help of the American embassy and the AFL-CIO, he went to the Harvard Business School for a seminar of several weeks. He absolutely loved it. One of the first things he noticed about Americans was that in comparison with the Japanese, they were not afraid to make mistakes. It was almost the first thing he noticed about his classmates at Harvard—they felt free to try anything they wanted. If they failed, that was their fault. But the restraints were those they placed on themselves, not invisible ones placed on them by the society. The Japanese, he felt, were afraid to take chances, for they were terrified of failure; the Americans tried, failed, and then tried again. In that sense it was a more open, less cautious society. Men openly coveted success, and if they achieved it, it was their own; that too appealed to him.

But what impressed him more than anything else was the role of the labor leader in America. There a labor leader had a position of authority, and with that position went respect. He was a public man. Many people, not just workers and employers but average citizens, paid attention. While he was at Harvard, Walter Reuther came to make a speech, and Shioji was awed. Reuther was his great hero. A small hall had been set aside for Reuther's speech, and it soon became apparent that it was much too small, and people scurried around and managed to get access to the Harvard gymnasium. Shioji was astonished. The entire Harvard gym was filled with students. There was standing room only. The idea that a labor leader had so broad a following struck him forcefully. No one in Japan had a following like that. If a labor leader went to Todai or Keio, only a handful of students would show up. After Reuther's speech there was a reception, and Shioji met Reuther. He had been warned the night before by an American friend that if he shook hands with Reuther he should use his left hand, since Reuther had lost much of the movement in his right hand when he was shot years before during Detroit's labor troubles. So Shioji stuck out his left hand, but Reuther waved him off and insisted on shaking with his right and then said, "Let's see which of us is stronger." They matched grips in a quick test of strength that to Shioji sealed the friendship. Shioji was struck by Reuther's openness. Reuther wanted to talk about Japan and about Shioji's problems there.

That summer, after leaving Harvard, Shioji went to Detroit and stayed with the UAW people at Solidarity House, and the Americans became his friends—Reuther and Leonard Woodcock and Pat Greathouse and Doug Fraser. Years later, even after Greathouse retired, he always came to the airport to meet Shioji whenever Shioji visited Detroit. They were the top people in the union, and they had all treated him as an equal. He worked hard on his English, and he could understand almost all of what they said. In fact he could soon speak fairly good English (though he preferred to use an interpreter, since it gave him added time to hear a question and ponder his answer). When he returned to Japan his confidence was greater; he was now a good friend—an equal—of the most important labor leaders in the world. From then on it was clear in his mind who his role models were: the UAW people, and particularly Reuther. He was proud that he was now Walter Reuther's friend. When Japanese officials visited Detroit or Washington and met Reuther, Reuther always asked them to send a message back to his great friend in Tokyo, Ichiro Shioji.

The trip to America confirmed him in his goal, which was to be a union leader. He did not want to go into management, as many of his contemporaries hoped to do. Nor did he want to go into some esteemed but to him essentially powerless and boring position in the Japanese Diet. He would be like Reuther. The American, he noticed, for all his democratic manner ran a very tight ship and kept dissent to a minimum. Shioji decided to do the same thing in Japan. So when he gained power he ran his union like a personal fiefdom. Anyone rising in the union who was a potential rival soon found himself dispatched to a meaningless job in a supplier company. Another potential adversary might be farmed out to the Diet. Shioji demanded complete loyalty. Those who crossed him, even in the smallest way, were soon gone. He played very tough. If a worker who was somewhat to the left of Shioji tried to distribute leaflets criticizing company policies, he was likely to find himself attacked by goon squads. Shioji was always kept well informed about any political stirrings of which he would not approve. Criticism of the company (as long as Kawamata was president) was the same as criticism of the union. If a worker complained about his wages to another worker, he was likely to be brought into a room with a foreman and have his words repeated back to him in the most ominous manner. The threat was both overt and covert. Without words the foreman was conveying: You are unhappy, and we know exactly what you are thinking and saying. But, to be certain, a warning was issued against any subsequent violations. It was barely needed. The union was clearly omniscient.

Shioji dealt with Kawamata and only Kawamata on any issue of importance. They decided what the raises would be. He was the union, and the union was he. He was to be neither questioned nor doubted. He believed in democracy, but, like many powerful men, he favored democracy of the most personalized sort. In 1962 a young man named Shunichiro Umetani joined the company and went to his first union orientation meeting. There he heard Shioji make a speech about the union and the company. It was during a period of some trade liberalization. This, said Shioji, was a difficult time for the company, and so the union had decided to cooperate by asking for only a fraction of the normal wage increase. Umetani, who did not understand the politics of the union and the company, stood up and asked what Shioji was getting in return. He could understand the need for sacrifice, but he knew that if the risk paid off, the company was going to receive considerable benefits. Was there anything for the union in this deal, since its salaries were relatively low?

"This question is not even necessary," Shioji said.

But Umetani did not let go, and he asked again if there was any quid pro quo.

"We don't have to get anything back," Shioji answered.

"But if you're giving them something when they're in trouble," Umetani asked, "isn't it natural that they have to promise to do something for you when they're in better shape?"

"Why do you talk like this?" Shioji asked. "We have their word." He looked hard at Umetani. He did not like the way the debate was going. "I do not need a piece of paper, I have their word and I trust them," he added.

Umetani, not knowing that he crossed some sort of line, persisted. "What guarantees are there?" he asked.

"I guarantee it," Shioji said, openly angry now. "I, Shioji. Is that good enough for you?"

Umetani for the first time heard the total silence in the room, and he looked around him and saw the other workers trying to look away from him.

Umetani thought Nissan a very difficult place in which to work in the early sixties. He suspected that later it became a little easier. After all, in the early sixties the shadow of the 1953 strike still hung over the factories. No one was allowed even to talk about it. What bothered him about the company was not so much the atmosphere of poverty but the atmosphere of fear. His fellow workers were curiously mute about their jobs; he was sure there were many grievances, but almost none of them were ever articulated. Indeed, it was a mark of the company at that time that if a man was unhappy and he sensed that a coworker was also unhappy, he would not, as in most other places of work, seek out that kindred spirit; rather he would stay as far away from him as possible for fear of being accused of politicizing discontent and forming a clique. Umetani thought his fellow Japanese workers were in many ways thoroughly admirable. But he also thought their participation in programs like quality control was less voluntary than many people liked to think. They participated not just because they wanted to but at least in part because they were afraid not to.

About a year after Umetani joined Nissan and confronted Shioji, Shioji and his people made a move on him. The union officials knew that Umetani was more intelligent than most other workers and that he was a holdout, at least spiritually, from the authority of the union. One day he was summoned to a meeting with the local union people. He was smart and skilled, they said; therefore they wanted him to run for union representative. He knew immediately that they had been shrewd enough to understand his doubts and that he was being tested, that they were calling on him to decide, one way or another, what his course was. The union, as far as he was concerned, did not so much represent the workers to the company as it delivered the workers to the company. The workers might get some benefits from their participation, for the salaries were by now acceptable, but the union was about political *control* more than anything else. He turned down the offer to run for union office, knowing that as he did, his career at Nissan was ruined. He got out of Nissan as quickly as he could, and he went ahead with plans to get a graduate degree and teach. He thought he was exceptionally lucky, for it was a rare man in Japan who was able to get out of a job in a big company and go on to something different and more satisfying. Most of his colleagues were not so fortunate. Many of them for whom the work and the workplace were intolerable simply slipped away into the night, to less remunerative but more congenial work; others, for whom the paycheck was critical, simply drowned their grievance in alcohol each night. Some fifteen years later, long after he had become a professor, Umetani ran into Shioji at a conference. "I used to work for you at one time," Umetani said.

Shioji gave him a very long look and said, "So you're one of the ones who escaped." It was a cool look, not at all friendly, Umetani thought. It was clear to him that Shioji did not like men who had escaped from his net.

It was Nissan's merger with Prince, another auto company, that showed just how tough Shioji was and what a force he had become within not just the union but the company. Mergers were extremely rare in Japan, but this one was part of the rationalization being urged on the auto industry by the Ministry of Trade. MITI felt, somewhat justifiably, that there were too many domestic auto makers in Japan; it also felt that this would hurt the Japanese in their competition with the Americans. (Actually, the fact that there were many car makers made the competition so frenzied that when the Japanese finally met the Americans, their companies were leaner and tougher by virtue of the domestic struggle than the American companies, whose competition had become increasingly marginal and whose survival seemed almost government-guaranteed.) MITI's request had generally fallen on deaf ears, except at Nissan and Prince. Nissan was delighted to go ahead; it wanted the extra financing that MITI would throw in as a sweetener. In addition, already short of facilities, Nissan coveted Prince's two plants.

But Prince was a weak and troubled company. While the Nissan people were merely contemptuous of the Prince management, they truly feared the Prince union, which they considered radical, far more like the old Masuda union than the new, more company-oriented unions that existed at the other major auto firms. The union affiliation of the Prince workers was to the Sohyo federation, thought to be left-wing and alienated, while Nissan employees belonged to Domei, which the industrialists regarded as more cooperative. Thus Shioji never considered any kind of amalgamation with the Prince union; instead from the start he sought to destroy it. The sides were never even. Prince was failing, and the Prince management desperately wanted the merger. That meant they were dealing with the Nissan executives hat in hand. In the negotiations between the two unions the Nissan union was backed completely by its management, while the Prince management, sensitive about offending its new partners, never helped its labor people.

Takashi Suzuki, leader of the Prince union, had never seen anything like Shioji before. He walked into his first meeting with the Prince union people not like a labor leader but like a board member. He opened no doors himself. There was always someone to open a door. No one walked in front of him. Someone carried his attaché case. Even the way he introduced himself, saying only, "I am Shioji," had a certain presumptive style, as if nothing else need be said. During the meetings he loved to come up with small errands on which he could dispatch any of the numerous assistants who were sitting around him. Everything was about the exercise of power. In all this confrontation between the two sides, Suzuki met Shioji only once, at a meeting early in the negotiations. "Shouldn't we compare our records," Suzuki suggested, "to find out how much each company pays?" Shioji grumbled his assent, but he was angry, and Suzuki knew immediately that he had made a mistake.

The announcement of the merger came in May 1965. The Prince labor people at first were somewhat pleased by the news. Nissan was a stronger company, and that was an asset. The Prince union people had checked around and found that their own wages and benefits were greater than those of Nissan workers. That pleased them and made them confident of their ability to hold on to their own members and survive the merger in some form, but it also lulled them into complacency. As a result they had not done very much organizational work.

The Nissan people, by contrast, had done a lot. Shioji had been through all this during the Masuda strike, and he had learned that the critical factor was organizational skill and peer pressure. He had notes on every worker at Prince, compiled with help from Prince labor executives who had switched over at the start, and with the aid of these notes he broke down the entire Prince work force into five categories. An A worker was already pro-Nissan and would work for Shioji. In the B category were men who were good workers and whose politics were coming around. The C workers were in the middle; attention had to be paid, for they could go either way, but they were generally solid workers. D workers were considered political and probably on the other side. Some of them might be flexible enough to come around, though if they did, it would be not until the end. E workers were the enemy, likely, in Shioji's opinion, to be radicals or even covert Communists.

The tactics were not unlike those used during the crushing of the Masuda union. The upper level of the Prince union, the executive board members, were taken to good restaurants, and they were promised a bright future in the new company if they cooperated and switched unions. If they did not, they would almost certainly be out of jobs. Shioji worked hardest on the leaders; he was sure if he reached them, the average workers would come along. His pitch was very elemental: At Nissan the union and the company were the same thing. Those who crossed Shioji were crossing Kawamata as well. Most got the message. Those leaders who resisted soon had toughs harassing them.

As for the average workers, Shioji's men simply took them to the local noodle shops and worked on them. There they suggested that when the merger was completed, perhaps not everyone who had worked at both companies would have a job. It was hard to tell about mergers, because they were funny, and there was likely to be a lot of overlap. In that case it would be a great mistake to be with the wrong union. The jobs would go to the men who came over to Shioji's union; the good jobs would go to those who had come early and brought their friends. Loyalty was important at a great company like Nissan. Shioji's people said they could understand resistance on the part of someone who did not intend to work at Nissan after the merger; but for anyone who wanted to keep a job, there was no point being in the Prince union. They would be out of jobs very quickly. Each worker who came over was asked to bring five colleagues with him to the next meeting. It was the same tactic that had worked before: an educational process, Shioji called it, the Nissan school. But it was more than a school, Suzuki thought, and he quite bitterly called it a "Nissan education."

It was over almost before Suzuki realized what had happened, that he had been caught asleep, and that he was fighting a brilliantly organized adversary. He tried to fight back and form an instant metalworkers school with which to indoctrinate his men, but it was too late. Even his best people were afraid to come. He tried to hand out leaflets exposing Nissan's tactics and showing that the Prince workers had better contracts, but Shioji's people intimidated his men and tore up the leaflets. None of the physical violence came from Shioji himself, and Shioji made no threats. But the threat of violence was always there, and the prospect was very real. Once when Suzuki started to protest to some of the Nissan people about their handling of his people, one of them, a real bully, turned to him and said, "Watch out or I put my hand in your mouth and shake you." That was pure gangster talk, Suzuki thought. On another occasion Suzuki went to his own management people to ask for some help or at least some protection, but they simply turned away in embarrassment. He had disgraced them, he realized, by showing that they had failed, first in not running the company well enough to prevent the merger and second in not being able to protect their own working men as the merger was taking place.

When it was all over Suzuki realized how skillfully it had been handled, that the man who had sat across from him was an immensely gifted organizer and a great street fighter. He was also hard and remorseless. He had absolutely destroyed the Prince union. Of Suzuki's top policy group of eleven men, Shioji had captured five; of the even more important forty-five-man central deliberating body, which actually decided practical policy for the union, Shioji took forty-three. He had cut the core right out of Suzuki's union. With that strength at the top it had been relatively easy to take over the rank and file. Of the 7500 workers, Shioji had gotten more than 7300 and left Suzuki with 150. Suzuki decided he had not been defeated so much as conquered. It was not just Shioji's union, Suzuki finally decided, it was his company, and he was so good at it that the man he supported, Kawamata, probably never even knew it.

Those were hard years for the workers at Nissan. The workplace had gone from chaos to absolute control, with no dissent possible. There was inevitably a considerable amount of grumbling among the hourly employees.

But Sanosuke Tanaka, the worker who had left his village in Kamagawa prefecture before the war and had taken a job at Nissan and thus had been there for many years, was not very sympathetic to these complaints. He did not like it when younger workers would go out for drinks after work and criticize their working conditions and their lack of freedom. They were not respectful enough, he felt. Tanaka was convinced that this was a far better, more orderly company than it had been. What did these men want? This was not some club, this was a place where you went to work and made cars. No one had ever said it would be easy.

Tanaka would not put up with complaints about the union either. He liked Shioji and trusted him, and he had in fact become one of Shioji's most valued men. The longer Shioji ruled, the more committed to him Tanaka became. He had been relieved when the 1953 strike ended and Shioji won. It was not that he had preferred Miyake and Shioji to Masuda, not at that point, for he had not really known which of the two unions was telling the truth; everything that each of them said always sounded right to him. But there was no doubt in his mind that the Masuda union was causing disruption and was making it almost impossible for him to work, and so he had been quite willing to join the new union. He never knew Miyake very well, but he liked Shioji from the beginning, because Shioji was so confident.

The younger workers did not know how lucky they were. They did not know how hard life could be. Sometimes he wanted to tell them that, and what he, Tanaka, knew about hardship and loneliness. His own brothers' lives had been more difficult than his. One brother died in the war in China before he was thirty; another had wanted to farm but had ended up with such a small sliver of land and so much debt that he was forced to sell it right back to the landowners. But Tanaka did not argue with the younger workers. Sometimes after he left them he would wonder why they had come to work in the first place.

He was proud of what he had accomplished at Nissan and how successful he had become. During the 1953 strike he had hoped the company would do well once the strike was finished, and in fact he had been one of the early beneficiaries. In 1954, with Shioji's help, he was able to borrow 200,000 yen, about $600, from the company, which he added to his modest savings and used to buy a house. The house was very small, but it was larger than his previous one, where all five family members were forced to sleep in one room. Now there were three rooms, and he and his wife had a room of their own. He regarded the ownership of the house as a major accomplishment, and he was sure that it made him seem worthier to the rest of his family. The food on the table was, he knew, better than what most of his neighbors were eating, and there was nothing now that his family needed that he was not able to buy for them. In 1957 he bought them a black-and-white television set. He was pleased with his life.

1954 was probably the last year when he worried about the future of the company. The strike had so badly shaken the company that it was thinking of laying off two thousand workers. But the union intervened and suggested that wages for everyone be temporarily lowered so that no one would have to be laid off. That helped save jobs and strengthened loyalty to the union among many workers. To Tanaka it proved the union's validity. Soon the company was doing well, and the wages were back to their normal levels. For a time Tanaka thought that there might be too little work, but in the late fifties, as Nissan began to become more prosperous, he wondered if the reverse was not more likely, that the danger might be too much work and too much pressure. Those years, the late fifties and the early sixties, he remembered as the most physically punishing in his life. His body was always sore. It was the moment when the company was exploding into the new age, expanding its production, changing its lines, and trying to modernize. The workers had to drive themselves to keep up with the machines. Each year, Tanaka remembered, they seemed to double the production of the previous year, and he would think, that is it, that is all a man can do, it is impossible for a man to do more. Then the next year they would double the production once again. He was proud of the fact that Nissan was becoming a modern company. In 1957 when they finally gone to five thousand units a month there was a celebration and a 5000-yen bonus, and then a few years later, in 1960, when they reached ten thousand a month, there was a 10,000-yen bonus. He felt that he was a part of that victory. Ten thousand vehicles in one month! No one on the line really believed it could be done until they did it. They had gone out that night and had a few drinks, and they said to each other, as if repeating the unbelievable, *Ten thousand cars a month.*

But the price was enormous. At first Tanaka welcomed the new machines that Nissan was installing on the line, not just because they were good for the company, a sign that the company was up-to-date, like the great companies in America, but also because he was sure it would make the life of the workers easier. That had not turned out to be true, however. Instead, those years of enormous growth proved even harder on the workers. There was always more to do, and it had to be done faster, in pace with the machines, which never tired. Always, just when you reached what you thought was your absolute limit, some young management man came along and set even higher goals. These young men seemed to Tanaka to be like people from a different planet. The work they were discussing had nothing to do with the work he *did*. The work they talked about was easy and comfortable and painless and above all logical. They were very polite as they outlined what they needed, and they talked about the good of the company and the exports to America. He wondered if they really knew what they were asking for. Words were so easy for them, but when he had to carry out their instructions, it was so much more difficult than the mere words implied. Sometimes he wondered if the management realized that there were limits to what human beings could bear. *I am not a machine!* he wanted to scream.

The company was changing fast. He knew hardly any of the faces anymore, and sometimes, looking around him at work, he no longer felt that he was in an old familiar place surrounded by trusted colleagues; he might have been in some train station at rush hour. At the beginning of the decade of the sixties there had been around seven thousand workers, and by the end of the decade there were sixty thousand. Once he had known and liked almost everyone he worked with. Then almost overnight it was as if he did not know anyone in the company. Now he could no longer depend on his colleagues. The company was expanding so quickly that it was hiring all kinds of untrained, incompetent workers. Tanaka and his friends, the few old-timers left, liked to joke about the newly hired.

"Why was he hired?" one would ask.

"Because he was alive," came the answer.

"What makes them so sure of that?"

The turnover was incredible. People were coming in on Monday morning, and Tanaka barely had time to learn their names when, by the end of the week, they were gone—gone, Tanaka liked to say, before they even had time to find out what they didn't like about the job. The turnover in the middle of the sixties was almost 90 percent annually. At one point, Tanaka remembered, some three thousand young trainees joined the company at once, none of them with any experience. He was now the section chief, so he had to teach them. He did not mind teaching them; it was exhausting, but if the company told him it was his duty, then he accepted it. What he minded was that it was so wasteful, for these young men were not serious. They would accept their lessons and their first paychecks and then quit. It was like dealing with intruders in your own home, and he disliked that. When Tanaka talked about the job, he was talking about something he loved. Yet he could see in their eyes that it did not matter to them.

Management kept apologizing to him for sending him so many green kids, explaining that the company could no longer find the workers it wanted. Management was wary of city boys, because they were likely to be spoiled and sophisticated. Anyone who was ambitious and intelligent and who was from the city would not work in an auto plant for long. City boys complained too much and caused problems and tended to be political. The ideal worker as far as management was concerned was a country boy, ambitious (but not too ambitious), with a ninth-grade education. That description fit men like Tanaka. Even young men from the rural areas were often a problem if they had graduated from high school. They seemed grateful for the job at first, and the salaries seemed immense to them in comparison to what they might make back home in Kyushu. But by the end of six months they were always complaining about how boring the work was, and many would quit and go back home and to do something else. So ninth-graders it was, neither more education nor less than that. This was, of course, what every other major industrial company had also discovered, and so there was an intense search for these solid, trusting, somewhat malleable young men. Golden eggs, the executives at Nissan called them, because they were so scarce. There were never enough. In desperation, the company began to hire more high school graduates and to pay them more. As a means of making the job more interesting and giving the workers more sense of community, it organized quality-control circles—discussion groups—throughout the plants. They took some of the impersonality out of the job and were as much an attempt to improve the social fabric of the workplace as to improve quality.

All of this pressure was becoming a psychological strain on the foremen as well as a physical one. Once a manager came to Tanaka's friend the foreman Saburo Watanabe and chastised him. "You have the most inefficient operation in all of the Orient," the manager said, and Watanabe apologized and said that he would work hard to make it only the most inefficient shop in all of Japan. At night, men like Tanaka and Watanabe and their friend Tadayoshi Enju would sit around and talk about how difficult it was to work with such green help. They spent so much time training, replacing, and training again that they were barely able to do their own work. That wasn't all. Under the pressure the machines were frequently breaking down, and because most of the workers were new, it was again the older hands who were having to do much of the repair work.

But in all his travail Tanaka always remembered that he was working for one of the most important companies in Japan, that his work was appreciated (he had a house, a television set, and all kinds of new appliances to show for it), and that he was making Japanese cars that were now being bought by people in faraway places like America. His superiors kept talking about that all the time, that *Americans* were buying these cars, and that they were in a great competition not just with Toyota, but with

666

Ford and General Motors as well. Tanaka understood that he had a personal obligation—he had to excel and to make those cars even better. A great deal depended upon him and the men underneath him.

In 1963 he became a real consumer, no longer just a laborer but a member of Japan's middle class, for that year Sanosuke Tanaka, former indentured peasant, bought his first car. It was a Nissan car, of course, a Bluebird. He had owned a motorcycle for several years, but he had always wanted a car, for commuting to work and for taking his family for rides. A car would make him a completely free man, free to go where he wanted to go. In 1963 the company announced that those in certain levels of management, the kachos and above, could apply to buy cars. Tanaka was a section chief, a kakaricho, technically below the required level, but since he had the same qualifications as a manager, he was permitted to apply. He wondered for a time whether he was being presumptuous in applying, since in those days only the richest and most powerful people owned cars. But then he decided he was a Nissan worker and it was a good thing for a worker to own a car; it would show the other workers that they did not have to be rich executives to have a good life. The car was expensive for a working man, but because Tanaka did not smoke and rarely drank, he had some savings. On an overall price of 680,000 yen (roughly $1800) he made a down payment of 150,000 yen. The rest came from his salary; it took two years to pay off what he owed. In order to own a car he had to show that he had a place to garage it. Though he did not have a garage himself, there was an old farmhouse about a hundred yards from him. The owner was a friend, and he allowed Tanaka to build a small shack at the corner to house the car. Tanaka built it himself with the help of a friend. As soon as he could after receiving the car, he drove his entire family to Kawasaki Taishi, a famous shrine. There he prayed for the safety of his family and the car, and the priest chanted to get all the devils away so that they would never have any accidents. For 1500 yen he also bought a charm at the shrine which he hung in the car to prevent accidents. Twenty years later he was convinced he had done the right thing, for there had been no accidents. He was not sure which gave him more pleasure, the freedom that the car offered to go and come as he pleased, or the pride he felt that he, a poor workingman, had earned so extraordinary a vehicle in his lifetime.

Tanaka was a perfect reflection of the middle-class surge taking place in his country. For it was 1964 that marked Japan's debut as a middle-class society. Probably Japan even during the hard times of the forties and fifties was much more middle-class than the average Westerner realized —poor in the fruits of the middle-class life, perhaps, but rich in its social structure and its ambitions. But now the fruits were available too. For twenty years the entire nation had sacrificed. The results, in industries like steel, had been evident not just to the Japanese but to any Westerner paying attention, and now the domestic economy was showing signs of great vibrancy. 1964 was for the Japanese a benchmark year. It was the year the Olympics were held in Tokyo, in effect a national coming-out party for a nation ravaged both by war and by the national sense of shame that had followed defeat. With the Olympics, Japan was being accepted back into the family of nations. It was the year that Japan confirmed its new international reputation for efficiency and quality instead of cheapness and shoddiness.

The prospect of hosting the Olympics had dominated the Japanese imagination for more than a year before the games themselves opened. Buildings went up in Tokyo, and highways were built on a massive scale. For a time, in the early days of the construction, the city looked once again as if it had been torn asunder. Gerry Curtis, then a young graduate student of twenty-four, later a distinguished Japanologist at Columbia, remembered that year with special affection. A foreigner moving around Tokyo in those days, he recalled, could almost feel the swelling confidence of the Japanese. It was not just the Olympics, he remembered, but the fact that the city's first skyscraper was being built at the same time, the Kasumigaseki building; every day at lunchtime scores of Japanese would show up at the building site, many of them having ridden the subway vast distances simply to marvel at this rarest of edifices, a skyscraper that was *Japanese*. Clearly this was additional proof that Japan could indeed become a modern and great nation.

Everywhere that year there were construction teams and cranes and bulldozers and traffic hassles. Then almost miraculously it was done, and, even more miraculously, right on schedule. The Olympics buildings were completed, a superhighway now cut through the center of the city, and the bullet train, the fastest and most comfortable train in the world, connected Tokyo to Osaka. The thousands of doubting gaijin who arrived for this particular athletic festival were stunned by the efficiency and courtesy with which they were treated, but no one was more impressed than the Japanese themselves. It was an electric moment for them; they were amazed by their own performance, and they became in that moment remarkably un-Japanese. They welcomed the foreigners and embraced them. The gaijin were all right, the gaijin seemed to approve of Japan. Because television sets in the home were still relatively rare, people gathered in bars to watch the games, and foreigners like Curtis found themselves hugged and toasted and virtually unable to buy a drink in this outpouring of Japanese pleasure. Given how uncomfortable most Japanese were with foreigners, it was most unnatural behavior. It was as if three centuries of reserve had dissolved. What he was observing was the entrance of a nation into twentieth-century affluence.

For Tanaka and his fellow workers at Nissan it was just as well that there was some material reward, for this was exactly the time that the company underwent the single most difficult challenge in its modernization. It went to two shifts a day. Orders were increasing at a remarkable rate, but the plant facilities were limited. The only solution was to do what companies in other industrialized nations did—operate on more than one shift. Shioji understood this sort of thing. When he was in America, he had visited American auto plants and was amazed to see that the Americans ran their factories not just sixteen hours a day but on occasion twenty-four. Shioji found that very impressive, that there were regular night shifts. What was even more remarkable was that the American workers did not seem to mind.

But the Japanese minded a great deal. It was mainly a matter of housing. In America a man working the night shift suffered a certain amount of social hardship in that his hours did not coincide with the hours of most other human beings. But at least he had a bedroom that could be sealed off from the rest of the family, so that he could sleep during the daytime hours. In Japan the houses were small, the walls were thin, and rooms often served two functions; a room could be a parlor during the day and a bedroom at night. How could a Japanese worker on the night shift sleep during the day with the rest of the family going about its business in the very same room? There were simply too many people in too small a space, and there was almost nothing that could be done about it. Housing was Japan's great national problem and America's great blessing. Food was no longer scarce for the Japanese by the mid-sixties; nutritionally the two nations were moving toward parity. But in housing, the richness of America and the comparative poverty of Japan were reflected. Shioji had visited the homes of workers in Detroit and was surprised to see how well ordinary people lived. They all seemed to have big kitchens filled with dishwashers, clothes washers and dryers, and freezers. They all had dining rooms where nobody dined, and they all seemed to have dens with pool tables. The Americans took their housing for granted, he thought. Even in Europe workers lived in small, though comfortable, apartments. But Japan lacked the resources and the space for large, expensively built apartments. Its housing was small and flimsy. Normally that was not a problem, for the

Japanese accepted limits, but the need to work at night and sleep during the day would cause acute disruption.

Shioji, told by Kawamata that Nissan had to go to two shifts, ran into immediate trouble with his own men. He pointed out that it was the Americans who had pioneered in the use of multiple shifts. His workers refused to believe it. No civilized country, they insisted, would permit its workers to be so mistreated. Shioji tried to explain how the Americans worked their system, but even his top aides bristled. Americans, they replied, work too hard, and we do not want to be like them. (Shioji thought of that with some irony twenty years later, when Americans decided that it was the Japanese who worked too hard.) They argued, and Shioji told them they would have to try it, that it was not a matter of choice, that the only way Nissan could become a major car manufacturer was with two shifts. The investment in machinery was such that it could not sit idle for two thirds of the day. He explained, and they listened, but they did not accept what he said.

Everyone hated the early experiments. No one could sleep. There were always children in the room, making noise. The schedule of mealtimes was upset. Even men as tolerant and durable as Tanaka, who believed in work, believed in the company, and believed in Shioji, resisted. When Tanaka was at work he wanted to be asleep, and when he was asleep he wanted to be at work. He was always tired. When he rode the train instead of driving, he often fell asleep on the train and went right past his stop to the end of the line. Then he would have to ride all the way back, trying not to fall asleep again. Food was always a problem. He was either too hungry or not hungry at all. Sometimes he ate four times a day. His stomach began to give him trouble. He tried not to be cross with his children. He was aware that his wife was working very hard with the children, trying to keep them quiet. He would come home from work early in the morning. The children, just getting up, would be noisy. It was just becoming bright out; he could not sleep, but he knew it was his duty to sleep.

He finally complained to Shioji. He was embarrassed to be doing that, but all of his friends felt the same way. Nissan and the union went back and forth on it for more than four years, trying to find a way that might work. They tried alternate weeks, and then alternating every two weeks, and then alternating every month. No one liked any of the arrangements. They tried three weeks of day and one week of night shifts and no one liked that either. Then they tried paying 50 percent more for the night shift, and it barely soothed the anger. Nothing seemed to work. Shioji had never seen such a reaction among good workers. He decided after about three years of experimenting that there was not any way that would be satisfactory.

They ended where they had begun, alternating day and night shifts each week. They gave night workers 50 percent more pay. Shioji concluded that the misery of it was part of the burden of being a Japanese worker and having poor housing and difficult hours. It was inevitable, because the exterior conditions were not going to change. The housing was never going to get very much better, and children were never going to make less noise, and there was never going to be a time when Nissan did not want to run two shifts.

24.
THE PIONEER

In early 1960, Yutaka Katayama, who two years before had forced Nissan to enter the auto rally in Australia and then led the team to victory, was told to look at Nissan's operations in California. The job was as much banishment as reward. After his win in Australia and his triumphal year as a national hero, the company had no job for him, for he was not really a company man. His old job as advertising manager had been given away to a union loyalist. There was no place for him in Tokyo, and he was not the kind of person to accept a lesser job. Kyoichi Harashina, his friend and sponsor, had lost out in a power struggle to Kawamata and been exiled to Nissan Diesel. Katayama's future looked bleak. Another friend in the Nissan hierarchy, trying to help him, suggested that he be sent to the United States to survey Nissan's brand-new American endeavor. It was an unimportant task at the time, so no one objected. He was assigned on a temporary basis, without his family.

Katayama knew that he was being banished, but he was delighted nonetheless. What his superiors thought was his exile he thought of as his liberation. He had been to America once before, as a student, sent by his father to expand his horizons, and he had loved it. He had been struck even as a boy by the freedom that Americans, even young Americans, enjoyed. They always seemed to be able to make their own decisions. Even the Nisei, the Japanese-Americans who were second-generation, were less dutiful; they were also open, like the Americans, given to telling sudden, impulsive truths about themselves. That startled him at first, but he soon became comfortable with the greater personal candor. Now, going back as a grown man and living in Los Angeles, he was struck even more by the freedom in America and the sense of possibilities. Americans believed they could do whatever they wanted, the way they wanted, when they wanted. The lack of ceremony and formality, symbolized by the absence of blue suits, cheered him. In Japan, if you were to transact serious commerce, you wore a blue suit. If you were not entitled to wear a blue suit, you wore laborer's work clothes. There seemed to be no middle ground. But in America and particularly in California, there was no telling what a man did by looking at his clothes. The head of a company, he soon found out, was likely to be wearing an open-collared sports shirt while the fastidious man in suit and tie might well be a relatively minor clerk. Katayama, who had no desire to wear blue suits himself and hated dealing with a world of blue suits, was relieved. Here men dressed for the office and for the golf course in the same way.

In addition, and most miraculously, it did not seem to matter to the Americans whether he was a Japanese or not; what mattered to them was what he was selling and what the terms were: Was it a good deal? An American trying to do business in Japan, he was sure, would never have found so many doors open as Katayama was finding open to him. In Japan the cultural and bureaucratic barriers to helping a foreigner were high, as were the innate suspicions of what a foreigner was up to. The only legitimate role for a gaijin in Japan was to teach English to Japanese. But America seemed to welcome foreigners. Yutaka Katayama, to his amazement, found himself more at home in California than he had been in Tokyo. Soon the American job became a permanent one. No one else seemed eager to go to America, that alien, often terrifying place, so he was placed in charge of Nissan's operations in the Western United States. He sent for his family. What was supposed to be a brief tour lasted seventeen years.

He was poor in America at first, barely able to survive on his salary, yet he knew that every dollar of hard currency he was spending represented real sacrifice for the company. To save money he developed an economical system for having his regional salesmen report in: They called every day at certain prescribed hours by long-distance phone; if the phone rang three times and then stopped, it meant that the salesman had nothing to report. It was typical of their early operation. Every penny mattered.

Katayama's big problem in the early days was that the car he was selling, the Datsun, was simply terrible, crude and underpowered. No one knew it better than his salesmen, who called Datsuns "mobile coffins" because of the unbearable heat inside the cars. There was no real heater; the car was heated involuntarily by the engine, and anyone who drove all day in a hot climate, such as the American Southwest, would get baked. This was merely one of its deficiencies. There were many others, none of which Tokyo would admit to.

But Tokyo was beginning to send engineers to America to modify the car for American requirements. They came in small study groups known as U (for United States) teams. Katayama pounced on these engineers, relentlessly indoctrinating them in his view of the Datsun's shortcomings and the need for improvements, creating allies for the debates he was already carrying on with the home office. He worked them over so hard that they called their sessions with him Katayama University. He thought the task ahead was much more difficult than Tokyo realized, and he had already found Tokyo very slow to accept the gravity of its problems in America. (Frustrated by Tokyo's failure to do something about the problem of overheated interiors, he began on his own to deal with an air-conditioning company in America; only then did Tokyo pay heed and come up with a Japanese system.) What Americans wanted in a car was different from what was right for the Japanese domestic market. Yet at first the company was not rich enough to produce a Japanese car *and* an American car; there would be only one, and it would be a compromise. But everything that would make the car better for America conflicted with what Tokyo wanted for the car back home. Katayama felt strongly that Nissan should adjust more to American needs and tastes, the American market was where the great new opportunity was. Convincing Tokyo of that, he knew, was going to be a long, hard job. However, though the company bureaucracy might be hopelessly political, eventually it would have to listen to its engineers. Besides, he and his peers at other Japanese companies had one major advantage over those in comparable positions elsewhere, for they represented a country that had a controlled economy and was eager to export. Japan did everything it could to facilitate exports while making sure that its own citizens were careful to save—slowing them down, if need be, with heavy commodity taxes. Thus in the seventies a Datsun or Toyota might cost as much as $750 less in Los Angeles than it did in Tokyo.

Katayama's counterpart on the East Coast was Soichi Kawazoe. He had far better connections at home than Katayama did; for example, he had done the English translation of the paper that Shioji wrote for his Harvard Business School course and also translated a speech Shioji had made for a ceremony honoring Walter Reuther. Tokyo assumed that the East was a bigger, richer market than the West and that it had therefore given Kawazoe, its favorite, the choicer assignment. Not surprisingly, a distinct rivalry developed between the two men.

Katayama moved more slowly than Kawazoe. He decided that the first thing to do was to study the American market and find out what it would take. He learned a number of things very quickly. The first was that he was probably lucky to be on the West Coast rather than on the East, for people in California were less fixed in their habits, including their buying habits. In most cases they were people who had already severed their connection with some part of their past, the place where they had grown up, and had gone west to try a new place. Thus they would be more willing to take a chance on something new, like a Japanese car. The second and more important thing he learned was that in America, unlike Japan, the dealer network was critical. In Japan dealers played almost no part in the sale of cars. Japanese firms farmed exiled managers to the dealerships, paid them poorly, and largely disregarded them. It was a passive job there. In America it was a crucial job, for the dealers were the true customers of the company. If the dealers were strong and vital, then the company might succeed. Katayama came to understand this immediately, and gradually he created a network of dealers along the West Coast that he was very proud of. Tokyo, already disapproving of the power that dealers had in America, was uneasy about Katayama's network. They were, in truth, a most unlikely group, with a high incidence of eccentricity. Many of them were men who had been around cars all their lives, often as repairmen, but had never been able to come up with the large amount of money required for an American dealership. There was, for example, Ray Lemke in San Diego, who as a boy of sixteen had repaired Model Ts and who had once handled the Go-Go-Mobile, one of the country's more exotic automotive attempts. "There was no way someone like me—a mechanic —was ever going to have a Ford dealership," Lemke said years later. "The best I could hope for was a used-car dealership, and a lot of us Datsun dealers had been in the used-car business, and we knew the poorer customers very well." Katayama quickly decided that Lemke was the perfect new Datsun dealer; he was hungry and he knew cars. Katayama gave him one car and told him to sell it; when Lemke sold it, he said, there would be another. "It was pretty raw at first," Lemke remembered years later, "just me and the wife. On Sunday I'd be in the office writing up sales, and the wife would be out on the lot trying to hold on to the customers until I could finish." In 1984, as a very rich man, Lemke finally sold his dealership. By that time he was selling nearly two thousand cars a month.

Many of Katayama's dealers seemed to have been sent over by central casting for parts in a movie about how to fail at business. Katayama judged them on two things: how eager they were and whether they had enough automotive savvy to hold the trust of customers. For those he chose, he made the deal quite profitable, giving them between 18 and 20 percent of the gross profit. The American companies, by contrast, were paying dealers only 12 or 13 percent, which was one reason that they all preferred selling large cars, and why America both manufactured and sold more big cars than little cars. It was a habit based on the difference between 13 percent of $2000 and 13 percent of $5000. Katayama paid them considerably more partly because he had no alternative; good men were not knocking down doors to represent a company that no one had ever heard of from a country that most Americans distrusted. But it was also because he had analyzed American business and come to realize that the only way the company could prosper was if the dealers got rich. "If you make money," he told them repeatedly, "we make money." They were, he told them, his partners. He let them know he was grateful to be doing business in their country, and he readily acknowledged that they knew things about doing business in America that he did not. Tokyo, unhappy about the cut the dealers were getting, went along with Katayama, but reluctantly, never quite forgiving him for it, either for paying so much or for becoming so successful by paying so much.

From the start, Nissan in Tokyo judged Katayama negatively. The managers remembered his old affronts, and, worse, they decided that he had gone American. That did not bother him. He was having too much fun. Even when business was awful, when the cars were bad and his prospects bleak, he had no regrets. He thought himself lucky. He had gotten his job largely because no one realized at the time how important a job it was going to be; it was for that reason he had evaded the veto power of his enemies within the company. He was lucky too, he thought, because, as it turned out, he was far better suited by temperament to do business in America than in Japan. Many Japanese, sampling the great personal freedoms of America, were unsettled, and they could not adapt to a country where decisions were usually made quickly. He, on the other hand, felt comfortable from his first day in America. In Japan, where he had always been perceived as incautious and somewhat aggressive, he made enemies; in America people responded to his openness and exuberance, and he made friends. Almost immediately, for the first time in years, he was enjoying his work. It was an odd definition of pleasure, perhaps, for sometimes he went house to house in the Japanese sections of Los Angeles trying to sell pickup trucks to Japanese gardeners. Many of them were among the city's poorer citizens, but they were usually sympathetic and also alert to the possibility that the pickup truck was a good buy. If he was having a hard time himself in those difficult days, making only about $700 a month, he was nonetheless always aware that no one was impeding his way because he was a foreigner. His English was not very good; as one friend noted, he spoke a language of his own, a kind of Janglish. But he was so winning that many Americans reached out to help him. If the businessmen he approached could not do anything for him themselves, they found themselves trying to think of someone who could. He loved showing up at the opening of Datsun dealerships, loved the hoopla of these American ceremonies, a barbecue in Texas (he would inevitably show up in a ten-gallon Texas hat), a fish fry in Louisiana, or a Mexican dinner in San Diego. The Americans did not call him Katayama—that was too long and too foreign—but Mr. K, and he loved that too.

Amid all the fun he was taking careful sights on the national market. Importers, he reasoned, would have to leave the center of the country alone for a while; it was a vast, underpopulated region of great distances where people needed big cars, and that was what the American companies did best. If the Japanese poured their energy and resources into every section of the country, they would surely fail. The Japanese should begin, on the coasts, creating their beachheads there, slowly earning the money to spend on advertising, and only then expanding into selected areas of the heartland. "What we should do," he told his American associates, "is get better and creep up slowly, so that we'll be good—and the customers will think we're good—before Detroit even knows about us."

He was absolutely convinced that the most important factor in gaining success was providing adequate service. The American market, he decided, was in some ways a prisoner of the country's richness. The nation and the people were so rich that they simply did not really repair cars. That mentality governed Detroit, its dealers, and their more affluent customers, who might replace a part, but did not really want a car *repaired*. The system was designed to produce a car that would last about three or four years and then, when it began to deterioriate, would be shuttled off to a poorer segment of the population. This was marketing based on the premise of a steadily ascending middle class for whom a car must always reflect status. Because the companies and their dealers were doing so well, they had become casual about repairs and cavalier about service. They not only believed as an article of faith that they made the best cars in the world, they also believed that their customers had nowhere else to go. The companies and dealers did not make much of an effort to service cars, because they could just as easily sell a new car. Something new was always the answer in America. Katayama could not argue with that system. He knew the American numbers, and they were very good; clearly the system worked well. But he also knew that there were a good many less affluent Americans who were unhappy with it, resentful that they were not getting the service they needed. These Americans were potentially good customers. They included young people, elderly people, and some poorer people, all of whom badly needed durable, fuel-efficient cars. They were the victims of a dynamic that dumped the tired, broken-down, oil-burning vehicles—expensive to buy and even more expensive to maintain—on the very people who could least afford them.

Already Volkswagen was doing well with these customers, the ones ignored by Detroit, providing a reasonably priced alternative source of good transportation, good mileage, and good service. Katayama, listening carefully to American voices in the early years, realized that Volkswagen customers believed that they were treated better, *respected* more, than they would be if they were trying to buy at the lower end of the American lines. (Generally the first thing that happened when they tried that was that some salesmen tried to talk them into buying something grander.) VW became the model for Katayama. At that time, 1961, when Katayama was just starting out, Volkswagen seemed invincible. It was at the height of its success (it would be another decade before it began to slip), and it was doing everything right, selling 177,000 cars a year, a remarkable 46.8 percent of the import market. The fact that the essential car remained unchanged for years meant that the repair and parts people developed great expertise. (What was eventually to become a burden was then still an asset.) The other imports he thought more vulnerable. The Renault was a good car, and it should have been doing well in America, but the dealer network was weak, and Katayama had a feeling that many of the Renault dealers were eating their advertising money—that is, not spending it, keeping it for themselves. The British had once been formidable competitors in the small-car market, and Katayama was surprised by their decline; but they were endlessly burdened by labor problems. His eye was on Volkswagen—if not to beat it, then at least to emulate it. The other European imports were ready to be taken.

His problem, of course, was that the first Datsun in America was a disaster. It sold for $1616, and both Katayama and Kawazoe often wondered why anyone bothered to buy it. Kawazoe later recalled that he sometimes looked on as a young couple was deciding whether or not to to buy the car, and part of him, knowing the troubles they would have with it, wanted to warn them off. Katayama and Kawazoe had direct personal knowledge of the car's problems, for in the beginning theirs was truly a shoestring operation; if a Datsun broke down—and one often did—and everyone else was busy, the sales manager himself might have to drive the repair truck to pull it off the road. Katayama and Kawazoe, in fact, sometimes ended up doing the repair themselves. If worse came to worse and the car could not be fixed, they might even lend the enraged owner their own cars. Nor was it just the Datsun that was terrible; the first Toyota to enter the American market, at about the same time, was such a bomb that Toyota took it off the market, went back to work on it, and did not come back into the U.S. market until 1964. There were those who worked for Nissan in America who believed that Tokyo, realizing how bad its car was, had declined to put the company's name on it, calling it not the Nissan but the Datsun, so that if the car failed, there would be less loss of face. Only twenty years later, when their cars were demonstrated successes, did the company go through the clumsy and expensive process of changing its American name.

The worst thing about the Datsun was that its engine was simply too small. Its displacement was only 1000cc. Even the VW's was 1300, and the smaller American cars in those heady pre-oil-crunch days were coming in with engines of 5000 and 6000cc displacement. With the Datsun's little engine, its acceleration was poor, a real problem on the entrance ramps of the California freeways. Also, the brakes were weak. That was not all. The Datsun was designed for Japanese winters, which by and large were milder than American ones, and the car was very difficult to start in the winter, in part because the battery was too small. For the Datsuns in the northern sections on each coast, this morning sluggishness was a major problem. In the East, the Datsuns were selling mainly to blue-collar people who could not afford better cars. Generally, these were people who got up early, when the engines were coldest and the batteries weakest. Masataka Usami, one of the Nissan executives, who lived in Greenwood Lake, New Jersey, and whose own car would not start in cold weather, reported back to his support team in Tokyo that Nissan could not have a car that started only two out of ten times. Tokyo was not very helpful. The alleged starting problems were impossible, they insisted, since they had checked and Hokkaido—the norternmost of the Japanese home islands, where Datsuns started without difficulty—was just as cold as New Jersey. Usami replied that in Hokkaido those few Japanese who were privileged to own cars lovingly put blankets over the hoods every night. Tokyo asked why Americans didn't do the same thing. Usami explained that whereas to the Japanese a car was a privilege, to Americans cars were an appliance, and they expected them to work without pampering. Soon a study team of engineers arrived, and Usami led them to Greenwood Lake, New Jersey. There, starting at four every morning, everyone freezing cold, they would check the effect of the temperature on the battery, the voltage levels, and the viscosity of the oil. They did this day after day for an entire week. The engine almost never started. Finally one of the Tokyo engineers turned to Usami and said, "You know, Usami-san, I think you may be right."

Katayama's attempt to get Tokyo to upgrade and Americanize the car was a constant struggle. Even on the small matter of the floor carpets there was a problem. The Japanese tended to clean their cars incessantly and exhaustively and thus preferred to take the floor mat out, the better to pursue every last speck; the Americans were more casual about cleaning their cars, at best giving the floors a quick vacuuming, and they wanted the mats permanently attached, an attitude the home office found inexplicable. Whatever Katayama asked for, whether it was a more powerful motor, better acceleration, or better brakes, Tokyo resisted. What the Americans wanted above all, power and particularly styling, the Japanese were not yet ready for. Americans liked styled, hot-looking cars, while for the Japanese, to whom transportation was an end in itself, something more functional, a simple piece of machinery, was quite adequate. Katayama knew Tokyo had to change, that Nissan would never be successful in America until it understood the importance of styling. Virtually everything, in fact, had to be changed, and changing *anything* was going to be a fight. This meant Katayama was constantly assailing the bureaucracy. He knew that every time he asked for something new he was making enemies. He was not, however, without allies. Mostly they were engineers, who understood what he wanted, liked the challenge, and wanted to improve the cars. But even with their support, he was going against the grain. In 1961, the year after he arrived in America, he estimated that it would take until 1970 to get the right car for the American market, one with at least a 1600cc engine, real performance, and some style. He was off by a year. The first really viable Datsun arrived in 1969.

What saved the company in the meantime, though Tokyo was loath to admit it, was Nissan's little pickup truck. It was small, it was inexpensive, and, unaffected by the Japanese weaknesses at the time such as lack of style, it exploited the singular Japanese strength—durability. Even more significant was the fact that, as Katayama soon learned, in Western America and especially California the pickup truck had a function different from the one it had elsewhere. Here it was both truck *and* passenger vehicle. Many Americans worked their small patches of farmland for an hour or two in the morning before driving off to a factory job. Some who no longer worked on the farm kept a pickup nonetheless as if to sustain their sense of self; rural they had entered this world, and though they might no longer work the land, rural they could believe they had remained, if they owned a pickup. Some older Americans preferred pickup trucks because they held up well; some younger ones liked them because of the image of ruggedness they projected. (Unlike most Americans, whose car conveyed their status and for whom the biggest and fanciest car signaled the greatest prestige, there were those who enjoyed the antistatus in having a little pickup truck parked in front of the house.) People who owned small companies, maybe just one or two employees or maybe just themselves, needed a pickup for work and liked the Datsuns because they were cheap and tough. Many of Datsun's best dealers signed up in the early days not because they wanted that ugly little car or because they were so prescient that they knew that this odd Japanese company previously unknown to them would do everything right and produce an increasingly sophisticated auto, but because they knew that the pickup truck was a winner in California.

The pickups sold right from the start. They sold without advertising. They sold because the men and women who came in to look at them could sense that they were well made. They sold because the word-of-mouth was phenomenal. These funny little trucks, owners told their friends, lasted forever, and nothing ever went wrong—they were a real buy. The sales were so good that Nissan's West Coast office soon had twice the total sales of the East Coast. In 1963, for example, a critical year, when Datsun was just beginning to get a foothold in the American market (late that year it moved into the top ten importers in terms of monthly sales), the western division outsold the eastern 2781 vehicles to 1151. Of the western divisions total, 1597 were small trucks.

Tokyo was ambivalent about this desperately needed success. Tokyo had wanted to arrive in America and be classy and sell cars and make a reputation; it had not wanted to come and sell trucks. Yet here were the trucks doing better than the cars. So when Katayama kept talking about the need to improve the trucks, management refused to listen. Katayama was trying to tell the home office that more than half of these Datsun trucks were used for commuting, that they were in effect being used as cars, and that the market would explode if Nissan would simply upgrade them a little. But Tokyo would not budge. A truck was a truck. Katayama was relentless. If only, he asked, they would add some decent upholstery, better springs, perhaps even an air conditioner. The answer was always the same: A truck was a truck, and Americans had no right to use them to drive to work, particularly to offices. It was wrong of them. The trucks should be used for carting heavy goods around. Katayama suggested certain changes that would permit owners to convert them rather readily for family use, and again Tokyo vetoed him. Families had no business riding around in pickup trucks. Japanese families that could afford cars would never be seen in a truck. Katayama sometimes wondered how many more pickups might have sold if Tokyo had listened. Even so they carried Nissan in America from the beginning.

What also helped carry the company in those days was Takashi Ishihara. He too, like Katayama, was in a form of genteel exile, although he was a far more senior and powerful figure in the company, the heir apparent at one time to Kawamata himself. Until very recently he had been the rising star of Nissan, the best of the new generation of management, the most promising young executive in the company. He had been made a director at an exceptionally young age, and he was considered a sure future president of Nissan. The younger managers in the company especially admired him; to them, he was a modern, confident executive, quick to make decisions, and not a creature, as Kawamata was, of the bank. His generation considered itself the first auto generation in the company—as opposed to those whose experience was primarily elsewhere and who were never entirely comfortable in their decision-making, since they made decisions according to lessons learned elsewhere. "This company," Asahara once told his son, "will not be a real business until Ishihara and his generation take over."

For a long time Ishihara managed to stay out of the bitter internal factionalism that scarred Nissan. He belonged to neither Kawamata's side nor Asahara's side. He was probably the only executive in the company who managed to straddle the chasm between the two men. Asahara was fond of him and thought of him as a protégé. Kawamata, for whom he worked, was fond of him too and seemed to be encouraging him as a potential successor. But he had serious private doubts about the power being usurped by the union; it was not something he complained about or fought, but he did not like it, and it was an invisible barrier between himself and Kawamata. When Asahara mounted his coup against Kawamata, Ishihara stayed on the sidelines. (There were, in fact, those who thought he had given tacit consent to the move against Kawamata.) Kawamata had not forgiven him, and a breach between the two men opened.

Ishihara was a formidable-looking man. More than any other Japanese auto executive, he looked like an Asian counterpart of his burly, forceful Detroit peers. In Detroit, in the tough world of auto making—going back to the days when a foreman, as a matter of job specification, had to be able to whip the men working for him—physical strength had always been an asset to advancement. In Japan that was somewhat less true, but Ishihara was the exception, undoubtedly benefiting from his imposing appearance. He was a former rugby football player, and there was an almost pugnacious physical quality to him, which he flaunted. Watching him, Keith Crain, the Detroit auto editor, once told friends that if he ever got into a back-alley fight, Ishihara was the one man of all auto executives he would like with him.

Although he looked like an auto man, in truth he was an accountant, a man of finance. After the failed coup, Ishihara's career seemed in suspension. He was given an assignment in Mexico, hardly a prized one. Not long after that he was placed in charge of exports to the United States. That assignment was not exactly a plum either, and most of his friends warned him against taking it. It was, they claimed, the riskiest posting there was. "You will go there, and we will never see you again," one of them said, "unless we arrive in America one day and get in a cab and find you driving it." When his friends cited the dangers, he answered that yes, he knew of them, but not taking the post was dangerous as well. He pondered the question a long time, finally deciding it was impossible to turn it down and still have a career at Nissan. He accepted it for that reason and also because he thought it had to be done, because he of all the top executives was most likely to be able to pull it off, and because if he failed, he did not deserve to run Nissan anyway. Besides, since the company was starting from scratch in America, if someone made a real success of it, then he would forever be placed ahead of the rest of the crowd of potential presidents. It was a calculated risk, and Ishihara took it. There was a Japanese proverb that Ishihara remembered: If you sit patiently on the stone for three years, you will be rewarded. It meant that either you would get what you wanted, because you were so patient, or, failing that, you would benefit from those years of adversity.

He was export manager of Nissan in the fall of 1960, when he was made president of the American branch. Though there was no love lost between him and Katayama, his colleague in America, for a time their purposes coincided. There was, after all, an ocean between them, because Ishihara chose not to live in America. To Katayama he seemed just one more of that legion of insular Japanese businessmen who looked upon America as a place from which to take something, either knowledge or technology or perhaps some hard currency, but not as a place in which to immerse oneself. There was more than an element of truth to that, for though Ishihara was by Japanese standards an internationalist, a man who wanted to bring Nissan to the world, his internationalism was essentially very Japanese. He was quite willing to be an internationalist—meeting regularly with foreigners and doing business with them—as long as he could live in Japan and be surrounded at almost all times by other Japanese.

Nonetheless he was an extremely powerful ally for Katayama. For though they might differ on specific tactics, and though their ambitions might be very different too, and though Katayama might be more willing to adopt a truly American business style, they were as one on the central goal, which was the success of the American enterprise. That gave Katayama a lever he otherwise sorely lacked. For Ishihara's troubles with Kawamata notwithstanding, he was *of* the company as Katayama was not. He was a powerful force there, he was still considered a potential president, and he had supporters both beneath and above him. Though his background was in finance, he was still considered more of a car man than Kawamata. Thus his recommendations had a great deal more impact than Katayama's. Katayama might complain that a Datsun would begin to shiver and vibrate when it went over forty miles per hour, and Tokyo would disregard it, but when Ishihara said it—that they would fail if something were not done—then Tokyo listened.

Besides, and this was critical, Ishihara was from the financial side. The engineering and the production sides were never the problem. They were car people, and though they might on occasion be a little annoyed that American automotive habits were different from those of the Japanese, there was not an engineer at Nissan who did not thrill to the idea of building a faster, higher-performance engine and a sleeker, more stylish car. It was the financial side that was always the obstacle. The financial people were conservative—all they could think of was that immense sum they owed the bank—and their instinct about any new venture was reflexively negative. To their mind the company was already stretched too thin, too many new factories were being built, there was too little cash, and America remained an uncertain world dominated by automotive giants. Only Ishihara, an Ishihara living in Tokyo instead of New York, could handle them. His requests were not the requests of some distant, lowly manager who had gone native in America and who was probably trying to create his own empire at Nissan's expense; these were the requests of one of their own, a man of profit. He knew all the numbers, all the games that the financial people played, and he had their trust. Because Katayama was living in America, he was perceived as alien. Every time he challenged Tokyo, it was additional proof that he was more American than Japanese. Ishihara's word would be trusted as Katayama's would not. Ishihara was acutely aware of this. Once, early in the course of the American venture, during a visit to the California offices he took Katayama and Nobe Wakatsuki, the trading company executive who in 1957 had urged Nissan to send cars to the Los Angeles auto show, to dinner. The question of Tokyo's reluctance to accept suggestions from America hung heavily in the air that night. It was very hard to make Tokyo respond to American needs, Ishihara said. "I am the only one who can do it, who can push it through," he told them, "and I can do it only from Tokyo. Always remember that."

There was soon ample evidence of it. Nissan capitalized the American company at $1 million. To the Japanese that seemed an enormous amount of money. There were strict governmental limits on how much a company could spend overseas. They were sure $1 million would last five years. But America turned out to be a terribly expensive place. Breakfasts at a hotel could cost the unwary traveler several dollars. Advertising on radio and television was like burning money. Even arranging dealerships turned out to cost money, for lawyers were expensive. Nothing was cheap in this country. There was no way to save. Within two years there was only $100,000 left from the original $1 million. In late 1962 Ishihara went back to the board, hat in hand, and asked for another $500,000. They had, he acknowledged, spent more rapidly than anyone had anticipated, but doing business in America had proved far costlier than imagined. He had done everything he could to save, but it was impossible to save in the Japanese sense of that word. If they held back now, the American company would come to a complete stop, and Nissan would have to retire from the American market, which meant in effect from the export market.

When he made his presentation at the board meeting, there was no real challenge to him. The board voted the money rather readily, and he felt very little heat. But the American operation continued to be costly, and results remained hard to come by. A year later he had to go back and ask for another $500,000. This time he knew he was going against the wishes of the board. Some board members suggested he had been careless and that for so much money there ought to be more to show. Ishihara replied politely that he was still confident they could attain their objective, that Nissan could make a car that would do well in the American market. Again he repeated what he believed, that if Japan was to have any world export market in autos, it had to prove itself in America, against the best. But they had all underestimated how expensive starting out in America was. He was positive that if they held on a little longer they would succeed. Indeed, he was willing to bet his career on it. If we don't make it with this request, he added, I will resign from the company. When he made that promise, no one, he noted, tried to talk him out of it.

The eyes on him at the meeting, he thought, were as cold as stone, and he could even see a small amount of pleasure in the faces of some potential adversaries. The board again gave him $500,000, but it left no doubt that he was not to come back again, and that his promise should be a serious one. If he failed, he might as well quit, for he would have no future at Nissan.

It was, he often reflected later, a very close call. In 1964 the company began to show a profit, about $200,000. Years later, when Ishihara was president of Nissan and was frequently congratulated on the brilliance of Nissan's performance in America, he was always mildly amused, for he knew how near they had come to failure.

25.
THE LIBERATION OF YUKATA KATAYAMA

To Katayama, Ishihara was simply someone in Tokyo who had responsibility for America. He was an asset, and an ally, but not a colleague. To most of the people in America who had any encounter with Nissan's American operation, it was still Katayama's company. He was there every day, impassioned, pushing for dealers, trying to sell cars. He often delivered cars himself to the dealers, because it was cheaper and because it gave him a chance to hear what they were saying. Once on a Saturday morning when a customer came to headquarters needing a particular part, Katayama was there alone; he went back into the parts department and found it. Not knowing how much it cost, he charged the customer $1.

America, he said later, was his paradise. There, everything was possible. He had never felt so free in his life. He had nothing but scorn for most of the other Japanese businessmen he met in America. When younger Japanese businessmen came to Katayama for guidance, he scorned the insularity of his own countrymen. Too many of them, he said, when they came to America, knew only the map of Japan, and thought only of the people in the home office, and trusted only other Japanese. Sometimes, out for a meal with American friends, he would spot a group of Japanese businessmen seated nearby, five or six of them, no Americans. "Look at them," he would say, "afraid to be in America." Worse, when Japanese like these talked about Americans among themselves, they still used the hateful Japanese word for foreigners, gaijin. Did they not know that they were the gaijin now? They did not go out and get to know the market; they sat in their offices being very Japanese, trying not to make mistakes. Timid rabbits, he thought. He would do business like an American. He would take chances, and he would say what he thought.

"I am Katayama of Nissan," he would say when checking into a hotel or arriving at a meeting, and that was enough. He was the head of a company just as Lee Iacocca and Pete Estes were heads of companies, though of course he made about $25,000 a year or about one thirtieth of what they made, and soon about one thirtieth of what most of his own dealers made. This did not bother him. The other auto executives traveled with great retinues, and there was always someone to meet them at the airport, someone to get them a drink, someone to light a cigar, someone to make sure that when they went to their favorite restaurant they got their favorite table. He preferred to travel alone; he could learn more that way. He could meet people on planes and in restaurants and bars, and not be separated from them and the truth by underlings eager to protect him from the truth. He ventured forth constantly, savoring and studying the country. There was not a sports event in Los Angeles that he did not find interesting, and he became a devoted football and baseball fan. He was a great hiker, and there was no mountain worthy of the name in the West that he did not climb. He became a devoted fisherman and he worked the rivers and lakes in the state of Washington, fishing there with his dealers and their friends. He was a good amateur painter, and wherever he went he took his paint kit and sketched the American landscape. Each year he would take the sketch he liked best and make it into his Christmas card. By the end of his tour his Christmas list had ten thousand names. Nothing, his friends thought, told more about him than this; here was a man who had come from a country where there was no Christmas and no tradition of Christmas cards, and he had compiled what surely must be one of the nation's longest lists. Few Americans understood the modern American Christmas-card ritual as well, or practiced it as personally. He wanted all of his American friends to eat at a nearby restaurant called Masukawa because it was good, it was Japanese, and the owner had been to Keio University. At first, it had been almost empty at lunch; a few years later, largely because of his efforts, there were long lines there every day.

Katayama was a man, thought his friend and speechwriter Mayfield Marshall, who wanted nothing more than to shrink the Pacific Ocean. Like many Japanese, he loved flying kites, and those Americans who worked for him had to be prepared to leave the office at almost any hour and fly kites (just as the Japanese who came to work for him had to be prepared to go to a barbecue for dinner or to watch a professional football game—to most of them a semibarbaric sport only dimly understood). When, after a few years in Los Angeles, he bought a large plot of land on the San Diego freeway, someone asked him what it was for. "One day it will be our headquarters building," he replied, "but for now it is our field for flying kites." He corresponded with innumerable American kite freaks, and one of his proudest days was when the editors of *Road & Track* invited him to their offices near Newport Beach, held a kite-flying contest in his honor on the beach, and then awarded him an inscribed winner's trophy. The trophy was of a bird dog and was supposed to go to a dog breeder, but the editors had gotten a small brass kite and stuffed it in the dog's mouth, which pleased Katayama immensely. That day, he told his friends, the East had met the West. He was fascinated by the difference in the way Americans and Japanese flew their kites: Even here, he thought, the Americans were frontiersmen, finding the wind current and charging into it as fast as they could, challenging it. The Japanese were more delicate about it; they would find the wind, turn their backs to it, and then gently let their kites out.

He was a rare man. He brought a face to the Japanese mercantile presence; meeting him, Americans felt that they knew, understood, and liked the Japan that was behind his products. If he took pride in the growing success of Nissan America, it was a quiet pride in showing what modern Japan could do, and in the success he had helped bring his dealers. He seemed to gain special pleasure from his work with them. After all, he had taken these ordinary and indeed often unsuccessful men, who had had nothing but their ambition and their willingness to take a chance, and helped turn them into millionaires. They were millionaires, he liked to say, many of whom had never owned a suit until they had joined up with Datsun. Years later in Tokyo in his tiny office he liked to point at a map of the Western part of the United States. It was covered with little dots. "Each dot is a millionaire I made," he would say. The dealers loved him because he listened to them and fought for them. He wanted to find out not so much what the sales were but what they meant—what was behind them and how ordinary people in America really felt. The only thing about America he really did not understand and truly hated and feared was lawsuits. When even a minor suit was filed, he began to shiver. Suitcases, he called them, because his lawyer was always talking about the suit and the case. "You have to save me from these suitcases," he would say. "They want to kill me with them."

Suitcases aside, the mid-sixties were joyous years for Katayama. Slowly, the Datsun was getting better. At first he thought it was not jaunty enough, and he argued with Tokyo to make it sportier, but Tokyo was stuffy, regarding him as too much of a sports-car buff. He also argued with the home office over naming the cars. Tokyo kept coming up with terrible names like Bluebonnet, Cedric, and Fair Lady. Katayama, who increasingly fancied himself an expert on American taste, wanted more virile names, like Lion or Tiger. The problem, of course, was that Tokyo's names were the personal choices of Kawamata, who seemed to have some odd hidden streak of Anglophilia running through him. Fair Lady had been so decreed because Kawamata had once seen and apparently liked the musical *My Fair Lady*. Generally Katayama accepted his defeats on nomenclature reasonably well, but in 1970, when the first Japanese sports car arrived in America—the car that Katayama had always wanted—and he saw with horror that it had actually been called the Fair Lady, he and his men simply pried the nametag off the car and replaced it with one using the company's internal designation for the car, 240Z. It was far more appropriate, they decided, and using the company's own designation was the only way he could change the name without being insubordinate. Generally, however, he had lost out on names in the beginning, and normally on sportiness as well, but he was winning on almost everything else. The car was adapted to American conditions, it was economical to drive, and servicing was very good; there were always parts.

Katayama was convinced that the major American companies were not listening to their customers—or, if they were listening, then those voices were badly filtered through the dealers. The Big Three's dealers, he knew, hated selling compacts because they made so much less money on them and because they believed, probably accurately, that for every compact sold, a full-size model wasn't sold. The Big Three went into the compact market only when the import total began to rise beyond their estimates, and even then they did it half-heartedly. When in 1968 General Motors brought in its own foreign import, the Opel, an exceptionally well engineered car, it never put its institutional energy behind it, never pushed it with a major advertising campaign. The Opel was handled by the company's Buick dealers, who had neither the knowledge nor the desire to sell it properly. For them, each Opel that sold was a Buick that would not sell. When the imports had reached 5 percent of the market in 1959, Detroit struck back with its own compacts, and the foreigners immediately lost ground. But, having fended the foreigners off, Detroit responded in its own Pavlovian way: It immediately escalated the size of its compacts and added on equipment. By 1963 the foreigners had started making inroads again.

In the sixties, Katayama began to sense a change in customer attitudes, an increasingly powerful undercurrent of resentment. The objections to Detroit, he and some of his American people (and their counterparts at Toyota) decided, were different now. They were no longer just about the size and the price of the cars but about the quality and, even more important, about Detroit's response to legitimate complaints. If something went wrong on a car, no one seemed to be responsible. Not that there wasn't an acknowledgment that the customer's complaint was justified; the dealers were rather straightforward about that. They might wink and say yes, they were having a lot of problems with the ignition system or the rear-window cranks on these models, the factory seemed to be a little sloppy; but the burden of repair, often not very successful repair, seemed to fall on the customer. Detroit's attitude seemed to be that if the customer was truly a good American, he would stop complaining and do the right thing, which was to buy a new car. In those years, Philip Broman, a Ford man who quit and went to work for Toyota, once said, the Japanese companies read the various magazines like *Consumer Reports* as if they were Bibles filled with absolute truth, and the American companies dismissed them as the product of hostile do-gooders. Volkswagen was treating its customers with respect, Katayama thought, and because of that VW was building the kind of loyalty that had once been reserved solely for American companies. The customers were becoming more sophisticated; for the first time there was a basis of comparison, and they demanded to be listened to.

That observation was borne out in the next decade. It had always been a part of the basic theology of Detroit that it could roll back the foreigners anytime it wanted. The idea had always been that the imports could have 5 percent of the market, nothing more; if the foreigners went above that magic figure, Detroit would strike back. But in the late sixties, mostly because of Volkswagen, the imports' share was beginning to rise, and Detroit, though it did not yet realize it, could not so readily roll it back. For in part it was a reflection of the fact that the country was changing, and many middle-class people were changing their ideas of why they wanted a car and what kind of car they wanted. In 1968 the figure reached 10 percent, with VW getting 60 percent of the total import market. Slowly Detroit executives began to take notice again. They were not really worried; they were all making too much money for that. All they had to do whenever they wanted, they assured each other, was tool up some small cars. Soon the Detroit companies were bringing out their new compacts and subcompacts; Ford had the Maverick in 1969 and the Pinto in 1970, and GM had the ill-fated Vega in 1970. But the import sales did not, as in the past, collapse. What Katayama and others had suspected was becoming true. Bonds of loyalty were being severed. It was no longer, as in the past, just an issue of size and price. The issues now were also quality and integrity. Detroit, among many of its less affluent customers, was losing its reputation and not doing very much to try to regain it.

Katayama gave a small party in March 1964, when total Nissan sales reached five hundred a month, the target that had been set when the company first opened its American operation. Gradually there was a little money for advertising. In the beginning there had been by American standards virtually nothing, simple black-and-white brochures printed in Tokyo with florid English-language descriptions of the cars. Katayama hired a Los Angeles advertising man named John Parker because he was young, did not cost much, and seemed bright. Parker was delighted to take the Nissan account, unlikely though the future for it seemed, because it offered a rare entry into the automobile field. In the beginning it was fairly primitive work, convincing Tokyo, for example, that its handouts should be printed in America. The budgets were tiny, perhaps $50,000 a year at the start. When Nissan needed to shoot still photos for advertising, Parker, his wife, and their son and daughter had served as models. For a long time there was no money for television. The first television commercial was shot in 1963 for a four-wheel-drive wagon called the Nissan Patrol. Parker had no television studio in his company and no film equipment. Hiring a friend who was an L.A. police photographer and who had a 16mm camera, he drove a Patrol into the canyons and they shot a sixty-second commercial for the vehicle; to save money Parker himself was again the model, his film debut. The next year they heard that Roy Rogers, the cowboy actor, liked the Nissan Patrol, and Parker called him up and asked him to do the company's first full-fledged commercial. "I can't offer you any money, Roy," Parker said, "but we'll give you a Patrol, two pickups, and all the glory a man could want." To his surprise Rogers was delighted to participate. As the cars began to sell, there began to be a budget for TV ads.

In the fall of 1964 Datsun made it into the list of the top ten importers for the first time, a list absolutely dominated by Volkswagen. VW had 63 percent of the import market with 307,000 cars sold, an average of over 25,000 a month. In July of 1965 Datsun's sales reached 1000 a month. Back in Japan sales were rising quickly, which allowed Nissan to keep cutting the price; success was begetting success. The American market now looked more and more promising, though VW still appeared awesome. Steadily Nissan and then Toyota gained on the other imports. In 1966 Nissan was sixth with total sales of 22,000, while the VW Bug sold 420,000. By 1967 Nissan was fourth with 33,000; in 1969 it was still fourth but with 58,000.

The cars were getting better, but he still needed one critical addition —a jump to a 1600cc engine. At 1400cc, the current cars simply were not powerful enough. Eventually, he kept telling Tokyo, if they did not improve and upgrade the engine, they would level off in the market. Worse, if they leveled off, they would not stay level; they would inevitably decline. On this Tokyo remained surprisingly resistant; if 1400cc was good enough for Japan, it was good enough for America. Katayama pleaded. His cars, he said were underpowered, and there was no way Nissan would ever have the right car for America unless it went to 1600cc. He tried shock tactics, pointing out that Toyota, with a 1900cc model, was making sizable inroads where Datsun had once been strong. Even this failed. He had never felt so frustrated within the company. "Why does no one listen?" he asked those around him. He had a terrible feeling that Datsun was going to come to the edge of a great success and fail, and fail not because it was unable to make a superior product but because it was so psychologically isolated.

Then he got an extraordinary break. In the fall of 1965 a man named Keiichi Matsumura joined Nissan. He came over from MITI, where he had been the ministry's man on automobiles. There was a tradition of this in Japan—a high MITI official, his career completed, would go over into the industry where he had served; the Japanese called it descending from heaven. Kawamata had brought him in to secure a better line of communication for Nissan to the critically important world of the high ministries. But Keiichi Matsumura turned out not to be Kawamata's man at all. He proved exceptionally independent. Soon it became clear to insiders there was genuine tension between the two men. In the spring of 1966 Matsumura visited America, and he and Katayama began a series of endless conversations about the problems the company was having.

Katayama had never before met anyone like Matsumura in Nissan, someone at so high a level who was so smart and who was not playing political games. He was sure within one day that this man would become president of the company and that Nissan would quickly pass Toyota. All he wants is the truth, thought Katayama. Very quickly they became, if not friends, at least allies. Matsumura made it his business to go to the United States as often as he could in no small part to talk to Katayama. They were soon discussing not just the technical problems of Nissan America but the larger problems that were burdening the company. For Katayama it was like a great burst of fresh air in a company where everything was so dank, and of hope where there was so much fear. Unlike everyone else Katayama had dealt with, Matsumura simply was not afraid of Kawamata and Shioji; if Kawamata had the bank behind him, Matsumura had MITI behind him. Like many of the top MITI men, he seemed the best of the best, a chosen soul of the nation, a man without doubt, absolutely confident of his decisions and his purpose.

Katayama knew immediately that this was his great chance to upgrade the engine, and so he pushed as hard as he could with Matsumura about the need for 1600cc. At the end of their first long session Matsumura said, "Write a letter for me, and I will sign it." Then he changed his mind. "Make it a telex," he said. "There's a board meeting coming up soon." The next day a long, impassioned telex message went out over Matsumura's name, which everyone at Nissan knew was from Katayama, not Matsumura. Almost immediately, Katayama got an angry message from Yuji Shimamoto, who was a key man in the export department. Shimamoto had been his chief tormentor in the past and had strenuously fought him on his repeated requests to upgrade the engine. This time Shimamoto was complaining bitterly and publicly of Katayama's failure to ask him for the 1600cc engine any earlier. That night, April 8, 1966, Katayama wrote in his diary: "I do not know how many times I have asked the head office for more [engine] power. In fact I have been begging for it, but we always had to shut up because their answer was that it was impossible. Now Shimamoto tells me that everyone including Kawamata was shocked by Matsumura's telex. It is we who should be shocked, not him." Without Matsumura, the 1600cc engine would have been delayed another year and possibly longer, he wrote. Why did people in a private company, he wondered, have to act as timidly as those in a government bureaucracy?

A few days later Kawamata arrived in Los Angeles with his wife. Katayama was nervous that the president might be angry with him because of the Matsumura telex. But Kawamata seemed not to mind it at all; indeed he affected to take it as a normal request. It was, of course, immediately approved, and the 1600cc engine went into production. That meant that in 1968 the engine was ready for the new Datsun called the 510. It was a remarkable car, in any real sense Yutaka Katayama's car, a personal victory of exceptional magnitude in any auto company and particularly in a Japanese one (a point of some sensitivity later with Tokyo). For years he had been pushing Tokyo to use its growing skill in engineering and manufacturing to leapfrog ahead of the American and European small cars. Nissan was at the point, he kept telling the home office, where it was capable not just of improving its small, durable little cars, but of going ahead, giving the low-end customer something that had never been available before, an inexpensive, sporty, mass-produced sedan. Nissan could do it now because its production costs had dropped so low and its engineering was becoming so good. Finally, reluctantly, the home office had listened.

The 510 marked the beginning of the end of the small car in America as a clumsy, flimsy econo-box. It was the fulfillment in that sense of Katayama's vision, of taking the best of modern European engineering and marrying it to Japanese manufacturing expertise to produce an inexpensive, small, rugged car that was also high-performing. That vision was special to him, for Katayama was above all else—and this made him unique in an increasingly bureaucratic company like Nissan—a man who loved cars and who loved to drive. The BMW 1600 had immediately excited him; it had taken the pleasures and advantages of a sports car and placed them in a sedan. This was the future. The Japanese, he was sure, could match this. The technology was available, and the ability to manufacture well. Why not do it, then? It was, of course—and this was hard for Tokyo to accept—largely a car for the export market, since it leaped ahead of Japanese domestic needs at the time. Gradually Tokyo came around, probably as much because people there were ready to come around.

In the months when the car was in its final engineering design, Katayama was on the phone to Japan constantly; one of his American associates thought he was more like an expectant mother than an auto executive. He went sleepless the night before it arrived, and when the ship was finally docking in San Pedro, he was more nervous than anyone had ever seen him. As soon as the first one came off the ship, he himself drove it out of the parking facility. "Finally!" he exclaimed to the friend riding next to him. "Finally they did it!" The car was white with a red interior. "I thought it would take ten years to do it," he told his friend. But they had really done it in seven. He was impressed by how good Japan's engineers were; in practical, functional work like this, building a car, they were possibly the best in the world. He had suspected that they were that good, but here now was the proof.

That night he again could not sleep. He was for the first few months like a kid with a new toy. He made everyone drive it, first his colleagues at the office, then journalists, then anyone who walked near the showroom. He loved the car, and it was inconceivable to him that anyone who touched it would not be equally excited. Taking personal charge of the advertising campaign, he demanded something different—not the usual commercial that would show the car and rattle off lots of words about its extraordinary features. It was a beautiful car, he said, it had high performance, and it should be shown simply for that, and people would know. So he helped design a commercial in which a beautiful girl drove a 510 through the Big Sur country on a dark, stormy night. The windshield wipers kept working against the rain, and the car worked against the terrain. In the background was the music of Vivaldi. It was known at Nissan as the Baroque commercial. Not a word was spoken. It was, thought Katayama, all that anyone needed to understand the car.

The 510 was a landmark car in many ways. Datsun promptly jumped into third place among the importers, with 100,000 pieces sold. The 510 alone sold over 300,000 pieces in five years, and for anyone paying attention it was a sure sign that the Japanese had arrived. They were now able to build not just small, solid cars, but cars with high-tech, high-performance capability. It was not just the first very good Japanese car to hit the market; more significant, it was the first inexpensive, ultramodern, high-performance small car on the American and European market. Its arrival showed that the Japanese were ready in auto making, that the explosive surge that they had already made in so many other industries was now about to take place in this industry as well.

In essence, as one high Nissan executive admitted at the time, the 510 was a brilliant knockoff of the BMW 1600, the main difference being that the BMW cost roughly $5000 and the Nissan 510 about $1800. The 510 bore witness to the great Japanese admiration for the skills that had gone into the BMW 1600. The 510 had four-wheel independent suspension, an overhead camshaft, and a 1600cc engine with ninety-six horsepower. It was very strong, well put together, fuel-efficient. It was almost immediately a hot car. The professional auto magazines were unusually enthusiastic. Car nuts loved the new Datsuns. Dealers could not keep them on the floor, and for a time there were the inevitable charges that some dealers were taking bribes in order to save cars for customers. In Detroit few of the people at the top of the auto companies took the 510 very seriously, though among the engineering people there was a sudden realization that the Japanese could be more than functional, they could be *good*. It was, thought Mayfield Marshall years later, a Yuppie car before the Yuppies had been properly identified, a car for bright young urban professionals who were not tied to the past.

Within weeks of the date the 510 went on sale, Katayama and his associates noticed a new phenomenon: VW dealers who wanted to come over and handle the Datsun cars. The following year, for the first time in two decades, VW's share of the American market did not increase. Like Henry Ford with the Model T, Volkswagen had stayed with the Bug too long. In the next five years Volkswagen's share of the import market dropped from 62 to 46 percent, almost all of the lost ground going to the Japanese. In 1968 the Japanese passed the West Germans to become the number-two producer of motor vehicles in the world.

26.
THE EMPEROR SHIOJI

The friends of Ichiro Shioji, the men with whom he regularly played golf, noted the change in him. He had never been exactly shy, but he had become a man of the world. His new self-confidence was startling to them. Suddenly, it seemed, he was always just on his way to some international meeting or just back from one. On the links with them or in the locker room after one of these business trips, he would talk expansively of the Americans he had just spent time with, Reuther and Woodcock and even some American politicians whose names apparently meant a great deal to him although somewhat less to them. As he became ever more influential he brought them gifts from abroad— cigarette lighters (personalized, with his name on them), golf clubs, bottles of Scotch—the gifts of Shioji, they called them. Presented immediately after a trip, they helped contribute to the image that began to grow in their minds, of Shioji as a man on the move, and finally as a man of power. His yacht did not detract from that image. Some of them were invited on weekends to sail with him on this huge beautiful boat with its crew of eight, all of them Nissan employees during the week, working now on their days off. On these occasions his sense of power was even more obvious. He commanded, it seemed, not just the boat, but the company.

He was always connected. He had placed some of his people in the Diet. He had close friends in the prime minister's office, and it seemed not to matter who the prime minister was. Many who knew the structure of Nissan well thought that by the early seventies he was its single most important figure. It was Shioji who supplied the muscle during those hard and difficult years when the auto industry was defining itself. He at once represented labor and brought it into line. Not only had he played a key role in breaking the Masuda union, not only had he helped arrange the Prince merger under terms satisfactory to Nissan, but in the sixties he had played a critical role in one other area. For though it was not something that the high executives of Nissan liked to admit, it was Shioji as much as anyone else who had helped bring the supplier companies into line.

That step was important to the modernization of the company. As the sixties started, the leading assembly companies were themselves emerging for the first time as fiscally sound enterprises. But the supplier companies were another thing. Many were in terrible shape, appalling little shops, often with dirt floors, their wages much lower than those at companies like Nissan. The competition was ferocious between them. They were seriously underfinanced and teetered constantly on the edge of bankruptcy. Some of them would bloom one year and go bust the next. Their quality was erratic, and when it was not high, it limited the quality of the assembly companies. In those days MITI, perceiving that this was the glaring weakness in the Japanese auto industry, was pushing for stabilization and rationalization of the supplier companies. It wanted fewer but more profitable supplier companies, and it wanted them to have closer ties to the assembly companies. These newly stabilized companies would have the kind of access to banks normally denied smaller companies, and they could count on long-term relationships with the main companies. That would allow them to upgrade their facilities and, eventually, their quality.

Soon Nissan developed a formula. On a vital piece of equipment, something without which the line might shut down, Nissan wanted the supplier company to be a direct subsidiary and wanted 90 percent of the stock. For all intents and purposes, these companies became part of Nissan itself. On parts for which there were alternative suppliers if needed, Nissan wanted 40 percent of the stock. That in itself was a virtual takeover. It allowed family companies to remain family companies, but it made sure they fit the specifications of Nissan and that the will of Nissan would be decisive. If the company refused to accommodate, Nissan—or Toyota or one of the other bigger companies, for the same process was going on throughout the industry—simply went elsewhere.

Many supplier companies found Nissan's proposed arrangements tempting. For a relatively small company whose principal nonautomotive products might be kitchen tools or children's toys, businesses in which the competition was ruthless and often fatal, the future was always uncertain. A connection with Nissan was a guarantee of success. It was an offer that few turned down. Almost as soon as the deal was done, however, the owner learned that he was no longer master of his own shop. Now he was taking orders not just from Nissan but from Shioji as well. For if Nissan was to become modern and highly technological, the new supplier companies had to be disciplined, their pay scales adjusted, their owners and workers introduced to their proper place in the hierarchy. That became Shioji's job. Again, he was the muscle. He was to make sure that they and their workers joined Nissan on terms acceptable to the head company. If he thought they paid their workers too much, he let them know. If he thought their workers were insufficiently respectful to him when he visited their factories, he let them know. Once when he visited a supplier company, he became angry because, in his opinion, the workers there did not render him the proper deference.

"I apologize for any disrespect they showed you," the owner, Akira Sugita, told him, "but they're only kids—not even high school graduates."

Shioji persisted. "You are too soft on them," he retorted. "Your workers are demanding tremendous increases in their bonuses."

"It is not their demands," Sugita said. "It is what I choose to pay them."

They argued for a while, and later one of the other supplier-company presidents took Sugita aside. "You can't do that—fight with him. Your job is to say yes. You are the only one of us who argues."

Shioji's purpose went beyond saving Nissan money. He wanted to keep the subsidary companies' presidents on constant notice that he represented Nissan, and that he was above them, and that, if they crossed him, they might lose their contracts with Nissan. He was not subtle in his reminders. If the association of supplier presidents was about to have its monthly golf game, he would sometimes call one of the presidents and demand that the president play golf with *him*, letting them all know that a golf game with Shioji was more important than playing with one another and deliberately casting a pall over the day. They were being taught their place. Once Shioji was to speak at a meeting of supplier companies; so were Kawamata and Sohei Nakayama, head of the Industrial Bank of Japan, and other Japanese executives. The others had already spoken, and it was Shioji's turn—but there was no Shioji. Eventually Shioji drove up.

"We must hurry," said the supplier-company president who was his escort. "Everyone is waiting."

"No," said Shioji. "I haven't eaten yet."

"But they are all waiting," the president insisted.

"I am hungry," Shioji said, "and I am going to eat," and he did, while the presidents of all those companies waited. The message was loud and clear.

Soon everyone who had any connection with Nissan had received that message. They came to understand, for example, that at certain Nissan meetings only Kawamata and Shioji spoke. Board members, technically Shioji's superiors in the hierarchy, never dared challenge him. The supplier-company presidents realized that he was the company; Kawamata was becoming a distant figure in the background whom they rarely saw. Shioji was the man to deal with. Some took him to dinner and flattered him. Knowing that he had spent time in America and was proud of having learned to mix cocktails, a rare skill in Japan, they passed the word among each other that at dinner in the Ginza Shioji liked to be asked to mix drinks for them, and to be told how exceptionally good his drinks were. At dinner Shioji was to be given the seat of honor: in front of the scroll.

For Nissan, dominating the supplier-company managements was not sufficient. Their workers had to be controlled as well. They all belonged to the Suppliers Union, which was supposed to be distinct from Shioji's Japan Auto Workers. But Shioji had installed his own man, Hideo Kuze, as head of the Suppliers Union. Kuze was a Shioji protégé, one of his most trusted assistants. He had been part of the Miyake-Shioji union from the beginning, and when Shioji made his trip to the Harvard Business School, Kuze had written up Shioji's adventures in the union newsletter, making them seem duly glorious. During the early sixties it was as if Kuze were Shioji's personal deputy, and some union members assumed that Kuze would be his successor. In the late sixties, Shioji placed Kuze as head of the Suppliers Union. It was assumed that he would follow Shioji's wishes in detail. But it soon became clear that Kuze intended to run a somewhat independent union. Presently there were small disagreements between them, and then minor tensions. Shioji rebuked Kuze for being not quite respectful enough on the phone, then of not clearing his policies with Shioji. At one point a contract came up with two supplier companies. On his own, without telling anyone, Shioji negotiated contracts. It was Kuze's misfortune then to go to the same two companies and ask for larger pay raises. That humiliation sealed his fate. Quietly, supported by Nissan management, Shioji squeezed Kuze out. Defeated, Kuze came apart, going into hiding and making several unsuccessful suicide attempts.

With Kuze's destruction the independence of the Suppliers Union was over and Nissan's domination of its suppliers was complete. It was a crucial step. Now the supplier companies, as extensions of Nissan, could be modernized, and there would be no strikes at the suppliers to disrupt Nissan production. Now Kawamata could control both quality and costs to a degree not previously possible. From its relatively impoverished beginning Nissan could now move into boom years, with enough flex to sustain the high rate of capital investment the company required, while giving the workers salaries that placed them at the very top of the Japanese pay scale.

The subjugation of the suppliers was not an accomplishment anyone at Nissan liked to talk about very much; it came to be regarded as something that simply had occurred. MITI had envisioned it, and Shioji had made it happen. That he had achieved it confirmed his special position within Nissan. Already Kawamata's closest confidant, he became almost like his son. Nothing important took place without his clearance. The Prince labor union leader whom he had destroyed, Takashi Suzuki, found Shioji a fascinating man in contemporary Japan, the outsider who had done the work of the establishment. Suzuki was reminded of the time-honored adage that Miyoji Ochiai had used to caution Nissan union leader Tetsuo Masuda: The nail that stands out gets hammered in. I was the nail, thought Suzuki, and he was the hammer. He wondered, however, if Shioji, powerful as he was, would become a nail himself.

PART
EIGHT

27.
WAR AND OIL

The equation that permitted the United States to survive on cheap oil was growing ever less stable. The Middle East was becoming increasingly turbulent, and the signs of rising Arab nationalism (and a declining Western ability to control that nationalism) were clear from the mid-fifties on. In 1954, Gamal Abdel Nasser had come to power in Egypt, in a coup engineered by young army officers. More than any other figure in the Arab world he seemed to have a vision of Arab nationalism. He had read in American books that it cost the oil companies only 10 cents to produce a barrel of oil in the Middle East, and that the average Middle Eastern well produced four thousand barrels a day, far more than the average American well. Oil, then, he perceived, was at the center of Arab power. His power base as a pan-Arab leader was undermined, however, by the fact that Egypt lacked oil. Other Arab leaders were wary of him and hesitant to share their oil revenues with a country that had none, led by a man they might not be able to control. Still, Nasser loomed as the first of the truly important nationalist leaders in the Arab world.

In 1956 he seized the Suez Canal. French, British, and Israeli troops moved against him; on the verge of victory, they were forced to call off their expedition by pressure from the Americans, who were nervous about what seemed to them virtually a restoration of colonial power in that region. After Suez, the former colonial powers in the area would not again use force there to try to change governments. The Americans had vital economic interests there, but for thirty years nothing short of ensuring the survival of Israel or keeping the Saudi fields open would compel them to back up those interests with their military power. That meant that in this postcolonial era there would be an inevitable surge of nationalist feeling, much of it anti-Western; the West would be reduced to trying to protect those more conservative Arab nations that were its friends, principally Saudi Arabia and Iran. If the West was not actually in decline, its

military and political power in the Middle East was no longer as great as
its economic interest.

The next important crisis came in 1958 in Iraq, where the military
revolted against a particularly brutal and autocratic regime installed by
the British. Gradually, the nationalism that Nasser symbolized was spreading throughout the area. Even the more moderate leaders that the West
regarded as allies portrayed themselves now as nationalists. The Shah of
Iran, clearly America's man, dared not look like a Western puppet. On
occasion he was harder to deal with than other Arab leaders, in part
because the West had installed him and therefore had to play to his
megalomania. Besides, no matter how conservative and autocratic a Middle East leader was, there was a subsurface rage against the Western
nations for taking so much out for so little. That feeling grew stronger
during the sixties. There was growing frustration with the power of the
oil companies, a sense that the companies were not fair in their dealings,
and an equally important frustration with Western support of Israel.

Nevertheless, for about twenty years the companies were able to stabilize the posted price of oil—in effect, the price at which they chose to
sell (vastly above the cheap price at which they bought). It was a price
pegged not to the ease of taking oil out of these lush new fields but instead
to the higher cost of oil that came from the Gulf of Mexico. The right hand
was doing a very good job of protecting the left hand. From about 1948
to 1971 the price was remarkably even, staying near $2 a barrel. But
beneath the seeming stability there was volatility. For the first time the
Arab nations began to talk of unity. Given the political, religious, social,
and historical differences in the region, as well as the awesome egos of
the leaders themselves, that they even spoke of unity was surprising, and
a measure of their discontent.

In 1967 the Egyptians and the Syrians attacked Israel in what became
known as the Six-Day War. The speed and completeness with which the
Israelis defeated their Arab opponents only made the Arabs more aware
of their weakness and deepened their rage. In the aftermath there was a
brief and somewhat pathetic attempt to use oil as a weapon. The only
victims were the nations themselves. Some of the Arabs tried to shut down
production. (Iran did not join in.) The Saudis shut down their fields for a
month and lost $30 million in revenues. Later Sheik Ahmed Yamani, the
Saudi oil minister and a forceful spokesman for the Arabs, admitted that
they had used their power poorly. "We are behaving like someone who
fires a bullet in the air, missing the enemy and allowing it to fall on
himself," he said. The impotence of the Arabs simply created more contempt for them in the West. But it was this demonstration of their own

ineffectuality that prompted real change, at last compelling the Arab nations to cooperate with one another.

At the same time the buyer's market in oil was beginning to become a seller's market. The Six-Day War took place twenty-two years after the end of World War II. By then Western Europe had become a full-fledged member of the oil culture, despite the counsel of some planners, like Jean Monnet, who had urged coal, in which Western Europe was rich, as the basis for the European economy. Instead, with American encouragement, Europe had become increasingly dependent on oil. From 1950 to 1965 the six Common Market countries' reliance on oil as an energy source increased from 10 to 45 percent while coal decreased from 74 to 38 percent. Japan's economy, a scaled-down replica of the American model, became ever more oil-based, and countless smaller countries were also beginning to demand oil. In 1973, for example, Jim Akins, one of the top American experts on the subject, forecast that in the ensuing twelve years the world would use more oil than had been used in all the years up until then.

Another factor acting inexorably in the Arabs' favor was that the American reserves had gone flat. In 1970, for the first time, American production began to decrease; in that year 28 percent of America's oil was imported, even though there were restrictions on imports. With any other commodity that might have profoundly affected the price; but because of the Middle East reserves and the seeming ability of the cartel to control things, the price remained the same. That meant oil was seriously undervalued. The market for it had exploded, and normally the price should have risen dramatically. But the companies prevented it. They might have their rivalries, their internecine bitterness and feuds, but the stakes were so large that they had managed some exceptionally ingenious methods of accommodating to each other in order not to be divided and thus lessen their control. They had managed to keep out the more vulnerable independents (they never wanted a country to have too much leverage over a company; the cartel must be mightier than the state), and they had managed to keep down the price of oil. The countries might be immensely bitter about it, but they had no choice. The cartel could deny access to markets to any oil-producing country that challenged the arbitrarily low price.

The first substantial break came in 1969 in Libya. In September of that year, King Idris was overthrown by a group of radical officers headed by a young army colonel named Muammar Qaddafi, a fanatic moralist, bitterly anti-Israel, fiercely anti-Western. His first act after coming to power was to outlaw liquor. He soon banned the use of Latin print in Libya and forbade the use of non-Arabic words like "helicopter" and "taxi." He had

taken power to avenge the past, to rid his country of any vestige of colonialism and the corruptions he believed the colonialists had inflicted on
his country. He had also taken power in the country where the major
companies were most vulnerable. For unlike most other Arab countries,
where the government dealt with only one main concessionaire, Libya
had opened itself up to a variety of companies, and its fields were allotted
among them. Thus someone like Qaddafi could exert considerable leverage
on a single firm he chose to isolate. Advised by experts that his oil was
underpriced, he sought an increase; the companies rejected his request.
In May 1970, his patience exhausted, he took on Occidental Petroleum,
an independent and, among the many companies doing business in Libya,
the weakest link. Occidental was already unpopular; the people who staffed
its engineering contractor, Bechtel, were disdainful of its Libyan workers,
referring to them not by their names but by their payroll numbers. Qaddafi
ordered Occidental to cut its production back by 300,000 barrels a day.

It was probably the first time one of the oil countries did to a company
what the companies had been doing to them. Occidental quickly offered
a modest increase in the price, but it was too late. Knowing how helpless
he was, Armand Hammer, the head of Occidental, flew to New York to
cut a deal with John Jamieson, the head of Exxon; he would stand firm
against Qaddafi if Exxon would make up for his Libyan losses from other
sources. In the past, despite antagonisms between its members, com-
monality of interests had always held the cartel together, but Hammer
was an outsider, and Jamieson distrusted him. (When Peru had nation-
alized some Exxon fields, Hammer had volunteered to step in and operate
them. Jamieson had not forgotten.) That decision, without anyone realizing
it at the time, for at first it was only regarded as a rebuff against Hammer,
was the beginning of the break in the cartel.

The relations between Occidental and Qaddafi grew worse. Qaddafi
squeezed Hammer a little more, cutting Occidental's production another
60,000 barrels a day to a low of 440,000, a figure just above half what it
had once been. He had Hammer now and could do what he wanted with
him. Isolated from the big boys who might have protected him, unable
to share in their solidarity, utterly dependent on the Libyans, Hammer
cracked and agreed to pay 30 cents more a barrel and an increase of 2
cents a year for the next five years. In return Hammer won the right to
pump 700,000 barrels a day.

Soon Qaddafi was picking off the other companies taking oil from Libya.
It was an immense triumph for him, as much political and psychological
as economic. At a meeting of OPEC in December 1970, the new Arab
confidence was obvious. No longer could the companies so readily control

the price. The oil countries were more confident, more demanding. Not just the leaders of the radical countries but even supposedly moderate leaders like the Shah were behaving in a new way. Now the Shah was openly critical of American practices in Iran. The conditions that once existed in Iran no longer existed, he said. The companies had used the protection of the American government to practice economic imperialism, he went on, and he threatened to kick them out. "The oil-producing countries know they are being cheated," he declared. "Otherwise you would not have the common front. . . . The all-powerful six or seven sisters [the big international oil companies] have got to open their eyes and see that they are living in 1971 and not in 1948 or 1949." The negotiations between the companies and the Iranians became intense. The Iranians wanted 54 cents more a barrel, and the Americans offered 15 cents. They finally settled on 30 cents, increasing to 50 by 1975. Although in comparison to what was soon to happen it was a relatively small increase, it was regarded at the time by the companies as ruinous.

It was in fact ruinous for the oil companies, in that it showed they could no longer control the price. In March of that year the companies doing business with the Libyans agreed on a posted price of $3, an increase of 76 cents. Word of that price, and a sense of the new possibilities it signaled, spread swiftly through the Arab world. The Shah, hearing the news, was furious; he realized how much more he could have gotten. The companies, warned Walter Levy, an authority on oil, faced a "hurricane of change." Quickly the Arab countries escalated their demands. Sheik Yamani reflected their new confidence. The Americans, he insisted, had to see that their realities had changed and that they now had to accommodate. Soon the Americans began to concede to Yamani on a number of points. Essentially he demanded a real partnership. "The oligopoly of the companies has now been joined by the oligopoly of OPEC," Anthony Sampson wrote.

As OPEC's spokesman, delivering the bad news to the developed world, Yamani was now an international figure. He was a far cry from the greedy sheik into whose hands the Western prospectors once could slip a few gold pieces. He was the symbol of the modern man in a feudal state. Young, educated at New York University and Harvard, he had intended to be a lawyer. Instead he soon became the Saudis' principal negotiator with the companies. He was intelligent, self-assured, comfortable with Westerners and Arabs alike. He was aware of the delicacy of the Saudi position—the Saudis, as a conservative nation in a radical part of the world, must not offend their radical neighbors but must also remain friends with the West. Yamani played his cards with great skill. His position was made more fascinating by dint of the fact that his country, with the vast deposits at Ghawar, had the world's largest reserves; thus the other countries could do nothing without the Saudis. Yamani, to the consternation of the companies, kept asking for larger and larger shares of the profits, and the countries grudgingly conceded. At the same time the Saudis, among others, increased their warnings that they would join with other more radical states to use oil as a weapon against American support of Israel.

In June 1973 there was another OPEC meeting, at which the countries announced an additional 12 percent increase. What they really wanted was complete control of the pricing. Yamani told reporters that this was the last time the countries would negotiate with the companies on price; instead, from now on they would meet among themselves, work out the price, and announce it unilaterally to the companies. That September, for the first time, the market price of oil rose above the posted price. Nothing showed the new power of the countries more than that single fact; it also marked the coming of market forces to a region previously immune to them.

In early October the leaders of OPEC prepared to leave for a meeting in Geneva. There, on October 8, they intended to meet with the representatives of what were by now extremely nervous oil companies. In effect the companies intended to tell the OPEC people that they had gone too far too quickly. The oil producers intended to explain that the old era was over, and they would now dictate terms. On October 6, even as they were leaving for Geneva, Egypt and Syria invaded Israeli-occupied territory, lending the meeting a special drama. Yamani demanded a doubling of the going price—from just over $3 a barrel to $6. George Piercy of Exxon instead suggested increasing the price 15 percent. Yamani made a gesture: He would accept a $2-a-barrel increase, or a total of $5. Piercy, on behalf of the companies, refused to go above 25 percent—roughly $3.75 a barrel.

Some of the Westerners negotiating with OPEC knew how fragile their position was—there was a potential now not just for an increase but for something far more threatening, a boycott. They cabled their home offices, suggesting that Yamani might come down somewhat lower than the $5 he was demanding. But the men in the home offices were made of sterner stuff and told their representatives not to budge. The Arabs were incensed, and the next day, without even bothering to notify the representatives of the companies, they flew home. Yamani told the Americans that if they wanted more news "listen to the radio."

Now two powerful currents came together—a changing market value for oil and an outraged Arab sensibility over American support of Israel. Four Arab foreign ministers flew to Washington to warn the Americans of the possibility of a boycott. The most important of them was Omar

Saqquaf, the foreign minister of Saudi Arabia. On the day that Saqquaf hoped to see President Nixon, the President pleaded too busy a schedule, and that angered the Saudis. At a press conference an American reporter suggested to Saqquaf that the Saudis might have to drink their oil, and Saqquaf retorted, "All right, we will."

The Americans assumed that the Arab world was too divided, too faction-ridden, to mount an effective boycott. But on October 21 the boycott, aimed primarily at the Americans, began. The embargo, of course, helped drive the price per barrel of oil skyward, for those allowed to buy. It seemed a particularly cruel irony that only a few weeks earlier the companies had sneered at Yamani's request for a $5 price. Yamani now spoke of the market price as the only price he believed in. The West was stunned. Unsuccessful efforts were made to pressure Japan, which imported all its oil, to restrain itself in bidding on the open market.

On December 16, 1973, the Iranian State Oil Company for the first time conducted an auction of its oil. The highest bid was $17 a barrel. Most of the bidders were independents. Shell was said to have bid at $12. Another auction in Algeria produced bids of $22. It was clear that the posted price and the market price no longer had anything to do with each other.

On December 22, representatives of the six Persian Gulf nations in OPEC met in Teheran to discuss what they should do at so important a moment. The Iranians were the most militant about pushing the price up, for the Shah's resentment of the West and the way he had been treated by the oil companies was growing all the time. ("Why should I let you waste my oil?" he once said to a group of Westerners.) He wanted a price of $14 a barrel, which, he said, was less than the Arabs could be getting on the free market. Yamani was more cautious. He was wary of setting a price so high that it could cause a worldwide depression. ("I knew," he said years later, "that if you went down, we would go down as well.") At the meeting Yamani was getting conflicting advice. Some American oilmen who happened to be in Teheran at the time, worried about the short-range impact, told him to have the Saudis keep the price low and break with OPEC, but other Americans were worried that if he did, the Saudis would never be forgiven; they would be under siege in their own part of the world, thus endangering the stability of the Arab state richest in oil and friendliest to America. Yamani decided not to break (for which he was later reprimanded by King Feisal). Even as the other ministers were still meeting, the Shah on his own announced that the new price would be $11.65 a barrel. It had been reached, he said, on the basis "of generosity and kindness." It would be good for the West to economize, he said.

"Eventually all those children of well-to-do families who have plenty to eat at every meal, who have their own cars, and who act almost as terrorists and who throw bombs here and there will have to really think of all these privileges of the advanced industrial world, and they will have to work harder."

In just two months the price of oil had quadrupled, and the key agents of that stunning change, the Iranians and the Saudis, were moderate or conservative states, perceived as allies of the West.

The embargo that the Americans had once mocked was surprisingly successful. Before the embargo, the United States had been importing 1.2 million barrels a day; by February that figure had dropped to virtually nothing. The companies had caved in completely; they were now the junior partners of the Arabs—"their marketing experts and their tax agents," one skeptic said. (They would, however, ironically, become much richer because of the whopping price increase, which they simply passed along. Their profits went skyrocketing.) It had been a truly historic victory for a region that had been suffering under a kind of economic neocolonialism. The victory was as much psychological as it was economic. What had held the oil countries back in the past, the Shah said, was "the mystical power of the companies." By that he meant the mystical power of the white man—a holdover from colonial days—to make Arabs believe that he knew more, was stronger, and had some sort of divine sanction that had been denied to them. "Until we realized our strength," said one Saudi official, "we did not have it."

The American economy and the American people were completely unprepared for the change. The squandering of oil was built into the very structure of American life. Everyone had become dependent upon cheap energy. Almost all American cars, for example, had automatic transmissions, which used 25 percent more gas than the old manual transmission. With many American brands of car, if a buyer wanted a manual shift, he had to say so in advance so it could be ordered from the factory. By the time of the Yom Kippur War, 85 percent of the job holders in America drove to work every day—and as a result, public transportation had atrophied. Suddenly gas was expensive and scarce. In a short time it went from 36 cents a gallon to 60. People lined up for hours at every service station. There were fights as drivers tried to jump the line, reports of bribes, and even one murder committed in a struggle for gas. In the neurosis created by the boycott there was a new craze called "topping off," which was an attempt to keep one's tank perpetually filled. At one service station in Pittsburgh a motorist came in and bought 11 cents' worth, and the attendant spit in his face. The Boston police department came up with an interesting statistic: The number of cases of automobile arson went up dramatically, from 149 to 330, in the year when the gas prices jumped; most of those torched cars were gas guzzlers. In the first quarter of 1974 the use of gas dropped 7 percent in the United States instead of rising the normal 7 percent.

In March 1974, just five months after it began, the boycott was over. The Arabs had flexed their new muscles, had made both their political and economic points, and were now being richly rewarded by the high price of oil. The oil began flowing again, though much more expensively, and many soon came to view the boycott as a brief nightmare, not a serious historical benchmark. In August of that year, five months after the end of the boycott, President Ford cut in half the $20 billion that Congress had appropriated for mass transit. The country had been momentarily jolted, but it soon was back to business as usual.

28.
HENRY FORD BESIEGED

Even before the Yom Kippur War, the danger signs were already there. Oil was certainly part of it; almost every credible expert in the energy field was warning of the limits of American domestic oil reserves and the risks in becoming too dependent upon foreign sources. But it went beyond oil. Even as new and formidable competitors like the Japanese were preparing to make major assaults upon the American market, it was clear that the American wage scale, both for managers and workers, was seriously out of synch with the rest of the world. The gap between American and Japanese scale, for example, should have been closing as the Japanese became more prosperous. But the settlements that Detroit kept making with the UAW were as inflated as ever, and the differences, particularly in benefits, remained considerable. Corporate profits too were greater than ever, and so were corporate salaries, in some cases reaching $1 million a year. The companies could not ask the union to discipline itself when their own officers were indulging themselves that way. Discipline had to begin at the top, and no one wanted that much discipline. Besides, each company feared a strike that would shut it down and let its customers go elsewhere.

The ironic result of this was that it created not an affluent and harmonious company but one devoid of harmony, where management and labor remained suspicious of each other, particularly on the question of quality. The workers thought that management's talk about quality was essentially a sham and what the company really cared about was pushing as many cars down the line as possible and maximizing the profit. Some junior Ford executives agreed with them. They were especially offended by a program known as PIPs, or Profit Improvement Programs, which began in the late sixties and lasted several years. It was an Iacocca plan, and it showed the increasing accommodation of the product men to the norms set by finance. The purpose of the PIPs was to bring down the costs of making a car by taking them out of an existing budget; an example might be the decision to equip a Mercury with Ford upholstery, which was cheaper. Some traditionalists were convinced that the PIPs systematically reduced quality, that it was automotive sleight of hand, and that the covert philosophy behind the program was that the customer would never know the difference. PIPs quickly became part of the vernacular, turning into a verb.

"What happened to that hood ornament?" a product man might ask.

"Oh," his superior would reply, "it got pipped."

It was the same essential theology that led to the disaster of the Pinto, a small car that came out in 1970. With its exploding gas tanks and subsequent law suits, it became a mark of shame for Ford. Years later, there was a serious attempt by the top Ford people to blame the Pinto on Iacocca, and he bears partial responsibility, particularly since he earlier had killed the Cardinal. But the Pinto was not his car; it was the kind of small car Ford was producing during a time when corners were being cut even on luxury cars and when, if a small car was being done, it was imperative to do it on the cheap. Ford was not good at taking weight *off* a car then, and the testing of cars for safety was underdeveloped compared to what it became later (under pressure from outsiders, all of whom Detroit's giants scorned).

There were other problems now. For the first time quality was in doubt. Iacocca was talking more candidly about the difficulties Ford was having making good cars. His people, he said, could design wonderful cars, but they couldn't count on the work force. "Look," Iacocca said, "I went out last week to our Wixom plant. We build our Continentals there—our best cars. And I'm looking at the line and I see some young guy who's going full-time to school at Wayne State, his mind is elsewhere, and he doesn't give a shit what he builds, he doesn't care and he isn't involved in his job, and when that car comes off the line, maybe it'll be okay and maybe it won't. We can't change a man like that anymore; we don't have the leverage. So what we're going to do at Ford is create a dealer organization that will fix up the cars and guarantee that they'll function right. We'll give you a dealer who will repair what we produce." Kurt Luedke, then an editor of the *Detroit Free Press*, was stunned by what Iacocca was saying. In effect, Luedke thought, he was admitting that Ford could no longer control its work force, and so it was pushing onto the dealers the burden of supplying customers with an acceptable car.

Still, these signs were small. Those at the top were still confident of what they were doing and confident that they knew the customers. Iacocca was the embodiment of that confidence. He believed he could sell anything. *Anything*. His spirit was contagious, for as he believed, so did others in the company. In these, the last years of Detroit's immodesty, American products were the best because they had always been the best. Perhaps, Iacocca might concede, the Italians were better designers, but no one made or marketed cars better than the Americans.

Iacocca was speaking not just for himself but for the company and the man he worked for as well. "Americans," Henry Ford once told an interviewer, "like to blast along over interstate highways at eighty miles an hour in big cars with every kind of power attachment, windows up, air conditioning on, radio going, one finger on the wheel. That's what they want, and that's what they buy, and that's what we manufacture. We build the best cars we can to meet the taste of the American people." Ford felt a contempt for European cars that was almost personal. Small cars were, in his phrase, "little shitboxes." If a friend drove a small car, no matter whether it was a Volvo or a Fiat or a Renault, it was to Henry Ford "a goddam little Volkswagen."

That truculence revealed as much about Henry Ford as it did about Detroit attitudes. By 1970 there were more and more indications that he was tired of running the company. There had been the possibility of his going to work in the Johnson administration as a kind of ambassador to the business community, but that had fallen through when Johnson had been driven out of office. So he had kept on at Ford, and though he refused to think of retirement, the job was clearly wearing him down. He much preferred now to travel and do business in Europe rather than in America, and he probably spent more time at the European plants than at those in the United States. In Europe he was treated like royalty (and spent much of his time with royalty and semiroyalty). Crowds might gather outside a restaurant where he was dining just to catch a glimpse of him —the personification of a great industrial empire, whose name was on a famous product. In America it was different; when he visited a factory, it was unlikely that even the local mayor would turn out, and indeed any meeting with a local official could turn quickly into a recitation of petty grievances. He seemed increasingly interested in the fact that he had a place in history, and above all in his connection to the first Henry Ford. The men around him soon learned that one of the easiest ways to win him over to a particular idea was to mention that, oddly enough, it was something that his grandfather had been interested in. He liked that. They were linked, the two of them, for they were the only two men who had run the Ford Motor Company. When he talked about the Ford Motor

Company with close friends, he referred to it as a sacred trust. It had been created by his own family and handed to him in terrible shape, and he was proud of the fact that he had resurrected it and sustained it as a great and successful enterprise for a quarter of a century. His era was far less congenial to privilege and authority than that of his grandfather. It had been his contradictory duty not just to preserve and extend the best of the past but to undo the darker part of the past as well. It was important that he not look like a bigot, that he be as humane as possible in his treatment of labor. He must be a modern, enlightened businessman, alert at all times to the new social complexities required of that role. The UAW understood this about him quite well. It was sometimes said that when the union wanted more money it threatened to strike GM because GM was so shamelessly profitable, but when it wanted a social principle it threatened to strike Ford, because young Henry Ford was haunted just enough by the past to make the company vulnerable. He prided himself on having the common touch, and he did have it, an almost intuitive sense of how to talk to ordinary workers in a language they were comfortable with. But no one privy to that part of him, that *role*, particularly the men around him, was to mistake it for a genuine expression of self. He might be the seigneur with the common touch, but he was first and foremost the seigneur, and the terms were always his.

He wanted strong and forceful men around him, but his relationships with them were always imbalanced: They had to earn their position with him and charm him, but he did not have to earn his position with them or charm them. Few men in American business were so spoiled. The toys were always his, and the rules were always his. Men rose and fell in his favor. He played them off against each other with skill, and it was often said of Ford that it could be a great company if half the top people there did not spend most of their time plotting against each other, usually with Henry's encouragement. Executives watched carefully to see who had Henry Ford's ear, who dined with him, who traveled abroad with him. Some young men coveted the chance to make those trips, the opportunity to be with the chairman in the 747 for six or seven hours, talking intimately with him; but others, more experienced at the game, warned their more junior colleagues against them. The trips, they warned, were minefields, all that intimacy over many glasses of Pommard. They tended to loosen the tongues of the younger men, not the tongue of the chairman. Even if the chairman was indiscreet, the next morning he would still be the head of the Ford Motor Company. For the company was different from other industrial firms in that the founding family still ruled. It was governed, one observer noted, by an odd combination of the most sophisticated of management techniques that the Harvard Business School could supply and a regal whimsy reminiscent of Versailles, the capriciousness of an erratic although intelligent king attended by ambitious courtiers.

For a long time he had managed to keep his behavior as head of the company distinct from his behavior in his private life, but in the late sixties and early seventies that began to change. Perhaps it was the increasing pressures from the government, from citizens' groups, and from labor unions; there were too many people telling him what he could not do, he said to friends, and it was simply no longer fun to be a business executive. Sometimes, he added, he felt besieged. In any case, his personal life was beginning to deteriorate.

When he was a younger man, it had been fairly staid. In 1940, at the age of twenty-two, he had married in the class from which he had sprung. Anne McDonnell, daughter of moneyed New York Irish, one of fourteen children, was perfect for a man who wanted his social life to be an extension of his professional life and perfectly in order. No one, her friends thought, would run a great house better. She was attractive, knew the correct thing to do, and suited Henry's station in life precisely. Theirs was a formal home. Dinner parties were often black tie. They did not see people from the company socially, or, with a few exceptions, from the auto world. They saw, as his parents before them had seen, the good and civilized people of Grosse Pointe, people like themselves. Henry and Anne were considered a lovely couple, respectful of each other, though there was a certain restraint about their relationship, as if they did not quite know each other.

It was a servant-dominated world. (Henry's son, Edsel, once said in an interview that the most influential person in his life was his French nanny, Zellie—a nickname taken from Mademoiselle—a statement that irritated his mother no small amount.) The rules for his children, as they had been for him, were rigid. They could be seen but they would not be heard. Dinners with them were served by butlers in tailcoats, the tables beautifully set and candlelit, the food presented course by course—all of it precisely the way children do not want to eat. Henry and Anne, as leaders of the community, often went to benefits and fund-raisers.

During the early 1960s some of Henry's friends began to sense he was growing restless with this routine. When he went to the charity benefits that she sponsored, he managed now to signal to his buddies that he had attended under protest, that he was there in body but not in soul. "What a bunch of shit this is," he told a friend at one affair. The friend sensed that the era of Henry Ford as the stalwart of Grosse Pointe fund-raisers had come to an end. He was engrossed every day in the work of the company, and he was bored at night. For all its incalculable comforts, his life was typically suburban. He wanted more fun and excitement. He began to feel entitled to mix with more interesting people, the most interesting people anywhere, and not just on occasion but all the time. His role model, his closest friends thought, became Gianni Agnelli of Fiat. There were parallels between the two. They had both taken over their family's auto companies, they had both done well. But there the parallels stopped. Agnelli had fun. He was an international celebrity, not just because he owned an auto company but because he was a figure in European social circles. He had houses at all the most exclusive watering holes of Europe, saw the most sophisticated people of two continents, and was a part of the emerging world of beautiful people. Henry Ford was not part of that world. He was a social leader of Detroit and Grosse Pointe. He was tired of it.

In the mid-1960s he fell in love with Cristina Vettore Austin. An Italian, she was beautiful, vital, exuberant, and a member of the jet set. His wife watched their increasingly public affair with mounting distaste, hoping that it would soon run its course. When it did not, when the two kept seeing each other quite openly in New York (where Cristina stayed at an apartment he paid for), Anne Ford did what was repugnant to her—she was a serious Catholic—and filed for a divorce. It was an acrimonious and expensive parting. Estimates placed the settlement at around $15 million. Years later, after she had married a lawyer named Deane Johnson and moved to California and was starting a new life, she told an old friend that she did not know what to do with her time.

"Why don't you get involved in things like benefits?" he suggested. "After all, you were so good at that in Detroit."

"Oh dear," she said, with some pain in her voice. "That's what cost me Henry."

Henry and Cristina were married in 1965. For a time that marriage was enjoyable. But his old life and his new life were not easily merged. When a large party was given in their honor in Detroit, all his old friends attended, and many of their new friends flew in from New York. Each group stood on its side of the room, and no one seemed eager to cross over; it was, said one person present, like a chess game where no one moves any of the pieces. His own family never accepted her. "The pizza queen," Edith Ford, wife of Henry's brother Benson, called her. Soon the people they saw were younger. Ford cars went to Le Mans and won there. Henry Ford was seen at the fashionable spots of Europe, being raucous, having more fun than Agnelli had ever had. It was, it now seemed, not so much that he had been restless with a woman but restless with a life.

His first marriage had lasted more than twenty years, but his second marriage soon turned sour. He had married Cristina because he was fed up with his Detroit life. But having gained a faster one, he was no happier. The disintegration of the marriage was surprisingly quick. Within three years he was complaining openly about her. He sometimes seemed embarrassed by her and her friends. Once on a European trip he called down to the hotel room where Bunkie and Florence Knudsen were staying. "Can you come up here and have dinner with me?" he asked, somewhat plaintively. "I need you—I've got nothing around me but Italians." The jet-set life, he told friends, was less fun than people thought. A lot of these people were pretty empty. In those years he was sometimes like a lonely little boy, often eating by himself in his huge Grosse Pointe house as Cristina traveled in Europe. When she was home, things weren't much better. She had begun to grate on him. What had once pleased him about her, her willingness to break convention, her candor, now began to pall. She was too open, too exuberant, too intrusive; she wanted too much of him.

She was no happier. She had married a jet-setter, but her jet-setter lived in the American Midwest. She had tried liking Detroit, but it was not an easy city for her. There was nothing in the city that would have drawn her there of her own accord. She had come because of a man, but when Henry Ford was in Detroit he worked very long hours and had little time for her. In Europe she had found him amusing. In Detroit he seemed less amusing. When he came home he wanted to eat simply and watch television, she complained to friends. Her life, she added, was one of exercising, walking the dogs, and going to beauty shops. She tried sculpting, with no success. She started showing up in the company of Imelda Marcos, the wife of the Philippine dictator. The Ford staff in New York complained that she was giving immense amounts of wine from the Ford apartment at the Waldorf to Mrs. Marcos and her security people. As Henry Ford with his vast power had been able to scorn conventional attitudes, now she, from her comparable position of power, was paying just as little attention.

For someone who took his manliness as seriously, indeed as self-consciously, as Henry Ford, who liked to boast in classic locker-room style of his conquests and of the appetites of his women, it was a humiliating time. Their fights, often fueled by alcohol, were ugly. High Ford executives tried hard not to be caught between the two of them, for a business-social luncheon might end with a ride during which Cristina would start yelling at him. "Why are you always traveling?" she once screamed at him. "Why don't you stay home at all?"

"Why don't you go play with your new Greek friends?" he answered.

He was becoming boorish in public more frequently now. In 1966 he joined a group of other leading corporate executives for a tour of Eastern Europe sponsored by *Time* magazine. The idea was that the businessmen would meet important officials, various diplomats, and American and foreign journalists, and come away with a more sophisticated view of the Soviet bloc—and that they would also be duly grateful to *Time*. From the start Henry Ford was a nuisance, behaving like a boozy sophomore. One executive had a memory of Ford drunkenly careening down the main street of Budapest shouting, "All I want is to be loved." He seemed preoccupied not with the problems of détente but with the functions of the body. At a certain point he decided he had fallen in love with a young woman in *Time*'s Vienna bureau, and he insisted that she make the rest of the tour with the group. Peter Forbath, who was then the Vienna bureau chief, informed him that the young woman would not be able to go to Bucharest, for she was needed in Vienna and did not speak Rumanian. Henry Ford then threatened to cancel all of the Ford advertising in *Time*.

"I think you should cancel all of your advertising in all of our magazines," Forbath said, undaunted. Forbath and a somewhat mutinous Ford drove to the airport together, where Ford sought out Dick Clurman, who was *Time*'s chief of correspondents and in charge of the tour. Again Ford announced his intention of canceling his advertising.

"That's certainly fine with me, Henry," Clurman answered. Ford stalked off, still quite angry.

Ten minutes later he came back to see Clurman. "Doesn't anyone in this damn operation care if I cancel all my advertising?" he asked.

"Well," said Clurman, "there's Bob Gordon over there, and he's in charge of advertising, and I'm sure he'd be interested. Powerless, probably, but interested certainly."

"Oh, the hell with it," Ford said and stomped off. That night, however, he told Clurman he knew he had been behaving badly, that it was a valuable trip, and that he was going on the wagon.

On another occasion, after a board meeting, he had indulged in some heavy drinking and then decided that he needed to attend to his friend Sidney Weinberg's sex life. Weinberg was well into his seventies then. Ford had turned to a bright rising executive and pointed to Weinberg and said, "I want you to go out and get a girl for him." The young man had looked puzzled. "Goddammit, I said go out and get a girl for him," the chairman of the Ford Motor Company insisted.

The young man searched until he found a more senior colleague. "What the hell do I do?" he asked.

"You go to bed, and you hope like hell that when Henry Ford wakes up he's forgotten about it. If he hasn't forgotten, you tell him you looked far and wide, but there were no ladies worthy of the honor. If he doesn't accept that, you start looking for another job."

That sort of dilemma, as another colleague later explained to him consolingly, was part of the special privilege of being at Ford. There were many moments like that, and they were hard on those who worked for the company.

Ford's drinking and carousing seemed to increase, putting even more stress on his system. He had started seeing an attractive young woman named Kathy DuRoss. She was a local girl who had had a very hard life —she had been widowed at nineteen and left with two young children when her husband was killed in an auto accident—and who did some modeling in the city. She was both strong and earthy—earthy American, unlike Cristina, who was earthy European. ("My father," said Charlotte Ford, "falls for strong, tough cookies.") A handful of his close friends knew he was seeing her, but others didn't. Don Frey noticed that the company was frequently hiring a certain brunette as a model in auto shows. "Why do we keep using that same girl?" he asked a colleague.

"Don," was the reply, "there are some questions you just don't want to ask and that I don't want to answer."

Ford's double life ended one night in February 1975, when a California highway patrolman saw a car swerving back and forth, pulled it over, and arrested its driver, Henry Ford, for drunken driving. In the car with him was Kathy DuRoss. The secret was out, and the marriage to Cristina was effectively over.

In the final days of the marriage there was considerable meanness displayed on both sides. Cristina, humiliated that another woman could do to her what she had done to Anne Ford, threw him out of the Grosse Pointe house, and Henry was forced to use the apartment in the Glass House, the Ford international headquarters. Unfortunately the apartment was rather small, and there was no room for his immense wardrobe. So his valet kept his clothes in a Ford van parked down in the lot and simply moved a few suits up for his perusal each day—it was somewhat as if the head of the Ford Motor Company were living out of a recreational vehicle. Henry sneaked into their house while Cristina was in Rome and took out about $2 million worth of their best antiques; she sued to keep him from selling them at Sotheby Parke Bernet. He won; he explained that he was only trying to make his holdings a little more liquid.

His divorce from Cristina threatened to be a good deal messier than that from Anne. Cristina subpoenaed a vast variety of people who knew about her husband's personal life and about Kathy DuRoss. But just as the case was to go to trial a private settlement was made. Each, it seemed, had a good deal to hide. The star of the trial turned out to be neither Cristina nor Henry but an inspired process server named Wylie Cossar, who explained in considerable detail how he had served the great of Detroit with their subpoenas. He had, for example, rung Kathy DuRoss's door carrying an enormous gift-wrapped box, asked her to sign for it, and, when she did, told her she had just signed a subpoena to testify in the divorce proceedings. In the end Cristina Ford received about $16 million, almost the same amount as her predecessor, albeit for a far shorter time with Ford. Henry was now free to marry Kathy DuRoss.

At Ford in those years he was still in charge, but more sporadically, coming and going, making a show of running the company, then disappearing, if it suited him, much to the annoyance of Iacocca and others who were actually running it. There would be bursts of energy followed by prolonged absences. Some of his top people thought it would have been better if he let go of the company completely, but he was unwilling to do that. Much admired by his executives when he was in his forties and early fifties, he now struck some of them as more of a dilettante. He no longer listened to a wide variety of voices; he would pick out only two or three men—courtiers, some of his critics within the company thought, chosen more for their social grace than their auto expertise—and listen to them exclusively. Others, less fortunate, felt cut off, for people whom Henry Ford did not listen to did not have power in the Ford Motor Company.

His friends thought he was worn out. He was conservative in part because he was tired. There was, his friends thought, a certain inevitable erosion from that many years as the head of so large a company. Other chief executives, in the new managerial age, spent five or at the most ten years at the top and then were gone. The burnout rate was very high, and a man who gave a company ten years was considered unusual. The fatigue of running so big and complicated a company in so difficult an atmosphere was beginning to show. He was tired of dealing with the government and even more with the new consumer groups. Business was harder to conduct in the seventies than it had been in the fifties. There were more pressures, more claimants demanding to share his power, less room for him to maneuver in. That which had been fun was less fun; that which was exciting had all happened before. Gradually, Henry Ford had grown old running his own company.

Within the company he became more churlish and contentious. His attention span seemed briefer. In the past at critical meetings he had always enjoyed playing the negative role, the devil's advocate, making the younger men around him prove their point. That was fine, it placed them on the defensive, and they had to work that much harder to prove their cases. In the end he would come across, he would almost always say, *Okay, but you'd better sell 'em.* Now, however, he was becoming much more conservative, his opposition to innovation was stronger, and there was less play-acting in the querulousness. William Clay Ford, his brother, became worried about him. Because he had never divorced and never had had to split up his holdings, Bill Ford owned more stock in the company than Henry, but he had chosen not to be a power there on the theory that there should be only one Ford making decisions. Now he began to talk to his close friends about his brother's drinking and impulsive behavior and wavering attention. He was in great anguish about it, but he could not bring himself to move against Henry or to use his stock as a genuine lever of power (despite the urgings of Iacocca, who at the very least later wanted him to use it to take out Philip Caldwell).

Henry Ford, on his part, sometimes seemed now to resent the burden put on him, the responsibility not just for the company and his own immediate family but for all the Fords. Occasionally, with close friends, he would slip into monologues touched with self-pity. *He* was the one who was doing all the work, carrying the family, while his brothers and sisters did damned little except take their dividends. Everyone, he said, claimed he was the playboy, and that was unfair. He was the one who worked while the others played. The worst thing, he would say, was the next generation, which had more power than his. Thirteen grandchildren, seven of them girls, and only six boys. Women will fuck up everything, he said. Then he would enumerate companies which he believed had been destroyed by the ascent of women to power. A few minutes after one of these monologues, he would be himself again, the conservator, responsive to the call of duty. Although he had less grasp of the company's day-to-day affairs, partly because he was not on hand as much, he nevertheless wanted to be as controlling a figure as in the past, when he had worked hard.

Inside the company, both Iacocca on the car side and Lundy on the finance side were consolidating their power. They were strong men moving in a partial vacuum. They were very careful not to offend each other; Iacocca was especially careful, for he knew that Lundy spoke for Henry Ford's real interests and those of the Ford family. Yet others watching them, knowing how different the two men were and how opposed their real interests were, Iacocca wanting to spend money and Lundy wanting to save it, believed there would be a time when their two armies would meet. Iacocca was unceasingly working to expand his authority, dominating the product side, becoming more visible all the time. He had never been a man to turn away from power and visibility, and now people checked things with him rather than with Henry. He had always been connected to the dealers, their man in Detroit. Then the production people, frustrated by the conservatism of finance, depended on him. Now even the board members, increasingly concerned about Henry, would take him aside and confide their doubts. There were more and more meetings where Iacocca was the central figure, in complete control of all aspects of the subject under discussion, and where Henry Ford seemed to dissolve into the background.

In any real sense, although Iacocca and Lundy might struggle over product and investment, Lundy had already won. Iacocca was working not off norms that he set himself but off norms set by Lundy. The PIPs were a good example of that; they reflected almost perfectly a product man, working within ever narrower confines, carrying out finance's mandates. Iacocca's best cars in that period, even going back to the Mustang, were patched cars. He was at once frustrated and successful. He got on surprisingly well with Lundy on the personal level, and there were those who knew Lundy well and thought he was a man of divided loyalties as the tensions between Ford and Iacocca mounted. His nominal loyalty was to Henry Ford, whose behavior was bothersome and often unsavory, but he knew Iacocca was saving the company. Iacocca for his part was even more divided. He had the job he had always wanted, he was handsomely rewarded, and yet his power was in decline. From 1971 through 1973, before the first oil shock, even as his relationship with Henry Ford began to disintegrate, he averaged $800,000 a year in salary and bonus.

That was also the period in which Lee Iacocca, who had prided himself on loyalty, began to feel scornful of Henry Ford. In Iacocca's mind, he, not Ford, was running the company. This was confirmed to him regularly by everyone he knew, including members of the board and Ford's own brother, Bill. Where once he had been grateful to Ford for reaching down and picking him out, now that gratitude had lapsed. There was some lingering bitterness over the Bunkie Knudsen affair, and that too had diminished Iacocca's sense of obligation. Less and less did he think, as he had some fifteen years earlier, that he was lucky that the company had treated him so well; more and more he felt that the *Fords* were lucky— that he was there operating the company for them while they indulged themselves. He was carrying them, making them look good. In any other company save this one, he would tell close friends, he would have been running the show completely. Ford would be gone. No non-family-dominated company would tolerate behavior like his. The dynamic, to some observers, was not a happy one. For a variety of personal reasons Henry Ford was pulling back from the company, and the more he pulled back, the more dominant Iacocca became in its daily affairs. Then, when Ford noticed that everyone was checking with Iacocca, going to him for decisions, Ford became annoyed. Henry Ford was not going to stop Iacocca from running the company—he had come to depend on him—but he was not going to like him for doing it.

At first the signs of tension between the two men were barely detectable even to those at the top level of the company. Only a few men who were unusually close to one or the other picked up on it. It was not much, perhaps just a quick cutting comment that one might make about the other in an atmosphere of total privacy. Soon the signs grew a bit more obvious. They were picked up by the respective retinues, those who not only worked with each of them but traveled with them. It was a change in body language—Iacocca no longer quite as much at ease with Henry Ford, straining to please him, working harder to be himself in Ford's presence. In the past, when Iacocca had deferentially referred to the chairman as Mr. Ford in front of everyone else, it was deference born of confidence. Now when Lee called him Mr. Ford, there was a certain artificiality to it, as if he were somehow groping for the right tone. They seemed like men apart.

Nothing emphasized this more than their trips to Europe. Ford of Europe was important to the company because it represented important revenues, but it was important as well because it was territory that Henry Ford enjoyed visiting and where his prestige and fame seemed more tangible. Within the company the jobs in Europe were always considered plums, because they provided exceptional access to Henry Ford, far beyond what comparable jobs in America might offer. In Detroit, Iacocca and Ford would work long hours and then at the end of the day go their respective ways; if there were great social differences between them, they were largely invisible. Traveling abroad, however, where work and social life were mixed, the differences of class showed themselves. Ford went by commercial 747, which he considered safer; Iacocca took the customized 727, because he loved its elegance and loved being in charge, delighted in telling the friends who accompanied him that when he was a kid growing up in Allentown he would never have dreamed that he would be flying across the ocean in his own jet, being served a perfect steak and a perfect drink by his own steward. In that moment it was *his* plane, not Henry Ford's.

Once they were on the ground, the differences were even more sharply drawn. Henry Ford would sit night after night at dinner in various Ford company dining rooms with his favorites from Ford of Europe, who, the Iacocca people complained, tended to be tweedier and more social than the American executives and who, because of Ford's love of Europe, seemed to have his ear more than they did. At the same time and often in the same dining room Iacocca was having dinner with his buddies from Detroit—Hal Sperlich, Gene Bordinat, and Bill Benton—whom he had brought along, and as often as not, with the pilot and the crew of the plane. It was as if Lee had taken his own slice of Detroit with him to Europe. Iacocca, so formidable at home, went to Europe with his own troops because he was ill at ease there. For him it was an alien place, and he was oddly shy, once again the little Italian kid and thus in need of the reassurance of his own men. But that irritated Henry Ford, for it raised again the issue of a company within a company. The sight of these two men with their two separate retinues, sitting apart in a Ford dining hall in Europe, was, thought one Iacocca friend, a reflection of a split between the men of function and the men of class. Ford and Iacocca, who shared responsibility for one of the greatest industrial empires in the world, seemed at these moments two strangers who had been thrown together by chance. It was clear only in retrospect, the Iacocca friend noted years later, that Henry Ford wanted to spend as little time with Lee Iacocca as possible and that Iacocca, highly sensitive to any slight, realized he was failing some kind of social test.

The first shot in what was to become an increasingly bitter seven-year struggle between them was fired in 1972. At issue was the question of who would head Ford of Europe. It was an important job within the company, especially since Iacocca, now reigning in Detroit, regarded Europe as a rival and as yet unconquered principality. Iacocca tried to put in his own man. It was an aggressive move and an exceedingly political one, for it showed that Iacocca was not content with the status quo and wanted even more power. Iacocca's choice for the job was Hal Sperlich. Sperlich, with the departure of Don Frey, was the most important product man within the company. He was fiercely committed to making good cars and equally committed to Iacocca, willing to take on anyone, including the chairman, in the passion of his cause. He was a good, sound engineer who did little in the way of original engineering (he had almost no patents to his name), but he could talk with the engineers and could visualize a car as readily as they; at the same time, he was at least as much a businessman as a product man. Sperlich had played an important part in the birth of the Mustang, watching over it day and night as it neared production, living in his office, seldom going home. He had always been boyishly eager and ambitious. In 1957, relatively new to Ford, he worked in product planning with a man named Jim Cappolongo under him. Cappolongo came in at seven-thirty one morning only to find that Sperlich had arrived at seven twenty-five. The next morning Cappolongo arrived at seven only to find that Sperlich had gotten there at six fifty-five. The next morning Cappolongo, determined to beat him, arrived at five forty-five only to find that Sperlich had come at five-thirty. Finally they made a truce, agreeing on a joint arrival time, and they joked about it for years, the zeal of the young.

Sperlich came from a family where hard work was a given. His grandfather had been a skilled carpenter, his father a plumber, good Germanic men of tools. Sperlich himself had been born on the east side of Detroit, but the family had moved to Saginaw, Michigan, when he was young. His mother had been orphaned when she was very young, and she was a conservative person who, having known difficult times, was leery of anybody who promised an easier life. She was strong, diligent, and careful; a nickle was to bring five pennies' worth of value and nothing less. His drive, he suspected, came from her. She might have married a plumber, but her son would be more than that. The most basic premise in her strict Lutheran household was that her son Hal was going to do very well in school so he could go to college. "I knew that I was going to go to the University of Michigan and become an engineer," Sperlich once said, "before I knew where the University of Michigan was and what an engineer did." He had fulfilled the ambitions of his parents in no small part because he did not dare fail this woman who had invested so much in his life and who monitored his progress in meeting her standards so carefully. Upon graduation he had taken a job with Alcoa in Kensington, Pennsylvania, and then he had gone off to the navy for three and a half years. When he returned, he had tried Ford.

Sperlich's rise meant that Iacocca was protected on the technical side. His connection to Iacocca served both of them well. Sperlich's skills shored up Iacocca in the area where he was weakest, the actual engineering of product, and Iacocca offered Sperlich the best chance within the company to turn new ideas into automotive reality. It sometimes seemed as if there was a father-son relationship between the two of them, even though Sperlich was not that much younger than Iacocca. Sperlich, at once so talented and so loyal, was almost singular in the company in that he was allowed to argue openly with Iacocca. The others, even those in Lee's own gang, if they wanted to dissent, did so privately, but Sperlich, fearless and impetuous in everything, did it openly and joyously. He was even, upon rare occasion, allowed to make fun of Iacocca. One morning Iacocca walked into the design room wearing an unusually loud checked suit. Sperlich turned and said, "What kind of a clown wears a suit like that?" The others in the room shivered, for *no one* talked to Lee like that. But Iacocca even managed to smile. It was impossible for the other product men to get angry with him. He was simply too enthusiastic. Even as a young man he had a special ebullience, the pure pleasure of someone who is doing exactly what he wants to do. Once, coming upon two subordinates arguing over whether to go ahead on a particular part, he had asked them what the cost was. Fifty thousand dollars, one of them said. "That's nothing but pocket change," he had said. "Go ahead." All good designs, his and those of competitors, excited him. "Look at that," he once said, pointing to a new hot GM car. "Lovely, just lovely—like a bowl full of tits."

Sperlich sometimes even seemed to mimic Iacocca: If Iacocca was angry with a colleague and cut him off, then Sperlich did too; if Lee began to warm a little again, so did Hal. Sperlich was Lee's favorite, and his trust in Iacocca was complete. He had been protected in the past, and, he presumed, would be protected in the future. Because he was shielded by Iacocca and because he was so gifted, Sperlich was an anomaly at Ford. Ford was a corporate place, and Sperlich was the antithesis of the corporate man. The company was filled with more and more bright young men from the nation's business schools, careful and cautious and able, who knew how to play the game and knew when to talk and when not to, who never made mistakes and above all avoided combat. They could destroy a car or a career without any confrontation, without even raising their voices, while in fact seeming to praise the car or its architect. Sperlich was different. He argued with everyone, spoke when he had not been spoken to, and seemed to have no respect for the pecking order. He did not modulate his voice if he was addressing superiors, including Henry Ford. The finance people, almost to a man, hated him, not only because he fought with them but because he did not fight in the modern style, as they often did, deftly and coldly, behind closed doors; he fought openly and furiously. The exception was Lundy, who, far above Sperlich in rank, seemed almost amused by his combativeness. He took, however, a small revenge by pretending he could never quite remember Sperlich's name. "I like that young man of yours, Lee," he would say. "You know the one—tell me his name. He's certainly feisty."

Warnings failed to moderate Sperlich. He believed that if the Ford Motor Company was to be truly open and regenerative, it had to be receptive to ideas, and that meant people should feel free to push ideas that might seem strange as well as the orthodox ones. Unless the company at least considered them seriously, no one would know which had been the good ideas and which the bad. (Once years later, after Sperlich had left Ford, David E. Davis, the auto writer, mentioned his name rather positively to Don Petersen, a top Ford executive. Petersen sneered. "Sperlich," he said. "I protected Hal Sperlich from hundreds of mistakes. When he was leaving Ford, I called him in and I showed him a desk drawer filled with ideas that I had saved him from, bad ideas, and I told him wherever he went next he'd better be more careful, because there would be no one to protect him from his own mistakes.") Sperlich was combative by nature, and when it was clear that a certain idea was dead and that the subject was closed, Sperlich would pursue it—almost, his friends thought, for the pleasure of provoking the finance people. It was as if, although he knew they were going to win and the dice were loaded, he nonetheless liked to taunt his opposition and expose the weakness of their positions.

Many of the finance people truly hated him. In the Ford company there were all sorts of unwritten rules about the acceptable level of confrontation at meetings, and Sperlich alone never seemed to play by the rules. Under normal circumstances he might have perished in the company much earlier, but his connection to Iacocca made him untouchable. To some of the financial people his abrasiveness was the true symbol of Iacocca's arrogance. Thus Iacocca's attempt to place Sperlich in the top job in Europe was a fascinating political gambit. It was not just an attempt to insert his own man in this rival kingdom; it was also an attempt to keep Henry Ford and finance from having their man there.

Henry Ford quickly shot the nomination down. He was already nervous about Iacocca's power within the company, and he did not like Sperlich. Henry Ford had felt Sperlich's disrespect in the past (and disrespect it was, for Sperlich disliked a man who, in his view, cared so little about making cars), and he was in no mood to give him the European crown. It was, he suspected, a frontal challenge disguised as a routine matter. Instead he appointed Phil Caldwell as chairman of Europe and Bill Bourke as president. Both were potential rivals of Iacocca (who saw Bourke as a threat and scorned Caldwell). This was the first open move in the grim chess game that now began between the two men. It revealed the limits that Henry Ford intended to impose upon Lee Iacocca: He could continue to do what he was doing, and that would be all.

Iacocca no longer saw Ford as the man who had advanced Lee Iacocca's career; he had become the man who stood in Lee Iacocca's way. Because Iacocca was so much the embodiment of the self-made man, it was difficult for him to appreciate anyone who was not, even someone who, though he might have had greater advantages, had equally exhausting responsibilities. Iacocca spoke to close friends now about spoiled Wasp bastards and about little prick princes born to the cloth who had never opened a fucking door for themselves in their entire lives. Within the company, even among his closest friends, Iacocca was still relatively discreet. Few members of his inner group realized the degree to which a breach had opened. He spoke openly, however, with a man named Alejandro De-Tomaso, an auto executive of Argentinian and Italian origins who, operating out of Rome, had put together several small European automobile companies in Europe, which Ford had subsequently bought. Henry Ford had then turned against DeTomaso and had forced Iacocca to sever Ford's relations with him. Iacocca had done that, but the incident had strengthened his own personal relationship with DeTomaso, bonded as they were by their feelings about Henry Ford. When Iacocca was with DeTomaso and a few associates in Rome, he seemed to be freer of the restraints of Detroit, and he was more rancorous about Henry Ford. Ford didn't know a goddam thing about the business or what he was doing, he said. The problem now was in minimizing the damage he did to the company. He was dumb, goddam dumb. The problem with the auto industry, Iacocca complained, was the dumb third-generation people like Henry Ford, family representatives trying to run their companies long after the brains had been bred out of them. Then he would complain about the minor humiliations visited upon him—he had to check in to use the airplane, like a goddam schoolboy needing a pass to go to the bathroom.

Nor was this all idle talk. Iacocca and DeTomaso were talking about Iacocca's leaving Ford and setting up a rival company. At first they spoke of combining several small European companies and connecting that unit to American Motors as the flagship company with Iacocca in charge. The result would be a huge international company with an expandable American base. Iacocca was interested, but he did not think American Motors was an adequate foundation. He suggested they go after Chrysler instead, and for a time they seriously considered it. Chrysler was strong enough in its essential resources—its plants and its dealer system—to be attractive, and at the same time sufficiently mismanaged to be available. They did some sniffing around, and for a time they spoke about making a run on the Chrysler stock. Then in 1973 Chrysler started coming back, its stock went up, and the plan fell through. But the idea had been seriously entertained, which showed how restless and alienated Iacocca had become.

The Ford company, as the critical decade of the seventies began, was a divided company, much of its energy wasted in power struggles. It was also a sterile company living smugly off its past. The people running Ford were saying in effect that they were so good and their own customers so satisfied and docile that they had only to meet their own existing levels. It was a static world, premised on standard volume. Ford's customers would stay faithful because they had always stayed faithful.

As Henry Ford became more conservative, Ed Lundy inevitably became even more powerful. He was the beneficiary of the age they lived in. The company was no longer young, it was middle-aged, and as it grew older its bureaucracy grew far faster than its creative parts. Besides, this was becoming a more difficult time in which to make money. The Vietnam War had produced a sharp increase in inflation, and as the cost of doing business rose, the price of a mistake also rose; therefore it became easier to continue to do what you were doing and innovate as little as possible. When an expensive new line of cars was proposed, Ed Lundy could talk about Wall Street's reaction or about what this might do to the bank rating—the danger that Ford might lose its triple-A rating with the banks. Those were magic words, and they stopped all discussion. Anything that made the Street nervous or threatened a bank rating could not be tolerated. The stock was particularly important in a company like Ford, where so much of the stock was family-owned. In other companies there were a variety of ways to measure success, but at Ford the stock was the very index of the family's wealth; if it was up, the family was richer, and if it was down, the family was poorer. In addition to the normal pressures for stock performance, an enormous new one appeared in the early seventies when the Ford Foundation began to diversify and to sell its Ford Motor Company stock. It was all done deftly, $1.37 billion in shares, unloaded with great skill so that the stock would not be depressed. In 1971, Ford shares worth $349 million were sold; in 1972, $466 million; in 1973, $275 million; and finally, in 1974, the last $282 million, emptying the foundation's portfolio of Ford stock. It was not a subject much talked about while it was happening, but it was something that everyone in the company was aware of; it hung over other deliberations, a reminder that this was not a time for Ford to be reckless and make mistakes.

Iacocca had his clique, and they were talented and loyal, but Lundy had something more powerful and cohesive—he had a genuine cadre. He had control of the personnel system, and over two decades he had placed his people in many key positions. His people were very good, and they knew the company as no one else did anymore. They were brilliant at getting the reports from the other departments, culling through them, and giving Lundy extraordinarily complete rundowns, so that when he went to meetings, he and his top deputies could always ask seemingly spontaneous questions that cut right to the core of any issue. The great sin for an aspiring finance man was to permit his boss to look unprepared at a critical meeting. Those who served him well were well rewarded. Lundy was a very tough taskmaster, but he was also extremely loyal to his own people. If a Lundy man made a mistake, even a serious mistake, he would be protected, it was believed, if the mistake reflected loyalty to finance. Lundy might switch the man to another area or recycle him in some way, but there would be a second chance.

What these cool young men were good at was the game of the company, for they were gifted gamesmen. They knew first and foremost how to keep their superiors happy. They understood the bottom line, and they understood how to find the weakness in any new proposal. They did not really know cars, but they knew the language of the company, and they were all quick studies. They were particularly skillful at putting the product men on the defensive. They were, said one product man years later, great counterpunchers. They never had to suggest or create, only to show the faults in others. They never stood for anything. They had no record.

Even within the world of finance they were unusually conventional and fearful of taking risk. Outsiders looking at the approaching dilemma of the Ford Motor Company, its rising labor cost, its incipient Asian competition, were puzzled that the company did not diversify more, hedging its bets and making itself less dependent on a whimsical, cyclical, and potentially endangered business like auto. Part of that reluctance came from Henry Ford, and part of it came from Ed Lundy. Ford himself was always wary of diversifying. "My grandfather made cars," he liked to say when the subject came up, "and I make cars." With Lundy it was a suspicion of worlds he did not know and could not readily quantify. Even the company's own financial advisers worried that Ford's investment policies were too cautious. One of the most trusted of these was Sidney Weinberg of Goldman Sachs, the man who had done the public offering. He came to Ford in the sixties with the suggestion that the company buy a very large share, perhaps as much as 49 percent, in an impressive but underfinanced Japanese company named Honda, which then made motorcycles. Honda, the outsider in the old-boy network of Japanese manufacturing, was always having trouble getting adequate financing. The idea of a connection to Ford appealed to Soichiro Honda, as it did to some of the Ford product men, for the originality of Honda's work was already well known, and Honda considered himself a disciple of the founder. But the finance staff turned it down cold. They wanted nothing to do with a motorcycle maker, least of all a Japanese motorcycle maker. Weinberg, they reported, was crazy; the motorcycle business was a dying one, the machines were unsafe, and it was highly likely that they would soon be banned in the United States. "Well," Weinberg said a few years later as Honda, without Ford financing, blossomed, "they always have so many facts, those finance people. I don't know. Maybe they have too many facts."

Ford also turned away, in the late sixties, from a chance to buy ABC at a bargain price. Henry Ford had no interest in it; if he was going to buy anything like that, it would be a large newspaper. Lundy wanted no part of it; he wanted to husband the company's resources, and he was nervous about the world outside, which was filled with secret dangers; opening the company to them might cause a dilution of his control. So on the rare occasion when Ford did buy a property, like Philco, the decision came as much as anything else from the fact that it was for sale very cheap. Philco, of course, became a disaster of the first order.

Their lack of a record elsewhere, their lack of practical experience, might have brought with it a certain modesty on the part of the finance people. This, however, was not the case. Few of them were afflicted by modesty. To the finance men their work was not abstract or their experience different from that of people who actually made things; in their minds they *were* the company. What they did was what the company did; they had only to look at their own superiors to see who held power and which values the Ford Motor Company rewarded. What they did not know they did not respect.

The result was a company living to a considerable degree off its past. But the great days of Detroit, when its success was almost automatic, were nearly over. The world was changing, and the American market was also changing. The men being hobbled by the financial people were the very ones upon whom the future of the company would depend. Ford was not responding, but its leadership was hardly alone. In the late seventies Jim Abegglen, the prominent American consultant in Japan, tried repeatedly to warn American firms of how good the Japanese had become. Eventually, at his suggestion GM executives deigned to meet with him and a few of his fellow Japanologists to talk about the Japanese automotive surge. His group included several men whom Abegglen considered stars—writer-historian Frank Gibney, Harvard sociologist Ezra Vogel, and Columbia sociologist Herbert Passin. GM had laid down the ground rules: Abegglen and his group could not talk about automobiles, since the GM people already knew about autos; instead they should tell the GM executives what Japan was like, the climate and so forth, and what the Japanese were like and why they worked so hard. The GM attitude, Abegglen remembered, was that there are these funny little people out there, and they're doing pretty well, better than we expected, so tell us a little bit about them. The meeting was all very pleasant; the visitors were picked up at the airport, driven to the GM headquarters, allowed to make their presentations, given a pleasant lunch, thanked very politely, and driven back to the airport. That was that. There was no give and take. The GM people never had to respond to what was being said—and indeed never heard the principal thing that, but for the ground rules, would have been said. Their world was about to crash down on them, Abegglen thought, and they didn't even know it.

29.
THE ALIENATED

By the early seventies there were a number of high executives in the auto industry who had detected what they considered to be clear signals that the industry was changing for the worse and about to enter a new and far more difficult era. These men were still a minority, for it was not an industry that lightly bred or promoted pessimists, but it was hard to argue with some of their calculations. They saw foreign competition becoming more serious as the Japanese gradually replaced the West Europeans as challengers to the United States. They saw American costs, especially labor costs, as increasingly burdensome. They were also worried about the new, more alienated generation of American workers.

Company executives were not the only ones concerned about the workers. Ironically, the UAW's leadership worried as well, for as the younger workers seemed more estranged from their jobs than were their predecessors, so too they were often more estranged from the UAW leadership. No one in the early seventies was more aware of the change in worker attitudes than Doug Fraser, then a UAW vice-president and, in everyone's mind, a sure president of the union when Leonard Woodcock, who had succeeded Reuther, reached mandatory retirement in 1974. Fraser was considered the most politically astute of the union's leaders, and he was well tuned to the growing iconoclasm of the new generation of workers as the powerful social forces then loose in America began to influence blue-collar workers.

It was part of the new American industrial dilemma: If the golden years were over, the social environment they created was not; there was a dynamic of high expectations that still existed among both managers and workers, and it was extremely difficult at every level of the company to change those expectations after almost thirty-five years of unbroken affluence. It was an industry where both sides, workers and managers alike, had come to expect an ever increasing market and ever higher pay. Coming off that extended cycle was like coming off a narcotic.

The workers whose memories went back to hard times were by and large, Fraser thought, easier to deal with; the workers who were the children of affluence, the young men who had come into the work force in the sixties, were different. As Fraser watched the change in the younger autoworkers during the seventies—the almost skeptical acceptance of their benefits from the union, their lack of gratitude, their alienation from aspects of American life that he revered—he sometimes thought that it might be a good thing if for a short period they had to lose what they had as union members and live as their predecessors had lived some forty or fifty years earlier. If they could stand in the shoes of a worker from the twenties and the thirties, Fraser speculated, they might value their benefits and their jobs a little more, and it might be healthier for everybody. Too much, he believed, was being taken for granted. What pained him most was not merely that the younger workers had no sense of what the older generation had won for them, but also that they frequently seemed to think that these benefits had been given to them by the company. Just handed out by benign companies.

Fraser was one of the men who spanned the generations at the UAW. Son of an old-fashioned socialist, he had suffered through the worst of the Depression as a boy, coming to manhood at a time when the union was just being formed. As a top aide to Reuther he watched as the UAW became one of the most powerful and admired institutions in America. He became its head just as the profound economic changes of the late seventies began to undermine both the industry and the union. (In the early eighties, a friend observed that Fraser had spent most of his adult life as Walter Reuther's unofficially designated successor, sitting next to the president through all those years of glory and expansion and waiting for his own chance to run the union, only to take over just as the good times were done and the job of the union leader became to minimize losses.

("You're like someone who takes over a great army just as it's in retreat," the friend said to Fraser, "and whose task is to carry the wounded off the battlefield."

(Fraser pondered the observation for a moment. "That is not a bad description of what happened," he finally said.)

His father, the son of a British officer in the Indian army, had been brought to America when he was seven. A socialist and trade-union man, he raised his son in a union home. Young Doug watched his father fired from job after job in Detroit and saw the family evicted from a house because his parents could not pay the rent. He lived as boy in a neighborhood of Polish and Irish immigrants, where, during the Depression, no one's father had a job. No one he knew as a boy ever went to college. Food was a problem in those years; the family was always a little hungry but, he decided in retrospect, never *very* hungry. On the worst days his mother bought stale bread for two cents a loaf (the storekeeper would slice through the wrapping paper so that you couldn't resell it), and she would soak the stale bread in water and then fry it with sliced onions. That was dinner. Years later, after times became much better, Fraser remembered those bread-and-onion dinners with considerable nostalgia, and once, a successful labor leader, he asked his mother to cook the dish again for him. She complied, and it tasted absolutely rotten. So much for nostalgia.

He was fired from his earliest jobs, first at Bryant Motors (where men were made to report every day without knowing if they would actually have work; often they sat around and waited and did not even make their carfare) and then at Everhot Heating, a company that made hot-water heaters. He often reflected that the greatest thing that the union had done for its members was not in the area of wages or pensions but in bringing a basic dignity to the daily lot of the worker. When he thought back to his days at Everhot, he did not think so much of the terrible pay, 33 cents an hour, or even the arbitrary way in which men were fired. He thought of the toilet. It was located in the center of the workplace, and it was made of glass above the waist so that a supervisor standing twenty yards away could tell how long a man had been inside. Fraser hated the glassed toilet. Compared to some of the other abuses in that age it was a small thing, and yet it symbolized to him the inhumanity inflicted on workers, as if they were subhuman. He hated working at Everhot. In 1936 right before the election the boss assembled all the workers and launched into a vitriolic anti-Roosevelt tirade. At the end he asked if there were any questions. No one said anything. A few weeks later, however, when Roosevelt won by a landslide, the workers came in early and papered the entire factory with headlines from the local papers.

Fraser was fired from Everhot for union activity. The work force was filled with stool pigeons in those days, and he had obviously talked to the wrong man. A foreman told Fraser he could save Fraser's job if Fraser would only stop working for the union. Fraser thanked him and instead started looking for another job. He found one with Chrysler, first at Dodge Main, and then at the DeSoto plant, where he was a metal finisher. In his first year there he worked one month and was laid off for the next eleven. He arrived at the height of the New Deal, when the autoworkers' union was just coming to power. Because he was young and literate and well-spoken, he quickly became a union leader. Most of his fellow workers were Poles and Italians who had trouble with the language, and they were less confident of their place both in America and in the factory. They were nervous about challenging authority; he was not.

In 1939, Fraser became the shift steward, the representative of some two hundred people. His job, he knew from the start, was to stand up to Ed Remsnyder, the general foreman in charge of all the other foremen. He was an intimidating figure. He kept his desk not in an office but on the plant floor. He never talked to the workers, and he never smiled. His power came from his silence, from the way that he sat at his desk, always scowling, his eyes surveying the plant. Periodically he would summon one of the foremen and point to a worker, and the foreman would return and either bawl out the worker or fire him. Everyone in the place, foremen and workers alike, was afraid of Remsnyder. It was not unusual for workers to switch to the second shift, with worse hours, in order to escape his gaze.

The New Deal had given far greater protection to workers, but it was as if the reach of Franklin Roosevelt and the New Deal fell just short of the territory governed by Ed Remsnyder. This was his domain. The laws here were his, as yet undiluted by modern labor legislation. If you came to work here, you left the New Deal outside. Only if Fraser could stand up to Remsnyder, he knew, would the workers take heart and would this plant become a civilized place. In 1940 he got his chance. Fraser's shift was working on fenders, and because of the poor quality of the steel and the poor stamping machines, the fenders always came out badly wrinkled. The job of Fraser's shift was to take the wrinkles out. It was the worst kind of backbreaking work. There was no shortcut to it. They could do fourteen a day, and barely that. Then Remsnyder announced that they had to increase their production and turn out sixteen a day. The anger among the men was intense; it was more than they could do. Fraser had an idea. He decided they should go to twelve fenders a day. It was critical, he told the other workers, that they give Remsnyder no excuse to retaliate against them and fire anybody. There could be no early quitting, no prolonged trips to the men's room. Everybody had to work as hard as before, but this time they would produce only twelve. For a week everyone on the shift followed Fraser's game plan to the letter. It was an invisible slowdown. The men all seemed hard at work, there was no detectable drop-off, and yet only twelve fenders a day were produced. Out of the corner of his eye Fraser could see Remsnyder watching the floor more closely than ever, scowling, calling his foremen over. Yet they could not pin anything on anyone.

After a week Remsnyder called Fraser over. He gave him a hard look. "Okay," he said, "you can keep it at fourteen."

It was Fraser's first victory as a labor leader, and his most precious one. From then on he knew that that was what he was going to be. He was smart and tough, and, unlike Reuther, who was always so serious, he had a deft charm that served him well. By the time he was twenty-six he was the head of a local.

That, Doug Fraser often thought, was a very different era. It was one of the ironies of American society that success and affluence loosened the ties that bound men and institutions. When he was young and poor, everyone had been united by hardship. He first started noticing the change in the attitude of the younger workers in the late sixties and early seventies. It was not something, he knew, that had happened overnight, he was sure it was cumulative, but at some point he and a few other members of his generation realized there was something of a crisis. Part of the change, he believed, was the effect of Vietnam and Watergate; there was a new skepticism, even cynicism, about all institutions. It had begun with the children of the upper middle class and had taken a little less than a decade for itself to work into the children of the working class. By the early seventies it was a problem for factory managers and union representatives. There was a new iconoclasm, a change in the nature of loyalties, and a new view of work and of money.

The older generation of workers had seen in their lifetimes the fruits of the UAW's negotiating victories. They owned their homes, had two cars and all the most modern kitchen appliances, and often owned boats and summer cottages. All this they associated with the UAW. The new generation, Fraser began to learn, was less thankful and more suspicious. Their alienation extended not just to the workplace but to the union as well. They accepted the results of negotiations not as victories but as a given. The comparison they made in their lives was not with a harsher America and a brutal workplace but with others who to them seemed to have a better deal—the college students who protested a war they did not have to go to, the company executives who made hundreds of thousands of dollars in salary and bonuses, the people they saw on television sit-coms who were rarely blue-collar and who seemed to have pleasant, middle-class jobs, nice suburban houses, and pretty wives and never had to go to work in a noisy, exhausting, spiritually depressing factory. Work seemed less important to these young people, and money seemed less important too. They complained above all of too many hours of work, of too much overtime. It was as if the local UAW officials were no longer their friends but their enemies.

Nothing brought it home more clearly to Fraser than an incident at Chrysler in the early seventies. Fraser was the head of the UAW's Chrysler division, Leonard Woodcock was still president of the union, and a UAW official named Cliff Earl had the job of meeting regularly with the membership listening to grievances. In the past that job had been prized, but by the early seventies, Earl was becoming increasingly shaky. The meetings, he said, had turned ugly. There was no pleasure in going before the locals. These men were supposed to be Cliff Earl's allies, his fellow workers, but they were treating him as a representative of a hostile force. The tone was surly, the mood often mutinous, and the anger often seemed focused on things the union was powerless to control. What these young men were complaining about—the larger frustrations of their lives—was beyond the reach of the UAW. What he actually could attain for them seemed unimportant to them. Finally he went to Fraser. "You've got to find me another job," he said. "I can't take it anymore." So Fraser had told Woodcock that that they to do something about Earl, that he was about to have a nervous breakdown, and a switch was made: Earl was given a job dealing with the problems of retired workers. He had in one moment switched not just jobs but generations. A few weeks later Fraser ran into Earl. "How do you like the new job, Cliff?" he asked.

"Wonderful, Doug," Earl said. "I was at a meeting for six hours yesterday, and would you believe it, no one called me a son of a bitch."

Fraser had plenty of evidence that a major change was taking place in attitudes toward work—for example, the company statistics displaying a sharp rise in absenteeism. But the glaring case in point was what happened in 1974 after he helped settle a strike against Chrysler at the Sterling Heights stamping plant. Because of the strike the Chrysler pipeline was dry, so Chrysler scheduled full shifts for both Saturday and Sunday, double time for everyone, which meant on each of those two days a worker could pick up an additional $100. That Saturday, Bill O'Brien, the Chrysler labor vice-president, called Fraser at home.

"Doug, you won't believe this goddam thing," he said, "but we're paying double time, and we've only got a fifty percent turnout."

"Jesus Christ, Bill, get me a pair of gloves," Fraser answered, "and I'll get out there myself."

The incident was important, for the indifference of the new worker toward the job and toward that much money was as much a puzzle to the employer as it was to the union leader. The new workers were less materialistic in a pure sense than the old ones, and less accepting of authority. Because of new techniques of birth control, they were not, as their parents and grandparents had been, heavily burdened by family responsibilities at an early age. Their wives often worked. There was often less dependence upon the paycheck. Around them a new white-collar, college-educated service society was rising, people who did not get their hands dirty or pay many dues, who made more money while never loosening their ties, and that tempered whatever gratitude they might have otherwise felt. A job on the line in an auto plant had always been a tough one, a son-of-a-bitch job in the vernacular, a job one did because there was no alternative and celebrated only because it paid much more than anything else that was available. Now more than ever it seemed to suffer by comparison with other work possibilities in America. More and more the men on the line suspected that everyone in America but them had some sort of deal going. The younger workers either had more options in life and were willing to exercise them or, in other cases, like that of the black workers at the Jefferson Avenue plant, they had very few options and were bitter about that.

Fraser himself liked to tell the story about a worker in the Chrysler stamping plant at Twinsburg, Ohio. A young diemaker there, who had just graduated from an apprenticeship program, had a terrible attendance record. He worked faithfully, but only four days a week. But the plant was on a full schedule, going seven days a week, and because of that there was a desperate shortage of diemakers. If it hadn't been for that shortage, Fraser was sure, the young man would have been fired. The foreman at the plant argued with the young man, cajoled him, tried everything. He finally turned to the plant manager in desperation. "You'd better talk to him," he said. "I can't get anywhere." So the plant manger went over to the young machinist and found him, in full working regalia, grinding down a part. The manager tapped the worker on the leg, indicating he wanted to talk to him. The worker flipped down his face shield.

"Why do you work only four days a week?" the manager asked.

"Because I can't make a living working three days a week," the young man said, and he flipped the shield back up and returned to work.

Attitudes like those were hard for men of Fraser's generation to understand. They had fought for the right to work every day, and for the benefits. On the carefully planned budgets of men and women with Depression mentalities, a day worth $100 was something to be cherished. It was hard for the UAW in the seventies to deal with the rising absenteeism and the rising alienation of its own people, their rebellion against the union itself. To the younger men, some critics of the UAW said, the union was the same as the company, simply the junior partner in a relationship filled with resentment, one more large, distant, insensitive institution.

Fraser was struck by the change. In the old days the role of the union leader was relatively easy. The times were harder, the rules more primitive, and it not been hard to rally the workers with a kind of us-against-them approach. Now it was different. Now you didn't try to be a labor boss, you tried to be a leader, and you listened more. You looked at the membership, he said, and hoped they were following you, not chasing you. He had a sense that the problem that the union faced was something that the nation as a whole faced; his life in the UAW had taught him that the factory was no different from the rest of the country but in fact was a microcosm of the country. That did not augur well, for these alienated, complacent workers, whether they knew it or not, were under challenge from purposeful, disciplined workers around the world, and their jobs and their whole way of life were in the balance. One memory kept recurring to Fraser. He was walking through a plant in Tokyo with a Japanese labor leader and a management official just as the workers were about to take their lunchtime break. Fraser checked the clock and could see that the workers were readying their lunches. Then the whistle blew. In America their little group would have been stampeded as the workers scrambled to get away from the workplace and go eat. But here the manager simply raised his hand as if to say stop, and everyone around them stopped. It was if they were frozen, no longer people but lifelike statues. Fraser's group passed through, and only then, when it was gone, did the workers come to life and go off to their break. In America, Fraser reflected, half with pleasure and half with melancholy, if a manager had tried the same thing, the members of the group all would have been knocked on their asses by the workers.

30.
CITIZEN NADER

One of the problems afflicting Henry Ford in those years was that he felt himself under attack, particularly by a government that he considered intrusive, one that seemed more and more determined to tell him what to make and how to make it, a government that seemed to prefer the word of outsiders—meddlers, in his view—to that of good professional businessmen like himself. Nothing symbolized that to him more than the rise of a young reformer named Ralph Nader. When Henry Ford was truly angry and speaking his inner truth, not the sanitized truths that came out of his public relations machinery, he turned to the subject of Nader with special vehemence.

Ralph Nader was thirty-two years old in 1966 when he took on General Motors. He was a solitary, distant, wary person who confided in no one and whose closest friends were amazed at how little they knew about him. A complete loner, without an institutional base such as a university appointment or an office in government, he was the most unlikely of young men to challenge a giant industry. Yet his timing was perfect. The auto industry was ripe for criticism, and many Americans, without knowing it, were ready for a citizen's challenge to an entity that for them had come to symbolize an increasingly haunting aspect of American life—bigness and power without apparent accountability.

In 1966 the American auto industry was at the absolute height of its power, so rich and mighty that its arrogance, its certainty that it *was* America, was almost unconscious. Its leaders were so carefully shielded from the world around them that when they sinned in the construction of the cars, they did not seek to correct the sin but rather sought to find the flaw in their accuser. At the same time the society had become so affluent that a broad-based consumer's protest—unthinkable in more difficult days, when people were grateful for jobs—had become a genuine possibility. Nader himself later described the consumer revolution he led as nothing less than a qualitative reform of the industrial revolution. It represented that to many members of the middle class and particularly to the upper middle class. (Almost all of Nader's most passionate recruits were from the upper middle class, in effect the children of the management class with which he was contending.) For them, more was no longer necessarily better; it was the quality of life that mattered—that and the responsiveness of large institutions, whether public or private.

It was as hard for Nader to understand the titans of Detroit as it was for them to understand him. He was constantly puzzled by their lack of feeling for their consumers, as he termed their customers. He could not see why they did not make cars safer or why they did not listen to their own engineers. They in turn were puzzled that someone so talented, so well educated—Princeton, Harvard Law—would want to knock the very system that was now open to him instead of taking his rightful place inside it, as they had taken theirs. Part of the conflict was generational. The top executives of Detroit were mostly men who as boys had suffered through the worst of the Depression, and many of them had lived difficult boyhoods. (Jim Roche, the head of GM, who was to be Nader's chief adversary there, had been orphaned at twelve and furthered his education by taking correspondence courses; Lynn Townsend, who was the head of Chrysler, was also an orphan; and Philip Caldwell, who was soon to head Ford, as a boy watched his father lose the family farm.) They were only too glad to join large, prosperous companies and trade some measure of personal freedom for the remarkable security these companies offered. That someone from the class they worked so hard to join would dispute its privileges was to them almost un-American. Roche once referred to Nader as "one of the bitter gypsies of dissent who plague America." The remark showed how someone at the top of the Detroit power structure, like Roche, perceived Nader: To Roche, Nader was a rootless, insubstantial person who owned no property, had never married, and contributed little to those around him in the conventional sense. He was not a citizen as the executives of GM defined citizenship. By the GM definition, a good citizen took the best job he could with the most powerful company around, bought a lovely suburban home (which he could not quite afford, leaving him even more dependent on the corporation), had two, possibly three children, and owned at least two fairly new cars, one of them a station wagon. He hoped to buy an even better home. He was a pillar of the community, serving on Community Chest drives with his wife alongside him. That, of course, was not the only definition of a citizen. To many others Nader himself became the quintessential all-purpose national citizen. One of the several biographies of him was in fact entitled *Citizen Nader*.

Ralph Nader was born in Winsted, Connecticut, in 1934, the son of

Lebanese immigrants who gravitated to that small mill town of eight thousand after their arrival in America. Native-born Americans might have taken the American dream for granted and become somewhat skeptical of its promise, but not Ralph's father, Nathra Nader. "When I went past the Statue of Liberty," he once said, "I took it seriously." That was the understatement of the year. Nathra Nader was the most passionate of Americans, idealistic, involved, contentious in a joyous and enthusiastic way. He owned a small restaurant-bakery in Winsted, which he had started just at the bottom of the Depression, and to keep it going he had labored longer hours than anyone else in that small town. "I never thought of working for anyone but myself," he once said. At almost any hour, anyone in Winsted wanting either fresh pie or an argument about civics needed only stop in. From that small shop during the worst of times he had managed to send three of his four children not only to college but to graduate school. Indeed, Nathra Nader, though he was hardly rich, refused to let Ralph, the youngest of the four, apply for a scholarship to Princeton, on the theory that scholarships should go to others far needier.

It was, in the best sense, a completely politicized home. Nathra's own example and that of his wife, Rose, were tangible ones. They led lives of involvement and sacrifice; they believed that the true dreams of their household would be realized by the children, once they were able to attend the best of American schools. If America failed to live up to its promise, Nathra Nader liked to say, then it was the job of Ralph's generation to make it better. All of the young Naders worked in the store. "The children," their father later said, "were made to understand that the family was a bank. They put in work, duty, and trust. Then they could take out what a child must have—education." He and his wife taught his children that the more they were given, the more they were obligated to give to those less privileged.

Ralph Nader had always done well in school. He was a serious, studious boy, somewhat apart from the others. In elementary school he had started bringing the *Congressional Record* home from the local library. He was easily admitted to Princeton. As an undergraduate he wrote letters to the *Daily Princetonian*, never published, criticizing the college for spraying DDT on the campus and thus endangering the birds. Princeton had been fun for him, a physically attractive, intellectually open school of endless academic resource and no narrow career focus. Harvard Law School, by contrast, he hated from the start. In the mid-fifties it was a fiercely competitive place with a self-consciously Darwinian culture of its own, dramatically at odds with everything Nader had known. "Look at the man on the right side of you and the one on the left of you," first-year students were often told at an opening-day convocation. "One of the three of you will not be here at graduation." It was about success in the meanest sense; the students were supposed to fight each other for their place in the class rankings. The highest-ranking graduates would go off first to serve the most famous judges and eventually to join the most powerful of American law firms. There, it was assumed, they would see to the needs of the largest companies in America. For all of his young life Nader had been taught a kind of American-civics-book idealism; now, at this most elegant trade school, he was being taught the inner secrets of American society. He was appalled.

"Harvard Law School," he said later, "never raised the question of sacrifice. Nothing! . . . The icons were Holmes and Cardozo and Learned Hand. Those were the heroes—the staid, the dry, those who were respected by the power structure. Who the hell says a lawyer has to be like that?" The success Harvard Law School offered had nothing to do with the kind of life Nader intended to live. (His mother, asked once what made her son tick, answered, "What is more important is why some other people do not tick.") For the first time it was clear that in some way he was different. He would not seek material success, and he would not respond to the impulses that Harvard Law assumed he would. He became the outsider.

An odd, somewhat skeptical, sober young man who had unorthodox interests, he would travel on his own to distant places without ever explaining even to his closest friends exactly where he was going or why. He compartmentalized his life so that no one knew much about him. He did not seek security—as did most successful young men, still touched by the Depression. He rejected his place in the mainstream, the certified kind of American success. Instead he sought involvement and, more than anything else, a role. A tall, ascetic person of great intelligence, he moved mysteriously in his own almost subterranean world and at his own pace, and had his own vision of America. To that vision he intended to sacrifice his life; he has never married because, as he later explained to friends, to be a husband and father would take too much time away from his causes. The normal material pleasures of life meant absolutely nothing to him.

In 1985 one of his former employees, Michael Kinsley, wrote an affectionate tribute to Nader in the *Washington Post*, in which he asserted that no living American had done more to improve life for his fellow citizens. Kinsley went on to say that although Nader was warm and funny in person, "his is the classic zealot's world view, paranoid and humorless, and his vision of the ideal society—regulations for all contingencies of life, warning labels on every French fry, and a citizenry on hair-trigger alert for violations of its personal space—is not one many others would care to share with him." The pleasures of a hot dog, Kinsley added, meant nothing to Nader; "he tastes only the nitrates."

Upon graduation from Harvard Law, Nader worked briefly for a law firm in Hartford, but his interests were elsewhere. Whenever he could, he traveled, on his own, to underdeveloped parts of the world. He wrote articles for magazines, more often than not magazines that paid little. In the early sixties he became interested in, among other issues, auto safety; a classmate at Harvard Law School had been crippled in an auto accident, and Nader started writing about the subject. He began spending more time in Washington and became friends with Daniel Patrick Moynihan, who, as an assistant secretary of labor, was also interested in the subject. In the glamour of the early Kennedy years, Nader was a somewhat eccentric figure, living apart, in a rooming house, no mark of his education in his simple clothes, the epitome of which was what his friend Nick Kotz would later call "that ridiculous scarecrow raincoat." It became his trademark.

Washington, as far as he was concerned, was the perfect place to be. The country had changed; there were all kinds of burning new issues to which the society did not address itself. He scorned friends who told him that the great time for reform had been the thirties. The great time for social reform, he declared, was just arriving. There had been no genuine reformist zeal in Washington in some twenty-five years, since the early part of the New Deal, and in Nader's opinion those New Deal agencies, which had originally been founded to help consumers, had gradually become part of the establishment, dominated by lobbyists from special-interest groups. Many of the old New Dealers, who had arrived in Washington to do good, had stayed on to do well. The city, he decided, was ripe for a new kind of challenge.

He made contact with some of the new muckrakers who were beginning to assemble in Washington, and did some more writing. In 1964, for the grand sum of $2000, he signed a contract with a publisher named Richard Grossman to write a book on auto safety. Grossman had been looking for a writer to delve into the subject. A year later Nader published *Unsafe at Any Speed*, an unsparing critique of Detroit's lack of concern for safety and its preoccupation with styling and profit. At first it appeared that the book would disappear with few traces. But it was extremely critical of the Corvair, GM's latest compact, and its publication happened to coincide with a large number of suits filed against GM based on Corvair accidents.

If Nader was looking for a larger constituency, then GM soon helped him find it. At the time that Nader was readying his book there were 103

Corvair lawsuits pending against GM. Already skittish about these suits, GM officials became even more nervous with the appearance of the book by this new troublemaker. They were suspicious: He was so passionate about the issue, and yet he did not hold a job. Whom, they wondered, did he really work for? What was he after? Was he in some way connected to these lawsuits? Failing to understand Nader's motivation, sensing that he was in some unacceptable way different, GM inevitably concentrated on his personal life—sending out investigators to find something to discredit him. The investigation was unbelievably shabby and crude and provided an insight into the reaction of a mighty institution challenged in a way which it did not understand. It began rather innocuously by trying to learn about Nader through an insurance company in Boston that specialized in product-liability cases. That investigation turned up the fact that Nader was clearly a model of probity. Soon another investigation was made. Eileen Murphy, a member of the General Motors legal staff who had once worked in the Justice Department, called a man named Richard Danner, who worked in a Washington law firm. She asked him for a thorough probe of Nader. Danner in turn went to a private investigator named Vincent Gillen. Gillen, a suspicious man in a suspicious business, taped Danner's instructions (which was fortunate for him, because later it appeared that GM wanted him to take the fall for the entire affair, and he was able to protect himself with his tapes). Gillen's tapes recorded the following notes he made on his conversation with Danner:

> This is a new client. . . . Could be a very important one. They came to me and I'm anxious to do a good job because they have had trouble getting investigators. . . . They want me to work with someone I trust. . . . It concerns this fellow who wrote this book. . . . They have not found out much about him. His stuff there is pretty damaging to the auto industry. . . . What are his motives? . . . Is he really interested in safety? Who are his backers, his supporters? . . . Some left-wing groups try to run down all industry. How does he support himself? . . . Who is paying him, if anyone, for this stuff? . . . Was he put there deliberately? . . . Is he an engineer? . . . No evidence of it: He went to Harvard Law. . . . They made some half-baked investigation in Connecticut. . . . He is not there and apparently is or has been in Washington. . . . I don't know where he is. . . . Strange but he doesn't show anywhere in any directory. . . . Apparently he's in his early thirties and unmarried. . . . Interesting angle there. . . . They said, "Who's he laying? If it's girls, who are they? If not girls, maybe boys, who?" . . . He seems to be a bit of a nut or some kind of a screwball. . . . Well, they want to know no

matter what. . . . They want to get something, somewhere, on this guy
to get him out of their hair and to shut him up.

The ensuing investigation was almost comic, as if conducted by Keystone
Kops. Nader, wary in the best of times, soon sensed he was being followed.
Then friends of his phoned to report that private eyes seemed to be
tracking him. He began to receive odd phone calls which, he was sure,
were designed to discover whether or not he was at home. Then there
were provocative approaches from young women. Two particularly inept
investigators managed to follow the wrong man, a reporter for the *Washington Post* named Bryce Nelson. That put the *Post* onto the story. In
time General Motors was obliged to admit that it had placed Nader under
investigation. At the same time Senator Abraham Ribicoff of Connecticut
was about to hold hearings on auto safety. Nader and Jim Roche of GM
—the one voluntarily and the other involuntarily—became the stars of
the show. GM found itself publicly apologizing to Nader, the man it had
set out to discredit, and eventually settled with him out of court for
$425,000 for invasion of privacy. It was an incident that reflected the worst
of a giant institution and the best of a solitary American citizen.

GM had made Ralph Nader a national figure. He was launched as a
consumer advocate, and he soon expanded into other areas—to the delight
of numbers of educated Americans angered by assaults on the quality of
life and frustrated by dealing with large, impersonal institutions. Bright
youngsters from this group became Nader's shock troops, Nader's Raiders,
as they were called, and Nader became the consumerist-journalistic midwife of Washington.

The Washington press corps in the sixties was growing fast as the nation
began a communications revolution. People suddenly spoke of communications as an *industry*. A new generation of reporters and lawyers, some
of whom shared the same interests that motivated Nader, were arriving
in Washington, spurred by the excitement of the Kennedy years and their
own desire to be a part of great events. Washington began to resemble
the Washington of the early thirties, and Nader became a critical part of
this new capital city. He found irate bureaucrats who were buried deep
in federal institutions and who felt their work was being killed for political
reasons by their superiors, and he connected them to an increasingly
restless and iconoclastic press corps. Others, professional engineers, equally
restless, became highly informed sources for him and were soon known
as whistle-blowers. Nader used the Washington press corps with skill. He
could focus on complicated issues and make them understandable. His
influence constantly expanded.

Ralph Nader brought Detroit kicking and screaming into the age of auto safety. Where it should have moved long before of its own volition, the industry now slowly and reluctantly moved, forced by mounting public demand as the Nader reform movement of the sixties became the government pressure of the seventies. For that he was not loved by Detroit; to that city he was alien, the symbol of a nation that was changing and that Detroit understood less and less. He was neither engineer nor businessman but a relentlessly attacking gadfly. Detroit's reaction was similar to that of generals in Vietnam who were soon to find their versions of events contradicted by young reporters; it was as if privates and corporals were challenging the rightful leaders of the nation and getting away with it—insubordination. It was as if what was at stake was not just their professionalism—how good they were at making cars—but the very dignity of their station. They had worked hard all their lives, waited patiently until they finally headed these immense organizations, and now they were finding themselves, and their sacred word, judged by this strange, unsmiling young man whose only real job had been a brief tour as a lawyer in Hartford. Worse, to their dismay the press corps now seemed to take him more seriously than it did them.

The government, prodded by Nader and his movement, was slowly but steadily beginning to impose new standards of safety and emissions controls on the auto industry. Soon after Nader's charges, there was a series of recalls, most notably of the Ford Pinto, that not only were costly but seemed to validate the case of Nader and his disciples, that the companies were careless about safety as they were not careless about styling. The rise of Nader, the resonance that his charges found in the government and the press, added to the rising foreign competition, gave Detroit's leaders the growing feeling that in some way or another they were coming under siege.

At Ford in the late 1960s the manufacturing men regarded themselves as engaged in a constant struggle to get money for the plants. The plants were low-priority, and no one at the top seemed to speak for them. The company was immensely successful, for these were very good years, but there seemed to be so many demands on it—money for the stockholders, money for the bonuses, money for the workers—that in the end the factories were always shortchanged. Marvin Runyon, one of the top manufacturing executives, thought there was a certain defeatism among the men from the factories. They were not paid as well as the men in finance, they were not as well educated, and they had not risen as quickly or as high; they were, inevitably, always on the defensive in high-level meetings, trying to justify their expenditures, being cut down.

Gradually they had come to doubt themselves. Repeatedly beaten on certain kinds of request for their plants over the years, they came to realize that some items would not go through, no matter how legitimate, and so they began to practice a form of self-censorship. They would think of something they needed, realize they could not get it through, and cut the request down so severely that the original purpose was sacrificed.

They also learned how to use others to help them get what they wanted. Sometimes they used the UAW; they would take the union's complaints about conditions at a plant and offer them as a rationale for more spending. Or, noting that a good deal of money was going to product, they would piggyback their requests onto the budget for a new product. The moment a new product line was approved, they would jump in and use it as a means of upgrading the plant, diverting as much money as they could to the improvement of their facilities. Without that sort of maneuvering, Runyon knew, they would starve. The product people, of course were aware of this gambit, and it made them furious, for it pushed up the price of a new product line. They too felt themselves undernourished, and they were angry when they sensed that manufacturing was slicing into their part of the pie. "You son of a bitch," Hal Sperlich, the chief product man, would say to Runyon, "you did it again," and Runyon would simply smile. One of the worst things about those years and about being in a finance-driven company, Sperlich later decided, was that it took the men from manufacturing and product, men who should have been natural allies, and made them into constant antagonists.

Part of it, Runyon understood, was finance's need to keep the stock up, to create an adequate return on investment. Another part of it, never really spoken of but tacit among those in the upper regions of management, was the bonus system. The bonuses were based on profit, and for the men at the top they were the critical part of the annual reward, often greater than their salaries. Thus the bonus dynamic became implicit in the theology of the company, a powerful personal inducement for middle-level managers as well as the leading executives to go along with the push for maximum profit and not to fight either for product innovation or for better physical facilities. It was hard to get money for them unless the lines completely broke down. General Motors, by contrast, always seemed to have a lot of extra production lines, but at Ford the maxim seemed to be that when you had a hot product you just kept running the line, maximum amount of overtime, until the line—and the men—wore out. The policy was bad for the line, the workers on the line, and also the cars.

Runyon knew it was impossible to *prove* that quality suffered in situations like that, but of course he and every other man who ran a plant knew that it did. It was impossible to *prove* that if they took a couple of hours off to maintain the machines, it was better for the company in the long run. In a situation like that, quality, above all, suffered. Runyon liked Ed Lundy and thought him a decent man. Whenever something was so important to Runyon that he was willing to invest his own personal credibility, put his own neck on the block, then Lundy would almost surely accommodate him. The trouble was, it had to be a matter of life or death to get to Lundy. On anything less than that, Lundy's system prevailed, and the system was dominated by endless concentric circles of bright young finance men who placed the manufacturing men perpetually on the defensive. During the sixties it became more and more difficult for the manufacturing men to get money for their plants, and the situation steadily became worse. Hard in the sixties, Runyon thought, even harder in the seventies.

Nothing reflected this—the low priority of manufacturing within the company, the lip service paid to quality—more than the struggle during the sixties and seventies to get a process called E-coat into the plants. E-coat was a technique that the Ford manufacturing-development people themselves had invented in 1958 to improve the quality of the paint jobs, particularly the rustproofing of the underbellies of the cars and trucks. It was an ingenious process. In the past the manufacturing people had tried all kinds of gimmicks to get paint to reach the nooks and crannies of the cars, but it had always been a hit-or-miss proposition, and the cars remained vulnerable to rust. E-coat could remedy that. In effect it was like painting a car the way metalworkers plated metal with silver or chrome. In the process, the car body was completely submerged in a tank of paint and given an electrical charge; the paint received the opposite charge. Thus the paint, electrically attracted to the car, was pulled into the tiniest, hardest-to-reach crannies of the body. From the first the process was a stunning success. No one had ever dreamed of paint coverage like that before, and Ford was first with it. Very soon it became the industry standard. Ford of Europe, being in an extremely competitive market, quickly installed it in all of its facilities. General Motors picked it up, paying a royalty to Ford based on the amount of paint it used. The Japanese also went to it. Nothing embittered the men of Detroit more than the knowledge that an invention as precious as this—which they had developed—was given to Ford of Europe and withheld from Ford North America. To them it was the ultimate proof of the arrogance of their superiors toward their customers.

Ford itself moved very slowly in installing the process in its American plants. It was an expensive technique, to be sure, requiring a huge dip tank and supporting paint ovens. Nonetheless the reluctance of the company to adopt a technique so clearly superior and so critical to basic soundness symbolized for many in manufacturing Ford's indifference to quality. E-coat was moved into the Wixom plant immediately, in 1961, for that was the company's prestige plant, where its expensive Lincolns and Thunderbirds were being manufactured. But getting it into the other plants was much more of a struggle than anyone had expected. Even in those pre-inflation days of the early sixties it would cost about $4 or $5 million a plant. Since there were twenty plants, the total figure was large, just under $100 million. The men who had developed E-coat and the plant men who pushed for it considered it the key to a great increase in quality. Unfortunately, there was no way to quantify that improvement in terms of sales. That it was a much better process no one doubted. But when the manufacturing and product men pointed to its virtues, the finance men would point to the price. Somehow the manufacturing men would be unable to *prove* that E-coat would make a $4 million difference. How, after all, asked one of its proponents, did one put a price on a happy customer? It took four years to get it into the next plant, which was St. Thomas, a brand-new one. Runyon, urged on by other manufacturing men, asked that it be put in every factory. He would keep saying that it was incomparably better, and the finance men would say, oh it was better, no doubt of that, finance would take his word for that, but was it really *that* much better, was it worth all those millions, could he *prove* the benefits? No, of course he could not. At those meetings he always ended up, like others before him, on the defensive; he would go in confident of what he intended to say, and when it was over he had somehow failed. In 1973 he was in a styling meeting with Iacocca when suddenly Iacocca exploded in rage over the quality of the cars they were making, especially the way the cars were rusting. The kickback Ford was having to make on their warranties was getting alarming. "Goddammit," Iacocca yelled, "when are we going to do something about this damn problem? We've just got to fix these goddam plants." Runyon talked to him after the meeting, and they decided they would try to get E-coat into a few more factories if they could. But the experience that day left Runyon shaking his head. Iacocca, he thought, is the president of this whole operation, and yet he's as much a prisoner of the system as I am.

By 1975, E-coat was in only half the Ford plants. Only then, as the competition from the Japanese mounted and as it became increasingly clear that one of their assets was superior quality, including fine steel and excellent paint jobs, was there a real drive to get E-coat into more plants. In 1984, more than twenty-five years after Ford had invented it, the company got it into its last two plants, one in Norfolk and the other a truck factory in Kansas City. The failure to move on something like E-coat, Runyon thought, was as sure a sign of a monopoly mentality within the industry as anything he could think of.

The Ford system, he decided later, was not just an imbalanced one— in which finance and marketing were the favored divisions—but one with clearly delineated class lines. The manufacturing people were, he decided, politically and economically disenfranchised within the company. The finance people had their careers laid out for them: They never had to go out in the field and actually deal with the reality of making cars; instead, they found sponsors and they went right up through the ranks. If they were good, the company did not want to lose them, and within a short span they would be at grade 16, where the executives' list started. By comparison a young manufacturing man would encounter a subcurrent of condescension and disrespect. If he had spent twice as long in the field and excelled at what he did, he would move very slowly into the grade 13–15 range and remain there for a long time. At grade 15 in the early seventies, a relatively prosperous time for the industry, a manufacturing man might make a salary of $40,000 with a limited bonus. Someone in finance who was the same age and performing equivalently would more than likely be several levels above him in grade and drawing much larger bonuses; the total package might be three or four times as much.

The men in the factories were under constant stress; there was always too much to do and too little to do it with. The plant managers, unlike the finance men, were caught in the brutal contradictions of the modern-day Ford Motor Company—high volume, diminished resource from Detroit, diminished leverage in dealing with workers. The plants, more than any other place in the company, were where men burned out. In the old days under the original Henry Ford and Charley Sorensen, the plant men had talked of the Ford Stomach, which was inevitably ulcerated. It was said of the manufacturing men that retirement benefits were unnecessary because few of them lived to retire; heart attacks and serious abdominal illness struck them down in their fifties and sixties. It was not surprising that by the mid-sixties the level of alienation among the men who ran the plants was exceptionally high. When they got together away from work they spoke bitterly about Detroit—not about product, not about their mission, which they loved, but of the frustrations of dealing with people who seemed so removed from the reality of their daily dilemma, and who treated them so badly. Even the best of them had little chance of making vice-president. They were men of Ford, it was true, but their autonomy had been whittled down every year for almost twenty years, and they felt themselves second-class citizens within the company.

It was widely believed in Ford manufacturing that the two ablest plant men in the late 1960s were Marvin Runyon and Don Lennox. At that time Xerox, upgrading its management and looking for a new head of manufacturing, became interested in both men. It finally offered the job to Runyon. Restless at Ford, discouraged about the lack of opportunity it offered, fed up with the frustrations of his work, excited by the Xerox offer—he would immediately become a vice-president—Runyon accepted it. The deal was done, but later Runyon had a feeling that Xerox was softening the terms, and he pulled back. Xerox then offered the post to Lennox, who eagerly took it.

The message of the incident was sobering to those who bothered to consider it: The two most talented young plant men at Ford could be lured away, something that would not have been possible in another era. Runyon stayed on at Ford, eventually becoming a vice-president. But ten years later, his frustrations as great as ever, he finally left. Much to the annoyance of many of his superiors, Runyon did not go to another American company (Xerox had been bad enough) but took a job—a much-coveted job, actually—as the head of the first Nissan plant in America.

The first thing Runyon noticed about working for a Japanese company was the much greater autonomy of a plant manager. The second thing he noticed was the much greater prestige of manufacturing men within the company. The board of directors of Nissan, in direct contrast to Ford's, was filled with men who had spent a great deal of time running plants.

31.
DATSUN SAVES

Ⅰf the first oil shock, after the Yom Kippur War in 1973, enraged and discomfited the Americans, who suddenly had to pay more for gasoline, then it truly frightened the Japanese. For it was not some temporary inconvenience; it was a crisis imperiling their modern society. Their economy was entirely built upon oil, of which they, unlike the United States, had no domestic supplies. What followed was pure panic. There was immediate hoarding of nearly everything, stores were mobbed, and the government had to promise that there would be enough toilet paper for everyone. A quickie book entitled *The Oil Is Cut* instantly became a best-seller. A great debate commenced on the future of the Japanese economy. Some intellectuals argued for a foreign policy more sympathetic to the Arab nations and less supportive of Israel. Others favored a more primitive economy less dependent upon foreign oil; Japan, they argued, could go back to its old traditions, and live once again as it had in the past, around the kotatsu, which was the brazier where the entire family gathered, sitting with quilts over them so that they could catch the heat from the fire. Companies decreed emergency measures to conserve energy; the paint ovens at most of the auto factories, for example, were redesigned so that they needed less heat. Steel production was cut back because of the lack of energy. Throughout the world of business, faucets in the lavatories produced only cold water. During the shock a visiting American executive touring the headquarters of one major company sensed the supreme irony of modern Japan: lights off in the halls, passageways so darkened that visitors could not see the Chagalls and Picassos mounted in the halls.

The entire experience confirmed to the Japanese how vulnerable and how isolated they were as a nation. Soon another book became a best-seller—*Japan Sinks*, in which a geological catastrophe causes Japan to begin to sink into the Pacific Ocean. The plot focuses on the matter of which countries agree to accept allotments of Japanese as the island goes under. (It is a fascinating study in national paranoia on the part of a nation that has been almost unique in its unwillingness to take refugees from other countries, most notably Vietnam.) The debate over what Japan should do in its new energy-deprived circumstances continued endlessly. One of the first things the Japanese did was tilt their foreign policy away from Israel to greater support of the Arabs.

The recovery came slowly. Eventually the effect of the shock was to enhance Japan's position in the international economy (because it was more disiplined, less wasteful, and thus better prepared for harder times), but in the beginning it was probably harder on the average Japanese worker than on workers elsewhere. There was a flurry of small bankruptcies. Many people were laid off, others went to shorter hours. Soon, however, it became clear that Japan was going to be the beneficiary of this crisis. Some Nissan executives claimed it was actually a blessing, because it had badly shaken the younger workers who had taken the company's success for granted and had become arrogant and spoiled, and it had made them properly grateful for their jobs. It was not just that there was now a greater need for smaller, gas-efficient cars. It was also that the yen fell. As the yen fell, exporting became easier.

In the summer of 1973, a few months before the first oil shock, Nissan was about to mount a major upscale advertising campaign on behalf of its new and, for a Japanese car company, luxurious model, the 610. The 610, which had more standard equipment than any predecessor, was the first attempt by Nissan to emulate GM and move up with its customers as they became more affluent. The campaign was agreed upon and the theme, "Datsun Originals," approved. The campaign featured original pieces of art by Peter Hurd, Peter Max, Robert Rauschenberg, and Salvador Dali. (An approach had even been made to Pablo Picasso, but he had little interest in doing a poster to help a Japanese company sell cars in America.) Katayama, an avid amateur painter, loved the campaign, but the dealers, when consulted, were underwhelmed by it; to them it was about status and snobbery—the company was going to advertise itself instead of its cars. Then, just as the campaign began, the world started to change. In October 1973 the Yom Kippur War took place. No one in Nissan America knew what the impact of that war would be, but it was obvious that it would affect the price of gas. At virtually the same time, in November 1973, the people at Nissan found out that the U.S. Department of Transportation had completed its first mileage test and that the Datsun 1200, the company's smallest car, one that had been around for several years and that the executives were anxious to phase out, had scored the best mileage. Mayfield Marshall, Katayama's friend who worked in advertising, took a crew and started filming the 1200 going across the country, from Palos Verdes to Maine, where it finally drove up to a lobsterman standing amid a pile of lobster pots. A team of independent authorities went along to check how much gas the 1200 used. The Department of Transportation study had rated it at thirty-three miles to the gallon; the independent officials certified that on this trip the 1200 had gotten forty. The last line of the commercial was simply: "Datsun Saves."

Then the Arabs, furious over Israel's victory, imposed their oil embargo. Originally Nissan's ad was planned to be only a small part of its overall campaign. Katayama immediately called a meeting of Nissan's advertising people. Marshall showed the film, which was quite striking. "This will be our campaign," Katayama declared.

Even if there were few 1200s left to sell, Datsun was able to push its low-cost replacement, the 210. Fifteen years of hard work and of constant upgrading of both performance and quality now paid off. This was the moment at which the Japanese consolidated their position. The Germans, because they had stayed with the Beetle, were unable to exploit the new opportunities. The boycott ran until March 1, 1974.

For the American auto companies, 1974 was beginning as a terrible year, what with the trauma of the embargo, the uncertainty over how long it would last, and the pending fateful question of whether the future belonged to big cars or small. Production was down 23 percent. The Japanese had trouble too, in finding the oil to keep their factories going, coping with depleted steel production, and shipping the cars they were making. But in due course the Japanese began to adjust to the crisis. The real benefits came in 1975. That was an important year for them, the year Toyota passed Volkswagen as the leading import car.

In 1973, VW had still been selling almost as many cars as the two Japanese companies combined. By 1975, however, Volkswagen was competing against cars in the same price range that had higher performance. In addition, the Germans were having exchange-rate problems with a strong deutsche mark, which made VW prices steeper in America. VW fell behind Toyota (283,000 to 268,000) and was only 20,000 units ahead of Nissan. (In fact, Nissan was some 67,000 vehicles ahead of VW if truck production was included.) Even more significant, imported passenger cars went to 18.3 percent of the market in 1975, and half of those cars were Japanese.

Yutaka Katayama watched this startling success and knew that it marked the end of his freedom. As long as Nissan America was small, profitable, and making progress (but not too much progress), he was relatively safe in his job. If he had been very unsuccessful, Tokyo would have paid attention, and now that he had become very successful, Tokyo, he realized, would pay a great deal more attention. If anything his growing accomplishment and the considerable publicity he was receiving were reminders back home that he was getting out of control and accepting credit for things that were not, it was felt, rightly his to take credit for. He had no sponsor in Tokyo, no one to speak up for him. Over the years as he had begun to do well in America, friends had begged him to go see Shioji during his visits to Tokyo and pay homage. The phrase they used, for in the old days the labor office was right across the river from the old Nissan headquarters, was "go across the bridge." Shioji was susceptible to courtship, they said; the relationship could still be patched up. But Katayama stubbornly refused to try. Kawazoe, his opposite number on America's East Coast, who was not doing as well in sales, had maintained his strong connection to Shioji and thus was still well-thought-of. Kawazoe, Katayama once said, had always had a gift for playing poker with the right people. Finally, somewhat reluctantly, on one trip home Katayama went across the bridge to see Shioji. Shioji was an hour late for the meeting. In a country where people are extremely prompt, there was no doubt of the lesson Shioji was teaching Katayama.

As the American operation became increasingly successful, more and more bright young men began to arrive from Tokyo to help him out. Katayama was extremely wary of some of them. "This one," he might say, "is here to spy on me. Watch out for him. Tell him nothing." At first some of Katayama's American associates thought he was being a little paranoid; later, as they learned more of the complexity of the politics of the company, they were not so sure. When Kawamata or Ishihara or Okuma showed up in America, they seemed cold and disapproving, and Katayama, in turn, usually so exuberant, became reserved. The Americans in the office thought Katayama was doing a brilliant job, and they found it odd that when they took these visiting officials out to some appointment and, making small talk, mentioned something about how well Mr. K, as they called him, was doing, the visitors never responded, never said a kind word about him. For Katayama had been much too visible in America, had taken too much pleasure in what he had done, had not played the role of the modest Japanese businessman who owes all to his superiors. They would not lightly forgive him for that.

Katayama himself knew that from their point of view, there had been too many articles in American newspapers and magazines about this wonderful entrepreneurial Japanese businessman in Los Angeles who had made Nissan such a success, and who had become so Americanized, and who was, it seemed, an honorary sheriff in half the counties in Texas. Too many people had said that it was Katayama's company and that the 510 was Katayama's car. All that, he knew, would hurt in Tokyo, but he did not care. He knew that they thought he had gone too American, that his clothes were considered too sporty and his manner too informal, and that every request he made to modify the car, no matter how valid, and no matter that Tokyo followed up on it, would eventually help to undo him back home. There he was seen as a spokesman for America against Japan, a man who had been implicitly critical of the existing Datsuns. He had had no illusion about his position from the start. "Everything I do right here," he told his closest American associates, "will be considered something I did wrong by Tokyo."

When he bought a house in Palos Verdes, he knew it would be held against him, that he would be charged with high living. He knew he would never be able to make Tokyo understand that whereas in Japan—because housing was so bad and perhaps because women were not a part of the business world—businessmen entertained by taking one another out for extravagantly expensive nights on the Ginza, in the United States, with its wonderful housing, Americans entertained in their homes. He paid a mere $25,000 for the house, and he loved entertaining there, barbecuing steak like an American but serving sushi beforehand. By American standards the house was very nice, but by Japanese standards it was extraordinarily grand, far grander than those in which his superiors lived at home. The house was always a sticking point. Tokyo never really accepted the idea of the house. A steady stream of high Nissan executives passed through California, looked at the house, and held it against him, concluding that if Katayama had a house this splendid, he was in some way ripping the company off. When Katayama retired, his successor sold the house at a profit of about $50,000 (and was much applauded for being a good conservative Japanese), and if he had held on a few years more, it would have been worth more than $1 million.

The end for him began when Hiroshi Majima showed up in 1975. He became president and Katayama became chairman. There had been Japanese executives who had arrived in the past, but Katayama had always been able to deal with them. Majima was different. He was Ishihara's man, a vice-president back in Tokyo, an executive with clout and connections. It was clear from the start that he was there to replace Katayama, and that his coming signaled the close of the era. There were two main offices in the Nissan headquarters, Katayama's office and another one that was used mostly for ceremonial occasions. Majima moved into the ceremonial office. It was an uncomfortable time for everyone. Katayama, of course, knew a lot more about America and doing business there, and

Majima, just as clearly, outranked Katayama by light-years and was under orders to take the company back from him. Majima did not speak English, and to the Americans at headquarters his manner seemed chilly and evasive. It was hard to get a quick and clear answer from him. He was not comfortable with Americans, only with other Japanese, and he brought more and more of them into the Los Angeles office. For some of the Americans it was their first real recognition that they were working for a Japanese company.

Katayama knew his time was running out. He had stayed on in America past retirement anyway, and now Tokyo was catching up. In early 1977 he received a cable summoning him home, without explanation. It was as if he had suddenly disappeared. On arrival in Tokyo he was informed that he had retired a few days earlier. His friends back in Los Angeles did not know what was happening, but feared the worst. Mayfield Marshall, who did the advertising and was probably Katayama's closest friend in the company, cabled him in Tokyo. "Hope they give you more than a gold watch," he said. A few weeks later Katayama returned. He looked at Marshall and held up his wrist. On it was a gold watch. It was about the only thing they gave him.

He did not particularly want to return to Japan and for a time considered staying on in America in a different business. But he returned home, and in Tokyo Nissan wanted to hide him. It was almost as if he had come home in disgrace. There was no reward for the job he had done; Nissan was not about to honor him. He was not put on the board, though normally the executive who had held his job and done it so well would have been on it. He did not make vice-president. He was given a minor job in an advertising subsidiary. "I was farmed out," he wrote his friends in America. "At least I am beyond the reach of the union." Nissan tried to minimize any publicity in Japan about the role he had played. When American writers wanting to talk about the American operation showed up, the Nissan public-relations people would come up with a short list of names, and though Kawazoe's was on the list, Katayama's was notable by its absence.

Not everyone ignored him; in April of 1977 Katayama was awarded a blue ribbon by MITI for his work in behalf of Japanese trade in America. That was a particularly high honor, and it pleased some of his friends back in America, for to them it was as if he had won it in spite of Nissan. But he took little pleasure in the award; to him it had a slightly bitter taste. He sensed that the Nissan people, embarrassed by his success in America and their own failure to recognize it by putting him on the board, had gotten MITI to do their work for them. It was partly a scam, he thought, and he felt oddly detached on the day of the award. Later he could not even remember whether or not he had celebrated with a few friends that night. A few months later there was a party in his honor given by about 150 of his friends and colleagues; they had had to pay for the party themselves he noted acidly.

In America, Nissan moved quickly against those who had been his nearest associates. Within a few months it got rid of John Parker, who had been in charge of the advertising. (Tokyo had always hated how much Parker made.) But in a way Katayama got his revenge. For in America he had become not just popular, not just admired, but mythic. In 1983, *Car and Driver*, lamenting that Nissan products, though still durable, had become boring ("Nissan remains innovative only in financial matters," the magazine noted), published a special tribute to Katayama as a human being and as a car man. By dint of a rare human vision, he had helped make a small, incompetent Japanese company an exciting one, pushing it relentlessly to produce its best. What Nissan needed most now, *Car and Driver* asserted, was another such man. The title of the article said it all: "Where Have You Gone, Yutaka Katayama?"

32.
THE STRUGGLE
AT THE TOP

There were clear signs in the early seventies that the domestic market was changing. Some of the more iconoclastic people at Ford and GM had been bothered by Volkswagen's success with the Beetle in America, not so much by the sales numbers as by the fact that comparatively affluent and sophisticated people were buying it. There were other signs of alienation. In California by 1970 the Japanese cars were beginning to sell vigorously in the lower echelons of the market. The cars were relatively inexpensive and were winning an enviable reputation for quality and economical gas mileage. Franklin Murphy, who was on the Ford board and who was the head of the *Los Angeles Times*, would mention the Japanese invasion to his fellow board members when he came to Detroit for meetings, but they would always put him down. It was serious, he insisted; the Japanese were doing very well in California, a state that tended to signal trends to the rest of the country, and doing well with an educated, young, expanding part of the market. But his colleagues seemed to feel that if the people of California were buying Japanese cars, then it was because California was an unreliable place, filled with health faddists who did not eat meat, worshiped strange gods, and preferred to play in the sun rather than work all day at a real job. The people who bought Japanese cars, one Ford executive said, probably all lived in communes. It was simply very hard for Americans to take the Japanese seriously. If the Japanese were doing well, the feeling seemed to be, it was only because the Americans had never really paid much attention to that segment of the market.

Iacocca embodied that feeling. In 1971 when his friend Carroll Shelby, the race driver, called and said that he had been offered a big Toyota dealership in Houston, Iacocca laughed and told Shelby, "Let me give you the best advice you'll ever get. Don't take it."

"Why not?" Shelby asked.

"Because we're going to kick their asses back into the Pacific Ocean," Iacocca answered.

Shelby listened and turned down the dealership. Later he decided it was the worst business decision he had ever made, one that in the decade that followed cost him roughly $10 million.

It was at this time, starting in 1971, that the Ford Motor Company faced a decision that would have profound long-range consequences. It was the question of whether or not to go into small, fuel-efficient front-wheel-drive cars. In the past Detroit's attempts to produce small cars had generally been halfhearted. The cars were afterthoughts, chopped-down editions of bigger cars, almost always underpowered and disappointing. But the Europeans were beginning to move toward cars that though small were fun to drive. The world was changing, and the company had to think about designing a radically new small car, a costly step. The issue cut to the very existence of the company, for Ford, with its existing salary scales, both for management and the union, was all but locked into an untenable dynamic. Because it paid out so much, it had to show constantly bigger profits, and bigger profits meant bigger cars. Without anyone realizing it, the wage scale, from the top down, had become geared to big cars and premised on an absence of real foreign competition. The profits that big cars generated had become addictive.

This crucial decision had to be made in the worst of contexts, an all-out power struggle between the company's two top executives, Henry Ford and Lee Iacocca. The struggle was already bitterly personal, and now it was to become economic and philosophical as well, with all three aspects interwoven. It began with Iacocca's attempt to make Hal Sperlich head of Ford in Europe. He had failed at that. So now, in 1971, he sent Sperlich there on special assignment. Iacocca believed that Ford was weak in the lower half of the European market. He also regarded the continent as alien territory. Except for Italy, he felt uncomfortable there, and he felt none of the principal Ford people there were loyal to him. He sent Sperlich to Europe with instructions to sniff around for six or seven months and learn everything he could and try to come up with a small car. It was a delicate assignment, for Sperlich, an indelicate man, would be working behind the lines in territory belonging to Philip Caldwell.

Sperlich's mission occurred just as the Europeans were bringing out their new front-wheel-drive cars. Sperlich immediately fell in love with them. Soon after he arrived he test-drove a Fiat 127, and he was stunned by the sheer pleasure of handling it. It was the smallest and yet the best-handling car he had driven in years. The word that came to mind was nimble. Driving it was pure fun. He then knew that these front-wheel-drive cars were about to happen. The customers would want them. This was progress, and it could not be held back. The only question was how well and how quickly the American companies would respond.

Sperlich was a good friend of David E. Davis of *Car and Driver*. Soon Davis's magazine referred to Sperlich as a born-again car lover. For Sperlich had regained the purer automotive faith that he had lost during fifteen years in Detroit. He was above all else an engineer, with the engineer's passion for efficiency. Now he had an epiphany, which was that Detroit was a crippling place for engineers because it was deliberately inefficient. Slowly, without even realizing it, he had become subverted by that philosophy. He remembered how excited he had been fifteen years before when he had first seen the VW Beetle. It was so different from anything he had known before; it had the qualities that engineers worshiped. It was simple, and it was efficient. It used a minimum of resources and produced maximum results. But the world of Detroit, the world of power and size for their own sake, had pulled him away from the elemental truths that the Beetle represented, and before long he had found himself regarding the German import contemptuously. He wondered now whether Detroit's ethic was one of intentional excess because that was the American ethic, or whether Detroit led the country. It was as if for twenty years the Detroit companies had competed to see which could be the most wasteful. In Detroit everything had to be bigger than last year. The cause of it all, Sperlich realized, was cheap gasoline. As long as gas was 30 cents a gallon, there was no incentive for good cars and good engineering.

The small cars that Detroit had produced, he believed, had been bad ones, reluctant efforts at best. If anything the companies had brought out inferior, unappealing small cars to prove their own thesis that small cars were in fact inferior and unpopular. The cars were not very good, were weak and underpowered, and the companies had not pushed them, and that had proved, the industry argued, that Americans did not like small cars. When the market for big cars finally went sour in the late seventies, during the energy crisis, the Detroit people argued that it was not their fault, for they had produced small cars in the past and their customers had turned away. That was true, Sperlich believed, but it was far from the whole truth, which was that the industry had never given its customers *good* small cars. Rather, he was convinced, Detroit had produced its small cars in precisely the wrong way, not as a labor of love but as a defensive necessity, to fend off at least momentarily the European invasion. It had been done by men whose hearts had never been in it.

The technology for small front-wheel-drive cars had been available for years, and though various innovators had tried courageously to push the idea through various Detroit bureaucracies, their efforts had gained them reputations as eccentrics, dreamers, to be indulged but not listened to. At GM a gifted engineer named Frank Winchell had from time to time over twelve years trotted out plans for a front-wheel-drive car and been scoffed at. At Ford in the fifties there had been an old-line engineer named Fred Hooven who had had a similar reception. Hooven, an outrageous, talented man, had been something of a godfather to the engineering people. He had come from outside the company and had always belittled the Ford bureaucracy, which in turn had no idea what to make of him, especially when the company's senior executives learned he had even voted for Adlai Stevenson when virtually every other good son of the company had voted for Dwight Eisenhower. When at one point he had invented a better steering system, the finance people lost no time in asserting that it was too expensive to be put into use. (Hooven felt that anything that was better always justified itself.) That was the way it went for Hooven at Ford. He was an early proponent of front-wheel drive for the Thunderbird, and was disregarded. Nonetheless he continued to push the concept without fear for his own career. Ideas died quickly at Ford, Hooven knew. Once, frustrated by the refusal of his superiors to listen to him on the subject of front-wheel drive, he wrote a satirical letter in which he reversed the issues. In the letter, Hooven wrote as if the industry were already using front-wheel drive and he was proposing switching to rear-wheel drive. He enumerated all the advantages of rear-wheel drive: It was heavier, more cumbersome, more costly, and used far more energy. The letter created a minor sensation at Ford, not least among the finance people, who at first took it seriously and spent several days trying to figure out how to reply. The letter made a deep impact on the young Hal Sperlich, because it had taken the existing world, turned it upside down, and made it look ridiculous. Hooven eventually left the company for a professorship at Dartmouth College. From there he continued to amuse his friends (and confirm the Ford Motor Company's view of him) by winning a national paper-airplane contest, taking a single sheet of paper and folding it simply but with such ingenuity that, launched, it seemed to stay aloft forever.

The issue of the front-wheel-drive car therefore was an old and smoldering one. The closest the product people had come to it was the Cardinal, which McNamara had approved and which Iacocca had killed in 1961 because he thought it would sell poorly and produce tiny profits per piece.

(Years later he absolved himself of responsibility for killing the car by noting that the Cardinal was ahead of its time.) The arguments he raised against the Cardinal then came back to haunt the company now, voiced by the finance people. The corporate arguments against the small front-wheel-drive car were powerful. A small car was likely to make less profit, but more important, they stressed, going to front-wheel-drive involved more than just some minor adjustment to the production line. It meant an entirely new car and power train. So it was a wildly expensive proposition.

It was relatively easy to design big powerful cars, and considerably more difficult to design smaller ones. That was where the craft of engineering became important, and that was what challenged the engineers. Few understood how different a front-wheel-drive car was. It was not just a car with the drive wheels in the front. It was a completely different car in terms of its basic design. Not only the engine but the entire power train and the transaxle were in front. Because it was all in front, there was no large, humped tunnel running through to the rear axle, taking up space and adding weight. That meant that the cars could be smaller and lighter. Because the car itself was now physically smaller, the engine could also be smaller, and because the engine was smaller, there was still less weight to pull. Everything was smaller, and everything could be reduced in scale. Smallness begot smallness. As David E. Davis, Jr., put it, "Lower mass is its own reward." Sperlich thought of it as the classic engineering triumph, the better mousetrap.

Sperlich had always been interested in front-wheel drive, but in the past he had believed it was for eccentrics. Now, based in Europe, he remembered all his earlier studies of it. It was the pure mathematical superiority of front-wheel drive that obsessed him. He was for it simply because it was better. The fact that the era of cheap energy was about to end in America had not occurred to him. Like most auto executives he had a general belief that the prophets of gloom on energy were wrong and would continue to be wrong. But he did know that front-wheel-drive cars were superior, and if America did not move quickly to build them, it would be out of business in Europe in a very short time. Ford was doing well in the medium-sized market in Europe, which meant the northern and more industrialized half of the continent; but in the less industrialized southern tier, where people were poorer, Ford was barely in the market. There a front-wheel-drive car might do very well.

In his first seven months in Europe Hal Sperlich lived like a gypsy. He never rented a house. He simply kept moving, from factory to factory, designer to designer, talking, studying, and sketching. In those seven months, with the help of some others, he designed a small front-wheel-drive car—precisely the kind of car men like Hooven and Winchell had been talking about years earlier. It was completely new. Sperlich felt himself under pressure all the time he was working on it; he knew that Volkswagen was about to come out with a comparable car, which would be known in Europe as the Golfe and in America as the Rabbit, and VW was already a formidable competitor. He was pleased with his early designs, as was Iacocca, and when the people in consumer research ran tests on them in Europe, they tested unusually well. The studies showed that not only did customers respond well but they thought the car would be a good deal more expensive than was actually projected.

Sperlich's position reflected the mounting divisions within the company. He was Iacocca's favorite, and he had gone on a special Iacocca mission into the alien world of Europe. He was clearly under orders to force something through there. But in truth he had only partial clout in a divided company, and the creation of his car did not go easily. The head of Ford of Europe was Phil Caldwell. Caldwell was not a finance man in the strict sense, but the others in the company considered him as true a reflection of the finance mentality as anyone around. He had been to the Harvard Business School, and he was a man of systems, orderly, thoughtful, extremely careful when making a decision. His advocates, like Henry Ford, thought him an intelligent, fastidious man with a broad understanding of the world, but many of the people who worked with him thought he was more pedantic than careful, and that much of his tidiness and orderliness bespoke an essential unwillingness to make a decision. He did not really seem a man of the auto industry. He seemed worldly and sophisticated compared to many of the men of Detroit, more eager to talk of European politics than of the company. He appeared to be the exact opposite of Iacocca. Iacocca seemed to be all instinct, the gunslinger as executive (though he was actually careful in business). Iacocca, said one colleague, looked at the design of a new car and thought of its possibilities; Caldwell looked at the same design and thought of all the risks. Iacocca was willfully profane, and Caldwell was consciously urbane. Of the perks that the company offered, Iacocca loved the private plane and the dining at good restaurants and the drinking of good wine; Caldwell—like the founder of the company but few of his descendants—was a teetotaler. This greatly annoyed the Ford of Europe people; there was always the possibility that the annual Ford Christmas party might not have alcohol at it, and some Ford executives tended to drink somewhat heavily before they arrived at Caldwell's house as if to arm themselves. Caldwell preferred Catawba grape juice, and he liked bottled water, favoring one brand in particular. Whenever he traveled for the company, his staff was obliged to be sure he was well provisioned with that brand of water. It was part of Ford lore that coinciding with one Caldwell trip to a Ford plant overseas there had been a strike at the bottling works, and in desperation the local Ford people simply used another bottled water but poured it into empty containers of the favored brand; according to the story, the deception went unnoticed.

Caldwell did not smoke either and made it very clear to those around him, especially subordinates, that he did not want them smoking in his presence. Once a few years later, when he was vice-chairman, he called Bill Bourke and Ben Bidwell, two of the company's top executives, to his office for a meeting. Just then he was summoned to Henry Ford's office. He excused himself. Bourke and Bidwell, both smokers, looked at each other and, taking strength from numbers, lit up. After a few puffs they looked for an ashtray in which to put their cigarettes out. The office was filled with beautiful antiques, but it had not a single ashtray. In desperation they put the cigarettes out in a very expensive-looking bowl. Caldwell returned. He smelled the smoke. His eyes went to the bowl, and his face twitched with anger, but he said nothing. Great self-control, thought Bidwell. It was just like Caldwell, he also noted, to have a very expensive ashtray.

Antiques were Caldwell's mania. He was a serious collector, and his purchases in New York were often transported to Detroit aboard a company plane. Iacocca liked to tell of a memo (which he said he planned to use in his next book) that Caldwell had sent to Henry Ford asking if he could spend $1.25 million to redecorate his office; his memo came back from him with a note in Ford's handwriting: "Make do with three quarters of a million."

To many of his critics, he embodied the problem of the modern Ford company as created by the men of the Harvard Business School: too much information, too many options, too little feeling about the cars. "The trouble with you, Phil," Iacocca once told him, "is that you went to Harvard, where they told you not to take any action until you've got all of the facts. You've got ninety-five percent of them, but it's going to take you another six months to get that last five percent. And by the time you do, your facts will be out of date because the market has moved on you." When he had headed the Ford truck division, he had insisted that he be given not just three or four different models from which to choose, but countless ones. He always wanted additional information, and each meeting seemed to end not with a decision but a call for yet another meeting, where there could be even more information and more options. Working with him was exhausting. Even after all the questions had been asked and all the answers had been given, the decision-making process would go on and on. After months of this his product people would go to what they had been led to believe was the final meeting only to hear Caldwell say, "Well, gentlemen, I have a lot of reservations about this. There are certainly a lot of questions still unanswered, and I have to say that I don't feel you've done anywhere near the proper amount of homework on it."

The worst thing about dealing with him, Sperlich's aide, a product man named Erick Reickert, thought, was that there was no aesthetic sense there, no feel. That made it nearly impossible for the best product men to deal with him. He could not explain to them what he wanted because he did not know, and as they offered him possibilities, they felt the chill of his discipline. "We'd go in, pleased and excited by something we had come up with," Reickert remembered, "and Caldwell simply would not respond. There was no way we could generate excitement in him. We wanted enthusiasm, and what we got was constant negative energy." To Reickert it was a deadening environment. (When finally, after designing two of Ford's best cars of the early eighties, Reickert quit in frustration to go to Chrysler, Caldwell, upset that he had left, said fittingly enough, "What went wrong with the system that we could lose a man like that?") Another Ford product man, Tom Feaheny, once characterized Caldwell as someone who liked to go to bed at night still thinking he had not made his first mistake.

To men like Iacocca and Sperlich, confident of their taste and judgment, Caldwell was the prototype of the Ford system, a man both created by it and protected by it. Iacocca regarded him, with thinly veiled contempt, as a man who could not make a decision. But Iacocca's disdain was nothing compared to that of Sperlich, who, when he had succeeded Caldwell in trucks, had gone around quite publicly complaining how little he had found on the drawing board or in any sort of planning stage. "An empty cupboard," Sperlich had called it. Caldwell, he said, had fought against or slowed down every major product in trucking, and then, when some of these same products had eventually materialized and been successful, had taken credit for them—had in fact gone around masquerading, in Sperlich's phrase, as "Mr. Truck." Sperlich, as was his manner, had been very candid about how demoralized he had found the truck people, and how little in the way of planning there was. This had not gone unnoticed. Sperlich had made a serious enemy. Those who had watched Caldwell and Sperlich together after that had seen something that had apparently eluded Sperlich, which was that when he was talking, a look that was close to hatred sometimes passed over Philip Caldwell's normally expressionless face. Now Sperlich was pushing for a new product line for a region where

Caldwell was his superior, and Caldwell was wary of both the man and his car.

Sperlich had no trouble selling the car to Iacocca. Iacocca was a big-car man, but he understood Sperlich's passion, and Sperlich was his man. Furthermore, he believed that there was a need for the car, in Europe, and that it might eventually be brought over to America. Henry Ford was not so easily moved. A completely new car like this was expensive; some of the estimates for producing it ran up to $700 million. The finance people projected a meager return. The issue began to go back and forth within the company. Both Iacocca and Sperlich argued that the finance people were wrong, that the car would bring a larger return. But they were also arguing something else: that the car was good, that it was the wave of the future, and that it had to be done, despite any assessment of costs, because their competitors were bringing out comparable models. To falter now, to leave Ford out of so dramatic a breakthrough in small-car engineering, was to concede not just a slice of the market but perhaps the market itself. Ford might also miss crucial lessons in applying new technology, since what was learned on this car would be vital to the manufacture of future cars not only in Europe but also in the United States. If you were in the car business, Iacocca declared, you had to produce the best cars possible, and you could not simply doll up last year's model if your competitors were breaking new ground. Certainly GM had been as conservative about moving to small cars and front-wheel drive as Ford, but if the Europeans were leaping ahead, then the Japanese would follow, and the American companies would inevitably be forced to act.

In the end the argument carried, and the Ford Motor Company went ahead with Sperlich's car for the European market—the Fiesta, which was perhaps the best small car Ford or any other American company had ever made. But it was a surprisingly close call. Probably, Sperlich thought, if the Fiesta had been judged on its own merits, they would have lost the car. Only two somewhat extraneous factors helped carry the day. One was that Henry Ford wanted to get into Spain and produce cars there for what was seen as an expanding market, using Spain's relatively cheap labor. Instead of the expensive retooling of an old factory, then, they could build a new factory in Spain designed to produce the Fiesta. The other factor was a shift in West German currency that added considerably to the cost of the Rabbit, which in turn allowed Ford to charge a little more for the Fiesta and make a larger profit.

Thus Sperlich was free to go ahead. He felt that Caldwell had fought him all the way, and fought him brilliantly in that he had never been able to catch him in the act. There had never been any tangible evidence of

Caldwell's opposition—no fingerprints, as Sperlich later put it—but none-theless he clearly felt Caldwell was slowing him down at every juncture, demanding more information, postponing decisions, making decisions more rather than less complicated. His aide, Reickert, felt there were all these obstacles to the Fiesta, but they were never quite tangible; there was an undercurrent pulling against the car, but no one could quite locate it. It was as if they were fighting an invisible enemy. Whenever Reickert made a presentation at a meeting, he found himself being chopped up by the Ford of Europe people. What did he know about Europe, they kept asking, or about the European market? It was clear to both Reickert and Sperlich that this was not routine challenging, that everything had been worked out in advance, that it was carefully orchestrated. It was all very deft, Sperlich thought, the presentation of endless obstacles rather than op-position itself. If Caldwell was for the car, Sperlich thought, it was the best-kept secret in Europe that year. It became so bad at one point that Iacocca pulled Sperlich back to America and told him, "Screw those sons of bitches in Europe. If you can't do it there, then we'll do it in America first."

But they were also slowed down by Henry Ford. He was not their ally on this car. Certainly the finance people were making Ford nervous with their estimates of the cost of the car and their projections of its dubious profitability. But even more influential upon Ford was the fact that by the time the debate over the car took place, the struggle between him and Iacocca had become intense. What Lee Iacocca wanted, Henry Ford was no longer sure he wanted. In the next six years, as the market changed dramatically, the company faced a series of historic decisions on small cars versus big cars. In those decisions it grew harder and harder to separate philosophical difference from personal animosity.

In 1974 the paths of the two men finally and irreversibly parted. The personal tensions had been bad enough, but now they were exacerbated by the aftereffects of the first oil shock. In October 1973, on the eve of the holiest of Jewish religious observances, the Arabs had attacked Israel, starting the Yom Kippur War, which Israel won. The subsequent economic fallout was devastating to an unprepared West. Oil at that moment was very underpriced. The Yom Kippur War drove the Arab nations together against Israel and its Western supporters and provoked the first oil em-bargo. That event had a traumatic effect upon Henry Ford; it was as if his own nightmare had come true. Big cars had become a liability jeopardizing the entire future of his company. Conservative and somewhat tired, he chose the most dangerous of options, to save his way out of the crisis. He quickly took $2 billion out of the new-product development program. For Iacocca that was a crushing blow. He had accommodated in the past to what Ford and Lundy wanted, surrendered again and again on vital product issues, but this was an unacceptable withdrawal. He neither liked nor respected the man he worked for, and now he saw him as afraid of the present and future, ill equipped to do business in a period of hardship. The result was a dramatic escalation in enmity. Some of the scenes were quite ugly. In early 1974 the top Ford people went to New York for a meeting with the auto analysts from the investment houses. It was not something Henry Ford liked to do. He had inherited some of his grandfather's feelings about Wall Street, and he was not comfortable going before a group of young analysts and pushing his own stock. In the past Sidney Weinberg at Goldman Sachs had told him he didn't need to do this, that by his deeds and the success of the company he would be known. But Gus Levy, who now headed the firm, said that times had changed, that it was harder for an auto company to compete for capital, that the new breed of analysts were different from the old, and that the Ford Company would have to adjust its attitude. New York, in fact, was just the first stop on a tour of three cities, and in company with Henry Ford were Ed Lundy and Iacocca.

The first session in New York was to be a dinner at the University Club. Henry Ford started drinking heavily before dinner, and when the dinner started it was clear he was in bad shape. We're headed nowhere, he told the assembled analysts, we're going to die. At the head table Lundy leaned toward Iacocca and said, "I don't know how you do it, but you'd better save us." Iacocca did speak, doing the best he could. The next day, Henry Ford, cold sober, canceled the two remaining cities on the tour. "You're talking to too many people outside," he told Iacocca. Less visibility was clearly preferable. Walter Murphy, Iacocca's public-relations man, dated his decline within the company from that day.

Now more and more it was not so much a professional critique that Henry Ford was making of Iacocca but a personal one. He spoke of him now in uglier and uglier terms. Iacocca became "that goddam wop." That goddam wop was not going to take over Henry Ford's company. Iacocca in turn became more and more blatant with his close friends in his expressions of contempt for Henry Ford. Ford became "that dumb spoiled bastard." Part of it was class. Henry Ford did not really *like* Iacocca, he did not like his manner, the way he dressed, his friends, or the way he talked. It was all right for Ford himself to use rough language; it was not all right for anyone else to do it. ("They were never *friends*," one of Henry Ford's

PR men said later of Iacocca. "Mr. Ford always regarded Mr. Iacocca as a rather vulgar Italian.") The only thing they had in common was appreciation of Iacocca's ability to make profits at the Ford Motor Company. Iacocca had his soaring ambition, he wanted to have it all; but Henry Ford saw him as merely a hired hand, a skilled and very highly paid hired hand, to be sure, but nothing more. He was simply too crude. (Henry Ford, Gene Bordinat once said, forgot that before the Italians were the hod carriers in this country, that job had been held by the Irish.) Indeed, the one time Henry Ford had ever dined at Iacocca's house, it had only dramatized their social differences: Henry and Cristina had joined Iacocca's parents, and they all had sat and watched home movies in Europe.

But the larger part was loyalty. The social transgressions might have been forgivable had Iacocca been less ambitious. For Iacocca was able— there was no doubt that he was the ablest man within the company—but Henry Ford had come to think that Iacocca was not content with that, that he sought more, that he wanted not just to run the company but to make it his. This conviction was particularly troubling for Ford because it raised an important internal issue. For this company above all else was a family company, and yet the difference between Henry Ford's age and his son Edsel's age was considerable, some thirty-one years, Ford's own health was shaky, and there was no way he would be able to hand the company over directly to Edsel.

There were ways of ensuring continuity even if Henry Ford died, means of guaranteeing that a Ford, perhaps Edsel, perhaps William Clay Ford's son Billy, would head it. Still, Iacocca was too strong, and his loyalties to the Ford family seemed questionable to the chairman; his true loyalty was to himself. Because of his age and health, Henry Ford thought, he would have an ever diminishing ability to control Iacocca. The man was becoming more influential within the company all the time, even with the board, and, unlike the shier, more grateful young man of ten years earlier, he showed little willingness to be controlled. Ford could see more and more signs that Iacocca was not content with his present position. Clearly he wanted grander things, things that no one other than a member of the family should even think of.

As before, the tensions between them were likelier to flare up in Europe than in the United States. In the spring of 1975 there was a meeting in West Germany. All the top people from Ford of Germany were there, as well as the Iacocca coterie. As the dinner was about to start, the Iacocca people sat down at one table. At the other tables were scattered Americans from Ford of Europe and the Germans. As the evening wore on, Ford's face seemed to darken, and he began to drink. Earlier he had told his aides that he would not speak that night, and when dessert was being served, Bill Bourke, the number-two man in Ford of Europe, got up and said that although Ford did not feel like speaking on this occasion, he wanted everyone to feel welcome. Just as Bourke finished, a rather angry Henry Ford got to his feet and began to talk. He was, he said, goddam well tired of those Americans who came over to Ford of Germany and wouldn't socialize with the Germans, and as far as he was concerned he'd like to goddam well put them all on one plane and send their asses back to Detroit and let the Germans run their business their own way. It was a terribly embarrassing moment, but it was more than that: It was the most public display so far of the split at the top of the company.

For the sight of Iacocca and his buddies gathered on occasions like this always raised in Henry Ford's mind the question of loyalty, the one question that was never even supposed to come up. Were these men loyal to the Ford Motor Company, or were they loyal to Lee Iacocca? And if they were loyal to Lee Iacocca, was he in turn loyal to Henry Ford? Did Iacocca think of it as the Ford Motor Company or as the Iacocca Motor Company? Shortly after that, Henry Ford attended a meeting of top-level European executives where Iacocca and his group were also present. Afterward, Ford was driven back to his hotel. With him were Bourke and one other executive. Henry Ford was very quiet during much of the ride home. Suddenly he turned to Bourke and asked, "Bill, do you have any doubt in your mind who is the boss of the Ford Motor Company?" Bourke assured him he did not. Then Ford turned to the other executive and asked him the same thing, and the man said, no, he had no doubt either. "Well, I'm glad to hear that," Henry Ford said. It was a question that Ford had never asked before; that it was now being posed was as much an answer as a question.

Even the 727 became something of a sore point. It was essentially Iacocca's plane in terms of the company and Cristina's plane in terms of family, and gradually Henry Ford was becoming less fond of both of them. It had been outfitted to make transatlantic flights, but Henry Ford wanted no part of it. He had once left Kennedy on a big plane on which two of the engines had caught fire—the jet had quickly turned around and come back to the airport—and from then on he wanted to make his transoceanic flights only on 747s, planes with four engines. The 727 had cost $5 million and then it had taken an additional $250,000 to style it, and it represented one of the few times that the finance people had played a little loose with cash. Anything over $5 million was supposed to go to the board, but in this case it had been decided to put it in as two smaller authorizations, so that it did not need to go to the board. Iacocca loved the plane. Though later he wrote bitterly of Henry Ford's exploitation of company privilege, no one liked having his own customized jet more than he did. Iacocca could always find business in Rome, and though Bologna was not one of the automotive centers of the world, there was usually a stop in Bologna, for lunch and for the purchase of some shoes, on the way from Rome to a meeting in Germany. Henry Ford became unhappy about Iacocca's use of the plane, but within the company it was generally believed that what sealed its fate was his increasing irritation with Cristina and her travels and her relationship with Imelda Marcos. Finally, in 1974, Henry Ford decided to sell the plane. The Shah of Iran seemed the most likely buyer. A top Ford executive named Will Scott was dispatched with the plane to Teheran with orders, which had come down from a very irate Henry Ford, not to come back until he had a check for $5 million in his pocket; otherwise he was to sit on the runway and wait. That ended one of Lee Iacocca's prize perks and signaled to those who watched closely just how badly things were faring in Henry Ford's second marriage.

Shortly after that, in the summer of 1975, Iacocca had a painful demonstration of how badly his relationship with Henry Ford had deteriorated. He learned that Henry Ford was conducting a legal audit of him and particularly of his friendship with a man named Bill Fugazy. Fugazy was in effect Iacocca's man in New York. He was in the travel business, and he was well known as a friend of celebrities, someone who introduced the famous to the other famous. He gloried in his associations: He had known Cardinal Spellman and knew Cardinal Cooke, as well as Bob Hope and Frank Sinatra and Roy Cohn. He seemed to specialize in the art of being known and being seen and of doing favors large or small without seeming to ask anything in return. He was likable and irrepressible, and among his other skills was an ability to charm the secretaries of all the people he wanted to deal with; thus he knew their schedules and when they coming to New York and where they were staying. When they arrived, there would be a call—could Billy get them tickets for a show or a sporting event? The Catholic Church leaders in New York liked him, because, among other things, when there was a fund-raising drive, Billy was brilliant at getting large donations from people not always perceived of as charitable. His church connections extended well beyond New York, all the way to the Vatican. In 1964 when Pope Paul VI had come to New York and had driven triumphantly through the city's potholed streets, he had done it in a Lincoln Continental, a great coup for Ford within the auto industry, arranged by Billy Fugazy. When Iacocca had gone to Rome there had been an audience with the Pope, again the work of Fugazy.

Fugazy's world—of first-name relationships with the famous, dinners with celebrities, and entré at the city's most glittering nightclubs—was immensely attractive to Iacocca, who wanted not just industrial and business success, which Detroit could give him, but something larger that Detroit could not bestow: the *recognition* that went with success. The news magazine cover stories had given him some of that, and now Billy Fugazy was giving it to him as well. Iacocca was grateful. When he was in Billy's hands, he had fun, and he was around stars. There were those in the Iacocca circle who worried about the friendship with Fugazy and who thought that Iacocca's gratitude was misplaced—that when Lee had first started coming to New York he had underestimated his own drawing power as a star. Rather than Fugazy opening doors for Lee, they believed, Billy was piggybacking on Iacocca's own rising fame, while giving the impression that he, Fugazy, had created this environment for Iacocca. For whatever reason, however, the friendship was close. When Iacocca checked into New York, he checked in with Billy Fugazy.

Once in the early seventies Iacocca flew into New York on company business, and he took with him Sperlich and Bordinat. They planned to have dinner at Romeo Salta, which was Lee's favorite restaurant in New York. As a rule when Lee and his buddies went on the town, they did certain prescribed things; they went to the same restaurant, and they took the same post-meal walk (the route chosen by Iacocca) to work off the same number of calories. On this occasion they were all looking forward to eating at Romeo Salta, but Fugazy said no, it would not be Romeo Salta this time, they would eat at the Christopher Columbus Club, which was an association of prominent New Yorkers of Italian extraction. There was a small groan from some of the group, for the food surely would not be as good. Worse, it turned out that this was the annual dinner for the club, which meant that the evening was likely to be long and tedious. Someone surely would be named man of the year, and there would be speeches hailing him. The speeches would be long.

In all this they were not disappointed, but midway in the evening Iacocca was introduced, and he immediately became the star of the affair. After the dinner was over everyone there seemed to want to line up to meet him, and many of them, as they shook his hand, showed him the keys to their cars, which were Fords. It was clear that Iacocca meant something special to those men, meant more to some of them than even Frank Sinatra. Sinatra had triumphed on a grand scale, but in the world of entertainment, where many other Italians had triumphed and where the prejudices against Italians were less formidable. Iacocca, however, had triumphed in the mainstream of American industry and in the most American of companies, against what they all knew were great odds, and he had done it without giving up a part of himself. Thus the line to shake his hand was a kind of homage, one of his companions thought. The others with Iacocca were bored to tears by the evening, but they noticed that Lee loved every minute of it.

Over the years, Fugazy had done a great deal of business with Ford. Like most big companies, Ford offered a series of incentive programs for successful dealers—trips to Hawaii or the Caribbean. This was very big business for the travel industry, and the competition for these contracts was intense. As far back as the late sixties under Bunkie Knudsen, other travel agencies had lodged serious complaints with the Ford company against Fugazy. They complained that the Fugazy company had the habit of coming in at the last minute with a bid just under the lowest bidder. The Ford finance people, too, had reported that it was harder to do the Fugazy accounts than those of other companies. Some of the complaints had gone to Henry Ford directly.

Several of Iacocca's own friends were uneasy about the Fugazy liaison. Sometimes, among themselves when Lee was not present, they would talk about it. Fugazy always seemed to know so much about the company, too much—or at least, if he did not really know that much, he had a way of making them think he knew a lot. Perhaps that was his real skill, to appear a little closer to the throne than he actually was. Henry Ford did not like the idea of Billy Fugazy's being associated with his company; indeed, he did not like anything he heard about him. Fugazy at one point had been in the boxing business, and to Ford that was a sure sign of dark forces at work. He often complained about that. Nor did he like Fugazy's friendship with Roy Cohn. (There had been a complicated federal trial in the early sixties during which Fugazy had testified that in an earlier trial he had perjured himself on Cohn's behalf in a case that involved a major Las Vegas gambler, Moe Dalitz.) Ford was seeing Kathy DuRoss by that time, and he was convinced that Fugazy was talking about her and her past in New York in terms less than admiring, and that enraged him. But once again the real issue was loyalty. Was Iacocca more loyal to a buddy like Fugazy than he was to the Ford Motor Company? That was the kind of question that bothered Henry Ford about Iacocca.

Early on, Ford had tried to warn Iacocca off the Fugazy friendship, but Iacocca had been curiously adamant. He was damn well going to choose his own friends, and Henry Ford was not going to dictate who those friends would be, he told those around him. When it became clear that this was not some small problem with Henry but a genuine sticking point, some of Iacocca's friends, men who took his side almost every time, urged him to listen to his superior and to put some distance between himself and Fugazy. But that made him more intractable than ever. His friends were surprised; some of them thought Ford's concern legitimate. They were puzzled that Lee, who had been willing to jettison people in the past, was taking such a hard line; after all, the gambit designed to bluff Henry into dumping Knudsen had depended on other men leaving the company. They finally decided it was a sign of Lee's growing contempt for Henry Ford, and of his own mounting resentment at his status as a hired hand rather than a proprietor.

The audit at Ford, however it was presented, was clearly aimed first and foremost at Iacocca. It went on for several months and cost more than $1 million. Nothing against Iacocca was ever proved ("I'm clean," he told friends), and indeed it was said that the audit inadvertently found more expense-account indiscretions on the part of Henry Ford than of Iacocca. But Ford was never completely satisfied with the audit and its lack of results. Iacocca was ordered to sever all of Fugazy's connections to the company. The audit had been a terrifying experience for those caught up in it. One rather junior Ford executive, loyal to Henry Ford but also fond of Lee Iacocca, had found himself summoned to the office of the chairman. "I'm going to ask you a lot of questions," Henry Ford had told him, "and if I don't get the answers I want, I'm going to throw you to the lions."

What the audit did reveal was that Henry Ford wanted Lee Iacocca out of the company but did not feel strong enough to dislodge him by himself. Iacocca now had too much power for him to be fired without true cause. The audit had been a search for the cause. If a cause could not be found, then at the very least the audit would weaken Iacocca by showing others in the company that his power was about to be curtailed.

In that sense it was a successful move, for it seriously wounded Iacocca. Everyone in the company knew what had happened and knew that the chairman was out to get the president. Iacocca's great strength in the past had been his reputation as an enabler, a man who could force a car through the bureaucracy and who had the confidence of Henry Ford himself. But now that the estrangement was public he was a marked man. He did not have the backing or the ear of the chairman. He was the chairman's enemy. Soon after the audit there was a meeting in which Henry Ford bitterly criticized the company's performance. Iacocca was never mentioned, but everyone in the room, including Iacocca, knew that the assault was directed at him. It was as if some great, all-powerful, and often unseen being had declared that it was open season on Iacocca. There was always, in a highly politicized place like Ford, fighting among the factions. Now Iacocca was more vulnerable than ever. His opponents in finance now felt free to attack him, though the attacks must be deft. One line went like this: *How long can the company expect to live on the success of the Mustang? The Mustang was more than ten years ago.* Or, and this was a particularly telling one: *Yes, Iacocca is good, there is no doubt about that*—there always had to be the disclaimer; it was much more effective if the disclaimer was there, if the person made it appear he was on Iacocca's side—*but if he is so good, why does Ford's share of the market never go up, why does it seem locked in at 23 percent?* The worst time for Iacocca was always right after the ten-day reports came out. They never seemed to go up very much—they just held the existing territory—and that fact was seized on with no small amount of glee.

In all of this Iacocca remained silent. The Lundy men were cutting him up, and he rarely responded. Once by chance he got hold of one of the backup books that finance had produced to prepare Lundy for a crucial meeting; for finance, that in itself was a major security leak, for while it was all right to give the opposition the drift of finance's intended positions, the books themselves were tightly held. At that meeting, when Lundy pressed him on point after point, Iacocca said, "Look, Ed, I've got all your questions here, and if you want, I'll just read you the answers that your own people have prepared. That might save us some time." It was a rare moment of victory, short-lived but sweet. Iacocca believed passionately that the company was not investing enough in its cars, that the oil shock had traumatized Henry Ford, and that the company was trying to save its way out of his problems. But he kept it to himself. He knew the rules of the game: If he went after finance openly, he was going after Henry Ford's support system. So he held back, becoming increasingly withdrawn. It was a bad time for him, and for his friends a silent Iacocca was unnerving. When he was himself, they could calibrate the noise. Shouting and cursing and general belligerence were essentially the signs of his good health. That was just Lee letting off steam, Lee being Lee. But it was harder to calibrate the silence. That was scary.

All this might not have mattered—simply a normal factional struggle —except for the timing. The impact of the first oil shock upon the company would have been overwhelming. The company was flagrantly unready, with fuel efficiency the farthest thing from its mind. In fact, it had been preoccupied with catching GM in the big-car range. Inroads against GM's Cadillac had always come slowly. The Lincoln Mercury division *always* lost money. Finally, in 1968, the company had come up with a hot car, the Mark III, a sporty model in the luxury class which young people could buy without looking like premature retirees. It used a Thunderbird base and a grill derivative of the Rolls. It had a long hood and a short rear deck. It was an immediate success. The car promptly outsold the Cadillac Eldorado. Ford made a profit of $2000 per unit, and Iacocca liked to boast that in one year the Lincoln division made a profit of almost $1 billion. It was a tantalizing kind of success, and Ford was thus looking one way as the market was about to go the other. In the phrase of Ben Bidwell, one of Ford's senior marketing men, Ford had learned to do the dance just as the music ended.

But Ford was not alone in this. The average gas mileage for the American motor industry on the eve of the Yom Kippur War was a dreadful thirteen miles a gallon. Nor was the government being very much help. It had finally pressured Detroit into trying to reduce fuel emissions, and Detroit's engineers were working on it, attempting to figure out how to cut down the pollution that their cars were pumping into America's air and lungs. It was something the industry should have done voluntarily twenty years earlier; now it was doing it under threat of regulation. It meant that much of the technological resource and talent of the city was being poured into meeting emissions tests rather than making the cars more economical. Then the government decided that it wanted fuel efficiency too, and set high standards for the auto makers to meet. But what the government had done was to provide the industry only half a policy; it demanded fuel efficiency but, despite the volatility of the oil-producing world, it never moved to stabilize the price of gas at the pump. A quick, firm decision to tax gas seriously at the pump might have signaled to Americans that the wasteful old era was over and that America would now have to be economical with fuel, like Europe. It would have instructed American consumers on what the future price of energy would be, and it would have shown them that what they preferred in a new car was not as important as what they could afford. It might also have provided a warning to the Arab nations, denying them the ability to raise the price of oil at will. But that tax was never forthcoming. America at that critical moment was immobilized. Its political mechanism was unwilling to pass on basic truths to its constituents. So instead of the U.S. government taxing the consumer, and stabilizing both the auto industry and the dollar, America in effect allowed the Arab nations to tax it.

Soon the nation was hit by a powerful inflation, and the cost of all the most basic items—housing, food, transportation, health—shot up. At the same time the government finally came up with specifications for long-term future conservation measures. In December 1975, some two years after the Yom Kippur oil shock, Washington announced its standards: It mandated an eighteen-mile-a-gallon fleet average—that is, the average for all the cars a company manufactured—for 1978 (the 1978 cars were being designed in 1975) and a twenty-mile-a-gallon average for 1980. It was a far-reaching decision: It committed the companies without necessarily convincing the customers. It meant that the companies would have to redesign their cars under terrible deadline pressure and suffer greatly inflated new costs. One think tank in Cambridge, Massachusetts, estimated that to meet the new standards the companies would have to spend some $60 to $80 billion—virtually all their capital assets. This placed an ominous burden on the industry, and, even more ominous, the burden fell on the companies in inverse proportion to their strength. Because of it, said Maryann Keller, one of the smartest of the auto analysts, "The rich will be richer, and the poor will be poorer." Indeed, that was what happened: American Motors simply opted for engines made by other companies; Chrysler, already in serious financial condition after years of being mismanaged by financial experts, edged toward bankruptcy; and even mighty Ford underwent trauma so severe that by the end of the decade there was a question of whether it would survive or not, at least as it had been constituted in the past.

It was all too apparent that Ford, like the others, would have to reduce the size of most of its cars and make its entire line more fuel-efficient. The question of *how* it would downsize dominated the company for two years, starting in 1974. It was a time of total confusion. The price of gas, after the early panic, had seemed to stabilize, and no one knew what effect that would have on the consumer's desire for smaller cars. Detroit seemed to have no idea of what the consumer wanted. Indeed, did the consumer know what he wanted? But Ford had to make a decision, and it was likely to be the most expensive decision in the company's history. The cost of downsizing, particularly if Ford went to a brand-new line—that is, a new body, new engine, and new transaxle—might be as much as $3 billion. It was in effect the biggest bet on the roll of the market that anyone in the company had ever had to make. It was a figure so large that, as one executive said, either way it was like betting the company.

In the past, the men in the auto business had guessed wrong from time to time, and the consequences had not been that serious. The numbers had always been so much smaller. Even in 1957, when Ford, in its most famous attempt to imitate General Motors, had brought out the ill-fated Edsel, the loss had been more one of pride than of resource. The Edsel had lost some $250 million, but, far worse, it had embarrassed the company enormously. Indeed the word "Edsel"—and that was most painful for the young Henry Ford, for it was his father's name—had become a synonym for clinker. Ernie Breech, who was then the head of the company, had privately blamed his old friend Lewis Crusoe for the Edsel decision, and their friendship had never been the same afterward. Others thought Breech was being unfair. "We all slept with the stenographer," Del Harder said later. But the Edsel fiasco had taken place in another time, when it was much easier to do business. Now a wrong decision had far graver implications. Retooling an entire line was far more expensive, borrowing money was harder, and the competition was more severe.

The debate took place when the Ford-Iacocca factionalism was at its height. Pushing for a small, completely new car, an American version of the Fiesta, were Iacocca and Sperlich. Sperlich was absolutely obsessed with the idea of doing a small, state-of-the-art car just as he had done in Europe. It would have all the benefits of the Fiesta, but to accommodate larger American bodies it would have a little more leg room inside. "A blown Fiesta," Iacocca called it. Sperlich was convinced that if Ford did not make a state-of-the-art small car, someone else would. He had easily persuaded Iacocca. However, whatever his skills as a car man, Sperlich was almost uniquely ill prepared for the immensely complicated bureaucratic game that was about to be played. He was an endangered species who was too innocent to know he was an endangered species.

Iacocca's motives were somewhat different, those close to him believed. Sperlich was his product man, and there was the instinct to go with his best man. He knew that you had to listen to your talent, not perhaps on every issue but certainly on something that mattered as much as this. To do otherwise would be to say that he had made a mistake and chosen the wrong people in the first place. Of Sperlich's talent he was sure; he felt he knew the market better than Sperlich, but he had no doubts about Sperlich's ability first to see and then to create a car. But in his heart, pressure from the government or no, Iacocca was still a big-car man. He liked his cars large, with lots of options. He had just learned how to make Lincoln more competitive with Cadillac. Now here was Sperlich, demanding a car that would be exceptionally expensive to tool up and that, worst of all, was small.

He knew the financial people would tear Sperlich's car apart. But he also felt he could justify the car on two grounds: first, that Ford at this critical moment simply had to bring out the best small cars possible; and second, and perhaps more important, the government was mandating a fleet *average*. That meant that Detroit could no longer simply sell what it wanted to sell but had to sell a mix. If Ford produced a very good small car with good gas mileage, that would bring up the average mileage for the company and permit the company to sell that many more bigger, heavier, more profitable cars. Each Fiesta might allow them to sell one more Lincoln. Lee Iacocca liked the Fiesta, one of his closest aides quipped, because he was a big-car man.

Allied against them in this struggle were Henry Ford and Ed Lundy and his finance people. Henry Ford opposed the new front-wheel drive for a variety of reasons. He was a product of his age. He did not like small cars himself and thought Americans did not like them. Worse, this was an unexplored future. It might cost a great deal of money, and even if the cars succeeded, even if they were good and they sold, they might not really make the company very much money.

He was also an increasingly conservative man. He had been at the company thirty years now, he was tired, and his health was bad. In 1976 he started suffering chest pains that were the first sign of a serious heart condition, angina pectoris. He saw several doctors and they all seemed to recommend bypass operations. But although bypass operations were relatively commonplace, Henry Ford wanted nothing to do with one. One of his friends said that it was a very simple operation these days. "Yeah, but every once in a while they lose one," Ford answered, "and I don't want it to be me." Because of his health he was extremely worried about the future of the company and about keeping it in family hands. That made him more cautious about spending and more contentious when asked to. It was an odd transformation, John Bugas, his longtime friend and ally, thought: When Henry first came to the company, it was teetering on the edge of collapse. What there was of it was virtually beyond preserving; in a sense it had had to be completely re-created. In those days Henry Ford had been filled with hope and ambition and enthusiasm. Everything was possible. Nothing daunted him. Now he was older and weary, feeling more mortal and vulnerable, and plagued by doubt and pessimism. For the first time in Bugas's memory Henry Ford was making references to the fact that it was *his* money they were spending, coming right out of the family's pocket. Optimism had been replaced by extreme wariness. All of this worked against a car that if successful might not make very much money.

The other thing that worked against it was Iacocca's sponsorship. The animosity was now so intense that if Iacocca had been for bigger cars, some Ford executives thought, then Henry might have come out for small and front-wheel drive. It made him more susceptible than ever to the arguments of the finance people. They were extremely negative about so expensive a venture. Nowhere in their calculations was there ever any provision for the profound change that was taking place in the price of energy and what that change might do to the market. They simply refused to project. Faced with crisis, they became more conservative than ever, less willing to take a risk. Years later some of their opponents on the product side took a certain modest pleasure in gloating over finance's failure to predict that the market might change and that the sources of Arab oil were unstable. To many of them it was proof that the finance people were, as these opponents had always claimed, small-bore bureaucrats without vision, who had poured all their skill into controlling the company by the most trivial numbers. The smaller the issue, the more skillful they were. Now, the critics claimed, the oil shock showed that the larger the issue, the more immobilized they were. The comparison with bureaucratic army officers who are brilliant in the gamesmanship of the peacetime army was now especially apt, for Ford was now at war and they were no help. "The vaunted Ford finance department," said Don Lennox, "completely blew the most important call of the modern era."

33.
BIG CARS AGAIN

In the two-year struggle over downsizing, Sperlich started as a proponent and became an angry, impassioned prophet. He was so convinced of the rightness of his arguments and so contemptuous of his opponents that month by month his tolerance diminished and his disdain became more visible. He was surrounded by men whom he had crossed in Europe, when his protector, Iacocca, had been more powerful. His own power was on the wane because Iacocca's power was on the wane. That did not matter to Sperlich. What did matter was that Iacocca had told him to make it happen. "I was," he recalled, "a good German son of good German parents, and I had been brought up to obey and never disagree with my superior, and Lee was my superior." That in itself was an important insight: Iacocca, not Ford, was his boss.

The car under debate, beginning in late 1974, would come out in 1978 or 1979. Sperlich was certain that by then the American market would change and that people were going to want small cars. In this belief he stood against a sizable portion of Ford's inner executive corps. Henry Ford himself made it clear from the outset that he did not want a small new front-wheel-drive car; he did not think the market would change that much. What he wanted to do was take an existing middle-level Ford car, strip it down, and make it lighter. That car was known in the debate as the Panther, and it was Henry's favorite. Sperlich thought it a bastardized car, and he felt both anger and sadness as he dealt with Ford and his forces. In Sperlich's view, Ford was an almost paralyzed man, a man who had lost all sense of what was right or wrong for his own business. To Sperlich the Panther was simply more of the same, a very expensive lightening of the same old vehicle. It was a half-assed car, he thought, one more belated shot at a market that was dying. It would be costly, and it would not be a very good car. It was the kind of downsizing that had traditionally been done in Detroit when there was a need for a smaller car, and it had invariably produced mediocrities.

Those months for him were a nightmare—of hearing objections to his proposals, of going back to the drawing board and working the problems out, and then of finding that it made no difference, that the reason stated was not the one cited but another one, never before mentioned. Getting rid of the first obstacle, he would simply uncover a new and more complicated one. If he heard the phrase "small cars mean small profits" once during that struggle, he heard it, he was sure, one hundred times. If he heard talk once about what the Street would think, and about the triple-A rating, he heard it two hundred times. Often he thought he was in the wrong place: He was there talking about cars, and they were there talking about some other activity, perhaps banking. They kept telling him about the lack of profitability per car, and he kept saying that profitability on a car was not the only thing, that Packard had had the highest margin of profit per car in automotive history the year it went out of business. There was a time, he would tell them, when you just had to follow the market whether it was going where you wanted or not. Sperlich used charts that showed Ford's world share declining in recent years because Ford had not done particularly well in the compact market. What had happened in the world, he now argued, was going to happen in America, because America, like it or not, was becoming like the world.

He was aware, as the battle progressed, that Iacocca did not have much leverage anymore. He also noticed that for the first time Henry Ford was turning down the recommendations of his line people. By then, totally engaged in the struggle, he had come to see Henry Ford as the personification of everything he hated about the business. At night Sperlich and Iacocca would talk over what had happened during the day. "What the hell can you do?" Iacocca would say. "You can't fight the man. It's his company." They both were convinced that Henry's Panther was going to be an expensive car—it was not new, but it involved enough changes to burn up perhaps $1 billion—and that, as Ford himself pointed out, would use up all the available money and preclude doing a new car like the Fiesta. What Iacocca and Sperlich wanted was to do the small Fiesta and then, to satisfy Ford, a downsizing of a medium-sized car. It would be a relatively simple downsizing, one that would leave most of the money for the small car. That modestly downsized car was known during the debate as the Tiger.

In late 1975, tired of hearing the arguments about how costly a new small line would be, Iacocca had an inspiration. He had been impressed with Honda's engineering, and Honda was far ahead of Ford in front-wheel-drive technology. Quietly, without tipping off what he wanted to do, he flew to Japan to see Soichiro Honda. His agenda was secret. He had a marvelous time with the old man, the true maverick of the Japanese auto world, a man who despised the Japanese business establishment. For a high-level Japanese-American meeting, theirs was unusually warm. Honda had gotten permission for a great fireworks show, and the entire neighborhood gathered around his house. He presented Iacocca with a handsome vase, and then, as dramatically as he could, Iacocca rolled a brand-new white Mustang down from a van and presented it to Honda. Then Iacocca made his pitch: He wanted Ford to build the Fiesta, but with a Honda engine and transmission in it. Honda was delighted: He would like nothing better than this joint production with an American company whose very name he revered. The price of the Japanese parts would be only $711. He could deliver 300,000 and do it quickly. Iacocca was even more delighted; he had an instant car and an unbeatable one at that. It could be in the dealers' showrooms in only eighteen months. He had also, he was sure, ended Henry Ford's objections to the Fiesta. The car would be cheap, and no Ford factory need be retooled. The idea was so good, they thought, it was faultless. When Iacocca told Henry Ford about the deal, he was indignant. "No Jap engine is going under the hood of a car with my name on it," he said. That killed the Honda idea. Even more, it proved in some final way that no matter what they came up with, no matter what the cost or how strong the arguments, they would lose. It was not just an issue, though certainly Henry Ford was anxious not to invest very much in a small car; it was personality as well. "What the fuck can you do?" Iacocca told Sperlich. "You just can't win."

The hopelessness of the struggle, in its last few months, seemed to intensify the fury with which Sperlich fought back. He was relentless, combative, insistent. He let nothing pass unchallenged. Watching him, one friend thought, was like watching someone commit corporate suicide. He bowed to no one, not even Henry Ford II. As for Ford, he had shown little affection for Sperlich, who seemed less tweedy than the new, smoother MBAs, and lacked their panache. Now, as Sperlich argued with him regularly, almost as an equal, Ford's distaste grew. At one point Iacocca took Sperlich aside. "Hal," he counseled, "I know you don't think you're telling the chairman that he's full of shit, but it sounds to him—because of your tone and because of what he's accustomed to—like you're telling him he's full of shit." He was sealing his doom, not just on this car but on his fate within the company. When finally in 1976 it came time for the showdown between the Tiger and the Panther, it was a struggle without a struggle. All the questions had been asked, and all the answers given. It was as if only one person in the company still thought Sperlich could win, and that was Sperlich.

His own memory of that time was that it was eerie. He had believed all along that the company was genuinely divided over the issue, that there were two sides fighting almost equally. Then suddenly the word came down, and there was only one side. All during the final week, people whom he and Iacocca had regarded as allies bailed out. What he heard in the last days before the final meeting was the sound of silence—people not returning calls, not responding to memos. It was odd, he thought, how lonely you could be in a crowded dining room at moments like this. Right before the meeting, Ben Bidwell, who was sales group vice-president for North America, sent Iacocca a letter: He was withdrawing his support from the Tiger. That stung, because Bidwell was regarded as a good product man and an unusually independent executive, no one's person but his own. There was no way, Sperlich was sure, that Bidwell could believe in the Panther. His defection, then, showed the power of the other side. If Bidwell could not stand the pressure, no one could.

The atmosphere just before the meeting was strange. Usually before a big meeting the company was filled with special energy; there was a flurry of preparation as each side consulted with its troops, working on its arguments, and tried to enlist new supporters. He had always liked that feeling, the excitement and the challenge. This time that feeling was gone. It was replaced by an odd stillness. No one was stroking anyone, no one was coming in for last-minute briefings so he could get his strategies right. It reminded him of the moment in the movie *High Noon* when all of the good townspeople who were supposed to help Gary Cooper disappeared.

Just before the meeting Henry Ford phoned Lee Iacocca and told him he could not go for the small car because there wasn't enough money. That was probably a sign to head Sperlich off, but it did not stop him. For that day he saw himself as the surviving spokesman for product and for the future. If he was to be a martyr for small cars, a martyr he would be. He was the only man in the room who did not seem to know that the ball game was over. Both Iacocca and Bill Bourke, his principal allies, had become very quiet, but Sperlich plunged ahead. He was so tough and relentless in martialing his facts that finally Henry Ford, enraged that Sperlich was fighting so hard when the decision had in fact been made, enraged that Sperlich was violating the unwritten law, turned to him in his fury and, in as hard a voice as anyone had ever heard from him, said: "I don't want to hear another damn word out of you. Just shut up, dammit."

That was it. The two-year fight was over. Ford had chosen to produce a partially downsized car. That car, as it would happen, would appear on the market in 1979 just as events in Iran came to a head and the price of gas went skyrocketing again. Iacocca would eventually say of the decision that with it Henry Ford had lost not just the battle but the entire war, because he had left the company so ill prepared for so important a turn in the market. Later that day, when they all went to lunch, Ben Bidwell sat next to Iacocca.

"Lee," he said, "the Panthers beat the Tigers in the Super Bowl today."

"Yes," said Iacocca. He seemed down and had little taste for Bidwell's humor.

"They were lighter and faster," said Bidwell, "and besides, they had a hell of a coach."

Henry Ford's friends thought that decision was one of the hardest of his life. He was keenly aware of its gravity and the possible consequences. The investment involved was massive, and although he did not for a minute underestimate the arguments that Sperlich had presented, they ran against everything he had learned about the industry. The only market he knew and trusted was the American market, where buyers wanted bigger cars. So at the moment of decision he had felt cornered. Two years later, talking about another, similar situation, he revealed the kind of thinking he had brought to the Panther-Tiger decision, the way he looked at things when torn between a new, changing, volatile market and the need to protect his family's firm and its finances. This time, in the spring of 1978, he was under pressure to put out two front-wheel-drive cars, one a smaller car called Erica during the debate and eventually called the Escort, and a medium-sized car known as Monica in the in-house code. After one long meeting he spotted Ben Bidwell in the parking lot. Bidwell had been arguing vigorously for both programs, despite the chairman's resistance. Ford walked over to Bidwell's car and started to talk. It was Henry Ford as Bidwell had never before seen him—so disturbed about the matter that he felt he had to explain his position to someone, if only an underling. He chattered for a few minutes, then grew introspective, and because it was very hot, he got inside Bidwell's car. "Listen," he told Bidwell, "I'm going to buy the Erica program. I don't want to do it, because it's accounted break-even at best, but I'm going to do it because I have to. But I'm not going to buy Monica. I know it's a good car, and it makes sense for someone like you to push it. But it's too much for me and the family. Just too much money being spent. If I were a manager like you, I'd look at it the way you look at it, and I'd be for it. But I'm an owner, this is my family's company. My grandfather didn't go into big debt, and I'm not going to go into big debt. This is my family's company. The stock represents our real wealth. I'm sixty-one years old, and I'm not going to take this company into big debt. We just don't have the billions it will take to do both. I wish we did, but we don't." With that, having revealed much more than he ever wanted to, Henry Ford shook his head and walked away.

About six months after the battle over the Fiesta was finished, Sperlich was fired, but not as most senior executives had come to be—with a grander title, and a laudatory statement written in the public-relations office which obscured what had happened, or a golden handshake that took care of the departing executive for life. In Sperlich's phrase, he was the beneficiary of an old-fashioned, hard-hearted firing. He had offended the chairman in the most personal way, so in November 1976, Henry Ford phoned Iacocca, who happened to be in New York. Ford told him that he wanted Sperlich dismissed by the end of the day. Iacocca argued briefly with him. Ford said that if Sperlich was not fired, then Iacocca would be too. Iacocca then called Bill Bourke in Detroit—Bourke was head of North America—and told him to fire Sperlich. Bourke told Sperlich he was fired, and Sperlich, innocent that he was, was stunned. The blood seemed to drain from his face. So Sperlich was gone, and now the entire company knew that Iacocca could not protect his favorite son. It was proof of his impotence within the company. Later that day Sperlich talked to Iacocca, and there was not much that either of them could say. "I'm sorry," Iacocca told him. "There was just nothing I could do about it . . . just nothing."

Sperlich very quickly became a nonperson. He cleaned out his desk and went to a distant office where he would not see old colleagues and embarrass them by his presence. He asked for a final meeting with Henry Ford, and a few days later it was granted. It was an odd, inconclusive encounter. Sperlich asked what he had done wrong. He had, he said, given twenty years of his life to the company, he had been a part of several of its most significant successes, and he had always been completely loyal to product. "I have never," he said, "done anything I was not supposed to do." Henry Ford looked at Hal Sperlich a long time, and then he said in words that echoed partings of executives past, "I just think it works out better this way."

Lee Iacocca's own days at the Ford Motor Company were now numbered. The firing of Sperlich had been an open humiliation. His authority had been thoroughly undermined. Though Ford was chairman and Iacocca president of the company, they barely communicated. Bill Bourke could not believe the enmity between the two men. He found himself relaying messages from one to the other, like a child whose parents are getting a divorce and no longer speaking. Henry Ford became more forthright than ever in his complaints about Iacocca. A friend told him if he felt that strongly, then he should let Iacocca go and end the turmoil.

But Ford still seemed to be looking for the right excuse. He had failed with the audit on the Fugazy connection. Now he hired a team of outside consultants, from the McKinsey company, to do a study on the future requirements of the company. Iacocca understood the move from the start, and he loathed the McKinsey people from the moment they walked in the door. "What is this shit?" he asked. "What the hell do we need outsiders coming in to tell us who we are?" The consultants, he said, were stupid goddam double-domes who had never built a car in their lives, and they were advising the Ford Motor Company on what to do. Predictably, within a year, adopting a McKinsey recommendation, Henry Ford announced the creation of a new post, the Office of the Chief Executive. He gave that title to himself and gave the second-ranking job, vice-chairman, to Phil Caldwell. That placed Caldwell, whom Iacocca despised, over Iacocca. Henry Ford, very conscious of the importance of the smallest of social rites and amenities, now began to twist the knife into Iacocca. He was careful at major dinners to place Caldwell at table two (he himself was at table one) and Iacocca at table three. The signal he was sending to the company thundered out. Even so, Iacocca would not quit. Instead he searched desperately for allies; in the past he had feared Bill Bourke as a rival, but now, with Caldwell rising above both of them, he sought out Bourke's friendship.

In the day-to-day exercise of authority, his power diminished. That had always been part of his real love of his job, the ability to move things and make them happen. Now he had lost that as well. The people in the bureaucracy knew that his strength was on the wane, and men who never would have challenged him in the past were suddenly standing up to him. Others who had once been his friends now put distance between them. He visited his daughter at Middlebury College, in Vermont, and while there he attended a football game and watched a man who headed an advertising agency that did millions of dollars' worth of business with Ford come within ten feet of him and manage not see him. He took careful note of who did and who did not come to his birthday party, which had always been an annual event among his buddies. He turned on a friend named Bill Benton, widely regarded as an Iacocca protégé, and accused him of betraying him and going over to Caldwell; among Benton's sins was that he had just bought a house that happened to be on the same street as Caldwell's. Now when Lee Iacocca wanted a company plane, he had to ask for it in advance and submit a manifest of who was going to accompany him.

At times, it seemed to his remaining friends, he was in a deep depression. Some told him to quit and get out, but he stayed on. After work he would simply go home and sit by himself in a room with the shades drawn, not talking to anyone, brooding in a world all his own, pondering how it had all gone wrong. His wife, who hated what this was doing to him, urged him to quit. Years later, talking about his last months at Ford, he admitted that his one regret was that he had not walked into Henry Ford's office and told him to stuff it. But he did not. He seemed immobilized, unable to believe that he had lost control of a company that he had so completely mastered, and unable as well to give up the income of nearly $1 million a year.

For a year he stayed and took it, and then he made his move, in effect a frontal challenge to Henry Ford. He went to the board of directors. Over the years his power with the outside board members had grown; in their eyes during the last decade Henry Ford had not been particularly effective, and Iacocca had run the company well on limited resources. As Henry's behavior had grown more erratic, these board members had confided their doubts to Iacocca. Among those who particularly liked Iacocca were George Bennett, a Boston financier, Joe Cullman, the head of Philip Morris, and Franklin Murphy, the chairman of the *Los Angeles Times-Mirror* company. In addition, Iacocca was close to William Clay Ford, Henry's younger brother, who had even more stock than Henry. A reformed alcoholic himself, Bill Ford had misgivings about Henry's drinking. Without knowing it, by confiding their misgivings to Iacocca, they had also fed certain fires within him. In 1977 and 1978, as Iacocca became more restless, he reflected on the misgivings that these men had voiced to him and the admiration they had expressed for his leadership, and he mistook what they were saying and what they felt, their *sympathy*, for what, in a confrontation with Henry Ford, they would actually do.

Early in June 1978, more than a year and a half after Sperlich had been fired and a year after the McKinsey people had institutionalized his decline, Iacocca was treated to one more increment of humiliation. Caldwell was made deputy chief executive, and Iacocca was ordered to report through him. That change had caused some reverberation on the board, and a three-man subcommittee of the board composed of Cullman, Bennett, and Murphy had been formed to look at it. A few weeks later, frustrated, depressed, Iacocca did the unthinkable. He took the company plane and flew first to Boston to see Bennett and then to New York to see Cullman. He talked with Murphy over the phone.

Going to the board was the act of a desperate man, for Henry Ford would take it as the ultimate act of defiance. To Henry Ford the board was, in the most personal sense, his. The Ford Motor Company might be publicly held, but in his mind it was still a private family company. The outside board members were not to challenge him; they were to show up, be wined and dined, receive their annual free cars and their fee—up to $50,000 a year—and make no untoward noises. He carefully monitored who went on, lest there be the possibility of a future challenge to the family. In going to the board, Iacocca was crossing a sacred line, and it was probably the mistake Henry Ford had long been waiting for, the act of disloyalty he wanted. The very act displayed the hopelessness of Iacocca's position, for he was forcing a confrontation he had no chance of winning. The outside board members might like him better than Henry Ford, they might think him an abler and more effective auto executive, but unless Ford's misconduct became considerably more egregious than it had been so far, they were not going to allow an executive, no matter how able, to challenge the sitting head of the family.

Iacocca was very careful in what he said to the board members. He did not talk about Henry's personal problems. He said that the company was in deep trouble, that he was the only one who could put it back on its feet, that Henry had not been the same since his heart trouble, and that the company was now leaderless. Most of them agreed with him, at least privately. Henry Ford, however, knew exactly what had happened within hours of Iacocca's moves. A few days later when the board convened again, Henry Ford said that he intended to get rid of Iacocca, because they were not comfortable with each other. This time, some of the board members, notably Bennett, argued with him. Bennett was a State Street Boston financier, and he believed not only that Iacocca was the most capable man in the company but that his value was reflected tangibly in the company's stock. Both Wall Street and State Street respected Iacocca's stewardship. If Iacocca was fired, he told some colleagues, it could affect the stock, for the action could undermine investors' confidence in the Ford Motor Company.

The firing was headed off the first day. The next morning the pro-Iacocca board members worked frantically to find some sort of compromise that would allow him to stay on. It was a peculiar scene. There was Henry Ford in his office, waiting to hear from the board, cool and aloof, the game now very much in his hands, and there was Iacocca down the hall in his office waiting to hear the results, and there were the board members, pulled between these two men, trying to put the fragments of the company's leadership back together. The board urgently wanted some kind of compromise, and only as the minutes passed and they shuttled back and forth between the two offices did they realize that Henry Ford did not want compromise, he wanted Iacocca out of his company. More, it was clear that Ford was underwhelmed with the part that the directors were playing. He did not, as they did, consider their role helpful. He believed that they had placed themselves above his law, and as a result he treated them with a certain disdain. He was perfectly polite, but he did not bend at all. They kept coming back to him with compromises, such as one that would switch some of Phil Caldwell's duties and give Iacocca more line responsibilities, and Ford smiled and said, "No, it's him or me." Then he added: "Look, I'll leave the room and you can figure it out without me."

"No, Henry," Franklin Murphy said, speaking for them all, "you don't need to do that."

They were members of the *Ford* board, and in any showdown they were not going to challenge the sitting representative of that family, who was, in his own way and most particularly in moments like this, as tough as his grandfather. So they folded. Not even Bill Ford could help Iacocca. He, even more painfully than the other board members, was caught between loyalty to the company and loyalty to the family. Blood was stronger. That afternoon he sat in on the meeting when his brother fired Lee Iacocca. Iacocca asked what he had done wrong, and Henry Ford answered, "I just don't like you." At the end Iacocca told Ford he was making a mistake, that they had just earned $1.8 billion after taxes in the previous year. "You'll never do it again," Iacocca said. The meeting was short. As Bill Ford, by now in tears, walked out of the office with Iacocca, he turned to him and said, "I'm sorry, Lee. I'm sorry." It was all over. At the end of the work day some of the other top executives, who had known vaguely of the meetings, went to the parking lot and found on their steering wheels notes that said they would now report to Phil Caldwell instead of Lee Iacocca. "He finally did it," Bill Bourke told Don Petersen. The Iacocca era was finally ended.

"Thank God all the bullshit is over," Iacocca told a friend.

Late in the day Henry Ford met with members of the board. The unpleasantness seemed in the past. He scarcely mentioned it. Some of the board members had never seen him so relaxed. Then near the end of the meeting he brought up the subject of compensation. "You know," he said offhandedly, the seigneur once again, "we ought to be very generous

with Lee." Then he added, almost as an afterthought, "He was very good to this company." That was it: Iacocca had come and toiled and fought and manipulated and risen and triumphed and then he was gone, and Henry Ford was still there. But he had been very good to the company.

For a time Iacocca was overwhelmed by his bitterness. The firing was the final mortification. It was as if in the last few years Henry Ford had confirmed all Iacocca's darkest suspicions, that despite his immense salary, his lavish perks, his title of president, he was the employee, the crude little Italian who worked for and had been tolerated by the Wasp owner. Later he told friends that his great mistake had been failing to get out sooner, that in the early seventies, when the relationship had soured, he should have told Henry Ford what he could do with his cars. His great mistake had been waiting until he was fifty-five and entitled to even greater retirement benefits. It was his own goddam greed that had done him in, he later admitted, which was stupid because he did not even care that much about money, he already had more than he needed.

34.
A VACANCY AT CHRYSLER

Lynn Townsend, smart, facile, and abrasive, became president of Chrysler in the first place because the company was in serious trouble. He was purely a numbers man. (An early, admiring profile of him in *Fortune* began, "The figures talk to Lynn Townsend. . . .") He had had a hard childhood. As a boy he kept the books in his father's auto repair shop. He was orphaned at fourteen and worked his way through the University of Michigan, where he was considered a truly gifted accounting student. Upon graduation he worked for a Detroit accounting firm, then went off to World War II. When he returned he joined Touche Ross, then new but eventually one of the nation's largest accounting firms, where he was soon put to work on the Chrysler account. By 1957, Chrysler was undergoing increasing stress, and he made a lateral move to become its controller. No one, it was clear, understood the company as well as he did. In 1961, a time of crisis within the company, George Love, in effect an acting chairman and himself the head of a coal company ("I don't know what a carburetor is and I'm too old to learn"), picked Townsend to run the company. "He is the right man because he is figure-minded," Love said. "It used to be possible to control the company through personal contact. But when a company gets this big, you no longer know all the people. You can't see that so-and-so is loafing. So you need a man for whom figures live. You control the company by a knowledge of figures. Townsend can spot trouble through them." Traditionalists in Detroit were shocked by the decision to give that much power to an accountant. They were convinced it would never have happened in the days of Walter Chrysler or K. T. Keller. These were not the days of Chrysler or Keller, however; they were the days when George Romney's earlier warnings about a monopoly industry were beginning to come true.

Romney had envisioned an industry in which a rich, powerful GM set the norms in all areas, including labor settlements, putting unbearable pressure on the weaker companies. By the late fifties that had become all too true at Chrysler; it had to match the salaries of GM without being able to match its economy of scale.

At forty-two, Townsend seemed at first the wunderkind of Detroit. A forceful and magnetic personality, he brooked no interference from anyone, whether product man or board member. Those who questioned his authority, no matter how gently, quickly regretted it, for he would lash out at them, demolishing their ideas and humiliating them in front of their peers. Because of his knowledge of the company's finances, he arrived at the top with a sure sense of its weaknesses. He knew where to cut and where to use the company's limited resources. He consolidated the Chrysler and Plymouth divisions, closed plants that duplicated functions, cut the white-collar staff, and decreed that Chrysler give a five-year, fifty-thousand-mile warranty on every car it sold. Together these steps stabilized the company. It was the era of the multinational corporation, so Townsend also internationalized Chrysler, buying some foreign companies outright and buying shares of others. The European companies he bought into—Rootes of England, Simca of France, Barreiros of Spain—were all dogs, he confided, but they were all that was left, so he had to deal with them or stay out of the international market. His goal was a "world car," a base model that could be used everywhere, and he was confident that his talent could turn even those dogs around.

At the time he took over, Chrysler could not have been shakier. By 1962 it was down to a low of 8.3 percent of the market share. The standard bad joke in Detroit at the time, journalist Nick Thimmesch wrote, went: "My wife's divorcing me, my girlfriend is pregnant, my son has been expelled from Yale, and now I've just been promoted to vice-president at Chrysler." Townsend seemed to shape it up quickly. By the end of 1963 it was up to 12.4 percent, and by 1968 it reached 18.1 percent.

On paper what he was doing looked good; that was part of the problem. Subtly and inevitably, more energy went into what would look good on paper than what was good for the cars. He was preoccupied with what would drive the stock up; therefore, so were all the men around him. There were lots of incentives and bonuses for those who could make the numbers look good—all of them short-range in their effect. It was as if the real customers of the company were the stockholders, not those who bought cars. The preoccupation with the stock had its penalty. Chrysler gradually became caught in a vast and lethal self-deception. It happened because one of the first rules of production, that there were supposed to be real orders before cars were built, had become a sham there. Waiting for orders might slow down the numbers game. Tom Killefer, who served as treasurer at Chrysler, once said that Townsend's policy was to "stack cars like cans of beans on a shelf." The unordered and therefore unwanted cars, created in order to inflate Chrysler's numbers, were trucked to what was called the "sales bank," the code name for the inventory. It was in effect one giant Detroit parking lot. At first the Chrysler people used their own grounds; when they ran out of space they rented some from Ford. Then they used the Michigan State Fairgrounds. Then the Windsor Raceway in Canada. The sales bank, begun in the early sixties, contained some 60,000 cars by 1966. By February 1969, the number of cars produced without dealer consent had risen to 408,302. Rushed through with less and less attention to quality, the cars sat there while the sales people pushed them at the dealers, who in turn would try to palm them off on customers. The policy was destroying the company's relationships with its dealers, who, forced to accept cars, soon learned that if they waited until the company was truly desperate, they could get cars at vast discounts. The cars that couldn't be unloaded on the dealers were assigned to something entitled the Chrysler Financial Corporation, to give them the semblance of a home and something that could pass for an order sheet. Often they were left standing outside in the sales bank for months, even through the Detroit winter. It was ruinous to both the cars and the company's morale.

While the sixties were a wonderful decade for Townsend at Chrysler, a time in which he was almost universally praised, things changed for the worse in the early seventies. The company was overextended; its international commitments were beginning to drain rather than strengthen it. Townsend had always been volatile. He could be utterly charming one moment and then turn unaccountably mean. Even on his good days he was capable of behavior that fell just short of corporate cruelty. Stories circulated of Townsend grilling high Chrysler executives for hours about real or imagined flaws, letting go only to return to the subject later. The night before board meetings in New York, Townsend made a ritual of going to Christ Cella, an expensive midtown steak house, with some of his top people, including the inside directors and a few outside directors. There they would eat a long, raucous dinner at the big table in the kitchen, a privileged location; on occasion they were joined by absolute strangers who, to their astonishment, found themselves included in intimate corporate discussions and ravaged by Townsend if they disagreed with him. The evening would continue until the restaurant closed in the early morning, whereupon they retired to the Waldorf Towers. A few hours later, at the board meeting, Townsend would be in total control, as cool and commanding a presence as ever.

As the company's trouble intensified, however, he became more irascible. He began to drink more. Close friends thought they understood what was the matter: Townsend realized that Chrysler's situation was such that he had to get rid of all his international acquisitions, the foreign companies he himself had bought; in effect he had to undo his most treasured handiwork, and he could not bring himself to do it. Thus, the shadow lengthened.

Chrysler, for all of its shakiness, had not been in debt when Townsend had taken over in 1961. By 1970, however, its debt had reached $791 million, even more than GM's, and was growing all the time. After Penn Central went bankrupt in 1970, officials at various financial institutions, in order to avoid losses from another, similar disaster, tried to guess what the next major casualty might be and fastened on Chrysler. So Chrysler's top executives, accompanied by their bankers from Manufacturers Hanover, flew around the country pressuring Chrysler's other lenders for more money. That raised $180 million, but it did not solve the problem. Even in the boom days, Chrysler had been a sick company, buying time at the expense of its future health; it became particularly vulnerable when the oil embargo hit in 1974. Much of the market share gained by early imports from Germany and Japan had been at Chrysler's expense; now that the entire industry was threatened, Chrysler was in real trouble. There were mass layoffs—not only of workers but also of engineers—accompanied by reduced investment in tools and facilities as well as research and development. A year later, in July 1975—at the suggestion, it was rumored, of the board and at the direct urging of Louis Warren, the outside counsel—Lynn Townsend resigned.

Hal Sperlich was crushed by his firing. It had never occurred to him that Iacocca would not be able to shield him. His life had been Ford, nothing but Ford; even the defeats, he realized after he left, had been exhilarating. It seemed to him that his life was over. Colleagues who came to see him would find him depressed and alone, convinced he was a failure. "Hal," one of them said, "you've been one of the two or three top men in one of the biggest companies in the world. You were Ford's best product man. Everybody in this business knows your value. You got hit by a truck. The truck was a Ford, and the man driving it was a Ford. You'll be successful again." At first these pep talks had little effect. Sperlich spent several months trying to decide what to do. Friends advised him to try an adventurous new company where he would not be crushed by a resistant bureaucracy. He received good offers from substantial companies like Xerox and Bendix, but he did not want to learn how to design photocopiers or small engine parts. "I'm a car man," he told friends. "That's all I know."

Unfortunately, there were few openings for a man like him in such a restricted industry. He was finished at Ford, and GM—whose well-ordered managerial system was bursting with men his age already tired of waiting in line for promotions—was out of the question. If he had offended the bureaucracy at Ford, his friends trembled to think of what he might do at GM. Although he was offered the presidency of the DeLorean Motor Company, he was leery of DeLorean. That meant Chrysler was his only hope. Iacocca called Gil Richards, the president of Budd, one of the major supplier companies, and asked him to help Sperlich at Chrysler. ("I think Lee felt a certain amount of guilt that he had not been able to protect me," Sperlich said later.) In November 1976, a month after his firing, he began talking with Chrysler executives. He went to work there in March 1977 as vice-president of product planning.

Sperlich knew the company was in trouble, but he had no idea, he later remarked, that it had terminal cancer. After all, in both 1975 and 1976 it had made money. He was stunned by the decay and apathy he found. Whatever his frustrations at Ford, he had become accustomed to its comforts and resources. At Ford there were always plenty of talented people, and the plants, while perhaps not sufficiently modernized, were always in reasonably good condition. At Chrysler, morale was terrible, many of the company's best people had already left, and the plants were in bad shape. Sperlich suspected he was the first person above the level of supervisor whom they had hired in years. Because no knowledgeable people had come in from the outside, the people there had no idea what they were doing wrong. Furthermore—and he was sure this was the worst thing about the company—Chrysler had utterly lost its sense of accountability. Early on he asked Gene Cafiero, by then the president, for the name of the person in charge of quality.

"Everybody," Cafiero answered.

"But who do you, as president of the company, hold responsible when there are problems in quality?" Sperlich asked, persisting.

There was a pause. "Nobody," Cafiero said.

Sperlich went back to his office and closed the door. Oh shit, he thought, we are in for it now.

A constant sense of crisis pervaded the company. The problems were so great and the lines of division so badly blurred that it was, in Sperlich's phrase, management by swarm. Whatever problem arose on a given day, the entire managerial staff piled on top of it as if it were a fumble. The factories were filthy and often unheated. In many of them the windows were broken, and the wind swept through in the winter. Racial tensions ran high. Drugs were used openly in some plants. The cars themselves were boring, weak imitations of GM and Ford. Quality had become a joke. Finally, to Sperlich's chagrin, while the finance people, as they did at Ford, had power, they had failed to create any of the protective systems that the Ford men had. The company enjoyed the burdens of the finance men, without any of their strengths.

Chrysler, even more than Ford, was the embodiment of what had gone wrong with American heavy industry in the last twenty years. As more was required, less was put in. Always near the top of *Fortune*'s list of the top five hundred companies, it had appeared for some twenty years to be the prototypical successful corporate giant. But it was rotting. In good years a company like Chrysler might do well, but there would be more and more bad years, when the entire company would hang in the balance.

Worse, the weaker it was, the better target it presented to the UAW. Although the union did not want to drive Chrysler under, it had a shrewd sense of how far to tighten the screws. A typical example of this occurred in 1964 when the UAW negotiating team, led by Walter Reuther and Doug Fraser, went to see Lynn Townsend, then president of Chrysler. Since the company was in the midst of one of its periodic comebacks, the UAW was thinking of going after it that year. Townsend's first mistake was to condescend to both Reuther and Fraser, treating one of their junior aides as if he were the most important person there and virtually ignoring the senior UAW officers. His second was to become expansive about Chrysler's circumstances. Never modest about his accomplishments, Townsend became even more boastful than usual. Chrysler was really coming back, he said, and he, Townsend, was personally pulling the company together.

"Just give me nine more months," he told them, "and we'll have fifteen percent of the market. All we need is nine more months. The stock will take off when that happens."

The UAW leaders played it very cool through the rest of the meeting, their expressions never changing, but when they got outside Reuther turned to Fraser and asked, "Did you hear what I heard?"

"Yes," said Fraser, knowing as well as Reuther did that Townsend was a man so desperate to achieve his goals and so full of himself that they had him.

"Let's sleep on it," Reuther said.

Sleep on it they did, and the next day Reuther said, "Let's go after Chrysler." They went back to Townsend and told him that if he met their demands they would spare him a strike and he could get his precious 15 percent. Townsend, realizing they had him, conceded.

Sperlich's first months at Chrysler were spent trying to patch some cars together for the 1980 product cycle, but he was soon involved in what was to be the most important decision in Chrysler's future: whether or not to go for front-wheel drive in its 1981 models. No decision could have been harder. The company was acutely short of cash, and when the choice fell to John Riccardo, who had succeeded Lynn Townsend first as president and then as chairman, he was staring at the possibility of a $1 billion deficit. At the same time Chrysler, like Ford and GM, was under great pressure to meet government-mandated emissions standards. The government had prohibited any sharing of technological expertise on the question, even though the eventual beneficaries would be the American people. While the expense would be monumental for all three companies, the ban on cooperation indirectly benefited GM and Ford by burdening their already faltering competitor.

In essence the company had to replace its small-car line. Everyone knew that the next model had to be lighter, more compact, and more fuel-efficient. On one hand there was the H car, which used rear-wheel drive. Of the two possible models, it promised to be the heavier and less efficient, but it could use the existing power train and suspension and thus would cost only about $400 million. The cost of the front-wheel-drive model, the K car, was figured at $700 million because it required a new power train and far greater expenditures on new technology. For a company facing the genuine possibility of bankruptcy, it was an almost unbearable call, and it was John Riccardo's responsibility to make it. Riccardo was a finance man. Like Townsend, whose protégé he had been, he had come from the accounting firm of Touche Ross, and he felt himself unprepared to make fateful, perhaps fatal, decisions for Chrysler. He was, thought Sperlich, as unready for his position as Henry Ford had been for his, with the important difference that he was not burdened by ego. The best thing about Riccardo, Sperlich decided, was that he knew what he did not know and did not pretend otherwise. Henry Ford, to Sperlich, reflected the arrogance of power, John Riccardo the modesty of power. Riccardo clearly wanted to make the right decision.

By the time Sperlich entered the controversy in mid-1977 it was clear that the product people almost unanimously favored front-wheel drive, and the managers, to a considerable degree, favored the rear-wheel-drive car and saving the $300 million. Front-wheel drive, of course, was what

Sperlich had been wanting at Ford for more than five years, and slowly he began to tilt Chrysler's management. He faithfully presented both models, but his heart belonged to the K car. His friends believe he changed the decision by changing John Riccardo. He emphasized that front-wheel drive unlocked the future for Chrysler, and that under short-range conditions, the K car might save as much as two and even three miles a gallon over the H car. For a shaky company threatened by a government mandate which would set standards for a company's entire fleet—an average of eighteen miles per gallon by 1978 and twenty miles per gallon by 1980 —that difference was considerable. Sperlich insisted there was no real alternative to front-wheel drive: The government standards were permanent; they demanded long-range thinking. For Sperlich, emerging from the wars of Ford, Riccardo's tolerance was a welcome change; he never fought back, he simply listened. In the end John Riccardo opted for the K car.

It was a courageous choice. Old-time Chrysler product men like Jack Withrow, who had been passionate about the K car but until Sperlich's arrival had considered it almost hopeless, felt that Sperlich's intervention had clearly made the difference. Taking place before the crisis in Iran, more than a year before Lee Iacocca arrived at Chrysler, the decision to go with front-wheel drive placed the company ahead of its American competitors. Years later, when Chrysler's health was good and its stock was booming, Jack Withrow would often say that it was Hal Sperlich more than anyone else who had saved the company.

Riccardo made other exceptional decisions as well. He decided to sell the European empire, removing a major drain on the company and making about $300 million in cash. Then he decided, knowing that it was a threat to his own leadership of the company, to hire Lee Iacocca.

Sperlich, naturally, helped persuade Lee Iacocca to come to Chrysler. Knowing that Iacocca was considering the job, Sperlich drove over to see his old mentor. He showed him all Chrysler's best new designs, the K car, already in preparation, and the sketches for a small van they had never been allowed to do at Ford. As much as Sperlich's encouragement might have meant to Iacocca, however, his decision to go to Chrysler already smacked of inevitability. When he had been fired at Ford, he had been flooded with offers. Being fired had in no way damaged his reputation; it was instead regarded by the business world as an act that revealed more about the whimsical nature of Henry Ford's business practices than about Iacocca's competence. But he had hesitated to accept any of the jobs he was offered, no matter how handsome the deal. He wanted to stay in the auto industry. It was what he knew best; he liked the scale of it. And, not least, he wanted revenge against Henry Ford. He knew Chrysler was sick, and he had a sense that he might be offered the top job there, so on his own he had some financial analysts prepare a report on its finances. They were even more dismal than he had thought. Eventually the offer from Chrysler came through. On November 2, 1978, Lee Iacocca joined the company. That same day John Riccardo announced that it had lost a record $158.8 million for the third quarter.

From the start Iacocca was appalled by what he found. After he took his first tour of the operation he turned to Sperlich and said, "You son of a bitch, why didn't you tell me it was this bad?"

"Because if I had, you never would have come," Sperlich answered.

Their always tempestuous relationship became edgier than ever; although they admired and respected each other, their friendship had its limits, for, alone among Iacocca's closest aides, Sperlich had always fought back. Both at Ford and later at Chrysler, Iacocca managed in a rage, often bludgeoning those who worked for him. Some learned how to take it. For others it was simply too much, and they drifted away. Only Sperlich responded in kind, pounding Iacocca back. The problem, Sperlich concluded, was that Iacocca was genuinely angry at him for having helped lure him to Chrysler, for now that he was there he was by no means sure that even if they could eventually get federal help, they would make it.

"You know," Iacocca would sometimes say to him during those first few years, "I'm not sure we can pull this off."

Iacocca held his first product meeting in the Rotunda, which was the styling room. The acoustics were terrible. "It sounds like we're talking in a tomb," he finally said, adding, "I wonder if someone is trying to tell us something." He could joke about it, but his fear of failure was real. Whether it was his fault or not, he would be blamed for Chrysler's collapse. He would have survived the humiliation of being fired by Henry Ford only to have Chrysler sink under his feet. For a man as proud as Lee Iacocca, who hated to lose in public, that would be unbearable. Worse, it might seem to prove that Henry Ford had been right. So it was that all through 1979 Lee Iacocca and Hal Sperlich went at each other in a constant fury. Very few outsiders watching them would have guessed that they had been the closest of professional allies for more than fifteen years.

Some who knew Iacocca well thought that when he first arrived at Chrysler he not only misunderstood the full extent its sickness but the nature of it. He was aware that the company was ill, but he believed it was ailing because of bad decisions, not because of fearful systemic pressures that had forced bad decisions. Thus, fairly quickly, the coming of a good management team, the Iacocca team, would turn it around. Good decisions would replace bad decisions. Soon it would be like Ford in the old days, except with a slimmer, better team. One incident seemed to prove that. For a meeting with Chrysler's product planners, Bernard Robertson, one of the more senior product men, had put together a paper that said that Chrysler had to concentrate its limited resources on small cars, that it had never made any money in big cars, that its credibility (limited though that might be) was with the smaller, less expensive ones, and therefore in these difficult times what little resource the company had should be concentrated in an area where the company already had some trust. When Robertson finished, he and the others in the room were treated to a patronizing lecture from Iacocca about how much money Ford had made on its big-car lines on quite limited investment, how you could take a basic chassis, add on a good grille and a few doodads, and the profits went off the chart.

That story had spread quickly through the company and the automotive world, and it had convinced some people that Iacocca did not really understand the horror at Chrysler and that he had not really changed. It also prompted a furious exchange between two old friends, David E. Davis of *Car and Driver* and Hal Sperlich, both of them critics of the old Detroit, both of them proponents of the new front-wheel-drive cars, both of them evangelists for an industry that would use its mind as well as its muscle. One night soon after Iacocca had taken over Chrysler they had a bitter argument in which Davis, having heard the story about Iacocca's big-car lecture at Chrysler and some others before it, told Sperlich that Iacocca was just the old Detroit in a new office and, worse, that Iacocca did not really believe in Sperlich's wonderful front-wheel-drive, fuel-efficient cars, he was merely using Sperlich. That was painful for Sperlich, and he turned to Davis and said, "All I ask is that you have lunch with him. One lunch. Then you make your own decision. Maybe he's not the philosopher-king that I claim he is, but at least you'll find out he's not the barbarian asshole that you think he is."

The lunch was duly arranged, and Davis came away impressed. Iacocca, he decided, had by that time perceived the full extent of the malaise of Chrysler (and thus the industry), and Davis had liked the indignation with which Iacocca regarded the Chrysler sales bank. That was not put on, it was real passion, directed against a kind of evil within the industry. More, unlike most of the auto men of his generation, who were wedded to the past, Iacocca seemed to Davis a man capable of real change. Davis later admitted as much to Sperlich, and he talked of the possible reasons Iacocca was different. Part of it was probably that he was smarter than most of his contemporaries and had risen in the company against greater odds. He had probably never accepted the conventional wisdom the way men with more conventional backgrounds had. But part of it was also that he simply was not programmed to do things as they had always been done, not tied to platitudes. Many of his contemporaries had learned the rhetoric of change and could talk a good game, but whenever they made decisions they inevitably reverted to form. This was not true of Iacocca. He not only talked change, he *had* changed. He was willing to take risks and to pay attention to new realities and adapt his thinking to them. He was, Davis decided, a completely pragmatic man.

Nothing at Chrysler offended Iacocca's pragmatism more than the sales bank. He was appalled that a company could try to do business by cheating and lying to itself. R. K. Brown, the outgoing vice-president for marketing, explained the system to him soon after he took over. Later, Brown came and asked Iacocca for some money for an advertising campaign to sell the sales-bank cars. It was March, the last month of the quarter. The sales bank, he said, had 100,000 cars in it. Iacocca was stunned. Sell 100,000 cars, millions of dollars' worth? And sell them under deadline pressure? But Brown was quite confident they could do it. They'd always done it this way, he said. Just look, he told Iacocca, at the last ten days of March for each of the past ten years. Everyone in the sales force, he explained, went to the Tank, a large room, and divvied up the regions and the dealers and the number of cars. Sure enough, in Iacocca's first year some 66,000 cars were pushed right through. But it took time to do that, and meanwhile every day that Iacocca went to work he drove by the old Ford plant at Highland Park. Chrysler was renting it from Ford to use for the sales bank, and the sight of his cars wasting away, the weeds growing among them, made him almost ill. He later figured out that it took about $125 a car to fix them up again for sale. It was immediately clear to him that the dealers were simply waiting each year until the last minute and then buying their cars at these fire sales.

The company's disease was endemic. To cut costs in the mid-seventies Townsend had laid off the people who were critical to the company's future, the engineers and the research-and-development experts. Now, in the late seventies, the company was paying for it. There were also the problems with the government safety and emissions standards. In December 1978, at the height of Chrysler's frantic struggle for survival, John Riccardo went to the White House to argue for a two-year respite from some of the federal regulations. He said that Chrysler otherwise might fall more than $1 billion behind in the next two years in its capital needs, and he blamed many of its problems, particularly its expensive retooling to meet new fuel-efficiency requirements, on the federal government. Stuart Eizenstat, the Carter administration domestic-policy adviser with whom he met, made no promises, and his superior, President Jimmy Carter—who privately regarded Detroit executives as greedy in good times and whiny in bad ones—was not sympathetic.

Nothing in Iacocca's first year was easy. Chrysler lost $205 million, and the next two years were to be a great deal worse. "We have quite detailed accounting that shows we have lost one billion dollars in this past year," Jerry Greenwald mordantly told his fellow senior executives soon after he joined the company as controller. "The only trouble is that the systems are so bad we don't have the foggiest idea why or where we lost the one billion." Recovery would have been difficult under the best of conditions, but within a short time the crisis in Iran began. GM and Ford were shaken by it, but Chrysler nearly died.

Probably no one but Iacocca could have pulled off what followed, the government rescue of Chrysler and the slow, painstaking process of resuscitating a dying company. Many other talented men like Greenwald, Sperlich, and Steve Miller played critical roles, but what legitimized the rescue operation first in the business community and then in the Congress was Iacocca's name and reputation. (The political muscle of the UAW during a Democratic administration did not hurt, of course.) He was aided not only by his strengths but by his tendency, not always attractive, to take everything personally. In this struggle, it was a major asset. To him, the battle to save Chrysler was not just an especially difficult job that it would be nice to succeed at; it was a chance to vindicate himself. It impelled him to work harder, to push everyone around him harder. Some of his closest friends believed he could not have pulled it off if it had been a mere corporate struggle. But to him it was the moral equivalent of war; it was Lee Iacocca against Henry Ford. It was the perfect role for him. Uniting his cause with the nation's cause, he made it seem that he was bringing back not only Chrysler but also America itself. His skill at merging personal destiny with corporate destiny dated from the Mustang, when the car had become *his* car and he had ended up on the covers of both news magazines; now he exercised it on a scale that no one else in corporate life could ever have imagined.

There were two more Iacocca assets that proved crucial. The first was that he was probably the only man in the world of automobiles who could have attracted talented people to so sick a company. He brought in some of the most promising young men from Ford, offering them a chance not at riches but at the excitement of turning around an ailing company and doing some of the things they had been forbidden to do at Ford. (For a time all of the top executives at Chrysler seemed to be Ford exiles—

Sperlich, Greenwald, Paul Bergmoser, Gar Laux. Some in Detroit started calling Chrysler "Little Ford." One day early in Iacocca's reign they sat around discussing a certain segment of the market. "Listen, in this segment there's only GM, Chrysler, and us," someone said.

"Wait a minute," said Laux. "*We're* Chrysler now.")

The second asset was more basic. In an industry where leadership had become increasingly cautious and finance-oriented, he was market-driven: He could respond to product. Even in the darkest days at Chrysler he retained his instinct for product, for what the customer wanted.

More often than not in those critical months, Iacocca was an absolute monster to deal with. Not only had the task of salvaging Chrysler turned out to be ferociously difficult, but also his wife was dying. He was forced to spend too much time away from her by the constant need to be in Washington lobbying Congress or the banks. Everything in his life at that moment must have seemed impossible to him, one close friend thought. As far as he was concerned, no one knew how to do anything at Chrysler. All of the amenities he had become accustomed to at Ford—the people who were always there to smooth his way, who knew what to do for him even before they were asked, drivers, pilots, secretaries, batmen—were all gone. Once, upon checking into the Waldorf and finding that his room wasn't ready, he pointed at the high Chrysler executive trying to help him check in and said to him, "I want you to call those guys at Ford and ask them how they do this." He had left a world of private jets to come to a company where he was lucky if someone met his plane. These inconveniences seemed to symbolize the deficiency he sensed everywhere around him at Chrysler.

His friends and employees became accustomed to his bursts of fury and profanity, his tendency to blame everyone but himself for his problems. The moods had always passed quickly, and he would neither apologize for them nor even acknowledge them. But now sometimes an eerie moodiness settled upon him; in his study with his closest friends, whether he was smoking a cigar or watching television, he was clearly alone—building, as one friend said, a wall around himself. He snapped at everybody, including, to everyone's surprise, his mother.

Fortunately for Iacocca and Chrysler, Sperlich was already there when he arrived, and the K car was already on the drawing board. Otherwise, the company would never have made it. From the moment John Riccardo approved the K, Chrysler entered a race to fend off bankruptcy until it reached the marketplace in the fall of 1980. There were times during the next two years when it seemed as if the company would not last until the K car appeared. All the normal channels of financing had dried up. No bank was interested in lending more money to Chrysler, no financial house anxious to do a public issue of its stock. Its only hope was the government. Even with Chrysler's best efforts—the most brilliant and expensive lobbyists in Washington, the strength of organized labor, the added force of black power (Chrysler was the largest industrial employer of blacks in America), and the energy of all Chrysler's dealers—the program was often in doubt. To satisfy critics in Congress who wanted a scapegoat, Riccardo resigned as chairman. He had not endeared himself to them by criticizing federal regulatory programs. In September 1979, Iacocca became chairman of Chrysler. In the weeks after that, the company edged perilously close to bankruptcy, and in December the bills to rescue Chrysler went to both houses of Congress. The government moved slowly, and the banks, which were already supporting Chrysler, moved slower, but eventually an immensely complicated bail-out program was approved that brought the company $1.2 billion in guaranteed funds, enough to keep the K cars in the pipeline.

For long periods in 1980, the company actually was bankrupt and existed only at the mercy of its thousands of suppliers, which it was gently and politely stiffing. For about four months the suppliers carried the company; any one of them could have pushed it over the brink by demanding payment. Chrysler's internal bloodlettings were terrible. On the day in August 1980 when the K car went into production, Chrysler laid off three thousand of its sixty-five hundred engineers. There was simply no money to pay them. It was one of the darkest days in Chrysler's history. Rarely had a company so large been suspended on a thread so frail.

The first K cars came onto the market in October 1980, with 100,000 of the previous year's cars still unsold. They were not the immediate success that everyone had hoped. The prime rate had just gone up again, and customers were cautious. 1981 was a bad year for cars, coming on the heels of the Shah's fall. Auto industry sales were down 27 percent overall; interest rates were so high it was hard to tell the difference between banks and loan sharks. Furthermore, the early K cars were loaded with too many options and priced too high. The basic stripped-down K was supposed to sell at $5880; instead, the average model in the dealers' showrooms cost some $2000 more. Iacocca, pushed by Greenwald, had opted to go for maximum profit per car. It was an attempt to gain additional cash, but in that economy it turned out to be the wrong move. The company, shellshocked, wanted to reverse its fortunes too quickly, but with interest rates often above 15 percent, many would-be customers held back and repaired their old cars. The haste also threatened the K's reputation; not everyone thought the cars were quite ready for the launch, that all the bugs were out of them.

Iacocca fought on, doing everything he could to hold down costs. He relentlessly slashed his white-collar staff, eventually cutting it in half. That was probably the most difficult aspect of his cost-cutting. When an aide once complained to him about how painful he found it to trim his own staff, Iacocca snapped, "Don't fucking bother me with your hard-luck stories about firing people—I fire a thousand people every goddam day, so don't come and tell me about your goddam problems." Labor granted concessions, perhaps in part because he forged a strong and mutually admiring relationship with Doug Fraser of the UAW, who became a member of the Chrysler board. Many suppliers continued to allow Chrysler to hold off on their bills, thereby giving the company an additional free loan of hundreds of millions. The check was always going to be in the mail. Chrysler stumbled through 1981, a terrible year in which it lost $479 million.

Iacocca made a decision at the height of the company's illness that was to have a considerable effect upon the long-term issue of quality. It had been a continual grievance among the Ford manufacturing people that the bonus or compensation system undermined quality, corrupting even the most moral of men into putting their short-range selfish interests over the larger interests of the customer, the product, and the future of the company. There was a financial reward for maximizing annual profit and no reward for foresight, and so inevitably decisions were tilted to profit because it was so directly connected to bonus. Iacocca had been a beneficiary of that system at both Ford and Chrysler—in the eyes of his friends, a ready and uncomplaining one. Quality had always been sacrificed. Now, at Chrysler, he moved to protect quality. In 1981, when the company was at its wobbliest, he told his inner circle that he wanted to go back to Lynn Townsend's five-year-or-fifty-thousand-mile warranty, which had been dead for ten years.

He was met with disbelief. Steve Miller, one of his top finance people, opposed him because the expense of covering such a warranty was terrifying—no one could predict what it might cost, perhaps $100 million a year, perhaps more. Steve Sharf, the manufacturing man, was quite unhappy about the idea. "Jesus, Lee—that's nothing but problems," he said. Even Jim McNaughton, the marketing man, was against it. As far as he was concerned, if there was that much money in the company, he would much rather spend it on advertising. "No," Iacocca said, waving away their objections, "if we have the five-fifty, if we have to live up to it, then I know damn well that finance is going to give us the money for the plants, and I know the marketing people will really use it in their ads, and I know that manufacturing, if it's a question of doing a thousand new pieces or doing a smaller number right, we'll do it right." He held the day. It was an important victory of the enlightened Iacocca over the old Iacocca.

Finally, tentatively at first, things began to improve. Hal Sperlich and his colleagues had done their work well, and the K car averaged twenty-five miles a gallon on arrival. Early in March 1982 Chrysler sold its tank division, for $335 million, to General Dynamics, and the cash immediately strengthened the company and eased the tension with the suppliers. The Japanese agreed to a voluntary limit on imports, and because they were using their restricted number of cars to move into the middle rather than the low end of the market, it took pressure off Chrysler and the K car. In the first quarter of 1982, Chrysler showed a profit, but only because of the sale of the tank division. Without it, the company would have lost $90 million. By the company's existing standards, however, that was virtually a profit. In the second quarter the profit actually came, $107 million. It was the first time in five years the company had posted two successful quarters back to back. That summer, interest rates began to come down significantly, and as they did, the market for new cars began to swell. The impact on Chrysler was instantaneous. "It looks like Lee dodged the bullet again," his old colleague Don Frey said that summer. But the bullet had come very close.

Soon Iacocca became the most unlikely of modern figures, the Detroit car maker as national hero, the one-time creator of big, luxurious cars at Ford who was bringing Chrysler back from the ashes with small, fuel-efficient ones. Someone had proposed using him in Chrysler's commercials. He had credibility, it was suggested, while the Chrysler Corporation did not. ("Why did they go to you, Lee?" a friend asked. "They wanted Walter Cronkite," he replied, referring to the most trusted man in the nation, according to polls, "but he wouldn't do it, so they asked me.") It was risky to use a CEO in commercials for a troubled company, because his career could be irrevocably damaged if the company went deeper in the red despite the campaign. But Chrysler was in such bad shape that qualms like this were unimportant. Iacocca himself, however, was ambivalent about the idea; while he knew it might help the company, it would also result in a considerable loss of privacy. Wendell Larsen, the company's top public-relations man, warned that even if the campaign was successful, it might somehow leave the impression that Chrysler had been saved only because Lee Iacocca was a fast-talking supersalesman who could persuade Americans to buy almost anything, even inferior cars. Although he was uneasy, Iacocca went ahead, and the first commercial with Iacocca as the company's main pitchman appeared in the fall of 1980. Slimmer than in the past, his suits less flashy, with fewer white-on-white shirts in his wardrobe, he was the new Iacocca.

For someone who had been so shy in the early days of his career, and who—appearances to the contrary—was in fact still shy, the transformation was remarkable. The people at Kenyon & Eckhardt, the agency that did the Chrysler commercials, were impressed by how quickly he picked up the technique and how good he became. He was much better than most of the professional actors they dealt with. The professional actors, trained in their work, frequently blew lines; Lee Iacocca, novice to the art, almost never did. He seemed to get it right every time, almost to the second. He always had the beat of it. Of course, the actors were mouthing alien words, while these words were his own, crafted by the advertising people from what he said at press conferences. But what set him apart was the almost feral intensity of his performances and of his concentration while he was doing them. No one at the advertising agency had ever seen anything like it. He had, of course, despite his ambivalence, always sought exposure. He liked to protest that he did not like doing the commercials. He would come in at the beginning and complain, "My kids say I look too fat." He worried that his nose might look too big, and the cameramen were told to be aware of that. Inevitably, however, he became a professional, giving direction to the directors, telling the writers what to write. He liked the celebrity that the commercials brought. In the old days, one of his friends noted, when you walked around New York City with Lee he was always checking the streets to see how many Fords there were. Now he checked to see how many people recognized him and turned around.

By the middle of 1982 he was pressing his aides to get him on the cover of *Time* magazine, as if that one fact could authenticate and assure the Chrysler turnaround. As other accolades poured in, the cover of *Time* became an obsession. He spoke constantly of men he knew in the publishing world who said they could help fix it for him. *Time*, however, skeptical as to whether the Chrysler rebound would last, hesitated. When John DeLorean was arrested in a drug bust in the fall of 1982 and *Time* put him on the cover, Iacocca was enraged. "Here I've saved this goddam company, and I can't get on the cover of *Time*," he said, "and that son of a bitch DeLorean gets caught dealing drugs and he makes it. What the hell kind of magazine is that? What the hell is wrong with those people?" *Time*, in its own good time, finally came around, and Iacocca, looking more like a huckster than he might have wanted, adorned an issue in March 1983.

As Chrysler's financial situation continued to improve, Iacocca became more egocentric than ever. In meetings he was often exceptionally hard on his old friends. He began to complain that it was difficult being at the top because everyone wanted something from him. There was no small irony in that, some of his old associates thought, for that was precisely the attitude he had detested in Henry Ford. If there was still a certain shyness to him, he had managed fairly well to overcome it. He obviously liked his new fame. It was hard, he complained, to fight off the networks that wanted to do specials and the magazines that wanted to put him on the cover. He was marvelous with the press—quick, funny, always, it seemed, on the attack. To a nation somewhat on the defensive that was particularly appealing. He was the man who had saved Chrysler. The more public recognition he got for that, the more he came to believe it.

The role of others in Chrysler's newly won success gradually diminished in his mind. He was less than generous about sharing credit with those —like Greenwald, Sperlich, and Miller—whose part in saving Chrysler nearly equaled his own. Of course, sharing credit had never been one of his strong points. In 1982 a small design company in Brighton, Michigan, named Cars and Concepts, which did highly specialized and innovative styling for the bigger companies, brought Chrysler the idea of bringing back the convertible. Unlike the other big companies, Chrysler was willing to take a risk, and soon the convertible, designed by Cars and Concepts and built on a K-car frame, was in production. It was a lovely small success for Chrysler. The public response was overwhelming, the car was remarkably profitable, and everyone had fun doing it. But when an automotive reporter called Cars and Concepts to get additional information on the genesis of the idea, he was told to cool it because the word had come down from Chrysler that the original idea was not theirs, it was Mr. Iacocca's.

He also played a crucial role in giving the go-ahead signal to a vehicle that the product planners at both Chrysler and Ford had long wanted, what eventually became known as the Minivan. Since 1974 Chrysler's product people had been working on plans for a relatively inexpensive, vanlike wagon which would be easy to drive, have a great deal of room, and get good gas mileage. So far they had been thwarted. From the moment Sperlich arrived at Chrysler he had pushed the program, but the K car was draining almost all of the company's resources, and by the time Iacocca arrived, the Minivan was almost dead. It was, however, something both he and Sperlich had wanted to do for a long time.

In the late 1960s at Ford, Don DeLaRossa, one of the best designers in the company, had mentioned an idea of his rather casually to Gene Bordinat, his chief, for a new, modernized, efficient wagon. Bordinat had picked up on it immediately. There were, thought Bordinat, a few times in a designer's life when he knew, *absolutely knew*, that he had a winner, and this was one of them. DeLaRossa had spoken of an all-purpose vehicle, neither station wagon nor van, which women as well as men could drive, a car for the suburban housewife during the week and for the family on the weekends, a sawed-off hybrid of a van and a wagon, with lots of interior room. The designers envisioned it as being more stylish than a normal van, and it would handle more like a car than a truck; it would get exceptionally good gas mileage, perhaps as much as twenty-five miles a gallon. It was, in short, to be the perfect vehicle for modern suburban living, a world of short hauls, most of them under fifteen miles, yet it would be capable of long trips.

Sperlich and Bordinat, more than the others in the company, loved the Mini/max, as it was called. Iacocca seemed interested in it, though he was hardly passionate about it, and never, in the prolonged battles that followed, did he make it his, as he had the Mustang. In the early part of the Mini/max's history, when Iacocca still had muscle at the company, his mind seemed to be elsewhere; later, when he was more interested in the product, he was a man of diminishing influence. Some of his subordinates thought his attitude toward the car reflected not so much a lack of enthusiasm for the wagon as for the battle necessary to force it through. Indeed, from the start the resistance within the company was considerable. The slow-walking, Bordinat thought, was the most deliberate he had ever seen. Sometimes it seemed to him like watching Death in the Design Shop. The finance people, he knew, had learned that you could kill a car there: Don't shoot the program down; shoot down the execution of it. Make them do it over again and again, so that the product never really gets out of the shop and never gets any exposure at a high level of the company.

The problem from the beginning, Sperlich believed, was that Henry Ford was against the Mini/max. It showed not so much in overt opposition but in a constant wariness and relentless grumbling. Sperlich suspected Ford was more negative in private with Lundy than he was with most other high executives. It was as if the signals given at the meetings were lightly negative but the signals given outside the meetings were *very* negative. Ford was distressed that the Mini/max would have to be a totally new car; it could not be a spin-off from an existing technology. For the Mini/max to work, it had to have front-wheel drive. The same van done with rear-wheel drive would have to be higher and heavier, more like a small truck; with front-wheel drive and a transaxle—a front axle incorporating a transmission—the car could be lower and lighter to handle; it would be, in Sperlich's phrase, a more friendly vehicle. He loved it because it had so many possibilities, and because, as the engineer designing it, he faced so many challenges. But the resistance because of the front-wheel drive was enormous. Henry Ford was still shying away from that commitment on cars, and now they were asking him to authorize still another front-wheel-drive vehicle.

Periodically the design people would bring it out again, and it would be shot down again. It was something new, therefore it was untried, and therefore it was likely to be risky and expensive. The finance people focused on that, and they stayed with it, despite overwhelming evidence that the new van was likely to be a brilliant success. That evidence came in from marketing research and was marshaled by a man named Norman Krandall, who was known in the company as something of a maverick, almost by choice not a member of the inner club. He was a Pole who participated actively in liberal Democratic politics and seemed to have taken pleasure over the years in defying the assumptions of the finance people. He was a natural comrade-in-arms for Sperlich, for Krandall believed that the company, now run by people who did not want to make cars, had become stagnant. By 1976 it was clear to Krandall that the possibilities for this van were greater than anyone's expectations, including, until then, his own. The research showed that the Mini/max might sell more than 800,000 pieces in its first year, or almost 400,000 more than the Mustang had. More, those sales would not subtract from Ford's other lines; they promised to come from people who owned traditional sedans, large cars that had been giving their owners ten or twelve miles a gallon. The Mini/max would give them twelve miles a gallon *more*— and carry just as many kids and groceries. Stunned by his research, Krandall decided to do it again; the results were the same. But that wasn't all. His findings showed that Ford could charge a great deal of money for it, between $8000 and $10,000, a large price back in 1976. Those figures made Iacocca really interested for the first time.

When some of the finance people challenged Krandall's numbers, he gladly gave way. Even if we're off by 50 percent, he replied, we're still talking about 400,000 pieces. Thus, he suggested, it still makes sense. In fact, he added, cut it in half again; use the figure of 200,000, and it *still* makes sense. Even the research findings for the Mustang, which had been remarkable, had never shown numbers like these. It was an exceptional market just waiting to be taken, Krandall argued, and if Ford acted quickly it could get in before anyone else and skim the cream off it for two or three years before GM could move. Bordinat, watching Krandall fight back at these meetings, was amazed by how audacious he was, how closely he stayed with his figures. Usually when the numbers were good and there was opposition, there was a normal tendency to soften them so that if the car was approved and did not pan out, the executive could protect himself. But in this instance Krandall was holding nothing back. It was almost as if he had a death wish, Bordinat thought.

Krandall was surprised by how little reaction there was to his research. This was a brand-new market he had uncovered, and the Ford Motor Company was supposed to react to the market. But the market, he realized, no longer mattered to most of the men running the company; they thought that they could dictate the market. Iacocca was clearly interested, he could see, but the fight seemed to be going out of him; ten years earlier with numbers like these he would have been unstoppable.

Krandall first unveiled his statistics in 1976. Two years later, with no action, he brought them forward again. At that moment the hard times had not yet hit the company, and there was at least $3 billion in the Ford coffers. At the critical meeting Krandall found himself challenging both Philip Caldwell, who was then deputy chief executive officer, and Ed Lundy. Krandall, looking at Lundy, knew he was probably in for a confrontation. For, as Krandall himself well knew, he had done the unthinkable within the Ford company: He had directly challenged the theology of the finance people and of Lundy himself. He had done this, two years before, with a paper. The paper had analyzed Ford's investment program in comparison with that of General Motors and had proved that Ford was now investing less in future models than it had historically. It had tried to show a direct relationship between investment and success in the market. In the past Ford had invested roughly 55 to 60 percent as much as GM, Krandall's paper showed; it then demonstrated that Ford had retrenched more than GM, and that the ratio of spending had fallen to 45 percent. Ford had to assume, he wrote, one of two things: Either its people had suddenly gotten much smarter than the General Motors people in the way in which they spent, or inevitably its fortunes would decline. Krandall had sent a copy of his paper to Iacocca and a number of other senior Ford people, and it had been passed around at the highest levels of the company. Lundy had written a very tough rebuttal of it and sent the rebuttal to everyone who had gotten Krandall's original—but not, of course, to Norman Krandall. That, Krandall was sure, was a sign that Ed Lundy was very, very angry at him.

At the meeting Krandall argued that Ford had to do not only the Escort program, which it had by then decided to go ahead with, but the Mini/

max as well; it had to do both. Lundy immediately countered that the company did not have the money to do the van. Krandall was obstinate. If there was not enough money, he suggested, why didn't Ford borrow the money to do the Mini/max?

"If we go out and borrow the money," Ed Lundy said somewhat sharply, "we'll lose our triple-A rating."

"If we don't borrow it and don't follow the market with cars like this," Krandall said, "we may lose it anyway."

He knew he was not playing the game; he was supposed to have surrendered much earlier. But his research was very good, and not only was his own integrity riding on that research but so, he believed, was the integrity of the company. The Ford Motor Company must tell the truth to itself, or it would be out of business.

Then Philip Caldwell joined in. "I don't mean to be offensive," he said, "but we just can't take on certain obligations. There's simply a limit to how much we can do."

At that point Lundy, normally the epitome of good manners, came back at Krandall hard. Krandall had crossed a line twice now; he had flagrantly violated the rules. "I *do* mean to be offensive," Lundy said. "We cannot do it, and we will not do it." The Mini/max was cooked, Krandall thought, and he was cooked as well; it was only a matter now of negotiating the terms of his retirement, for his career was over at Ford.

Now at Chrysler, Sperlich and Iacocca saw the Mini/max, or Minivan as Chrysler called it, as a chance for vindication. Beyond that, Iacocca firmly believed in its market possibilities. "The hell with what people say," he told Sperlich, "somehow we'll find a way to do it. For God's sake, let's not forget we're here to do cars." He managed to find just enough money and engineers to keep the program going. The decision to make the K car had kept the Chrysler company alive, and Iacocca's next decision, taken in early fall of 1980, while times were still terrible, to go ahead with the Minivan helped make the company prosper. Years later someone asked him how he had been able to make the decision when things were so bad at Chrysler. "When you're already losing your ass," he answered, "what's another billion among friends?"

Essentially it was produced by many of the same people who had tried to do it at Ford but who had since gone over to Chrysler—Sperlich, DeLaRossa, and Iacocca—along with some Chrysler people who had suffered through the same sort of frustration. Of its original Ford architects, only Gene Bordinat had not moved to Chrysler. Making it turned out to be not that hard. They had the front-wheel drive and the platform from the K car, and the market research had been generously supplied by Ford. Norman Krandall's research turned out to be generally accurate, for it was a wagon that proved to fit the needs of a good number of suburban Americans. In the fall of 1983 the Chrysler Minivan, long planned at Ford and always sidetracked, came out and was an exceptional success.

Ben Bidwell, the Ford marketing executive who at the last minute in the front-wheel-drive dispute had switched to Henry Ford, had left the company and gone to Hertz, then Chrysler. Near the end of the year he was dining in a suburban restaurant when he noticed that Bordinat, the former Ford designer, was seated across the room. He penciled a note to Bordinat and had the waiter hand it to him. "Gene," it said, "thanks for the Minivan. It was very generous of you. We'll do over 160,000 pieces this year."

A few weeks later someone asked Iacocca about the Minivan and its success. "It's really very easy," he replied, "when you've done it once before."

PART
NINE

PART NINE

35.
THE ARRIVISTES

It took Takashi Ishihara, once considered the boy wonder of Nissan, only forty years to become the company's president. He had joined it in 1937, when he was a young man of twenty-five trying to crash the old-boy network of Japanese business. He was not very well connected, having come from a second-level university, and he entered what was generally regarded in those days as a second-rate company. He got the job there in the first place, he liked to tell friends, because he was not talented enough for the first-rate places, the banks and the high ministries. He advanced quickly during the war, in which he did not serve. "I was lucky," he later said. "All the smarter young men had to go into the army, and so there was little competition in my generation." Some contemporaries thought he had not served because the authorities were suspicious of him for alleged left-wing activities as a student.

Because he went back so far in Nissan's history, he was well aware of the hard times. He had been director of the accounting department in 1945, when Nissan simply could not pay its bills and the company seemed perched close to bankruptcy. There were crises every Saturday, when the parts suppliers would show up to be paid. Nissan did not have the cash to pay most of them, and so it had to hold them off until Monday, the day its own desperately needed loans came through from the bank. Ishihara selected a young man named Yoshihisa Yokoyama to write all the Saturday checks. "But I am not very good at writing checks," Yokoyama protested. "Good," Ishihara replied, "the worse the better. Make as many mistakes as you can." So it was that on Saturdays the parts suppliers would line up, and Yokoyama, warned by Ishihara to write only a few checks, would sit, sweat pouring down his face, writing as slowly as he could, making as many errors as he could, until the clock tolled noon and Nissan closed up and the banks also closed.

Ishihara had an exceptional early career, and he was made a director

in 1954, when he was only thirty-three. For a time his career became
sidetracked because of the company's political divisions, but in the sixties,
with the success of the exports, he was resurrected. In the mid-sixties, as
managing director, he pushed for a small one-liter car for the domestic
market. Kawamata opposed this strenuously. The car was made, Ishihara
opened a separate sales channel for it, and it became Nissan's best-selling
model. In 1973 many board members thought it was his turn to be president, but Kawamata passed him over for a union loyalist named Tadahiro
Iwakoshi. Four years later, Ishihara's time finally came. He was sixty-five
years old.

His first major test came in 1978, just a few months after he took office.
It was some five years since the Yom Kippur War, which had triggered
the first great oil shock and quadrupled the price of oil. The Japanese,
with their smaller cars, had been the immediate beneficiaries of that
cataclysm, but over the five years American consumers had gradually
adjusted to the new prices. By 1978, the Yom Kippur shock was regarded
not as the beginning of a complicated, less stable era but rather as a
momentary aberration. Big cars were selling again. "Welcome to the year
of the Whopper," Ben Bidwell of Ford had said in introducing the new
Ford line to automotive reporters that year. In 1978 all the Ford factories
that fall were working overtime trying to get as many hefty V-8 engines
into the showrooms as possible.

The world automotive market, always fickle, now seemed more so than
ever. This time it was the Japanese companies that had been caught in
the changing tide. Their small cars simply were not selling; they were
piling up on the beaches of California. All fall, month by month, Japan's
problem had gotten worse: There had been a reversion to type in American
taste. In December 1978, Ishihara estimated that there was some five
months' worth of inventory waiting to be sold in America, about 150,000
cars. His only consolation was that the people of Toyota were in the same
predicament. It was unlike anything the cautious Japanese companies had
ever faced before.

Ishihara was desperate. He knew he was going to have to take drastic
action. All that stock, he thought, had to be liquidated. He did not know
what it was going to take to do it—what gimmicks, sales drives, rebates
—but it had to go. He decided to tell the Nissan directors that they must
prepare themselves to go to zero production for export, perhaps for the
entire period between April and September. The first move he made was
cutting back on overtime and holidays. Nissan workers usually got one
hour of overtime a day, which they badly wanted, and they often worked
on holidays. Starting in January and lasting through March there would

be none of either. But this was not enough of a reduction, he knew. He could close down one of his factories, each of which was producing about 170,000 cars a year, but closing down a whole factory would be terribly hard on its workers and its community; instead he would close the equivalent of one factory, spreading the reductions among all the plants. He intended to start doing this in April. Everyone in the company would have to share the burden.

Then the events in Iran began to unfold. At first it seemed inconceivable to Ishihara that the Shah, with billions of dollars' worth of the best American military equipment, could fall to a rabble, but soon his advisers were telling him that the Shah might not make it. At first Ishihara had little sense of the long-range implications of what was happening. Gradually he realized that these were not minor matters but transcending ones, which would profoundly affect the price of oil. That portent unsettled him, because any dramatic increase in oil prices would strike to the very core of his business. As oil jumped to $16 a barrel and then $20, still rising, he became alternately pessimistic and optimistic. Then he began to see that this was a comparative problem. If the world of autos was threatened by expensive gasoline, the big auto was threatened first, which constituted a great opportunity for the small auto. He was head of a company that produced some of the best small cars in the world.

The market obeyed his prediction. In March he did not have to give the order to cut back production; he gave an order to increase it. Years later the American manufacturers claimed that he and the other Japanese executives had been lucky, that they had been like beached whales until the collapse of the Shah's regime. Perhaps it was luck, Ishihara thought, but he and the others at Nissan had worked very hard for a long time to earn that luck.

Japan's success in automobiles came so fast it threatened to upset the long-accepted hierarchy of the nation's businesses. It was puzzling and bothersome to the Japanese establishment that the auto industry, which was not venerated or connected to Japan's past, became more powerful every year. Auto's spiritual place in the life of the nation was still uncertain. Was it wasteful? Did it pollute? Would it help create a softer, more materialistic youth? Despite these reservations, the power of the auto industry surged in the mid-seventies, while shipping and steel—under assault from poorer countries like Korea—went into minor slumps.

As auto's power grew, so did that of Katsuji Kawamata, the chairman of Nissan. He was now auto's representative in the Keidanren, the powerful business association, although chosen only by process of elimination. The Toyota people didn't want the job; they kept to themselves in Nagoya. Soichiro Honda was too radical, too much the outsider. The rise of auto privately offended many of the Keidanren traditionalists, who felt that the auto men were arrivistes, unaccustomed to their new power and insensitive in using it. (Their disdain was similar, in fact, to what some American industrialists felt toward Detroit executives, that they were too confident, selfish, and insular.) Kawamata, like the industry he represented, was considered too young, only in his early seventies while they were in their eighties. Furthermore, he was viewed as too arrogant and bumptious, insufficiently schooled in the art of false modesty.

In the past the leaders of the Keidanren were from industries whose role in the nation was absolutely clear. Steel, for example, had been of great importance in Japan ever since 1853, when Admiral Perry sailed his black steel ships into Tokyo Bay, impressing the Japanese. The steel men were perceived not as crude, bullying capitalists but as men who embodied the national spirit. This lofty image did not hinder their business practices in any way, however; steel was a genuine cartel. Once the fierce early competition had abated, executives from every company regularly convened to set prices, which they then announced to their customers. No other industry besides agriculture had enjoyed such complete government support in the early years of Japan's postwar recovery. Now that agriculture no longer played such a large role in the country's economy, steel was the government's favorite. It was full of top bureaucrats from MITI and the Ministry of Finance who went to work in the industry after their ministerial careers were completed. Thus aided by the government, the banks, and a rising new class of engineers, the Japanese steel industry was by the early sixties the best in the world. The excellence of the steel industry had been a major factor in the success of the automobile industry. It not only met auto's specifications but even surpassed the quality of American steel, particularly in rustproofing. The Americans had had the same technology available but had failed to use it. That was to grate on some American auto makers.

The steel industry's status was threatened in the seventies, however, and nothing demonstrated auto's ascendancy so vividly as its increased leverage in dealing with it. "We had to bow to them a great deal when we were younger," Kawamata once confided to a friend. "We do not have to bow so much anymore. It was not so hard for us to bow then, we never expected it to be different—but I think it is very hard for them now when we do not bow." Many of the steel men had been imperious when they had been more powerful than auto, and there was lingering resentment among auto executives. After the Yom Kippur War, as the balance changed, auto began criticizing steel for failing to modernize facilities quickly enough, for prices that were too high, for becoming lazy now that they were no longer challenged by the Americans.

In 1977 the steel men asked for a price increase. The auto men agreed but declared that they would no longer accept an annual increase. They began to buy in bulk, what one auto man called their own "cartel." The steel men did not like it, but there was little they could do. Slowly auto began to set the terms. "You are beginning to treat us," one of the executives of Nippon Kokan told an official of Toyota, "like one of the noodle caterers." He meant not only that steel was being demeaned but also that the auto industry was regarding the steel companies like any other supplier: telling them how much steel they wanted, when it was to be delivered, and how much they were willing to pay for it. To save everyone's face a ritual was conceived. In 1982, steel executives wanted a 10 percent price increase. They reconnoitered quietly and were immediately repulsed by the auto men. The auto men met and decided that $5\frac{1}{2}$ percent was their outer limit. They were not happy with even that large an increase, but they were worried that steel, which was suffering badly from foreign competition, might go in the red. In the long run, the weakening of the steel industry would harm auto. Therefore, they secretly communicated this figure to the steel industry before the public negotiations began. They were exceptionally polite about it, but there was no doubt that theirs was the hand that held the whip. At that point the steel men went public. They announced that they wanted an increase of $5\frac{1}{2}$ percent and they would fight to get it. In the following weeks the newspapers were full of speculation about whether or not steel would be able to muscle the increase. In the end, when $5\frac{1}{2}$ percent became the size of the increase, the appearance was given that steel, as always, had gotten what it always wanted, though auto had the satisfaction of knowing steel had gotten barely half. Its representatives were so powerful that they did not need to show their power in public.

That new power was symbolized by Katsuji Kawamata. Some colleagues thought he was openly politicking to become the chairman of the Keidanren. To them, that outcome was unthinkable. He was the upstart head of an upstart company. Many of the old-timers were offended by the nakedness of his ambition and his relationship with the union. Besides, the chairmanship of the Keidanren was not something one sought; it was something that happened. "He's the man," said one of the older members, a textile man, "who has a statue of himself in his own factory!"

36.
GREATHOUSE
IN TOKYO

The success of Japanese industry had made Takashi Ishihara's job infinitely more complicated than Katsuji Kawamata's had been when he was Nissan's president. Sometimes, speaking of his predecessor to his friends, he would say that Kawamata had had the easy years, when the Japanese were poor, when loyalty was easier to summon, and when Japanese goods were regarded with such disrespect that the Japanese were nearly invisible to their foreign competitors— Kawamata, he would say, had been there when no one was watching. He, by contrast, had taken over just in time to deal with the reaction to that success, when protectionism was on the rise in the West, when the Japanese were no longer seen as weak little brothers who were beneficiaries of the West's charity but as dangerous Oriental competitors, and when racial resentments against them were secretly and not so secretly harbored. Almost every decision he made was as much political as it was economic. Kawamata's job had been to be successful; his job, more difficult, was to be successful *and* not antagonize the foreigners. That was just one of the dilemmas that Ishihara faced as he began a new era at Nissan. For he was a man of the old order in a very new kind of situation.

He had come from accounting, not engineering, and the esteem he inspired among the company's best engineers was marginal. His strength was that he knew money and had the confidence of the men who ran the bank, and yet, unlike Kawamata, he had not come from the bank, so was not viewed by his executives as an outsider. His imposing size also had helped—he *looked* like a man of industry. But the principal dynamic of his success was ambition; he was zealous in the pursuit of his own interests, as befit a man who had waited so long in another's shadow. "There is nothing more ambitious in Japan," said one of his friends, "than a man who reaches sixty and has not yet attained his goals."

His life was the company, nothing else; he thought of virtually nothing but his work. That single-mindedness surprised some of his colleagues. It was not just that Ishihara and his wife did not have any children; it was that unlike most very successful Japanese they did not adopt any, even children from other members of their family, until late in their lives. A nephew of Mrs. Ishihara, named Tadashi Yoshikawa, came to live with them when he was a student and eventually went to work at Nissan. Only when he was about thirty did the Ishiharas adopt him. To the men around Ishihara, that was extremely puzzling.

Ishihara was sixty-five when he succeeded Kawamata, and in Nissan the tales of his maneuvers were many: stories of his doing deals directly with West Germans or Italians and not only cutting out the local Nissan people but never even mentioning the deals to them; stories of his competing with Katayama in the United States, undercutting the deals that Katayama had worked out with International Harvester for Nissan engines. It was not that his behavior was unusually self-interested for a Japanese executive; it was that he so nakedly wanted the credit. Within the company some who might normally have been his allies, finding they could make no connection with him, pulled back from him as he seemed to pull back from them. The Island, that was what some men called him.

Now Ishihara, like the heads of other Japanese companies, was under mounting pressure to become more international, to deal with foreigners in ways he had never done before, and to open plants overseas. That entailed an immense challenge for Ishihara, who for all his success in America was basically an isolationist Japanese businessmen, filled with the normal prejudices of his generation. What he would be seeking was a new kind of relationship with foreigners, which one American who closely monitored the auto industry in Japan called "no-fault internationalism": Nissan would flirt with places so desperate for a new factory that they would give Nissan exceptional benefits. For as the Japanese had become richer and more powerful, they had changed: They were no longer the supplicants in the world economic order; they no longer had to ask Westerners for favors. Westerners now asked them for favors. That change was reflected in the new attitudes of Takashi Ishihara and Nissan.

Among the first to notice the change was Pat Greathouse, who handled international affairs for the UAW. Greathouse was an old friend of Ichiro Shioji, and he had started visiting Japan in 1973, returning often. During his visits Greathouse began talking to the Japanese about their responsibilities in America: If they were selling that many cars there, they should start thinking of generating some jobs there as well. Obtaining a Japanese factory in America had surfaced as a major UAW objective. Greathouse, in fact, believed that Nissan had given him a commitment rather early on, and that the only unanswered questions were about what type of plant the Japanese would build and where they would build it. If it was an assembly plant, he gathered, it would be on the West Coast; if it was a manufacturing plant, it would likely be located near Kansas City.

In those early meetings Greathouse was pleased with the way things were going; he thought he was developing rapport with Masataka Okuma, who was the executive vice-president. Okuma, as far as Greathouse was concerned, made it clear that the Japanese were coming to America and that when they did, theirs would be a union plant. Someone better versed in listening to Japanese businessmen might have understood what Okuma was saying quite differently, realizing that it was what he was *not* saying that mattered. But the UAW people, like most Americans new to dealing with the Japanese, heard the answers they wanted to hear. In 1978, on what he hoped would be a decisive trip, Greathouse was warned by his friend Shioji to be less optimistic. Nissan, he confided, was pulling back from its original plans for an American factory. The mood was shifting, he said, and because of personal conflicts with Ishihara, his own ability to help Greathouse was declining. Greathouse therefore spent a fair amount of time warning the Japanese executives he met of a rising tide of protectionism in America, and that the best way to defuse it was to build a plant in the United States. At the end of his trip he and Shioji held a joint press conference at which they both endorsed the idea of Japanese production in America. Almost off the top of his head, Greathouse suggested the 250,000-car rule: A company that sold more than 250,000 cars a year in the United States should build its own factory there. The figure was based on the optimum production for a two-shift, sixty-cars-an-hour factory.

Greathouse felt that the Japanese were toying with him. Ishihara, for example, was always extremely polite, but he was not as forthcoming as Okuma. An evening would end pleasantly, but when Greathouse later tried to assess what was promised, there was nothing tangible. Besides, Greathouse sensed for the first time that underneath the courtesy was a disdain for America. Ishihara left him with a feeling that he, Ishihara, considered himself the representative of a superior culture talking to a man of a lesser one. Greathouse, as a representative of a powerful union in a dominating industry in the world's richest country, was not accustomed to the disdain of anyone he met, let alone foreigners.

Shioji, with his strong connections to the UAW and men like Woodcock, Greathouse, and Fraser, his friends and sponsors, wanted a plant in America, he wanted to make autos, not trucks, there, and he wanted it to be a union plant. The UAW had supported him when the Japanese auto industry was small and fragile, and now that it was strong he owed them comparable support. Besides, a union plant in America would enhance his own position as an international labor leader. What was particularly frustrating for Shioji, and was probably responsible for some of the extreme bitterness he was now exhibiting toward Ishihara, was that on this most crucial issue he, for so long virtually the most powerful man in Nissan, was unable to deliver. Shioji was always sure that no matter how wary Kawamata would have been on this issue, if he were still president, Shioji could have brought him along. Now with Ishihara heading the company, not only was his own influence diminished but his weakness was being revealed. Shioji's position was awkward, Greathouse thought. More than anyone else in the company he was committed to an American plant, and among people as chauvinistic as the Japanese, that position could easily be used against him. An alliance with the Americans, once a major asset in Japanese life, was now something of a liability.

Ishihara had always regarded the United States as a place of customers rather than workers. He had a fairly typical Japanese businessman's attitude about a pluralistic, multiracial society with aggressive, highly independent unions. Despite his years of doing business in the States, he had no ties to America. Once when an American reporter asked him for a list of his American friends, Ishihara had not even paused to reflect. "I have a few counterparts that I do business with," he said, "but I have no friends there." In private he had always derided the skills of American workers and the quality of their products, his criticism bordering on contempt. When he visited American factories, he said, he always found them dirty; the workers, by comparison with Japanese workers, looked indifferent and always seemed to be taking a break. America, which was such a paradise in which to sell, was as far as he was concerned something of a hell in which to produce. Since he did not know America in any depth, he feared it and so was uncertain about which way to go. The issue had been before the Nissan board, in one form or another, for almost ten years, and everyone was leery of it. The solution had always been to delay the decision.

In the days after the oil shock, the equation changed. Now the pressure to build a plant in America mounted. Because the American industry was so clearly in trouble, protectionist feeling began to increase in America, and those feelings were always magnified in Japan. Because of the intense nationalism of Japanese society, a nationalism reflected in even the best of Japanese journalism, every incident in America, whether it was a congressman complaining about Japan or Detroit workers smashing a Toyota, was amplified in Tokyo. To the Japanese it seemed that what they had always feared was now beginning to happen; they were being resented for their success—and their race. None of this, in Ishihara's view, made his decision any easier. Ishihara also feared that if he made a huge commitment to produce cars in America, the Americans might then put their companies back in order, produce cars of excellence again, and strand the Japanese on American shores. That was not a singular fear; Toyota, which was even more nervous about moving into America, was troubled by the same scenario.

What made the negotiations more difficult still was that they coincided with the growing feud between Ishihara and Shioji. The antagonism between the two men went back more than twenty years. Ishihara had always regarded the relationship between Kawamata and Shioji with misgivings; in 1957, during the move against Kawamata, he had not only stayed on the sidelines but been prepared to step into the vacuum the coup might create. Like many senior managers he came to resent the union's influence in the higher levels of the company and the fact that Shioji often seemed better informed about what Kawamata intended to do than the board did. Indeed, it was said, Ishihara had first heard of his own promotion to the presidency when Shioji, stopping him in the hall outside of Kawamata's office, said, "Congratulations—he's going to name you president."

When Ishihara became head of the company, it should, he felt, have been his to run. Kawamata had become chairman, and normally in Japanese companies chairmen let the presidents do the actual running of the company. But Kawamata refused to let go of his power. He had in fact become closer to Shioji than ever, for now, more than ever, they needed each other. Their alliance, based on opposition to Ishihara, strengthened. For Kawamata, now somewhat removed from the fray, Shioji was a link to the active daily company life and a brilliant source of information. As long as Kawamata was allied with Shioji, it would be hard for Ishihara to move against either of them, hard for him to make the company his own. For Ishihara it was terribly frustrating. By 1977 he had been with the company for forty years, and yet he still could not put his own mark on the company. He groused to friends about the difficulties he was having, about Kawamata's stubbornness, and especially about the malign power of the union. "It is like a cancer growing right in our body," he would say. Of the ability of Kawamata and Shioji to dominate decisions at every level of the company, he once told a colleague: "It will take us thirty years to undo what they have done in thirty years."

What started as a territorial rivalry with Shioji became a full-blown feud. Though the basic issues that divided the men were often real—Ishihara's desire to control all personnel decisions, Shioji's desire to locate a Nissan plant in the United States—what truly divided them was ego and love of power. People who knew them both thought them too much alike. Both were domineering. Neither knew how to share power. Each felt he was the rightful heir to Nissan. Each thought he would never be able to hold the power he craved as long as the other was there. So the struggle, ever more ferocious, went on for some eight years. There was no doubt that it damaged the company, if not to the naked eye in America, where Nissan seemed strong and successful (though with increasingly dull cars), then certainly in Japan, where it began to slip well behind Toyota. At the height of the tension between the two men, one of Shioji's old friends, a writer named Saburo Shiroyama, stopped to talk to him one day. "How long can this go on? Things are getting very bad."

"They might get worse," Shioji answered.

"Can't you work things out?" Shiroyama asked.

"No," said Shioji. "Ishihara must quit."

That reply did not surprise Shiroyama, who believed that if he had asked the same question of Ishihara, he would have gotten the same answer.

Thus in addition to the other problems they were encountering with Nissan, the Americans inadvertently were running into this one as well. Their principal ally was Shioji, and what Shioji wanted, Ishihara almost certainly did not want. That did not help Pat Greathouse, who continued to visit Japan regularly. He began to identify two potentially dangerous and conflicting currents in nations that were supposed to be allies. In America, where the auto industry was showing early signs of decline, he sensed a growing resentment against the Japanese and a rising protectionism, not on the part of the UAW leadership, which was still essentially internationalist, but on the part of the workers themselves. At the same time, he detected in the Japanese something approaching cockiness. Things that they really thought about America but had once kept veiled they now were expressing more openly. It was as if now that they were making better cars than the Americans, they were sure that they had a better society. One reflection of that was a decreased interest on the part of Nissan in building a plant in the United States. It was not surprising then that by 1980 Greathouse was thoroughly tired of dealing with the Japanese.

That February, Doug Fraser, president of the UAW, was scheduled to go to Japan as part of a special group of American leaders who had been encouraged by U.S. Ambassador Mike Mansfield to meet with their Japanese counterparts and solve some of the vexing mutual problems. Greathouse kept warning Fraser that dealing with the Japanese was different from dealing with other foreigners. Their manners were better than their follow-through, he said. At Fraser's first meeting with Ishihara, however, good manners were not the problem. The UAW people brought up the subject of how difficult it was to export goods to Japan, and Ishihara said that the Japanese market was open. That immediately severed the bonds of civility, for the UAW people would not tolerate a polite ceremonial dustoff; they were offended by the implication that they were so stupid that they did not know how intricately protectionist a society Japan was. The meeting went downhill after that. Fraser tried to talk about the impact of the flood of imported cars on America's economy, and he became furious when in his opinion Ishihara juggled the figures. Fraser insisted on the figure that had become the generally accepted one, roughly 360,000 cars a year from Nissan alone. But Ishihara, seemed determined to use the figure adjusted for the slowdown that took place in those months just before the crisis in Iran. Have I really come all the way to Tokyo to have this man cook the books on me and treat me like an idiot? Fraser wondered. Soon they were shouting at each other.

"Your problem in America," said Ishihara, "is of your own making. It is your work force—it is your whole American system. Nobody wants to work."

To Fraser this was a surfacing of the scorn that he had always suspected men like Ishihara felt for America. "You wouldn't understand America," he answered, "because you're so undemocratic a man, and you come from so undemocratic a country. But if I had to choose between the two countries, even with all of our problems, there would never be any problem. You wouldn't even know how to exist in a free country."

Greathouse, sitting in on the meeting, wary of whirlwind American visits to Japan, felt that Fraser's very anger would only confirm in the minds of the Japanese how contentious the union was. Fraser, on his part, believed that Greathouse had been too soft on the Japanese. The Nissan and UAW groups were supposed to go to dinner together that night, and for a time it looked as though the dinner would be canceled. It was finally held, and the atmosphere was a bit more relaxed, and two days later another meeting was called, and at this meeting the Japanese said they were going to construct a plant in the southern part of the United States. A few months later Nissan announced that it would build a truck factory in Tennessee. The commitment that Pat Greathouse thought he had won, that the plant would be a UAW one, was clearly not a commitment at all. This plant, if Nissan had anything to do with it, would be nonunion.

The episode was a bitter one for Shioji. Later he apologized to Fraser. He said that he had tried as hard as he could to make sure that the factory was in the north, but that from the start, despite his promises, or his seeming promises, Ishihara had no intention of dealing with the UAW. Of Ishihara he said, "He looks like a lion but he has a heart the size of a pea."

Fraser was at first somewhat pleased by that outcome, although he never knew whether his burst of anger had helped persuade the Japanese to build the plant or had killed any chance of its being union. But any job, he believed, union or nonunion, that went to an American was better than one that remained overseas. The more Fraser learned about the Tennessee plant, however, and the degree to which Nissan intended to resist the UAW, the angrier he became. Anger was not his style. More than almost anyone else in the union Doug Fraser was regarded as unflappable; his trademark in the rough world of American unionism was his ability to get along with almost anyone. It was not surprising that he was the first UAW member to sit on the board of directors of one of the Big Three auto companies or that his fellow board members often spoke of him with greater fondness than they spoke of each other. But from then on, when he referred to Ishihara he did so with genuine venom, not just because Ishihara had insisted on a nonunion factory in America but because Ishihara, who had delayed so long the decision on building a plant in the States, was now pushing as hard as he could to place a factory in England. Even worse, Ishihara had said that Nissan would be willing to deal with British labor. For Fraser that was a particularly personal affront, like a slap in the face. "It's such a goddam double standard," he said, "I really can't control my anger. I can understand that the American model is hard for the Japanese, that it is a very different kind of labor relationship. I can almost accept that argument, though it is hard for me not to argue with it. But to go to the United Kingdom! To deal with five unions there! Five British unions! What the hell kind of excuse is there for that? Just what the hell kind of excuse is there for that?"

That confrontation with the Japanese—especially their obvious contempt for American workers and the fact that they believed it was the UAW that had weakened American industry—was extremely painful for Doug Fraser. As much as anyone in the union he had, in his own lifetime, seen the relationship between management and union come full circle, the workers go from utter poverty to blue-collar affluence. But now a variety of experts were criticizing the union for its very success. In their opinion the union had lifted UAW salaries too far above those of other industrial workers in America and of autoworkers overseas. What had largely been applauded in the past as a symbol of true American economic justice had become almost overnight, because of the Japanese competition, a symbol of American wastefulness. He thought it unfair that many critics, looking for villains in the auto industry, blamed primarily the union. For to his mind UAW salaries had never been disproportionate in terms of the profits of the companies or the salaries and bonuses of the industry's chief executives. What had once been a source of pride had now become a sticking point.

PART
TEN

PART
TEN

37.
A MAN OF THE SYSTEM

Philip Caldwell seemed at first an odd choice for the first nonfamily member to head the Ford Motor Company. Unlike Henry Ford and Lee Iacocca, he had no air of drama about him. He was careful and cautious—in the words of one contemporary, a man without a signature. In his early years at the company few of his colleagues had thought of him as a potential chief executive, but after his ascent they grudgingly acknowledged that the very qualities that had annoyed both his subordinates and his peers had commended him to Henry Ford as the ideal successor. Ford, anxious to lay aside his exhausting responsibilities but not entirely sure how much power he actually wanted to hand over, decided to retain a certain veto power, however invisible. In turning his company over to an outsider, particularly during a difficult era and immediately after the trauma of the Iacocca years, he did not want a swashbuckler. He wanted a conservator of the company and the family interest. Far from threatening to go outside the system, Caldwell *was* the system. The company was filled with talent—let the men of talent work a little harder to push their ideas and cars through a bureaucracy headed by Phil Caldwell, who would always play by the rules.

His climb to the top had been opposed bitterly by his two competitors for the job, Iacocca and Bill Bourke; Bourke, later squeezed out, was executive vice-president for North America. They insisted Caldwell was too deliberate and pedantic for such a troubled company. "Plain vanilla" was what Bourke called him in private, which was the ultimate Ford Motor Company putdown, meaning blandness in style and manner. Caldwell's relationship with Bourke was particularly sensitive, because they had worked together at Ford of Europe, Caldwell as chairman and Bourke as president. They had both been rising stars in Henry Ford's best-loved duchy, and it was widely believed that Bourke had in general fought for product while Caldwell had delayed it. It was believed that somehow Caldwell, who had supported the Fiesta only at the very end, had gotten much of the credit for it.

Caldwell's position as chief executive officer was always ambiguous, and Ford did his best to keep it that way. Henry Ford might have moved his office to the Renaissance Center downtown, but it was his company. Caldwell, as one senior executive said, was free to do anything he wanted so long as Mr. Ford did not disagree with it.

Caldwell had been extremely deferential to his bosses on the way up, and now that he had become a high executive, he expected nothing less from his subordinates. He took executive protocol very seriously. Before a Ford dinner he wanted to know exactly where everyone was to be seated, where the doors were, where the servants' entrance was. He insisted on being escorted to the table first. His position had to be manifest in every detail, no matter how small. In the past senior people had usually been allowed to hitch their way aboard the company plane if it was going in their direction, but not under Caldwell. He preferred to travel with his own entourage or in imperial loneliness.

When Caldwell became chairman, he even established a departure ritual. The moment he was ready to leave at night, his secretary would pack his attaché case and call down to his driver, who would be waiting in the garage of Ford headquarters. Then she would deposit the case in the executive elevator, in which it would travel down to the garage by itself. The chauffeur would enter the elevator, pick up the case, and put it in the car. A little later, Philip Caldwell would descend, empty-handed. He would then remove his suit jacket and pass it to the driver, who would spread it carefully on the seat so it would not get wrinkled. There was considerable speculation on the part of his senior colleagues about why the attaché case went first, and they eventually came to this conclusion: Caldwell thought that if people saw him going through the corridors with the attaché case, they would know he was going home and would no longer work as hard; if he left without it, they might think he was still in the building. That kind of thing, among other qualities, bothered his subordinates. They knew he hated them to smoke, and meetings under his leadership were tobacco-free. Nor did he drink. His notable abstinence had become obvious fairly early in his career when Henry Ford pressed some excellent red wine on him at an executive dinner in London.

"I don't drink wine, Mr. Ford," Caldwell said. Ford gave him a puzzled look. "As a matter of fact, my wife and I don't drink beer or any hard liquor," Caldwell continued. Henry Ford, a man who enjoyed his own vices, looked even more baffled. "In fact, we don't drink coffee or tea, and we don't smoke," Caldwell said.

"Well, then," said Henry Ford in disbelief, "what the hell do you do?"

Caldwell was not an easy man for whom or with whom to work. Any project in which he was involved, no matter how simple, was attacked with infinite, painstaking thoroughness. As a young man rising in middle management, he had quickly signaled that he was different by the way he treated routine requests, the kind that had formerly gone right though his office to the next level. More often than not, after sitting on his desk for a week, they were sent back with a note asking for more information or bearing the words "See me." The lesson was that nothing was routine, and nothing was going to get past his desk unless he thought it was perfect. A pattern was established: His superiors would value his work, but his subordinates would be drained in the process. It was management by exhaustion, one deputy thought, a relentless search for the one last bit of information that might yield the perfect car or truck. Some of his colleagues believed this approach was not a quest for truth so much as an evasion of decision-making; it was not, they thought, the method of a secure man. (When Caldwell rose to the top, some of his senior executives became convinced that his exaggerated caution was more than a fear of making mistakes; it was a form of wielding power, a way of keeping experienced men who felt more at home in the auto business than he did constantly on the defensive.)

As a young executive in the truck division, he became known as the A-J Man because of his insistence upon having options A through J. On one occasion during these years a superior noticed he had not yet produced plans for the new model and began to press him. Weeks passed, and the deadline drew closer. Finally the superior went over to the truck shop; in the design room endless drawings of countless different trucks were pinned to the wall, with Caldwell in the midst, mired in indecision. "Phil," the man said, "why don't we just walk over and pick one before we leave the room today?" And so they did, the complex suddenly made simple. Even something relatively straightforward, like delivering a speech at an automotive seminar, became a monumental task—ten different men from ten parts of the company would sit around for three weeks making suggestions, canceling each other out, protecting their superiors' territory, until they came up with a completely neutralized recommendation of the let's-get-a-committee-of-the-best-minds-in-the-country-to-study-this variety.

Caldwell's meetings seemed to last forever. The joke went that it wasn't bad enough that Caldwell kept them there for six hours at a time, but that because he never drank coffee or tea, he never had to go to the bathroom. Some men claimed he pissed chalk. Others said that if a colleague stubbornly resisted something Caldwell wanted, Caldwell waited until his opponent went to the bathroom and then called for a vote. When he was head of Ford of Europe his wife would occasionally return to the United States to visit their children. Then the meetings would be even longer, continuing late into the night. The theory among his subordinates was that he assumed that since he had nothing to go home to, they did not either. He was least at ease with the creative people, for whom decisions were almost a matter of instinct and reflex. Dealing with him, they in turn felt he regarded them as careless and facile. He had made it up the hard way and was wary of brilliance and impatience. The more creative the people he dealt with, especially designers and engineers, the more frustrated they were. They would come to a meeting filled with a vision for a new car, and he would respond in numbers, refusing to discuss it on their terms, to share their excitement even for an instant. Instead he would always find the weakness in their presentation and send them back to do more, letting them know of course, that they had failed him.

Some of their passion and energy would die in that room. "You live and die product, you burn with excitement when you're working on something new, and you were always dealing with a man who did not seem to hear a thing you were saying, and who could only answer in the most rigid numerical formulation," said product planner Erick Reickert, who helped design the Topaz and Tempo cars and then resigned and went to Chrysler. "It was the ultimate frustration."

Hal Sperlich, eventually an enemy, had a similar reaction. "For a long time I thought we simply could not understand each other, that we were from such different backgrounds that we might as well use different languages," he said. "And then later, when it was all over and I was gone, I realized it was more than that. It was a struggle between men for whom a car was an end in itself, an object of passion, and someone for whom a car generated no excitement but was a means to success and power. It wasn't different languages, it was different businesses."

Caldwell reminded some of the bright young men at the Ford Motor Company of their fathers, possibly because he had more in common with men who were molded by lean times than with those raised in an affluence that encouraged risk-taking. His childhood had not been easy. The Great Depression of 1929 had hit the small farmers of America first, during the early twenties, and his father, Robert Caldwell, was one such farmer. Most men who have survived hard times and go on to great success tend to exaggerate the harshness of the past. Philip Caldwell, however, was guarded on the topic of his youth, seeming to regard his father's reverses as an embarrassment. Caldwell's wife, Betsy, would caution friends that Philip had had a very difficult and painful childhood, and it was not something he liked to talk about. Sensitive it was. Not only did he fend off all questions in interviews about his family's hard times, but when a young reporter for the *Detroit News*, Michael Wendland, wrote a story about Caldwell's childhood, a largely gentle and warm piece about Caldwell's triumph over adversity, Caldwell was enraged, and some Ford employees tried to find out who had talked to Wendland. Wendland, thinking he had written sympathetically and unaware of Caldwell's reaction, saw Caldwell a few months later and introduced himself, saying that he had written the article. Caldwell turned on him in instant fury. "That was going too far," Caldwell said to him. "There was no need for that, no need to stir that up again."

The Caldwells had come to America in the middle of the eighteenth century and settled rich Ohio farmland a hundred years later. Some stayed and farmed, and others ventured forth, people with broad vision who traveled to far places and did romantic things. A cousin had been the first dean of the humanities at MIT. Other Caldwells had been prominent missionaries in China, one of them president of Nanking University. A college education had always been an assumption, and despite the family's straitened circumstances, Philip Caldwell and all three of his brothers went to college. The family traditionally sent its youngsters to Wooster, an excellent church-connected college in Ohio, but Philip, something of a rebel, went to Muskingum, another small church-related school. It was not, he said on one of the rare occasions he spoke of it, a deprived childhood. It was, instead, one in which there was a fierce sense of the priorities of life and no luxuries.

As a boy, Caldwell dreamed of being a businessman. He loved the early issues of *Fortune*, which were filled with stories about the country's foremost industrialists by the nation's best writers. He spent the end of the Depression in college, and in 1940, aided by a scholarship of $300 a year provided by a Harvard club in Cleveland, he went off to Harvard Business School. That was the beginning of his real life. He loved the school from the beginning, years later clearly recalling his first day there and the nice second-year student who offered to carry his suitcases up the five flights of stairs to his room (and thereupon sold him laundry service). He enjoyed the classes and admired the professors, who knew the most influential business executives in the country. George Doriot asked the students at the start of the year whom they would like to have lecture and produced everyone they requested. A speaker of another kind, a naval recruiter, spoke to his class on Monday, December 8, 1941. The entire class, it seemed to him, enlisted.

Caldwell loved being in the navy too. It was a fascinating war, and his task suited his talents. Sometimes, he liked to say, positive things can come out of terrible ones. Certainly it was true in his case that the navy opened up vistas for him. When he talked about those years, he became a different person. The man who could barely recall a detail of his childhood remembered each experience in all particulars even though he was far from the field of battle—the lessons learned, the men to whom he was apprenticed, the excitement of being near the center of command. He had been assigned at first to a captain named Radford Moses. It was Moses's job to preassemble the bases and men required by the forces as they conquered a succession of islands held by the Japanese. The bases were miniature cities with military functions, complete not just with hospitals but with fuel depots and ordnance areas as well. They needed to be ready to be shipped from Oakland, complete with men, at the moment each island was liberated. In due course Caldwell became Moses's man in Pearl Harbor. His war was not one of combat but of learning to make a giant institution function like a small one. The work was exacting but provided the thrill of being connected to great men in charge of great events. Caldwell remembered Admiral Chester Nimitz calling in the top officers on D-Day to explain what Overlord, the invasion of Europe, was really about. When Curtis LeMay took over command of the B-29s in the Marianas and implemented the stunningly successful low-level bombing of Japan, Caldwell's job was suddenly to make sure there were enough bombs. LeMay went through so many of them they had to stack them right on the beaches.

Caldwell was doing staff work on the invasion of Japan, set for November 1, 1945, when the war ended. Because he did not have enough points to get out immediately, he had to stay in the navy until May 1946. He loved it so much, however, that he stayed on and worked as a civilian officer for eight years, eventually becoming the country's highest civilian executive in military procurement. In 1953 he joined Ford, a decision that had nothing to do with cars but with his experience in ordering, moving, and tracking vast quantities of supplies in a giant organization. When he arrived at Ford, procurement methods were remarkably primitive—the division was still run, in his words, by glorified shipping clerks. Jim Wright, one of the early Whiz Kids and a McNamara protégé, needed support in bringing systems to the procurement operation and quickly reached out to him. Caldwell did very well there. Though he was not a member of finance, his roots and viewpoint were similar and he soon had finance's support in internal political struggles.

He had held many different jobs in the company and seemed to do well at all of them, although there were those, like Sperlich, who claimed that he was just lucky, and that he had opposed or delayed the very products that made his reputation. He became a vice-president when, as head of the truck division, he went to Bunkie Knudsen in 1968 and mentioned, first, that Ford did not seem to be taking the truck business too seriously, and second, that he had a very good offer from Rockwell. "I'll go talk to Henry," Knudsen had said. Iacocca, master of the same kind of move, later said that Caldwell blackmailed the company into a vice-presidency.

But the largest factor in Caldwell's rise was probably what he did for Philco. A company that mainly made radios, Philco was a notorious disaster area within the Ford Motor Company. Unaccustomed to corporate expansion outside its own business, Ford had bought Philco in 1961 and had never been able to run it properly. A series of managers had ruined their careers trying. At Ford it was known as Siberia. Its reputation was so bad, in fact, that Caldwell's teenage daughter Desiree knew from the school grapevine how dangerous a job it was. "Daddy," she asked her father, "if it doesn't work out, will Mr. Ford throw you in the discard pile?" In one sense Caldwell was fortunate, however; by the time he was sent to Philco Henry Ford's expectations for it had diminished. Caldwell was not required to be a miracle worker so much as a terminator. "Either fix it up or get rid of it," Ford told him. Caldwell quickly streamlined the company. He improved its car radios so that skeptical Ford engineers would accept them, unloaded a number of underused older factories in the United States and Europe, and began to expand overseas production in places like Taiwan and Brazil. Costs soon came down, and the company became profitable enough for Ford to have little trouble selling it after Caldwell went on to run North American manufacturing.

Henry Ford had called Philco the principal management problem in the company when he had given the job to Caldwell, and the problems facing Philco in 1970 closely resembled those facing the Ford Motor Company a decade later. Philip Caldwell had proved himself to be a good manager for a troubled company. Not a brilliant or original man, it was said at the top, but a careful, relentless, and thorough man—good for cutting costs and shepherding a company through hard times. That he would now have to do, for by the time he took over Ford at the last moment of the 1970s, the company was in trouble again. Its costs were out of line, its products lacked quality, and they had lost their appeal. All the unfavorable trends had come together at once.

"He held all the tough jobs," Henry Ford once said of Philip Caldwell, "and he held them at the tough times."

On the evening of October 1, 1979, the day Caldwell took over as chief executive officer of the Ford Motor Company, Henry Ford rode down in the elevator with him and said, "I'm really sorry about leaving you with all these problems—it's an awful time, and it doesn't seem fair to dump this on someone else."

"Well," Caldwell said, "you've been through it all yourself."

"Yes, I suppose so," said Henry Ford, "but it was different then. Even at its worst, in 1946, we could sell everything we made. But you don't have the market with you anymore. It's changed on us."

The company was losing $1 billion a year. But that figure hardly reflected just how badly Ford was doing. In its North American operations, the traditional center of Ford's strengths, the company was losing more than $2 billion a year; over the three most difficult years, from 1979 to 1982, it lost about $7 billion. Only Ford of Europe kept the company afloat. Decisions in those days were fraught with danger; in the newly inflated economy, mistakes were measured in billions rather than millions, and it seemed impossible not to make them. The Ford line was bland and full of heavy cars that customers refused to buy. Worse, there was ample hard evidence that Japanese cars were not only smaller but better. Hertz Rent-a-Car supplied Ford with its maintenance reports, which displayed the staggering fact that Japanese quality was almost twice as good as American.

Caldwell had to restructure the Ford Motor Company under desperate conditions. The company needed to fend off the Japanese (which it did in part by throwing its weight behind protectionism), improve quality, get labor to consent to new, less adversarial agreements, develop lower-priced cars with front-wheel drive, and—most pressing—cut back its fixed costs. Nowhere did Caldwell show more skill or deserve more credit than in the last area, and no one was better qualified to do it. As a man of the system he knew how to trim the system. Harold "Red" Poling, the finance man in charge of North American operations, was his chief executioner. It was bloody work. In March 1980 they cut 250,000 cars out of the schedule for the following five months. That meant layoffs, reduced hours, closed factories. Eventually seven plants were closed, the decision to close each of them filled with the anguished awareness that great numbers of families were being devastated or, at the very least, dislocated. Thousands of middle-management workers were let go. Old friends were told to look elsewhere. Formerly prosperous men were suddenly unemployed and unable to sell their houses. Fewer and fewer managers worked ever longer hours. The company was filled with rumors of who was going next. A thousand people lost their dealerships in those years. Over a period of eighteen months in 1980 and 1981 Caldwell cut $2.5 billion out of Ford's fixed costs. One high executive called that time the winter at Valley Forge. A year later the board of directors gave Caldwell a copy of the famous painting of Washington crossing the Delaware in the midst of the worst winter of the war—with his face substituted for the general's.

38.
HARD TIMES
COME HOME

In the fall of 1978, thirty-three-year-old Joel Goddard, a die-cast diemaker for Ford at its plant in rural Rawsonville, Michigan, was aware that the company he worked for was in a depressed condition, and that his plant, which made housings for small parts like windshield wipers and carburetors, was cutting back its work force. A number of diemakers had already been laid off. At first Goddard did not take the layoffs seriously because he was part of an elite within an elite. Most diemakers made ordinary parts, but the *diecast* diemakers were the true artisans—they made the molds for the most important exterior auto parts, like the grilles. In the six years he had worked at the plant, his type of diemaker had always been immune from layoffs. When he heard union men from other companies discussing layoffs, he envisioned a world where unskilled workers in marginal industries worried about their jobs. By contrast, his position seemed strong and secure. The automobile industry was a powerful one, and he was a skilled artisan who had, if anything, too much work—at least forty-eight hours a week. His professional situation had never seemed better, and 1978 had begun as a very good year in the auto business. He was sure that he was quite all right. He worried about smaller things, such as whether he was working too much overtime.

Goddard also worried about the quality of the apprentices in the diemaking shop. He was sure it had fallen off. In the past, diemaking had been a closed world into which entry was gained only by family connection. Being a diemaker was considered a privilege. Then the government became involved, pushing minority members into the program (Goddard was convinced they were being coached on how to pass the certification exams). The work done by these new apprentices, he believed, was not as good, and neither was their attitude toward their seniors. Before, the word of a journeyman had been law, but the new apprentices, in his opinion, lacked the proper respect, often challenging and criticizing the more senior men. Joel Goddard was not amused by the attempts of less experienced men to correct him. Still, that was Ford's problem, not his. In general he was feeling good about his life. That year he went out and bought a new Thunderbird for $10,000. But already the company was beginning to respond to events in Iran, and because the diemakers did the molds for other Ford factories, they felt the early shock waves before the men on the line. Since the prognosis at the top of the company was that 1979 was likely to be a bad year, the company quickly began cutting back among the die casters. Had Joel Goddard known a little more about the international economy, he often reflected later, the last thing he would have done was buy an expensive new car.

There were sixty people in his department, in a plant that had fifty-two hundred workers. The layoffs started in the spring. In April about ten of his fellow diemakers were laid off by reverse seniority, those hired most recently being the first to go. Although he knew the seniority of every man around him and thus knew that his own number was coming up, Joel Goddard refused to worry. He was quite sure that even if he was laid off, it would be for only a brief time, part of a short downturn that would soon end, whereupon he would be one of the first called back. The idea that he and others like him were living on the edge of an abyss never occurred to Goddard. He even looked forward to being laid off. In his mind it was going to be an extra paid vacation, long overdue.

Since he had gotten out of school some thirteen years earlier, Goddard had worked hard to live like a proper member of the middle class. To afford the life-style that others seemed to attain working only five days a week, he often had to work on both Saturdays and Sundays; he had to work while his neighbors were out barbecuing hamburgers or cutting their lawns. Unlike them and most other members of the middle class, he went to work at odd hours, more often than not at midnight. So he felt entitled to the time off. For all those years, he had paid out some $30 a month in union dues, and now finally he was going to get some return on his investment. The money in benefits would be only what the union owed him. When, just before Thanksgiving, he was told that he was laid off, the twelfth in his department to go, he was delighted. He had carefully planned a six-week vacation in Florida, where his wife's parents lived. His children would miss about a week of school, but that was all right; this was a once-in-a-lifetime opportunity. Soon it would be over and he would be back at work—in about six weeks to two months, he figured. Three and a half years later, in March of 1982, he was called back to work. He returned a different man.

Thus began the real education of Joel Goddard, born on July 5, 1945, a true child of postwar American affluence. Until the layoff, Goddard later said, he never realized how fortunate he had been. Nothing had ever really gone wrong for him. Neither he nor his wife had ever had any sense of what genuine poverty and genuine fear about getting a job meant. He was good at his work, and he liked it. He was a highly skilled man whose talents were greatly in demand, and he was well compensated for them. In the last year before the layoff he had made about $35,000. This figure, which was close to Goddard's norm for the few previous years, compared quite favorably with what the men on the line at Ford made, $22,000, which in turn compared nicely with what other American workers earned. As a die-cast diemaker he was a member of the blue-collar aristocracy, more nearly middle-class than most of his colleagues. He had gone to college for two years, and he had never spent a day on the line as a production worker. He owned a handsome split-level house about thirty miles from the factory, in Pinckney, a lovely town in southern Michigan. He commuted that far because he liked living in the country and living on a lake. Rich in the toys favored by American adults, he had two cars and a boat and four snowmobiles. His wife, a college graduate, did not have to work and busied herself with raising their two children. Although the cost of education was rising at an alarming rate, Joel and Joyce Goddard never considered the possibility that either of their children would not go to college. By 1978, some seven years before Kim, their older child, was to enter college, they already had more than $10,000 in savings accounts marked for education; furthermore, Joel was confident that if he needed to borrow additional money all he had to do was walk into a bank and utter the magic words "I work for Ford," which almost guaranteed a loan. Until the fall of 1978, as far as Goddard was concerned, his was an American success story.

The first indication that his layoff might be something grimmer than a paid vacation was word of another major layoff of die casters shortly after his departure. That shattered his illusion that he was going to be the first to be called back. Now men with considerably more seniority were also out of work. So it went over the next weeks; every bit of news from the plant was bad. Once bustling with three shifts, it was already down to two and soon would be down to one. A few months after his own layoff, he was number fifteen among die casters waiting in line for a recall, and it was clear that things were going to get worse before they got better. Goddard's department, once sixty men strong, was cut to about twenty people of high seniority before it stabilized, which meant the economy and the company were going to have to improve dramatically before he returned to Ford.

Goddard was aware, however, that he was luckier than many other Ford workers who had been laid off. His skill as a diemaker was a marketable commodity. A number of his friends from the production line had nothing comparable. In a state where the unemployment rate was soaring, they had no skill to offer. Goddard could sense their desperation. The official unemployment rate for Michigan was around 20 percent, but Goddard was sure it was much higher, probably well above 25 percent. He was better prepared than most for the hard times ahead. He owned his house, and, since it was not in Detroit, he had a better chance, in a soft market, of selling it. The house payments were not that great (soon, as the price of oil rose, the heating bills were greater than the house payments). Even so, his world, so carefully pieced together, came unglued. At first the strain came from not working, and then from working at jobs he did not like and for men he did not like. He did not realize until then how important his job had been to him, his success in it representing a victory of considerable proportions within his family.

When Joel Goddard was growing up, his family had been among the elite of Lakewood, a suburb of Cleveland. His father, a banker, with what Goddard assumed was the natural class prejudice of a successful small-town businessman, had looked down on blue-collar workers as a lesser species. He constantly chided his teenage son to work harder and achieve more, lest he end up with a wasted life. Blue-collar people, men who worked with their hands, were different, his father seemed to be saying, almost like garbage. When Goddard was in his teens, the father of one of his friends worked in an auto plant, and Joel spent a lot of time at their house, much to the displeasure of his own father. "You want to be careful—you don't want to end up like that," his father often said. It was clear that Joel was supposed to become a banker too. The problem was that he had no affinity for it. During the summers of his high school years he worked in various office jobs and hated them; in particular he hated wearing a jacket and tie. He disliked businessmen, who seemed to feel that because they wore suits and ties they were more important than other people. Offices seemed sterile and boring to him. One summer an uncle who worked for Inland Steel got him a job working on its boats, and he had loved it—it was a wonderful, crummy, humanly rich world.

He went off to Bowling Green College in Ohio and did fairly well there, but he was still somewhat rebellious, not in the way much of the youth of America was, dissenting from the war in Vietnam and wearing its hair long, but pulling away from the life of a banker's son. His first real act of rebellion was leaving college to elope with Joyce Ford, a college classmate from Toledo. His parents were furious, and not just because he had quit college. Joyce's people were blue-collar. The senior Goddards barely sanctioned the marriage. Their son was marrying below them. Then Joel told them he was looking for a job as a blue-collar worker. "You might as well go to Toledo, because there's nothing here for you now," his father said, and to Joyce Goddard those words seemed to mean that she and her new husband were now a social embarrassment to his parents.

Married now and with a child on the way, Joel needed a job. Joyce's father, a diemaker for Doehler-Jarvis in Toledo, suggested that Goddard try to get work there. Goddard had no known mechanical skills. Nonetheless he went to Doehler-Jarvis. The personnel office, seeing that he had been to college, tried to push him toward a white-collar position, precisely what he did not want. Fortunately, he scored well on his mechanical tests. He argued for a chance to be a diemaker, and they gave it to him. He did not even know how to spell the word "die," spelling it "dye" on his application. His father was furious over his choice of job, and their relationship was for a time all but severed. "You're stupid and you're arrogant," his father told him. "You don't listen. The worst thing is, you're throwing away all your advantages." His father-in-law said that the job would at least get him by a hard stretch in his life.

When Goddard started work in 1965, diemaking was still an old-world occupation. Some of the diemakers were German immigrants who still wore white shirts and ties under their aprons, just as their fathers and grandfathers had done before them, as a sign of their craft and the status that went with it. There was a certain amount of hazing, and Goddard was aware that he was being doubly tested because he was merely an in-law and not a blood relation, and, more important, because he had been to college. In his first week, not looking where he was going, he walked into a crane. Everyone laughed. "Get your head out of your ass, college boy," someone yelled. Another time he did not know how to throw the switch to turn on a machine. "How goddam dumb can you be?" someone asked. The hazing also included pranks, such as putting spotting blue, a kind of blue dye, on his toolbox, which he got all over his clothes and hands. His apprenticeship lasted four years. Apprentices cleaned out the bathrooms, swept up the shop, and never challenged the word of a journeyman. Goddard went to night school two days a week to acquire the technical skills that had not been available to him as a child in a white-collar home.

He found to his surprise that he was good at making dies. Doehler-

Jarvis had its own system of raises. Every three months, a diemaker received a raise of 7 cents an hour, but if he was doing well he might get a double or triple raise. From then on doubles and triples were normal for him. He was gradually accepted by his fellow employees. He loved working with the metal, loved the fact that he was actually creating something. The dies might be huge, bigger than men, but they had to be made as precisely as Swiss watches. On his first job, he was apprenticed to an old-timer to work on a zinc grille for the Ford Thunderbird. They spent six months on it, and the pleasure he derived from converting a drawing, nothing but lines, to something made of metal was almost indescribable. More important to him was that there was no room for phoniness: He did it right or he did it wrong. He liked the camaraderie of the shop, the fact that the men encouraged and praised each other. This was a world of shared triumphs. He spent seven years at Doehler.

Doehler was a union shop, organized by the UAW, and while the pay was not as good as it was at the Big Three, it was better than that at most industrial plants in the region. When he had started, he made $1.81 an hour, almost $80 a week. (Years later at Ford he took pleasure in showing his old paycheck stubs to the apprentices assigned to him, who were starting out at $12 an hour.) By the time he finished his apprenticeship he was making $9 an hour. Even that did not appease his father. When Joel Goddard told him in the late sixties that he was now making $10 an hour, his father said: "You guys are all paid too much. That's why everything costs too much." It was, thought Joel Goddard, the classic response of the small-town Midwestern banker to the UAW worker.

Nevertheless, Goddard was making a living. He and Joyce rented an apartment in Toledo for $65 a month, and within a year they bought their first house. They paid $16,200 for it and, on a salary of about $90 a week, had to make payments of $110 a month, which required close budgeting. Four years later he and Joyce sold the house for $25,000 and bought a larger one. Goddard was proud of the success he was making of his life, the respect he had at the plant. Unfortunately, there were signs that Doehler-Jarvis was cutting back on its diemaking operations. The equipment at Doehler's, he realized, was getting old, and the company seemed reluctant to invest in new machinery. The company was hiring fewer and fewer apprentices. Just a few years earlier, when Goddard had joined it, there were some ten or twelve apprentices for forty journeymen, and now there were only two or three. The trouble, Goddard learned, was that creating dies was getting more and more expensive, and Doehler's old customers were now giving the work to smaller, nonunion shops. In the old days Doehler, as a supplier company, had made dies for Ford; now

Ford brought Doehler already completed dies to do minor work on. The diemakers felt they were being used as repairmen rather than skilled artisans. There was, Goddard thought, less pride around the shop, because the diemakers got little satisfaction from repair work. Goddard felt that way himself. When he was working on a new die, the full range of his talents was called upon, and he became excited and positive; when he was repairing a die, a job that challenged him far less, he became irritable. His wife could always tell whether he was doing new work or old. The future at Doehler's looked bleak, and it was time to get out. (He was right in his assessment: The die shop closed in 1976, four years after he left.)

Like many young workers at places like Doehler, Goddard had dreamed of working for one of the Big Three auto companies. The pay was $2.50 an hour more, and, even more important, it was the major leagues. What expedited his decision was an incident during a strike at Doehler. He and some other workers were trying to block the entrance to the plant. The head of personnel drove up.

"Hey, Goddard," he said as Goddard charged at his car, waving a sign, "what the hell's your real bitch, anyway? You're doing well. You don't have the hardest life in the world."

"I want to make as much as someone at the Big Three," Goddard answered.

"Well, then," said the personnel man, pointing in the general direction of Detroit, "better get up the road to the Rouge, because that's the only way you're ever going to make it."

After the strike was over, the idea of Ford grew in Goddard's mind. His father-in-law tried to argue him out of leaving. Goddard had a good secure job, he pointed out, and in two years he would be able to freeze his pension. The temptation was too great, however, and in 1972 Goddard took a job at a Ford plant in Toledo. That plant was doing experimental work on turbine engines. It was supposed to be a hot area, and everyone was excited about producing an engine that required less gas. Goddard was told by old hands that he had gone to the right place at the right time. About five months after he joined the company, he attended a large meeting at which a number of proud and happy managers congratulated everyone because word had just been received that they could proceed with Phase Three on the new turbine engine. The future was theirs. That meeting was on a Tuesday. On Friday, Ford closed the entire plant down. The Ford people were vague about relocating Goddard, and for a time he worked in a small job shop in Toledo. But he soon learned his lesson there—in a place like that, only one person, the owner, really benefits. Soon, hearing that there might be work at the Ford plant in Rawsonville, one of two Ford plants where diemaking was still done, he drove up on his own and found a job. That was in 1973. He had almost six good years at Ford, and then, late in 1978, came the layoff.

In early 1979, as the layoff continued, Joel Goddard began to pay more attention to the news. He did not like being prejudiced, but he could not help it. He couldn't stand the idea of a dinky Arab country like Iran being able able to stick up the United States of America, arbitrarily changing the price of gasoline and disrupting his own life. Iran was a shitty little ragamuffin country run by crummy people. Every day there were terrible stories on television about what was happening there, and his feelings about them connected, he knew, to the frustrations in his own life. He felt oddly powerless. He hated Iranians and Arabs. The Japanese were just as bad. We knocked them on their ass in World War II, he thought, and deservedly so, and then we helped them back up, and here they are taking jobs away from us. The more he followed the international news, the uneasier he felt about his job. The pleasure of the strike-as-vacation had long since disappeared, replaced by anxiety. The news from the plant became as discouraging as the news on television: Rather than hiring people back, Ford was thinking of laying off still more. All the same, he had his benefits, and that was rightfully his money, something he had earned.

Every two weeks he went first to the unemployment office to pick up his check for about $300, then to Ford for his SUB check—Supplemental Unemployment Benefits—equaling roughly 95 percent of his base salary. Since his base pay for forty hours was about $550, which after taxes came to $375, and his unemployment compensation was subtracted from the amount he received, he drew about $375 a week for the first year he was unemployed.

After about six months he became bored with fishing and daytime television. He read the want ads in the newspaper every day, but there was nothing there for a diemaker. Friends of his were starting to go to Texas, lured by the promise of a booming oil economy there. Goddard wasn't eager to join them. He loved where he lived and was reluctant to move. Still, his self-esteem was ebbing fast. He was a grown man, unable to support his family. After about six months he heard of an insurance company that would hire men like him to sell insurance. He tried it and soon came to detest it. His early sales were almost entirely to friends. He had always disliked the idea of selling; now, hopelessly miscast, he was succeeding only in exploiting his friendships. It was a misery for him to call strangers on the phone with a sales pitch and even worse to sell them in person. Only when he thought of his bills and his family's needs could he steel himself to do it. After several months he quit, his self-confidence badly damaged by the experience. Years later his wife, not a person much given to bitterness, still felt genuine anger about the way the insurance company had behaved. As far as she was concerned, it had taken a bunch of desperate neophytes, conned them into believing they could succeed in a very difficult profession, and left them to flounder. When they failed, there was no loss to the company. Quite the reverse. Having added the friends of the failed salesmen to its list of policyholders, it simply went on to find another batch of instant salesmen.

The Goddards by then had long since sold two of the snowmobiles. Then they had sold their boat for $2400, which covered their house payments for several months. Now, painfully, they drew on the money put away for their children's college educations. Yet for all the financial pressures, the fiercest stress Goddard was undergoing was more psychological than financial. His pride and dignity were at stake, as well as his family's survival.

Joyce Goddard went to work at K mart as a checkout supervisor. It was the first time she had worked since their marriage. She knew the money was critical to their household, and she thought Joel would welcome her help. She was making $5 an hour, bringing home $150 a week to a family that badly needed it. As long as she was working they were guaranteed food. But her success—she did well and was soon promoted—coincided with his failure and further undermined his ego. He liked to think of himself as a macho man, independent, afraid of no one, a man who could take good care of his family, whose wife did not have to work. An American success story. Now he began to feel that it was his fault he was out of work. For the first time the Goddards began to have serious marital problems. Unable to find work, Joel Goddard rebuked himself for failing to finish college; a degree would have given him an advantage at a time like this. He became angry at Joyce for working when he was not, and he picked fights with her. If she came back after a long day and said she was tired, he would snap at her, telling her he had done it for ten years, Saturdays and Sundays too, and he didn't need to hear any crap from her.

1980 was their worst year. The Ford benefits had run out, the news on television was always bad, and there was no prospect of work. He withdrew entirely, talking to no one, sleeping long hours. He became addicted to daytime television shows. Joyce, anxious to help and mindful that they had always had a strong marriage, reached out to him and was wounded by his rejection. In the past, they had always been able to talk about their problems, but now when she tried he refused to answer her. Days would pass without a real conversation. She found some solace in talking to a minister and disclosing the pain she felt because she could not reach her husband. "You have every right to expect Joel's love, Joyce," the minister said, "but you can't have it if Joel doesn't have it to give. Right now," he added, "Joel is empty."

That helped explain some of their difficulties, and she was grateful to the minister, but she was still preoccupied with what his problems were doing to her. She was sure their marriage was not going to last. Her guilt grew. Joel, she thought, was such a good and gentle man. She knew that her situation was not unique, was not even among the worst; she had heard the horror stories of other blue-collar men working out their frustrations by physically abusing their wives and children. What made Joel's suffering particularly painful for her was her sense that Joel's life was not necessarily one of his choice, that he had been diverted from an easier life, as a white-collar man with a college degree, by their early marriage and the coming of a family. Just as he had proved how good he was at his work, just as he had begun to value himself properly, this had happened. It struck her as unjust. Finally she began to think what for her was unthinkable: She would give Joel a divorce, if what he wanted was freedom from her and the children. Only then was she able to see her husband's dilemma clearly and give him the space he needed: When she mentioned the idea of divorce to him, he became terribly upset. There was some measure of relief for her in that.

Goddard was terrified of the future and doubted he would ever work at Ford again. In late 1980, now laid off for two years, he sent out résumés to companies in Texas and the Pacific Northwest. The idea of leaving Pinckney, the town he loved, was hard, but he was ready for the move. But first, he promised himself as part of his New Year's resolution, he would make one more effort to find work nearby. In January 1981 he was hired at a small job shop. He had been out of work for more than two years.

The hiring process was not particularly pleasant. He showed the boss his journeyman's card from Ford, one of his proudest possessions. "That doesn't mean shit here," the man said. "You can buy those papers on the street. We've had a lot of men from Ford here, and none of them could cut the mustard." Asked what he'd made at Ford, Goddard said fifteen dollars an hour. "My journeymen make eleven," the boss said. "I'll start you at ten."

On Monday Goddard bought new work clothes. On Tuesday he went to work. The first thing he noticed that morning was the icy stares of the workers as he walked from one end of the plant to another. There was no energy, no life, in that cold and hostile place. As Goddard later put it, they were men whose bodies were alive but whose minds and souls had died. The plant was a scene from the nineteenth century. The stench was terrible, the oil-and-grease-and-dirt smell of a place that has never been cleaned. The lighting was dismal. How, he wondered, can men work in light this bad? He was suddenly terrified. There's no way I can do this, he thought, no way I can make it here. It was as if he were professionally paralyzed. As he worked he knew the other workers were snickering at him, the big star from Ford who was having trouble hacking it. When he asked a worker for a piece of equipment, he would get no answer. No one would speak to him at all. It struck him that he was going to fail.

On the first day he was asked to align a part he had made, but because of the specialization at Ford, aligning had not been part of his job there, and he did not know how. The boss came over and said, "This ain't worth crap. What the hell are you doing? I thought you were a Ford-trained diemaker."

"I am," said Goddard.

"A Ford man, shit," said the boss. "Anybody could do this job."

That night Goddard went home and told Joyce he was not going to make it. She, of course, did not believe him. "I've lost all my confidence," he said. She told him to go back, that it would work out. The next day he went to work, and the boss called him in. "Listen," he said, "you're really screwing up. I'm not sure you can cut it here. You've got too much to learn. I can't afford to pay you what I've been paying you if I've got to teach you everything. I tell you what—I'll cut you to eight while you're learning."

That was one more humiliation. The morning went even worse than the first one. Finally Goddard took his three toolboxes and trudged out. The other men were sitting around having lunch, and as he walked he knew they were watching him and gloating over his failure. He felt demeaned. He wasn't sure if he had quit or been fired, but if he had been fired, he thought, it was from a shithole.

When he got home, he barricaded himself in his bedroom, and for the third time in his life (the first was when he broke a leg in a high school football game, the second was when his father died), he cried. Joyce Goddard felt just as bad. When the job first came up he had mentioned that it was not exactly what he had been trained for, but she had blithely told him that he could do it. He had been wiser than she, and now, because of her mistake, he had been brought even lower in his own eyes. For four days he stayed in his room. On Monday he came out, picked up the phone, and started calling his friends to see if they knew of any work. A friend working in a machine shop some thirty miles away had heard of a job there. Goddard went and got it. He started at $11.50 an hour.

Sanosuke Tanaka was pleased by the success of Nissan. When he had become a worker there more than forty years earlier, as a very young man, it had been a small company. Now it was a huge organization, and he was one of its most trusted and most senior workers. He had been through all the terrible times, the strike, the postwar years when there was not enough work, and the early sixties when there was too much work, the terrible years when he was working night shifts and he had not been able to sleep. He was very proud of his part in so great an enterprise, and while he did not exaggerate what he had accomplished, for he knew that it was small, he also knew that it was only because of men like him, thousands of them, that Nissan and Japan had been so successful. What he was really proud of was his generation, which had suffered so much during the war and then had come back to help restore Japan to a proper place in the world. It was not something he went around saying, for he was not an immodest man, but it was something that he quietly felt. That Japan had scored this remarkable triumph in America, that the Americans were now beginning to study Japanese means of production, made him very proud.

He felt, too, that he had been amply rewarded by the richness of his career; the company had even sent him to Mexico and other foreign lands to speak to Nissan workers there. To his great surprise, however, there was to be one additional reward. In May 1979, Tanaka, then sixty-four years old, was told by his superiors that because of the excellence of his work for so long a time and, above all, because of the model he had been to other workers, he would receive a special award. It was the Oju Hosho, the Medal with the Yellow Ribbon, and, most miraculously, it came from the Emperor himself.

This would of course be the most important moment in Tanaka's life. The day before the ceremony, he went to the barber. That evening he took the longest bath he could ever remember and scrubbed himself very thoroughly. He slept scarcely at all, and the next morning he was up at dawn. He put on the new white shirt his nieces had given him, and the new pair of shoes he had bought, and the formal morning coat and trousers that he had gotten from a rental shop, with his daughter's assistance. He felt a little awkward in these clothes—they were not, after all, proper for so simple a man—but he knew it was all right to do this, to rent the morning coat and wear it, because he was going to meet the Emperor. Then he went before the small altar in his house and thought of his late wife and told her he was ready for this day. Long before the chauffeur-driven sedan pulled up, he was ready.

He was taken first to the Ministry of Labor, where he waited with all the others who were going to receive an award. Some of the other men were quite famous, people whom Tanaka had read about in the newspapers or seen on television. It seemed incongruous that he was there waiting with them, as if some frightening mistake had been made and he would soon be found out. The minister of labor gave him a certificate and then the medal itself. Then Tanaka and the others were driven in a bus to the Imperial Palace, where they entered a great hall. Eventually the Emperor arrived and started to climb the stage. He was very old, and Tanaka was struck by how fragile he looked. He worried whether the Emperor could make the steps. If he collapsed and fell, Tanaka wondered, whose job would it be to help him? Then he concentrated on what was happening, on the fact that it was happening to him, that he was standing in front of the Emperor, and he thought again of his wife, wishing that she were alive and were with him on this special day.

The Emperor praised all the medal winners, and one of them in turn thanked him. Then they toured the palace garden. They were given cigarettes with the mark of the imperial chrysanthemum on them, and although he did not smoke, Tanaka kept the cigarettes so he could give them to his friends at work. That night there were parties. First there was one given by his family. All the members of his family told him how proud they were of him. Then there was a party given by Nissan at the New Grand Hotel, perhaps the fanciest in all Yokohama. Several hundred people had been invited, almost all of them Tanaka's superiors. At this party he finally began to cry. Some of his closest friends from work were also there, and they accompanied him to the third party of the evening, their own. It was a wonderful evening for Tanaka. Afterward he sometimes found it difficult to believe that it had happened, that his own life had meant so much, that although Nissan had been a company for fifty years, he was the only Nissan employee who had ever won the Medal of the Yellow Ribbon.

39.
THE FALL OF A
FREE TRADER

The shock waves of these great events soon brought considerable changes in both Ford's and the UAW's view of protectionism. The union's reaction was the move visceral; after all, its workers were immediately threatened. But the company was changing quickly too.

The Ford Motor Company had been a staunch advocate of free trade since the days of the founder, who had put his signature all over the world. His grandson had made some of his best early speeches on the subject and had symbolized to many in the postwar years the new generation of American business—liberal in its trade policy and enlightened in its dealings with labor. Of course, favoring free trade was natural to a company that was selling millions of dollars' worth of products abroad each year and was without serious foreign competition. In the mid-1970s, however, the company's position began to change.

One of the principal witnesses to that change was a young man named William Niskanen, hired in 1975 as Ford's chief economist. In the past, both at General Motors and at Ford, economists had been supremely unimportant. Often gifted men and women, they would sit in their offices coming up with brilliant projections only to find that no one paid the slightest bit of attention. There was no need to, in a virtual monopoly. A warning on their part that a particular labor settlement might be too costly simply did not matter, because there was no real competition and the cost could be passed on. Besides, no matter how talented the economists were, they were still minor figures in the chain of command, lieutenants warning the generals above them that the generals were courting disaster. Even when their judgments were independent, they themselves, in the eyes of their superiors, were not. Once the high executives of an auto company had learned to ignore an economist the first time, it was easy to continue.

Niskanen was different. While not necessarily more talented than many of his Ford predecessors, the forty-two-year-old Niskanen had a considerable reputation in both academia and conservative politics. He had been a professor of economics at Berkeley and was considered a possible candidate for the Council of Economic Advisers should Ronald Reagan or another conservative be elected President, which seemed increasingly likely. Niskanen was, by his own description, a serious conservative ideologue and free-market man. He found his position at Ford an unusual one. He was not powerful within the structure of the company, for he belonged to none of the various duchies of Ford, yet he attended all board meetings, had obvious access to the top people, and was a figure of genuine prestige within the company. Some Ford groups, such as the international people and the legal people, openly solicited his advice. However, he sensed immediately a certain wariness of him among a number of Ed Lundy's men because he had no established place in the hierarchy and might be prone to give unprogrammed, noncorporate answers. No group better exemplified the culture of Ford, he thought, than Lundy's: Be smart and quick and play the game right, and the momentum of your superior will pull you right up into the stratosphere. There were always tests, not lightly failed. One Friday, Niskanen—wearing a dark blazer, gray slacks, white shirt, and tie—dropped by Lundy's office on some business. "Starting the weekend a little early, aren't you, Bill?" Lundy remarked. No matter how pleasantly it was said, it was unmistakably a rebuke.

Niskanen was there at exactly the moment the easy years were ending, and thus when the company's economists were about to become considerably more important. For a variety of reasons, most notably the first oil shock, there was a surge in inflation, which hit Ford in several ways. For one, it made the company's health costs climb 10 to 15 percent a year. That immediately sent Ford's labor costs up, because the wages of both autoworkers and steelworkers were indexed to it. The formerly acceptable gap between autoworkers' wages and those of other industrial workers widened dramatically. At the beginning of the seventies, auto and steel workers made roughly 30 percent more than other industrial workers; by the end of the decade autoworkers made 60 percent more than the average of workers in other industries. (In steel, the difference was 70 percent.) Yet the company seemed oblivious, continuing to operate as if the economy had not undergone a drastic change.

At one board meeting in 1978, Bill Bourke, the executive vice-president for North America, made a strong pitch for buying Zincrometal, a processed steel coated with zinc that was better at resisting corrosion than ordinary steel. American steel companies did not yet make Zincrometal, but it could be bought from the Japanese, Bourke said, and, what was more, it was not only better than American steel but cheaper. The Canadians, he added, made it too. A heated discussion ensued. Bourke had clearly touched a nerve: He quickly realized there was obviously some kind of gentlemen's agreement between Ford and the steel companies. "Dammit," Henry Ford said, "we're a steel company ourselves, and we're part of the American steel industry, and I goddam well don't like us going and buying Japanese and Canadian steel." Finally a compromise was worked out: Bourke could buy the foreign steel until it was available from American manufacturers. Price was not to be a condition; availability was. Later Bourke decided that this was the last gasp of the old order, of the America immune to economic challenge from the rest of the world, and of cost-be-damned.

Yet already quality was becoming an issue, although something of a secret one. Ford's own warranty records clearly indicated mounting problems in manufacture and declining discipline in the work force, but these indications had long been ignored, and now there was blunt confirmation from Hertz of the superiority of Japanese quality. This news badly shook the people at the top of the company. What amazed Niskanen in 1979 was that despite such conclusive evidence on quality and despite the obvious fact that American pay scales were dangerously high, the people at Ford were going on as if it were business as usual. The agreements with the UAW in that year were, in his opinion, obviously inflationary. It was clear to anyone who faced facts that the Japanese had already become very tough competitors, and that one of their advantages was the lower cost of their labor. But Ford sailed along as if the world were still the same. Niskanen knew that the top Ford executives were in a poor position to halt the wage spiral. 1978 had been a very good year, and bonuses for those executives had been phenomenal. Both Caldwell and Bourke had received $630,000 in addition to their salaries. It was not exactly the right time to crack down on the workers. Discipline had to begin at the top, but there was no sign of it.

Gradually Niskanen watched a great free-trading company—threatened by the Japanese, caught in its own wage cycle—turn toward protectionism. The Ford leadership could see no other way out of its dilemma—a strike might cost $1 million a day. The company needed to revamp its product line, improve its quality, and modify its labor relations, but instead looked for external remedies against the Japanese. It was as if Ford's new dilemma had been caused only by Japan's wiliness, its own protectionism, and its skill in keeping the yen soft. Jack Barnes, Ford's principal Japan watcher, whose job had once seemed unimportant, took on new prominence in 1979. His ideas went right to the top now, to Phil Caldwell. In 1980 a decision was made to go for protectionist legislation.

As far as Niskanen was concerned, it was a quick-fix solution born of desperation, and he decided to fight it even though it was supported by Phil Caldwell and Will Caldwell—no relation—who had just replaced Ed Lundy as chief financial officer. In one memo Niskanen wrote: "A common commitment to refrain from seeking special favors serves the same economic function as a common commitment to refrain from stealing." He warned that if the government did help, it would exact a price; the more the government intervened, the more authority it would gain over how the Ford Motor Company did business. That point did not go over well with his superiors, nor did the rest of his dissent. He criticized the hypocrisy of Ford's calling for protectionism and domestic-content legislation at the same time it was escalating its imports of engines and transmissions from overseas.

Many executives told Niskanen confidentially that they agreed with his position, but the two Caldwells had a different opinion: In February 1980, much to his surprise, Bill Niskanen was fired. The closest thing to an explanation he got was from Will Caldwell. "In this company, Bill," he said, "the people who do well wait until they hear their superiors express their views. Then they add something in support of those views." That seemed to Niskanen a description not of how to do business but of how to amplify mistakes. Niskanen believed he had been fired simply for holding a dissenting opinion. Some of his friends thought he was fired for a different reason: He had come to embarrass those above him at Ford—because he still believed what they had believed in the past.

He was, one sympathetic colleague noted later, one of the early casualties of a rising new protectionism in America. For all of Japan's flaws, its own exclusive tendencies, it was hardly Japan's sins that had made Detroit vulnerable. Certainly Detroit had made only the most halfhearted gestures to open the Japanese market to its products; it had never lobbied very hard to open it, and it had never bothered to ship right-hand-drive cars, which the Japanese used, instead of left-hand-drive cars, which Americans drove. But at this terrible moment, with so much from the recent past to undo, it was a great deal easier to find the villains elsewhere rather than in the Glass House.

40.
AMAYA ENDS
AN ERA

It had been acknowledged at MITI early on that Naohiro Amaya understood the Americans and their politics better than almost anyone else in the ministry and had a highly refined sense of what, in any serious confrontation, America's most basic positions really were. At the same time, respect for him among the Americans steadily increased. There was a consensus that he played fewer games with them during important negotiations than other Japanese and did not insult their intelligence by poor-mouthing and exaggerating Japan's vulnerability. He made sure he understood their political realities as well as his own. Furthermore, unlike most Japanese, who seemed eager to gather information but reluctant to volunteer it, he was willing to be honest, and the more he told the Americans, the more open they were with him. Some Americans who had lived in Tokyo during the late fifties had monitored his progress over the year. At early meetings, awkward and diffident in a poorly tailored suit, he had read haltingly from speeches laboriously translated into stilted English. Gradually, however, as if he were a metaphor for his country, he became more confident in appearances before foreigners. Both his English and his clothes got better, and one day, an American diplomat said, he looked up to see an elegant man sitting across from him, poised and eloquent. Amaya had become a master of the verbal jousting that went on at these sessions. When Chalmers Johnson, a distinguished Japanologist and an expert on MITI, teased him about there being only two economics Ph.D.'s in the ministry, Amaya answered that this was true, for running MITI was too important to be left to economists. Then he cited a study he had conducted that showed that the more Nobel laureates in economics a country had, the more likely its economy was to go downhill.

Because of Amaya's growing reputation it was not surprising that Japan turned to him when it was time to deal with the burgeoning American pressure for some sort of protection in the field of autos. He was not looking forward to the task, however, since it was not going to be easy to deal with either the Americans or the Japanese. He had been surprised by the speed of the American auto industry's decline and had serious reservations about its ability to adjust to its new circumstances. As for Japan, he had a very clear sense of how well its resources had been allotted and utilized in the thirty-five years since the war, of how little had been wasted, of how everyone had played his part. Having to tell his countrymen to cut back on exports just as they achieved their goals was going to be painful as well as difficult. It was not the workers he was worried about; as far as he was concerned the Japanese had the best blue-collar workers in the world, men who worked hard, accepted the limits of their lives, and were at once proud of their accomplishments and modest about them. The trouble was likely to be with management, where ambition and ego had always been thinly concealed. With Japan's industrial rise there had been a comparable decline in their modesty. Many of the men who ran Japanese businesses had begun to believe that they, not the workers or the state, were responsible for Japan's success.

The delicate negotiations between the Japanese and the Americans over restrictions on importing Japanese autos to the United States began in 1979. The Americans themselves were divided over the issue of protection. Ford and the UAW wanted relief and were willing to say so, but General Motors, locked into its own free-trade rhetoric, was reluctant to advocate a limit; it might want one, for it was suffering too, but it was not going to go on the record as calling for one. The Carter administration was divided as well. The chief split was between those advisers who based their judgments on the economy as a whole and those who represented various afflicted constituencies. Charles Schultze, President Jimmy Carter's chairman of the Council of Economic Advisers, was particularly opposed to protection. As far as he was concerned, Detroit's problems were completely of its own making, and the blame fell on both management and labor. Labor contracts had become too inflationary in the last decade, he argued; he was indignant that the industry, aware of the new economic realities in 1979—higher gas prices, the growing alienation of American car buyers, tougher competition from abroad—had nonetheless given the union a settlement that placed it at 60 percent above the American manufacturing norm. Now he felt that Detroit was asking the government to validate its bad management practices.

Carter was also reluctant to aid Detroit. Not only did he have a populist's wariness of auto men, but he also felt frustrated by them because he had pushed them in the past to make their cars smaller and they had not been very responsive. On the other hand, Carter had human and political sympathies for the 250,000 auto workers who were out of work. While his administration did not carry as much of an ideological free-trade burden as the one that was to succeed it, some members were also strongly opposed to any intervention for fear that it would set off antitrust suits, brought by American dealers who handled imports.

It became obvious, however, that the crucial decision might not be made under Carter. His administration was soon forced to invest its final energies in the attempt to solve the Iranian hostage crisis. Dealing with the Japanese became the problem of the entering Reagan administration, which, although far warier of imposing trade restrictions, also held conflicting opinions. Ronald Reagan, the first truly conservative President elected in more than half a century, was a firm believer in free-market economics. Murray Weidenbaum, the chairman of the Council of Economic Advisers, shared the view of his predecessor Schultze that import restrictions were inflationary. However, some politicians with good connections—particularly former senator Bill Brock, who was the administration's international trade negotiator—held differing opinions. By early March 1981, Brock was saying that limited restraints on the Japanese might be politically acceptable. To add to the discord, Brock and Secretary of State Alexander Haig wrangled over whose domain the negotiations should fall in.

Toward the end of its time in office the Carter administration had given clear signals to the Japanese to come up with some voluntary restrictions. The Japanese, realizing it was very early in the negotiations and that a new administration might well be coming in, pretended not to hear. By the time Reagan took office the auto industry was in desperate trouble. Interest rates bounced between 15 and 21 percent, making it terribly difficult for Americans to buy cars, especially the more expensive domestic models. Finally the Reagan administration, too, despite Murray Weidenbaum's objections, decided to ask the Japanese to suggest a voluntary ceiling on their exports into America.

The Japanese auto industry had immense influence within the ruling party in the Japanese Diet. When American requests for voluntary restrictions grew more pointed in 1980, leading members of the party, pushed by the heads of the Japanese auto companies, made a trip to Washington to let the Americans know they could not be squeezed on this issue. The Americans had never been very tough on the Japanese in the past, and the delegation had no reason to believe that anything had changed. This time, though, the Japanese faced a new political climate. The troubles of the American auto industry were creating widespread anti-Japanese feeling, which was now reflected in Washington. The Japanese were accustomed to militant opposition in Europe, but encountering it in America was a shock. Their earlier adversaries, like Senator John Danforth of Missouri, were angrier than ever, and now there were many new ones. Previous allies, along with the top lobbyists the Japanese had been using to great effect, now claimed they could no longer protect the foreigners. The Diet members had gone to America expecting to make a stand; instead they were absolutely flattened. The American economy was momentarily in shambles. Much of the unemployment seemed to come from the auto industry. Because of that there was a swelling protectionism in Washington. Their own core economy in jeopardy for the first time since the war, Americans were looking long and hard at Japan, and they were dismayed by its own protectionism. Japan must bend, and bend quickly, on auto or risk harsh legislation, the Diet members reported back. With this threat, serious negotiations began between the two countries. Brock represented the Americans. He played it very cool. I'm as much for free trade as you are, went his line, but we have to face some very serious political realities here. I'm not asking you for anything, in fact I'm here to help you. People like Danforth are gaining support all the time, so your friends, like me, are worried about you.

The bargaining sessions were long and arduous. When Amaya had negotiated with the Americans before, it had always been over the issue of a troubled sector of an essentially vibrant economy. Now that so vital a part of the American economy was in peril, the Americans seemed to have lost the quality that had most impressed Amaya in the past: their complete confidence in themselves. Amaya estimated the figure needed by the two big Japanese manufacturers to keep their balance sheets in the black, and then he estimated the figure that would allow the Americans to salvage their pride and to repair their ability to make better cars. Then he decided the two points he would insist upon. First, he wanted the ceiling to be a fixed number rather than a percentage of the previous year's total—so the Japanese would not suffer if American sales plummeted further. Second, he wanted to keep the Americans from setting categories by size or price: The Japanese did not want to be locked into exporting small cars; they wanted a chance to move into the more profitable middle range.

Convincing the new Japanese titans was even less pleasant for Amaya than bargaining with the Americans. The people at both Toyota and Nissan, seeing themselves as self-made men about to be deprived of a success that was rightfully theirs, were enraged. They pointed out quite angrily that MITI had done a great deal for steel, shipping, and computers, but it had done very little for the auto industry—and therefore Toyota and Nissan owed MITI nothing. Toyota executives were particularly virulent. They assembled their friends in the press and unleashed against Amaya a barrage of the most acrimonious name-calling in recent Japanese memory, in which he was referred to as "a whore for the foreigners" and "Reagan's concubine." Nissan executives were almost as angry, although they did not go to the newspapers.

Amaya began to fear that the issue was getting out of hand, that there was a danger of its becoming a focal point of tension and hidden resentments on both sides of the Pacific. The name-calling did not bother him, but he was made nervous by any issue that could appeal to such emotions. So he invited Ishihara, the head of both Nissan and the Automobile Manufacturers Association, to a restaurant in the Ginza to persuade him to agree to a compromise. Until then Ishihara had taken a very hard line on the issue. He felt, in the most personal way, that he was being cheated out of his own success. It was not fair that his company should have to pay for the Americans' mistakes. Amaya heard him out, then bowed on the tatami mat and begged him not to repeat the mistakes of the past by fighting the Americans. Do not, he entreated, be like Yosuke Matsuoka when he led the Japanese out of the League of Nations and thus intensified Japanese nationalism. (Asked later about the moment when he prostrated himself, Amaya said a little theatrics never hurt.) It had, however, been a difficult night for both him and Ishihara. Amaya had not doubted for a moment that he would win. He knew that Ishihara would have to concede, that his obligation to his country was greater than his obligation to his company. Ishihara, for his part, was also aware that he did not really have a choice. If he and the other auto makers rejected this compromise (which was not that bad a deal, after all), the full power of the government, the press, and public opinion would be turned against them. The ceiling was set at a rather high 1.685 million cars.

The irony of what he had done did not escape him. When he, Naohiro Amaya, saw America at the moment of its ultimate strength in 1945, when he was young, the idea that he might participate in negotiations placing limits on Japanese auto exports to the land of Henry Ford would have struck him as the unlikeliest of events. But it had happened. The oil century had started with Henry Ford, and it had been ended in part by

Naohiro Amaya. Nor was the profound symbolism of what he had accomplished lost on his fellow countrymen. Some commentators referred to it as the reverse of Japan's signing the surrender aboard the battleship *Missouri*. But Amaya took no particular pleasure from it. The world as he knew it depended on a strong America. There must be a strong America to help sustain a strong Japan.

PART
ELEVEN

41.
THE DEFECTION OF
MARVIN RUNYON

By 1978, Marvin Runyon had pretty much decided to take early retirement from Ford. Aside from personal considerations—his wife was not happy in Detroit and he wanted to find a job in the South for her sake—he was frustrated by the difficulty of keeping up the plants and with the overall problem of trying to build a good car in America. He was also disturbed by the firing of Iacocca and Bourke, two of Ford's best product men. He found Philip Caldwell, Iacocca's successor, extremely hard to deal with. Caldwell, he thought, understood the rule book but not the true essence of the Ford Motor Company. Runyon was coming up on fifty-five, which was a good demarcation point, for he could retire with considerable benefits. He began looking for work in the South and soon was considering offers from various supplier companies. As he neared his own appointed date for retirement, Nissan's officials, having decided to open a factory in America, were looking for an American to run it. They learned through headhunters that Runyon, then vice-president in charge of assembly plants, was thinking of leaving Ford and approached him. Runyon let them know he was interested, and newspapers soon reported that Nissan was talking to a high Ford executive. Runyon's superiors knew it was he, and they made their distaste for what he was doing—going over to the enemy at the height of the battle—quite apparent.

By his last day at Ford, Runyon still had not made up his mind. Normally when an executive at his level left Ford, he was given an inscribed silver tray and a Ford car of his choice as a going-away present. This time an emissary from Caldwell appeared in Runyon's office asking for his signature on some papers saying that he would not go over to a competitor. Runyon asked if this was standard procedure for all departing Ford executives.

The emissary hedged. Runyon refused to sign. Later Runyon was informed that he would not be given a car. He was also told that there would be no silver tray because Ford had run out of them. At the last minute someone reversed the decision and he was notified that he could have a car. Runyon said not to bother, he had already rented two Lincolns from Budget. At his going-away party no silver tray was presented, although again there was a change of mind, and he received it later. So it was that Marvin Runyon made his departure from the Ford Motor Company.

Runyon did decide to join Nissan, but he did not leave Ford after thirty-eight years because he was offered a job by a Japanese competitor; he left because of accumulated frustrations and because he was angry over the firing of Iacocca and Bourke. He believed, furthermore, that he was taking a job in an *American* company, one that would provide Americans with jobs, even though its parent company happened to be in Japan. It seemed unfair to him that he was judged so harshly by the very men whose pedantic style and unwillingness to take manufacturing seriously had made Ford so vulnerable. The new Nissan plant was located in Smyrna, in a lovely rural area of middle Tennessee. (Tennessee was just one of the states competing to get the Nissan factory by offering various incentives, including tax benefits and state-subsidized training for the workers. The competition had been so intense that Jim Thompson, the governor of Illinois, had flown to Tokyo twice to woo Nissan, and Governor Jim Rhodes of Ohio had gone to the Columbus airport with popcorn to greet Mitsuya Goto, the Nissan representative, and then had flown him around the state in his own plane, while making sandwiches himself for Goto and the other Japanese.) Smyrna was selected by the Nissan people because of its good rail connections and its right-to-work laws and because it was assumed to be far enough from the industrial North to be beyond the reach of the UAW. Runyon was eager to be free for the first time in his life of the limitations imposed by the UAW as well as the bureaucracy and heavy centralization of Ford. He was looking forward to working for a company that believed in the primacy of manufacturing.

Nissan asked him to make an estimate of what it would cost to run the plant. When he finished it, he typed it up, signed it, and—according to the procedure he had been taught at Ford—brought it to his new boss, Takashi Ishihara, president of Nissan, to sign. Ishihara seemed surprised when he looked at it, and said nothing. A few days later he brought it back to Runyon with his signature at the bottom. "Frame this," he said, "because it is the last piece of paper I will sign for you." Runyon looked puzzled. "We searched very carefully for the man to run our factory," Ishihara continued, "and we picked you, and you are our man and we trust you. We don't have to sign papers anymore. From now on it is just yes or no with us."

The Japanese had been slightly startled by Runyon's initial figures, which they thought were too high. When Runyon asked how much too high, they suggested cutting them 10 percent. Then the Japanese discussed it some more and finally came back to tell Runyon not to cut anything he really needed; they did not want him to start a factory and then make himself and their product vulnerable. The Japanese, he thought, differed from the Americans in this respect, at least. They had learned long ago that manufacturing was basic to quality. They were aided in this respect by their relationships with their banks, which allowed them to make long-range investments in expensive machinery that would have been impossible for an American company. Nissan budgeted the plant for $500 million and accepted that it would not turn a profit for five years. Runyon was sure that while an American firm might have pledged to wait just as long, management would have announced a year later that the stock analysts said the company needed a greater profit in the coming year. He had altogether too many memories of being at Ford and winning approval of a $50 million project and then, halfway into it, $25 million already spent, receiving a series of hold-downs from the Glass House, so that in the end the guts of the project would be cut out.

Ishihara had always been nervous about coming to America and doubted the quality of American workers and their capacity to make cars. Thus, to minimize the potential weaknesses of American workers (and the potential power of a union), Nissan wanted a highly automated factory; it also was decided to manufacture only trucks at Smyrna, at least in the beginning. When Runyon asked Ishihara why he planned to build trucks rather than autos, Ishihara replied, "Because we are unsure about the American workers and we are concerned about quality—and if the vehicles are not going to be up to our quality, then at least we want them to be our lowest-selling item."

The man, thought Runyon, is nothing if not blunt. "We can build a car as good as the Japanese," Runyon said.

"Perhaps," said Ishihara, "but we have not seen it yet."

"You haven't seen us build to Japanese design," Runyon answered, and they let it go at that.

Smyrna became the most automated car or truck factory in America, a quick look into the future. In other factories, men operated machines that made vehicles, but at Smyrna, in vast areas such as painting and welding, machines did the work and men simply cared for the machines. Instead of the classic blue-collar line worker of limited education and skills, Nissan was hiring a new breed of worker, people who often had electrical and electronic skills and could repair immensely complicated machines. Some of these employees had not finished high school but had been electricians for fifteen years; others had attended junior college or spent four years as maintenance and repair men in the air force. Nissan administered a battery of psychological tests designed to pick up any predilection on the part of a new worker to join a union. The pay was good, virtually the equivalent of UAW money; by Tennessee standards, it was very good.

Runyon's management style was very much his own—a combination of the best of Japanese and American methods. He spent only about twelve hours a year in board meetings and eliminated the endless red tape in which, to his mind, Ford had specialized. At Ford there were twelve layers of management; in Smyrna he cut it to five. He himself became a fixture on the factory floor. Rather than a suit, he wore the Nissan worker outfit, a kind of blue fatigue uniform. He was not Mr. Runyon, but, as it said on his shirt pocket, Marvin. He simplified the executive hierarchy so that his managers were on the floor as well. Because he was free of UAW restrictions, he was able to move his workers around and expedite plant procedures. Morale was unusually high among the workers, men and women who were grateful for jobs that had almost instantly lifted them from the lower middle or even working class to middle or upper middle class. They were called technicians, and, with overtime, they made as much as $29,000 a year, wages equal or superior to the salaries of college professors in the same region. On the Smyrna factory floor, it seemed as if fifty years of labor-management bitterness had been wiped away, as if there had never been a Henry Ford or a Harry Bennett, who had treated workers with such cruelty. It also seemed as if there had never been a UAW, which had grown unwieldy in building itself up to combat those same indecencies. The Nissan workers got the benefits of UAW pay without being unionized, for Nissan had to meet the going rate, and Runyon and the Japanese had the benefit of learning from the mistakes of both American labor and management in their new streamlined plant.

The Nissan plant was an almost immediate success. It began truck production in June 1983 and a year later had the capacity to build ten thousand trucks a month. Encouraged by its early success, Nissan decided in 1984 to begin manufacturing cars. That year the plant was named by *Fortune* magazine as one of the ten best-managed factories in America. The first cars rolled down the line in March 1985, and by the end of the year the factory, with a total of three thousand workers on two shifts, had produced a total of 240,000 cars and trucks. Some critics in the Japanese press claimed that the level of profit was not nearly as high as that of the

Honda factory in Ohio. But the Nissan people pronounced themselves pleased with the early results and Ishihara went so far as to claim that the American trucks were of higher quality than the ones being made in Japan.

Although he made an effort, it was difficult for Runyon not to be critical of the system he had just left. Sometimes he would mention to the press that steel and auto unions had succeeded so well in driving up wages that one day they looked around to discover there were no jobs left. At other times he would remark to community groups that for twenty years management and labor had spoken only with each other while they kept the customers cooling their heels outside, until one day they opened the door to the waiting room and found it empty. On other occasions—as when he went before the Detroit Economic Club in February 1986 to give a speech entitled "Has Detroit Gotten the Message?"—he chided his former colleagues for abusing the opportunities granted them every time they received a tariff advantage against the Japanese. Instead of using the edge provided by the tariffs to charge less than the Japanese, Detroit had raised its prices to maximize profits. It was shortsighted and ill advised, he said (implying that it was greedy as well), since the Americans could not compete with the Japanese on quality. They should therefore, he argued, exploit the advantage in price. They were giving away an advantage just won for them by their government.

Nissan's approach, thought Runyon, was much more sensible. The board was full of former manufacturing men; the importance of making things *right* permeated the company. Designers worked to the specifications conducive to high-quality manufacturing. Finance people were aware that machinery had to be maintained properly. Runyon felt he was no longer talking to the deaf.

One autumn evening in 1982, millions of Americans turned on their television sets and were treated to an extraordinary sight. They saw black-and-white FBI films of John DeLorean, once the fair-haired boy of Detroit, participating in a colossal drug deal, bartering part of his dying auto company for a large share of the $60 million transaction. The background of the story was complicated. Federal agents had been pursuing other dealers when suddenly DeLorean, in desperate trouble with his car company in Northern Ireland, had walked right onto their stage. He had seemed, to those watching the government films, a willing, indeed eager, participant in the drug deal, or what his onetime friend David Davis called his "new career as an importer of controlled substances." He had been set up; the men he thought were his newest partners were in fact federal agents.

Though he was eventually acquitted of the charges, many who had watched the case felt that he was free not so much because the jury believed him but rather because ordinary Americans did not like the idea of their government setting up its citizens, no matter how tawdry their behavior. The film seemed oddly indelible, as if although acquitted he had not been cleared.

The trial itself was the end of DeLorean's long, slow fall from grace. Earlier that year his new car, the DeLorean, had appeared, and it had been a disaster. The cars were more expensive than expected, the quality was unacceptable, orders began to decline, and the company was in ruins. Serious questions about DeLorean's personal and corporate finances remained, particularly about $18 million that seemed to have mysteriously disappeared from the company's coffers.

The city of Detroit had watched with fascination as the entire saga of John DeLorean unfolded. No one had ever doubted his talent, for he was one of the most creative young men of his generation. Many thought, that his was the most plausible attempt by an American at a start-up company since that of Henry Kaiser, even if it was being undertaken in Ireland rather than in Michigan. Since Henry Kaiser had failed in the fifties, the auto industry had become ever more closed. Dominated by the three large firms—oligopoly was the term for it—and free of fresh challenges, it grew increasingly cautious and conventional. As the number of automobile companies continued to decline, with old names like Packard and Studebaker and Nash and Hudson disappearing from the highway, the cost of doing business kept going up, which guaranteed that it would be harder and harder to create a new company. The ticket was simply too high: If the price had been $300 million in 1945, when Kaiser tried it, then by now it was many times that. Certainly $2 billion, said one Detroit expert, was the minimum. That requirement was sufficient to scare off would-be entrepreneurs. Thus in the late seventies when DeLorean tried to create his own auto firm, the city of Detroit watched with utter fascination. Nothing else told more about the society and the industry—the changed values of both—than DeLorean's quest.

DeLorean had become celebrated, justifiably or not, as a rebel within the ranks of the industry. His self-proclaimed rebellion against GM, his ability to charm the media, his good looks (which with the help of modern surgery he worked to improve much as one restyled a car, replacing a weaker jaw with a stronger one), and his flamboyant life-style had made him something of a national figure. Like Iacocca he was that rarity in contemporary Detroit, a star, an audacious man who liked to deal with the press and who sought *personal* publicity. The media buildup of him in the good days was exceptional; in the words of Hillel Levin, a Detroit writer, DeLorean had become "a Gary Cooper industrialist in a movie scripted by Ayn Rand." The fact that he was so public and exciting a figure eventually helped him when it came time to build his own car. The ironic likelihood was that a more serious person with a better professional background might not have been able to raise the money for a new company, while someone like DeLorean, who had caught the public's eye (more often than not for the wrong reason), could.

DeLorean combined the worst of two cultures: He was the swinger as car man and the car man as swinger. The original entrepreneurs of Detroit had been true Calvinists, men obsessed by their visions, who worked long into the night in their kitchens or garages and sacrificed all their time and money to bring those dreams to life. DeLorean was different, the company founder in an age when narcissism had replaced Calvinism. He was a modern man, obsessed more by his own looks, fame, and luxuries than by his product. He had been a poor blue-collar kid in Detroit, his father a Rumanian immigrant who had toiled on the Ford line. The son's dream was to escape the harshness and monotony of that life. He had studied engineering at local schools, and when his skills and charm propelled him to a level where for the first time he encountered the prospect of living in a fantasy world, he found it irresistible.

As a young man working for GM, DeLorean was clearly gifted, full of good ideas. Sponsored by Bunkie Knudsen, he rose quickly in the Pontiac division. Soon, as head of Pontiac, he had his first contacts with Hollywood, and he was seduced by it. At this point, in his early forties, he reinvented himself. He was no longer what he had been—in Detroit's lexicon, a damn good car guy, an engineer that the old-timers would have approved of; he became the styled and stylish voice of youth in a middle-aged corporation. It was the sixties, and Pontiac was pushing cars for young people. He not only knew how to appeal to the new generation, he became part of it. He shed his first wife. He redesigned his hair, which became noticably less gray. (He went gray years later, when it was time to raise money for his own company and he needed to look more distinguished.) His ties disappeared. His suits, on those occasions when he dressed formally, were of fashionable Italian cut. He wore loafers without socks and carefully shaved the hair around his ankles. He lifted weights to build up his body, and changed his diet to lose weight. His marriages increased his celebrity: His second bride, a girl of nineteen, was Kelly Harmon, daughter of the famed football player Tommy Harmon. (The match gave him Ricky Nelson, son of Ozzie and Harriet, as a brother-in-law.) That marriage lasted two and a half years. (When he seemed depressed by its breakup, some of his good buddies in Hollywood hired a bunch of what might generously be called starlets, got makeup men to style their look as much like Kelly's as possible, and made them available to the saddened auto executive. The message was implicit: There were a lot more fish in the sea.) His third wife was Cristina Ferrare, one of the most beautiful models in the country. In an environment where ego was always supposed to be controlled, his burgeoned: As a kind of Christmas card he sent General Motors dealers thousands of posters of himself posing with his adopted son, Zach. His friends now included the great and famous of Hollywood, all of whom lived lives faster than those of his Bloomfield Hills colleagues. For his new business friends, he chose self-made men of minimal restraint, maximum glitter, and extraordinary access to money. Unlike the titans of Detroit, who had to hide their pleasure as part of the covenant of Detroit success, his new friends had *fun*.

It soon became obvious that DeLorean was bored with Detroit. He took to insulting his GM superiors first by his manner of dress—blue jeans, cowboy boots—and then, when that seemed inadequate, with the condescending profanity of his tongue. Soon he was gone from GM. (His business practices had become bothersome to GM officials, and he did not leave of his own volition.) General Motors, which always took care of its own, particularly its own senior executives, was extremely generous to DeLorean; it gave him a Cadillac dealership in Florida, which in those days was like giving someone the right to print money. Nonetheless he promptly collaborated on a scathing indictment of GM as an institution, which confirmed most of the darker visions the company's critics had long harbored. (When, during his brief tour as the head of a company, his own behavior seemed to fall considerably beneath that of the GM executives whom he had denounced, one of his colleagues, Bill Haddad, said of DeLorean, "He is what he condemns.") His post-GM business ventures did not do well, and he left behind a trail of bad feeling and litigation.

Having been ousted by GM, he longed now to return to the automobile world and create his own sports car. His would be, he announced, an ethical car company. He played Britain, which wanted the factory for Northern Ireland, off against Puerto Rico—the underemployed of the world competing desperately for the right to have those jobs. The British won, if that is the word, and put up some $90 million for him in start-up money. His predecessors some seventy years earlier had been passionate men who had poured their entire savings into their mechanical dreams and who had literally lived out the creation of their cars. DeLorean was different. He put relatively little money of his own into his car, and though he was starting a company, he continued to live in high style. As he readied his car, he bought expensive property for himself—a duplex in Manhattan, and a twenty-five-room house on a 430-acre spread in the most exclusive part of New Jersey. (They were worth by 1985, when they became the center of a keenly contested *third* divorce, an estimated $9 million.) He already owned an expensive spread in Southern California. He rented a Park Avenue suite in Manhattan for his corporate headquarters. His top people received credit cards for Tiffany's and the 21 Club. He billed the company some $78,000 for his move to New York, though in fact he was already there. He drew a consultant's fee of $300,000 a year. The company bought a $53,000 Mercedes for Cristina. One Christmas, even as the company was getting started, he bought her three sable coats, average cost about $30,000, each of a different length. "I forgot which length you wanted," said his note to her.

There had been a great deal of hoopla at the beginning of his attempt to create his own company and car—DeLorean appearing in Cutty Sark Scotch ads; DeLorean lending his name to a men's cologne that sold in chic stores—and his colleagues in Detroit watched it all with more than normal curiosity. In 1981 there were reports from Belfast that the car was in serious trouble, that DeLorean visited the factory only on the rarest occasions, and that there were grave financial questions about his use of money. As much as $18 million had mysteriously vanished into some secret account in Switzerland. Still the car was yet to come, and Detroit was willing to give DeLorean the benefit of the doubt; high liver though he might be, no one had ever doubted his talent. That summer, just before the car was launched, a reporter called DeLorean to talk in general about the problems of Detroit. DeLorean, who liked dealing with the press, was friendly and lingered on the phone.

"What about the problem of worker productivity?" the reporter asked.

"The problem, I'm afraid," said DeLorean, "is the 'me generation.' "

42.
THE HAMMER
AND THE NAIL

Finally, by the mid-eighties, Ishihara had accumulated enough power so that he could move against Shioji and, some eight years after becoming president, take command of the company. The split between the two men had been private at first, but gradually it became more and more public. Shioji seemed to take particular pleasure in flaunting his vendetta with Ishihara. At first his demonstrations of disrespect were rather mild; he used phrases that deprived the president of normal conversational respect. That was shocking enough. Soon, however, he was telling journalists that Ishihara was a stupid ass, adding that if he, rather than Ishihara, were president of the company, it would not be lagging so badly behind Toyota. In Japan, where it was one's duty to esteem one's superior, such blatant disrespect was unthinkable; defying that convention made it all the sweeter for Shioji when he hurled an especially sharp barb at Ishihara. He felt it showed the world that he was Ishihara's equal.

They had fought over the American plant, and Ishihara (with Kawamata's support) had won that round, making it a truck factory instead of auto and placing it in Tennessee with a manager, Marvin Runyon, who was determined to keep the UAW out. If that victory was Ishihara's, then Shioji was determined to get his revenge in other ways. But Shioji's own freedom of movement was circumscribed by the very nature of the union system in whose development he had played so important a part. He could not lightly take his workers out on a strike. In Japan a strike was a grievous thing. It was one thing to have passionate rallies, to accuse the bosses of insensitivity to the working class, to wear armbands, and blare out messages on a bullhorn, for a zen labor struggle was usually quite enough, and an embarrassed management quickly got the message. But a real strike—in which workers walked off the job—had a terrible finality to it. Japanese harmony, so crucial to the survival and the success of the state, so carefully put together, could disintegrate very rapidly, and if it did, everyone would suffer. Even a modest strike meant not only that the company's profits would decline but that the workers would lose their annual bonuses. In Japan, unlike the United States, when the company did poorly, the workers did poorly as well. So in protecting the workers' interests, Shioji could not lightly lead them out on strike. He had to negotiate their interests deftly. That meant that there was often an elliptical quality to his struggle with Ishihara. It was never about the things it was supposed to be about, and it was rarely frontal. It was verbal, and about protocol, and it divided the company (to the delight of the people at Toyota), but it did not result in a strike.

In the early eighties, for the first time in more than twenty-five years, there were work stoppages. These were not strikes—they had not been voted by the workers; they were part of an ongoing test of will. An assembly line, usually run by someone very close to Shioji, might shut down for a a few days. The explanation for the stoppage would be that there had been an accident at the working station. Work, Shioji's people announced, could not continue for reasons of safety. The message was clear: The company needed Shioji's cooperation.

In the end the struggle between the two men, one that had been building for some twenty years, came to a climax not over an issue of wages, or the issue of installation of robots, but over the decision to place a Nissan factory in England. Ishihara wanted the factory, and Shioji, still angry over his inability to influence the American factory, opposed it. The struggle spanned several years, and during it the members of the British embassy in Tokyo felt, as one member said, like a child whose parents are always about to get divorced—caught in a family squabble over which they had no control. The decision was made no less stressful by the fact that it was being made by a company that was steadily losing ground to its main competitor, Toyota.

The British factory became a heated issue in the early eighties. Having gotten by the first hurdle, the decision to build in America, and having figured out how to do it for a relatively low cost, Ishihara was trying to turn Nissan into a more international company. The Japanese market was fast becoming a mature one, and anti-Japanese protectionism was on the rise throughout the world. To his mind the only way for Nissan to continue its success was to get into other areas; he passionately wanted to enter the defense industry and build rockets, and at the same time he wanted to expand the auto market beyond Japan's frontiers. To that aim he became a constant traveler and salesmen. ("I think," said Shioji, "he is never in Tokyo, but he is this traveling Japanese gentleman who prints up a lot of calling cards with his name on them and goes throughout the world stopping off at every country and handing them out to everyone he meets, asking to do a joint venture with them.") In particular Ishihara wanted to penetrate the Common Market, where anti-Japanese feeling, be it suspicion or prejudice, was considerably stronger than in the United States. To Italy the Japanese were allowed to export only two thousand cars. The French, whose tolerance for Japanese trade practices was almost nonexistent, kept the imports under 3 percent and, even worse, deliberately forced Japanese goods to enter through a port manned by a minimal number of inspectors all of whom seemed distinguished by the slowness of their procedures—a process that mimicked the one that exporters to Japan found themselves undergoing. In England the suspicions of Japanese intentions were immense; the Japanese were limited to 11 percent of the market, and there was serious talk of cutting even that figure back. In West Germany the market had been relatively open, but the Germans were said to be thinking of a 10 percent cap.

To evade these worrying restrictions, Ishihara wanted to build a Nissan factory *within* the Common Market, and he aimed to do it by starting with a toehold in England. But his position within his own company was vulnerable. If there was a wariness on the part of the Japanese of doing business in America, then their attitude was one of pure terror where Britain was concerned. "The British disease," the Japanese called England's condition, and for them it was the summation of all that was wrong with the West, an overtaxed society collapsing of its own indifference, both labor and management willing to destroy a company rather than find common ground. In their own professional lifetime most senior Japanese managers had seen England fall from its position as one of the world's foremost manufacturing centers, its craftsmanship universally admired, to its present condition as one of the world's weakest ones. When the Japanese noted things about American society that they did not like, they talked about the Americans coming down with the British disease, and when the smallest domestic signs were detected of what they considered decline, be it juvenile delinquents beating up a park bum or the desire of one Japanese family to sue a neighbor over a domestic squabble, they spoke of the danger of Japan's coming down with the British disease. Now Ishihara was suggesting that Nissan manufacture cars in England, the very place that was the exporter no longer of fine finished industrial goods but of the British disease.

He was largely without support in his own company other than that which came from the power of the presidency. Kawamata, Nissan's chairman, far more leery of international expansion, was opposed, if not actively, at least passively. Shioji was furiously against it. Frustrated and embittered by Ishihara, he chose this struggle as a vehicle for his revenge. He had no love for British labor in the first place. Unlike American labor leaders, the British union officials had paid no attention at all to him before, and as a young Japanese attending international meetings, he had felt their snobbery. Nor did he admire their politics; he thought them far too left-wing, too much interested in ideology and too little in work. In his view they stood for factionalism in the workplace as a way of life.

The British badly wanted the factory. They were the tired men of the Common Market, much scorned by other industrial countries both old and new, and this, the coming of a new Japanese factory, would be an immense vote of confidence for an industry that seemed to be dying. They also saw it as a chance—if the union agreements could be worked out—for a nation that had virtually choked itself to death on its labor troubles to achieve a new, less contentious kind of industrial order. To the surprise of British officials desperate for Nissan's approval, they were getting preliminary assent from various labor leaders to labor agreements for the Japanese that would be virtually strike-free. But within Nissan itself, despite growing evidence of how flexible, indeed malleable, the British intended to be, the struggle was intense. In the beginning it appeared that Ishihara would lose, that the opposition to him was too great.

Shioji's lobbying was zealous. On his own he went to the Ministry of Foreign Affairs and spoke against the project; on his own he attended meetings at the British embassy where he berated British unions—he had respect for the people of England, he said, but not for their unions—and Ishihara. For an influential Japanese to sit in front of foreigners and attack the president of his company was extraordinary, but there he was, doing it. No mention was ever made of Ishihara's name. "There are people in this company," Shioji told the British, "who do not seem to understand that this company is about making motor cars, and that is special. There are people in this company who want to speculate and diversify, to build rockets and boats, but that would be a mistake because we are the makers of automobiles, and that makes us unique. There is a mystique to making motor cars, and these people do not seem to understand it." The British listening to him were astonished. It did not bode well for their chance at a factory. At the same time Kawamata's opposition was a serious problem. The old man, the British thought, was always in the way. Privately (with other Japanese but never with foreigners), Ishihara spoke of his frustration with Kawamata and the problems he had, because of this, in running the company.

What seemed to strengthen Shioji's position was the fact that in its domestic competition with Toyota, Nissan was steadily slipping. In 1980 the two auto makers had been fairly close in domestic sales: Toyota held its customary edge, with 1.49 million cars sold as compared with 1.22 million for Nissan. But then Nissan seemed to grow weaker while Toyota gained. By the end of 1983 Nissan had 1.12 million and Toyota had 1.59 million, and was climbing. Nissan was in serious trouble, not just from Toyota's growing strength and endless resource (it was reliably reported in 1983 that Toyota made a greater profit than all the other auto companies combined), but from the challenge beneath it of Honda and Mazda, which were much more innovative and creative companies.

By 1983 those who knew Nissan well thought that Ishihara was about to lose the British deal. That would mean a considerable loss of face in addition to failure to complete his own international strategy. In 1983, Margaret Thatcher visited Japan. High on her priority list was the Nissan factory. She was greeted in Tokyo by Kawamata, who opposed the deal, while Ishihara, who favored it, was conveniently out of the country at the time. That to Nissan watchers was a sign that the deal was in jeopardy. In the spring of 1983, shortly after the Thatcher trip, one of Ishihara's close friends told reporters he thought the deal was dead. But then, at almost the same time, there were small signs that Kawamata might be shifting. The old man was uneasy about the scope of the deal, to be sure, but he was also wary of being seen by his peers in the Keidanren as the man who had stopped so important a deal. He began to argue for a more limited approach to England, in effect a trial run to see whether anything was possible with British labor. Perhaps, he proposed, they could begin with a small assembly plant rather than a manufacturing plant, and perhaps they could *lease* rather than buy the land at first. Though the softening of his position did not then seem that important, for the first time it gave the advocates of the project, both British and Japanese, a lever with which to move him. "I am not so opposed to this project as some people think," he told one of Ishihara's people in June 1983. "I know there are differences—if you enter the factory from the Kawamata entrance it looks very small, and if you enter from the Ishihara entrance it looks very large—but in the end it will be pretty much the same."

What began to emerge was a rare view of the interior politics of a Japanese industrial company. Much of the strength of contemporary Japanese society came from the modern application of Confucian tradition—

of the respect for authority and the obligation of people and groups with vastly differing objectives to reconcile their differences and eventually come together. To the Westerner this always seemed to happen without any real contention or dissent. The Japanese appeared to be part of one big happy family, instead of one filled with constantly competing factions. What was unusual about the struggle at Nissan was not that something as harsh and complex as this was taking place, or that the company was so divided, but that because the British were involved, Westerners could witness the normal disputes that went on in a Japanese company.

In 1983 the struggle between Shioji and Ishihara began to take place in the press. Shioji became convinced that Ishihara was the source for articles that were being written about him, some of which criticized his night life in the Ginza, his finances, his yacht. Shioji in turn ridiculed Ishihara for the way he handled *his* yacht. "He knows nothing of the sea," Shioji told a reporter. "He just wastes fuel out there. It is as if he is working for the oil companies." He sought a private audience with Prime Minister Nakasone, berating him for returning from a meeting with Margaret Thatcher and declaring that he hoped the British factory would go through. Nakasone, Shioji said, was interfering in a private business matter. Shioji's own statements about the project were increasingly militant. "You do not start building a second home when the roof of your first house is falling down," he said, a reference to Nissan's domestic problems.

Ishihara viewed Shioji now as an open dissident and believed that what was at stake was not just a factory in England but his own control of the company. That spring he finally moved against Shioji. He decided to break Shioji's hold on the personnel department, the key to his power, and he did it by moving his own man in there. He held the board together on this issue by treating Shioji's man well, sending him to an unusually good job as the head of a body plant. Still, by summer Ishihara seemed no less embattled. (A year later he would say somewhat ruefully, "I have been president for seven years, and somewhere between seventy and eighty percent of my time has been spent dealing with the union.") Then late in autumn things began, ever so slowly, to change. There were reliable reports that influential people in the Keidanren were pressuring Kawamata to support Ishihara. That the head of the company and the head of the union were feuding so openly on so important an issue, the Keidanren members felt, was bad for the company. They particularly disliked the fact that the head of the union was operating against the president with the tacit support of the chairman. There was also good news from England about the site: The land could be leased with an option to buy. That wiped out a major reservation on Kawamata's part. In late 1983 Kawamata publicly reversed course; the struggle between Ishihara and Shioji, he said, was hurting the company, and since the only important thing was the future good of Nissan, he therefore would no longer stand against the UK project. The admission that there was such a deep chasm within the company was remarkable enough, but Kawamata's public change of direction was even more remarkable. That day the phone at the British embassy rang off the hook with congratulatory calls. "My God, man," one American said, "you've got it—don't you see that? You've split Kawamata off from Shioji. It's only a matter of time now."

Even so, the months that followed were difficult. The British had a sense that they were closing in on the deal, but it was like trying to steer a ship through dangerous waters in dense fog. A request would come in from Nissan about the deal, and the British could not tell whether it was a serious request or a trivial one, whether it was, in the words of one diplomat, "major face saving or minor face saving." The British gathered that Ishihara was winning, but they were never entirely sure how strong a hand he held.

Now Ishihara, more confident of his control of the company and even surer of the British deal, began to move more openly against Shioji. Though there were concessions to Shioji, most principally the confirmation in 1984 that Smyrna would produce not just trucks but, as Shioji had wanted, cars as well, Ishihara was slowly isolating him within the company. In the fall of 1984 the Tokyo branch of the union, mostly white-collar headquarters people and thus somewhat more sympathetic to Ishihara in the struggle than the average worker, dissented from a union proposal. The proposal, though vaguely worded, challenged management on the issue of labor-management relations and authorized Shioji to confront management. Too late Shioji realized that Ishihara had turned Haruki Shimizu, one of his own closest deputies, against him. There had been a subtle courtship, and Ishihara had played to Shimizu's vanity. Then he had split him off. That meant the end was in sight for the labor boss.

At the same time that fall, the Nissan management was encouraging and aiding Japanese reporters who wanted to write about Shioji's finances and personal affairs. His extravagance, thought Ishihara, was an area of vulnerability, for working men would not necessarily find it charming. Shioji, aware that these articles were being orchestrated by the president's office, was enraged. The culmination came in early 1985 with what one Ishihara friend later called "the famous *Focus* magazine article." *Focus* was a new and highly popular weekly magazine in Japan, a mélange of *Time*, *People*, and *Playboy*. On its cover a headline said: "The Emperor Shioji's Pleasure: A Woman on the Yacht Who Threatens Nissan's U.K.

Deal." Inside, the magazine printed a large photograph of Shioji aboard his yacht with a pretty young woman. "The man who is so proudly steering," said the article, "is the owner of a beautiful sailboat which would cost 40 million yen [about $160,000] to build now. Behind him is his guest who is a piano player in a Ginza bar. . . . The man is Shioji. His income for 1982 was 18.63 million yen [about $75,000]. He owns a seven-bedroom house in Shinagawa, drives a Nissan President and two other 240Z cars. On the day when the photo was taken he returned from sailing, had lunch with her and drove off with her (with a driver, though). The woman put her arms around his shoulder inside the car." The article then went on to say that at recent high-level meeting the Nissan executives had not been able to finalize their decisions on the British plant because the meeting had been devoted to attacks by Shioji on Ishihara for having the company monitor his personal life and follow him around with photographers. "Shioji," said the *Focus* article, "was furious because he thought the company was trying to sell him to the press. He refused to discuss the U.K. deal until he got an answer from the company about this." The connection of his personal life-style to the British factory was carefully calculated. Shioji was being portrayed as the man who was holding back not just the company but the nation. At the British embassy the *Focus* article was viewed as a considerable victory and a sign that more victories would soon be coming.

Then, one evening in late January, there was a phone call from Nissan to the British embassy. The deal was on. This was a Thursday evening, and the Japanese had a very specific scenario in mind: They wanted Kawamata to go to London on Tuesday, meet Margaret Thatcher, and make the announcement before Parliament. That clearly was part of the quid pro quo for Kawamata; he would end up in a cherished ceremonial role as the senior international statesman of Nissan. It was clear to the British diplomats that the time frame was important, that the deal had to be done and done quickly. The impatience showed that the consensus was very fragile and could come apart at any moment. The arrangements on the British side were not easily made, the prime minister and Parliament not so easily rounded up, but finally the plans were set according to the Japanese request. The next day there was another call from Nissan: Kawamata had caught the flu, and please delay the ceremony until Wednesday. No, the British answered, we cannot maneuver the PM and Parliament; fill him with medicine, bundle him up, and put him on the plane. But Kawamata did not seem to respond to the medicine, and so on Monday Ishihara was dispatched instead. In order to give Kawamata some share of the glory, joint press conferences were set up, one for Ishihara in

London, one for Kawamata in Tokyo. The Ishihara press conference was predictably very upbeat about the deal and the future; the Kawamata press conference, equally predictably, was downbeat. Originally the deal was supposed to be for production of 200,000 cars, but the figure had been whittled down considerably, as Ishihara had retreated before the opposition within his own company. Now it was now a good deal more modest: at first an assembly plant for 24,000 cars, and then, if things worked out, although there was no commitment, perhaps 100,000 cars manufactured there and possibly one day 200,000. At his press conference Ishihara, in an expansive mood, said that 200,000 was a quite viable figure. Back in Tokyo someone asked the same question of Kawamata, and he said there was no commitment to make 100,000 cars. What about 200,000 cars? someone asked him. You might as well say 300,000, he answered.

None of this boded well for Shioji. He had lost out in the very public struggle with Ishihara, and he now faced an additional problem: In a country with little tradition of individualism and with a time-hallowed instinct to be with the majority, Shioji had acted individually and found himself on the outside. He was perceived as the loser, and in Japan if someone was seen as a loser, a dynamic ensued and there was the likelihood of further attrition as ordinary people made sure they lined up with the winner.

Later that year Ishihara became chairman. He had made the company his at last, forty-eight years after he had first gone to work there. Where Shioji had held almost dictatorial authority in the past, for almost twenty-five years, now subordinates, aware of his vulnerability, were encouraged to move against him. Now it was as if an invisible signal had been given throughout the country: His power was in decline, and it was all right to defy him. Nissan management was openly encouraging reporters to write critically about him, and there were more hostile articles appearing in the popular press, including another photographic essay about him and a bar girl. The very publication of these articles showed how vulnerable he had become. In February others within labor moved against him, and his position completely crumbled. Once the hammer himself, he had become the nail that stuck out and had to be hammered in.

43.
A GRATEFUL
WORKER

When Joel Goddard was first hired at the nonunion machine shop in early 1981, after nearly twenty-six months out of work, he felt lucky. He was making an acceptable salary while the rest of industrial Michigan was on its knees. He lavishly praised his new boss to some of his fellow workers. "Listen, Joel," one of them said, "I know you're glad to get the work, but ease up—you'll learn soon enough this guy is far from perfect." Soon Goddard was torn between gratitude to be working again and resentment of the way he was treated.

For the first time in his life he was working without union protection, something he had taken for granted when he worked at Ford. It was not the money; it was the atmosphere of the plant that bothered him. In the nonunion shop, the boss was all-powerful, a virtual dictator, Goddard thought. He never let his employees forget that he had given them their jobs and could take them away. If a worker complained or if the boss took a dislike to him, he was soon fired. There was genuine fear in the shop: When the boss walked through, everyone jumped to attention. Workers were allowed five minutes to go to the bathroom. There were no chairs to sit down on. The boss watched them all the time. If he had to leave the shop for a sales appointment, he went around the shop first to check how far each worker had gotten on a particular job so he could monitor how much progress had been made while he was gone. "What the hell were you guys doing while I was away?" he would always ask. He constantly pushed them to work faster, yet Goddard and the other workers knew that he was charging his customers their time plus other charges.

To get more money, Goddard realized, people had to kiss ass. No one was supposed to know how much anyone else made. There were no benefits of any kind. If you wanted a 50-cent raise, you went in and begged for it, and you were lucky to get 25 cents. The workers had no leverage, and the boss knew it. Not as confident or educated as Ford workers, they couldn't get jobs anywhere else. When Goddard pointed out to his boss that he was making $2 an hour less than a colleague not nearly as skilled, the boss waved him aside. "He's more loyal to me," he said. "You're going back to Ford the first chance you get." A key ingredient of the boss's power was his ability to withhold praise. If he praised the men, he would have to pay them; his hold on them came from letting them know that they did not quite measure up. Since the language of the shop was deliberately negative, the mood paralleled the language; a negative place it became. When the boss sensed that the men were about to ask for raises, he would start saying he doubted he could make the payroll that week. If he gave them their checks on time, he would tell them to hold on to them until Monday or Tuesday just to be sure they cleared. Even one year when the shop did well and there were bonus checks, they were handed out secretly in the men's room, with dire warnings that no one else was to know how much the worker made.

Finally, in March 1982, Goddard was called back to the Ford plant at Rawsonville. The day he heard, he went to see the boss and told him, "You can take this job and shove it up your ass. I'm done here. I appreciate the fact that you gave me a job, but you ought to learn how to treat people. A lot of things here aren't fair."

"I'm sorry you feel like that," the boss replied. "I always thought I treated you well."

When Joel Goddard went back to Ford he was thirty-six years old. Suddenly he felt a new pleasure in driving to work. It was like being reborn. He had been through bad times, but he had always had a marketable skill and a strong marriage. Others were not so lucky. About twenty-four hundred workers from the Rawsonville plant were still out. Hundreds of men he had worked with, unable to find work, had just disappeared—crushed as he had nearly been crushed. Some of the wives, not as well educated as Joyce, had been punished by their jealous husbands for finding even $6000-a-year fast-food jobs. Goddard decided he had been a spoiled American kid but had just grown up in hurry.

Protected temporarily against the Japanese by the import restrictions, the auto industry was making a comeback. Goddard was aware, however, that his plant was in direct competition with the Japanese and the Koreans, because making parts was a great strength of the Asians. The other Ford diemaking plant, in Sheffield, Alabama, was closing down. He heard rumors that the Rawsonville plant might follow. Who needed expensive diemakers anymore in an automated world? The word—and in a place like Ford, the word was often reliable since the top union people seemed to be one step ahead of management—was that Ford was planning to transfer much of its diemaking to its plants in Mexico, where labor was much cheaper. Goddard had a piercing sense of his factory's vulnerability, and his own. A man, it had turned out, did not have a God-given right to work forty-eight hours a week for high wages at a Ford plant. To his surprise, however, he found that few of his colleagues shared his fears. Many of them had not been laid off, and they refused to believe the world had changed. The company often held slide shows emphasizing how stiff the competition was. Goddard's colleagues were not impressed with the photos of smiling, harmonious Japanese workers at Nippondenso, a threatening competitor that had just established facilities in Michigan to serve not only the Japanese manufacturers in America but the Big Three as well. He himself had a sinking feeling when he saw those presentations; he believed the quality was better at Rawsonville, but he knew how much cheaper Japanese manufacturing was, especially that of Japan's auto industry's suppliers. With mounting anxiety he read stories about the rise of the Koreans. But the men around him were blithe. "It's all bullshit," one of them told Goddard as they left one of those slide shows, "but if the company wants to pay me fifteen dollars an hour to watch it, that's okay with me." The man's sense of immunity from the world outside stunned Goddard. Was he unaware of the agonizing three and a half years Goddard and others had just gone through? He did not appreciate the privilege of working for Ford, of good wages, a comparative lack of harassment, the right to go to the bathroom and read a newspaper. The man reminded Goddard of somebody, but he couldn't quite recall whom. And then he said to himself, *He reminds me of me.*

After much consultation, Ford and the UAW chose the Rawsonville plant for a pilot program called Permanent Employment Guarantee (PEG). In exchange for a freeze in hourly wages and for giving the company quite a bit more freedom with job classifications, Ford said, it would protect the jobs of the Rawsonville workers during the three-year life of the contract. Under the proposal, through 1987, if Ford laid off workers, it would keep paying their salaries; a laid-off person might be required to contribute his time to public service, with the Red Cross for example. Goddard, wary of being laid off again, was thrilled to sacrifice immediate financial gain for security, and he became an early and enthusiastic supporter. To his surprise, however, most of his colleagues remained suspicious of the contract. Goddard knew that many of them were older and were concerned with retirement; since their pensions were based on their hourly wage at the time of retirement, they wanted it to be as high as possible. Although

both the union and the company had expected the contract to sail right
through, it was defeated almost two to one. The union's mistake, Goddard
thought, lay in its assumption that the pilot program was so good that the
workers could not fail to recognize its value. They did not realize that the
workers' suspicion of both the company and the union ran very deep.

By the time the proposal came up a second time, the UAW had lobbied
much harder. The old Joel Goddard had never been a very strong union
man; he had wondered why the UAW could not protect him if, for example,
he had gotten written up for leaving the job five minutes early. The new
Joel Goddard decided it was his own damn fault for leaving early. Somewhat to his surprise, he became one of the leaders of the movement to
accept the agreement. He tried to describe what had happened to him to
his fellow workers in the most personal terms and to convince them that
it might happen again. This factory, he told them, is right in the line of
fire of the new world economy; we workers are an endangered species.
One of the factors that influenced the workers' decision was Ford's promise
to spend $10 million on new diemaking machinery if the proposal was
approved; the workers believed that while they themselves were disposable, the company would not buy millions of dollars' worth of new machinery only to close down the factory. Eventually the proposal passed,
this time by almost a reverse margin. Those who had sold it were men
like Goddard who had seen the future and were terrified.

Joel Goddard was excited by the prospect of the twenty-one new diemaking machines, but when they arrived, he decided they were junk.
That they also happened to be Japanese junk angered many of the men
even more. They were furious that Ford had bought these machines from
the Japanese after it had made its great case against the Japanese and had
enlisted the help of the union in seeking domestic-content legislation and
voluntary restrictions from the Japanese. The workers felt it smacked of
hypocrisy, and it aggravated their suspicions about Ford's long-range intentions. They felt that the company would do what was good for profits
and stockholders, even if it hurt the workers. Company officials held a
series of meetings at which they tried to explain their actions, but the
workers were not satisfied. One of the things Goddard sensed from the
meetings was how diversified Ford was; he doubted Ford needed him as
much as he needed Ford. In fact, he was not sure Ford and he were in
exactly the same business. Ford had a connection to Mazda. Perhaps
Mazda would soon make the parts currently produced at Rawsonville.

The brief period of artificial prosperity ended in late 1985 when the
voluntary restrictions on Japanese cars were relaxed. As Datsuns and

Toyotas started flooding the country again, the increased demand of the last four years for American cars fell off, and so, of course, did production at Rawsonville. There were layoffs, but since the number of plant workers could not dip below the 2625 who were employed at the time of the PEG agreement, 500 men who would normally have been laid off were channeled into community service. They were guaranteed a minimum salary of thirty-two hours a week at their regular Ford wage. The shadow of the changed international economy hung over the plant, although even then not all of the workers perceived it. Goddard heard through the grapevine that Ford's management was not pleased with the PEG agreement and that it might not be renewed in 1987. So much for permanence, he thought. Certainly the new machines, which he hated, were an argument for keeping the plant open, but Ford had just closed down a brand-new casting plant in Flat Rock. There was more and more gossip about transferring Rawsonville's functions to Mexico.

Goddard knew that Lee Iacocca was boasting about Chrysler's advantage, that it could buy its parts cheaper than Ford and GM could because it was less vertically integrated, it didn't make as many of its own parts and so wasn't locked into expensive American suppliers. Goddard admired Iacocca a great deal, but words like those were particularly chilling. Still, Goddard was confident about the future, if not with Ford then on his own. He was sure the worst was over. He and his family had been tested, and they were better and stronger people now. If there was one lesson he and Joyce had learned in the last four years, it was that they had to depend on themselves and not on an institution that in his opinion cared first and foremost about profit.

He remained somewhat uneasy about his job. The plant had stabilized by early 1986; the men who had been lent to different social service institutions under the PEG agreement had been called back. But it was a plant under constant pressure from foreign competition, both Asian and Mexican, and the very existence of that competition had all but neutralized the union, which operated now, if not out of weakness, then certainly out of acute vulnerability. Beyond that, it was a plant with an old work force. There were no young workers; they had all been let off. Joel Goddard, much to his surprise, looked around one day and decided that, at forty, he was one of the youngest men in the plant. Most of the men were in their fifties and had twenty-five years of seniority. That brought home to him the fact that he was in a business with a marginal future.

That spring his seventeen-year-old son Scotty, a junior in high school, had come home with his college aptitude test scores. They were good but not as good as they could have been, and that night father and son talked about what Scott Goddard would do with his future if his marks were not good enough for college.

"I can always do what you do, Dad," the boy said. "That would be fine with me."

"No, you can't do what I do," Joel Goddard replied. "Those jobs aren't going to be there anymore."

44.
BONUS TIME AGAIN

Almost the hardest job in front of him, Philip Caldwell decided, was that of improving quality. For more than twenty years the company had paid lip service to the concept; now, its back to the wall, its customers disenchanted, Ford had to prove to its workers and the public that quality was important at Ford. It had to accept that production totals had on occasion to suffer for it, and short-term losses had to be absorbed in order to gain long-term benefits. But Ford soon found that it was easier to coin the slogan "Quality Is Job One" than it was to change so large an operation.

Manufacturing men like Marvin Runyon had complained that in the past, when Ford had a hot car, it always pushed too hard, to the detriment of both men and machinery. Now that was proving to be all too true. John Betti, who was in charge of manufacturing the power trains, reported that some of the lines were operating at only a 60 percent yield because the machinery was constantly breaking down. He asked for $25 million to improve the operation. Once a request like that would have been chopped up; now, emphasizing the seriousness of the issue, Caldwell pushed for immediate approval of Betti's request, and it was done. For almost two years, through 1981, there was no discernible improvement in quality. It was immensely frustrating to spend money and make no headway. Then, in 1982, they perceived from their own tests that things were improving. The warranty reports got better. Letters from owners became more positive. Soon Caldwell came to believe that he had rescued the Ford Motor Company.

That belief became evident after 1983, a year when Ford and GM made mild recoveries. Both companies rewarded their top executives handsomely, but Caldwell benefited most. In addition to his regular salary of

$520,000, he received a hefty bonus of $900,000 and, even more startling, took some $5.9 million in delayed stock options, for a total package of $7.3 million. No one disputed that the stock options were rightfully his or that he and other executives had gone without bonuses for several years, but the timing could not have been worse. Auto executives at Ford and GM became targets of a firestorm of criticism. Many Americans believed that for an unstable industry that had asked for and received protection (and that had raised the price of cars), such behavior was obscene. Some who had bought American cars partly out of patriotism, by no means sure they were as good as Japanese models, felt duped. Some economists and politicians called it an egregious mistake. They were certain that the American auto industry could become competitive with Japan only if its wages came down, and that an industry that awarded such large sums to its senior executives lacked the moral right to ask anyone else—the UAW, for instance—for long-term sacrifice. The senior American trade official, William Brock, publicly criticized the auto executives for their actions. In Tokyo, Naohiro Amaya of MITI, who had negotiated the voluntary tariff restrictions on behalf of the Japanese, ran into an American reporter who was an old friend. Amaya shook his head and said, "They have betrayed people like me." Japanese auto executives beamed. Someone who was with Marvin Runyon at the Nissan plant in Smyrna, Tennessee, the day the news broke sensed he was barely able to conceal his glee.

It astonished outsiders that so little thought had been given to the public reaction to these decisions. No one had tried to talk Philip Caldwell out of collecting his stock options. Walter Hayes, Ford's chief of public relations, had written Caldwell a memo beforehand suggesting there might be a problem, but he had by no means anticipated the virulence of the public's response. His memo was at best a light warning. Caldwell, however, far from regretting his actions, was enraged by the criticism he received. In his mind he had earned every cent. Angry at the press, angry at Brock, he called a press conference to vindicate himself. It was not a success. Unlike Henry Ford and Lee Iacocca, Caldwell was not a figure of great personal magnetism, and the sight of him saying he deserved the money, when he did not look as if he did, was not the pinnacle of corporate public relations. To some of his colleagues the incident helped to reveal just how seriously Caldwell took himself. A year after he left the company, old friends lunching with him were stunned to hear him begin to reminisce about how he had "saved the Ford Motor Company," a phrase that cropped up regularly during the meal. He had been so carefully controlled in the past that they were surprised at the extent of the ego now revealed.

Part of that was because Caldwell had given off no smell of power. A serious and scholarly figure, he seemed at first glance better suited to be dean of a small Midwestern liberal-arts college than head of a giant industrial corporation. He was, thought one of his friends, a good man placed in an almost unbearable position, heading so vast an industrial enterprise. He found himself in a job that tended to emphasize the conservative nature of his personality. When colleagues railed against him, they were really railing against Henry Ford. Caldwell's values were simple: He believed fully in the Protestant creed that if you work harder than anyone else, don't advertise yourself, and the right people will know and reward you. That had, after all, worked for him. Then and only then was he ready to accept the accolades due him. Unfortunately, he was neither respectful of nor comfortable with the press. He expected it to accept his success and worthiness as a given. The media men, however, failed to comply. They saw him as a cautious man of the system and much preferred more charismatic figures like Iacocca and Caldwell's own deputy, Don Petersen, who enjoyed a reputation in the Detroit press as a "car guy." Caldwell seemed to resent those executives trumpeted by journalists. "I don't like the cult of the personality," he would say, "men who think they are bigger than the company. . . . I don't like managers who feel they have to pound on the table and be colorful." When an emerging star in the Ford firmament named Bob Lutz came to Dearborn after great success in Ford of Europe, he quickly became the subject of considerable media attention. A man who loved to ride to work on a motorcycle, Lutz was so successful and popular in Europe, Don Petersen later liked to say, that when he himself was president of Ford and visited Europe, car buffs would come up to him and ask if he worked for Bob Lutz. Petersen was amused by incidents of this kind, but Caldwell was not. Soon he ordered Lutz to stop talking to the press.

Caldwell became increasingly irritated with the media's portrait of him, which appeared all the worse when compared to that of Iacocca—whose commercials were running at the time—and other media heroes. The press's portrayal of him confirmed his suspicion that it was shallow and concerned only with trivia. When journalists tried to ask him questions about himself, he immediately expressed not only impatience but disrespect for what they did: What he *was* was not important, he said, lecturing them; what he *did* was. That there might be some connection between the two was not something he considered relevant. That was just stuff for *People* magazine. Ironically, he left many journalists who interviewed him with the impression of a man who was unusually defensive. These sessions often ended with disappointment on both sides. During his years as chairman, he came to loathe the press. For a time he considered hiring a public-relations expert to bring him together with the media titans and straighten out his image. Headhunters were sent forth to look for a man like Herb Schmertz, who had orchestrated a highly successful campaign with the press, and against it, for Mobil. Some of the candidates suggested that Ford already had the ideal person on its staff in Bill Sheehan, who had in the course of a distinguished journalistic career served as head of ABC News and who knew both print and broadcast journalism. To Caldwell, however, Sheehan's value was diminished by his already being at Ford. His candor did not help his case either. Soon Sheehan was pushed aside, and the idea of a public-relations czar was put aside too.

One of the first steps Philip Caldwell had taken as chairman of Ford, along with improving quality and changing the company's attitude toward free trade, had been to go for a look that would make Fords radically different from other American cars. It struck many in the company as supremely ironic that it was he who was responsible for such a sharp break with the past. As one Ford man said, it was as dramatic a departure as Richard Nixon's decision to visit Communist China after using it for so long as a whipping boy. Caldwell's decision to venture into uncharted waters was a measure of exactly how bad a state Ford was in. When word first reached the design shop in early 1980 that top executives, including Caldwell, wanted a more modern look, the designers were understandably suspicious. One of the best of them, Jack Telnack, was ordered to put together a special team and create a completely new car, but he knew that management's desire for something new had always been more theoretical than real. Confronted with innovation, Ford executives always became nervous about straying from their own conventional patterns and, more important, from the patterns so safely established by GM. The result was constant disappointment in the design shop, a sense that it perpetually ended up with "compromised cars." The Ford designers displayed a mordant humor about their inability to escape convention: "We're no worse than anyone else," they said.

The Ford shop, Telnack thought, was filled with gifted young men who were as capable as any designers in the world of jumping into the future but whose ideas generally failed to go beyond sketches or, on occasion, clay. Instead, they were forced to imitate the boxy, hard-edged cars of GM, which were neither attractive nor aerodynamically sensible. He liked to recall a remark made by Alex Tremulis—an early innovator at Ford who favored a softer look—who had once asked a conference of designers, "When are all of you going to stop this torture of innocent sheet metal?" Telnack was quite sure he wanted a more rounded look as well, what became known among designers as the Aero look or, to some, the eggshell look.

As the weeks passed in 1980 and he and his team advanced on the design for what was to become the Taurus and Sable program, Telnack slowly became more optimistic; perhaps his superiors really had given him the freedom they had promised and withheld so many times before. It was, he decided, the perfect time for innovation, because the company had no choice. In the past the creative men at Ford would discuss among themselves the question of who was the enabler of a particular car—as Iacocca had been with the Mustang and Lewis Crusoe had been with the Thunderbird. In this case the enabler was disaster. The company hit rock bottom in April 1980, the month it instituted the Taurus and Sable program. The largest gamble in the history of the company, the program was initially budgeted at $5.7 billion, although in the end the figure was closer to $3 billion for a five-year plan.

Nowhere was Ford's changed attitude toward innovation more evident than in Caldwell's support of the Aero look. Telnack had never dealt with him personally, but he knew his predecessors had been wary of him; in the design shop the very mention of his name caused grumbling. It astonished the product planners and the men in the design and engineering shops that Caldwell backed Telnack and his colleagues. If anything he pushed them to go further, to outdo themselves. Very early in the program he took Telnack aside and asked, "Are you reaching far enough? Are you really different?" Telnack said he thought so. "Be absolutely sure you are," Caldwell said. "Don't hold back." Later Caldwell resumed his normal distance and seemed more neutral about the car, but he had made it clear that he wanted a real departure. So had Don Petersen, the top product man and then president, who startled Telnack in 1979 when he came into the design shop and looked at some models Telnack was making of the 1983 Thunderbird.

"Is that really the best you can do?" Petersen asked.

"No, it's not," Telnack answered.

"Would you really want to drive that car yourself?" Petersen persisted.

"No," Telnack replied.

"Then show me what you can do."

That was what Telnack had always wanted. Forty-three when the Taurus program began, he was a true native son of Detroit. He had been born there, and the only thing he had ever wanted to do was design cars. As a boy he often went to the Ford Rotunda to look at the new models. When it closed during World War II, he would bicycle over regularly in the hope that it had reopened. After the war, he and his friends would sit on the wall of the Ford test track watching the new models until someone shooed them away. He went to high school in Detroit, still determined to be an auto designer, though his father, a musician, was less than pleased with the idea. Jack Telnack's brother-in-law taught at the University of Detroit and knew people at Ford, so he arranged a meeting between Telnack and the auto designers, hoping that they would cure the boy of his irrational urge. The meeting had the opposite effect: He was introduced to Alex Tremulis, who was encouraging, and shortly thereafter Telnack headed off to the Art Center College in Pasadena, the leading school for auto designers. Upon graduation he joined Ford, where he began his somewhat frustrating career, never quite designing the cars he wanted. In his early years at Ford, Telnack exercised his creativity by moonlighting as a motorboat designer and even received a handsome offer to work full-time at a boat company. He decided in the end, however, that corporate restrictions or no, his true love was working on cars. Now he had his chance to create the car of his dreams.

The design went smoothly. Everyone in the shop had wanted for some time to develop a car that offered less wind resistance and therefore not only looked better but got better gas mileage. It was the rising cost of fuel, Jack Telnack believed, that had forced the Europeans to address the most important issue of all, function. The Aero look was more advanced in Europe because fuel conservation was more important there than in America. When he first spotted the emerging Aero look in the French Citroëns, Telnack had not liked it. But gradually it grew on him, and he also knew that bending sheet metal in the right way could save the company millions of dollars. He estimated that a 10 percent reduction in the car's drag could bring about a 3 or 4 percent improvement in fuel efficiency. In an industry where new government mandates had made the tiniest reduction so critical that companies were spending hundreds of millions to find a new carburetor that would save a tenth of a mile on a gallon of gas, this concept was rendered doubly important. Telnack estimated that Ford saved roughly two miles per gallon just from the design of the Taurus, even though two inches had been added to the wheelbase by the time it was finished.

Telnack liked working with Lou Veraldi, the chief engineer on the program, who had been one of his colleagues in Europe, and his superiors remained encouraging. The only problem, Telnack thought, was the designers' habit of self-censorship, born of hundreds of battles lost in the past. Sometimes Telnack detected a tendency to concede even before a meeting began. But morale was generally good. Although times were hard for the rest of the company, the crisis gave the designers a freedom they had always lacked.

They finished the Sable, the Mercury version, in the spring of 1981 and then concentrated on making the Taurus, the Ford version, slightly different. They had worked hard to come up with a look that was new without being shocking. After all, these were mainstream cars, not part of a small, elite line. They wanted to be just far enough ahead of fashion to excite the average buyer, not jar him. Telnack was pleased with the response to the early designs within Ford. He was aware of the considerable danger in startling your own company.

The product-planning sessions were as fraught with intrigue as the design shop was tranquil. The company was divided between those who wanted front-wheel drive and those who did not. What made the struggle particularly interesting was that the warring factions were represented by the two ambitious men who hoped to succeed Philip Caldwell as chairman, Red Poling and Don Petersen. At that time, Petersen was president of Ford; Poling, a rising star from finance, was the head of North American operations. Their roles were oddly reversed. Petersen, the product man, advocated rear-wheel drive, while Poling, the finance man, supported the more innovative front-wheel drive. Poling was distinguishing himself at the thankless job of trimming Ford's fixed costs. No one doubted that he was particularly well suited for it; he had always been known as a hard man, unsparing of those who failed to meet his exacting standards. Of his ability to save the company money there was no doubt. He needed to prove, however, that unlike Ed Lundy, he could handle operations as well. Thus the Taurus became a means of putting his signature on an exciting new program. He argued that front-wheel drive was indispensable in the wake of the oil shock. Furthermore, he pointed out, GM's massive advertising campaign for its new cars had led the public to expect front-wheel drive by identifying it with the mystique of new technology. It would be a mistake for Ford, said Poling, to bring out a car so radically different without reaching to every possible innovation.

Petersen's political position was quite different. There was no more supple player of the Ford system, no product man in the last twenty years who had shown as delicate a sense of which way the wind was blowing and as deft a knack for managing to be on the winning side. With the departure of Iacocca and Sperlich, he became the company's senior product man, and he knew how to take advantage of the legitimacy that position gave his opinions. He was eager to show, however, that he was not someone who spent money blindly. He argued that front-wheel drive was of little advantage in a midsize car and that skipping it could save a billion and a half dollars. For a company taking on the most expensive project in its history while in the throes of a financial crisis, that was a persuasive argument. Red's a good guy, went the line put by Petersen's proxies, and he's doing a damned good job getting the fixed costs down. But does he really know product?

It was probably the sales and marketing people who tilted the decision to front-wheel drive. They had loved Telnack's designs from the start and they wanted a completely modern car, not one that looked new but had an old-fashioned drivetrain. As the date of Poling's June 1982 presentation to the board neared and it became clear that the Taurus was going to go through—and go through as a front-wheel-drive car—Petersen's objections disappeared, and he embraced the project wholeheartedly.

The launch was delayed for several months, because there were still some manufacturing bugs to be worked out. That of itself, some product people felt, was the sign of a new era at Ford. In the old days, bugs or no, the cars would have been forced through. The actual introduction came in late December 1985. The Taurus and Sable were immediate successes. Auto writers were thrilled with them. Customers were, as promised, excited, and it was hard to keep them on the lots—they stayed there, on the average, only four or five days before being sold, compared to thirty days for the average American car. The factories simply could not turn them out quickly enough. By March 10, Ford had sold a total of 41,163 of both models, with back orders for 168,000. It was the company's most successful launch since the Mustang. There was a lesson in all of this, some of the more disgruntled product men felt—that the combination of hard times and severe competition had finally forced Ford to do what it should have been doing all along, use its immense reservoir of talent to build the best cars imaginable, instead of conservatively sitting on the sidelines, figuring out how to take the minimum amount of risk in a business where true success came only with risk.

Philip Caldwell was due to reach the retirement age of sixty-five in January 1985. That would give him a five-year tour as chairman. As that date drew near there was some talk that his term would be extended, and it was known within the company that Caldwell hoped to stay on. He had even suggested that he was available, but Henry Ford quickly dispatched the idea. Instead, he named Don Petersen chairman, and on February 1, 1985, Petersen replaced Caldwell.

When the news reached the Ford design and product people, the relief was visible. For despite Caldwell's support of quality and of the Sable and Taurus program, Petersen was considered more sympathetic to product, more innovative, and quicker to make decisions than anyone else in the upper echelons of the company. Petersen himself was relieved, since it was well known that he was not Caldwell's choice as a successor. The two men had never gotten along. The tension between them was constant, although it seldom showed in public. Petersen was careful not to let it. At a press conference held to celebrate Ford's 1983 comeback, some reporters saw a quick flash of their animosity. As Petersen, who then was president, prepared to enter the dais from one side, he saw Caldwell, the chairman, entering from the other. Noticing simultaneously that there was only one chair on the platform, Petersen deftly slipped into the audience. After the press conference a couple of reporters went over to ask Petersen some questions, but he waved them away, saying, "I'm sorry, this is Phil's show." In private and away from the office, however, it was clear that he had no love for Philip Caldwell. To close friends he would complain about how maddening it was to try to move Caldwell ahead on decisions.

Of the two men, Donald Petersen was certainly the more interesting. Caldwell was the conventional administrator who had been produced by the system, Petersen the creative product man who had made his peace with it. He was an ambitious, creative man who had come to terms with the organization and adapted himself to its dictates for over twenty-five years. His personal discipline was remarkable; he was ever the good soldier. He was a product man, and a good one, but he was a skilled survivor as well. He had negotiated his way through Ford with great agility and had never been bloodied in one of those interior struggles that took so many casualties at the high levels of the company. He wasted no energy on lost causes, no matter how strongly he believed in them. His self-control was absolute, his colleagues thought: He never at any meeting said anything he did not intend to say or later regretted saying. He had always been apart at Ford, a member of no clique. Though he was a friend of many of the Iacocca people and had, like many of them, worked on the Mustang—which at the Ford Motor Company was like having a PT 109 tieclip, a sign of having joined the winning side early in the game—he had never been a member of Iacocca's group, nor had he been an anti-Iacocca man. He had done something nearly miraculous: He had managed to be a friend of Iacocca's but not his satellite. Nor was he connected with the finance people or the Ford of Europe people. Because he was not a member of any clique, he did not rise with the clique and—this was more important in the volatile world of Ford—did not fall when that clique no longer pleased Henry Ford. He was, thought one friend, simply more astute politically than most of his contemporaries. He knew that factions came and went, and therefore he stayed deliberately outside them.

He was rationally for product, but he was not going to put his life down in any meeting for it. He was not an engineer—his graduate degree was from Stanford Business School—but almost as soon as he joined Ford, he became a product planner. He was about the same age as Hal Sperlich, and his talents were seen by many people as potentially at the same level as Sperlich's. But Sperlich remained almost ingenuous; he wore his talent and passion on his sleeve; he was exuberant, joyous, almost incorrigible in the pursuit of product. Petersen was the reverse. He was cool, distant, disengaged. If, unlike Sperlich, he made few friends, then, unlike Sperlich, he also made few enemies. His nickname within the company was the Smiling Cobra. At meeting after meeting he spoke for product, reducing whatever issue had been before them to a question of product. He had done that at a time when it was not fashionable, and he had thus created a reputation for himself as a car guy. Even so, although it was understood that Petersen was for product, it never got him into battles. If in some critical meeting an underling was being defeated by the finance people, Petersen had a way of signaling if not his support at least his sympathy. He was not a risk-taker himself, but he was on the side of those who were. It was as if he, better than almost anyone else of his generation, understood the Ford Motor Company and accepted it the way it was, with its conservative tilt because of finance, and, having decided to spend his career there, did not intend to fight dragons that could not be slain by mere mortals. The company was that way first because it was big and second because Henry Ford intended it to be that way, and so the best thing to do was work within the system, waiting for the moment when it would be possible to push product.

The quintessential Don Petersen story was about the time in 1983 when Erick Reickert, one of the best designers, frustrated by his failure to get a position he wanted, announced that he was thinking of leaving the company. Petersen checked out Reickert's position and reported back to him that though Reickert had done well in all his jobs, he had a problem: "You don't seem to have any supporters." Since that presumably included the president of the company, Don Petersen, Reickert decided to go to Chrysler.

He was very smart—the ablest executive to run Ford since Ernie Breech, in the opinion of his old colleague Don Frey—yet there was something just a little self-conscious to his intellectualism: He wore his Phi Beta Kappa key quite publicly and he not only belonged to Mensa, an organization for people with unusually high IQs, but listed the membership in his *Who's Who in America* sketch.

He had been extremely frustrated during the Caldwell years, and there had been long periods when he and Caldwell, president and chairman, barely spoke to each other. Near the end Caldwell complained to friends that Petersen was deliberately trying to embarrass him by posing for the media as a car guy. But by then Petersen's restraints had also worn thin. He too had begun to complain rather candidly, less cryptically, claiming that Caldwell's conservatism was damaging the company, making it stagnant. Some six months before the final announcement was made, Petersen told a friend, "I think I'm going to get it. It just depends on Henry Ford." But what about Caldwell? the friend asked, knowing of the bad feeling. "Decisions like this are still made by Henry Ford," Petersen replied, "and I think he feels the company needs to be more product-oriented." If anyone could run a topheavy, overly bureaucratized company in the modern era and at the same time champion product, many believed, then it was Don Petersen.

45.
THE SCION

The young man had gone to the Detroit Tigers baseball game with a few friends, and under normal conditions he might have attracted considerable attention, being as he was the heir to an exceptional tradition, the most prominent male member of the fourth generation of Fords. But no one seemed to recognize the heir, a pleasant young man of modest height with a slight tendency to put on weight—though he no longer, as he had when he was a boy, kept his own secret supply of the powder to make chocolate malts. Suddenly there was a stir, a VIP was arriving, and photographers and television cameramen rushed through the box seats toward the celebrity. People were pushed aside, including the young heir himself, as the photographers scurried to chronicle the arrival of Lee Iacocca. So it was with Edsel Bryant Ford II, son of Henry Ford II, grandson of Edsel Ford, great-grandson of Henry Ford, possessor of a name that reeked of automotive history. Not knowing who he was, the photographers did not bother to capture the moment when he and Iacocca greeted each other, awkwardly but politely.

It was fitting. He was both a marked and an unmarked man. To the world at large he was a figure of marginal fame, barely recognizable. In the world of insiders, however, of auto aficionados, his life and career were topics both fascinating and important. Sometimes it seemed that inner Detroit put him and his wife, Cynthia, under too much scrutiny. That was particularly hard on Cynthia, who was uncomfortable with any kind of public role. By the standards of Grosse Pointe's young matrons she was not as important a player as Edsel Ford's mother, Anne McDonnell Ford, had been since she was of a new generation and disliked the charity-ball fund-raiser work that had traditionally been assumed by the wives of the city's most powerful men. Cynthia Ford wanted to stay home and raise her children. Recently she and her husband had gone to a dance for the Children's Hospital; she had worked hard in the preparations, and she and Edsel had been proud of the part they had played. They stayed on through a good deal of the evening, but because their children were young, they left a little early. They were both stunned the next day when they were chided in one of the city's newspapers for their premature departure. No good deed, they were learning, if you were a Ford, would go unpunished.

Edsel Ford was the most visible family heir to what was no longer entirely a family company. His father was the last family autocrat. Some thirty years after it had gone public the Ford Motor Company was an odd mixture of family blood and family stock, on the one hand, and on the other, outside managerial talent and outside power. It was becoming a more corporate place all the time. That raised the inevitable question: Would the family power last long enough for yet another Ford to head the empire? "There are no crown princes at the Ford Motor Company," Henry Ford II said in 1979, hoping, of course, that there would be at least one more. He himself, strikingly ill prepared, had had to take over the company at twenty-six; by contrast his son Edsel, much admired by true auto buffs, well trained in every aspect of the business, was making his way far more slowly up the corporate ladder, a ladder that his family no longer entirely controlled. There was always the sense of his father deftly moving levers behind the scenes to enhance Edsel's chances, while saying publicly that there were no guarantees about his son's ascension. "It's very difficult in the total scheme of things to make predictions about a young man who is thirty years old, as to what his situation is going to be when he's fifty," Henry Ford had said a few years earlier. When a friend remarked to Edsel how hard it must have been for his father, taking over so chaotic a company at so young an age, Edsel smiled and said with surprising vehemence, *"I would have loved to have done it."*

Instead he had to wait his turn and keep hoping. He was in the company because of blood, and because of a singular passion for cars as well. He knew and loved cars as his father did not. In the late seventies, Henry Ford once dropped by his son's house in Grosse Pointe, looked in the garage at a particularly powerful piece of automotive machinery, and asked Edsel, "What the hell is that?" The answer was that it was an exact replica of one of the Ford GTOs that Henry Ford had taken to France in 1966 and with which the Ford Motor Company triumphed at Le Mans—a car that the son loved and the father no longer even recognized. His son's taste for high-performance cars was something of an irritant to the senior Ford, and on occasion he complained to Edsel that he spent too much time at auto races and with racers. "Well," answered Edsel, "you were the one who introduced me to it all." As a teenager he had been schooled by Carroll Shelby, the famed race car driver, at Shelby's operation in

California, where Shelby customized sports cars; Edsel had loved that. It was a total automotive experience—everything was about cars and performance. Edsel Ford eventually won that cherished Detroit accolade, the highest that a man like Shelby could bestow: "Edsel's a damn good car guy." Race car drivers were among his closest friends; as an impressionable teenager he toured Europe and hung around their world, and to him they seemed truly heroic figures. They were, he said, the last gladiators. Jackie Stewart, the famous British driver, became his close friend and was an usher at his wedding. Most of his friends in Detroit, too, tended to be auto buffs, lovers of the machines rather than of the business generated by those machines. He was intrigued by the fact that most of the city's auto journalists were true car nuts, while the companies themselves were increasingly governed by passionless businessmen. No wonder, then, he thought, that the journalists were often so frustrated when they wrote about the companies; it was as if, by some cruel trick of fate, those who should have been on the inside were on the outside, and those who should have been out were in.

Edsel Ford always knew he wanted to be in the company. It was, he once said, a proud heritage, and he wanted to be part of it. Even as a child his toys were large, powerful cars. At eleven years old he drove cars up and down the family's driveway—no small piece of track on a gigantic estate. On his sixteenth birthday he was given his first car, a Mustang with a governor rigged to it to keep the speed down. "The attitude," he said years later, "seemed to be, 'We'd better protect the crown prince some way.' " He managed to disconnect the governor.

He was raised in Grosse Pointe, a Ford, aware of his responsibilities but spoiled nonetheless. He was the youngest of three children, the first boy, and his sisters were much older. His parents were distant figures. In those days, he once recalled, high-level executives worked very hard and their wives did charity work, and servants raised the children according to intricate, demanding rules laid down by the parents. He did not mind being a Ford, but he hated being *Edsel* Ford. As a boy he longed for a nice regular name like those the other kids had. The name Henry would have been just fine, he thought. The name Edsel was not only different, it had an opprobrium to it. Other children taunted him about it, connecting it to the failure of that car. He was a lemon. "I wish," he once told his father, "that I had a different name. Anything but Edsel." Overweight, unsure, indulged, he was in his own words a wimp before his time.

At the age of fourteen, hardly thrilled by the idea of leaving home, he was sent off to his first prep school, Eaglebrook, in Deerfield, Massachusetts, where he was moderately happy. Then, after graduation at sixteen, he was, like Fords before him, dispatched to an exclusive Connecticut school called Hotchkiss. The first thing he saw as he approached his dorm was the Edsel B. Ford Library; with that he knew he hated Hotchkiss. He pleaded with his parents to let him come home. The answer was always that he must stay, that Hotchkiss was good for him. ("If you think Hotchkiss was bad for a family member in my generation with the Edsel Ford Library," he said years later, "imagine it now with the William Clay Ford Tennis Courts.") Finally the headmaster of Hotchkiss came to share Edsel's opinion that this was not the right school for him. He ended up at another Connecticut school, Gunnery, where he was less burdened by the family tradition. There a kindly faculty couple named Norman and Nancy Lemcke, sensing his misery, reached out to him. He was seventeen years old, lonely, loved a bit too remotely, a little unsure of who he was, trying to find his place amid the pressures of name, wealth, and privilege. The Lemckes' attention made all the difference.

He graduated from Gunnery and went on to Babson. None of the great colleges of the Ivy League had solicited his attendance, and Babson had the reputation of being a pleasant, acceptable college to which very successful men could send their not entirely successful sons. The possibility of failure for academic reasons seemed remote. He displayed no signs of academic brilliance at Babson; Edsel, said his close friend Billy Chapin, grandson of Hudson founder Roy Chapin, was a typical underachiever. In his own, blunter words, he was a typical screw-up. Edsel eventually graduated from Babson, and though it took him five and a half years, he became the first member of his direct line, going back to his great-grandfather, to finish college.

He discovered something about himself in college. He was not brilliant in class, but he was a good manager. People seemed to like him apart from the fact he was a Ford, and he was skilled at using his connections with influential people when necessary. Every year Babson honored Roger Babson with a founder's day ceremony, and normally these ceremonies were rather boring church services. Then Edsel Ford took over: he started holding symposia. One year the topic was movies, and Billy Friedkin, the director, Judith Crist, the critic, and Jack Valenti, the motion-picture industry's lobbyist, came. The next year it was professional sports, and Jack Kemp, the former quarterback, William Clay Ford, the owner of the Detroit Lions, and Howard Cosell, the sportscaster, took part. For the symposium on automobiles he was able to get Henry Ford II as a keynote speaker. He did not know how to study, but he knew about the real world and how to organize things concerning it. He could not wait to get out of college and get into the auto business.

He graduated in 1974, at precisely the moment when the auto business was about to go under siege. After graduation his father took him out to dinner.

"What do you want to do now?" Henry Ford asked his son.

"I thought I'd take three months off and then go to work for the company," Edsel Ford answered.

"Are you sure you want that?" the father continued. "It's a public company now, and you'll have to earn your own way. It's all much harder now."

Edsel Ford assured his father that it was the only thing he wanted to do. It was where he felt he belonged. He had never thought of doing anything else. He was a Ford, and he was part of a special heritage. (Once, meeting a man named Tom DuPont who published a magazine devoted to the buying and selling of antique cars, he asked a friend, "Is he a *du Pont* du Pont the way I'm a *Ford* Ford?") He knew the lineage in terms of character: His great-grandfather had been a raw, hard, brilliant man; his grandfather Edsel Ford been sensitive and creative, a good family man; his own father was stubborn, with a damn-everyone-else-I'll-do-it-my-way attitude. Edsel Ford II saw himself linked to his grandfather, the first Edsel Ford, because they were both passionate about cars. His father and great-grandfather, he thought, were also linked, both tough leaders with fierce drive who would have been successful in any business.

The young man who emerged into the middle level of Ford management in his mid-thirties was an agreeable person of considerable social grace. He seemed more at harmony with himself than his father had been, less weighted with ego. He could make fun of himself, a quality few detected in Henry Ford II. His interest was in product, and the company to him seemed burdened by too many layers of management, too many men who in the end had little affinity for cars. During the seventies he and his father had on occasion argued seriously, because Edsel Ford thought the company was not putting enough resource back into product. Henry Ford's answer was, in effect, if you knew what I know, you'd take my position, too. That was an argument that Edsel, along with all the others before him, lost. But he respected what his father had done with the company —Henry Ford, in his opinion, had been shrewd and strong, and he generally had measured people well. His attitude had been that he did not have to be brilliant because he could always buy brilliance. Most important, as far as Edsel Ford was concerned, Henry Ford thought constantly of the broad responsibilities of the Ford company. His stewardship had been a steady effort to do right by as many of the company's constituencies as he could. If there was one thing he felt bad about, it was that his father had not really had fun while running the company, that because he did not love cars, the job had always been business, a family obligation to fulfill. Edsel had seen the job wear his father out. When Henry Ford announced he was going to retire, Edsel asked him why. "I'm just tired," the chairman answered.

Edsel knew he was perpetually being watched, yet the first decade of his career had been a good one, and there was a general feeling that he had done well in his various posts. A number of executives believed that it would be a good thing if a Ford eventually ran the company, particularly this Ford, who loved cars. It made the company special in the great impersonal corporate world, gave it a quality that most other companies lacked.

Certainly his father was interested in his career. Though retired, he still played an important role in critical personnel decisions, but whether Henry Ford and the rest of the family would still be able to dominate the decision-making in another ten years was an interesting question. Besides, he was not the only potential family representative of his generation working in the company. Although he was nine years younger than Edsel, Billy Ford, the son of William Clay Ford (who owned more stock than Henry), was also working his way up through the ranks, and he was also admired by his peers. As for Edsel Ford, the clock was ticking against him; in 1986 he was thirty-eight and probably ten to fifteen years from the time when he might be promoted to the highest jobs, and every year the power of the family to control those promotions slightly diminished. He was racing, ever so slowly, against time. In that race he had certain large advantages as the boss's son, but there was the corresponding drawback: If he was promoted, people would always assume that it was because his name was Ford. Therefore when he achieved something, he would get less than the normal credit; in some people's eyes his only real possibility was failure. The other drawback was that his associates sometimes deferred to him because he was a Ford, bending their own instincts to what he wanted, or they thought he wanted.

He had always regarded the auto business as glamorous, and he had reported for duty precisely at the moment when the glamour was disappearing. Times were harder, the margins of pleasure and profit were slimmer. He observed the young men who were his contemporaries working longer and longer hours for less and less reward. He loved the business and found it very difficult on its people. It was, he thought, wildly destructive to marriages. Men went to work early in the morning and came home late at night, and then they worked on the weekends. Someone, he said, should write a book about the auto business and divorce. There were fewer perks, too, fewer frills in what had once been a world with lush conveniences. Recently his mother had phoned from New York to say that she had to come back to Detroit for the funeral of a friend and would like to stay with him. He said that of course she could, and then asked her flight number, saying he would pick her up at the airport.

"Oh, Edsel," said Anne Ford, "there's no need for you to come and pick me up. Just send your driver."

"Mother," he answered, "these days, *I'm* the driver."

He himself was staying in the company, he liked to emphasize, because he liked cars; he certainly did not need to work. On the day that he was married in 1975 the *Detroit Free Press* estimated the value of his portfolio at $54 million. He had gone into the marketing side, which he thought was an underdeveloped area, a reflection of the feeling among auto men that the cars could damn well sell themselves. ("Can you believe an ad campaign saying 'GM Sweats the Difference?'" he said. "Imagine a campaign saying 'Procter and Gamble Sweats the Difference.'") The work, because of the ongoing crisis in the industry, had turned out to be a lot harder than he expected. If he had not been a Ford, or perhaps if he had known when he graduated from Babson what he knew now, he said, he might have gone instead into a somewhat more contemporary business, like Federal Express. That was an exciting operation, he thought. The people there were always ahead of their competition; just about the time the competition caught up in one area, then Federal Express would come up with something new. Unlike many of his colleagues in Detroit, he believed that the modern service industries were the real future of the American economy. Their world was expanding, while the auto people were fighting harder and harder for smaller and smaller pieces of territory.

Still the auto business was his family's past, and it would be his future and, he hoped, the future of his children. He was, in fact, preparing yet another generation of Fords for it. He made it a point to bring new cars home and show them to his kids, and when he took his five-year-old son driving, they played a game of naming cars.

"What's that one?" he would ask.

"A GMC," his son would say.

"Who makes it?" Edsel Ford II would ask.

"General Motors," would answer Henry Ford III.

46.
THE NEW
AMERICAN HERO

Lee Iacocca seemed to burn with the fire of vengeance against Henry Ford. That as much as anything else was his driving motivation during the worst of times at Chrysler. His friends in the company were unnerved by the degree to which it dominated his psyche. When Iacocca was writing his book, he would begin sessions with his ghostwriter and his editor with the casual remark that he would not discuss Henry Ford that day, there was already too much about him in the book. Then, sooner or later, it would come pouring out, the rage over the injustice of his being fired by Henry Ford.

Sometimes he would talk about Henry Ford's son Edsel. Iacocca believed absolutely that he had been destroyed at Ford because he had been too strong, and that Henry Ford had sacrificed him in order to preserve the family ownership for Edsel. "It's all a damn shame," he would say. "There isn't a person in the whole goddam place who cares about Edsel. Those bastards over there kissing Henry's ass aren't going to take care of Edsel—all they can do is take care of themselves. If Henry had wanted Edsel to run the company, all he had to do was come to me and say, 'Look, Lee, I'm putting Edsel under your tutelage. I want you to teach him everything you know.' I would have done it. I could have taught him and protected him and set him up for the future. Now there's no way in the world he's going to be able to make it, because there's no one over there who gives a damn about him. They don't know anything about loyalty. The only one who could have done it and *would* have done it is me." That was a judgment that neither Henry Ford II nor Edsel Ford concurred in.

In Detroit, as Iacocca became the city's dominant celebrity, if there was a business or journalistic event at which his presence was desired, he would turn it down if someone else who was involved was, in his phrase, "too close to the Fords." When Bill Curran, a longtime Detroit advertising representative for Time-Life, was turning eighty, his associates decided to invite both Ford and Iacocca to a birthday celebration, a party of twenty-five old friends. Iacocca let it be known that he would not go if there was a possibility that Henry Ford was going to attend. Ford rather gracefully declined, to spare Curran embarrassment. When on the occasion of Chrysler's first good year the Chrysler board voted Iacocca a handsome bonus, Najeeb Halaby turned to his fellow board member Doug Fraser and said, "Wouldn't you like to see Henry's face tomorrow when he reads about the bonus for Lee?" Fraser, whose concerns at the moment were somewhat different, more about the future employment of hundreds of thousands of the members of his union, was slightly surprised, then thought to himself: Is that all it's about, ego?

The problem was that Henry Ford did not reciprocate. That made the war somewhat less satisfactory for Iacocca, for it was a struggle in which the enemy did not fight back. He did not fight back because he did not need to; he was Henry Ford. As far as he was concerned, there was nothing unusual about the decision to replace Iacocca. After all, he had done it to several others before him—Breech, Miller, Knudsen—and they had had the good sense, indeed the propriety, to understand what had happened, that it was time to go, and then had gone away quietly, or at least fairly quietly, handsomely rewarded in no small part for the decorum of their departures. With Breech it had been unusually simple. Breech had saved the company, but he had outlived his usefulness. "Ernie, I've graduated," Henry Ford had said, and Breech had known immediately what it meant. To the list of Lee Iacocca's other failings, then, was added one more: He had failed in his comportment as a firee. Henry Ford most certainly did not feel guilty about those firings. He had taken care of the men, paid them off well, helped them get new jobs if need be.

The more Iacocca attacked, the less Henry Ford responded. Lee, said Bunkie Knudsen, an authority on this topic, was wasting his time feuding with Henry Ford. He was just burning his guts out. It was a waste of energy, anyway. He's Henry Ford and you're not, Bunkie said, and you accept it and get on with your life. There was, of course, a line among the top company people around Henry: Lee's book, they noted, was a perfect example of the kind of thing for which Mr. Ford had fired Iacocca; the book revealed a man who let his ego get in the way of his job. Ford himself said nothing. Not only did he not respond to Iacocca's assaults, but there was a family policy on it. His son Edsel Ford, more comfortable and candid with the press than his father, nevertheless refused to talk about Lee. Within the family, the private position was that there were some families that had had power and money for a long time and whose members had learned the responsibility that went with such power and privilege, and there were other families, new to wealth and power, whose members did not know how to behave. Some of the Ford people hinted, however, that if Iacocca ever decided to run for high office, Henry Ford might go public and write *his* side of the affair. As those stories gained currency in Detroit, there was no doubt that a small shot had been fired, however discreetly, across Iacocca's bow. When others asked him about Iacocca's success at Chrysler, Ford became absolutely jovial. That was Chrysler, he said, things never changed over there, it was always a boom-or-bust place. Things were going well there now—a sure sign they'd head toward bust pretty soon.

What surprised most people about Henry Ford was the degree to which, when he began his retirement, he actually stayed away from the company. It was clear that he was exhausted by his long tenure, relieved to be away from the day-to-day responsibility, and that he could not wait to escape it all and leave Detroit. He was comfortable with what he had done. He had held the company together, as a family company, through very difficult years. He would not be judged by Lee Iacocca (from whom, in truth, he saw himself as having saved the company) but rather by the ghosts of Fords past, principally his grandfather. Not unlike his grandfather, he would turn his back on history even while living it. When two writers who were working on Ford histories checked the Ford archives for certain papers belonging to the first Edsel Ford, they noticed that these and other important papers were missing. They suggested to Henry Ford II that possibly he himself had gone there and taken the files. Ford later called one of his closest aides and repeated their accusation. "It sounds like the kind of thing I would do," Ford said, "but I don't think I did it. Do you think I did?" The aide investigated and discovered that indeed Henry Ford—who hated documented history, who warned aides to leave as little behind as they could in letters and memos—had done away with the missing files.

That he was very much retired did not mean that he did not watch the company closely. It was still the *Ford* Motor Company, and all things being equal or even a little unequal, he would like it to continue as a family company—in his branch of the Ford family, of course—so he kept a hand on major personnel decisions. Nobody went on the board whom he did not approve of, and the decision to choose Don Petersen as chairman was his, a reflection of a belief that the company needed more energy in product. But he was rarely in Detroit, and rarely around the Glass House now. He loved his country home in England, and he spent a lot of time there, frequently hunting, and when he was not there, he was more often than not in Palm Beach, fixing up a new house. (He lived in Florida, he told friends, because he could not afford to die in Michigan and pay the inheritance taxes there.) Some old friends who had been with him through his previous two marriages found that he was slipping away from them as he was pulled more and more into the orbit of Kathy DuRoss and her young friends. He was occasionally involved in real estate deals with his friend Al Taubman, a major Detroit real estate man, whose wife, Judy, was a friend of Kathy's. There was a general consensus among those old friends that on his third try he had probably found the wife he had wanted in the first place, one earthy enough to enjoy his world and strong enough to stand up to him. That feeling was bolstered by an incident that took place at, of all things, a fashion show in Detroit in 1982. Halston, the designer, had come to Detroit with a new line of clothes. There was considerable excitement in haute Detroit when it was learned that both Henry and Kathy Ford would attend, and attend they did, which was a conquest of sorts for Halston. It was noted that day that Henry Ford seemed pleased with the show, particularly with one tall, slim model. Although he was talking with a young television executive, he did not seem able to take his eyes off this one model, and he asked the young executive, "Who is that absolutely stunning young woman? Could you please find out who she is?" At that very moment Kathy DuRoss Ford appeared and quite gently and gracefully took him by the hand and said that it was time to leave the party.

Henry Ford himself had received a variance from the Grosse Pointe municipal authorities allowing him to turn his estate into eighteen single-unit dwellings. It was one more reflection of a stagnant American economy in which it was easier to make money dealing in real estate than producing something. He kept his eye on Grosse Pointe, however. A tour of Grosse Pointe was like a tour of automotive history as well as of Henry Ford's personal life. There was the house on Lake Shore Drive in which he had grown up and then the grand house, also on Lake Shore Drive, in which he and Anne had lived, and he and Cristina, and which he had turned into the eighteen small houses. Now there was the almost modest house in which he and Kathy lived, on Provencal, Grosse Pointe's grandest street. There was a house not very far away on Lake Shore Drive which in 1985 had come on the market, and it was reported that Lee Iacocca and Peggy Johnson, his fiancée, looked at it several times, though not together, and that as soon as they did and the word had gotten out, a call had been made (perhaps by Henry Ford himself, more likely by someone on his behalf), and that, in the strange way that these things were done in Grosse Pointe, the house was immediately taken off the market. Eventually it was put back on the market and was bought by Edsel Bryant Ford II. But not long after that another Provencal house (ironically, one owned earlier by the young Henry and Anne Ford and then owned, but never lived in, by Cynthia and Edsel Ford II) came on the market, and the Iacoccas bought it. A cartoon in the *Detroit News* showed Henry Ford looking out the window, saying "There goes the neighborhood."

If Henry Ford took little notice of Lee Iacocca, that was not true of many of his fellow citizens. In part because of Chrysler's dramatic resurgence, in part because of skillful television commercials, in part because what seemed in hard economic times a compelling need for champions, Lee Iacocca became the new mythological figure of the 1980s, a symbol of American industrial resurgence. He had rescued one of the nation's great corporations from bankruptcy, and he had become not just an exceptional businessman but a star. In 1983, *Time* had put him on its cover, with an illustration that suggested the huckster, and then, as Chrysler continued to be successful, it put him on *again*, this time with a more statesmanlike rendering.

His new celebrity status was affirmed by the astonishing sales of his book. He had decided to write it because there were, after all, a lot of things on his mind, mostly about Henry Ford. The advance payment from the publisher was nominal; the ghostwriter did not take a percentage of the action, a mistake he would not make again; and the literary agent was his New York barber, who connected him to Bantam Books and who later seemed quite annoyed that the people at Bantam did not see fit to pay him anything.

In ways that the author did not intend, the book was exceptionally revealing. It was pure Iacocca, and it was completely personal. It was similar not to the memoirs of Detroit industrialists past but rather to those of a new breed of American celebrity in what Christopher Lasch called the culture of narcissism. In tone it was remarkably like the memoirs of Ed Koch, the mayor of New York, and of Howard Cosell, the sports announcer, two other men of talent and insecurity who because of their insecurities had reached constantly for success, had become in time extremely successful, and had become famous through access to television. But the success had not made them more harmonious with themselves; it had made them worse, for it had diminished the need for normal human restraints while at the same time making them far more famous. Each had become a best-selling author because of his success a telecelebrity. The emotions and the psychic display of each author tended to obscure more serious discussion of issues and in Iacocca's case his very considerable abilities and achievements. Each book, reduced to its essence, was about being loved and unloved, so that inevitably each book ended up seeming, more than anything else, about getting even.

Iacocca's book was in no small part an assault upon Henry Ford, and within the inner world of Detroit, even among those who had been on his side and thought him essentially right in his struggle with Ford, there was serious, if private, dissent from it. Some people simply believed that he had broken unstated rules, that if Henry Ford was as sinister and distasteful a figure as described, then Iacocca should have left long before, voluntarily.

He had, after all, been a part of those years, he had been well paid (in his last ten years there he had received in salary and bonus—excluding stock options—some $6.8 million, even though because of the first oil shock there had been no bonuses in 1974 and 1975). In Detroit there had always been a phrase for a situation like this, the lavish payment for a dissatisfied employee or a large severance settlement for a fired executive, designed to guarantee future silence. It was called "stuffing his mouth with dollar bills." Certainly the Ford people thought they had done it in Iacocca's case; besides the immediate settlement Iacocca was to receive $178,500 a year until he was sixty-five and $175,000 a year thereafter. But in this instance it had not worked. Thus the virulence of his attack upon a former employer bothered some former colleagues.

For others the fault of the book was merely in the failure, in an industry where teamwork is so vital, to share credit. Neither of those alleged shortcomings, of course, hurt the sales. No one could have predicted the results: The book rose almost immediately to number one on the best-seller lists, and then it stayed there and stayed there. If before publication anyone had suggested to his publishers that the book would sell 200,000 copies, they would have been overjoyed. Instead it sold 500,000, then a million, then 1.5 million, then 2 million, then 2.7 million. It was not so much a book as an event. There were fifty-one printings by February 1985. Only *Gone with the Wind* and a book about a bird, *Jonathan Livingston Seagull*, had ever sold better in modern hardcover editions. It stayed on the best-seller list for more than a year. It did so well that another book on him, by an advertising man, which had done poorly on its own, was reissued in paperback. Entitled *Iacocca* and carried by the thrust of Iacocca's own book, it went to the top of the paperback list.

One day when Iacocca spoke to a large audience in Detroit, a close friend from Ford days came by to hear him. Iacocca was at his best, ingratiating, funny, hard but not too hard on the government that had just rescued his company. The audience loved it. "He's very good, isn't he?" the friend said to his companion. "Still the same Lee. Look—all that charm, all that bravado, and all that insecurity. Look at his hands shake." Some of his friends thought that he loved the speculation about his running for office more than he did the idea of actually doing it—that he was by nature too sensitive for the brutalizing world of presidential elections. Lee, one of his best friends said, would not run for fear of failure. If the Democrats could promise a draft, he would be glad to make himself available. Failing that, he would continue to toy with it. If the pain from the firing at Ford was still with him, then he was unlikely, they reasoned, to try so risky a course. He was well rewarded for his success at Chrysler. For 1984 he received $1.6 million in salary and a bonus plus $10.8 million in stock options—which he exercised on stocks bought very low.

He had become the national political flirt. In a field of relatively colorless candidates he seemed to be the most exciting figure, in no small part because it was assumed that the other candidates would run, whereas with Iacocca that was less readily assumed. He would have to start a whole new career, it was pointed out (although in truth it would be merely an extension of the old one, which had always been his ability to sell himself). The uncertainty of that appealed to political writers, just as the certainty of the ambitions of the other candidates did not appeal to them. The industrialist-as-politician, he seemed to have the best of both worlds. On the one hand he was the man who could claim to have brought back American industry despite the threat of Asian competitors, while on the other hand he was the man who went around telling stock analysts to buy Chrysler stock because his was the least vertically integrated auto company—which meant, of course, that he was freer than the others to sign up with the cheapest suppliers in Asia.

He had become, as if overnight, America's supercelebrity, replacing an exhausted Henry Kissinger. Those groups that had once sought Kissinger as their speaker now turned to him only when Iacocca was unavailable. Iacocca became the head of the drive to refurbish the Statue of Liberty.

Once during one of the early ceremonies involving the Statue of Liberty a group of his aides took a boat over to the island. They arrived to find Iaccoca missing.

"Where's Lee?" someone asked.

"He's walking over," someone else answered.

Told of the quip later, he was delighted. "Give that man a raise," he said. The full measure of his fame was hard to gauge. Not only was his face on countless magazine covers, not only could he, if he wished, give a major speech every night of the year, but in 1986 he attained the ultimate confirmation of modern fame—he was asked to do a small guest appearance on a top-rated television show, *Miami Vice*, and he accepted, though he mused later that it turned out to be much harder than doing his own commercials, and he kept blowing his lines.

His friends were intrigued by his transmogrification. He had once complained that Henry Ford spent too much time away from Detroit, but now Iacocca was away more and more, in New York as often as he could be. In the past he had complained that Henry Ford spent no time with people from the auto industry socially and all his time with his social friends; now that Iacocca was the head of Chrysler, old friends pointed out, the gang called Lee's Buddies had been dissolved and Iacocca spent as little after-hours time as possible with his Chrysler colleagues and as much as possible with his New York non-auto friends, Fugazy, George Steinbrenner, the baseball team owner, and Donald Trump, the builder. He had criticized Henry Ford's outside interests, and now, it was noted, he spent more and more time on the Statue of Liberty renovation and with people who might one day have political connections. He had faulted Ford for the way he played his top people off against each other, but now there were signs that he was doing the same thing with his own top aides. He had studied, they decided, at the knee of a master.

By 1984 there was more and more talk of him as a presidential candidate, or failing that, at least as a vice-presidential one. He stayed out of the 1984 campaign, but that did not diminish talk about him for 1988. He hired an expensive speechwriter, and he spoke more and more on public issues. In Detroit those who monitored him carefully thought his speeches seemed more political all the time. A Detroit magazine ran a cover story on his prospects for the presidency, and it published the results, which showed him doing quite well against most potential opponents. A well-known writer had already started working—without any authorization from him—on a book that sounded remarkably like a 1988 campaign tract. In private Iacocca said that the job of bringing back Chrysler had been tougher than that of running the country, and that Ronald Reagan, with his short working hours, was proof of it.

As the talk of an Iacocca presidential candidacy increased, Russell Baker, the *New York Times* humorist, wrote a column imploring him not to run. Iacocca, Baker took note, was a first-class car maker, and, because of Parkinson's Law, there was danger of his running, being elected, and becoming just another second-rate American President. Since the nation, in Baker's words, needed a first-class auto maker much worse than it needed a second-rate President, the race would be a mistake. Iacocca immediately wrote Baker saying that he was not about to run for the presidency. Baker, wise to the denials of politicians, called a friend, read him the Iaccoca letter, and said: "My God—a letter like that—it's a sure sign he's running!"

PART
TWELVE

47.
THE RAIDERS

It seemed at first the most unlikely of takeover bids. In the fall of 1985, a relatively small supermarket chain called Pantry Pride moved against Revlon, one of America's great companies. Revlon had brought in $2.4 billion in revenues during the previous year, and its net worth was estimated at some $2 billion while Pantry Pride's rested at $120 million—a differential of sixteen to one. Pantry Pride was about to pull off what in the eyes of some Wall Street observers was the quintessential hostile take over—that is, Wall Street's new brand of merger, in which companies were consumed without their consent. A deal like this could never have been attempted under normal circumstances, but Wall Street had conveniently come up with an acceptable form of financing known as junk bonds, which one stock analyst called paper whose worth lay somewhere below cash and above Monopoly money. Of the nearly $2 billion needed to take over Revlon, about $1.5 million came from junk bonds. Ronald Perelman, the head of Pantry Pride, was one of a deft new breed of corporate raider; he was particularly skilled at exploiting the cash value of a small company to acquire a larger, more profitable one. There was even a somewhat specialized signature to his work: Immediately after the conquest, he would strip down the vanquished company and sell off the divisions he did not want in order to pay for the very deal he had just consummated. At the time he moved against Revlon, the Pantry Pride supermarkets were for sale, the resulting profits to be used to pay for the acquisition of Revlon.

The very idea of it appalled the executives at Revlon. They were not innocents; they knew that no company was safe anymore. But if they were to lose their company, they had hoped it would be to an organization of size and excellence. Instead, it became clear that the unthinkable was about to happen. The canary (in the eyes of those at Revlon, a rather scruffy canary) was about to swallow the most elegant of cats. It was not just the loss of a beloved company that was so painful to the people who ran Revlon, it was the feeling that something must be terribly wrong with American capitalism for this to happen. At one point, Simon Rifkind, a board member, a former federal judge, and the man who, as a young attorney, had helped Charles Revson take the company public, turned to his colleagues and said in a mournful soliloquy, "What is it that we did wrong? We always ran a good company. We never gave our customers inferior products. We always worked to improve every line we sold. We never lived in the past. We never busted any union. We always treated our employees well. What sins have we committed to have this plague visited upon us. What has happened to this country?" In time Perelman won and soon began breaking up Revlon to pay for his efforts to buy it. The conquest of Revlon was the latest in an ever-escalating frenzy of adversarial takeovers that had fascinated Wall Street for a dozen years.

The first of the hostile mergers took place in 1974. The timing was significant. The tremors that followed the first oil shock had sent the Dow Jones down; the good times of the go-go years were over. While a number of companies, beneficiaries of a changing world economy, found them-selves with more cash than they had expected, other solid companies were, through no fault of their own, significantly undervalued and had depressed stock listings. At a number of large Wall Street investment and banking houses, business was lagging, and high executives of these houses, looking for new opportunities, were beginning to consider what they would not have dreamed of only a few years earlier: representing hostile raiders. In the past, a merger had been a voluntary act between two consenting companies. Now rich companies were willing to swallow dissenting or-ganizations, and they were abetted by Wall Street investment houses badly in need of the business.

At Morgan Stanley, a bright young man named Bob Greenhill was told to start a mergers-and-acquisitions department. By the standards of Wall Street, Greenhill was considered unusually tough and aggressive. He had gone into the navy after finishing Yale, and years later, when he started his series of hostile offers, he went at them with combat ferocity. "Bob," said a friend, "regards these battles as miniature Okinawas." At the time, Morgan Stanley, like other companies on the street, had a vague policy against aiding hostile offers; it was not something the company had done before, and no one seemed, in theory at least, to like the idea. A hostile merger was an ungentlemanly thing to do. Greenhill promptly set about changing the way the merger section was run. In the past there was a finder's fee for someone who came up with the idea for a merger that was consummated—which was too much like the world of ambulance chasers, Greenhill thought. From now on, he decided, the firm would operate on retainer; a company looking for a merger would pay Morgan Stanley for the time it spent searching for a deal. This step professionalized the process. It also meant that the investment houses, because they would now be handsomely paid, could afford to put their best young staff people on the merger cases. The era of the gentlemen's agreement, in which one company did not raid another, was about to end.

In 1974, representatives of International Nickel walked into Greenhill's office and said they wanted to buy a battery company, ESB (Philadelphia Electric Storage Battery). Inco was a blue-chip firm, highly respectable, with a board made up of some of the country's leading business statesmen. Its business was unusually cyclical, which made its managers want to diversify, and its scientists believed they had come up with a technological breakthrough that might be used in the battery business. The Inco people also felt that the battery business was a cartel, that there was no way for an outsider to get in because the other companies controlled distribution; they were a tight little group, successfully excluding any newcomers. So Inco had decided to buy one of the existing companies, ESB. Its managers were quite sure that ESB would not permit a voluntary merger. So when Inco's people came to Morgan Stanley, they wanted to know if Morgan would go along with a hostile merger. This was an important moment, for Morgan Stanley represented the ultimate in probity. But this was a new era, and the investment houses were persuading themselves that they would have to respond to their customers' needs. After a certain amount of debate the Morgan Stanley partners voted to do an unfriendly merger. Joe Flom, one of its lawyers, who later came to specialize in this kind of business, advised the partners that there was no legal reason not to go ahead.

Greenhill called Fred Port, the head of ESB, and suggested a meeting. Port, about to go on a trip to Africa, tried to put him off, but Greenhill was insistent. Port reluctantly agreed. Greenhill had a sense that Port believed he was merely some young Wall Street hustler who wanted to sell him some stock. Along with Chuck Baird, the chief financial officer of Inco, Greenhill went to Philadelphia to meet with Port. At first the meeting was friendly. Then Baird said that he wanted to make an offer for ESB.

"We'd like to do it in a friendly manner," Baird said, "but we're quite prepared to take it to the shareholders."

Port was startled. This sort of thing wasn't done. "Whether I agree or not?" he asked.

Baird and Greenhill nodded their assent. Then they left. Port was stunned. At first he simply couldn't believe that someone was trying to take his company away. What he wanted to do at first was to issue a series of outraged statements to the board members of Inco, saying that if they realized what was going on, they would know this was an indecorous way to behave. His own investment bankers had to try to calm him down and explain that emotions like that were futile, it was past all that, and that he could not win by waging a war of public relations. You are, said Steve Friedman of Goldman Sachs, who was defending ESB, summoning a past that no longer exists. Port, he said, could either try to argue that the deal should not go through for anti-trust reasons, or he could find a white knight, a third firm that was willing to pay an even higher price for the stock and thus rescue ESB. The advantages of the white-knight approach, Friedman explained, was that it meant a higher price and also that the merged company might be headed by a less hateful chief executive. Port went to Harry Gray of United Aircraft as his white knight. (Gray, ironically, soon emerged as one of the most ferocious corporate raiders in America.) Back and forth Gray and Inco went. The first offer was at $18. Soon it was $38. Inco went to $41, and United Aircraft dropped out. Inco won but it lost. ESB never turned out to be a viable part of its operation, and a few years later Inco wrote it off. But the deed was done. No company was ever that safe again. The merger business began to boom.

In fact, the merger business soon began to create a culture of its own. It appealed to the ego as few other aspects of business life did. Mergers had captured the fancy of the media—for there was drama, with winners and losers—to a degree that running a sound industrial company had not. Photos of the chief executives involved began to appear in the *New York Times* and *Fortune* and *Forbes*, and there were often small sketches of them in the *Wall Street Journal*. The chief executive who had pulled off a hostile merger became a figure to watch and in an odd way to respect. No one was to tangle with him. This world was about deals, and deals were fun and exciting. It became a world within a world, one where limousines always waited, and "power breakfasts" were held at Manhattan's Regency Hotel; there was light gamesmanship over the the quality of Cuban cigars, medium gamesmanship over the location of summer homes, and heavier gamesmanship about private jets; at one meeting a famed chief executive went on at great length because his corporate jet had soup that came out of a faucet. It was not necessarily a world of corporate statesmanship, but it had an irresistible attraction; it made ordinary business seem pedestrian. There was to the process, once it began, a kind of frenzy, a sense on the part of the participants that they were involved in a miniature war game. There was almost a macho quality to it; manhood was at stake. The attacker's competitive juices would begin to run, and those around him, the lawyers and the investment bankers, and the media, egged him on. The appeal was not just the acquisition but the act of acquisition, the hunt.

The Street, having helped created this world, was soon affected by it. The mergers-and-acquisitions sections of the investment banking houses became larger and more important. In the process, a new class of investment bankers was created. Because the world of mergers was so frantic, the risks and therefore the stress so great, those drawn to it were hungry, driven, and above all young. The burnout rate was extraordinary. A young man would rise as a star in M/A (mergers and acquisitions), his reputation would expand enormously, and for about five or at most ten years, he would be in demand; and then, because the pace was so demanding, the merger star at the venerable age of thirty-eight or forty would move aside into a more dignified position in his company. But in the beginning they were brash and quick, usually the brightest and most facile young men and women in the houses. All the best young people wanted to be in M/A. That was where reputations could be made. Most of them were the first members of their families to work on the Street, and, though well educated, they were in no way tied to the past; indeed, they were openly contemptuous of those who had gone before them. They boasted that they could work for either side, and when a big deal hit the papers, those firms that were on the outside openly peddled themselves to participants already engaged and to others contemplating entering. The self-promotion, in contrast with the customary staidness of the Street, was shameless. They wanted to make sure that no one thought of them or their occupation as stodgy, and there was little danger of that. Some of them liked to speak about their days as antiwar activists or Nader's Raiders, though roles of social conscience seemed well behind them. Almost no one, as far as they were concerned, was as smart as they were. The only people they seemed to respect were their opponents, people exactly like themselves in rival houses, the best of the best, and perhaps a handful of managers able and willing to pull off a big deal.

They spoke a brittle shorthand with each other, a language that seemed to reek of contempt for the world of business. Everyone, in their argot, was trying to "screw" everyone else anyway, and the only good people were those shrewd and tough enough to be "winners." Most companies were "garbage." They were located in "shitbird little towns." Most of what they built was "junk." Most managers were "schmucks." Defenders fighting off predatory assailants could use "shark repellant," swallow "poison pills," or go to a "doomsday defense" (which would destroy, if not the world, at least both companies). Attackers could feint at a company and opt instead for "greenmail"; that is, they could be bought out by the defenders, their vast number of shares greatly sweetened.

The Street soon became highly creative in devising ways to finance these deals. Junk bonds, for instance, were just another triumph of the new Wall Street, a manipulator's paradise. Less and less was the impulse to bring two companies together a desire to make both more efficient and productive. Now the impulse came more and more those for whom the fast gain was an end in itself, the raiders and, in due course, the arbs (for arbitrageurs), who were the new superrich of American finance. The arbs played the Street the way other men longed to play Las Vegas, making millions and millions on the right call of a merger.

The most brilliant of the arbs was a man named Ivan Boesky. No one was better at the modern game of betting on mergers than Boesky. Sometimes he would invest as much as $200 million on the roll of a merger; he had made as much as $50 million in a single day. His success—and his willingness to back his decisions with far greater amounts of money than most of his colleagues—did not make him popular on the Street, where his nickname was Piggy. Boesky typified the new winners on Wall Street in the age of mergers. He was all nerve ends, sleeping at the most two or three hours a night. He scarcely ate but it was said instead drank coffee throughout the day—it was, he said, his plasma. In his office was a phone system with 160 lines. He did not come to his job with a pedigree; he was from Detroit, the son of Russian immigrants, had attended Wayne State, and had a law degree from Detroit College of Law. What set him apart from the others who practiced the same trade was the relentless way he and his staff pursued information—he was, said one colleague, the best reporter Wall Street had ever known—and the audacity with which he was willing to back up his decisions. Others might hedge, Boesky did not. For a few minutes of work on a small deal, he often made what the manager of a relatively successful industrial company earned in a year.

If the era was a paradise for those leveraging these deals, then the opposite was true for those trying to run companies, and there was a growing split, indeed chasm, between what was good for Wall Street and what was good, in the long run, for productivity. The effect of all this was immensely negative on those poor managers trying to produce something. There were just entering a new international economy, against formidable competitors who because of their relationships with banks enjoyed considerable advantages in terms of long-range planning. Yet now Americans were under pressure not to run their companies well, or to produce a better product, but to maximize their stock and make the books look better. If they did not drive their stock up, the company was considered undervalued—the stock a bargain—and it became a likely plum for a hungry raider. All of this, of course, meant an emphasis on short-range managerial methods that maximized the stock. Some of this pressure had always been there. Now there was an additional pressure, that unless they maximized the stock and drove it up, often at the expense of thoughtful business procedures, their own companies might be taken away from them. The new threat created an even more predatory environment. Increasingly, American business leaned away from fields that emphasized productivity and toward those areas in which bright young men and women could exercise their talents ever more quickly and share in larger and earlier rewards. The deans of America's business schools complained privately that their best students—often as large a percentage as half the class—wanted to go to work immediately in investment houses or, failing that, consulting firms. None of the best students wanted to take jobs in large corporations, let alone in manufacturing. What was taking place, said one dean, was a brain drain of massive proportions.

If the American manufacturers were bothered by the hostile takeovers, then their counterparts in Japan were merely bewildered by it. In November 1981, Walter Mondale, the former Vice-President, and one of his advisers, Richard Holbrooke, a former assistant secretary of state for Far Eastern affairs, were touring Japan and visited a new Kawasaki steel plant. Mondale, Holbrooke could tell, was amazed by the visit, by the sight of a steel plant far more modern and efficient than anything in America yet driven by machinery largely designed by Americans. The Kawasaki people were very gracious that day, acknowledging a great debt to Republic Steel, which had helped them, but the trip was troubling for both Americans. At one point Holbrooke asked the Japanese what they thought of U.S. Steel, which had just acquired Marathon Oil in a giant merger. At first his hosts were polite, and therefore evasive, but Holbrooke pressed them. Finally one Japanese said: "Look, we respect U.S. Steel very much. It is the father of our industry. But we do not understand why a company that is supposed to make steel spends so much money to buy an oil company." What they were really saying in as polite a way as possible, Holbrooke decided later, was: We have different purposes in life. We are steel men, and they are businessmen.

48.
OPEC UNRAVELS

The fall of the Shah in 1979 and the consequent surge in the price of oil did not surprise Charley Maxwell, the oil industry analyst on Wall Street who, by dint of being prescient and connected to a suddenly hot field, had become something of a celebrity in his field. One of the things he later liked to point out in describing the feverish events of 1978–82, when the price of oil seemed out of control, was that the price set by OPEC never went above the spot (or market) price. It was not OPEC that was pushing the price up, Maxwell realized, but the consumer nations themselves, caught up in hysteria as the unthinkable took place. It was not a shortage of oil so much as fear of a shortage that caused the crazy escalation of prices. The OPEC ministers might believe they were the engineers of it, and in a minor way they were, but essentially it was a panic born of Western terror and Western lack of conservation. Having exploited the Middle East for years, having long taken out so much oil for so little and having feared in their darkest visions that something like this might happen one day, they now believed the apocalypse had arrived. Unprepared for what had occurred, each nation was consumed by greed as it tried to ensure its precious share. Maxwell was intrigued as the price continued to soar, for he was sure he was observing a psychological rather than an economic phenomenon. Normally solid conservative businessmen who had not panicked would go to lunch with colleagues who had and lose their perspective as well. It was contagious.

The OPEC nations, Maxwell believed, were initially as surprised as the West by the sudden price jump but soon began to believe that they had accomplished it through shrewd political maneuvering and that the resulting riches were rightfully theirs. Just as the consuming nations had thought a few years earlier that the artificially low price was real and final, so OPEC now took the current rate for the just and permanent one. Maxwell noted, somewhat wryly, that one does not view one's involvement with the fates too clearly. Bad luck is seen as whimsically inflicted by perverse gods, but good luck is hard-earned. OPEC, following the tradition, became greedy. As if there were a kind of historical transference at work, the avarice and cockiness that had for so long been the mark of the consuming nations was assumed by the producing nations. Of the major producers only the Saudis, while pleased, were nervous about the surge. They were rich enough, under normal circumstances, to have the luxury of worrying about the effect of the sudden price escalation on their fragile political base. Their nervousness was that of a conservative regime suddenly confronting the unknown. The market as they knew it was being changed, and they feared not only a depression in the West but the unknown into which they and their colleagues were now sailing. Within OPEC meetings they argued strenuously and vainly to keep some sort of a lid on the price. Losing those struggles, they repeatedly told the other OPEC nations that what was happening was madness.

Maxwell believed the price had gone up too quickly, at the end exceeding market realities, and would eventually come down, although perhaps not as quickly. He was certain that the economic impulse would soon overtake the psychological one. At the height of the fever, when the spot price was $34 a barrel, he estimated that the real price—if there was such a thing in a world gone mad—should be about $24. At an OPEC meeting in late March 1983 the Saudis pleaded with their colleagues to bring it down, and the price was reduced from $34 to $30. The spot price was then hovering around $28 or $29. Soon the price went to $22.

Maxwell saw a number of factors contributing to the steady decline in price that ensued. One was slower economic growth on the part of the industrialized nations. Numbed by the exorbitant price of oil, their economies had quickly slowed down. Another was the West's new consciousness of conservation, which began to show up in the market by 1983. A third was the increase of substitutions for oil: A world that had been blithely turning from coal to oil began to reverse that procedure. The last factor was considerable growth in production among non-OPEC nations like Angola, Denmark, Greece, Tunisia, and India. By 1985 roughly 6 percent of the world's total oil was being produced by new non-OPEC countries.

In September 1985 the Saudis, frustrated by what they felt was systematic cheating by other OPEC members and feeling serious pressures on their own domestic economy, announced that they would substantially increase their production. The effect of that on the price of oil had to be dramatic. In the first place, OPEC was held together by the most tenuous of adhesives; in fact, one reason the Saudis decided to move was to punish the cheaters in the producing cartel. But Maxwell knew there were many and varied other reasons. For example, the Saudis wanted to lower the price because they did not want to help support the war machine of Iran in its prolonged war with Iraq. Iraq was the Saudis' ally, Iran its sworn enemy, and Saudi Arabia wanted to make sure that Iran was economically pressed. There were still other considerations. A number of powerful Saudi families were finding themselves in serious financial jeopardy as massive construction and extensive real estate programs, commissioned in an era of plenty and high oil exports, suddenly floundered because of the limited OPEC-directed production. The Saudis in mid-1985, when the decision to increase their production was made, were pumping only 2 million barrels a day, down from a norm of 4.3 million. But that was not even a real 2 million: 800,000 barrels went for internal needs, 200,000 were ticketed for Iraq, and another 200,000 went to poorer countries, primarily Muslim, on notes the Saudis never expected to be paid. Thus in real terms the Saudis were pumping only 800,000 barrels a day, consequently depressing their economy. (When they went up to 4.3 million barrels, some skeptics argued that they were, because of the lower price, pumping twice as much oil to make the same amount of money. That was not true, Maxwell believed; in effect, the equation was 3.5 million barrels a day at roughly $16 a barrel against 800,000 barrels at $27, or $56 million a day against $21.6 million.)

In addition, the Saudis were made edgy by the number of non-OPEC countries that had decided to pump oil because of the inflated price per barrel—and by the degree that the West was both practicing conservation and turning to other forms of fuel. The cut was designed to drive out the peripheral producers by making the market price so low that it did not make sense to pump it (among the early casualties were a number of smaller American producers) and to make sure that oil was cheap enough to remain the basic commodity for industrialized states that otherwise might turn to coal.

The Saudi decision sent the price tumbling. It fell below $20. Then it feel below $15. It kept falling. Essentially it bottomed out at $10 a barrel in the late winter. By spring of 1986 it had begun to come back, to a price of $15 and $16 a barrel. OPEC seemed once again more divided than united over the most basic of its issues. It was like the OPEC of fifteen years earlier.

In the *Wall Street Journal* reporter Youssef Ibrahim told of the dire consequences for some of OPEC's more vulnerable members. Ibrahim was standing with Javier Espinosa Teran, the Ecuadoran minister of energy, during a recess in the Geneva meetings when Teran spotted his Venezuelan colleague Arturo Hernandez Grisanti looking at a display of watches for sale. "Hey, Arturo," he called, "oil is too cheap. Don't look at things we can't afford."

If the price drop depressed the economies of certain OPEC nations, it also depressed the economies of certain American states. In early 1986, as the price of gas began to come down, the pleadings of the governors of Texas and Oklahoma for federal assistance and the urgings of Vice-President George Bush that the Saudis put the price up did not go unnoticed in Detroit. It had been only four years since the oil states had been booming, Detroit had been depressed, and Texans had mocked the auto makers. The collapse of the Texas boom led to a certain amount of gloating in Michigan.

Among oil analysts there was talk about when and how far the price would come back. The new magic figure was $20 a barrel; some analysts believed the price would reach $20 in 1987. Charley Maxwell was more cautious than most; he thought the change would probably not come until the winter of 1988–89. In the meantime he wondered what this change would do to Detroit's long-range planners. He was sure that among the principal beneficiaries of the change was Japan, a nation without oil.

49.
THE UPSTARTS

Japan did not wear its new success gracefully. By the mid-eighties, its staggering victory in automobiles assured, it was the most insular of international giants. Trade with Japan was so one-sided as to smack of reverse colonialism: The Western nations shipped raw materials to the Japanese, who turned them into finished goods that they sold back to the West. What came back to the West was an uncomfortable sense of Japan's financial strength. The Japanese became the greatest customers for U.S. Treasury bills. Some of Japan's oldest friends were troubled that the power conferred by its success was not accompanied by the willingness to accept the diplomatic and political responsibilities that normally went with it. We Japanese, one Japanese intellectual told writer Frank Gibney, treat the world like visitors to one of these great outdoor animal parks, a place where they can drive around at will and stare all they want but must never leave their cars.

As the insular side of Japan showed more and more, so did resentment over its trade practices grow. The relationship between America and Japan became increasingly delicate. Significantly, the greatest concern was not among would-be Japan bashers but among those who had been Japan's oldest and most forthright friends. No one in postwar America had been a better and more committed friend of Japan than Edwin Reischauer, the distinguished Harvard professor of Japanese studies. He had served during the Kennedy-Johnson years as ambassador to Tokyo, where he had been unusually sensitive in representing Japanese as well as American interests, to the point where a number of American businessmen in Tokyo had become exasperated with him, feeling that he had been too soft in pressing the American case to make the Japanese open their market. But by 1985, even as true a friend as Reischauer was exhausted by the Japanese slow-walking on trade issues. Reischauer met with a group of fifteen traveling Japanese editors, and he warned them of the gravity of the trade situation and of the failure of the Japanese to move more quickly to open their markets. What stunned and angered Reischauer that day was the lack of response on the part of the visiting editors, and he became, as the session went on, angry, lecturing them in the end about how dangerous and explosive the trade imbalance had become and how politically untenable it was.

At almost the same time Henry Rosofsky, a former dean of Harvard, wrote a letter to the *New York Times* warning about Japan's protectionism, particularly in the areas of high technology and biotechnology. To many Americans these fields—where the best of American scientific research was married to the most vital part of America's venture capital system— reflected much of the future hope of the American economy. What was especially troubling about Japanese protectionism in fields like this, the tendency to fend off a foreign product until the Japanese could match it themselves, Rosofsky argued, was that it denied the newest and best of American companies the right to make a deserved profit on their entrepreneurial talents and then go on to develop other products.

The Japanese seemed not to understand that with their greater success had come greater scrutiny. More and more Americans were aware now of the duality of the Japanese modus operandi—how fast they could move if a particular decision was in their economic interest and how slowly they would move, citing always the need for patience in the Orient, if something was economically bothersome. The Americans were becoming wiser about a number of Japanese stalling tactics, and the Japanese were not adjusting to it.

Perhaps the classic and most clear-cut example was that of trying to export American cigarettes to Japan. Japanese tobacco was bad and expensive, American tobacco good and inexpensive. Yet it was almost impossible for the Americans to break through the endless levels of protectionism, official and unofficial, that guarded the national interest. Prime Minister Nakasone might meet regularly with President Reagan and announce new programs that would open up Japan's markets, but once the hoopla of the summit was over, almost nothing happened, and tobacco was a perfect reflection of it.

Japan Tobacco Inc. was government-owned. In 1982, with Japan under pressure to open up its markets, JTI had responded with a deliberate company policy to foil any chance the foreigners had of expanding their market share. There had been directives from the top to subordinate employees telling them to tear down advertising posters for the foreign brands and to put the American cigarettes behind the Japanese ones and keep them in short supply. For a country operating with a huge trade surplus, it was an ugly business, a rare revelation, many Westerners sus-

pected, of the protectionist hanky-panky that went on all the time. Once
the scandal broke, the president of the tobacco company offered to resign,
but he was told by the minister of finance to stay on. He promised it
would never happen again. It did. Though the tobacco market was supposed to be freed in April 1985, the change was almost imperceptible.

One of the most critical methods used by the Japanese in maintaining
protectionism was their control of distributorships. In this case the only
distributorship belonged, oddly enough, to the offending government
company, Japan Tobacco Inc. Not surprisingly, a year later the foreign
share had gone up only marginally, from 2 percent to 2.3 percent. The
representative of Philip Morris in Tokyo remarked that it was like having
Pepsi-Cola distributed by Coca-Cola.

Even more offensive was a subsequent move by the head of JTI. Knowing that the Americans and other foreigners were about to introduce additional brands, the government company had quietly applied for the
Japanese trademark rights to some fifty foreign brands. Newport cigarettes,
it turned out, was an old and time-honored Japanese cigarette brand. The
disgust among foreigners was extraordinary. Here was a nation with so
great a trade advantage that trade wars were imminent, doing something
so disgraceful. It was a reminder that in Japan it was not so much the laws
of the nation that were protectionist and exclusionary as it was its soul.

For despite its overwhelming new international success, Japan was a
nation turned largely to itself. "The electronic tribe," Donald Richie,
writer and longtime resident of Japan, called it, catching in that exceptional
phrase the culture's unique combination of high technology and spiritual
traditionalism. Although it borrowed constantly from the West in technical
matters, it tried to resist social influences. For all of Tokyo's neon veneer,
its air conditioners and modern fashions, it sometimes seemed a vast,
shiny tribal village where the past, smoothly updated, continued to dominate. Japan was racing from the nineteenth century to the twenty-first,
with barely time for a pit stop in the present.

Japanese insularity had always manifested itself in a variety of ways—
from the inability of an American baseball player who was leading the
Japanese league in home runs to get a decent pitch in the final weeks of
the season (the Japanese pitchers would simply walk him every time he
came up) to the difficulty foreigners found in getting their products through
customs or establishing distribution systems in Japan, something easily
done in other capitalist countries. Japan's economic success exaggerated
that insularity into arrogance: Not only was there a Japanese way to do
everything, but it also happened to be the right way; it was about time
the world found out that Japanese excellence was no fluke—they were

the best manufacturers in the world. So the Japanese went overnight from undiscerning admiration for things Western to contempt for them. A typical example of the Japanese attitude was a comment made by Norishige Hasegawa, the head of a committee to promote U.S.-Japanese trade: "We are already importing what we need: Parker pens, Cross pencils, and French neckties. The Japanese people are satisfied with Japanese goods."

A certain amount of self-mythologizing went into the Japanese mystique. There had been signs of it as early as fifteen years before, when the American futurist–political scientist Herman Kahn had prophetically analyzed the forces at work in Japan—the social coherence, the primacy of education, the low birthrate, the skillful weaving of personal, communal and business goals, the delicate supportive balance between private and public sector—and predicted that the twenty-first century would be the Japanese age. That thesis, of course, made Kahn an eminent figure in Japan almost overnight. Americans visiting Japan were amazed by how often the Japanese asked them what they thought of Professor Herman Kahn. The answer in many cases was that they had not thought a great deal, if at all, about Professor Kahn. What the Japanese were really asking was, What do you think of Japan?

By the early eighties many influential Japanese were proclaiming that the next century belonged to them. Europe was perceived as decadent, and America, if not actually decadent, was certainly tired. Sometimes when they spoke candidly with Americans, Japanese executives said America had weakened itself by tolerating hostile unions and granting special treatment to blacks and women.

Beneath Japan's sudden affluence and arrogance, the fragility of both its economy and its psyche were only thinly concealed. One of the difficulties of dealing with the Japanese, some foreign experts observed, was how quickly they could swing back and forth from arrogance to insecurity and arrogance again. Unlike some nations whose wealth came readily from the ground (the Saudis with their oil, the South Africans with their gems and ores, the Americans with their bountiful farmland and minerals), Japan's economic power was not a natural condition. It bore no guarantees and had to be renewed every day. Poor planning and poor work habits could easily undo what had been so arduously gained. Therefore, Japanese affluence was in one sense shallow. The Westernized sections of Tokyo—the Ginza, Roppongi, and Akasaka—were stridently modern and the Japanese businessmen who dined there each night were handsomely dressed, but their prosperity was superficial. A successful Japanese might have fifteen expensive suits to his Western counterpart's six, but at night he might ride for an hour and a half, first on a subway and then on a commuter train, to a tiny, cheaply constructed apartment in the distant suburbs. Many highly paid businessmen owned relatively little; they had perks, but most of what they enjoyed belonged to the company. The system deliberately made it difficult for Japanese to pass on wealth to their children, in order to limit the psychological damage wrought by too much affluence.

All of these factors fed the tension between Japan and its Western trading partners. The West saw Japan as a powerful, monolithic society concerned exclusively with its own economic aggrandizement: Japan Inc., as the phrase went. The Japanese were thrilled with their success, but they were acutely aware of how tenuous it was and preferred to think of the nation as dependent and put-upon. Knowledgeable Westerners in Tokyo called it the Little Orphan Japan Syndrome. The Japanese wanted to be both powerful and weak. If a foreigner remarked on Japan's economic strength, the Japanese were quick to plead their vulnerability. If, however, a foreigner was suspected of failing to appreciate their remarkable gains since the war, they were duly offended.

Japan's ambivalence about its role in the world fostered a tendency to magnify each trade development with the United States. On alternate days America was viewed as so rich and smug it was not worthy of its world position and as so desperate to penetrate the Japanese market that it was ready to start a trade war because of the smallest import barrier. Another manifestation of Japan's insecurity was an exaggerated fear that its young people would become weak and soft, "victims of the American disease." Because of this anxiety, every incident of juvenile delinquency was played up, and trends such as the rush of younger workers to leave their offices at closing time instead of staying on into the night, the desire of young Japanese to own a car while still in their early twenties, and the inability of girls to tie kimonos were discussed as symptoms of decline. At the same time, of course, competition was intensifying for the young, and they had to work even harder to get into the right schools so they could get the right jobs. The greatest fear, however, and the most justified, was of the ascent of less-developed Asian countries. Because the Japanese—through ambition, desire, and discipline—had triumphed over wealthier and presumably lazier societies, they dreaded that the same thing would be done to them. As they had pursued the Americans, so other Asian nations now pursued them, using the same formula. The middle-aged Japanese worried that their children, reared in homes that were heated in winter and air-conditioned in summer, would be no match for the hardship-driven children of Korea and Taiwan and Malaysia. They were also aware that with success had come higher salaries, which might make Japan vulnerable in the world market to lower-cost producers. Therefore, automation was a serious issue, for it offered Japan at least a partial hope of retaining an advantage over countries with cheap-labor pools. In the late seventies the business historian Peter Drucker was given a tour of a Japanese auto factory by a management official and a labor leader. The manager explained that the difficulty of automating an industry was that the first 35 percent was relatively easy, but that it got harder and harder after that. It was going to be extremely tough, he said, to reach the high proportion of automation everyone wanted.

"What happens if you don't reach it?" Drucker asked.

For the first time the labor leader spoke up. "His successor," he said, referring to the manager, "will run a plant in the Philippines."

50.
THE JOBS DEPART

In the late seventies no one watched the reaction of the American auto industry to the Japanese challenge more closely than Harley Shaiken, a young professor at MIT. Shaiken, an expert on technology, had gained exceptional insight into the dramatic changes taking place in the American workplace, in part because of his formidable intellect and in part because of the years he spent, before finding his place in academia, as a worker on the line at a GM plant. By 1980 Shaiken had become very pessimistic about the future of the American blue-collar worker.

Most other academics and industrial experts, concerned with the decline of American heavy industry, were focusing almost exclusively on Japan. But Shaiken believed they were looking in the wrong place. The loss of jobs to Japan was just a part of a vast new change in the American work force, albeit the most obvious and dramatic part. The concentration on Japan, he said, reminded him of the story of the man who had lost a coin. His friend asked him why he was looking in one area when he had said he was sure he had lost it in another. "Because the light is better here," the man answered. Shaiken felt that those who had become obsessed with Japan were neglecting other changes—subtle but crucial—such as the export of jobs, under American corporate seal, to other countries in East Asia and to South America, and the coming of high automation both here and abroad.

Gradually, in the early eighties, Shaiken came to believe that the Japanese challenge had given many American companies an excuse to do something they had always longed to do, which was to locate their factories in underdeveloped countries, beyond the reach of American labor unions. Until then only the most labor-intensive industries, such as the garment industry, had been able to escape the nation's borders. Until then abandoning the American worker had been socially and politically unthinkable. But now, because of the coming of the Japanese, the tactic had become acceptable. No one could protest the opening of a factory in Singapore or Taiwan anymore, because it was held to be the only way to compete with the Japanese. What surprised him, as the transformation began to take place, with one major American company after company setting up plants abroad or signing contracts with low-wage Asian firms, was how little domestic protest there was. Great and powerful unions like the United Auto Workers were clearly on the defensive, the UAW fighting as hard as it could to hold on to jobs in the Big Three auto firms, but steadily losing its leverage.

Shaiken, in this period, evolved his theory of superautomation. Superautomation was a reflection of profound recent changes wrought as powerful computers became small and inexpensive, and could guide robots. One result of superautomation was to permit an American company to export technology, and thus in effect a factory, much more readily. In the past, American executives, looking eagerly across the ocean, were restrained not just by domestic political forces but by the fact that third-world countries had few skilled workers and weak mechanical and industrial traditions. One did not lightly set up an engine or a transmission factory in one of these countries, for fear of all the things that might go wrong. Shaiken estimated that in the past it had taken as long as ten years to build a factory in the third world and make it truly profitable, to get out all the extra bugs that turned up in a factory in places like that. Now, he realized, the advance of computer technology had cut that time drastically, to as little as two years. In addition, the surge of competition from East Asia had shown American managers that other countries had enviable work ethics and systems of authority.

For one thing, in the new world of superautomation, factories required fewer skilled workers. The level of skills among those few had to be even higher than in the past, but training them was worth the money, because many other jobs could be automated. For another, there were no powerful local unions to argue against the introduction of high technology. Finally, because of the power of modern, highly computerized communications, one didn't have to put so much faith in the local managers who were so far away. The factory could be run (or at least monitored) from the home office, say Detroit or Stamford, Connecticut. Thus in the early eighties the exporting of factories had become at once technologically feasible and politically legitimate.

Shaiken was struck by what happened when in 1981 Chrysler opened an engine factory in Mexico. At first it decided not to manufacture the camshaft there because it was such an important part and had to be machined within such fine tolerances. So the camshafts were made in the

United States and shipped down. But in about two years the level of skill at the Mexican plant was so high that Chrysler started making the camshafts there as well.

By 1982, Shaiken was convinced that something quite profound in terms of the migration of jobs was already taking place. It was not yet noticeable to the naked eye, but he was sure that in top managerial offices across the country, the decisions were being made, and that the men who were making them were not even aware that they were a part of something basic, of a new industrial revolution, the slow but steady de-industrializing of America. He was not sure where this would all end up, which country would emerge as the major winner as the satellite American manufacturing base, but he was convinced it was going to happen.

There were, that year, some 250,000 autoworkers on indefinite layoff from the Big Three auto companies, in addition to a vast number from supplier companies, and he believed that most of those jobs were never coming back. These workers had not been laid off because of technology, but the layoffs would become permanent in no small part because of technology. He also believed that within five years there would be an erosion of employment in the companies that supplied the auto companies, and that the general work force would become older, with fewer and fewer young workers hired.

Shaiken started with the belief that the men who headed these large American industrial companies would not stand and fight against the Japanese, or at least would not fight very hard. They had not stood and fought before, when other important issues were at stake. Indeed, the degree to which they had conceded the low end of the market, the market in small cars, had been astonishing. In his opinion they had virtually quit the battlefield without firing a shot. It was significant, Shaiken thought, that they were not men of the plants, not manufacturing men who, finding that they had lost the lead, would push hard and fight to regain it. Rather they were men of finance, and they were trained to think in terms not of loyalties to product and to factories and locales and men who worked for them but of profit and profit alone. It was not that they were bad men, it was simply that that was who they were and the way they reacted, to find the quickest and easiest way to generate profit.

Shaiken's studies showed that the Japanese had made their great surge in the sixties and seventies, by which time the financial men had climbed to eminence within America's industrial companies and had successfully subordinated the power of the manufacturing men. When the Japanese advantage in quality became obvious in the early eighties, it was fashionable among American managers to attribute it to the Japanese lead in robots, and it was true that the Japanese were somewhat more robotized than the Americans. But in Shaiken's opinion the Japanese success had come not from technology but from manufacturing skills. The Japanese had moved ahead of America when they were at a distinct disadvantage in technology. They had done it by slowly and systematically improving the process of their manufacturing in a thousand tiny increments. They had done it by *being there*, on the factory floor, as the Americans were not.

In that opinion Shaiken was joined by Don Lennox, the former Ford manufacturing man who had ended up at Harvester. Lennox had gone to Japan in the mid-seventies and been dazzled by what the Japanese had achieved in modernizing their factories. He was amazed not by the brilliance and originality of what they had done but by the practicality of it. Lennox's visit had been an epiphany: He had suddenly envisioned the past twenty years in Japan, two decades of Japanese manufacturing engineers coming to work every day, busy, serious, being taken seriously by their superiors, being filled with the importance of their mission, improving the manufacturing in countless small ways. It was not that they had made one giant breakthrough, Lennox realized; they had made a thousand and one quite modest ones.

When Ford and GM showed profits in 1983, for the first time in several years, Shaiken was not impressed. He believed it an illusory profit in terms of true industrial response, a profit based on built-up demand, on the temporary restrictions on the Japanese, on some accumulated tax credits, and on forcing their break-even costs way down. There was a lot of talk about improved quality, but, as far as he could tell, U.S. quality programs were still marginal compared to those of the Japanese. What the American companies had really learned, he felt, and in a brief time, was how to cut costs and how to make money while selling fewer cars. That was a triumph of accounting and middle management, and it could be only temporary. On the factory floor he believed the battle had barely begun.

He was sure, then, that the American auto companies would not respond the right way. The first bad sign, as far as he was concerned, came in 1982 when it became clear to him that they weren't really going to contest the Japanese on small cars. As a former autoworker he dissented from that decision. He had no doubt that it would be difficult to compete with the Japanese in small cars, that it might take as many as five years to turn the tide, but it would be worth it, not just in recapturing lost ground but because the lessons learned in fighting back would be applicable to making not only small cars but larger cars as well. The only way to learn, he believed, was to do it, to struggle through and make endless mistakes but, as you did so, constantly improve your process and your workers. That was what the Japanese secret had been.

Instead, the Americans in 1982 were using that new buzzword, robotics. But robots weren't what was making the critical difference. The American robotics craze, he realized, was about trendiness and wealth—we're not as good as they are, and we're richer, so let's go to robots. It was the panicky response of men who did not really know the factory, and who had little confidence, despite their public statements, in the quality and attitude of their workers.

In 1984, GM announced its plans for the Saturn program. That was precisely what Shaiken had expected, an attempt to beat the Japanese with high technology—the creation of the superfactory. The intriguing, revealing thing about Saturn was that its union agreement, though complex and sophisticated, was clearly intended eventually to eliminate as much human labor as possible. It was GM's vision of 1995: Very expensive machines would do everything. It was a high-tech-and-money solution, the natural one for GM because in high tech, America was still more competitive than Japan, and because GM certainly was still richer than the Japanese companies. Saturn was a brilliant and unusual risk, a commitment of billions of dollars, but Shaiken remained dubious. To him it was an example of throwing money at a problem. It reminded him of the American response to Vietnam; confronted by a clever, relentless, dedicated enemy they could not understand, the Americans had tried to win by throwing their technology at the war, smothering both ally and enemy with it. That had not worked, and to Shaiken these auto executives seemed the lineal heirs of that Vietnam approach—virtually the same men, in some cases—coming up with the same responses, drowning a problem with money and technology.

That was the beginning of the American reaction. Shaiken watched the American companies carefully and, despite their advertising and their public statements, he decided that almost none of the American executives believed that America could be competitive anymore, either in the small-car field or in parts supply. They would not say that publicly, but they said it privately among themselves, and their every financial move pointed that way.

By 1985, Shaiken decided what the real American response to Japan was going to be: an escalation in joint production with emerging nations, which he spoke of symbolically as the Korean connection. The Americans would either buy or build their own factories there outright, or they would make joint deals with Korean companies. Indeed, he began to call Korea

"Saturn Two," because of the avalanche of deals and the prospect of even more. The hot new phrase for it was "outsourcing." He saw the following scenario: The American parts supplier, pressured by one of the Big Three (which of course was pressured by the Japanese), would seek a joint-production deal with a Korean company. It would supply badly needed technology, badly needed expertise, and badly needed capital; the Koreans would supply the work force. The cost of the worker would drop from $20 an hour in a union shop or $12 an hour in a nonunion shop to $3 an hour. The American companies would contract with the Koreans for auto parts made by high technology at exceptionally low cost; the parts would be assembled in America; and no union could throw up roadblocks to the installation of the high-tech, labor-saving machinery as had happened in America. Besides, the more manufacturing work the American auto men moved abroad, the greater their leverage on the American workers they still employed, who would be told to take the contract management offered or see their factory exported. There was already a great deal of that going on. It was the ultimate weapon against both the American unions and the Japanese. The part of Shaiken that was blue-collar had thought, "America to these managers is going to be just a place where they'll receive their mail."

The rise of Korea as an American industrial satellite in just a few short years had stunned Shaiken. In 1979 and 1980, Korea had been merely one of several countries that the Americans were thinking about. If anything, countries like Mexico and Brazil, with a more sophisticated skill base, seemed to be more likely to succeed. But Mexico and Brazil, after all, skills and other strengths aside, were still Latin countries; their peoples, it was believed, were of volatile temperament, the nations themselves vulnerable to revolution and political upheaval at the worst and uncontrollable inflation at best. Then Korea began to catch on. American executives, looking at Korea, saw the coming of the next Japan—the dutiful, hardworking, ambitious Confucian workers who were willing to labor for little. The Koreans, like the Japanese, seemed born to manufacture, seemed to have innate industrial energy, and their society was even more controlled than the Japanese. Korea was not some small Asian country limited to textiles and ceramics; it had a good steel industry and a good shipping industry, among others—and it acutely needed foreign capital. It was also full of desire to compete with its historic rival, Japan. For that reason American companies that had often been frustrated in their attempts to do joint ventures in Japan found that Korea was far more receptive to their investment.

Throughout 1985, Shaiken watched as the number of deals between the

American auto companies and the Koreans mounted. Sometimes the American company bought a Korean factory outright. More often than not, there was some form of coproduction. GM had Dae Woo producing some eighty thousand small cars for 1987—a small deal but a beginning, a test run of sorts. Ford signed a Korean truck manufacturer to produce cars for export to America in 1988—not many at first, but there were plans to expand the relationship. At the same time, Ford announced plans to build a radiator factory in Korea; a radiator factory was not the ultimate in sophistication, but it was a way of finding out how good the Koreans were, what these workers were like, whether they were a match for the Japanese, and whether their skills could be applied in the more refined levels of auto manufacturing.

Nor were Ford and GM alone. Lee Iacocca visited Korea in 1985 and tried to work out a deal with Samsung, a general manufacturing company not yet in the auto business. The deal was to be basic: Iacocca offered Chrysler's expertise and technology and said it would provide the plant, and the Koreans would make some 300,000 small cars for shipment to the United States. The Korean government, wary of overextending the nation's industrial capacity, at first blocked the deal, though eventually it was expected to go through. But Iacocca's attempt left no doubt that Chrysler, vulnerable as it was, saw its future in increased relationships with suppliers in East Asia. At meetings with stock analysts, Iacocca now boasted that what had once been a weakness—the lack of vertical integration of Chrysler, the dependence upon outside suppliers—was actually a strength in the new age. He did not need to mention East Asian suppliers; everyone there knew what he was talking about. In sessions with their American parts suppliers the Chrysler people were more blunt: If you want to supply Chrysler in the future, the message went, you have to get your costs down and your quality up, so you'd better start exploring joint ventures with someone in East Asia.

None of what Ford or Chrysler was doing surprised Shaiken. The only thing that surprised him was how quickly it had happened.

51.
INSTANT REPLAY:
THE RISE OF KOREA

They came to Seoul not for pleasure but for their future. They were nervous on arrival, for by and large they were small-town Midwesterners, owners of modest companies, and many of them had not traveled very much. Now not only were they in a distant and strange land but they had arrived there vulnerable, almost beholden, needing to make a deal, and they might have to give away part of their company in the process. They came because they feared they could no longer compete at home, and they had been told by their most important customers, the giant American assembly companies, to get their costs down. Korea was to them, like it or not, their best hope. Korea, they had been told, was the new Japan and for them a way of holding off the Japanese challenge.

What had once been a trickle of them had become by the spring of 1986 a torrent. In Seoul they met their new partners, men with whom they could not communicate at all. William Vaughan, a Chrysler representative in Korea, had watched them come and witnessed their desperation, knowing they were there to survive, for if they could not work something out, they were convinced, they would soon be out of business. Vaughan had an unusual job; he represented Chrysler in its continuing negotiations to complete the massive deal with Samsung, the vast South Korean manufacturing combine, but in addition to that he was a kind of matchmaker between the American parts manufacturers used by Chrysler and the Koreans, trying to find Korean companies who could succeed in this alien new world of autos. It was not always easy, for few of the Korean companies, their eagerness and ambition and low labor costs notwithstanding, had tried anything on the scale of, or as demanding in specifications as, auto manufacturing. More often than not the owners ran the most primitive of operations, sometimes literally dirt-floor. They typically had been manufacturing fairly simple consumer products which were put to intermittent use in the home. The jump to the world of auto, where what they made would undergo constant stress, was enormous. Chrysler, like the other American assemblers, was now in the business of arranging the marriages, and Vaughan, a longtime overseas operative for Chrysler, hearing of one of its American suppliers who wanted to make a deal, would put together a list of potential Korean companies. Then a team of four or five Chrysler technical experts would fly out to evaluate the factories, eventually recommending the one most likely to succeed in auto parts—a decision made not so much on achievement as on potential, on the Korean manager's instinct for organization. Then the American supplier would fly out to meet his intended, and with that, like as not, the deed would be done.

To the suppliers, pressured, nervous, Korea increasingly seemed the most attractive option remaining. Japan was too exclusionary, too hard to penetrate; too much was demanded and too little given. In Mexico, a country that generated a certain unease on their part, potential partners wanted a sixty-forty division of the relationship. Taiwan and Singapore seemed too small for the scale of auto, better suited to high technology. Korea, by contrast, was relatively open, eager for foreign investment, and somewhat experienced in big-time industrial production. It was a country, in effect, with muscle. Those unaware of that were directed to the example of Hyundai, which had entered the world of auto export only recently but was already good and improving at a remarkable rate.

Hyundai was not just the largest of Korea's new conglomerates but a nation within a nation. It was a classic East Asian hybrid—a family-owned capitalist giant but state-supported and state-buttressed, more a creature of the state in some ways than even its Japanese competitors. The advantages of its special position were remarkable: It was the state that decided which Korean firms could compete with Hyundai, and the state had an immense financial and emotional investment in Hyundai, the epitome of Korea's industrial surge and an object of national pride. In an American conglomerate, one Korean businessman noted, if the shipbuilding or construction division was depressed, the company might be forced to sell it off; but during bad times Hyundai needed only go to a Korean bank for more money—in effect a national subsidy for a private company. Yet even discounting its advantages, Hyundai was impressive. It had mastered the process of taking Korea's great human potential—all that raw energy and desire for a better life, so long suppressed—and giving it modern economic form and expression, moving workers not just from farm to city but from the old century to the new, changing their lives dramatically. Its accomplishments were staggering: its enormous construction projects in the Arab world, its ability to compete with the Japanese head-to-head in shipbuilding. Now Hyundai had entered auto. In 1984, with a small rear-wheel-drive car called the Pony, it penetrated the Canadian market; by the end of 1985 it had become the number-one exporter of cars to Canada, with seventy-nine thousand cars sold. In 1986, with a small front-wheel-drive car called the Excel, it moved into the American market, and the early sales were well above expectations. Hyundai had talked of selling 100,000 subcompact cars in the United States in 1986, but by midyear it had to revise the forecast to 150,000.

It was not until 1985 and 1986 that numbers of Americans began to sense that Korea was becoming the new Japan, another thrusting Confucian nation where traditional values and hierarchies had been deftly transferred into a modern, highly disciplined industrial workplace, another challenger with superior workmanship and seemingly unbeatable labor costs. Even as Japanese wages were at last beginning to parallel those of American workers, Korean salaries remained ominously low, approximately $3 an hour in the heavy industrial sector. Informed people in the American auto industry, watching Hyundai's early success, were struck by how much faster it was happening than Japan's had. Remembering, for example, that when the first Japanese cars had arrived in America they were poorly designed and of doubtful quality, auto insiders were struck by the good looks of the Korean cars—Hyundai had hired Italians to design them—and by how well they were made. They were struck too by the fact that whereas the Japanese, when they arrived, had spent almost no money on advertising, Hyundai was budgeting some $25 million for 1986 and, to spend it, had retained Backer & Spielvogel, the creative American advertising agency that did the inspired campaign for Miller Lite beer.

For South Korea the explosion into the modern era was accompanied by considerable stress. Seoul, the capital, had swollen to a city of ten million as hundreds of thousands of Koreans left the farm annually. Countless high-rises formed a new skyline over a city that as late as the early seventies had been something of a wasteland. Now Seoul was preparing to host the 1988 Olympics, believing that just as the Olympics had represented a coming-out party for the Japanese twenty-four years earlier, allowing them to step confidently into a new world position, so would the Olympics confirm Korea.

Yet amid all the change and excitement there were constant reminders that this remained a poor country, trying to go even farther than Japan in a shorter time, and that the burden of achieving industrial eminence would fall directly and unmercifully on today's workers. "The workers understand that it is the duty of this generation to sacrifice for the good of the country," said Chung Se Yung, the president of the Hyundai Motors Company and the younger brother of the founder of the Hyundai complex. "If we are lucky, because of their sacrifices, in fifteen years the workers will make $10,000 a year, they will own their cars, and their children will have it easier than they did. Already our lives are getting a little better. In the old days we worked both Saturday and Sunday. Now we have Sunday off. That is the first sign of progress."

The sacrifice notwithstanding, there was now a powerful optimism in South Korea. The country had suffered painfully in this century, first under the Japanese and then in a bitter and costly civil war, which not only bled the whole peninsula but provided what to some seemed additional justification for South Korea's autocratic rule. (Some Americans saw an irony in the Korean economic challenge: Having fought to keep Korea from being overrun by the Communists in the 1950s, the United States subsequently supported an oppressive government in Korea, one so strong that it could exclude unions and impose a wage scale so low that it was almost impossible for America to compete with.) Now, thanks to the new economic success, the lives of ordinary Koreans were improving, the first early fruits of their hard work were being tasted, and there was an absolute conviction throughout the land that more would follow, that all it took for a better life was hard work. As Michio Nagai, the former Japanese minister of education, observed, there were few national forces more powerful than the belief that things could get a great deal better within the span of one's lifetime.

The surge of Korea left the Japanese somewhat ambivalent. Part of it was the traditional antipathy of the Japanese for the Koreans, a people they regarded as primitive and uncultured, garlic eaters. The relationship between the two countries, one American noted, was not love/hate but hate/hate. Having colonized and exploited the Koreans for the thirty-five years ending in 1945, and quite brutally at that, the Japanese well understood that the Koreans would now rival them with special passion. Key to the cultural-social contempt for the Koreans as a lesser people, a belief not unlike that which many Americans had about Mexicans, was the conviction that they could not do anything really sophisticated. There was also a more empirical view among many Japanese, that Korea simply lacked the scope to become an true competitor. But for all that there was a growing Japanese nervousness about the Koreans—that they were so ambitious, that they would now work harder than young Japanese, that their wages were so low. If the combination of Japanese government and business had been able to control Japanese labor so that what passed for labor-management harmony was really a steel fist in a velvet glove, then the authoritarian Korean government dominated its workers even more nakedly; in Korea, the steel fist wore no glove. As a matter of policy the Korean regime used force to compensate for the nation's lack of industrial and technological sophistication. Also, though Japan was a disciplined society, it seemed hedonistic and insubordinate compared to Korea, where leisure and domestic consumption and dissent were severely restricted.

At every step the Japanese could see their own challenge to the Americans reflected back at them. Furthermore, although the learning curve for the Japanese, as they worked off the American example, had been brief, the Koreans, using the Japanese example and the devices of modern technology, were shortening the curve even more dramatically. They had moved into shipping and steel much faster than the Japanese had thought they could, and now, much earlier than expected, were readying themselves for an assault on the market for autos. In Japan, these developments provoked a mixture of fear and respect. Some older Japanese did not merely complain about the work habits of the younger Japanese; they began to contrast their own young people unfavorably with Korea's. "The Koreans' IQs are on the rise, while Japanese IQs are slipping slightly," said Michio Nagai. "Their family units are stronger than ours. The children study hard and listen to their parents. The Koreans are very confident of their future. Five or ten years ago they did not have that confidence. They are very impressive."

Impressive was an understatement. For Stewart Kim, a young American of Korean ancestry who had attended the best American schools and who was in Korea for graduate studies, the way Korean students used their college libraries was awesome. American students had worked hard, he thought, but their habits were nothing like those of the Koreans. The libraries normally opened at six in the morning, but during exam time they opened at four; at four, there were always long lines of students waiting to get in, and by five there were often no seats left.

Along with the respect among the Japanese there was a tendency toward what could be described as Korea-bashing. Korean companies applying to make things off outmoded Japanese patents found that the Japanese companies they wrote to neither approved nor denied the requests. In 1983, when Exxon of Japan asked for bids on the construction of an immense drilling rig, Hyundai, the giant Korean conglomerate, competing against a number of Japanese companies, made the low bid and won the contract. The reaction in the Japanese press was extremely ugly; there followed several weeks of articles about the danger of the Korean threat and how terrible the Koreans were in general. Finally the Korean ambassador in Tokyo went to the foreign ministry and said that he thought the vituperation was getting out of hand. The bid, however, was eventually rescinded, and it was announced that the Koreans could not meet the specifications. No one was fooled. No other company in the world had done as many massive seawater projects as Hyundai.

In the spring of 1983, Robert Cole, a Japanologist from the University of Michigan, an expert on Japanese labor, met with some of his friends in the Japanese labor movement. Times were very hard, a man from the steel union told him; steel was operating at only 60 percent of capacity. "I am afraid we're going to have to cut back and let people go," the union man said. The problem, he explained, was the Koreans. They were right on the heels of the Japanese. "I keep telling the Koreans that they've got to get their wages up," he said, "because what they're doing now is destructive to everyone." The shoe, Cole thought, was finally on the other foot.

The shifts are very long—twelve hours a day, ten of which are intense, concentrated labor—and Park Jin Kean works six days a week. His life is about his job and little else. Every evening he goes home exhausted. He had to force himself to talk with his family at dinner and, afterward, to pay attention to his two young children and not to slip off into sleep. Park is a foreman at Hyundai Motors, in Ulsan, South Korea, in charge of stations 139 through 164 on the final assembly line, where, among other things, the engine is placed into the body frame. He is proud of his job, and he is also proud of his salary, which, though small by American industrial standards, is exceptionally large by Korean standards. In a nation just emerging from centuries of rural poverty, where the average wage has finally reached $2000 a year, Park makes about $9600. He accepts the long hours without complaint. There is no union to represent him, and he accepts that readily too. It does not occur to him that he is not greatly favored by fate. The work is hard, but the alternatives to his life are much harder.

Park grew up on a farm. His father, Park Kyung Won, though a farmer, was an educated man who taught Chinese characters to neighbors as a sideline. In his youth Park's father had been conscripted into the Japanese army and forced to fight under the Japanese flag. He worked his tiny plot of rice land with great skill, but the plot was one of the smallest in an area where most of the farms were too small. Even when things went well there was little surplus at the end of the year, and when things went badly, the family suffered. When Park was eight there was a terrible harvest because of heavy rains, and because the Park farm was already so poor, the hard times that resulted for the family lasted for three years. During that time the Parks were even poorer than usual, and they were forced to eat barley instead of rice. His father always talked with pride of his life as a farmer, but for young Park it was harsh and wearing, each day the same as the one before, the hours endless. Park's father sometimes beat him for his mistakes, and Park later came to believe that the real cause of those beatings was the hard life inflicted on his father.

As a boy Park liked to make things; when he was seven he made a bicycle out of wood, with wooden wheels, and it worked rather well, he remembered, as long as he was going downhill. Long before finishing high school, he began to think of leaving the farm. He decided that there had to be a better and more exciting life. He knew Korea was changing, that there were industrial jobs for bright young men like him with a high-school education. His father was outraged when Park told him of his intention. Park was the oldest son, he said, and had responsibilities. Un-spoken was the assumption that a father had a time-honored right to determine a son's life, and Park must respect that. But it was more than those things. The son's desire represented the decline of the Korea the father knew and valued, an agricultural land of traditional values, and the rise of a Korean he neither liked nor understood, an urbanized, indus-trialized nation of confusing modern ways and diminished respect for the past and for one's elders. The younger Park and a friend at work, Yoo Mal Bok, also a foreman, often talked about the pain their decisions to leave the farm had caused their fathers. "And what will happen now to our people when all of you young men leave?" Yoo's father had asked angrily. "I will tell you. Everyone goes to the city, and we all will starve."

Park had no desire to be a bad son, but he was determined to have a more modern life. In this he was encouraged by his mother. Over the years he had learned that he could talk to her as he could not talk to his father, who tolerated no dissent and responded to whatever displeased him with physical force. She, good Korean peasant woman, had worked side by side with her husband every day, year after year, "like a slave," said Park. She had never questioned the authority of her husband, but when she understood that her oldest child wanted a better life, she took his side. Park's final decision, involving the defiance of his father, was difficult. His father loved the farm because it was the only thing he knew; the Korea of his generation had offered nothing better than farming. But Park lived in a world where there were other choices. When he made his choice to leave, his father did not speak to him for a year.

It was his mother who heard that there were jobs at Hyundai, in the city of Ulsan, and at her urging he went there, one of four hundred men trying for fifty jobs. He was so nervous that he was sure he gave the wrong answer on one of the oral questions ("If something bad happens inside the company, would you tell anyone from the outside?"), but he got a job nonetheless. He had a chance to go into the shipbuilding division of Hyundai, which was then the grandest part of the company. But Park did not want to build ships. It seemed too much like farming, too much time on one project, too little sense of accomplishment. He took a position in Hyundai Motors, then a small, struggling auto company, as an ordinary worker on the production line, and he was sometimes taunted by the shipbuilding workers because auto was much less powerful and the pay not as good.

The early years were very hard. In a world where most auto assembly was at least partially automated, the Korean line was at first primitively manual. The workers were new and inexperienced, there were few to teach them, and many of the parts they received from the suppliers were poorly made. They were like men working in the dark, for they had no real knowledge of what they were supposed to accomplish or what modern automotive standards were. The line was often down; Park remembered that it functioned about 20 to 30 percent of the time. A shift could make only twenty cars. The workers knew that the cars were not good, but they were told by their superiors to keep working hard and eventually the cars would become better. It was their obligation to persevere, and they did.

Slowly they improved. Hyundai, which sold 15 percent of its stock to Mitsubishi in exchange for, among other things, considerable technical assistance, used technicians from Mitsubishi to help teach its people. (Other Japanese companies, it was said, were angry with Mitsubishi for giving technological aid to the upstart Koreans and complained frequently to Mitsubishi executives.) Gradually the workers began to understand what was expected of them. The parts suppliers improved too. Then the company bought machinery that made the line more efficient and the work easier. The critical year, Park recalled, was 1979; until then they had been making a car every four minutes and thirty-eight seconds; in 1979 they were making one every two minutes. That pace was very hard on the workers, but even when he was at the extremes of exhaustion Park never thought of his new life as difficult, for he could always compare it with that of his parents.

Shortly after he went to work at Hyundai, Park married a girl from Ulsan. Sometimes, as he became more successful and earned more money, he would remind his wife of how much easier her life was than that of his mother. She did not, he pointed out, have to work in the fields all day.

A city girl, she became infuriated with the comparisons. "That's enough," she would say. "I do not want to hear that anymore. You've said it before, and that's enough. I am not going to live like that. Do not bother to tell me about it again." He was pleased, however, that he was married to this city woman and could support her so well. Occasionally he would confide to his friends that she was asking for more clothes and more jewelry and that she claimed the other wives had more than she did. His friends confided that their wives said the same thing. All of this, they decided, was proof of how well they were doing. They knew, in fact, that many young men were leaving the farm and coming to work at Hyundai in order to get married. Farm boys soon learned that the most attractive young women would not marry farmers; they wanted to marry a worker at Hyundai. They did not want to work the farms like their mothers; they wanted to live in the city and be new modern women of Korea.

Park came to realize that he was a prosperous man. His wife was in truth careful with their money, and they saved about $500 of his $800 monthly salary, enough, in due course, to buy a small house in Ulsan. They did not live in the house—they still lived in company housing—but rented it out to others for nearly $100 a month. Park's goal was to save enough to buy a car himself. That would make him one of the first workers in the company to own a car. In Korea cars were being made primarily for export; the few that were not exported were used as company cars or purchased by successful middle managers. Park had almost enough money to buy a car but not enough to operate one, since gas was very expensive in Korea. He hoped to have the money by 1988. When he bought the car, he would move out of the company housing, which was very near the factory, and live in his own house, which was farther away, on the other side of Ulsan. Most of his friends hoped to buy cars, too, and thought they could do it in five or six years.

Ulsan, Park knew, was now a symbol of the new Korea and of the fact that the challenge to the West was not just Japanese. Once just a fishing village with a fine natural harbor, it had become an instant city of more than 550,000. It had the feel of Detroit in the early 1920s, flooded by immigrants desperate to escape hardship and share in the fruits of the industrial age. In Ulsan everyone moved fast, no one ever seemed to rest. It was not a beautiful city, and its amenities were marginal. It was not about enjoying things but about making things—ships, containers, cars —and exporting them quickly. From Ulsan, the company town of Hyundai, the Koreans were mounting the latest assault upon American industrial supremacy, competing for the low end of the American auto market. Barely a factor in 1981, when it made about 60,000 cars, Hyundai hoped to manufacture more than 400,000 cars in 1986 and one million in 1990.

Park thought his life had already exceeded his dreams. His father had somewhat grudgingly accepted the value of Park's job, and Park himself was proud not only of what he earned but what his labor contributed to. He took considerable pleasure from the fact that Korea, a small, poor country, was exporting cars to a great nation like America, and he was confident that Korea would someday outstrip Japan as an automobile manufacturer. The Koreans, he liked to say, were obviously more inventive than the Japanese. He knew from talking to the technicians that the production line at Hyundai was not nearly as modern as those in Japan, which were highly robotized, and that Korea, because it was weaker in capital investment and rich in human labor, used extra manpower to make up for technological shortcomings. (In fact, American auto industry experts were comparing the Korean assembly lines favorably with those of Japan in the early seventies.) Three years ago, after seven years as a regular worker, Park was made a foreman, and he liked that job, though it was much harder than being on the line. When he was on the line he had to worry only about his own work, but now he was responsible for all the men under him, and he felt constant strain because of that.

But the men who worked for him were very good. What struck him about the younger men who had just entered the company was that they were considerably more ambitious than men like himself and the others who entered in the seventies. When he had first shown up at Hyundai Motors, it was a small company. Now it was very large, very successful, making an important product and paying high wages, so it was attracting the most ambitious young men of a nation filled with ambitious young men. The company's older men—the foreman like Park, in their mid-thirties—were beginning to complain that these younger men were perhaps *too* intense. A sign had been posted in the factory warning the workers not to rush their tasks, urging them to take their time. Still, at Hyundai Motors the president, Chung Se Yung, his managers, and the workers themselves enjoyed referring to the Japanese as "the lazy Asians."

52.
THE VENERABLES

In October 1985, Yutaka Katayama returned to Los Angeles. He was seventy-six years old now, more than a little overweight, quick to lose his breath. He was returning because one of his old colleagues had noticed earlier that it was twenty-five years since Katayama had first arrived in America, and it would be nice to give a party in his honor. All around him, as he arrived, were the signs of his success, the giant billboards portraying hot new Nissan sports cars, the deluge of beautifully crafted television commercials suggesting that America's youth try these terrific new models. The commercials were a far cry from the first ones, in which John Parker had used himself and his family instead of actors and which were shot by a police photographer. In the twenty-five years since he had first come to America, Nissan had sold eight million cars, and there were in Southern California alone half a million in current use. Given the unlikely beginnings of the endeavor, those figures were truly astonishing.

The morning of the reunion, Katayama had breakfasted with his old friend Mayfield Marshall, and they had reminisced about the old days, how Katayama at first had kept all the bills in an old shoebox, how they had pushed Datsun in Hawaii through aggressive promotion, renting them for only $5 a day, and how in the early seventies Katayama had pushed Marshall to buy the first Seiko watch he had ever seen or heard about. "Here, you'd better buy one of these," Katayama had said. "They're going to sell millions." Marshall had forked over $15, knowing that he was not only buying a watch but undoubtedly helping to cover the expenses of some young Japanese salesman who was living on virtually nothing and was almost certainly a graduate of Keio University, Katayama's alma mater. That night the dinner was very emotional. Old memories were stirred. No one from Nissan headquarters attended.

Katayama did not linger in Los Angeles. He had just returned from Finland, a country he loved to visit because the light was so remarkable and he enjoyed painting there, and he was soon off to Paris to continue to push for one of his dreams, the restoration of the old Paris-to-Peking auto rally.

In 1985 Sanosuke Tanaka was seventy years old and living in partial retirement. He missed working regularly, but he often appeared at Nissan factories, where he would teach motivational classes and explain to young people just entering the company the importance of work and of loyalty to their fellow workers and the company. He regularly returned to Takabeya village, where he had grown up, to visit his family. The land that the family had gotten during the land-reform period had been sold back to the landowners during hard times, but the family still owned a small plot on which two very simple Japanese houses stood, and in them lived his two brothers and their families.

On a visit in 1985 he briefly visited his brothers and then went to his parents' graves. Then he took a visitor to see the house of the largest landowner in the area. The landowners, he said, had once been rich, and they had remained rich without working. Before, they had people like us working for them, Tanaka said, and then, just when they might have had to go to work, everyone began to move out here. They got rich by selling off their land. They became real estate men. So they still did not have to work hard.

Takabeya village had changed dramatically in the last thirty years, and Tanaka was not sure he liked many of the changes. Once it had been purely rural farmland, untouched by the cities. Now Isehara city, the small neighboring center, had reached out and swallowed up Takabeya village, and Isehara city itself had become nothing more than a suburban extension of Yokohama. He was driving a new Nissan car, a Laurel, big and fancy and loaded down with electronic gear. He drove through areas that had been farms, and they were completely developed and, what was worse, populated by spoiled young sons and daughters of Japan. As Tanaka drove past the main street, a teenager in a punk-rock outfit walked past.

"Look at that!" he said. "Did you see that? In my village! Look what he is wearing." He drove a little farther, and a teenage girl, dressed as an American bobby-soxer of the fifties, her contours explicit, passed by. "Another one," he said, outraged. "When I was a boy we dressed as modestly as we could. We did not want to call attention to ourselves. Now that is all they want to do, cry to the heavens to look." He was not pleased.

The visitor asked him if he worried about the direction of Japan's young people. He paused for a long time. The question clearly bothered him. The Japan of modern affluence was difficult for him to accept. "They will wear their jazz clothes today," he said, "and then tomorrow they will do what they have to do."

In the spring of 1985, with the tensions between Japan and the United States rising again, Naohiro Amaya was once again taking on a powerful, entrenched part of the Japanese establishment. In addition to his other battles, he was on a committee which was trying to reform the rigid Japanese educational system and to make it so that less learning was done by rote and more by the student's using his analytical abilities. Nothing cut more to the core of Japanese life, acceptance of authority, than the school system. The obedience the child learned there and in the home became the same obedience one showed to all forms of authority for the rest of his life. To make a student more independent was to make an entire society in the most profound way independent. But Amaya and others felt that Japan's entry into the world, and the nature of the new economy, demanded a different kind of citizen, a more modern one who could think for himself. The graduate of the rote system was a wonderful worker in a blue-collar manufacturing economy—"We have the best blue-collars in the world," Amaya said—but a new economy of high technology demanded more creativity and thus more independence of young men and women, who must move readily in and out of foreign cities and adapt to and understand different conditions.

Amaya was frustrated but not surprised by the mounting trade tensions between the United States and Japan. He put much of the blame on his own country. The inability of the Japanese political system to adapt to new realities and to open the nation up to Western markets was distressing to him. America, he thought, for all its flaws in manufacturing, might prove to have a more flexible political system and thus might eventually make the adjustments necessary to the new world economy better than Japan. The quickness with which the Reagan administration had deregulated certain industries and the success of that deregulation had impressed him. In his opinion it was the sign of a political system adapting successfully to new economic realities. In his opinion, America, having gone through a prolonged period of self-obsession which began with the Vietnam War, was only now emerging and taking stock of the rest of the world again. He was impressed at this moment by the degree of flex in the American system, and in the essential American pragmatism.

By contrast, what was required of Japan was a period of major political readjustment. That would not be easy, for Japan was locked into a particularly narrow vision of itself and its relationship with the outside world, and imprisoned politically by the power of its vested interests. Every sophisticated modern Japanese knew the nation needed to export, and knew in addition that it had to be fairer in accepting imports, and that it was coming under far closer scrutiny from the West. But the political system, an extension of powerful existing interest, was proving to be surprisingly rigid. Because Japan's farmers were so vulnerable, they were an especially regressive force politically. The rest of the world, already sensitive to growing Japanese economic power, need look no farther for its anti-Japanese rationales than its agricultural protectionism.

Perhaps that was another reflection of American affluence, he thought, that its richness was so diverse and spread so broadly across the country that no sector in decline could hold the nation hostage against larger communal interest. In Japan, on the other hand, agriculture represented a classic example of domestic economic obstruction. It was old-fashioned and bad, but its political power was unchallenged. Nakasone, the prime minister, understood the dilemma, but his power was limited in his own party, whose members were tied more to their petty narrow connections in agriculture than to the good of Japan. Thus, much was being risked for very little, in the larger balance, and the Americans, quite predictably, were becoming angrier and angrier. The prime minister would periodically meet with Reagan, promise to do something about it, and then find that his own party would not budge. It was a political system married to vested archaic interests.

Amaya believed that as the world entered its new economy with very different political and economic relationships, each nation had what he defined as hardware and software. Hardware in his sense was the ability of a nation to produce—the sum of its engineers, its workers, its essential skills, plus its natural resources. Of Japan's strength in the area of hardware, he had no doubt. There could be no greater willingness to work, nor could there be more or better professional engineers on a factory floor. Japan's problem would be with the software, which he saw as the ability of a nation's political system to adapt to new realities, to tell the truth to its own population about the way the world was instead of the way they would have it be. The Russians had probably the worst software in the world.

But he was worried by Japan's software. Our politicians, he said, are rigid, very rigid. He spoke with palpable disdain for elected politicians who scurried around gaining favor with a group of insular farmers whose interest did not necessarily coincide with the national interest. Their Japan was the Japan of the nineteenth century. His was no longer the twentieth century; now it was the twenty-first. He did not share their nostalgia for either a feudal past or a highly nationalistic past. Amaya wanted to hold on to the essence of the nation but help it change and adapt to a new era, lest its exclusionary spirit end up isolating it from those who were its friends and allies. There was too much talk about regaining a samurai spirit in a nation that more than ever before needed to be supple. He was aware of the singular danger of Japanese insularity, which was traditionally its strength but like many strengths could quickly become a weakness. Fighting Japanese insularity was like fighting its history. Throughout its history, Japan had coveted the hardware of foreigners—other people's toys—first those from China, then those of the West. But it had pulled back from any possible contamination from their software, or, in effect, from the political and social consequences of its modernization. The yearning for the old Japan, for a way of life that no longer existed and could not possibly exist, he thought, was powerful and potentially quite destructive.

America, he believed, would do well in the new economy. Its hardware was quite good. Not as good in manufacturing as the Japanese, but the Americans would make adjustments there; a company based in America would have more of its manufacturing done in Asia. American technology was likely to be more inventive than Japanese for a number of years because of the nature of the American educational and entrepreneurial systems. America's weakness was that it was less tied to the past than were other societies, like Japan, but it was the American strength too. It was ironic, he thought, that the heads of American companies were not very knowledgeable about their own factories, but they were educated and broadgauged and knew the world—whereas Japanese manufacturers knew their factories very well, but did not know the world. Because of this he was inclined to believe that American software, in his use of the word, America's ability to adapt its economy and political system to new circumstances, might be superior to that of the Japanese.

He was not amazed in 1985 by the sudden force of the American anger over Japanese protectionism. If it did not go too far, if it did not flare into the dangerous kind of nationalism that had dogged both countries in the thirties, it might even be a good thing, for it would help force Japan to modernize. Twice before, he believed, Japan had been dramatically changed by pressure from America—in 1853 when Matthew Perry sailed into Japanese waters, and the Japanese, seeing his black ships, knew that the only way they could preserve their society was to modernize; then again after World War II, during the Occupation, when the Americans forced the Japanese to change and modernize. Perhaps pressure from the Americans would eventually force the Japanese political system to do what it could not do for itself.

53.
THE RECKONING

Starting in 1983, there was in the auto industry a kind of euphoria. American cars were selling again, interest rates were down, the price of oil was beginning to go down. The advertising campaigns seemed to reflect it. America was coming back. We might have made some mistakes in the past, but we had learned our lesson. Quality was job one. Even the beer commercials seemed to get into the swing of it, and there suddenly seemed to be an onslaught of commercials showing good hardworking blue-collar Americans putting in a long hard day, good guys who got along with their foremen as long as the foremen were square about things, drinking a well-earned beer that was brewed the American (not the foreign) way. As with many things in America the trend was celebrated by Madison Avenue and turned into videotaped myth before it was fact. Within the industry itself there was a sense of celebration and a belief that the customers had returned, that the bad days were over and the industry had righted itself.

Wall Street analysts and others, however, took a colder look at the sudden bonanza. They judged the temporary wall against the Japanese to be of critical importance. It was hard to estimate something like this exactly, the dollar benefit to Detroit of the temporary restraint—just as it was hard to estimate how much of an advantage the Japanese had in the production of a car—but shrewd analysts who knew something about Detroit's cost and price structure put it near $1000, per car an almost sure difference between red ink and black. In effect the great lever that Detroit had had before the Japanese onslaught—the ability of GM to set the price and of the other companies to stay in the lee of GM—had momentarily returned, with the Japanese, now able to charge even more for a car, among the principal beneficiaries. For conservative economists, free traders who believed that protection created inflation, the jiggling with the prices of American and Japanese cars in that period seemed to be perfect proof of their arguments.

Ford was a good example of what had happened. In 1979, the last good year, the one before the crunch, it had made a profit of $1.2 billion on sales of 4.7 million cars while employing a work force of about 500,000 people worldwide; in 1983, the year of the company's first turnaround (after some $2.4 billion in losses over three years), it made $1.1 billion on sales of only 3.6 million cars (more than a million fewer) with a work force of 380,000. The comeback, some skeptics sensed, was not an industrial resurgence but rather a skilled financial rearrangement. The essential problems remained. It was an industry desperately trying to improve itself. But to take a giant industry, one that had grown careless and sloppy over more than twenty-five years of virtual domestic monopoly, and restructure it under combat conditions was not easily accomplished.

At Ford, Don Petersen pushed a serious new quality-control program. He had brought in Edwards Deming, the quality expert the American auto people had once scorned and the Japanese had taken so seriously, and he had placed some Deming disciples in key positions. In 1984, in what was a gratifying victory for Deming, the Society of Automotive Engineers asked him to address its convention in Detroit. He accepted on the condition that the presidents of both GM and Ford sit with him on the platform, and they did. He was now officially a prophet with honor in his own country. Ford even made a training film in which a Ford executive held up a part from a transmission made by Mazda, its Japanese sister company, and said, "We thought our part was good, and it is, but theirs is damn good." Some of the Deming people privately complained that it was hard to push the essentially egalitarian Deming principles in large corporations like GM and Ford, which gave million-dollar bonuses to their highest executives. Still, there was no doubt that quality was receiving more than mere lip service and that American cars, particularly Fords, were getting better.

The problem was that the Japanese were not standing still. Pushed by their own demonic need for excellence and their own fierce domestic competition, pushed as well by the vision of an ascending Korea, pushed by the fear of a resurgent America—the battle of Midway all over again —pushed above all by a cultural spirit that made them more comfortable in adversity than in success, they were getting better at a striking rate. A number of studies by professional organizations showed that despite the improvements by the Americans, the Japanese were significantly ahead in quality. "The Japanese," said Keith Crain of *Automotive News*, "remind me of a racecar driver who's five laps ahead but doesn't know it and keeps driving as if he's five laps behind." Certainly many American executives were stunned with the ferocity with which the Japanese auto makers decided to thrust ahead once the voluntary trade restrictions ended in 1985. The Americans had expected a gradual assault, but the Japanese, fearing each other, the Koreans, and the Americans, had been ruthless. Some Americans thought that they would only go to 2.1 million cars in the first year, but they went instead to 2.3, and there were internal Japanese projections that went as high as 3 million. The Americans were stunned; they had no idea that the Japanese would push their advantage so openly. The figure was actually closer to 2.4 million, which meant an increase of more than 25 percent.

At the same time, the Japanese were opening factories in America, first Honda, then Nissan, then Mazda, then Toyota and, planned for the future, a joint deal between Fuji Motors (Subaru) and Isuzu. More often than not these new factories were located in the South, outside the reach of the UAW; that meant that the Japanese could come to America and retain some of their cost advantages. For the Japanese, building an American factory was a way of fending off future trade restrictions. It allowed them to make small cars in America (and eventually, if they wanted, to move into the coveted middle and upper levels of the market), and it allowed them incidentally to pick up increasing American political support, for when they came to a new area, its congressmen, newspaper editors, and workers immediately became more sympathetic to the Japanese industrial vision. Some of the Japanese suppliers followed the Japanese auto companies to America, confident that they had a guaranteed relationship with Honda or Nissan and eager to sell to the American assemblers as well.

In this new phase of the drive on the American market, thought Maryann Keller, the Japanese had an advantage: They had so many companies, and such intense domestic competition. It meant that their quality was always high. It also meant that if one or two of them came out with weak models, there was nonetheless always going to be another manufacturer who had the right car for that season. A related advantage was that the Japanese did not need the scale that the Americans depended upon. To Detroit a car was not a success unless the company could run some 500,000 pieces over the cycle of a few years. But the Japanese were accustomed to different scales, their increments of everything were smaller, and they could make a profit on much lower numbers. One Japanese manufacturer, she noted, was coming up with a miniature four-wheel-drive vehicle. Though a car like that might capture a rather limited market by American standards, it might be extremely profitable for a small Japanese company. By contrast, she noted, all the new money being spent in Detroit was for giant, old-fashioned production lines, what she called dinosaur lines.

All of that new competition made the future look grim. In the bad times between 1980 and 1983, six American assembly plants had been closed. Now, with the obvious jump in foreign production in North America, some experts predicted that the Big Three would have to close no fewer than six and perhaps as many as twelve assembly plants in the next few years. A cloud of desperation hovered over workers about the future of their jobs, as the personnel office of Mazda in Flat Rock, Michigan, could testify: The new Mazda plant in construction there would not open until September 1987, but some twenty months beforehand, there were some ninety-one thousand applications for the thirty-one hundred jobs.

In the early eighties, American executives, because of joint production deals, were often visiting Japanese factories, and they were finding out how good the Japanese were, especially at the basics. One executive who had made that trip and reached that conclusion a decade earlier was Hal Sperlich, then of Ford. Touring a Japanese auto factory in the early seventies, he had noticed that there were no repair bays alongside the line, areas into which defective cars in the process of assembly were pulled for fixing.

"Where do you repair your cars?" Sperlich asked the engineer with him.

"We don't have to repair our cars," the engineer answered.

"Well, then," Sperlich asked, "where are your inspectors?"

"The workers are the inspectors," his guide answered.

Sperlich left that factory somewhat shaken: In America, he thought, we have repair bins the size of football fields.

In 1985, Sperlich, by then at Chrysler, was talking about what he called "nonconformance." That was the difference in what it cost to do a car right the first time and what it cost to do it wrong and then have to compensate—the money spent on the scrap metal, the manpower wasted on repair, the problems on the warranties, the insidious costs spread throughout the company associated with paying attention to something that you should not have to pay attention to. By Sperlich's estimates the cost of nonconformance for an American auto company was some 20 to 40 percent of revenues. That, in turn, he thought, meant that if you did the car perfectly, if all the parts came in right and everything was done correctly the first time, not only would the cars be better and the company's reputation better, but you could reduce your costs by, say, 25 percent, or finally about $2500 a car, which was close to the Japanese price advantage.

A critical part of the answer, he believed, was to put far more pressure on supplier companies. What was startling about Detroit up until then was how casual the major companies had been about their suppliers. When he came to Chrysler he checked with his colleagues who dealt with the supplier companies, asking, What is our standard of purchasing? He was startled to find that there was none. That had been true, he was sure, at Ford at well. There was, in his phrase, no report card. One of the best things about the challenge from the Japanese was that this aspect of the business was changing and changing quickly. The suppliers were being pushed hard to improve quality.

In 1985, very quietly, a symbolic event took place in the American automotive industry: Honda passed American Motors as the fourth-largest maker of cars in America. Honda, perhaps because it was the most entrepreneurial and the least bureaucratic of the Japanese companies, and the one most dependent upon its export market, had done everything right in this country. While the other Japanese companies dragged their feet on the issue of building factories in America, Honda in 1979, just when the American industry began to collapse, decided to build its Marysville, Ohio, factory; in December 1982, as the other Japanese companies struggled with import restrictions, Honda started American production. It managed to keep the UAW out—though that was a sore point, and there were constant struggles with union organizers. It pressured its American suppliers to raise their quality. By 1983 it was producing 50,000 cars a year, and by 1985 the total reached 150,000. (American Motors in the same period was falling from 200,000 to about 120,000.) With the 400,000 Honda was allowed to import, it was selling by the end of 1985 over 550,000 cars a year in America. More, though producing in a foreign country with foreign workers, it retained its mystique, as much from word of mouth as from advertising, that for the money Honda cars were the best-engineered and best-made in the world. In late 1985, badly shaken American manufacturers resorted to special promotional deals, including carefully adjusted credit rates, but Hondas were selling well above the sticker price throughout the country. Nor was Honda content to stand still. In 1986 it was planning to expand its facilities and make 300,000 cars at Marysville, and there were serious plans to build yet another factory, which would give Honda the capacity to sell a million cars a year in America by the end of the decade. At the same time, it was moving into the middle range as well, with a car called the Acura Legend, which sold for about $18,000.

That was just Honda. In May 1985 the first passenger cars came down the line at Nissan's Smyrna factory. That same year, Toyota, the dreaded Toyota—so skillful (some competitors would say brutal) in its industrial process and its capacity to pressure suppliers that it alone made a profit in the crowded Japanese domestic field; so deliberate in its corporate strategy that it was almost invariably the last of the Japanese companies to try a major move, such as locating in America—chose a site for its first factory in the mid-South. By 1985, Toyota was seeking nothing less than to replace General Motors as the foremost producer of autos in the world. It was likely, thought Maryann Keller, to become America's low-cost producer, and it was clear to her that Toyota would not have come to America unless it was planning to make a million cars a year there eventually, many of them in the middle of the market.

By 1985 it was apparent that the events of the past two years, especially the surge of profits, did not signify a true comeback and that the auto industry remained very vulnerable. The creation of all those new Japanese plants—and supplier plants—in America seemed to promise an even more difficult struggle in the years ahead. To many American executives surveying the battlefield, a real competition with the Japanese seemed unwinnable. More and more the Americans were turning toward cooperation with the Japanese, making deals in which small cars carrying American labels were produced by Japanese sister companies, or in which American labels went onto cars with an ever-higher percentage of Japanese component parts.

In the fall of 1985, Lee Iacocca gave an interview to John Holusha of the *New York Times* in which he said that according to his projections, in two years the Japanese would have 50 percent of the American market, counting component parts, Japanese cars, and Japanese cars under American label. Some of his old colleagues in Detroit thought it was significant that in the same interview Iacocca managed to put the blame entirely on the federal government (which had just helped rescue Chrysler) for its tax policies and the way it valued the dollar. "That's why I went to Japan," he said. "I've got to build some of my stuff in yen and sell it for dollars. That's the magic of it." There were others who thought that the magic was a great deal more complicated, and that if there was a flaw in Iacocca it was his inability to admit his and the system's culpability and the constant need to blame someone else.

In early 1986, Don Frey, one of the fathers of the Mustang and now head of Bell & Howell, went back to Detroit to visit his brother Stu, a senior executive in Ford engineering. At one point they began talking about the Mustang, a subject close to Don Frey's heart. He told his brother that he thought it was time for a new model. "The one you have now is getting a little long in the tooth," he said.

"I just signed off on the program for the new one," Stu Frey said.

"Tell me about it," Don Frey said. "Who did it?"

"Well," said Stu Frey, "we're doing the clay, which we'll send to Mazda in Hiroshima, and they'll do the body design and drive line on a Mazda chassis to be shipped to Mazda's Flat Rock plant, where it will be assembled with a Ford engine." Something hung in the air between them, so Stu Frey added, "We can't make any money on it doing it here."

The Mustang, Don Frey had thought, my Mustang. The most American of cars. Now made by Mazda. He felt a special sadness for the car, for the company he knew and cared about, and finally for the country.

All of this showed in 1985, as the barriers started falling, that the auto industry remained deeply troubled. But perhaps the most dramatic evidence, to people in the industry, was that in the summer of 1985, Maryann Keller, widely regarded as one of Wall Street's most astute analysts of the industry, testified in Congress in favor of limited protectionism. In the world of auto men, that was a surprising development. As accurately as anyone else in her field, Keller had prophesied and tracked the rise of the Japanese industry, acquiring a considerable reputation on the Street, in the press, and in the industry internationally. So often was she painfully right that many American auto executives considered her anti-American and pro-Japanese. She was nothing of the sort. She was a virtuoso analyst, the kind of person whom the CIA, when it is lucky, places in charge of a vitally important country, someone whose estimates are a shrewd blending of a deep and powerful knowledge of the area and very adept daily reporting based on impeccable sources. There were few if any journalists or auto executives who had contacts like hers in Japan. Her skepticism about most of Detroit's managerial skills was legendary. Because she had understood the Japanese surge so early, she was highly esteemed in Japan, where executives and journalists took her assessments extremely seriously, and where she had, for an American and woman, remarkable access. There what she said was often front-page news. When in 1983 she was thinking of moving from Paine Webber to another firm, named Vilas-Fischer, that was major news in Japan, and one night, into the early hours, her phone rang off the hook as Japanese journalists called to ask if it was true.

Thus her testimony on behalf of protection was important news in both countries. She so testified because she thought that with the Japanese in such a strong position and the Americans so weak, there was a significant danger of the entire American industry collapsing. While it was one thing, she thought, for a nation to lose its color-television industry, it was quite another thing to lose something so crucial to its industrial well-being and its potential national defense. She had regarded the American comeback of 1983 and 1984 a good deal more dubiously than had the men of Detroit.

It was, she thought, a brief honeymoon in a very hard time. Far more important than the good balance sheets for those years, in her opinion, were two critical developments. The first was that the Japanese, faced with quota limitations, had quite predictably escalated the size and profitability of each car and were now beginning to do very nicely in the middle range, which had previously been the exclusive property of Detroit. We had, she thought, with the temporary quota, forced them to get better even faster. The other was that the Japanese had not only arrived on American shores but, because of the benefits bestowed on them by local politicians, had been able to transfer from Japan to America their ability to produce at low cost. That additional capacity to produce would surely come at the expense of the American companies that were already shaky.

What finally jarred Maryann Keller into testifying, however, was a Department of Commerce report that said that by 1988 the Japanese would be able to produce nearly 800,000 cars in America and would have 44 percent of the market. Between cars imported and cars manufactured in America by the Japanese, that would eventually mean that American companies would sell 1.5 million fewer cars a year. Detroit by 1988 might be selling only 6.3 million cars—well down from industry hopes, which were closer to 8 or 9 million as low figures. The earnings for the entire industry would be significantly down. Factories would have to be closed, more workers laid off. A decline like that would roll through the entire American economy. So somewhat reluctantly, as if going against her own beliefs, Maryann Keller told Congress she favored a limited protection which might give the American industry time to become competitive. She proposed a three-tier system: a free market on all cars under $6500, a free market for anything above $20,000, and a 25 percent tariff on all imports between $6500 and $20,000—that or a 65 percent American-content law. The Japanese, she noted, were so good that they would be able to overcome the disadvantage of a 25 percent tariff in six or seven years. That meant the pressure on the American industry to become competitive would be extreme. Her testimony, coming from someone so innately critical of the sins of the industry, someone so naturally committed to a free market, was perhaps the most damning forecast of all.

54.
THE PAST
BECOMES
THE FUTURE

J. Edward Lundy had retired as the chief financial officer of the Ford Motor Company in June 1979. He remained not just active but powerful, however. He was the vice-chairman of the finance committee of the board—the chairman was Henry Ford himself—and he continued to wield influence through his network of bright young men, some of them not so young anymore, who had advanced into key positions throughout the company. His life, as befit a man with so many friendships, was uncommonly rich. It was the carefully arranged life of a nineteenth-century man who fended off the pressure and crudeness of the late twentieth century so that he could do the things he wanted to do. As a company executive he had loathed trips to Europe; now he enjoyed traveling to Europe with his friend Arjay Miller and Miller's family, visiting the better restaurants and vineyards. He had also become more deeply involved in private philanthropy. Beyond his very generous support of St. Joseph's Catholic Church in Dearborn, he had given a great deal of money, over forty years, to a long list of people in need, especially to the wives and children of Ford men who had died when they were young. As in all other things, he was meticulous in this giving; if a recipient passed on and there was no more need of support, there were legal arrangements whereby the money would go to a residual beneficiary such as the Henry Ford Hospital. His social life, which was conducted primarily among Ford finance people whose careers he had encouraged and who had in time become part of his extended family, was at once busy and skillfully controlled. There was an unwritten protocol for those who were part of that family by which they understood how often to invite him over for dinner, for while it was important for them to maintain the friendship, it was also important not to seem to be pushing it, not to look as if they were exploiting the relationship. In May 1985, at the age of seventy, after twenty years on the board of directors, Ed Lundy retired from that body as well, and for the first time in forty years had no official connection to the Ford Motor Company.

His imprint, nevertheless, was everywhere upon the company, studded as it was with his progeny, all of them obsessed with the bottom line. Red Poling, a Lundy man, was now president of Ford, and Allan Gilmour, a special favorite of Lundy's, had become chief financial officer. Once again, in fact, the company was seriously divided between the product people and the finance people, in a way that resembled the small-car/big-car struggles of the 1970s. This time the issue was even graver: whether or not Ford would turn over production of all its compact and subcompact lines to Mazda. The Japanization of the small-car line, according to Ford insiders, was Red Poling's pet project. It was simply too hard to make money producing small cars in America, he argued, what with the competition from the Japanese and the Koreans. He had become preoccupied by how much money the company might save if cut loose from so draining a part of the business. If Ford took that step, no less than two and perhaps as many as four more factories would be closed.

Holding the line against Poling, at least for the moment, was Don Petersen, the chairman. He and his people argued that it would be a tragedy to vacate the battlefield without more of a fight. Ford, they objected, was in the business of *making* cars, not just marketing them. Besides, said Petersen, the step would make Ford alarmingly dependent upon Mazda. Who knew what the future was for Mazda and the Japanese? Would Mazda be as good a car company in 1990 as in 1986? Look at what had happened in the last year, with the yen rising so quickly against the dollar. That rise had profoundly affected Japanese competitiveness in America, they pointed out. Through the spring of 1986 the battle raged. It lacked the personal animus of the Iacocca-Sperlich-Ford struggles of the 1970s, but in terms of the future of American industry, and of America, it was every bit as important.

Even as the combatants at Ford hammered away at each other, Lee Iacocca scored a major coup against his former company. In June 1986 he announced that he had hired away Bob Lutz, who for a number of years had been considered the rising star in the Ford firmament. Flamboyant, cocky, with a touch of the jet jockey to him, Lutz had been credited with much of the success of Ford of Europe, which had helped rescue Ford North America during those long, hard years of the early eighties. Lutz was the car guy personified. But his style, his magnetic effect upon both subordinates and the auto press, had kindled memories of a young Iacocca, and it was not just Philip Caldwell who was unamused by Lutz's growing cult of personality but Henry Ford himself, who did not like the idea of another Iacocca-like figure within his company. Henry Ford had become more and more hostile to Lutz and had said at one meeting when Lutz arrived a few minutes late, "Well, here comes our movie star." In desperation Lutz pleaded with his friends in journalism to stop writing about him. Even that had not helped, and Lutz's career had been put on a slower track. Snatched away by Iacocca, Lutz was placed in charge of Chrysler's international operations and the company's truck lines. He was a vice-president and Sperlich was president of Chrysler auto, but those knowledgeable about Detroit politics noted that Lutz reported to Jerry Greenwald, not Sperlich. Sperlich was said to be stunned, then wounded, by this move by Iacocca, the man whom he had followed and believed in more than anyone else over the last thirty years.

In March 1986, Katsuji Kawamata, former chairman of Nissan, suffered an aneurysm and was rushed to the hospital in critical condition. A week later, at the age of eighty-one, he died. The Japanese press hailed him as one of the founding fathers of the modern Japanese auto industry. There were to be two funeral services, one a relatively private ceremony for family and close friends, the other larger and more public. The funerals posed something of a problem for those in charge. The question was what to do about Ichiro Shioji, Kawamata's closest professional associate, the true source of his power. Shioji might have been expected to attend and perhaps to speak at the second ceremony. But that was not to be. Shioji had recently fallen from grace, and the management people did not want him there. Ishihara, Nissan's chairman, let him know through proxies that if he attended he would be hounded by photographers from his journalistic nemeses, *Focus* and *Friday*. Shioji took the warning seriously and stayed away, choosing to attend Kawamata's cremation instead. He was somewhat amused by the fact that the speakers at the second ceremony—Nakayama of the Industrial Bank, Inayama of the Keidanren, and Ishihara of Nissan—were all men who had in one way or another been rivals of the deceased and on occasion had done all they could to thwart his will. Since his fall, Shioji had been trying to figure out what to do with the rest of his life. He was considering setting up a travel agency that would specialize in serving the unions, but friends warned him that Ishihara might block him there too. He was also planning to become an international consultant on union affairs. He was well off; money was not a problem. Getting his yacht out on the water was now the problem. His crew, after all, had been made up entirely of Nissan employees, and they could no longer sail with him. He told friends he hoped they would come sailing with him in a few months, when he had recruited a new, non-Nissan crew.

In the late winter and early spring of 1986, serious tremors ran through the Japanese economy. The nation went through an immense crisis as the yen, which for most of the postwar period had been deliberately floated as softly as possible (among other reasons to spur exports and discourage imports destined for Japan's consumer economy), suddenly strengthened against the dollar. That process did not begin by chance; in the fall of 1985 there had been a decision by Japan's Western trading partners to try to weaken their currencies against the yen and thus bring some measure of fairer trade into play. That move had been somewhat successful, and by November the dollar, which had been worth about 230 yen, had fallen to 200 yen. The Americans probably wanted it to fall a little more but were pleased to hit the 200 mark. At just the moment when the two currencies were leveling out, however, the Saudis began to manipulate their oil production, and the price of oil fell dramatically.

The impact on the Japanese economy was phenomenal. Because the Japanese, of all the major industrial powers, were the most dependent upon imported oil, they were the greatest beneficiaries of the drop in price. As a result, the yen was strengthened even more. In 1979 the fall of the Shah had weakened the yen and thereby reduced the cost of Japan's auto exports, boosting sales; now the reverse had taken place. The Japanese currency had become stronger—the dollar now bought only 160 yen—which abruptly made exporting that much more difficult. That struck terror into the hearts of many Japanese industrialists. Japan had manipulated its currency with great skill for some thirty years; now the strength of its currency was proving a burden. "Don't you Americans realize what this will do to your economy?" one Japanese friend asked auto industry analyst Maryann Keller. "It's going to ruin your standard of living." Prime Minister Nakasone, nervous about the strengthened yen, intended to make it a major issue at the May 1986 Tokyo summit, but that conference was dominated by the issue of terrorism, and the issue of the yen was largely neglected by Western representatives, who were hardly sympathetic to the economic plight of the Japanese in the first place.

Things therefore became much harder for all Japanese exporters. Auto companies had to raise their prices again and again as the yen fell. No longer were Japanese cars, in addition to their other virtues, the cheapest on the market. The Japanese now had to stress other advantages, most notably quality and styling. American and German manufacturers reacted in different ways to the Japanese crisis. "Watch," Keith Crain of *Automotive News* told a friend. "GM will now put its prices up." Shortly thereafter, GM did announce a 2.9 percent price increase; Ford and Chrysler wisely held back. Volkswagen ran a commercial in which bewildered Japanese businessmen had to admit they faced a terrible price problem. The pressure this put on the Japanese companies to save elsewhere was immense. The senior executives of Nissan all took pay cuts. Throughout Japan factories commenced what were in effect speedups, as if to make up for the hardening yen. But all of this, in the view of many analysts who had long observed Japan, was temporary. It was a momentary obstacle in their way, and the Japanese would surely treat it as they had others: They would work harder than ever. They would streamline their system even more and press for every tiny gain. Suppliers and workers would be squeezed, banks would ease their terms, new processes of manufacturing would be implemented, and other adjustments would be made, and in time they would compensate for their losses and come back tougher and more determined than ever.

If there was any one fact that could destroy doubts that the Japanese challenge remained as formidable as before, it was that, in the first quarter of 1986, the trade imbalance between Japan and the United States reached $60 billion. Concealed within that staggering and portentous statistic was still another awesome fact: The Japanese were steadily moving away from the earlier, more primitive forms of their challenge, and not just from steel and auto into high-technology goods; they were reaping the benefits of their Calvinist era of hard work and diligent saving. By 1985, thanks to all those years of extraordinary sacrifice, the Japanese had accrued great amounts of capital. Now, very quietly, they were becoming new, powerful world financiers.

In America, despite the seeming resurgence of its economy in 1985 with the decline in the price of oil, there was the unsettling sense that a crisis existed and had not been faced. Jobs were being lost, the industrial core was weakening, and no real attempt was being made to do something about it. America, after all, had been so rich and successful in the postwar years that it could put much of its public energies into the political rather than the economic definition of the nation. In 1984, in the most recent presidential campaign, there had been more talk about school prayer than about the Japanese challenge. Even under a conservative administration pledged to major fiscal reform, the national debt mounted. America, facing competition from hungrier, more disciplined Asian nations, seemed unable to discipline itself. Everyone in America, it appeared, believed in sacrifice, so long as it was sacrifice by someone else. The budget director of the Reagan administration, frustrated by his President's appeasement of special-interest groups, left the government to write a book describing his defeats. It seemed symbolic of the new triumph of personal well-being over public virtue that he was given an advance by his publisher of $2.5 million for chronicling the decline of the latter. At a commencement address at Duke University, Lee Iacocca suggested to the assembled graduates that they try to do a better job of balancing the books than his generation had done, since they were being left with a two-trillion-dollar deficit. "We've been using your credit card," he said, "and you didn't even know it."

These attitudes contrasted sharply with those of Japan, a carefully focused nation concerned first and foremost with economic rather than political success. America had taken its economic success largely for granted. There was no small amount of irony in the fierce American arms race with the Soviet Union, which so seriously drained the American economy, both by adding debt to it and by taking many of the nation's most talented scientists out of the consumer economy. In a competition like that, the Soviets, with their crude, sluggish state economy, had something of an advantage; after all, their domestic economy did not work, and the only thing that did work was the defense sector—they could make missiles but not cars. By competing all-out in arms, the Americans were taking on the Soviets at what the latter did best, weakening an otherwise very sound and dynamic economy in the process and, of course, making the way much easier for the Japanese, who were under the American military umbrella. Those were Toyotas, Hondas, and Datsuns driving down the American highways, not Moskvas, and that was East Asia that America was losing jobs to, not Eastern Europe.

Some Americans talked knowledgeably about the new economic era as being one of a service economy, rather than an industrial one. But there were clearly two kinds of service jobs—high service ones for privileged Americans with good educations, whose careers reflected a considerable degree of choice, and low service. Low service was for those without much education in a society that increasingly was delineated by access to education. Those in the lower service economy had little leverage in terms of their career decisions, and their salaries, when adjusted for inflation, were barely comparable to those of the pre-New Deal period. As the blue-collar sector of the 'economy declined, there was danger of the nation's becoming more sharply divided along class lines, with a diminishing middle class and a chasm between the educated few and the unlettered many. That obviously had long-term implications; for one thing, it seemed likely to undermine the social harmony that Americans had enjoyed in much of this century. There was also some question, still to be answered, as to whether a strong service economy could stand on its own, for many analysts believed that a society was at its healthiest when the service economy was ancillary to a vibrant core economy, not an end in itself.

In some ways, as America faced the future and prepared to find its place in the new and uncertain international economy, it was, contrasted to other leading Western industrial nations, still remarkably blessed. It was rich in land, and its agriculture was productive, modern, and bountiful. It had more mineral resources than any potential industrial competitor. Its venture capital system was probably the most vital in the world. If the hostile mergers reflected, in Harold Wilson's phrase, "the unacceptable face of capitalism," then the world of the start-up companies, of talented men and women willing to leave secure jobs with larger corporations to bet on themselves, was the most exciting and most promising face. Its higher educational system was probably the finest in the world, although even here there were disturbing signs, for approximately half the engineers being trained in America's graduate schools were foreigners; in effect, states like Michigan and California were subsidizing the challenge to the United States from Japan and Korea and other striving nations.

There were two real weaknesses, however. One was the public school system and the low level of literacy. (A recent study said in its conclusion that if a foreign power had wanted to undermine the United States of America, it would have given it the public school system it currently had.) Even here, the drive and energy and ambition of the new Asians was apparent. Whereas the top graduates at the Bronx High School of Science, one of New York City's great democratic yet elite high schools, where admission was based on merit, had some twenty-five or thirty years ago been the children of Jewish immigrants, now they were the children of Asian immigrants, often in fact young Asians themselves born in the old country. There was something about that fact that spoke of both the best and the worst of modern America, for it showed simultaneously that it was an open and regenerative nation, where a better life was still possible, and that all too many native sons and daughters had taken their standard of living for granted.

The other respect in which America was ill prepared for the new world economy was in terms of expectations. No country, including America, was likely ever to be as rich as America had been from 1945 to 1975, and other nations were following the Japanese into middle-class existence, which meant that life for most Americans has bound to become leaner. But in the middle of 1986 there seemed little awareness of this, let alone concern about it. Few were discussing how best to adjust the nation to an age of somewhat diminished expectations, or how to marshal its abundant resources for survival in a harsh, unforgiving new world, or how to spread the inevitable sacrifices equitably.

AUTHOR'S NOTE

I decided to do this book in the spring of 1980. In the wake of the fall of the Shah of Iran it was clear that the entire American industrial core was vulnerable to relentless challenge from a confident, disciplined Japan. How and why that had happened seemed to me a story worth telling. While there were a number of experts on both sides of the Pacific, it struck me that there was no book that tried to tell the parallel stories of the Japanese ascent and the American malaise, and that it was a perfect opportunity for a writer willing to spend the five years or so it would take to report the critical events closely. The story was what I would call soft drama—that is, something profound that has taken place so quietly, in such small increments, that it is barely visible to the naked eye—as opposed to hard drama, something so obviously dramatic that it is on the network news that very evening or on the front page the next morning. In any case, the story of Japan's ascent and America's subtle industrial decline seemed to me drama of the highest order and consequence. I chose the auto rather than steel because it was a consumer item, familiar to every reader, and the symbol of America's surge into the middle class—indeed, to the rest of the world, the most American of products. I decided to tell the story through the personae of two companies. On the American side, I picked Ford because at that moment Chrysler was too fragile, too near bankruptcy, and GM so large and rich as to be impervious to all but the vastest changes. Having selected Ford, the number two American company, I chose Nissan, the number two Japanese firm, after Toyota, as its Japanese counterpart. At that moment I knew precious little about either; I had absolutely no idea, for example, that critical to Nissan's modern history was the settlement of a hundred-day strike in 1953.

This book was harder for me to do than *The Best and the Brightest* and *The Powers That Be*. Those books were about events that were already part of my life; when during interviews sources told me about important occurrences, I knew immediately what they were talking about, and the context. Here, however, I had to familiarize myself with a completely different and often quite alien world. I was not only reporting, I was learning different languages, those of industry and of auto. As I entered this world, a number of Detroit officials and journalists were generous with their expertise and wisdom. I have listed many of them among my interviews, but I should note that Keith Crain and David E. Davis (each first among equals) were particularly helpful, and I turned to them again and again. I would also like to note that though I covered the men of Ford in what were the company's most difficult years, they were as a rule gracious and cooperative.

The Japanese section was harder to do, not because of language problems but because the Japanese have a very different attitude toward divulging what they know. As Frank Gibney, a leading writer on Japan, says, "It takes a very long time to get someone who really knows something to say something that really matters." Or as the Japanese intellectual Tadao Umesao points out, in terms of communications Japan is like the black hole of the universe: It receives signals, but does not emit them. Tadao also observes that in Japan, the getting of information has a positive social value while the *giving* of it is considered worthless or even harmful. I spent eight months in Japan, six of them accompanied by my family. Nissan was at best slow to help me. Like many American writers in Japan I felt no overt resistance, just a constant undertow that seemed to work against me. The downside of that problem was a great deal of wasted time; the upside was that it forced me to put even more effort into finding unofficial sources.

The officials of Mazda, in part because of the far more sophisticated attitude of Bunzo Suzuki (and his greater leverage with his superiors), were far more useful, as were many other Japanese in unofficial positions. A number of American Japanologists were extremely generous in sharing their lifetimes of knowledge with someone new to the subject. I feel especially grateful to Gerry Curtis of Columbia, Ezra Vogel of Harvard, Chalmers Johnson of Berkeley, James Abegglen, Frank Gibney, Donald Richie, and Tracy Dahlby. I am also indebted to my two interpreters, Hideko Takayama and Nobuko Hashimoto. Miss Takayama, dedicated and fearless, was splendid in her ability to keep working at certain loose strands after I left Tokyo and to continue interviewing. Her participation was critical to the completion of my project and my esteem for her knows no limits. She is one of the most talented members of Tokyo's press corps. She and Miss Hashimoto also did a number of translations for me, most notably the works of Satoshi Aoki and the memoirs of Katsuji Kawamata.

At the start of the book, Alex Kotlowitz was extremely helpful in compiling a journalistic history of the subject for me; at the end, Roddy Ray of the *Detroit Free Press* was equally helpful in checking a number of things. Nancy Medeiros typed my notes and was unfailingly positive about one of the hardest aspects of this book. At Ford, Tom Foote was very kind, and at Nissan, Yukihito Eguchi worked diligently at his melancholy task of bringing my requests to his superiors. Baron Bates of Chrysler persevered in helping to arrange interviews for me with his own best-selling boss. David Crippen of the Ford Archives was resourceful and supportive. Marty Lipton of Wachtel, Lipton was invaluable in discussing the changes on Wall Street and suggesting other sources. I would like to thank the on-the-scene reporters of two fine newspapers whose stories from both Tokyo and Detroit were a constant source of information for me when I was on location and, even more valuable, when I was not. Writers like myself often tend to take the work of reporters on the beat for granted; in this case especially that is not acceptable, so I warmly acknowledge my debt to *The New York Times*'s reporters in Tokyo, Susan Chira, Clyde Haberman, and Henry Scott-Stokes; its Detroit bureau chief, John Holusha; and its labor reporter, Bill Serrin. Also to *The Wall Street Journal*'s Tokyo reporters, E. S. Browning, Chris Chipello, Masayoshi Kanabayashi, John Marcom, Bradley Martin, Bernard Wysocki, and Stephen Yoder; and the *Journal*'s staff in Detroit, Amanda Bennett, Dale Buss, John Bussey, Damon Darlin, Melinda Grenier-Guiles, Paul Ingrassia, Doron Levin, Amal Nag, and Bob Simison. I am much obliged to Urban Lehner, who managed to serve as the *Journal*'s bureau chief in both Tokyo and Detroit during the period when I was working on the book and who is to me the prototype of the complete journalist. The work of Hillel Levin and Kirk Cheyfitz in Detroit's monthly magazines always seemed to me to be of a very high order, well above that found in many national magazines, and like many another journalistic visitor to that city I found it of great assistance.

On a more personal level a book like this demands a great deal of logistical support. I would like to express my gratitude to John Murphy, Henry Kehlenbeck, and John McMahon, to Peter Grilli and John Wheeler of the Japan Society, and to Walter Anderson of *Parade*, whose interest and generosity were vital. My most heartfelt thanks go to Neil Dunlap Hughes, Stevie McCarthy, Amanda Earle, and Carolyn Means (who made the trip to Tokyo with our family). I am indebted to the staffs of the

Pontchartrain in Detroit and the International House in Tokyo, and also owe thanks to Dr. Ben Kean, Michael Hecht, Alan Fruchter, and Gary Schwartz.

My editor at Morrow, Tom Congdon, working under highly pressured circumstances, had from the first day a fine sense of what the book needed and, equally important, what it did not. For more than six difficult months we were not so much writer and editor as partners. I am also grateful to Dawn Drzal, Lori Ames, Sherry Arden, and Larry Hughes.

With the exception of the portrait of the first Henry Ford, the book is primarily the product of my own research. I post the following list of interviewees with some caveats. First, it is incomplete. At least fifteen critical sources, a few in America and more in Japan, asked that their names not be used, because listing them would make them vulnerable professionally. Second, while a list like this sketches out what a writer has done and where he has gone, it may well be misleading. The name of one well-known source will jump out at readers as someone who helped the writer a great deal, while a less familiar name may have been indispensable. A good example is the late John Bugas. I saw him seven times at great length. No one in the company went as far back with Henry Ford II as he did; few insiders—since Ford had fired him at one point—had as much reason to be angry with Henry Ford. Ford himself was extremely nervous at one point because I was spending so much time with Bugas. Yet while Bugas was certainly helpful to me, and knew a great deal about Ford's personal life, he was only mildly revealing as a source. I spent so much time with him largely because we enjoyed each other's company; both serious baseball fans, we usually held our later appointments in his box seats at Tiger Stadium, where he would reminisce more about the days of Hank Greenberg than of Harry Bennett.

Interviewed for the Japanese section: James Abegglen, Naohiro Amaya, Satoshi Aoki, Fumiko Araki, Hideo Asahara, Yaichi Ayukawa, Merrick Baker-Bates, Pete Brock, Phil Broman, Mark Brown, Frank Cary, Otis Cary, Jay Chai, Bill Chapman, Atsuko Chiba, Tetsuya Chikushi, Bill Clark, Gerald Curtis, Midori Curtis, Michael Cusumano, Toshiko Dahlby, Tracy Dahlby, Peter Dennison-Edson, George DeVos, Bill Dizer, Takeo Doi, Jack Eby, Yukhito Eguchi, Takuro Endo, Tadayoshi Enju, Roy Essoyan, Bob Fisher, Glen Fukushima, Yoichi Funabashi, Barbara Gewirtz, Elliot Gewirtz, Alex Gibney, Frank Gibney, Donald Gorham, William Gorham, Koichi Goto, Mitsuya Goto, Joseph Greenwald, Peter Grilli, Clyde Haberman, Eleanor Hadley, Fumiko Halloran, Richard Halloran, Tsuneyuki Hane, Teiichi Hara, Michio Hatada, Tsuyoshi Hayashi, Gerd Hijino, Shigeki Hijino, Takuzo Hiki, Tadashi Igarashi, Tatsuya Imai, Robert Immerman, Munemichi Inoue, Takeshi Isayama, Hideo Ishihara, Tadashi Ishihara, Kaoru Ishikawa, Sam Jameson, Chalmers Johnson, Sheila Johnson, Naotake Kaibara, Kaiichi Kanao, Hajime Karatsu, Mikio Kato, Hideaki Kase, Yutaka Katayama, Katsuji Kawamata, Kinji Kawamura, Soichi Kawazoe, Dusty Kidd, Eric Klestadt, Chizuko Kobayashi, Noritake Kobayashi, Yotaro Kobayashi, Kazuo Koike, Tetsuo Komatsu, Masataka Kosaka, Takahiro Koyama, Bernard Krisher, Tokuichi Kumagai, Masao Kunihiro, Sadayuki Kuriyama, Jim Laurie, Masako Laurie, Nancy Lehner, Urban Lehner, Ray Lemke, Tim McGinnis, Ichiro Maeda, Hideshi Maki, Shin Maki, Mike Mansfield, Mayfield Marshall, Bradley Martin, Kathleen Martin, Jurek Martin, Keikichi Matsumoto, Yukio Matsuyama, Masaru Miyake, Tom Mori, Yoshihiko Morozumi, Masumi Muramatsu, Kiyoaki Murata, Michio Nagai, Hideya Nakamura, Yoshikazu Nakashima, Sohei Nakayama, Hideo Numasaki, Sadaaki Numata, Miyoji Ochiai, Dan Okimoto, Saburo Okita, Keigo Okongi, Masataka Okuma, Shoji Okumura, Shintaro Ota, George Packard, Wingate Packard, John Parker, Anne Pepper, Tom Pepper, John Curtis Perry, Tait Ratcliffe, Ed Reingold, Edwin O. Reischauer, Donald Richie, David Riesman, Johnnie Rinard, John Roderick, Jun-ichiro Sakura, Henry Scott-Stokes, Isaac Shapiro, Yonetaro Shimatani, Ichiro Shioji, Rei Shiratori, Saburo Shiroyama, Janet Snyder, Akira Sugita, Bunzo Suzuki, Tadashi Suzuki, Takao Suzuki, Takashi Tachibana, Sadao Tachikawa, Rennosuke Takeda, Yasuo Takeyama, Katsuo Tamura, Kinichi Tamura, Kuniyuki Tanabe, Akinori Tanaka, Kanichi Tanaka, Minoru Tanaka, Sanosuke Tanaka, Yasumasa Tanaka, Michael Tharp, Gordon Togasaki, Tamiyo Togasaki, Shigehiko Togo, Kisaburo Tsubura, Tadao Umesao, Shunchiro Umetani, Masataka Usami, Ezra Vogel, Susumu Wakamori, Nobe Wakatsuki, Saburo Watanabe, Robert Whiting, Jack Yamaguchi, Kenichi Yamamoto, Nobuyoshi Yoshida, and T. F. Yukawa. Korea: Ahn Sung Chan, Chung Se Yung, Kang Oh Ryong, John Kim, Stewart Kim, Y. S. Kim, Kwon Ki Chul, Stan Lee, Park Jin Kean, H. B. Suh, Bill Vaughan, Greg Warner, Ed White, and Yoo Mal Bok.

Interviewed for the American section: Tom Adams, William Agee, Bob Alexander, Roger Altman, Martin Anderson, Lee Bach, George Ball, Ken Bannon, Jack Barnes, Baron Bates, Calvin Beauregard, Clay Bedford, George Bennett, Bill Benton, Ben Bidwell, Barry Bluestone, Irving Bluestone, Michael Blumenthal, Ron Boltz, Gene Bordinat, Bill Bourke, George Brown, Holmes Brown, Warren Buffet, John Bugas, Philip Caldwell, Jim Cannon, John Chancellor, Roy Chapin, Sis Chapin, Richard Clurman, Shirley Clurman, Dolly Cole, Robert Cole, Jack Conway, Andrew Court, Keith Crain, Mary Kay Crain, David Crippen, Mike Cronin, Paul Crowley, Ron Daniel, Sam Daume, David E. Davis, Jeannie Davis, Don

DeLaRossa, John DeLorean, Ron DeLuca, W. Edwards Deming, Jake Diaz, Chuck Dotterer, Peter Drucker, David Eisenberg, John English, Tom Feaheny, David Fine, Arthur Fleischer, A. P. Fontaine, Jack Fontaine, Charlotte Ford, Edsel Ford II, Henry Ford II, Doug Fraser, Donald Frey, Stuart Frey, Sheldon Friedman, Steve Friedman, John Kenneth Galbraith, Ray Geddes, Roswell Gilpatric, Joel Goddard, Joyce Goddard, Jack Goldman, Pat Greathouse, Bob Greenhill, Gerry Greenwald, Bill Haddad, Bill Hambrecht, Walter Hayes, Jay Higgins, Dick Holbrooke, Hudson Holland, Jr., Fred Hooven, Robert Hormats, Joseph Hudson, Jr., Lee Iacocca, Bill Innes, Don Jahncke, Don Jesmore, Edward Johnson III, Arvid Jouppi, Joseph Juran, Sandy Kaplan, Eugene Keilin, Leo Kelmenson, Tom Killefer, Bunkie Knudsen, Florence Knudsen, Norman Krandall, Wendell Larsen, David Lawrence, Don Lennox, Robert Lenzner, Walter Levy, David Lewis, Martin Lipton, David McCammon, Arch McCardell, Amy McCombs, Paul McCracken, Gillis MacGill Addison, Sid McKenna, Matt McLaughlin, Don Mandich, Nancy Mann, Karl Mantyla, David Maxey, Charles Maxwell, Ted Mecke, Kay Meehan, Arjay Miller, Elaine Mittleman, Ron Moen, Chase Morsey, Franklin Murphy, Walter Murphy, Ralph Nader, John Nevin, John Nichols, William Niskanen, Norman Pearlstine, William Perry, Don Petersen, Nick Pileggi, Bob Pisor, Richard Rainwater, Erick Reickert, Ralph W. E. Reid, Felix Rohatyn, George Romney, Dick Royal, Marvin Runyon, Paul Schrade, Steve Schwarzman, Bill Scollard, Fred Secrest, William Serrin, Brendan Sexton, Harley Shaiken, Irving Shapiro, Bill Sheehan, Victor Sheinman, Carroll Shelby, Bill Scherkenbach, Herb Segal, Martin Siegel, Sue Smock, Bob Spencer, Hal Sperlich, Arthur Stanton, Philip Stearns, Don Stillman, Gordon Strossberg, Bob Teeter, Jack Telnack, Jerry terHorst, Michael Thomas, Myron Tribus, Gerald Tsai, Raymond Vernon, Phil Villers, Tom Volpe, Bruce Wasserstein, Neil Waud, Michael Wendler, John Whitehead, Jerry Wiesner, Bill Winn, Jack Withrow, Leonard Woodcock, Pat Wright, and Ian Zwicker. (Of the principals both Robert McNamara, who cited the frailty of his memory, and J. Edward Lundy, who kept to his rule of giving no interviews to anyone from the press, declined to be interviewed for this book. There were of course others who declined to see me, or simply did not return my phone messages.)

BIBLIOGRAPHY

In my reading certain books were particularly helpful and I used them as pathfinders: John Brooks's *The Go-go Years*, Ed Cray's *The Chrome Colossus*, William Manchester's *American Caesar*, Michael Moritz and Barrett Seaman's *Going for Broke*, the Allan Nevins and Frank Ernest Hill three-part history of the Ford Motor Company, William Serrin's *The Company and the Union*, Keith Sward's *The Legend of Henry Ford*, and John Toland's *The Rising Sun*.

Abegglen, James. *Management and Worker: The Japanese Solution*. Tokyo and New York: Kodansha, 1973.
———, and Stalk, George, Jr. *Kaisha: The Japanese Corporation*. New York: Basic Books, 1986.
Abernathy, William. *The Productivity Dilemma*. Baltimore: Johns Hopkins University Press, 1978.
———; Clark, Kim; and Kantrow, Alan. *Industrial Renaissance: Producing a Competitive Future for America*. New York: Basic Books, 1983.
Allen, Frederick Lewis. *Only Yesterday*. New York: Harper, 1931.
Aoki, Satoshi. *The Crisis of the Nissan Group*. Tokyo: Chobunsha, 1980.
———. *Secrets of the Nissan S-organization*. Tokyo: Chobunsha, 1981.
Bainbridge, John. *The Super-Americans*. New York: Holt, Rinehart and Winston, 1972.
Barnard, John. *Walter Reuther and the Rise of the Auto World*. Boston: Little, Brown, 1983.
Barnet, Richard J. *The Alliance*. New York: Simon and Schuster, 1984.
Beasley, Norman. *Knudsen*. New York: McGraw-Hill, 1947.
Bennett, Harry (with Paul Marcus). *We Never Called Him Henry*. New York: Fawcett, 1951.
Bluestone, Barry, and Harrison, Bennett. *The De-industrialization of America*. New York: Basic Books, 1982.
Brooks, John. *Once in Golconda*. New York: Harper and Row, 1969.

————. *The Go-go Years.* New York: Weybright and Talley, 1973.

Burlingame, Roger. *Engines of Democracy.* New York: Scribners, 1946.

————. *Henry Ford: A Great Life in Brief.* New York: Knopf, 1955.

Chandler, Alfred D., and Salsbury, Stephen. *Pierre du Pont and the Making of the Modern Corporation.* New York: Harper and Row, 1971.

Chinoy, Eli. *Automobile Workers and the American Dream.* New York: Doubleday, 1955.

Christopher, Robert. *The Japanese Mind.* New York: Linden Press, 1983.

Chrysler, Walter P. (with Boyden Sparkes). *Life of an American Workman.* New York: Dodd, Mead, 1950.

Clarke, James, and Halbouty, Michel. *Spindletop.* New York: Random House, 1952.

Cole, Robert. *Japanese Blue Collar.* Berkeley, Calif.: University of California Press, 1971.

———— (editor). *Automobiles and the Future: Competition, Cooperation, and Change.* Ann Arbor, Mich.: University of Michigan Press, 1983.

Conot, Robert. *American Odyssey.* New York: Morrow, 1974.

Cormier, Frank, and Eaton William. *Reuther.* Englewood Cliffs, N.J.: Prentice-Hall, 1970.

Courdy, Jean Claude. *The Japanese.* New York: Harper and Row, 1984.

Cray, Ed. *The Chrome Colossus.* New York: McGraw-Hill, 1980.

Cunningham, Mary. *Power Play.* New York: Linden Press, 1984.

Curtis, Gerald. *Election Campaigning Japanese Style.* New York: Columbia University Press, 1971.

Cusumano, Michael. *The Japanese Automobile Industry.* Cambridge, Mass.: Harvard University Press, 1985.

Dahlinger, John C. *The Secret Life of Henry Ford.* Indianapolis, Ind.: Bobbs-Merrill, 1975.

Doi, Takeo. *The Anatomy of Dependence.* Tokyo and New York: Kodansha, 1971.

Dore, Ronald. *City Life in Japan: A Study of a Tokyo Ward.* Berkeley, Calif.: University of California Press, 1958.

Dower, John. *Empire and Aftermath: Yoshida Shigeru and the Japanese Experience, 1878–1954.* Cambridge, Mass.: Harvard University Press, 1979.

Drucker, Peter. *Adventures of a Bystander.* New York: Harper and Row, 1979.

Fallon, Ivan, and Srodes, James. *Dream Maker: The Rise and Fall of John Z. DeLorean.* New York: Putmam, 1983.

Fine, Sidney. *Sit-Down: The General Motors Strike of 1936–37.* Ann

Arbor, Mich.: University of Michigan Press, 1969.

Flink, James. *The Car Culture*. Cambridge, Mass.: MIT Press, 1975.

Ford, Henry. *My Life and Work*. New York: Doubleday, 1923.

Galbraith, John Kenneth. *The Great Crash, 1929*. Boston: Houghton Mifflin, 1961.

Gibney, Frank. *Five Gentlemen of Japan*. New York: Farrar, Straus, 1953.

————. *Japan: The Fragile Superpower*. New York: Norton, 1979.

————. *Miracle by Design*. New York: Times Books, 1982.

Giddens, Paul Henry. *The Birth of the Oil Industry*. New York: Macmillan, 1938.

Gordon, Maynard. *The Iacocca Management Style*. New York: Dodd, Mead, 1985.

Halliday, Jon. *A Political History of Japanese Capitalism*. New York: Pantheon, 1975.

Halloran, Richard. *Japan: Images and Realities*. New York: Random House, 1969.

Herndon, Booton. *Ford: An Unconventional Biography of the Men and Their Times*. New York: Weybright and Talley, 1969.

Hewins, Ralph. *The Japanese Miracle Men*. London: Secker and Warburg, 1967.

Hickerson, Mel. *Ernie Breech: The Story of His Remarkable Career at General Motors, Ford and TWA*. Des Moines, Iowa: Meredith Corp., 1968.

Hofheinz, Roy, Jr., and Calder, Kent. *The East Asian Edge*. New York: Basic Books, 1982.

Howe, Irving, and Widick, B. J. *The UAW and Walter Reuther*. New York: Random House, 1949.

Iacocca, Lee (with William Novak). *Iacocca: An Autobiography*. New York: Bantam, 1984.

Jardim, Anne. *The First Henry Ford*. Cambridge, Mass.: MIT Press, 1970.

Jerome, John. *The Death of the Automobile*. New York: Norton, 1972.

Johnson, Chalmers. *Conspiracy at Matsukawa*. Berkeley, Calif.: University of California Press, 1972.

————. *MITI and the Japanese Miracle*. Stanford, Calif.: Stanford University Press, 1982.

Johnson, Sheila K. *American Attitudes Toward Japan, 1941–75*. Washington, D.C.: American Enterprise Institute, 1975.

Kahn, Herman, and Pepper, Tom. *The Japanese Challenge*. New York: Morrow, 1980.

Kawamata, Katsuji. *My Career*. Tokyo: Nihon Keizai Shimbunsha, 1964.

Kurzman, Dan. *Kishi and Japan*. New York: Obolensky, 1960.

Lacey, Robert. *The Kingdom.* New York: Harcourt Brace Jovanovich, 1981.

Lambert, Hope. *Till Death Do Us Part.* San Diego: Harcourt Brace Jovanovich, 1983.

Lasky, Victor. *Never Explain, Never Complain.* New York: Richard Marek, 1981.

Lewis, David. *The Public Image of Henry Ford.* Detroit: Wayne State University Press, 1976.

McCarry, Charles. *Citizen Nader.* New York: Saturday Review Press, 1972.

Manchester, William. *American Caesar: Douglas MacArthur, 1880–1964.* Boston: Little, Brown, 1978.

Marquis, Samuel. *Henry Ford: An Interpretation.* Boston: Little, Brown, 1923.

Marsh, Barbara. *A Corporate Tragedy: The Agony of International Harvester.* New York: Doubleday, 1985.

Moritz, Michael, and Seaman, Barrett. *Going for Broke: The Chrysler Story.* New York: Doubleday, 1981.

Nader, Ralph. *Unsafe at Any Speed.* New York: Grossman, 1965.

Nakane, Chie. *Japanese Society.* Berkeley, Calif.: University of California Press, 1970.

Nevins, Allan, and Hill, Frank Ernest. *Ford.* Volume 1: *The Times, the Man and the Company.* New York: Scribners, 1954.

———. *Ford.* Volume 2: *Expansion and Challenge.* New York: Scribners, 1957.

———. *Ford.* Volume 3: *Decline and Rebirth.* New York: Scribners, 1962.

Okita, Saburo. *Japan's Challenging Years.* Canberra: Australia Japan Research Center, 1981.

Packard, George. *Protest in Tokyo: The Security Treaty Crisis of 1960.* Princeton, N.J.: Princeton University Press, 1966.

Perry, John Curtis. *Beneath the Eagle's Wings: Americans in Occupied Japan.* New York: Dodd, Mead, 1980.

Rae, John. *Nissan-Datsun: A History of the Nissan Motor Corporation in the U.S.A., 1960–80.* New York: McGraw-Hill, 1981.

Rand, Christopher. *Making Democracy Safe for Oil.* Boston: Atlantic Monthly Press, 1975.

Reich, Robert. *The Next American Frontier.* New York: Times Books, 1983.

———, and Donahue, John. *New Deals: The Chrysler Revival and the American System.* New York: Times Books, 1985.

Reischauer, Edwin. *The Japanese*. Cambridge, Mass.: Harvard University Press, 1977.

Reuther, Victor. *The Brothers Reuther and the Story of the UAW*. Boston: Houghton Mifflin, 1976.

Richards, William C. *The Last Billionaire: Henry Ford*. New York: Scribners, 1948.

Riesman, David (with Evelyn Thompson Riesman). *Conversations with the Japanese*. New York: Basic Books, 1967.

Rothschild, Emma. *Paradise Lost*. New York: Random House, 1972.

Sampson, Anthony. *The Seven Sisters*. New York: Viking, 1975.

Sanders, Sol. *Honda: The Man and His Machine*. Tokyo and Rutland, Vt.: Tuttle, 1975.

Sansom, Sir George. *The Western World and Japan*. New York: Knopf, 1950.

Satoshi, Kamata. *Japan in the Passing Lane*. New York: Pantheon, 1982.

Seidler, Edouard. *Let's Call It Fiesta*. Newfoundland, N.J.: Haessner, 1976.

Serrin, William. *The Company and the Union*. New York: Knopf, 1973.

Servan-Schreiber, Jean-Jacques. *The World Challenge*. New York: Simon and Schuster, 1980.

Shaiken, Harley. *Work Transformed: Automation and Labor in the Computer Age*. New York: Holt, Rinehart and Winston, 1984.

Sick, Gary. *All Fall Down*. New York: Random House, 1985.

Sloan, Alfred P. *Adventures of a White Collar Man*. New York: Doubleday, 1941.

———. *My Years with General Motors*. New York: Doubleday, 1963.

Sloan, Allen. *Three Plus One Equals Billions: The Bendix–Martin-Marietta War*. New York: Arbor House, 1983.

Sorensen, Charles. *My Forty Years with Ford*. New York: Norton, 1956.

Stockman, David. *The Triumph of Politics*. New York: Harper and Row, 1986.

Sward, Keith. *The Legend of Henry Ford*. New York: Rinehart, 1948.

Thurow, Lester C. *The Zero-Sum Society: Distribution and the Possibilities for Economic Change*. New York: Basic Books, 1980.

Toland, John. *The Rising Sun*. New York: Random House, 1970.

Vogel, Ezra. *Comeback*. New York: Simon and Schuster, 1984.

———. *Japan as Number One*. Cambridge, Mass.: Harvard University Press, 1979.

———. *Japan's New Middle Class: The Salary Man and His Family in a Tokyo Suburb*. Berkeley, Calif.: University of California Press, 1963.

Weisberger, Bernard. *The Dream-Maker: William C. Durant*. Boston: Little, Brown, 1979.

Whiteside, Thomas. *The Investigation of Ralph Nader*. New York: Arbor House, 1972.

Whiting, Robert. *The Chrysanthemum and the Bat*. New York: Dodd, Mead, 1977.

Wright, J. Patrick. *On a Clear Day You Can See General Motors*. Grosse Pointe, Mich.: Wright, 1979.

Yamamota, Tadashi. *The Silent Power*. Tokyo: Simul, 1976.

Yates, Brock. *The Decline and Fall of the American Automobile Industry*. New York: Empire Books, 1983.

Yoshida, Shigeru. *The Yoshida Memoirs*. Boston: Houghton Mifflin, 1962.

INDEX